Juvenile Justice

D1210806

Juvenile Justice: An Introduction, 8th edition, presents a comprehensive picture of juvenile offending, delinquency theories, and how juvenile justice actors and agencies react to delinquency. It covers the history and development of the juvenile justice system and the unique issues related to juveniles, offering evidence-based suggestions for successful interventions and treatment and examining the new balance model of juvenile court.

This new edition not only includes the latest available statistics on juvenile crime and victimization, drug use, court processing, and corrections, but provides insightful analysis of recent developments, such as those related to the use of probation supervision fees; responses to gangs and cyber bullying; implementing the deterrence model (Project HOPE); the possible impact of drug legalization; the school-to-prison pipeline; the extent of victimization and mental illness in institutions; and implications of major court decisions regarding juveniles, such as Life Without Parole (LWOP) for juveniles.

Each chapter enhances student understanding with Key Terms, a "What You Need to Know" section highlighting important points, and Discussion Questions. Links at key points in the text show students where they can go to get the latest information, and a comprehensive glossary aids comprehension.

John T. Whitehead is a Professor and former Chair in the Department of Criminal Justice and Criminology at East Tennessee State University. He completed his M.A. at the University of Notre Dame and earned his Ph.D. in Criminal Justice from SUNY-Albany. He teaches courses in corrections, criminal justice ethics, and the death penalty.

Steven P. Lab is Professor and Director of the Criminal Justice Program and Chair of the Department of Human Services at Bowling Green State University. His research interests include victims of crime, crime prevention, juvenile delinquency, and school crime. He received his Ph.D. in Criminology from Florida State University in 1982. His primary research interests are in crime prevention and juvenile justice; he is the author of five textbooks and three edited works, and has published more than 30 articles on various topics.

Titles of Related Interest from Routledge and Anderson

Juvenile Justice

An Introduction

Eighth Edition

John T. Whitehead
Steven P. Lab

Routledge
Taylor & Francis Group

NEW YORK AND LONDON

First published in 1990
by Anderson Publishing, an imprint of Elsevier

Seventh edition published in 2013
by Anderson Publishing, an imprint of Elsevier

Eighth edition published 2015
by Routledge
711 Third Avenue, New York, NY 10017

and by Routledge
2 Park Square, Milton Park, Abingdon, Oxon, OX14 4RN

Routledge is an imprint of the Taylor & Francis Group, an informa business

Library of Congress Cataloging-in-Publication Data
Whitehead, John T.
    Juvenile justice : an introduction/John T. Whitehead, Steven P. Lab. —
Eighth edition.
    pages cm
    Includes bibliographical references and index.
    1. Juvenile delinquency. 2. Juvenile justice, Administration of.
    3. Juvenile justice, Administration of--United States. I. Lab, Steven P.
    II. Title.
    HV9069.W46 2015
    364.36—dc23
    2014034929

ISBN: 978-1-138-84900-6 (hbk)
ISBN: 978-0-323-29871-1 (pbk)
ISBN: 978-1-315-72563-5 (ebk)

Typeset in Giovanni, Stone Sans and Helvetica
by Florence Production Ltd, Stoodleigh, Devon, UK

To Pat, Dan, and Tim
and
To Bryce, Madison, and Rylee

Contents

List of Figures   xi
List of Tables   xii
List of Boxes   xiv
Preface   xvii

CHAPTER 1   **Introduction—The Definition and Extent of Delinquency**   1

     Introduction   2
     Defining Delinquency   2
     Defining a Juvenile   6
     The Extent of Delinquency   7
     Summary   26

CHAPTER 2   **The History of Juvenile Justice**   29

     Introduction   30
     Property and Person   30
     The Rise of Juvenile Institutions   33
     The Establishment of the Juvenile Court   37
     Benevolence or Self-interest?   44
     Juvenile Justice from 1920 to the 1960s   46
     Changes Since the 1960s   47
     Summary   49

CHAPTER 3   **Explaining Delinquency—Biological and Psychological Approaches**   51

     Introduction   52
     Theoretical Schools of Thought   52
     Biological and Sociobiological Theories   56
     Psychological Explanations   66
     Summary   77

CHAPTER 4   Sociological Explanations of Delinquency   79

Introduction   80
The Ecological Perspective   81
Learning Theory   83
Subcultural Theories   86
Routine Activities and Rational Choice   90
Strain Theories   92
Social Control Theory   95
The Labeling Perspective   99
The Integration and Elaboration of Theories   101
The Impact of Theories on Juvenile Justice   102
Summary   103

CHAPTER 5   Gang Delinquency   105

Introduction   106
Gangs Defined   107
Early Gang Research   110
The Extent of Gang Membership   112
Characteristics of Gangs   115
Why Do Youths Join Gangs?   122
Gang Behavior   123
Do Gangs Cause Delinquency?   128
Intervention with Gangs   129
Summary   137

CHAPTER 6   Drugs and Delinquency   139

Introduction   140
Gauging the Extent of Drug Use   141
The Drugs–Delinquency Connection   147
Research on the Drugs–Delinquency Relationship   149
Interventions   151
Alternative Responses to Drug Use   162
Summary: The Response of the Juvenile Justice System   168

CHAPTER 7   Policing and Juveniles   171

Introduction   172
Statistics on Police Work with Juveniles   172
Professional Policing and Juveniles   173
Community or Problem-Solving Policing   181
Citizen Attitudes Toward Police   185
Recent Issues in Policing Concerning Juveniles   189
Police Effectiveness with Juvenile Crime   200
Summary   201

CHAPTER **8**   The Juvenile Court Process   205

Introduction 206
Detention 209
Detention Alternatives 215
The Intake Decision 216
Processing Juveniles in Adult Criminal Court 223
Adjudication and Disposition 229
Summary 242

CHAPTER **9**   Due Process and Juveniles   245

Introduction 246
The Landmark Supreme Court Cases 246
Additional Supreme Court Rulings 250
Search and Seizure 254
Rights in School 256
Rights at Home and in the Community 269
Summary 275

CHAPTER **10**   Institutional/Residential Interventions   277

Introduction 278
Institutional Corrections for Juveniles 278
State Training Schools 279
Program Effectiveness 286
Institutional Life 289
New Directions in Institutional Interventions 298
Summary 303

CHAPTER **11**   Juvenile Probation and Community Corrections   305

Introduction 306
Probation 306
Aftercare 309
Supervision and Counseling 310
Current Trends in Community Supervision 311
Effectiveness of Juvenile Probation and Related Sanctions 321
Effective and Ineffective Treatment Interventions
   with Offenders 323
Continuing Concerns in Community Corrections 329
Summary 332

CHAPTER **12**   Restorative Justice   335

Introduction 336
Background of Restorative Justice 336
Precursors to Restorative Justice 339

The Theoretical Basis of Restorative Practices 341
Types of Restorative Justice 343
The Impact of Restorative Justice 351
Problems and Issues with Restorative Justice 354
Summary 357

CHAPTER 13 **The Victimization of Juveniles** 359
Introduction 359
The Extent of Victimization 360
Explaining Juvenile Victimization 368
Responses to Victimization 370
The Role of Formal Social Control Agencies 373
Summary: The Need to Recognize the Victim 379

CHAPTER 14 **Future Directions in Juvenile Justice** 381
Introduction 382
Proposals for Reforming Juvenile Court 382
Broader Issues 395
Capital Punishment for Juveniles 406
Life Without Parole for Juveniles 409
Jurisdiction over Status Offenses 412
Conclusion 416

Bibliography 421
Combined Glossary Index 477

Figures

1.1	Behavior Continuum	5
1.2	Trend in Juvenile Violent Crime, 1988–2012	12
1.3	Trend in Juvenile Property Crime, 1988–2012	12
1.4	Trend in Delinquency Cases Since 1960	16
5.1	Prevalence of Gang Problems by Area Type, 1996–2011	113
5.2	Distribution of Gangs by Area Type	114
5.3	Distribution of Gang Members by Area Type	114
5.4	Percent of Gangs with Female Members, 2009	118
5.5	Factors Influencing Gang Member Migration	121
6.1	Possible Relationships between Drug Use and Delinquency	148
8.1	Juvenile Court Processing of Delinquency Cases, 2010	207
8.2	Juvenile Court Processing of Petitioned Status Offense Cases, 2010	208
12.1	Restorative Practices Typology	344
12.2	Parties Involved in Conferencing	348

Tables

1.1	Number of Offenses Cleared by Arrest or Exceptional Means	8
1.2	Distribution of Juvenile Arrests, 2012	10
1.3	Number and Rates of Youths in Juvenile Court	15
1.4	Characteristics of Juveniles in Correctional Facilities: Average One-Day Count—2011	17
1.5	Monitoring the Future, 2011	21
2.1	Comparative Terms in the Juvenile and Adult Systems	39
2.2	Factors in the Growth of *Parens Patriae*	41
2.3	Categories of Juvenile Court General Purpose Clauses	48
3.1	Major Elements of Classicism and Positivism	54
3.2	Sheldon's Physiques and Temperaments	58
3.3	Common Objections to Biologically Based Explanations	65
3.4	The Freudian Personality	68
3.5	Interpersonal Maturity Levels	70
3.6	Kohlberg's Moral Development	71
4.1	Sources of Neighborhood Control	83
4.2	Sutherland's Differential Association Theory	85
4.3	Miller's Lower-class Focal Concerns	88
4.4	Sykes and Matza's Techniques of Neutralization	89
4.5	Merton's Modes of Adaptation	93
4.6	Types of Strain Related to Crime	95
4.7	Elements of Hirschi's Bond	97
5.1	Typical Elements of a "Gang" Definition	109
5.2	Number of Gangs and Gang Members, 2006–2011	115
5.3	Klein and Maxson's Gang Types	119
5.4	Reasons for Gang Membership	122
5.5	Risk Factors for Gang Membership	123
5.6	Gang-related Homicides, 2011	126
5.7	Gang Intervention Strategies	130
6.1	Lifetime, Annual, Past Month, and Daily Drug Use by 12th Graders, 2013	142

6.2   Drug Use by 12–17-Year-Olds, 2012   143
6.3   Trends in Past Month Prevalence of Use of Various Drugs
         for 12th Graders, 1975–2-13   144
6.4   Percent Reporting Drugs Very Easy or Fairly Easy to Obtain,
         2013   145
7.1   Percentage of Schools with Full-time or Part-time Security at
         School at Least Once a Week, 2005–06, 2007–08, and 2009–10   190
7.2   Activities of Law Enforcement in Schools   190
11.1   Adjudication Offenses for Juvenile Delinquency Probationers   307
11.2   Effective Types of Intervention and Estimated Effects on
         Recidivism   324
12.1   Assumptions of Retributive and Restorative Justice   337
12.2   Common Traits of Dispute Resolution   341
12.3   Restorative Justice Objectives, Practice, and Typical Location   345
12.4   Restorative Conferencing Models Administration and
         Process   346
12.5   Charges Accepted by Type of Restorative Conferencing
         Program   355
13.1   Estimated Personal Crime Victimization Rates for Youthful
         Age Groups, 2012   361
13.2   Victimization at Schools, 2012   362
13.3   Homicides of Youths at and away from School   363
13.4   Student Reports of Bullying at School, 2012   364
13.5   Students Reports of Cyberbullying, 2012   365
13.6   Number, Percent, and Rate of Child Maltreatment, 2012   367
13.7   Avoidance Responses of Students to Victimization and Fear
         in School, 2011   371
13.8   Outcomes of CASA Involvement   378
14.1   Selected State Legislative Responses to *Miller* Decision   411

Boxes

1.1   A Criminal Law Definition of Delinquency   3
1.2   A Status Offense Definition of Delinquency   3
1.3   Criticisms of the UCR   14
1.4   Short and Nye Self-reported Delinquency Items   19
1.5   National Youth Survey Items   20
1.6   Criticisms of Self-report Surveys   25
2.1   Major Milestones/Events/Dates in Juvenile Justice,
      1825–1899   33
2.2   Major Milestones/Events/Dates in Juvenile Justice,
      1900–Present   38
3.1   Physical Trait Explanations   57
3.2   Genetic Explanations   59
3.3   Biosocial Explanations   61
3.4   Psychoanalytic Explanations   67
3.5   Developmental Explanations   69
3.6   Psychological Learning Explanations   71
3.7   Personality Explanations   72
3.8   Mental Deficiency Explanations   75
4.1   Ecological Explanations   81
4.2   Social Learning Explanations   84
4.3   Subcultural Explanations   87
4.4   Routine Activities/Rational Choice Explanations   91
4.5   Strain Explanations   92
4.6   Social Control Explanations   96
4.7   Labeling Explanations   99
4.8   Integrative Explanations   101
5.1   G.R.E.A.T. Middle School Curriculum   134
6.1   NIDA's 13 Principles of Effective Treatment for Drug Abuse   153
6.2   NIDA's 16 Principles of Effective Prevention for Drug Abuse   157
6.3   911 Good Samaritan Law   161
6.4   National Drug Control Strategy   162

6.5	Juvenile Drug Court Strategies	164
7.1	Ban on Police Use of Tasers in Schools?	180
7.2	The U.S. Supreme Court on Deadly Force	181
7.3	Racial Profiling: Do Only Outcomes Matter?	194
7.4	Does the Officer's Race Matter?	195
7.5	Curfews and Proms	198
8.1	Model Juvenile Delinquency Act	210
8.2	Example of a Risk Assessment Instrument	212
8.3	Detention Rewards and Fines	213
8.4	The Intake Process	221
8.5	Automatic Transfer (Direct File): One State's Experience	224
8.6	The Results of One Transfer Decision: Rape and Death	226
8.7	Transfer in the First Juvenile Court: Cook County, Illinois	228
8.8	One Lawyer's Observations About Juvenile Court	231
8.9	Judges' Attitudes About Rehabilitation for Juveniles	241
8.10	Suggestions for Reducing the Effect of Race on Court Dispositions	241
9.1	Excerpts from Justice White's Dissent in *Ingraham v. Wright*	257
9.2	Excessive Discipline/Cruel and Unusual Punishment	258
9.3	Free Speech in Schools: Posting a Website	259
9.4	Lewd Speech in School	261
9.5	Censorship of Student Publications	262
9.6	Cyberbullying and Schools	263
9.7	Prayer at Graduation and at Football Games	264
9.8	Is the Good News Club Good for School?	266
9.9	Excerpts from the Brennan–Marshall Partial Concurrence–Partial Dissent in *New Jersey v. T.L.O.*	267
9.10	Parental Tracking of Teen Driving	274
10.1	Sample of One Training School's Rules	280
10.2	Typical Weekday Daily Schedule at a Residential Placement for Delinquents	281
10.3	Typical Institutional Point System	282
10.4	Daily Schedule for Offenders in a New York Boot Camp	284
10.5	Conditions at Cottage Blue: Much Ado About Nothing or Something?	292
10.6	Human Rights Watch: Girls in Custody in New York	293
11.1	To Register or Not to Register: The Question of Juvenile Sex Offenders	314
11.2	Supervision Fees: A New Direction?	316
11.3	Summary of Research Findings About Successful Correctional Interventions	325
11.4	A Contemporary Vision Statement for Juvenile Probation	333
12.1	Key Concerns with Restorative Justice	354

13.1   Major Types of Child Abuse and Neglect   366
13.2   Excerpts from Ohio's Guardian *Ad Litem* Statute   377
14.1   A Uniform Upper Age for Juvenile Court   385
14.2   Some Arguments Against Capital Punishment   407
14.3   An Argument in Favor of Capital Punishment   408
14.4   Majority and Dissenting Opinions in the *Roper* Case   409

Preface

For this eighth edition of *Juvenile Justice: An Introduction* we have updated materials. We have included the latest available statistics on juvenile crime and victimization, drug use, court processing, and corrections. The gangs chapter provides updated information on the gang problem as well as on responding to gangs and ganging in the community. The chapter on drugs notes the possible impact of drug legalization in some states. The police chapter now includes mention of the school-to-prison pipeline and notes other recent experience with school resource officers in schools. The due process chapter includes the most recent Supreme Court case on juvenile life without parole and material on cyber bullying and related free speech on the Internet. The probation chapter discusses two recent developments: the use of probation fees and a deterrence model (Project HOPE) and their implications for juvenile probation. The restorative justice chapter contains updated information of the growth of restorative practices and the impact of those practices on future offending. The futures chapter has a section on the new balance (rebalanced) model of juvenile court, discussion of the implications of the research on adolescent development, and discussion of the impact of the latest Supreme Court decision on life without parole for juveniles.

Each chapter has a section entitled "What You Need to Know." This is a list that summarizes key pieces of information. Along with the Key Terms list, this section should help students focus on the key concepts and information in each chapter. We have also included website information at key points in the text showing students where they can go to get the latest information from such sources as the FBI *Uniform Crime Reports* and the Office of Juvenile Justice and Delinquency Prevention.

As with previous editions, there is instructional material that is available on the publisher's website for the book. There we have materials for both the instructor and the student. These materials supplement the book and can be incorporated into regular class activities or can be used by the individual for study and further exploration. Some of these materials are directed specifically to the student, while others are for the instructor. We thank all of the people at Taylor & Francis (Anderson Publishing) for their support and hard work, and those who reviewed the book:

John Reece, Colorado Mesa University
Michele Bratina, Shippensburg University
Gordon Crews, Marshall University

We are especially grateful to Ellen Boyne, our editor, for her excellent work in editing and producing the book, and to Mickey Braswell for his continuing support.

JTW
SPL

CHAPTER 1

Introduction—The Definition and Extent of Delinquency

WHAT YOU NEED TO KNOW

- Delinquency can be defined in terms of criminal laws just like for adults; status offenses, which are applied only to youths; or sociological/criminological definitions, which take on a specific meaning depending on the interests of the individual or group studying delinquency.

- Defining delinquency requires one to define who is a juvenile. Most states outline minimum and maximum ages as well as exceptions in which the youth can be handled as an adult.

- Measures of delinquency include official records of the juvenile justice and criminal justice system and self-report surveys.

- According to the UCR, roughly 11 percent of all arrests are of youths under the age of 18, with one-quarter of all property arrests being of youths.

- Court and correctional statistics also provide insight to the extent of delinquency, although the magnitude of the problem appears much less due to the funneling effect of system involvement.

- Self-report measures reveal that virtually all youths offend, although this is true only when status offenses are included. Otherwise, the results are remarkably similar to official figures when serious crimes are considered.

- Regardless of the measure used, the trend in delinquency has been one of large increases since the 1960s with some leveling off and decreases since the late 1990s.

KEY TERMS

dark figure of crime

delinquency

Index crimes

juvenile

Monitoring the Future (MTF)

National Youth Survey (NYS)

offense rate

panel design

self-report measures

sexting

Short–Nye instrument

status offense

transfer

Uniform Crime Reports (UCR)

waiver

INTRODUCTION

Discussions of the juvenile justice system cannot proceed without a clear understanding of the behaviors that it is tasked to address. The juvenile court and the juvenile justice system are relatively recent inventions, tracing their history back to the late 1800s. Prior to that time, youths who broke the law were handled in the same system and in the same ways as adults. "Delinquency" was born in the late 1800s when crime and misbehavior by youths were redefined as separate and distinct from adult offenses, and new mechanisms of social control were developed to address problem children.

Youthful offenders, who used to be seen as simply young "criminals," have been transformed into "delinquents." The label of "delinquent," however, represents a variety of different behaviors and means different things at different places and points in time. It is important to understand the diversity in definitions of delinquency in order to examine the workings of the juvenile justice system adequately.

DEFINING DELINQUENCY

As already noted, **delinquency** has a number of different meanings. These various interpretations appear both in state statutes and criminological discussions of juvenile behavior. State statutes typically offer two sets of definitions for delinquency—a criminal law definition and a status offense definition. Beyond the codified legal definitions are social/criminological definitions that are used in research on juvenile misconduct.

Criminal Law Definitions

A criminal law definition of delinquency delineates activity that is illegal regardless of the age of the offender. "Delinquency" is simply a substitute label for criminal behavior by a juvenile. The only distinction between being a delinquent and being a criminal is the age of the individual.

Criminal law definitions of delinquency typically define a delinquent as someone who violates the criminal laws of the jurisdiction (see Box 1.1). The key to these statutes is the idea that a juvenile violated the criminal law. The fact that a juvenile committed the offense means that a different label will be imposed (delinquent versus criminal) and a different system will handle the individual (juvenile versus adult). A criminal law definition explicitly extends the criminal statutes to the juvenile population.

WEB ACTIVITY

You can go to your state's statutes and look up the definitions of "delinquency," "status offense," and "juvenile."

BOX 1.1 A CRIMINAL LAW DEFINITION OF DELINQUENCY

"Delinquent child" includes any of the following:

- Any child, except a juvenile traffic offender, who violates any law of this state or the United States, or any ordinance of a political subdivision of the state, that would be an offense if committed by an adult;
- Any child who violates any lawful order of the court;
- Any child who violates [prohibitions against purchasing or owning a firearm or handgun (Section 2321.211)];

- Any child who is a habitual truant and who previously has been adjudicated an unruly child for being a habitual truant;
- Any child who is a chronic truant.

Source: Ohio Revised Code (2008). Section 2152.02. Available at http://codes.ohio.gov/orc/2152

Status Offense Definitions

Besides criminal actions that can be committed by a juvenile, there are other behaviors for which only juveniles can be held accountable. This type of behavior is usually referred to as a **status offense** because it is only illegal if it is committed by persons of a particular "status." Thus, juvenile status offenses represent acts that are illegal only for juveniles. Adults who take part in these acts are not subject to sanctioning by the formal justice system.

While "status offender" is the most common term for those who violate these acts, a variety of other names are applied to these individuals. Among the more common names are "unruly," "dependent," and "incorrigible," as well as acronyms such as PINS (person in need of supervision) or CHINS (child in need of supervision). One common criticism of status offense definitions is that they are ambiguous, and the language is so vague that they allow wide latitude in interpreting what is and is not a violation (see Box 1.2). Such statutes allow the juvenile justice system to intervene in the life of almost any youth.

BOX 1.2 A STATUS OFFENSE DEFINITION OF DELINQUENCY

Ohio Chapter 2151.022 defines an "unruly child" as:

- Any child who does not submit to the reasonable control of the child's parents, teachers, guardian, or custodian, by reason of being wayward or habitually disobedient;
- Any child who is an habitual truant from school and who previously has not been adjudicated an unruly child for being an habitual truant;

- Any child who behaves in a manner as to injure or endanger the child's own health or morals or the health or morals of others;
- Any child who violates a law . . . that is applicable only to a child.

Source: Ohio Revised Code (2008). Section 2151.022. Available at http://codes.ohio.gov/orc/2151.022

The behaviors outlined by status offense statutes make virtually any behavior of a juvenile sanctionable by the state. The definitions are all-encompassing and have been criticized for being overly broad (see, e.g., the President's Commission on Law Enforcement and the Administration of Justice, 1967). Arguments for eliminating such overly broad language have resulted in some courts ruling that the statutory language, such as that referring to "leading an idle, dissolute, lewd, or immoral life," is unconstitutionally vague (*Gonzalez v. Mailliard*, 1971).

Actions that typically fall under the heading of status offenses include truancy; smoking; drinking; curfew violations; disobeying the orders of parents, teachers, or other adults; swearing; running away; and other acts that are allowable for adults. Most, if not all, juveniles violate these statutes at one time or another. Normal youthful behavior includes many of these activities. It is possible that all youths could be subjected to system intervention under these types of "status" definitions.

Social/Criminological Definitions

The study of delinquency and juvenile justice often relies on definitions of delinquency that do not conform precisely to the legal definitions of delinquent or status offenses. The definition of delinquency often takes on a specific meaning depending on the interests of the group or individual examining juvenile misconduct.

In one respect it is possible to define delinquency in terms of who is officially recognized as such. Cloward and Ohlin (1960), for example, define delinquent acts as those "that officials engaged in the administration of criminal justice select . . . from among many deviant acts, as forms of behavior proscribed by the approved norms of society" (Cloward & Ohlin, 1960:2–3). This means that the police, court officials, corrections officers, and others determine which actions are to be considered delinquent when they decide to take action. This limits delinquency to those actions that are handled by the justice system. Juvenile behavior that is ignored by the system is not to be considered delinquent.

Most definitions of delinquency present juvenile behavior as either delinquent or nondelinquent, with no middle ground. In reality, most individuals fall in between these extremes,

School-aged children are searched by a truancy task force in Richmond, Virginia, before being loaded into a van to be processed at the truant center. Truancy is a status offense, as it is a behavior for which only juveniles can be held accountable.

CREDIT: AP Photo/ *Richmond Times- Dispatch*, Don Long

having violated some laws and conformed to others. Most juveniles are involved, to varying degrees, in some form of delinquent behavior. Cavan and Ferdinand (1981) offer a continuum of behavior that ranges from extreme delinquency on one end to extreme "goodness" on the other (see Figure 1.1). The shape of the continuum, a bell curve, represents the proportional distribution of juveniles along the continuum. It is assumed that the largest group of youths would fall into the middle category of "normal conformity." The left-hand portion of the curve represent youths who run the risk of being apprehended and labeled delinquent. Minor underconformity may include such acts as status and victimless offenses while the delinquent contraculture category includes serious acts such as murder and rape and suggests organized involvement in deviance. The right side of the curve represents individuals who do not become involved in delinquency. Few juveniles appear in either of the "contraculture" categories of extreme delinquent or extreme goodness.

Today, most criminological research considers delinquency in terms of Cavan and Ferdinand's continuum. It does not limit the researcher to a simple legal definition or an either/or dichotomy. Instead, it allows the inspection of various types of delinquent activity as well as activity that is highly over-conforming. Seen as a continuum, juvenile activity can be subdivided into various parts and phases that change over time and can be compared to one another.

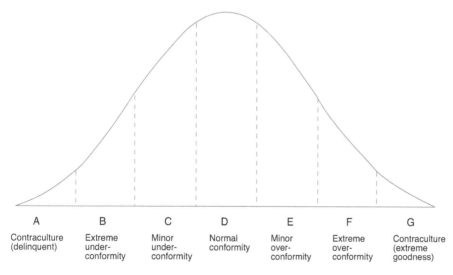

A	B	C	D	E	F	G
Contraculture (delinquent)	Extreme under-conformity	Minor under-conformity	Normal conformity	Minor over-conformity	Extreme over-conformity	Contraculture (extreme goodness)

FIGURE 1.1
Behavior Continuum

Source: Figure 2.1 from *Juvenile Delinquency* (4th ed.) by Ruth Shonle Cavan and Theodore N. Ferdinand. Copyright © 1981 by Ruth Shonle Cavan and Theodore N. Ferdinand. Reprinted by permission.

DEFINING A JUVENILE

In every definition of delinquency there is an implicit assumption of what constitutes a juvenile. Interestingly, the legal definition of a juvenile varies from jurisdiction to jurisdiction. This means that persons subject to the juvenile statutes in one location may not be in another place. The majority of states (40) and the District of Columbia recognize juveniles as individuals below the age of 18 (Butts & Roman, 2014). Eight states list the age of majority below age 17 and two states consider anyone under 16 as a juvenile. Under these ages the individual is considered a juvenile and is handled in the juvenile justice system.

Besides setting an upper age for juvenile status, other factors influence whether an individual can be handled in the juvenile justice system. Thirty-three states and the District of Columbia set no lower age limit for being subject to juvenile justice intervention. Eleven states set age 10 as the minimum for jurisdiction, three set age seven, two set age eight, and one sets age six. In those states with a lower age level, any juvenile below the minimum age who exhibits deviant behavior is simply returned to his or her parents or guardian for handling.

WEB ACTIVITY

The Office of Juvenile Justice and Delinquency Prevention's *Statistical Briefing Book* provides access to a wealth of data on juveniles, including juvenile justice jurisdiction. Investigate the criteria for your state using that information (http://www.OJJDP.gov/ojstatbb) or go to your state's statutes for this information.

A second age consideration is the termination of the juvenile system's intervention with an individual. Most state statutes allow the juvenile system to continue supervision and intervention with individuals who have passed the maximum age limit. Two-thirds of the states (32) set the maximum age at which juvenile court jurisdiction is relinquished at age 20. Four states allow jurisdiction until age 24. Maintaining jurisdiction occurs mainly when that person committed his or her act as a juvenile and/or is being handled as an extension of intervention begun when he or she was a juvenile.

A final factor influencing juvenile court jurisdiction involves **waiver** or **transfer** provisions that may send a youth to adult court. Waiver is a process by which an individual who is legally a juvenile is sent to the adult criminal system for disposition and handling. The minimum age for transfer varies from state to state, with 22 states setting no minimum age. The most common minimum age set is 14. The varying definitions of delinquency and the consideration of what age constitutes being a "juvenile" have a major impact on any study of juvenile justice. The definitions alter the type of behavior with which we are concerned, the practices and interventions used in the treatment of delinquency, and the number of problems and youths subjected to intervention and study. It is the effect of the definition of delinquency on the measurement of delinquency to which we now turn.

THE EXTENT OF DELINQUENCY

There are various ways to measure delinquency, each of which produces a different picture of the delinquency problem. The different methods for measuring delinquency result in different absolute levels of delinquency as well as different information on the offense, the offender, and the victim. The two basic approaches to measuring delinquency are the use of official records and the administration of self-report surveys.

Official Measures of Delinquency

Official measures of delinquency are based on the records of various justice system agencies. Consequently, the level of delinquency reflects both the activity of juveniles and the activity of the agency that is dealing with the youths. The degree of detail in the records also varies by agency. The police, courts, and corrections each have different sets of priorities and mandates under which they operate. As a result, the data compiled by the agencies differ from one another. The following pages will consider data from each of these official sources.

Uniform Crime Reports

The **Uniform Crime Reports (UCR)** provide information on the number of offenses coming to the attention of the police, the number of arrests police make, and the number of referrals by the police to the juvenile court. These data are collected yearly by the Federal Bureau of Investigation (FBI) and provide information on 29 categories of offenses. These counts reflect only crimes known to the police. Actions that are not reported to the police are not included in the yearly crime figures. The UCR is comprised of two offense subgroups. The first eight offenses, Part I or **Index crimes**, include murder, rape, robbery, aggravated assault, burglary, larceny, motor vehicle theft, and arson. All remaining offenses fall within the Part II category. It is within the Part II offense category that status offenses like running away and curfew violations appear. Extensive information, including demographic data on the victim and offender (if known), circumstances of the offense, the use of a weapon, and the time and place of the offense, is gathered for the Part I offenses. For Part II offenses, only information on offenses for which a suspect has been arrested are tabulated.

Age Distribution. Due to the fact that fewer than half of all violent crime and less than 20 percent of all property crimes were cleared by an arrest in 2012, and this is limited to the Part I offenses, little information is known about the offender in most crimes. (Table 1.1 provides data on clearances involving persons under age 18 for the Part I crimes.) Some idea about the participation of juveniles in delinquent/criminal behavior, however, can be gathered from an inspection of those cases in which a youthful offender can be identified

TABLE 1.1 Number of Offenses Cleared by Arrest or Exceptional Means

Percent of Clearances Involving Persons Under 18 Years of Age by Population Group, 2012

	Violent crime	Murder and nonnegligent manslaughter	Forcible rape	Robbery	Aggravated assault	Property crime	Burglary	Larceny-theft	Motor vehicle theft	Arson
Total clearances	442,506	7,384	26,474	76,985	331,663	1,383,878	215,979	1,096,464	71,435	9,253
Percent under 18	8.8	3.8	11.4	11.6	8.1	12.4	11.0	12.7	11.2	30.1

Source: Adapted by authors from FBI (2013).

and/or arrested. Table 1.2 presents arrest data for 2012. Roughly 9.5 million arrests were reported to the FBI. Of these arrests, 1,020,334, or 10.8 percent of the total, were of juveniles under the age of 18.

A closer inspection of the arrest data reveals the extent to which youths were involved in serious offending. For the violent crimes of murder, rape, robbery, and aggravated assault, youths comprised 12 percent of the total arrests. This represents more than 47,000 offenses. More striking is the fact that youths were arrested for over 230,000 property offenses. This reflects 18 percent of all property offense arrests in 2012. Taken by themselves, these figures are large. The problem is exacerbated, however, when you consider that youths between the ages of 10 and 17 (inclusive) make up less than 12 percent of the total U.S. population (U.S. Bureau of the Census, 2011). Youthful offenders are contributing more than their share to the level of arrests in the nation.

Sex Distribution. The UCR routinely presents breakdowns of crime by sex of the offender. UCR data for 2012 show that juvenile females made up 30 percent of all juvenile arrests, and 30 percent of female arrests were for Part I offenses. One-quarter of the juvenile male arrests were for Part I crimes. A much greater percentage of males are arrested for every Index offense category, as well as most Part II offenses. The only offense for which females are more often arrested is prostitution.

Race Distribution. The UCR also provides information on the race of juvenile arrestees. Table 1.2 presents data on arrests for white, black, Native American, and Asian/Pacific Island youths. White youths make two-thirds of all arrestees (65.2%), and account for roughly 47 percent of the Part I property crimes and 62 percent of the Part I personal offenses. Black youths, however, are greatly overrepresented in violent personal offenses (murder, rape, robbery, and aggravated assault). This overrepresentation of blacks in violent offenses (52%) is even more dramatic in light of the fact that blacks comprise roughly 15 percent of the youthful U.S. population (U.S. Bureau of the Census, 2011).

An examination of individual Part I offenses provides a more detailed look at the data. While a greater percentage of white youths commit every type of offense than blacks, except for murder and robbery, offending by black youths far surpasses their population representation for all Part I offenses. Arrests of black youths also exceed that of white youths in the Part II categories of prostitution and commercialized vice and gambling.

Trends in Delinquency. The trend in youthful crime has changed in recent years. The change in the number of violent offenses since 1988 appears in Figure 1.2. Arrests for both murder and rape have remained relatively stable, while

TABLE 1.2 Distribution of Juvenile Arrests, 2012

Offense Charged	Number			Percent of Juvenile Arrestees						
	All Ages	Under 18	Percent Under 18	Males	Females	White	Black	Am. Indian or Alaskan Native	Asian or Pacific Islander
Total	9,446,660	1,020,334	10.8	70.8	29.2	65.2	32.2	1.3	1.2
Murder and nonnegligent manslaughter	8,514	560	6.6	90.3	9.7	47.2	50.8	1.8	0.2
Forcible rape	13,971	1,954	14.0	98.6	1.4	64.1	33.9	1.1	0.9
Robbery	80,487	16,563	20.6	89.9	10.1	29.9	68.6	0.4	1.1
Aggravated assault	301,065	28,160	9.4	74.0	26.0	55.2	42.7	1.1	1.1
Burglary	220,284	42,075	19.1	88.1	11.9	59.1	38.8	0.9	1.2
Larceny-theft	1,000,496	175,261	17.5	58.1	41.9	62.2	34.6	1.4	1.8
Motor vehicle theft	53,244	10,185	19.1	84.5	15.5	57.9	39.3	1.4	1.3
Arson	8,882	3,282	37.0	86.0	14.0	73.5	24.8	0.6	1.1
Violent crimes	404,037	47,237	11.7	80.8	19.2	46.6	51.5	0.8	1.0
Property crimes	1,282,906	230,803	18.0	65.1	34.9	61.6	35.5	1.3	1.7
Other assaults	930,210	132,198	14.2	63.3	36.7	59.1	38.9	1.2	0.8
Forgery and counterfeiting	51,987	1,106	2.1	70.4	29.6	69.3	29.2	0.8	0.8
Fraud	118,374	3,610	3.0	67.1	32.9	58.0	39.1	1.6	1.3
Embezzlement	12,429	341	2.7	61.3	38.7	63.2	33.2	1.5	2.1

Stolen property	75,989	10,176	13.4	83.6	16.4	52.7	45.2	0.9	1.2
Vandalism	177,325	46,468	26.2	84.0	16.0	75.2	22.6	1.3	0.9
Weapons; carrying, possessing, etc.	115,464	18,856	16.3	90.5	9.5	61.4	36.4	0.6	1.5
Prostitution and commercialized vice	43,395	616	1.4	23.7	76.3	39.7	59.4	0.0	0.8
Sex offenses (except forcible rape)	52,768	9,570	18.1	89.9	10.1	71.5	26.4	1.0	1.1
Drug abuse violations	1,200,538	107,095	8.9	82.9	17.1	74.0	23.5	1.1	1.3
Gambling	5,976	732	12.2	94.1	5.9	10.6	88.4	0.1	0.8
Offenses against family and children	82,121	2,663	3.2	62.4	37.6	68.3	27.1	4.0	0.6
Driving under the influence	987,224	7,236	0.7	74.2	25.8	92.0	5.1	1.7	1.2
Liquor laws	341,328	62,611	18.3	60.2	39.8	88.5	7.0	3.1	1.5
Drunkenness	399,920	7,618	1.9	73.1	26.9	87.2	9.1	2.2	1.4
Disorderly conduct	422,382	92,017	21.8	64.7	35.3	56.0	42.0	1.2	0.7
Vagrancy	20,900	984	4.7	78.7	21.3	71.6	27.6	0.4	0.4
All other offenses	2,666,096	184,073	6.9	73.4	26.6	69.1	28.3	1.4	1.2
Suspicion	1,160	193	16.6	72.5	27.5	75.6	23.8	0.0	0.5
Curfew and loitering law violations	54,131	54,131	100.0	71.3	28.7	59.4	38.3	1.0	1.2

Source: Compiled by authors from FBI (2013).

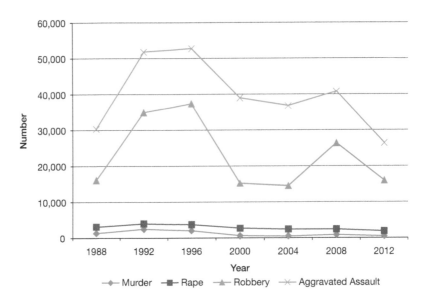

FIGURE 1.2
Trend in Juvenile Violent
Crime, 1988–2012

Source: Constructed by
authors from UCR data.

robbery and aggravated assault arrests increased from 1988 to 1996, dropped until 2004, rose until 2008, and dropped again over the following four years. Data on property crimes (see Figure 1.3) show general declines since 1988, except for a slight increase in 2008 for both larceny and burglary. Similar trends are evident when considering the **offense rate** (typically the number of offenses per 100,000), which eliminates the influence of any changes in the number of potential offenders on the delinquency data. One thing that is clear in both the raw number of arrests and the arrest rate figures is that official juvenile offending is higher today than 40 years ago, although the recent trend has been toward lower arrests.

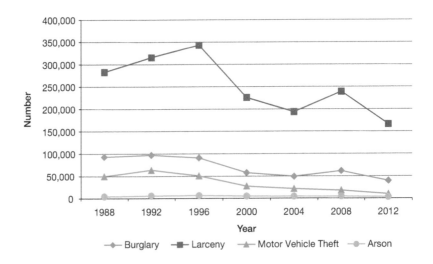

FIGURE 1.3
Trend in Juvenile Property
Crime, 1988–2012

Source: Constructed by
authors from UCR data.

A Critique of the UCR. The UCR is the longest running and most widely known and cited method of collecting information on crime in the United States. It began in 1931 and has continued on a yearly basis since that time. Despite this longevity and notoriety, the UCR has a number of flaws that must be considered when using the data (see O'Brien, 1985). The most frequent criticism is the fact that it reflects only those offenses known to the police. Many individuals, for whatever reason, opt not to contact the police when they are a victim or a witness to a crime. This failure to bring crimes to the attention of the police results in an under-count of crime in the United States. The unreported crimes are typically referred to as the **dark figure of crime**. In terms of juvenile behavior, the UCR focuses on more serious offending, since that is the focus of police activity, and it fails to consider the vast array of status offenses committed by youths.

A second concern with the UCR is that it is voluntary, and it relies on the individual agencies to report their data accurately. Each agency tabulates and forwards its own data to the FBI. Political and economic pressures have been known to influence the accuracy of counts submitted to the UCR system. For example, changes in police procedure due to political decisions can alter the amount of attention a police department pays to a certain form of crime. Similarly, the simple reclassification of offenses from one category to another (i.e., listing "rapes" as "other sex offenses," or "aggravated assaults" as "simple assaults") can alter the reported crime rates. Decisions like these can greatly alter the annual offense counts and have an impact on trend data over time.

Another concern in using the UCR is the lack of information on offenders in much of the data. UCR arrest data reflect only those offenders who were caught in the course of the crime or ensuing investigation. The fact that less than 20 percent of all crimes are cleared by an arrest means that little is known about the offenders in most crimes. It is possible that UCR figures are distorted in terms of the age, race, and sex distribution of the total offending population. The UCR provides no information about the offender in more than 80 percent of the crimes committed each year.

Another serious problem entails the fact that the UCR counts offenses and not offenders. It would be easy to claim that the number of offenders is equal to the number of reported offenses, but unfortunately, this would provide a highly inaccurate picture. Many offenders commit more than one offense over a period of time. Alternatively, some individuals may commit a single act (such as bank robbery) that legally constitutes more than one offense (robbery, assault, and possibly kidnapping). These problems make it difficult to estimate the number of offenders over any period of time using the UCR. The number of offenders is clearly not equal to the number of offenses.

BOX 1.3 CRITICISMS OF THE UCR

Dark Figure of Crime	Offenses that are not reported to the police and therefore are not reflected in UCR data
Voluntary	Agencies do not have to report their figures to the UCR and can manipulate the data that they do report
Limited Offender Data	Data available only on those offenders who are arrested; unable to know if those arrested are representative of all offenders
Focus on Offenses	Counts offenses and not offenders; fails to consider the fact that one offender can be responsible for multiple offenses
Changing Crime Definitions	Changes in the legal definitions of crimes over time and jurisdictions makes comparison of crime data difficult
Data Collection Techniques	There is a lack of knowledge on what impact changing methods for data collection (such as from hand to computers) can have on the data reports
System Bias	Impact of system policies on data collection is not clear

A variety of other concerns must be considered in using the UCR data. Among these are the fact that legal definitions of crime change over time and vary from place to place. In addition, the methods of data collection have changed over time (particularly from hand to computer tabulation). A further concern is the fact that any selective enforcement of the law or bias in making arrests can result in an overrepresentation of certain individuals (such as lower-class youths) in the UCR figures.

The most problematic aspect of official police data for the study of delinquency is the combined issues of the dark figure of crime and the failure to identify offenders in the vast majority of all cases. It is due to these problems that alternative methods of unofficial crime and delinquency data have been developed. Before turning to these types of data collection, we will look at two additional official measures of delinquency.

Juvenile Court Statistics

Juvenile court data present a picture of the cases and the juveniles who reach the adjudication stage of the system. The numbers of juveniles who appear in these records are smaller than those found in police data. This is due primarily to the fact that most juveniles reach the court through contact with the police who filter and screen cases. Relatively few youths are referred to court directly by their families, schools, or other associates. At the same time, court data offer more insight to status offending.

Table 1.3 presents data on delinquency cases in juvenile court. In 2010, more than 1.3 million youths reached the juvenile court for delinquent offenses. This translates into a rate of 43 out of every 1,000 youths. An additional 137,000

TABLE 1.3 Number and Rates of Youths in Juvenile Court

Offense Type	1985	1990	1995	2000	2005	2010
	Number of Offenses					
Delinquency						
Person	185,192	257,268	410,411	401,794	434,148	346,817
Property	708,964	780,648	919,958	705,803	612,707	502,440
Drugs	77,786	69,863	162,754	187,787	185,526	164,138
Public Order	196,614	232,998	333,441	413,952	446,889	354,756
Total	1,168,557	1,340,778	1,826,563	1,709,335	1,679,270	1,368,151
Offense Type	**Rate per 1,000 Population**					
Delinquency						
Person	7.0	10.0	14.3	13.1	13.5	11.0
Property	27.0	30.4	32.1	22.9	19.1	15.9
Drugs	3.0	2.7	5.7	6.1	5.8	5.2
Public Order	7.5	9.1	11.6	13.5	13.9	11.3
Total	44.4	52.3	63.7	55.6	52.3	43.4

Source: Constructed by authors from Sickmund, Sladky, and Kang (2013a) and OJJDP Statistical Briefing Book (2013).

youths reached the court for status offenses (a rate of roughly 4.3 per 1,000 youths). Information on type of offense, sex, and race is also available in the court statistics. The most prevalent form of offending is property crimes, followed by personal offenses and public order offenses (e.g., disorderly conduct and liquor law violations). Like the UCR data, males dominate throughout the juvenile court statistics.

The number of delinquency cases today far exceeds that of four decades ago. While the number of cases peaked in 1996–1997 and has fallen since that time, the number of cases increased from 1960 to 1996. The number of cases in 2010 remains more than three times that in 1960 (see Figure 1.4). In terms of sex, court numbers are dominated by male youths (72% of all petitions). While the trend in male data has been declining since 1996, female data have been level with a decrease only in the past year. Racial breakdowns show that whites make up roughly two-thirds of court cases, although the rate for black youths is almost two and a half times higher (87.6 compared to 36.4 per 1,000 youths). Blacks are clearly overrepresented in juvenile court. The rate for American Indians was 36.6 and for Asian youths it was 11.6 (Puzzanchera & Hockenberry, 2013).

FIGURE 1.4
Trend in Delinquency
Cases Since 1960

Source: *OJJDP Statistical
Briefing Book* (2013).

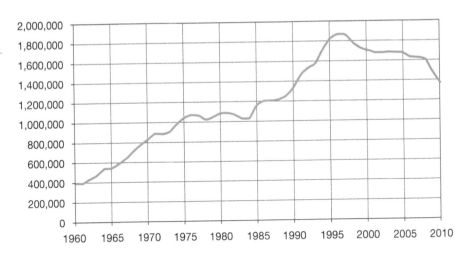

Juvenile Corrections Statistics

A third official source of information on juveniles coming into contact with the juvenile justice system is records kept on juvenile correctional facilities. The U.S. Justice Department routinely conducts a census of the population of juvenile facilities. As with juvenile court statistics, the numbers of youths who appear in these statistics are smaller than the UCR and court figures. Juvenile facilities rely heavily upon the juvenile court for their clients, and few of the youths coming into contact with the court are sentenced to confinement. Therefore, the figures found in data from juvenile facilities represent only a fraction of all the youths having contact with the juvenile system.

WEB ACTIVITY

Additional juvenile court statistics are available at http://www.ojjdp.gov/ojstatbb/ezajcs/asp/selection.asp

Table 1.4 presents data on youths in public and private juvenile facilities in 2011. The data in the table represent a one-day count, and the daily totals would vary around these figures. Public facilities handled more than 42,500 youths, and private institutions dealt with an additional 18,800 on any one day (Sickmund, Sladky, Kang, & Puzzanchera, 2013b). There are no differences between types of facilities in terms of sex of juveniles held, while private facilities handle a larger percentage of whites and a lower percentage of Hispanics. Few differences appear in the reason for admission when comparing public and private institutions. Each type of institution handles roughly the same proportion of youths committing different types of offenses. The only significant difference appears in status offenses, where 18 percent of the youths in private institutions are there for these violations, compared with only 2 percent of the youths in public facilities.

TABLE 1.4 Characteristics of Juveniles in Correctional Facilities: Average One-Day Count—2011				
Characteristic	Public Facility		Private Facility	
Number of Juveniles	42,584		18,839	
Sex:				
Males	36,975	(87%)	16,104	(86%)
Females	5,609	(13%)	2,735	(14%)
Race:				
White	12,783	(35%)	7,144	(44%)
Black	16,505	(45%)	8,069	(50%)
Hispanic	11,414	(31%)	2,559	(16%)
Other	1,882	(5%)	1,067	(7%)
Reason for Admission:				
Person Offense	16,650	(39%)	6,314	(34%)
Property Offense	10,352	(24%)	4,353	(23%)
Drug Offense	2,453	(6%)	1,862	(10%)
Public Order Offense	5,058	(12%)	2,259	(12%)
Status Offense	785	(2%)	1,454	(8%)
Technical Violation	7,286	(17%)	2,597	(14%)

Source: Compiled by authors from Sickmund *et al.* (2013b).

Not unlike UCR or court statistics, correctional figures show that most offenders are male. Females make up only 14 percent of the institutionalized youths. In terms of types of offenses, males greatly outnumber females for every category except status offenses, where females make up 40 percent of those in custody (Sickmund et al., 2013b). The racial breakdown for youths reveals that blacks are committed to a facility more often than any other group. Indeed, 40 percent of all committed youths are black, followed by whites (32%), Hispanics (23%), and all other racial/ethnic groups (Sickmund et al., 2013b).

The trend in correctional figures is somewhat interesting. Figures indicate that the number of incarcerated youths steadily increased from 1983 to 1999, with steady reductions since. The one-day count of youths in public and private facilities increased from 80,091 in 1983 to 99,008 in 1993 (a 24% increase) to 120,563 in 1999 (a further 22% increase), although the number decreased by 43 percent to 68,815 in 2011. The earlier increases may be due to the increased violence and drug problems in the late 1980s and early 1990s. Recent moderation in incarceration mirrors the reduction in arrest statistics.

Summary of Official Statistics

Each of the various official measures of delinquency presents a slightly different view of juvenile offending. In terms of numbers of offenses, the UCR presents

WEB ACTIVITY

Correctional data are available at
www.ojjdp.gov/ojstatbb/ezacjrp

the most disturbing picture due to the large numbers of offenses it reflects. In addition to the number of offenses, the UCR provides detailed information on a variety of demographic and crime-related characteristics. Unfortunately, as noted earlier, this source of data has a number of inherent defects that limit its usefulness, in particular its reliance upon offenses known to the police.

Juvenile court statistics and correctional facility data also present a picture of juvenile misconduct that is somewhat narrow. A large part of the problem with these figures lies in the fact that they are greatly dependent on the productivity of the police. Most youths entering the courts and institutions initiate their journey by way of police contact. Any failure at the police level, therefore, carries over to these other counts. The increased levels of status offenses in court and correctional data is one point where discrepancies with the arrest data appear. This is probably due to court referrals from sources other than the police. The problems and differences do not make the information useless, though. Rather, the data can be used to assess the workings of the institutions over time and provide insight into the juvenile system. They cannot be used to portray the extent of the juvenile crime problem accurately.

Self-Report Measures of Delinquency

Self-report measures attempt to gauge the level of delinquency by asking individuals to tell of their participation in deviant activity. This approach has a number of advantages. First, it is possible to measure both actions "known to the police" and those that are not known by official agents of social control. Second, it becomes possible to gather information on all offenders and not just those few who are arrested for an offense. Self-reports do not need an arrest in order to have information on the perpetrator. Third, self-report surveys can ask a variety of questions designed to elicit information useful in understanding why an individual violates the law. Information routinely collected includes data on family background (such as broken home, parental affection), economic status (occupation, income), education, attitudes (toward school, family, or work), friends' behavior, and others, as well as direct questions about the individual's behavior. This type of information is not available from most official delinquency measures. For these and other reasons, self-report methods have proliferated in recent years.

Self-report surveys have a fairly long history in juvenile justice. One of the earliest surveys was developed by James Short and Ivan Nye (1958; see Box 1.4). This survey asked youths to note the frequency with which they committed each of 23 items. The items in the scale were dominated by status and minor offenses. The few serious crimes included in the original list (such as stealing

BOX 1.4 SHORT AND NYE SELF-REPORTED DELINQUENCY ITEMS

- Defied parents' authority*
- Driven too fast or recklessly
- Taken little things (worth less than $2) that did not belong to you*
- Taken things of medium value ($2–$50)
- Taken things of large value ($50)
- Used force (strong-arm methods) to get money from another person
- Taken part in "gang fights"
- Taken a car for a ride without the owner's knowledge
- Bought or drank beer, wine, or liquor (including drinking at home)*
- Bought or drank beer, wine, or liquor (outside your home)

- Drank beer, wine, or liquor in your own home
- Deliberate property damage*
- Used or sold narcotic drugs
- Had sex relations with another person of the same sex (not masturbation)*
- Had sex relations with a person of the opposite sex
- Gone hunting or fishing without a license (or violated other game laws)
- Taken things you didn't want
- "Beat up" on kids who hadn't done anything to you
- Hurt someone to see them squirm

---

* Commonly used items in self-report surveys

Source: Short and Nye (1958).

over $50) were deleted in subsequent forms of the scales, which included only seven items.

Self-report scales like the **Short–Nye instrument** invariably uncover a great deal of delinquent activity. Indeed, various studies using these types of scales show that virtually every person is a delinquent. This is due to the fact that it is hard to conceive of anyone saying they never committed any of the behaviors asked, particularly the status offenses. Defying parental authority or trying alcohol at some time are rather universal activities by juveniles. Asking if the individual has "ever" committed an act contributes to the high levels of positive responses. Compared to official counts of delinquency, such self-reports show a great deal more deviance.

Criticism of early self-report surveys, particularly due to their focus on minor activities and their exclusion of major delinquent/criminal offenses, prompted some researchers to develop surveys that more closely mirrored actions covered in the UCR. Two of these early surveys were the **Monitoring the Future (MTF)** survey (started in 1975) and the **National Youth Survey (NYS)** (started in 1976). Both of these include many more serious offenses and elicit significantly fewer positive responses. These surveys include questions on hitting teachers, group fighting, use of weapons, robbery, and aggravated assault.

The NYS used a **panel design**, beginning with a group of 11- to 17-year-olds from across the United States. A panel design means that the same set of individuals are interviewed repeatedly over a period of time. In the case of the

---

BOX 1.5 NATIONAL YOUTH SURVEY ITEMS

Aggravated assault	Theft between $5 and $50	Skipped class
Sexual assault	Joyriding	Lied about age
Gang fights	Damaged family property	Had sexual intercourse
Hit teacher	Damaged school property	Cheated on school test
Hit parent	Damaged other property	Stole at school
Hit student	Drug use	Thrown objects
Strong-armed robbery of student	Prostitution	Carried hidden weapon
Strong-armed robbery of teachers	Drug sales	Stole from family
Strong-armed robbery of others	Hitchhiked	Threatened physical violence for sex
Stole motor vehicle	Disorderly conduct	Pressured someone for sex
Stole something over $50	Public drunkenness	Credit card fraud
Broke into building or vehicle	Panhandled	Used checks illegally
Bought stolen goods	Made obscene phone calls	Fraud
Theft under $5	Runaway	Arson

Source: K. M. Jamieson and T. Flanagan (1987) *Sourcebook of Criminal Justice Statistics*. Washington, D.C.: Department of Justice.

NYS, this was over a number of years. This allowed researchers to compare the number of offenses and changes in offending over time. Today, the NYS is called the NYS Family Study (NYSFS) and the subjects are now age 39–45. Consequently, current NYSFS results reflect adult and not youthful behavior for the original subjects. (A list of the kinds of behaviors probed by the NYS can be found in Box 1.5.)

The MTF project surveys a national sample of youths and young adults each year. At its initiation, the project surveyed 12th graders each year. In 1991, the survey was expanded to include 8th and 10th graders and young adults. The MTF focuses primarily on drug use, although it also probes delinquent behavior. While different respondents participate each year, it is possible to examine general trends and changes over time.

These and other self-report surveys find high levels of delinquency when minor and less serious behaviors are considered, but show reduced levels of serious offenses and behaviors. Interestingly, self-report surveys such as the NYS and MTF uncover much less offending. This is due to the inclusion of more serious offenses such as using a knife or gun in a robbery or hitting a teacher. Alternatively, items like arguing with your parents elicit much higher levels of behavior. Table 1.5 presents results for high school seniors in the 2011 MTF data. Only 3 percent report ever using a weapon to steal something, while 85 percent admit to arguing or fighting with parents. The data reveal similar levels

TABLE 1.5 Monitoring the Future, 2011

	Total	Sex		Race	
		Male	Female	White	Black
Argued or had a fight with either of your parents					
Not at all	14.7	16.6	11.9	11.2	23.9
5 or more times	37.5	37.1	39.5	9.5	27.4
Hit an instructor or supervisor					
Not at all	97.2	96.0	99.1	98.4	92.6
5 or more times	0.5	0.9	0.1	0.1	2.4
Gotten into a serious fight in school or at work					
Not at all	88.7	85.6	92.7	89.6	87.0
5 or more times	0.7	0.9	0.4	0.4	1.7
Taken part in a fight where a group of your friends were against another group					
Not at all	83.8	81.8	87.0	84.8	79.1
5 or more times	1.2	1.6	0.7	1.3	0.9
Hurt someone badly enough to need bandages or a doctor					
Not at all	87.1	81.0	95.1	88.8	86.3
5 or more times	1.5	2.8	0.2	1.1	1.8
Used a knife or gun or some other thing (like a club) to get something from a person					
Not at all	97.0	95.7	99.0	98.0	93.1
5 or more times	0.5	0.6	0.1	0.4	1.4
Taken something not belonging to you worth under $50					
Not at all	74.6	68.9	81.2	76.2	74.8
5 or more times	4.1	6.0	2.1	3.5	3.1
Taken something not belonging to you worth over $50					
Not at all	91.0	87.5	95.5	92.6	89.2
5 or more times	1.4	2.0	0.9	1.0	2.1
Taken something from a store without paying for it					
Not at all	76.1	75.3	78.0	79.1	71.8
5 or more times	4.7	5.9	3.6	4.0	5.5
Taken a car that didn't belong to someone in your family without permission of the owner					
Not at all	96.1	95.0	97.3	97.0	92.1
5 or more times	0.7	1.0	0.3	0.4	2.2

TABLE 1.5 *continued*		Sex		Race	
	Total	Male	Female	White	Black
Taken part of a car without permission of the owner					
Not at all	96.5	95.0	98.4	97.0	93.3
5 or more times	0.7	1.2	0.1	0.7	1.6
Gone into some house or building when you weren't supposed to be there					
Not at all	75.9	70.6	81.8	75.7	76.8
5 or more times	3.3	4.5	1.9	2.7	3.9
Set fire to someone's property on purpose					
Not at all	97.1	95.9	98.9	97.5	94.1
5 or more times	0.5	0.6	0.3	0.5	0.5
Damaged school property on purpose					
Not at all	88.9	84.4	94.2	90.1	86.5
5 or more times	1.6	2.3	0.7	1.5	0.1
Damaged property at work on purpose					
Not at all	96.3	94.2	98.8	96.4	95.2
5 or more times	0.8	1.1	0.2	0.4	0.9
Been arrested and taken to a police station					
Not at all	92.1	89.2	95.6	93.4	88.2
5 or more times	1.0	1.4	0.3	0.5	1.8

Source: Compiled by authors from Johnston, Bachman, and O'Malley (2013).

WEB ACTIVITY

Data from *Monitoring the Future* can be found at the MTF website at http://www.monitoringthefuture.org/pubs.html#refvols

of offending for males and females in most categories. Most racial breakdowns also reveal similar offense patterns.

Official and Self-report Comparisons

Self-report data show that, although many persons commit various deviant acts, the majority of subjects confine their activity to minor offenses. Indeed, when major, serious offenses are included, there is a great decrease in the level of reported offending. The figures become much more similar to those in official statistics.

The age distribution of offending in self-report data generally mirrors that of official data. Offending increases as individuals reach later teen and young adult years. Some variation emerges when the content of the self-report survey changes. Younger respondents tend to report less offending when serious offenses (such as aggravated assault and felony theft) are considered. Older youths report more serious offending and substance use. Unlike in official data, most differences in offending by race are modest in size. Data from the MTF project show only minor variation between black respondents and white respondents.

Self-report surveys display sex differences similar to those found in official data. Almost without exception, males report higher involvement in offending than females, although the differences are dependent on the type of behavior.

New Directions from Self-Reports

Self-report studies paint a different picture of offending compared to official figures. These methods also provide a means of examining youthful behavior that does not always draw the attention of the formal social control agencies, at least initially. Asking youths about their lives and behaviors can open up new avenues for exploration.

One major new topic receiving attention is **sexting**. Lounsbury, Mitchell, and Finkelhor (2011) note that sexting definitions include an array of behaviors. At the most basic level, sexting involves the transmission of sexual images across an electronic medium. The typical assumption is that this is by a cell phone, although it can be by e-mail, social networks, on-line postings, faxing, or any electronic means. What makes it explicitly problematic is when it is done by or involves juveniles. This does not require that the sexual images are of the individual. Indeed, they can be of some other person and are simply forwarded from person to person. The Youth Online Safety Working Group [YOSWG] (2009) defines sexting as "the sending of sexually explicit texts or nude or partially nude images of minors by minors."

Sexting has become a key topic of discussion in recent years, largely due to national news stories on the topic. Estimates of the extent of sexting vary greatly based on the definition and methods used in the analyses. Most data on sexting relies on surveys of youths. These surveys are usually a combination of a self-report survey on the extent to which respondents report being involved in sexting and a victimization survey where respondents are asked if they have been the target of sexting. Based on self-report survey data, one study reports that almost 4 out of 10 youths claim to have sent sexually suggestive messages, while almost 20 percent had been involved in transmitting sexually oriented pictures (National Campaign to Prevent Teen and Unplanned Pregnancy, 2009). Other surveys have reported sexting by only 4 percent of the respondents, and still others place the behavior as high as 40 percent and more by sexually active teens (Jolicoeur & Zedlewski, 2010). Higher estimates typically reflect older respondents and those who are more sexually active, while lower figures reflect data on younger juveniles. Females are more often the subject of sexting and report receiving more sexts than males.

The problem of sexting is multi-faceted. The first concern is the blatant transmission of pornographic images, especially those involving children. The fact that it is being done by children and that they see no problem with this activity is a major concern. A second related concern is the use of such transmissions as a form of bullying between youths. The accompanying shame and embarrassment, along with the bullying, has led to suicide, attempted suicide, and assaultive reactions. These topics have been the focus of several national media reports. A third concern is the fact that sexting is not easy for parents, teachers, and the juvenile justice system to see. It is an action that is easily hidden and, therefore, difficult to identify and address. In many jurisdictions there is no clear legal definition of sexting, which makes it difficult to address except under laws defining pornography (Jolicoeur & Zedlewski, 2010). The juvenile justice system must therefore utilize options not initially meant for this type of behavior between youths.

Critique of Self-Report Data

Self-report data pose separate problems for researchers. The most common concern with self-report data involves the truthfulness of the respondents. Interestingly, most investigations into the validity of the self-report data show that the figures are fairly accurate. This assessment is based on studies that compare self-report results to lie-detector tests, repeated measures, and cross checks with other forms of data (Clarke & Tifft, 1966; Gold, 1970; Hardt & Peterson-Hardt, 1977; Hindelang, Hirschi, & Weis, 1981; Lab & Allen, 1984). The greatest discrepancies between self-report and official figures can be attributed to the different domains of behavior that are tapped by the two methods. Official records focus more on serious offenses, while self-reports often probe more minor offending.

An additional shortcoming of self-report data is the focus on juveniles. Due to the problems of locating accessible groups of adults, most self-report research has been carried out on youths. Although the data are rich with information on kids, there is little opportunity to compare the findings to those found on adults. Typical adult samples found in self-report surveys deal with institutionalized adults or young adults in college settings. Neither of these two groups are representative of the general adult population. The method of selecting youths for self-report surveys may also bias the results. The typical use of school students in surveys may inadvertently miss high-rate offenders who are truants or dropouts and not present at the time of data collection.

Despite these shortcomings/concerns, there are great advantages to using self-report data. First, these data provide information on offenses not known by the police. Second, the method is able to probe the number of times each individual commits an offense. Much official data (especially police records) are not readily set up to track an individual over time. Self-reports, however,

BOX 1.6 CRITICISMS OF SELF-REPORT SURVEYS

Truthfulness	Respondents can falsify their answers, although research shows high levels of accuracy when checks can be made
Limited Respondents	Mostly youthful respondents; lack of adult respondents
Representativeness	Miss different groups in society, such as youths not in school, adults not in college; use of institutionalized populations not representative
Limited Domains	Focus on minor crimes; miss major offenses
Non-Systematic	With a few notable exceptions, self-reports are one-shot studies and there are no repeats against which to compare the results

can simply ask about the number and frequency of offending. Third, self-report surveys often ask a variety of questions about the individual's background, which provides a rich base of information on the demographic and social factors related to delinquent activity. Finally, the richness of the data allows for a more complete discussion of the reasons why an individual acts in a certain way than the data found in official records.

Comparing the Delinquency Measures

The different types of delinquency measures (official and self-report) show both similarities and differences. In general, they show that delinquency is a widespread problem. It is not restricted to any one group, area, or type of offense. The level of offending increased throughout the 1960s and early 1970s, leveled off and showed some decreases in the late 1970s and 1980s, increased in the late 1980s and early 1990s (particularly in serious personal offenses), and has been generally decreasing since 1999. There is a clear diversity in offending. Youths are involved in all types of behavior—from status offenses to serious personal crimes. Property crimes dominate in all measures, and personal offenses are the least common.

The differences between the measures are a result of the measurement techniques. Official records provide an ongoing look at the level and change in delinquency from year to year according to the formal justice system. These records reflect offenses that are brought to the attention of the authorities. Actions that are not reported but are withheld from public officials are lost to these records. Self-reports typically portray a larger delinquency problem than official figures. The cause of this is the type of activities that are probed in the survey. Surveys that inquire about minor status offenses will always find high delinquency levels. When more serious offenses form the core of the questionnaire, however, the number of delinquents falls to lower levels.

Most differences in the measures appear in the relative magnitude of offending and by offending subgroups in the population. Self-report measures uncover more offending than official measures. Official measures themselves differ in magnitude, with police figures leading court and correctional data. In terms of demographics, official figures show a much larger number of minority black offenders than self-report measures. Self-report statistics find little racial difference in offending. Similar discrepancies emerge when considering the sex of the offenders. While males dominate in magnitude of offending, official figures show the sexes committing different types of offenses. Self-report data, however, tend to portray the sexes as participating in the same types of behavior.

No single method of measuring delinquency should be considered better than the others. The usefulness of the measures depends entirely on the question that is being answered. Each method provides a different set of information about delinquency. Official records are useful for noting change in official processing and handling of youths over time. They also provide a long-term set of data that allows the inspection of changes over time. Official data are also rich in information about various demographic and offense factors not found in other measures. Self-reports provide a measure of delinquency based on the offender's viewpoint. They are capable of addressing behaviors that may not result in arrests and lead to official records. These measures are rich in data on minor crimes, the number of offenses an individual commits, demographics on offenders, and why an individual acts in a certain way.

SUMMARY

The study of delinquency depends heavily on the definition of delinquency and the measurement of the problem. The definition is not clear-cut and varies greatly from one study to another. Delinquency can be limited to those acts that are violations of the criminal code, signify those actions that are illegal only for juveniles, represent some combination of both criminal and status offenses, or be molded to fit the criminological question of each researcher.

The outcome of this search for a definition of delinquency is a vast array of different measures of delinquency and resultant claims about the level of delinquent activity. The major methods of measuring delinquency—official and self-report—rely on somewhat different conceptions of what constitutes delinquency. The UCR, for example, is oriented more toward a criminal law point of view and considers only two very broad status offense categories (runaway, curfew, and loitering) among the 29 offense categories. Conversely, self-reports often rely heavily on status offenses in their surveys and include only a few (mostly property) criminal offenses. Throughout this great confusion of definitions and measures there is no clear sign of arriving at a consensus on the issues.

Perhaps the reason behind the great discrepancies in definitions and measures can be found in the history of juvenile justice. The juvenile system has grown quickly over the past century and has seen many changes. Part of this is due to changes in the view society holds of youthful offenders. It may also be attributable to changes in the field of criminology and corrections. The changes in the juvenile system and the impact of various factors on the definition and extent of delinquency make up the substance for the next chapter on the history of juvenile justice.

DISCUSSION QUESTIONS

1. You have been appointed to write a definition of delinquency for the state legislature. You can either propose a new definition or rely on the existing definition. What is your definition? Why is it best, and why should it be accepted?

2. You have been asked to research each of the following questions or issues. What type of delinquency measure(s) will you use and why?

   • How much delinquency is there in the country?

   • What characterizes the typical juvenile offender?

   • Has the delinquency rate increased or decreased over the past 15 years?

3. A discussion has arisen over the best measure of delinquency. As an expert on such matters, you are asked to present an unbiased view of the strengths and weaknesses of official and self-report measures. Be as thorough as possible.

CHAPTER 2

The History of Juvenile Justice

WHAT YOU NEED TO KNOW

- Throughout most of history, youthful offenders were handled under the same laws and system as adults.
- The early institutions for handling juveniles (houses of refuge and reformatories) emerged in the 1800s as an outgrowth of concern over poverty and the need to train youths to be productive members of society.
- The first recognized juvenile court was in Cook County, Illinois, in 1899 with a focus on helping youths and not punishment.
- *Parens patriae* became the philosophical basis for the new juvenile court with a focus on handling youths as parents would handle their children.
- The early court cases of *Ex parte Crouse* and *Commonwealth v. Fisher* affirmed the right of the state to intervene in a child's life even if the parents objected.
- Platt and others argue that the juvenile court was not developed solely out of the benevolent intentions of those involved, rather it was developed as a tool of capitalism to ensure a complacent work force.
- Today, juvenile courts operate under a number of different rationales besides *parens patriae*, including punishment, deterrence, child welfare, restorative justice, and rehabilitation.

KEY TERMS

abandonment
apprenticeship
Bridewell Institution
Chancery Court
child savers
Commonwealth v. Fisher
cottages
dowry
Due Process Period
Ex parte Crouse
houses of refuge
infanticide
involuntary servitude
Kent v. United States
Lancaster State Industrial School for Girls
Lyman School for Boys
nullification
parens patriae
People v. Turner
probation
Punitive Period
right to intervention
wet-nursing

INTRODUCTION

There is no question that juvenile misbehavior is a major concern in modern American society. No matter which definition of delinquency or which form of measurement is used, the level of delinquent activity is high. Any understanding of the juvenile justice system must begin with an analysis of delinquency in a historical framework. Interestingly, the history of juvenile delinquency and juvenile justice is a relatively short one. While deviance on the part of young persons has always been a fact of life, societal intervention and participation in the handling of juvenile transgressors has gained most of its momentum in the last 100–150 years. This chapter will discuss the state of affairs leading to the development of a juvenile justice system and briefly examine the early workings of that system.

PROPERTY AND PERSON

An understanding of the development of juvenile justice must begin with an understanding of the place of children in society. Throughout most of history, there was no such status as "child." Youthful members of society did not enjoy a separate status that brought with it a distinct set of expectations, behaviors, and/or privileges. Rather, the young were considered either property or people. The very young, from birth to age five or six, held much the same status as any other property in society. They were subject to the same dictates as other property—bought, sold, and disposed of according to the needs of the owner. Once the individual reached the age of five or six, he or she became a full-fledged member of society and was expected to act according to the same mandates placed on all "adult" members of society (Aries, 1962).

The state of indifference toward the young and the absence of any separate status are easy to understand within a historical setting. First, the life expectancy of the average person was short. More importantly, the infant mortality rate exceeded 50 percent. The failure to develop a personal, caring attitude for infants, therefore, can be viewed as a defense mechanism. Indifference reduced or eliminated the pain and sorrow that would accompany the loss of the infant. A second explanation for the lack of concern over the young entailed the inability of many families to provide for the young. Families lived from day to day on what they could produce. Each child represented an increased burden to the already overburdened family.

The inability to provide economically for a child led to a variety of practices. **Infanticide**, or the killing of young children, was a common response to the appearance of an unwanted and demanding child prior to the fourth century (and continued in some places into the fourteenth century) (Mause, 1974). Mothers would kill their young in order to alleviate the future needs of providing for the child. The great chances that the infant would die anyway from disease or illness made this practice easier for the parents.

The killing of female offspring was especially prominent. Females were considered more burdensome than males. This was because they would not be as productive as a male if they lived and because of the **dowry** practice. The marriage of a daughter often necessitated the provision of goods by the female's family to the groom. The basic rationale was that the groom and his family were assuming the burden of caring for a marginally productive female. The dowry practice was especially problematic for the poor, who could not provide a sufficient enticement for a prospective husband. The killing of a female infant, therefore, not only removed the immediate needs of caring for the infant but also eliminated the future need of a dowry.

A practice similar to infanticide was **abandonment**. Parents would abandon their children to die for the same reasons underlying infanticide. Abandonment grew to be the more acceptable practice in the fourth to thirteenth centuries and appeared as late as the seventeenth and eighteenth centuries. Infanticide and abandonment were not restricted to the poor members of society. Historical records show that even the affluent accepted the killing of infants. One prime example of this is the story of Oedipus the king. Oedipus, the son of the Greek king and queen, was destined to kill his father and marry his mother. In order to avoid this fate, the parents had the infant Oedipus bound at the ankles, taken to the mountains, and abandoned.

Another method that appeared for handling youths was **wet-nursing**. A wet-nurse was a surrogate mother paid to care for a child (Mause, 1974). Wealthy families would hire other women to raise their children until they had reached the stage of "adulthood," at which time the child would return and assume a productive role in the family. Poor women, who assumed the role of wet nurses, would kill their natural offspring in order to save their mother's milk for the "paying" youths. The arrangement served a monetary purpose for the poor while relieving the wealthy of an unwanted responsibility.

Children who survived the first few years of life became subjected to a new set of activities. These new actions, however, retained the economic concerns that allowed for infanticide and other practices. The inability to provide for the needs of the family prompted the development of **involuntary servitude** and **apprenticeship** for the young. In essence, these actions were nothing more than the sale of youths by the family. The father, by selling the children, accomplished two things. First, he alleviated the burden of having to feed and clothe the person. Second, he gained something of "greater" value in return—money, a farm animal, food, or some other necessity of life. Such practices also were promoted as a means of providing labor for those in need. The rise of industrialization created a need for skilled labor, which could be learned by children through apprenticeships.

A second set of reasons behind the apprenticeship and servitude of youths was the general view that individuals who survived the years of infancy were simply "little adults." Indeed, children participated in the same activities as adults. Children worked at trades, drank alcohol, dueled, and participated in sex with adults and other young people. Part of this can be attributed to the lack of distinct expectations for youths. There was no period of schooling or education that separated the young from the actions of adults. Additionally, the living conditions of the family placed all ages within the same set of social conditions. The family home was typically a single room used for all activities. Eating, sleeping, and entertaining occurred in the same place and in view of everyone. The youthful members of society, therefore, learned and participated early in life.

The general view that children were the same as adults extended to the realm of legal sanctioning. Children were viewed as adults and were subject to the same rules and regulations as adults (Empey, 1982). There did not exist a separate system for dealing with youthful offenders. At best, the father was responsible for controlling the child and his choices for punishment had no bounds. Additionally, society could sanction youths in the same way as adults. The law made no distinction based on the age of the offender. In fact, youths could be (and were) sentenced to death for various deviant actions. While the law allowed for and prescribed harsh punishments, there is some question as to how frequently the more serious actions were actually used. Platt (1977) suggested that, while many youths could be sentenced to death, few received such a sentence, and most of those who did were never put to death. Similarly, Faust and Brantingham (1979) claimed that a process of nullification, or refusal to enforce the law against children, took place because of the lack of penalties geared specifically for juvenile offenders.

Throughout most of history, children held no special status in society. They did not receive any special, protected treatment. If anything, they were subjected to harsher treatment than adults. In terms of legal proscriptions, children could be held liable for the same actions and in the same fashion as adults. There was no legal term of "delinquency" under which the state could intervene with youths. Youths fell under the same statutes and guidelines that were used with adult offenders.

The concept of childhood began to emerge in the sixteenth and seventeenth centuries. It was during this time that medical advancements brought about a lengthening of the life expectancy of youths. Youths also began to be viewed as different from adults. They were in need of protection, assistance, and guidance in order to grow up uncorrupted by the world. This movement was led by clergy and scholars of the time. These leaders saw the young as a source of attack on the immoral and sinful aspects of society. Youths, who were not yet corrupted, had to be shielded from society and trained for their future role in the world. Children were seen as a catalyst for general social change. Childhood came to be seen as a period of time during which the young could receive an education and moral training without the pressures of adulthood.

Accompanying these changes were alterations in how youthful offenders should be disciplined. Responses to misbehavior began to be tailored to fit the age of the offender. In England, youths under the age of seven could not be held responsible for their actions, individuals between 8 and 14 could be held responsible only when it could be shown they understood the consequences of their actions, and youths age 14 and over were considered adults (Empey, 1982). While these types of changes began to recognize the difference between juveniles and adults, the actions taken against offenders remained the same, regardless of the age of the offender.

THE RISE OF JUVENILE INSTITUTIONS

Changes in the methods of dealing with problem youths corresponded to the changes occurring in American society of the early 1800s. During this time, there was a great movement toward the cities. Industrialization was drawing families out of the countryside and to the cities. The cities were growing in both size and density. In addition, the individuals moving to the cities brought with them a variety of outlooks and ideas. This growing diversity in the population was especially true of the cities in the United States, which were attracting immigrants from a wide range of European countries. The promise of a better life in the new world also brought with it a great deal of poverty.

Methods for dealing with problem youths grew out of the establishment of ways to handle poor people in the cities (see Rothman, 1971, 1980). The poor were seen both as a threat to society and in need of help. The primary response

---

BOX 2.1 MAJOR MILESTONES/EVENTS/DATES IN JUVENILE JUSTICE, 1825–1899

1825	Houses of Refuge established	1855	Chicago Reform School Act established reform schools in Chicago
	New York: 1825		
	Boston: 1826	1869	Massachusetts State Board of Charities takes control of juvenile probation
	Philadelphia: 1828		
1838	*Ex Parte Crouse* rules in favor of *parens patriae*	1870	*People v. Turner* rules against *parens patriae*
		1892	New York separates trials of juveniles and adults
1848	Lyman School for Boys established		
1841	Probation initiated in Boston	1899	First juvenile court established in Cook County (Chicago), Illinois
mid-1800s	Institution of reformatories		

for dealing with the poor entailed training them and making them productive members of society. Unfortunately, there was little that could be done with the adult poor. They were beyond the training stage and were set in their ways. The children of the poor, however, were viewed as trainable. A key aspect of this training was the removal of the child from the bad influences and substandard training of the poor parents. While this view became prominent in the 1800s, Krisberg and Austin (1978) noted that as early as 1555 the English established the **Bridewell Institution** in London to handle youthful beggars. The primary emphasis of the institution was the handling of poor and destitute youths, although in practice the institution handled all problem youths, including delinquents. The Bridewell Institution was envisioned as a place where the youths would be trained in a skill that they could use after they were released.

The establishment of institutions in the early 1800s in the United States closely followed the ideas of the Bridewell Institution. The institutions were viewed as places for training those individuals who were not productive and who seemed to pose a threat to society. There was a heavy emphasis on the problems of the poor. The establishment of institutions for the poor and delinquent also reflected a shift in the view of causes of deviance. Throughout most of history, deviance was viewed as a result of problems inherent in the individual. The 1800s, meanwhile, witnessed a growth in the belief that deviance was a result of poor environmental conditions. A change in the environment, therefore, should result in changed behavior. The earlier the individual was placed into a new environment, the better the chances of having a positive impact on the person's actions. The establishment of new institutions also provided the court with an alternative to doing nothing with juveniles or placing them in adult institutions.

Houses of Refuge

The establishment of institutions for children in the 1800s clearly conformed to these ideas. These early institutions were called **houses of refuge** and were envisioned as a place for separating the youth from the detrimental environment of the city. The first house of refuge was established in New York in 1825 and was followed by institutions in Boston (1826) and Philadelphia (1828). The rationale and setup of the houses of refuge closely followed the concern for the poor and the need for training discussed above.

Central aspects in the handling of youths were indeterminate sentences, education, skills training, hard work, religious training, parental discipline, and apprenticeships (Pisciotta, 1983). The use of education, skills training, hard work, and apprenticeships were clear indications that the goal was to produce a productive member of society. Indeterminate sentences allowed the institution to work with each person on an individual basis. Where one youth may benefit from a short period of intervention, another child may require extended work and assistance. The interest in religious training and parental discipline carried over the historical ideas that the best methods of training lay in the realm of the family and the church. The families of the youths in the institution were considered to be lacking in the ability to provide these basic needs. The houses of refuge were envisioned as shelters and sanctuaries that would protect and nurture their wards away from the corrupting influences of the city and the poor family (Rothman, 1971).

The establishment of the houses of refuge also was seen as a means of removing children from the criminogenic influences of the workhouses and adult jails (Krisberg & Austin, 1978). Reformers saw the prior methods of handling youths through the adult system as nothing more than placing poor and problem juveniles in contact with adult criminal offenders. The natural outcome would be "schools for crime" that produced more problems than they solved. The houses of refuge supposedly differed by offering education and training in useful skills within a setting that allowed for control and discipline of the children.

While the rationale and the goals of the houses of refuge were laudable, the daily operations and the impact of the institutions were questionable. Many of the activities were far removed from the real world. Inmates had little, if any, contact with members of the opposite sex. Military behavior was the norm. This included enforced silence, marching to and from different activities, the wearing of uniforms, and swift and habitual corporal punishment (Rothman, 1971). Apprenticeships often failed to be more than simple slave labor. Many of the apprenticeships were on farms in the country. Problem youths were apprenticed to ship captains and sent to sea. In general, there was no quality control or oversight for the apprenticeships. The institutional labor was often dictated by contractual obligations that led to exploitation of the youths by the institutional masters. Children were bribed, beaten, and even subjected to extended incarceration if the monetary interests of the administrators were at stake (Pisciotta, 1982).

Besides failing to provide the basic tools that they promised, the houses of refuge also failed in other respects. For the most part, these institutions were nothing but new prisons. They were tremendously overcrowded. This over-crowding was partly due to the admission of persons not suited for the goals of the institutions. The houses of refuge served the poor and destitute, and the delinquent youths. At the same time, they handled poverty-stricken adults and adult offenders. The overcrowding of the facilities by such diverse groups of inmates changed the focus of daily operations from the goals of education and training to that of simple custody and discipline. The establishment of institu-tions like the **Lyman School for Boys** in 1848 by the state of Massachusetts eliminated the housing of adult and juvenile offenders in the same facility but carried on the tradition of overcrowding and related problems. In general, the early houses of refuge failed to provide their stated goals and settled into a process very reminiscent of that of the adult prisons and jails that had previously been the norm for handling youths.

New Reformatories

The failure of the early houses of refuge did not lead to the end of juvenile institutions. The problems of the houses of refuge were well known by the mid-1800s. While the practice of the institutions had failed, proponents argued that the principles underlying intervention were correct. The issue, therefore, was in proper implementation of intervention. Emphasis on education, training, and parental discipline led to the establishment of "cottage" reformatories.

The **cottage** setup was intended to closely parallel a family. Concerned surrogate parents would oversee the training and education of a small number of problem youths. Discipline would be intermixed with the care and concern typical of family life. Most of the cottages were located in the country and emphasized work on the farm. This was supposed to separate the youth from the criminogenic features of the urban environment and instill a sense of hard, honest work in the charges. The idea of indeterminate sentencing carried over to the cottage approach.

Other changes in the handling of youths accompanied the growth of these cottage reformatories. Foremost among these features was the development of **probation** in 1841 by John Augustus. While the early use of probation was centered on adult offenders, by 1869 the state of Massachusetts dictated that the State Board of Charities would participate in, and take charge of, court cases involving youthful offenders (Krisberg & Austin, 1978). Probation officers would assist in the gathering of information on the youths, suggest alternative means of intervention, and oversee the placement of juveniles in reformatories and apprenticeships. Another method of dealing with youths, in accordance with the cottage idea, entailed the "placing out" of juveniles into foster homes. For the most part, these placements were the same as apprenticeships. Such placements were seen as an alternative to institutionalization and allowed for the training of youths in a worthwhile occupation.

Unfortunately, like the earlier houses of refuge, these new alternatives for handling youths faced many of the same problems. The institutions and cottages became terribly overcrowded to the point that custody became the primary concern. Apprenticeships proved to be little more than slave labor, and youths often fled at the first opportunity. One analysis of 210 apprenticed individuals found that 72 percent of the youths either ran away or returned to the institution (Pisciotta, 1979). The harsh treatment of the youths in the institutions led to running away, the setting of fires, and various sexual problems (Pisciotta, 1982). The inability to handle some youths prompted the establishment of special facilities such as the Elmira Reformatory in 1876. Unfortunately, Elmira accepted both juveniles and young adults and negated the premise of separating youths from criminogenic older offenders. A final problem with the institutions was the continued mixing of both deviant and destitute youths in the same facilities. The institutions considered that being poor was closely tied to deviant activity and, as a result, intervened in the lives of lower-class individuals regardless of the existence (or lack) of a delinquent or criminal act.

Institutions for Females

Throughout the development of alternatives for handling boys, little attention was paid to females. Problem girls were dealt with in the same institutions as males and adults. Part of the reason for this was the relatively small number of females officially handled by agents of social control. Exceptions to this situation began to appear in the mid-1800s with the establishment of separate institutions for girls. One of the most well-known facilities for females was the **Lancaster State Industrial School for Girls** in Massachusetts. The girls committed to Lancaster had the same basic background as boys found in other institutions. They were mostly from poor, immigrant families who were faced with the vagaries and problems of the urban environment (Brenzel, 1983). The institutions were set up as family cottages in order to deal with these problems.

The hoped-for end product of the institutions for girls was the production of females capable of fulfilling their place in society. Where boys were to become productive laborers, females were to learn how to be good housewives and mothers (Brenzel, 1983). Success with the girls was gauged by successful marriage and parenthood. Much of the concern centered on the plight of future generations that were to be raised by the problem girls and not on the girls themselves. Unfortunately, these institutions fared no better than those handling boys. While some girls successfully graduated from the institutions, married, and became mothers, others did not realize the goals set by the institutions. In addition, Lancaster and similar institutions tended to be little more than prisons for youths. They were characterized by overcrowding, lack of treatment, and strict discipline. The differing focus from male institutions did not result in different outcomes.

THE ESTABLISHMENT OF THE JUVENILE COURT

The juvenile court arose in response to the failure of the earlier interventions with juveniles and to address the issues of the era. The late 1800s continued to experience great levels of immigration by lower-class Europeans to the

BOX 2.2	MAJOR MILESTONES/EVENTS/DATES IN JUVENILE JUSTICE, 1900–PRESENT		
1901	Illinois State School for youths established	1912	U.S. Children's Bureau established
1903	Illinois expanded juvenile court jurisdiction to status offenses	1920	All but three states have separate juvenile courts
1905	*Commonwealth v. Fisher* upheld *parens patriae*	1966	*Kent v. U.S.* raises concerns about *parens patriae*
1909	Establishment of child guidance clinics		

industrial cities of the United States. Environmental factors remained at the head of the list of causes for deviant behavior. In addition, the emergence of psychological and sociological explanations for behavior suggested that the problems of society could be fixed. Finally, middle- and upper-class individuals (primarily women) were interested in doing something to help the poor and destitute. The new court system utilized many of the earlier intervention ideas. Consequently, the expansion of juvenile justice was subjected to many of the same problems of the earlier interventions, as well as new concerns.

The Growth of the Juvenile Court

The first recognized individual juvenile court was established in Cook County, Illinois, in 1899. While this represented the first official juvenile court, a variety of jurisdictions implemented and experimented with similar institutions. Between 1870 and 1877, the state of Massachusetts established separate court dockets, separate hearings, and separate record keeping for cases involving juveniles under the age of 16 (Ryerson, 1978). New York passed legislation in 1892 that provided for separate trials for juvenile offenders, although juveniles continued to be held in the adult system (Platt, 1977). Similarly, Judge Ben Lindsey of Colorado, a leading advocate of juvenile court, operated a quasi-juvenile court for a number of years prior to the establishment of the court in Illinois (Parsloe, 1978). Regardless of the initial beginnings, by 1920 all but three states had juvenile courts, and there were more than 320 separate juvenile courts in the United States (Ryerson, 1978).

The legislation that established the Illinois court reflected the general belief in the ability to alter youthful behavior. First, the court was to operate in a highly informal manner without any of the trappings of the adult court. Lawyers and other adversarial features of the adult system (such as rules of evidence and testimony under oath) were discouraged. The judge was to take a paternal stance toward the juvenile and provide whatever help and assistance was needed. The emphasis was on assisting the youth rather than on punishing an offense. Second, all juveniles under the age of 16 could be handled by the new court.

The court was not restricted to dealing with youths who committed criminal acts. Rather, the court could intervene in any situation in which a youth was in need of help. In practical terms, this allowed intervention into the lives of the poor and immigrants, whose child-raising practices did not conform to the ideas of the court. Third, the new court relied extensively on the use of probation. Probation continued to serve both administrative functions for the court as well as supervisory actions with adjudicated youths.

While no two juvenile courts could claim to have the same program, the courts all held the same general principles of providing assistance for the juveniles. Julian W. Mack of the Chicago juvenile court aptly portrayed the role and methods of the court when he stated:

> Most of the children who come before the court are, naturally, the children of the poor. In many cases the parents are foreigners, frequently unable to speak English, and without an understanding of American methods and views. What they need, more than anything else, is kindly assistance; and the aim of the court, in appointing a probation officer for the child, is to have the child and the parents feel, not so much the power, as the friendly interest of the state; to show them that the object of the court is to help them to train the child right . . . (Mack, 1909).

WEB ACTIVITY

Read the entire statement of Judge Mack at http://www.routledge.com/cw.whitehead

Within this statement, Mack noted the minor concern over the deviant act in the court, the goal of providing assistance to both the youth and the family, the place of probation in the court, and the typical youth who was subjected to court intervention. The shift from the adult orientation is evident in the new terminology that developed in the juvenile court (see Table 2.1).

The progressive reforms that led to the establishment of the juvenile courts also had other influences. One of the impacts was a gradual widening of the juvenile court's mandate. The original Illinois statute allowed intervention for criminal activity, dependency, and neglect. In 1903, Illinois added such actions as curfew violation and incorrigibility (status offenses) to the situations allowing intervention. A second area of change involved the development of new institutions for handling youths who needed to be removed from their families. One of the first new institutions was the Illinois State School at St. Charles, Illinois, which was funded in 1901 and opened in 1905 (Platt, 1977). These institutions closely followed the family/cottage model used throughout the

TABLE 2.1 Comparative Terms in the Juvenile and Adult Systems

Juvenile System	Adult System
Adjudication	Conviction
Hearing	Trial
Aftercare	Parole
Commitment	Sentence
Delinquent	Criminal
Petition	Indictment
Custody	Arrest

late 1800s. The greatest distinction was in the administrative unit (the juvenile court versus the adult court) and not in orientation. A move toward using full-time, paid probation officers also occurred shortly after the court's beginnings. By 1912, the federal government established the U.S. Children's Bureau to oversee the expanding realm of juvenile justice (Ryerson, 1978).

A final major movement coming from the progressive reforms was the institution of court-affiliated guidance clinics. The first of these was established in Chicago by William Healy, a leading proponent of the juvenile court, in 1909. These clinics relied on the new psychological and sociological explanations emerging during this time. Central to these explanations was the need for the expert analysis of each juvenile in order to identify the unique factors contributing to the individual's behavior. Following Healy's example, 232 clinics were established by 1931 (Krisberg & Austin, 1978).

The Legal Philosophy of the Court

Perhaps the greatest challenge to the growth of the juvenile system entailed debate over the philosophy of the court and the question of a juvenile's constitutional rights. Critics of the court and earlier interventions often claimed that the state was subjecting juveniles to intervention without regard to their rights and those of the family. In many instances the state was forcibly removing a youth from his or her parents' custody. These new interventions were viewed as an abrogation of the family's position in society. The problems of constitutional rights and the new juvenile justice system were deemed inconsequential compared to the possible benefits that could accrue from intervention. Indeed, the state relied on the doctrine of *parens patriae* for justification of its position. Table 2.2 presents key factors in the growth of *parens patriae* and its application to the juvenile court.

Parens patriae, or the state as parent, was based on the actions of the English **Chancery Court**. The Chancery Court was primarily concerned with property matters in feudal England. One aspect of the court's function was to oversee the financial affairs of juveniles whose parents had died and who were not yet capable of handling their own matters. The court acted as a guardian until such time that the youth could assume responsibility. In practice, the court dealt only with matters involving more well-to-do families. The offspring of the poor did not have any property to protect. As an arm of the state, the Chancery Court often converted much of the property to the ownership of the state. There would be little to gain in overseeing the needs of the poor. Regardless of the intention of the Chancery Court, the precedent was set for intervention into the lives of children.

Movements to intervene into the lives of children in the United States were quick to rely on *parens patriae* for justification. The earliest example of this

TABLE 2.2 Factors in the Growth of *Parens Patriae*	
English Chancery Court (Middle Ages)	Basis of state intervention for welfare of children, particularly in cases of property rights and orphans
Ex parte Crouse (1838)	Pennsylvania Supreme Court rules that *parens patriae* is sufficient basis for intervening in the lives of juveniles without parental consent
People v. Turner (1870)	Illinois Supreme Court rules against *parens patriae* in favor of parental rights to raise and care for offspring; largely ignored by the courts
Commonwealth v. Fisher (1905)	Pennsylvania Supreme Court rules that the court can intervene without impunity when the objective is to help the youth, i.e., if the intent is good the juvenile court can act
Kent v. United States (1966)	*Parens patriae* is seriously questioned in light of the lack of adequate help and treatment provided by the juvenile court coupled with the lack of due process applied in juvenile cases

involved the case *Ex parte Crouse*. Mary Ann Crouse was incarcerated upon her mother's request but against her father's wishes. Her father argued that it was illegal to incarcerate a child without the benefit of a jury trial. In rejecting the father's argument, the court denied that the Bill of Rights applied to youths. The Pennsylvania Supreme Court ruled in 1838:

> May not the natural parents, when unequal to the task of education, or unworthy of it, be superseded by the *parens patriae*, or common guardian of the community? It is to be remembered that the public has a paramount interest in the virtue and knowledge of its members, and that of strict right the business of education belongs to it. That parents are ordinarily entrusted with it, is because it can seldom be put in better hands; but where they are incompetent or corrupt, what is there to prevent the public from withdrawing their faculties, held as they obviously are, at its sufferance? The right of parental control is a natural, but not an inalienable one. It is not excepted by the declaration of rights out of the subject of ordinary legislation (*Ex parte Crouse*, 1838).

The *Crouse* opinion set the tone for intervention with juveniles in the United States. In essence, the state could intervene, regardless of the reason, if it found that the child was in need of help or assistance that the parents and family could not provide. The decision relied solely on the good intentions of the state and the need to provide the proper training for the child.

Intervention based on *parens patriae* did not go completely unchallenged. Critics charged that the state was overextending its rights by intervening in many minor matters that should be simply ignored. More importantly, the argument was made that the state provided little more than incarceration and was not providing the education, training, and benevolent care that was required under the *parens patriae* doctrine. In **People v. Turner** (1870), the Illinois Supreme Court stated:

> In our solicitude to form youths for the duties of civil life, we should not forget the rights which inhere both in parents and children. The principle of the absorption of the child in, and its complete subjection to the despotism of, the State, is wholly inadmissible in the modern civilized world. The parent has the right to the care, custody, and assistance of his child. The duty to maintain and protect it, is a principle of a natural law.

In this instance the court affirmed the rights of the parent to care for the child. The intervention of the state was to be reserved for instances in which the youth had violated a criminal law and after the application of due process concerns. The good intentions of the state and the needs of the youth were not enough to warrant unfettered intervention into the family unit. Despite this apparent shift in legal concerns, most jurisdictions ignored the opinion and continued to follow the general guidelines set forth in the *Crouse* decision.

The issues of a child's and parent's rights were largely settled in the 1905 case, *Commonwealth v. Fisher*. In this case the Pennsylvania Supreme Court directly addressed the question of a juvenile's behavior, his or her constitutional rights, and the intent of the juvenile system in intervention. The court said:

> The design is not punishment, nor the restraint imprisonment, any more than is the wholesome restraint which a parent exercises over his child. The severity in either case must necessarily be tempered to meet the necessities of the particular situation. There is no probability, in the proper administration of the law, of the child's liberty being unduly invaded. Every statute which is designed to give protection, care, and training to children, as a needed substitute for parental authority, and performance of parental duty, is but a recognition of the duty of the state, as the legitimate guardian and protector of children where other guardianship fails. No constitutional right is violated (*Commonwealth v. Fisher*, 1905).

The key concern was over the intent of the intervention and not the rights of the juvenile, his or her parents, or the effectiveness of the system. In essence, the child had a **right to intervention** and not a right to freedom. Moreover, the parents had little, if any, rights in the disposition of the child.

The juvenile court was viewed as providing help in the most benevolent fashion possible. The Pennsylvania Supreme Court was granting the juvenile system a free hand in dealing with youths.

The basic constitutionality of the juvenile system went largely unchallenged after the *Fisher* decision. Those cases that did arise were met with the same rationale and outcome of the earlier case. It was not until the mid-1960s that the courts began to alter their views and grant some constitutional rights to juveniles. Indeed, not until 1966 was the benevolent premise of the juvenile system adequately challenged. In the U.S. Supreme Court case of *Kent v. United States*, Justice Abe Fortas said:

> There is evidence, in fact, that there may be grounds for concern that the child receives the worst of both worlds: that he gets neither the protections accorded to adults nor the solicitous care and regenerative treatment postulated for children *(Kent v. United States,* 1966).

As will be seen in Chapter 9, the constitutional rights provided to juveniles in the last two decades are not equal to those provided to adults. The courts have continued to reserve various powers for the state and treat juveniles as a separate class of citizens with different rights and expectations.

Problems of the Court

Despite the swift adoption of the juvenile court and its related components, the new system was faced with a number of problems and failures. A major problem involved the extent to which the various operations were initiated. Many of the courts and agencies relied solely on untrained volunteers. The number of full-time, paid juvenile court judges, probation officers, and trained clinicians was small. Ryerson (1978) cited one survey (Beldon, 1920) that found that only 55 percent of the courts provided regular probation services and, of those with probation, less than 50 percent of the officers were full-time employees. The same survey reported that there were only 23 full-time juvenile court judges in the United States in 1918 (Beldon, 1920). The child guidance clinics experienced the same shortage of trained professionals. As a result, most youths did not receive any evaluation. Most evaluations that occurred took place after a child was incarcerated (Ryerson, 1978). This lack of adequate staff was accompanied by inadequate facilities and resources. While the juvenile court retained the use of institutionalization, the choice of placement usually rested on those institutions that had existed prior to the court's establishment. The problems of these institutions were the same as before. Harsh treatment, military regimentation, lack of training and education, high recidivism, and running away all continued. The new agencies, such as the child guidance clinics, similarly failed to provide the treatment and supervision they promised.

Criticism of the court also focused on its expanded jurisdiction. As noted above, new statutes outlined juvenile behavior that had previously been left to the family for correction. The expanded jurisdiction of the court based on *parens patriae* also led to an increase in unofficial dispositions and handling of youths. There is evidence that many proceedings took place without the presence of a judge or the keeping of records. Such actions were justified on the basis of relieving the burden of the court and the desire to avoid the stigma of a more formal procedure. While these reasons may have been laudatory, they encouraged the handling of more juveniles with very minor transgressions. Many trivial actions, such as making noise, sledding in the street, playing in the street, riding bicycles on the sidewalk, and throwing paper into the sewers, became the subject of these unofficial cases (Rothman, 1980).

BENEVOLENCE OR SELF-INTEREST?

The institution of the juvenile court has generally been held as a progressive, humanitarian development. Most historians refer to the time period from about 1880 to the 1920s as the Progressive Era. It was during this time that many laws were passed mandating apparently humanitarian reforms. Actions such as mandatory schooling, regulations on working conditions for both adults and juveniles, concern over the plight of the poor and immigrants, the growth of agencies dealing with health concerns, and the establishment of the juvenile court were listed as examples of the benevolent actions of the reformers and society. Coercion within the juvenile justice system, and other forms of intervention, were considered a necessary evil for improving the lot of those who did not know any better (Rothman, 1980). Schlossman (1977) went so far as to label the benevolent movement in juvenile justice as an exercise in love. He plainly stated that institutions and the court needed to provide the type of love, affection, and concern found in the family setting.

According to other writers, however, benevolence was not the driving factor. Anthony Platt (1977) referred to the persons involved in the development of the juvenile court as **child savers**. The issue he addressed was the rationale for saving the youths. Platt viewed the growth of juvenile justice as a part of larger social movements that attempted to solidify the position of corporate capitalism in the United States. Rather than being a humanistic endeavor to help the less fortunate societal members, intervention through the courts allowed the powerful classes of society to mold a disciplined, complacent labor force. The juvenile court was a means of preserving the existing class system in the United States (Platt, 1977). Krisberg and Austin (1978) essentially made the same argument. They saw the system as a vehicle of the upper classes for controlling the "dangerous" (lower) classes in society.

Both Platt (1977) and Krisberg and Austin (1978) pointed to a variety of factors in support of their contentions. First, the driving force behind the growth of the juvenile system, especially the juvenile court, were middle- and upper-class individuals. Middle-class women formed one key group in the system's development (Platt, 1977). These women were the wives and daughters of the industrialists and landed gentry who controlled production and had the greatest say in government. A second form of support rested on the fact that the system grew during the time when the lower-class ranks were swelling with new, poor immigrants. In essence, the lower class was growing to a point at which it could pose a threat to the status quo. Third, and related to the second, was the establishment of new laws that addressed the activity of the lower classes. Statutes governing youthful behavior primarily addressed the actions of the poor and immigrants. The government extended control over entirely new classes of behaviors in the juvenile justice statutes. A fourth indication of the juvenile system's inherent bias was the exploitive use of children who were incarcerated or under the care of the system. Youths were placed in involuntary servitude, indentured, and apprenticed, all under the argument that they would benefit from learning a trade. Realistically, according to Platt (1977) and Krisberg and Austin (1978), these actions supplied immediate cheap labor and indoctrinated the youths in the capitalistic ideology of the upper classes. It was upon these, and similar, arguments that various writers question the benevolent intentions of those individuals involved in the juvenile justice system movement.

Additional support for the argument that the system lacked the benevolence purported in many studies comes from an evaluation of the treatment of females and blacks. Pisciotta (1983) offered evidence that the juvenile justice system had been both racist and sexist. The author noted that most residential institutions in the early 1800s refused to admit blacks. Instead, black youths were subjected to continued incarceration in adult facilities until special institutions for blacks could be built. One of the earliest separate black institutions was opened in Philadelphia in 1848. Exceptions to this rule of separating whites and blacks were restricted to instances in which the admittance of blacks was economically advantageous to those in charge. Once admitted to an institution, little education was supplied. Intervention with blacks revolved around training them in menial labor and to learn their "proper place" in society. Females were handled in a similar fashion (Pisciotta, 1983). Academic education was minimized while religious, moral, and domestic training was emphasized. This view of proper training for women rested on the expectation that females were to stay in the home and raise the next generation of children (Brenzel, 1983; Pisciotta, 1983).

One possible problem with the proposal that the juvenile court was a self-serving invention of the powerful involves the place of the new professionals in the growth of the system. As noted earlier, the emergence of the new psychological and sociological explanations for behavior played a major role in the direction of the juvenile institutions and court. Why did these professionals not criticize the growth of juvenile justice if, indeed, it was simply a means for the powerful to control the masses? Platt (1977) addressed this issue by pointing out that the professionals received a great deal of benefit from juvenile justice, regardless of the driving forces. These individuals gained the reputation as experts, secured employment as either full-time employees or paid consultants, gained access to data and information otherwise denied to them, and found a forum willing to let them advance their theories and ideas. It was not that these professionals may not have objected to the biased premise of the system, they simply found more personal benefits in allowing the system to be instituted and advanced.

The debate over the intent of those forming the juvenile court has not been resolved. The usefulness of recognizing the difference in opinion is in opening the way for varied suggestions about dealing with problem youths. Individuals who assume the benevolence point of view turn to a variety of theoretical explanations and the accompanying forms of intervention. Advocates of the self-interest perspective focus on the actions of society and not the individual offender. Instead of looking for ways to help the youth, these writers suggest that changes in the social structure account for variation in the levels of deviance. This approach will be further explored in Chapter 4.

JUVENILE JUSTICE FROM 1920 TO THE 1960s

Most of the great movements and changes in juvenile justice were completed by the early 1920s. By this time, the juvenile court was solidly entrenched as the proper institution for dealing with problem youths. The problems and criticisms directed at the court and its institutions were passed off as the failure to implement the programs properly. The shortcomings were not inherent features of the system. Advocates called for increased resources, time, and patience. Society and the legal system were content to leave the juvenile justice system alone to search for effective interventions, provided the system continued to act in the best interests of its youthful clients. Changes in the handling of youths over the next few decades, therefore, were restricted to generating new theories of behavior, attempting new types of treatment, and evaluating their efforts.

Various new institutions were established for handling problem youths. These were necessitated both by increased numbers of youths entering the system and differing approaches to treating youths. Psychological explanations and perspectives led to the growth of various training and counseling (group and individual) programs. Psychotherapeutic interventions gained prominence in the 1940s and led to private and public institutions based on these ideas. The use of such interventions as guided group interaction and peer pressure formed the basis of programs such as the Highfields Project in 1950. Highfields was a short-term, residential facility that allowed the youths to visit their families and remain a part of the community. This type of program helped form the basis for halfway houses and other community interventions. Later chapters will address such actions in more detail.

CHANGES SINCE THE 1960s

Challenges to the *parens patriae* doctrine through a growing number of court cases in the late 1960s and early 1970s were early signals of major changes in society's approach to both juvenile misbehavior and adult criminality. The period from 1967 to the early 1980s has been referred to as the **Due Process Period**. The federal courts ruled in a number of key cases that juveniles had to be offered some procedural rights similar to those enjoyed by adults. The 1980s returned to an approach that was more punishment oriented and ushered in what is referred to as the **Punitive Period**. Actions during this period included increased use of waiver, mandatory sentencing, and less emphasis on rehabilitation and treatment.

Clearly, the strong reliance on and belief in rehabilitation and treatment that dominated throughout the twentieth century has given way to more punitive responses (Garland, 2001). Retribution, just deserts, and deterrence have emerged as the watchwords for both the juvenile and criminal justice systems. Rather than look for the causes of deviant behavior in the inequities of society or the surroundings of the offender, there is a stronger belief that individuals of all ages choose to commit offenses and need to be held responsible for their actions.

Garland (2001) views these changes in social control as a result of numerous changes and forces over the past 30 years. Among those influences have been rising crime rates, changing economic conditions that marginalize greater number of individuals,

Boys take part in group therapy at the Highfields Treatment Center, located in the former home of Charles A. Lindbergh, in Hopewell, New Jersey, in 1961. The boys seek a way to rebuild their lives away from the delinquency that landed them in the facility. Eyes masked in 1961 to guard juveniles' identities.

CREDIT: AP Photo/Dave Pickoff

challenges to the welfare state, growing concern for victims, the diversification of the population, the perceived inability of the state to control the citizenry, and the perception that families and other institutions have lost their ability to control the behavior of their members. Passing new laws, increasing the use of punishment, and similar responses have emerged as responses to these and other perceived problems. Changes in the juvenile justice system and society's response to youths are a clear reflection of these broad social changes.

Detention facilities for juveniles take several forms. The Hamilton County (Ohio) Juvenile Court Youth Center is a county detention facility that contains two court rooms, a psychological/psychiatric clinic, an intake complaint processing center, and a counseling center. It has received special recognition for its Suicide Assessment/Management program.

CREDIT: Ellen S. Boyne

TABLE 2.3 Categories of Juvenile Court General Purpose Clauses

Balanced and Restorative Justice Clauses:
- Juvenile court is to focus on balancing the needs of the youth, the victim, and public safety
- Typically includes an emphasis on treatment, care, and guidance of the youths
- Found in 17 states

"Standard Juvenile Court Act" Clauses:
- Emphasis on "care, guidance, and control" to ensure the welfare of the youth
- Offer care similar to that which would normally be supplied by the parents
- Found in nine states

"Legislative Guide" Clauses:
- Provide care, protection, supervision, and rehabilitation to children
- Maintain children in the home if at all possible
- Provide institutional protection to youths
- Found in six states

Punishment, Deterrence, Accountability, and/or Public Safety Clauses:
- Criminal court orientation
- Focus on community safety and offender accountability
- Found in six states

Traditional Child Welfare Clauses:
- Emphasis on welfare and best interests of child
- Focus on *parens patriae* philosophy
- Found in three states

Source: Adapted by authors from *OJJDP Statistical Briefing Book* (2013).

Despite the movement to include greater emphasis on retribution and punishment in the juvenile justice system, *parens patriae* remains the key philosophy underlying juvenile courts in the United States. This is illustrated in an analysis of the "purpose clauses" for juvenile courts found in state statutes. Griffin, Szymanski, and King (2006) identify five general categories of juvenile court purpose clauses (see Table 2.3). In only one of the five categories is *parens patriae* largely excluded and the emphasis shifted to an adult court/criminal law orientation for the juvenile court. The other four categories maintain *parens patriae* as at least a key component (if not directly named) in addressing problem youths.

WEB ACTIVITY

You can find out more about the general purpose clauses for juvenile courts and the purpose clauses for the different states at http://www.ojjdp.gov/ojstatbb/structure_process/qa04205.asp?qaDate=2012

SUMMARY

The growth of juvenile justice from the 1920s to the early 1960s followed a pattern of new programs, all within the original mandate and scope of the early reformers. The issues that fueled debate in the early years have returned to be debated in recent years. While there has been an increased emphasis on punishment and due process in the system, many of the rehabilitation and treatment ideas are still being tried and adapted in an attempt to live up to the *parens patriae* ideals that still underlie the juvenile justice system. The remainder of the text will look at the varied issues and the operation of the juvenile system, primarily since the early 1960s. Questions of theory, implementation, practice, and evaluation form the core of the discussion.

DISCUSSION QUESTIONS

1. Concern over child abuse has greatly increased over the past two decades. Many people argue that society's young are treated worse today than at any time in history. Based on your knowledge, place this view within a historical framework. That is, outline the historical view of children and some of the major practices for handling kids.

2. You are an administrator of an early house of refuge and are asked to give a dispassionate view of your institution. What are the strengths and weaknesses of this type of institution? What problems do you face, and how can you correct them?

3. The legislature is proposing to abolish the juvenile court. Argue in favor of the legal philosophy that is the basis for the court. What is the philosophy, why has it been legally upheld throughout the years, and why should it be maintained?

CHAPTER 3

Explaining Delinquency— Biological and Psychological Approaches

WHAT YOU NEED TO KNOW

- The Classical school of thought holds that humans are free-willed and choose their behavior, while the Positivist school sees behavior as dictated by outside causes beyond the control of the individual. Neoclassicism takes a middle ground where choices can be made from limited options.

- Early theories of behavior relied on biological explanations. Lombroso and others relied on physical features to identify criminals.

- Studies of genetics-inheritance and behavior find that there is some degree of heritability in behavior, although it is small and subject to a great deal of external influence.

- Modern biological theories are best considered as biosociology, which refers to the fact that there are both biological and environmental influences on behavior, and it is necessary to consider the interaction of these factors.

- While psychological theories have a long history, they are limited by three common features—they focus largely on early life experiences to the exclusion of other variables, they are highly individualistic, and they are most useful in treatment settings.

- Freudian psychoanalysis seeks the cause of behavior in the unconscious/instinctual parts of humankind, particularly in the battle between the id, ego, and superego.

- Developmental explanations argue that everyone develops through certain stages, with each stage contributing to the knowledge a person needs to be a successful conforming member of society. Deviance results when an individual fails to advance successfully through all the stages.

KEY TERMS

Antisocial Personality Disorder (APD)

atavistic

attention deficit hyperactivity disorder

biosociology

Classicism

concordance

determinism

dopamine

ego

epinephrine

free will

hedonistic calculus

hypoglycemia

id

Interpersonal Maturity Levels (I-levels)

IQ

medical model

meta-analysis

Minnesota Multiphasic Personality Inventory (MMPI)

modeling

monoamine oxidase A

moral development

multiple causation

nature–nurture controversy

Neoclassicism

neurotransmitters

norepinephrine

operant conditioning

orthomolecular factors

physiognomy

phrenology

Positivism

psychoanalysis

psychopharmaco-logical perspective

reactive hypoglycemia

serotonin

soft determinism

somatotypes

spiritualistic/demono-logical explanations

superego

theory

- Attempts to identify antisocial personalities have been common but have not succeeded in being able to assess adequately who will and will not be deviant.
- Low IQ has often been used as an argument for why some people break the law; however, a key unknown is the extent to which IQ is inherited or is a result of one's environment.

INTRODUCTION

Throughout the history of juvenile justice, criminologists and others interested in deviant behavior have sought to explain why certain individuals act in certain ways at certain times. The number of theories for deviant behavior has grown considerably over the past 100 years as the field of criminology has progressed and the level of research has improved. A theory can be described as an attempt to answer the question "Why?" Why does an individual violate the norms of society? Why do certain conditions seem to accompany deviant behavior? Why does deviance occur when it does? These and other "why" questions form the basis for the theories that have been proposed for explaining delinquent behavior.

The types of factors that have been used to explain delinquency take a wide variety of forms. Early spiritualistic or demonological explanations reflected the belief that deviant acts were the result of the battle between good and evil—God and the devil. Individuals who committed crimes were possessed by the devil. Consequently, the solution to deviance involved exorcising the devil and delivering the individual back to God. Often times this could only be accomplished through the death of the devil's vessel—the individual. The soul would then be freed to join God.

These nonscientific explanations gave way in the 1700s with the advent of Classicism and the movement into Positivistic approaches in the later 1800s. Classicism and Positivism are "schools of thought" rather than specific theories of behavior. These schools lay out general beliefs about people and the world that shape the form that individual theories will take.

THEORETICAL SCHOOLS OF THOUGHT

Every explanation of behavior, whether it be conventional or deviant behavior, rests on a number of implicit assumptions about individuals and the world within which they operate. These beliefs form the core of many arguments about the causes of crime and how to deal with offenders. For example, differences in opinions about the death penalty often boil down to different beliefs about whether punishment can deter people. Every science has schools of thought that organize its ideas. In criminology the two schools are Classicism and Positivism (see Table 3.1).

The Classical School

Classicism finds its roots in the writings of Cesare Bonesana Marchese de Beccaria (1738–1794) and Jeremy Bentham (1748–1832). Beccaria was an Italian aristocrat who broke with the ruling classes to condemn the methods of dealing with crime and morals in society. In outlining a new set of criminal and penal practices, he set forth a number of beliefs about humankind and the function of society in dealing with deviance.

Under Classicism, humans are viewed as having **free will**. That is, individuals choose to act the way that they do after calculating the pros and cons of an activity. Coupled with the idea of free will is the belief that humans are hedonistic. Under the **hedonistic calculus**, individuals seek to maximize pleasure and minimize pain (Bentham, 1948). Individuals, therefore, choose activities and behaviors based on their calculation of the amount of pleasure and pain that will result. Pleasurable behaviors will be undertaken and repeated, while painful activities will cease. Under Classicism, individuals make a conscious, *rational* decision to commit crime based on the expectation of a pleasurable outcome.

These beliefs about free will and hedonism suggest that the solution to crime requires altering the outcome of the hedonistic calculation. That is, increasing pain and reducing pleasure can reduce, and possibly eliminate, deviant behavior. Beccaria and other Classicists, therefore, focused their efforts on making laws and setting punishments that would alter the choices of individuals. Beccaria felt that individuals could not make an informed decision to avoid crime unless they were presented with a clear set of laws and punishments. The emphasis must be on the offense and the legal system, not the offender. There must be a set punishment for each crime, and the level of punishment must be sufficient to offset any pleasurable consequence of an individual's behavior.

Classicism seeks to prevent and deter crime by punishing the offender for the offense. Ideally, individuals should be deterred from crime by knowing the pain that would come from being caught and punished. Punishment is not meant to be a form of retribution or retaliation by society. Instead, punishment is solely for the purpose of altering the outcome of the "hedonistic calculus."

Classicism dominated discussions of crime, deviance, and the law in the 1800s. Indeed, changes in laws reflected the general belief in free will and attempts to deter individuals from becoming involved in crime. Classical elements still drive deterrence arguments in modern society. Certainly, the move toward incarceration, treating youths in adult court, and the emphasis on punishment today are based on Classicism. The fact that crime did not disappear under classical approaches led to new ideas about behavior in the late 1800s. Much of this movement toward a new "school of thought" grew out of the developing medical sciences.

The Positivistic School

The basic tenets of **Positivism** are diametrically opposed to those of Classicism. Rather than hold the individual responsible for his or her actions, Positivists claim that behavior is *determined* (caused) by factors beyond the control of the individual. Altering behavior, therefore, cannot be brought about through simply raising the amount of pain a person will receive if caught and punished. Rather, changing behavior can be accomplished only by identifying and eliminating the factors that are causing the individual to act in a certain way.

Positivism typically recognizes that there are multiple causes of behavior. Deviance may be the result of a single factor, multiple causes, or a series of events or situations occurring over a period of time. The same deviant act committed by different people may be the outcome of totally different causes. The fact that there is no single cause of crime requires examining each individual case for reasons behind that behavior. The approach used by Positivists to identify causes follows a **medical model** or uses a medical analogy.

Using a medical model, the scientist approaches deviance the same way that a doctor approaches a sickness. Just like a doctor considers coughs and fevers as symptoms of other problems, the Positivist views deviant acts, like burglary

TABLE 3.1 Major Elements of Classicism and Positivism

Classicism	Positivism	Neoclassicism
Free will	Determinism	Soft determinism
Hedonism	Multiple causation	Free will with limited choices
Rational offender	Emphasize offender/situation differences	Punishment or treatment
Emphasis on offense	Medical model—Crime as "symptom"	
Legal responses—Clear laws and procedures	Individualized response	
Punishment for prevention and deterrence	Rehabilitation and treatment	

and rape, as symptoms of other underlying causes or conditions. The Positivist attempts to identify what causes an individual to commit a deviant act and prescribes a tailored response to the person and circumstances. For example, two burglars may have committed their acts for different reasons, thus necessitating totally different interventions. The emphasis in Positivism, therefore, is not on the offense. Rather, the emphasis is on the offender, the unique situation, and the various factors causing the individual to be an offender.

The logical extension of the focus on **determinism** and **multiple causation** is the belief in rehabilitation and treatment. Instead of punishing an individual for his or her actions, Positivism seeks to remove the root causes of the deviant behavior. The proper rehabilitation or treatment strategies may be as diverse as the number of clients. For example, one burglar may need financial assistance for his or her family because the offense served to provide food for the family, while another burglar may need group counseling to address the specific animosity toward the victim that caused the action. Treatment and rehabilitation need to be tailored to the circumstances of the individual.

Positivism emerged from the 1800s as the dominant school of thought. Advances in medicine, psychology, and sociology presaged a more scientific approach to explaining and understanding deviance. The emerging juvenile justice system focused on identifying the causes of delinquency and sought ways to correct the inadequacies that led to delinquency. While the criminal justice system retained vestiges of Classicism and deterrence, the juvenile justice system and the emerging field of criminology embraced the ideas of Positivism.

Neoclassicism and a Summary

In recent years, the juvenile justice system has shifted back to a more Classical viewpoint, with mandatory punishments, deterrence, and the waiver of youths to the adult system. While Positivism has not totally disappeared, the dominant approach better fits a label of **Neoclassicism**. Neoclassicism takes the position that an individual exercises some degree of free will. The choices, however, are limited by factors both within and outside of the individual. Sometimes referred to as **soft determinism**, an individual can make decisions only based on the available choices. The available options determine the extent to which the person can exercise his or her free will. This compromise gives both the Classicist and Positivist a stake in the criminal and juvenile justice systems.

The balance of this chapter, as well as the entire next chapter, discuss a wide range of theories. The biological and psychological theories appearing in this chapter are primarily Positivistic in orientation. For the most part, they approach deviance as the outcome of forces beyond the control of the individual. The sociological theories appearing in Chapter 4, however, more often incorporate elements of free will in their arguments.

BIOLOGICAL AND SOCIOBIOLOGICAL THEORIES

Explanations of deviance based on biological factors are among the earliest and the most recent theories in criminology. Medical advances, particularly in the 1800s, led to explanations of behavior that focused on the biological makeup of the individual. The underlying assumption made by the early biological theorists was that if the biological makeup of the individual dictated his or her physical capabilities, these characteristics could also contribute to the type of behavior exhibited by the person.

A "phrenology head" on exhibit at a Special Collections Fair at the Beinecke Rare Book and Manuscript Library at Yale University. Phrenological thinking was influential in nineteenth-century psychiatry and modern neuroscience.

CREDIT: AP Photo/ Bob Child

Physical Appearance

Early biological explanations focused heavily on observable physical features of offenders. The basic argument was that offenders could be identified by their appearance, which often was described in terms that suggested an ape-like appearance. Among the earliest of these approaches were **physiognomy** (the study of facial features) and **phrenology** (the study of the shape of a person's skull).

Atavism

Cesare Lombroso, who is considered the father of modern criminology, based his ideas on Charles Darwin's theory of the survival of the species and viewed criminals as throwbacks to an earlier state of human existence. These individuals were not as physically or mentally advanced as the rest of society. Lombroso (1876) identified a number of **atavistic**, or ape-like, qualities that generally reflected the physical features of the apes from whom man was a descendant. Typical features noted by Lombroso included a protruding jaw, a high forehead, deep/close-set eyes, and excessively long arms and legs. In a study of incarcerated offenders, Lombroso (1876) noted that more than 40 percent of the criminals had five or more atavistic traits. These "born criminals" were a direct result of the lack of evolutionary progression found in the person.

BOX 3.1 PHYSICAL TRAIT EXPLANATIONS

	Key Idea: an individual's physical features can indicate/identify who is or will be a criminal
Physiognomy	Focus on facial features
Phrenology	Considers the shape of the skull
Lombroso	Atavism: idea that offenders are throwbacks to an earlier stage of human development; ape-like
Sheldon	Somatotypes: considers different body types and related temperaments as explanations for deviant activity

The remaining criminals fell into categories of "criminaloids" and "insane" criminals. Criminaloids were individuals who entered criminal activity due to a variety of factors including mental, physical, and social conditions that, when occurring at the same time, would trigger deviant behavior (Vold & Bernard, 1986). Insane criminals included idiots and mentally deranged individuals.

Lombroso's work led to a great deal of controversy. His failure to include a control group of noncriminals meant that he was unable to state whether the results would be different if he studied people in the general public. Goring (1913) found only minor differences in the physical makeup of convicts and a control group of noncriminal citizens. Subsequent research by Lombroso, including control groups, revealed great physical similarities between offenders and nonoffenders, leading Lombroso to consider nonphysical atavistic qualities, as well as environmental and social factors for explaining deviance.

Somatotypes

Despite the criticisms of Lombroso and his contemporaries, the relation between physical appearance and deviance has appeared in twentieth-century research as **somatotypes**, or body types. Sheldon (1949) identified three basic somatotypes and related temperaments (see Table 3.2). Based on his observations of delinquents in a residential facility, Sheldon (1949) found that meso-morphic characteristics were most prevalent and ectomorphic features were the least common. He concluded that mesomorphic individuals were more likely to commit delinquent acts than were other youths. Support for the relationship between mesomorphy and delinquency is also found in the studies of Sheldon Glueck and Eleanor Glueck (1956) and Juan Cortes (1972).

Not unexpectedly, somatotype studies share similar methodological problems. First, much of the research is based on subjective determinations of body type, often by simply looking at photographs of the youths. Second, the researchers do not consider changes in body type as the youths grow older. Third, the researchers ignore the possibility that mesomorphic youths are more often recruited into delinquency because of their physical build, rather than having

TABLE 3.2 Sheldon's Physiques and Temperaments

Physique	Temperament
Endomorph	Viscerotonic
Short, fat, round, soft	Soft, easygoing, extrovert
Mesomorph	Somotonic
Muscular, large, barrel-chested, thick, hard	Dynamic, active, athletic, aggressive, talkative
Ectomorph	Cerebrotonic
Bony, thin, skinny, small, delicate	Nervous, complainer, introvert

Source: Constructed by authors from Sheldon (1949).

a natural propensity to commit delinquent acts. Fourth, considering delinquents as only incarcerated youths may bias the results if mesomorphic delinquents are institutionalized more often because they are perceived as greater threats than are smaller youths. Finally, the determination that mesomorphs were somotonic (aggressive, active, etc.) rests on the fact that many delinquents are mesomorphs and delinquent behavior is considered aggressive. Based on these problems, physical type theories have fallen out of favor and are rarely addressed in contemporary juvenile justice.

Genetic-Inheritance Studies

Biological explanations often assume a strong genetic contribution to behavior. The fact that physical features are clearly passed on from generation to generation has led some to extend that same propensity to nonphysical factors, such as behavioral tendencies. Two basic methods for inspecting this possibility are comparing the behavior of twins and comparing the behavior of offspring to their biological parents. In both sets of studies, it is not the criminal behavior that is considered to be inherited. Rather, it is factors such as low self-control, sensation-seeking, and temperament that are inherited, which lead to criminality (Eysenck & Gudjonsson, 1989; Mednick & Christiansen, 1977; Rowe, 2002).

Twin Studies

Studying twins for the genetic propensity to be deviant requires knowing whether the siblings are monozygotic (MZ) (identical) or dizygotic (DZ) (fraternal) twins. Monozygotic (MZ) twins are the product of a single fertilized egg that separates into two individuals with an identical genetic makeup. Dizygotic (DZ) twins are the result of two separate eggs fertilized by separate sperm. While genetically similar, the two offspring will not be genetically identical and are no more genetically similar than any two siblings born at different points in time. An examination of the genetic propensity for deviant

---

BOX 3.2 GENETIC EXPLANATIONS

	Key Idea: deviance is at least partially a result of genetic factors that an individual inherits
Twin Studies	Compare twins and siblings for similarities and differences in behavior; assumes identical twins will act more similarly to one another than other twins or simple siblings
Adoption Studies	Compare the behavior of siblings or offspring and biological parents who have been separated and are living in different environments for similarities in deviance
ADHD	Attention deficit/hyperactivity disorder has a genetic base and is related to antisocial behavior
MAOA	Monoamine oxidase A gene impacts on an individual's response to stimuli

---

behavior rests on finding greater **concordance**, or similarity, in behavior for MZ twins than for DZ twins or common siblings.

Several studies of twins claim to find a genetic component to behavior. Newman, Freeman, and Holzinger (1937), for example, reported much higher concordance in behavior for the MZ twins than DZ twins. Similarly, using a registry of 6,000 pairs of twins in Denmark, Christiansen (1974) uncovered three times as much concordance between MZ twins than between DZ twins when criminal records were inspected. More recently, Lyons (1996), in a large-scale analysis of subjects from a registry of Vietnam-era veterans born between 1939 and 1957, reported higher concordance in adult criminality for MZ twins than DZ twins. Each of these studies suggests that genetic factors have an influence on the actions of the individuals.

Adoption Studies

While the twin studies suggest a genetic component, they are unable to control for any environmental influences that may be at work (Katz & Chamblis, 1995; Reiss & Roth, 1993). The concordance may be due to similarity in rearing, imitation between siblings, or other non-genetic factors. Studies of behavior and adoption implicitly add environment to the investigations. A second method of investigating the genetic contribution to deviance is through the comparison of the behavior of adopted offspring and their biological parents. Adoption studies assume that any similarity between the adopted offspring and the biological parent must be due to the genetic similarity between the subjects because the child has been raised in a different environment from the parent.

Various adoption studies find a genetic link to behavior. Schulsinger (1972) finds that psychopathic subjects have more psychopathic biological relatives than do nonpsychopaths. Crowe (1972), analyzing females and their offspring, reports only a 13 percent difference in the arrests of offspring of offending and nonoffending mothers. The results in both of these studies, however, are based on very small sample sizes. Hutchings and Mednick (1977), using a much larger sample, reported that 49 percent of criminal boys have criminal biological fathers while only 31 percent of noncriminal boys have a criminal biological father. Whether the adoptive father is criminal or not does not eliminate this relationship, although it does temper the results. Brennan, Mednick, and Jacobsen (1996) report a strong genetic component in their adoption study, but it is only true when considering property crimes.

Several large reviews of the research find a genetic component to behavior. Walters (1992) undertook a meta-analysis of 38 twin and adoption projects dating from 1930 to 1989. In a **meta-analysis**, the researcher uses the reported data from past studies and computes a common statistic for all studies, thereby allowing a direct comparison of the different results. Walters (1992) reported that there is a "low-moderate" correlation between heredity and crime. Ellis and Walsh (2000), reviewing 72 studies, note that 93 percent provide strong support for a genetic contribution to behavior. In another meta-analysis, Rhee and Waldman (2012) find that more than 40 percent of the behaviors in twin and adoption studies are due to heritability, and the relationship is strongest in property offending. In all of these reviews, the authors note that the behavior itself is not inherited, only a propensity to criminality is inherited.

Other Genetic Examples

The search for genetic influences on behavior has not been limited to adoption and twin studies. Beaver and Connolly (2013) note that roughly half of all behavior and traits are inherited. They support this by pointing out the stability of behavior over time in the face of changing social and environmental conditions. Owen (2012) points out that genetics impact a person's brain structure, how it functions, and how it reacts to social and environmental inputs.

Attention deficit/hyperactivity disorder (ADHD) provides one example of a genetic contribution to behavior. Children suffering from this disorder are persistently disruptive, act impulsively, are easily frustrated, experience wide mood swings, and act inappropriately (Fishbein, Miller, Winn, & Dakof, 2009; Ward, 2000). Anderson (2007) notes there is a strong genetic basis for ADHD as demonstrated in a number of studies. To the extent that ADHD is related to deviant and criminal behavior, it can be argued that there is a genetic contribution to criminality (Anderson, 2007). It is important to note that genetics and ADHD are neither necessary nor sufficient for deviant behavior.

Another potential genetic component to behavior involves the MAOA gene. **Monoamine oxidase A** (MAOA) has the ability to impact an individual's response to external stimuli (Guo, Roettger, & Cai, 2008). It does this by facilitating or inhibiting the transfer of information from neuron to neuron, thus altering possible reactions to inputs. A meta-analysis by Kim-Cohen,

Caspi, Taylor, Williams, Newcombe, Craig, & Moffitt (2006) uncovered a clear association between MAOA and delinquency/criminality.

Genetic Summary

Research on genetics and deviant behavior has grown over the past 20 years and the support for a connection has grown. Genetic research is still in its infancy, and future advances may reveal stronger contributors to a wide range of behaviors. The problem of separating the environmental influences from a genetic component, however, remains a major stumbling block in the research.

Biosocial Factors

A recent trend in seeking biological/genetic explanations of behavior involves what is known as biosocial approaches. **Biosociology**, or sociobiology, refers to the idea that the biological makeup of the organism and the surrounding environment are intimately related. The environment plays a part in shaping the organism, and the organism, through its daily activity and interpretation of the world, shapes the environment. Owen (2012) points out that genes impact the structure of the brain, but the environment has the ability to change the functioning of the brain. Biosociology sees deviance occurring when specific biological conditions coincide with appropriate sociological or environmental factors. For example, an individual with a congenital hormonal defect may be overly aggressive in situations that force him or her into a choice between fight and flight. This individual, however, does not seek out such situations or become aggressive without the external stimulus. The more modern biological explanations of behavior, therefore, accommodate both biological and sociological factors.

BOX 3.3 BIOSOCIAL EXPLANATIONS

	Key Idea: the interaction of an individual's biological makeup and the environment plays a role in behavior
Hormones	Natural chemicals that regulate the body have a role in behavior; testosterone; epinephrine/norepinephrine
Orthomolecular Factors	Chemicals that are introduced to the body or altered through diet or other influences; reactive hypoglycemia; alcohol; drugs
Neurotransmitters	Chemicals involved in the transmission of electrical impulses through the nervous system can alter behavior; serotonin; dopamine
Central Nervous System	Different parts of the brain regulate behaviors, and recognizing abnormalities and problems with the brain may help in addressing deviance

Hormones and Aggression

Among the normal functions of the body is the production and secretion of various hormones. These natural chemicals control many of the basic bodily functions, including growth, reproduction, and functioning of the central nervous system. In terms of deviant behavior, most attention has focused on reproductive hormones (Shah & Roth, 1974).

Androgen, the male sex hormone present in testosterone, has received a great deal of attention. It has been found to be related to aggressive behavior, particularly in animal studies. Studies on human subjects have found a relation between higher testosterone levels and aggression and more serious offending (Booth & Osgood, 1993; Dabbs, Carr, Frady, & Riad, 1995; Ehrenkranz, Bliss, & Sheard, 1974; Kreuz & Rose, 1972; Rada, Laws, & Kellner, 1976; Soler, Vinayak, & Quadagno, 2000). While such studies suggest that testosterone leads to greater levels of aggression, the evidence is not totally convincing. Among the problems are the fact that testosterone levels vary over even short time periods; testosterone is affected by diet, stress, exercise, and social factors (Booth & Osgood, 1993; Katz & Chamblis, 1995; Nassi & Abramowitz, 1976; Reiss & Roth, 1993); and aggressive behavior may cause testosterone levels to increase, rather than the other way around (Harris, 1999).

Two other hormones that receive attention are **epinephrine** and **norepinephrine**. Both of these are responsible for the fight or flight reactions in humans (Owen, 2012). Increases in norepinephrine lead to increased heart rates and energy levels. Increases in epinephrine mean an increase in adrenaline. Changes in either may result in fear, greater activity, and/or aggressive responses to external stimuli (Mezzacappa, 1999). The external stimulus is typically some form of stress (Owen, 2012). While epinephrine, norepinephrine, and other hormones are involved in behavior, they are triggered by the environment and are not necessary nor sufficient for deviance.

Orthomolecular Factors

Orthomolecular factors refer to chemicals that are introduced to the body or altered through diet or other influences. This includes alcohol and other drugs, as well as normal dietary substances such as sugar. One commonly discussed substance and its relationship to aggression is sugar. **Hypoglycemia** is the term most often used in these discussions. However, hypoglycemia, a condition of low blood sugar, manifests itself in a lack of energy, lethargy, nervousness, and, in the extreme, a coma. It is difficult to imagine hypoglycemic individuals taking aggressive, deviant actions against anyone. The proper term for the relationship between blood sugar levels and criminal activity is **reactive hypoglycemia**, which refers to changes in the blood sugar level, both higher and lower, as a result of dietary intake.

While various researchers claim to have found support for a relationship between hypoglycemia and crime (Bonnett & Pfeiffer, 1978; Geary, 1983; Hippchen, 1978, 1981; Podolsky, 1964; Schauss, 1980), their conclusions rest upon suspect research methodology (Gray & Gray, 1983). Much of the support comes from anecdotal accounts of physicians and psychologists who simply compare a person's diet to his or her behavior without establishing the different bodily needs or processes of the different individuals; or from the Oral Glucose Tolerance Test, which is not a definitive measure of blood sugar (Gray & Gray, 1983). When more accurate measures are used, the studies fail to support reactive hypoglycemia as an explanation for deviance. Given the state of the evidence, reactive hypoglycemia is considered a minor cause of deviance (American Dietetics Association, 1984; Gray & Gray, 1983; National Dairy Council, 1985).

Alcohol and illegal drugs are other substances commonly linked to deviant behavior. That alcohol correlates with delinquency and criminality is indisputable. There is evidence that alcoholism has a genetic component (see Bohman, 1996). Many would argue that alcohol is a disinhibitor, making it easier for an individual to commit crime. Reiss and Roth (1993) suggest a more biological connection, in which alcohol alters the processing of information and, depending on the dosage, may prompt aggression and irritability, or more passivity and sluggishness. The use of other licit and illicit drugs may also lead to criminal behavior. The mechanism underlying the correlation between drugs and deviance, however, is not clear. From a **psychopharmacological perspective**, drugs have a direct causal impact on crime by inducing the user to act out in a certain way (Goldstein, 1989). At the same time, drug use may be related to deviance as a result of crime and violence related to the need to purchase drugs in uncontrolled settings. Such systemic crime is the result of competition between drug dealers or the need to commit property crimes in order to obtain money for drug purchases (Goldstein, 1989). Whether the drugs–crime relationship is psychopharmacological or systemic may be a function of the type of drug and related factors (its addictive properties, its cost, etc.).

Neurotransmitters

Neurotransmitters are chemicals involved in the transmission of electrical impulses through the nervous system which are capable of altering an individual's behavior. This occurs as a result of changes in the body's ability to process information and communicate in the brain (Anderson, 2007). In turn, this impacts on the individual's behavior.

Among the neurotransmitters that have been investigated are serotonin and dopamine. **Serotonin** is an inhibitor of behavior, particularly aggressive and impulsive behaviors (Anderson, 2007). Low levels of serotonin have been found to be related to low self-control (Wright & Beaver, 2005) and aggression (Moffitt, Brammer, Caspi, Fawcett, Raleigh, Yuwiler, & Silva, 1998). Similarly, Virkkunen, Goldman, and Linnoila (1996) note that serotonin levels influence impulse control, hyperactivity, and other behavior related to deviance. **Dopamine** acts in the opposite way from serotonin. Specifically, higher dopamine levels result in greater action and pleasure-seeking behaviors. Aggression is similarly enhanced from higher dopamine levels in the body (Anderson, 2007).

Research has shown that it is possible to alter various neurotransmitters. This can be done purposefully with drugs and inadvertently through the use of alcohol and other substances. Such changes can alter social behavior (Brunner, 1996). While still in its early stages, this research suggests that there is a relationship between different neurotransmitters and deviance (Anderson, 2007; Brennan, Mednick, & Volavka, 1995; Reiss & Roth, 1993).

The Central Nervous System

A wide range of other factors related to the brain and central nervous system have received attention in studies of deviant behavior. Recognition that different parts of the brain are related to different behaviors has led some researchers to look at brain abnormalities, functioning, and deviance. Various methods are available for such analyses, including magnetic resonance imaging (MRI), positron emission tomography (PET scans), and electroencephalography (EEG). An MRI can show the physical makeup of the brain and reveal any physical problems (Rowe, 2002). A PET scan, however, reveals differing levels of brain activity when faced with varying stimuli (Rowe, 2002). Similarly, an EEG measures a person's electrical brain waves, which can be compared to those of other individuals (Rowe, 2002). Based on these new technologies, Raine, Venables, and Williams (1995) conclude that there is clear evidence relating brain functioning, especially frontal and temporal lobe problems, to deviant activity. The impact of these factors relative to other variables, such as the environment, however, is not clear.

Issues in Biosocial Arguments

Many biosocial arguments suffer from common problems. First, the identification of correlations is often touted as clear evidence of a causal relationship. Second, there may be reversed time order in many of the relationships (Reiss & Roth, 1993). For example, aggressive behavior may lead to physical confrontations that result in the head injuries and altered brain functioning that is used to explain the aggression. Third, the ability to generalize results of studies based on animals to human beings is questionable. Finally, the studies typically fail to consider other spurious factors, such as social status, diet, and the environment, in the consideration of biosocial influences. It is

TABLE 3.3 Common Objections to Biologically Based Explanations

Biological Theories are Deterministic and Socially Dangerous
- Ignores the fact that those espousing biology recognize the interplay of biology and the environment
- Does not assume single cause

Because Crime is Socially Constructed, There Cannot Be any Genes for Crime
- No claim of a gene for crime but genes do play a role in traits and subsequent behavior

If a Problem is Considered Biological, Therapeutic Nihilism will Ensue
- You can alter and influence biological factors that contribute to behavior
- Biological treatments are not enough in themselves

Crime Cannot Have a Biological Basis Because Crime Rates Change Rapidly While Changes in Genes Require Many Generations
- Of course environment influences change in rate, but individual factors influence when and who will start and stop offending

Biological Theories Tend to be Insensitive to People's Feelings
- If we find results that suggest one group or condition is more predisposed to certain behavior, should we ignore it just to be politically correct?

Source: Compiled by authors from Walsh (2009).

possible that these other factors are influencing both deviance and neurological functioning.

Walsh (2009) outlines five typical objections lodged by mainstream criminologists against biosocial theories (see Table 3.3). These objections reflect two underlying problems. First, most criminologists are trained in the social science tradition. As a result, there is a fundamental lack of understanding and ignorance about biological issues. Second, there is an assumption that biological explanations are being promoted as an alternative to sociological and psychological theories. Those making this objection are ignoring the fact that what is being promoted is "biosociology" or "sociobiology," which posit looking at the interaction between biological and traditional social science factors in causing crime and deviance. Indeed, biosocial theorists recognize that the biological factors often play a minor role in behavior, and that the environment is a key factor in understanding crime and delinquency (Walsh, 2009).

Biological Implications for the Justice System

At the present time, there is still relatively little known about the relationships between biological influences and deviant behavior. Despite methodological problems, studies have provided qualified support for biosocial explanations. At the same time, they raise many questions.

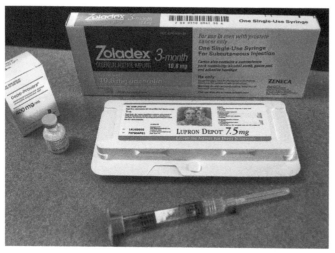

From left, seen clockwise, are the drugs Depo-Provera, Zoladex, and a Lupron-filled syringe, photographed at Atascadero State Hospital. Some experts believe that sex offenders can control and manage their deviant sexual urges with a combination of drugs and psychotherapy.

CREDIT: AP Photo/Ben Margot

The modern biosocial approaches have engendered interest in biological influences on behavior. Conditions that have a genetic component or behaviors related to hormonal or orthomolecular problems can be altered or modified by changes in diet or drug therapy. For example, both chemical and surgical castrations have been employed to reduce testosterone levels in convicted sex offenders. Depo-Provera is a drug that inhibits the production of testosterone. As biosocial research progresses, additional practical uses for curbing deviance will emerge.

The degree to which biological development and functioning can be influenced early in an individual's existence suggests that early interventions may be useful. Olds et al. (1998) and Lipsey and Wilson (1998) note that interventions as early as prenatal and during infancy can alter later behavior, including delinquency. The avoidance of early trauma can avoid later anti-social activities. As Brennan and associates note:

> Understanding of the interaction of genetic and environmental factors in the causes of crime may lead to the improvement of treatment and prevention. Several genetically based conditions are treated very successfully by environmental intervention (Brennan et al., 1995:90).

At the same time, caution must be taken when implementing programs based on biosocial research. These activities may also bring about more harm than good. For example, altering a diet to do away with "problem" foods may inadvertently damage an otherwise good diet. The most prudent direction for biosocial advocates to pursue at the present time would be expanded research.

PSYCHOLOGICAL EXPLANATIONS

A second general area of explanations for delinquency entails psychological theories. As with other types of theories, psychological explanations take a variety of forms and include a wide range of factors. The early base for psychological theories was biological/physical factors. Indeed, psychiatry, which is usually seen as a part of the general psychological field, is distinguished by its strong commitment to finding physiological bases for aberrant behavior. Psychiatrists are medical doctors who have specialized in the general area of mental disorders.

Many psychological explanations, however, do not look for a physical explanation. Instead, the psychological theories typically have the following distinctive characteristics:

- They generally view problems as arising out of early life experiences. Deviance is seen as a result of problems and flaws that were not recognized and corrected during the adolescent years.
- They are highly individualistic. While many individuals may display the same or similar behavior, different explanations or factors (such as incomplete socialization or poor personality development) may be at work for each person.
- They lend themselves to a treatment orientation. Rather than focus on who will become deviant, the emphasis is on working with individuals who are already having problems and assisting them to overcome the problem.

Psychoanalytic Explanations

Perhaps one of the most widely recognized names in psychology is Sigmund Freud (1856–1939). Freud pioneered the psychoanalytic approach to understanding human behavior. The major premise of **psychoanalysis** is that unconscious, and perhaps instinctual, factors account for much of the behavior displayed by individuals. In particular, deviance is the result of unconscious desires and drives being manifested in behavior. The goal of psychoanalysis is to identify the unconscious, precipitating factors and then develop conscious methods for dealing with them.

Freudian psychoanalysis outlines three distinct parts to the personality that are involved in behavior (see Table 3.4). The **id** reflects the unconscious desires, drives, and instincts within the individual. In simple terms, the id can be seen as the selfish, "I want" part of the individual. The **superego** entails learned values that form the moral character of the individual and help dictate what the person considers acceptable or unacceptable behavior. The superego is a result of early moral training. Where the id looks for satisfaction of desires, the superego responds with either a "can't have" orientation or a "must do" response. That is, the superego helps orient the individual's behavior away from

BOX 3.4 PSYCHOANALYTIC EXPLANATIONS	
	Key Idea: unconscious/instinctual factors cause individual behavior
Freud	Id/Ego/Superego; conflict between wants/desires and social values/morals leads to deviance when the id wins
Defense Mechanisms	Individuals respond to the conflict in various ways, including deviance and conformity
Goal	Identify the conflict, bring it to consciousness and address it

TABLE 3.4 The Freudian Personality	
Id	Unconscious desires, drives, instincts
Superego	Learned values, behaviors; moral character of the individual; outlines the acceptable and unacceptable; may be conscious or unconscious
Ego	Social identity of individual; actual behavior; conscious activity

simple desires and toward the value system that the person has incorporated. The actions of the superego may be both conscious and unconscious. The final part of the personality, the **ego**, is the social identity that is exhibited through behavior. It is often the manifestation of the conflict between the id and the superego. The ego is the conscious attempt to satisfy the needs of the id while continuing to abide by the mandates of the superego. This aspect is always conscious because it is the solution to the question of whether the individual follows his or her drives or the morally correct line of activity.

Psychoanalysis seeks to uncover the causes of behavior by bringing the unconscious conflict between the id and the superego to consciousness. Often, psychoanalysis is only undertaken when an individual develops criminally deviant behavior. The conflict between the id and the superego may be resolved in various ways. One response can involve acting in accord with the id, which may be deviant (such as stealing an item because you want it). Another could be denying the id and acting in another way which could also be deviance (such as hitting your spouse because you are mad at what happened at work). It is also possible to simply repress the id and maintain an acceptable behavioral pattern. Yet another response could be following the drive and rationalizing it as acceptable. It is the goal of psychoanalysis to uncover why the individual acts as he or she does.

Despite the development of a large body of literature, the psychoanalytic approach is subjected to strong criticism. First, it is very hard to undertake empirical tests of the theory because there is no clear method for measuring the id, ego, or superego. A second major criticism involves the fact that psycho-analysis is totally retrospective. That is, it is useful only for looking at what has already happened. It is geared toward uncovering why something happened and working to correct problems. A third criticism is that psychoanalysis em-phasizes early childhood and assumes that little change occurs after adoles-cence. Adult behavior is viewed only as a result of poor childhood socialization and not from factors appearing in adult life. Finally, psychoanalysis is criticized for ignoring social-structural factors in the determination of behavior. Indeed, with the heavy emphasis on the unconscious, psychoanalysis examines the social setting of the individual only to the extent that it failed to provide the necessary moral atmosphere during early adolescence.

Developmental Approaches

A number of writers identify the source of deviance in interrupted or arrested development. The basic assumption is that individuals develop through a number of stages. Each stage provides an integral part of the knowledge and understanding that a person needs to operate in society. The failure of an individual to complete any one of these stages or steps successfully may lead to some form of socially unacceptable behavior. This basic argument can be seen in Freud's psychoanalytic explanation in which the failure to develop appropriate superego and ego responses to the id takes place in early childhood. The child is born with the id but must learn and internalize the moral dictates of society as he or she grows.

BOX 3.5 **DEVELOPMENTAL EXPLANATIONS**	
	Key Idea: everyone develops through stages; deviance is the result of interrupted development
I-Levels	Interpersonal Maturity Levels; deviance committed by those stuck in early levels that focus on individual needs
Kohlberg's Moral Development	Six stages of moral development; failure to develop to the stage of recognizing the needs of society/others allows for deviant behavior

Interpersonal Maturity

One of the most well-known developmental approaches in delinquency research is the **Interpersonal Maturity Levels (I-levels)**. The I-levels represent a continuum from the most basic stage of development through the most advanced stage (see Table 3.5). The interruption of any stage makes the attainment of later stages difficult, if not impossible.

Most delinquency and deviance occurs in Levels 2, 3, and 4. Level 2 individuals operate primarily on the basis of their own need and use others only as a source of enjoyment or fulfillment. While Level 3 individuals begin to integrate rules, they are still oriented toward their own needs. As a result, they may realize what they are doing is wrong but cannot justify the rules with their desires. Finally, persons in Level 4 may resort to delinquent behavior as a means of striking out against what they perceive as contradictory demands. The inability to cope with competing demands may result in choosing delinquent activity. Individuals operating at lower maturity levels, however, tend to act in ways counter to societal demands.

Moral Development

A second well-known developmental approach is Kohlberg's (1981) **moral development**. Kohlberg's model notes that individuals progress through six stages of "moral development," which are arranged into three levels (Table 3.6).

TABLE 3.5 **Interpersonal Maturity Levels**	
Level 1:	The individual learns to discriminate between themselves and others.
Level 2:	The individual starts to separate things into persons and objects, partly on the basis of their own needs and what they can control.
Level 3:	At this level the individual begins to learn rules and can start to manipulate the environment for their own benefit.
Level 4:	The individual begins to perceive things from the standpoint of others. He/she sees conflicts between expectations of others and their own needs.
Level 5:	Here the individual becomes aware of patterns of behavior and relationships. There becomes an awareness of distinctions made between events, objects, and roles in society.
Level 6:	The individual is able to distinguish between himself/herself and the roles they play. These are not one and the same and can accommodate one another.
Level 7:	At this level, the individual begins to perceive a variety of methods for dealing with the world and makes choices based on his/her and other's past experiences and for the benefit of everyone.

Source: Compiled by authors from Sullivan, Grant and Grant (1957).

The Preconventional Level is characteristic of young children, while most adults fall into the Conventional Level. Only a small proportion of adults reach the Postconventional or Principled Level. Deviant individuals typically fail to display the same level of moral development as noncriminals with the same or similar characteristics. As in the I-level classification scheme, Kohlberg views deviance as a result of interrupted or incomplete development. For example, an individual at Stage 2 sees his or her own needs and feels that he or she does not get enough in return for what they do or want. As a result, that person may turn to deviance to "balance" the exchange.

Learning Theories

Implicit in developmental discussions is the idea that people learn right from wrong, and learning takes place over a long period of time. There is a cumulative nature to learning. In learning theories, the emphasis is on how an individual learns and what factors are effective in promoting learning. The failure of an individual to complete a developmental stage successfully, therefore, may be due to a problem in the learning process.

Modeling is perhaps the simplest form of learning. According to Bandura and Walters (1963), children learn by copying the behavior of others. Most modeling follows the behavior of significant others, particularly parents,

TABLE 3.6 **Kohlberg's Moral Development**

Level I. Preconventional Level

Stage 1	Right is obedience to authority and rules, and avoiding punishment. There is clear concern for one's own physical well-being.
Stage 2	Right corresponds to seeing one's own needs, taking responsibility for one's self, and allowing others to do the same. At issue is a fair exchange with others.

Level II. Conventional Level

Stage 3	Right is avoiding the disapproval of others, having good intentions and motives, and being concerned for others. Individuals are aware of others and their needs.
Stage 4	Right is doing one's duty to society and others, and upholding the social order. The individual is capable of looking at things from society's viewpoint.

Level III. Postconventional or Principled Level

Stage 5	Right is based on upholding the rules and values agreed upon by society. The individual feels obligated to society. There is a recognized social contract between the individual and society that outlines acceptable behavior.
Stage 6	Right is a reflection of universal ethical principles. The individual recognizes the moral rightness of behavior and acts accordingly.

Source: Compiled by authors from Kohlberg (1981).

siblings, peers, and other individuals close to the child. Modeling, however, is not limited to the people around the youth. Children also can learn from characters, both real and fictional. If the child continuously sees deviance, either real or fictional, the child may begin to copy that behavior. The child may not know whether it is right or wrong. He or she only knows that this is how people act. (Further discussion of modeling and identification will be taken up in Chapter 4.)

A more classical psychological learning theory is that of **operant conditioning**. Operant conditioning deals with the reinforcement of behavior through a complex system of rewards. Skinner (1953) and others view subsequent

BOX 3.6 **PSYCHOLOGICAL LEARNING EXPLANATIONS**	
	Key Idea: behavior is learned over a long period of time
Modeling	Basic form of learning where individuals, particularly children, copy what they see
Operant Conditioning	Behavior is molded through a complex system of rewards and punishments applied to past behavior

behavior as a consequence of past responses to behavior. Specifically, an individual repeats (or does not repeat) a behavior based on what happened when the behavior in question appeared in the past. For example, a child who does as he or she is told by his or her parents is given a treat for being good. The treat becomes a reinforcer for future good behavior. In operant conditioning the reinforcement comes after the behavior or action of the individual. Actions that result in a pleasurable response (positive reinforcer) or that eliminate painful or unpleasant situations (negative reinforcer) will be repeated. Learning, therefore, becomes an ongoing process, with every choice made by the individual resulting in some form of response. Future actions are based on the reinforcement, or lack thereof, of past behavior.

Bandura and Walters (1963) have combined conditioning and modeling in a general discussion of learning. They note that the degree to which a child models his or her behavior is mitigated by the level of reward or punishment that the model receives. For example, a child observing an act of aggression by another person or a fictional character is more likely to copy that act if the aggressive person is rewarded or not punished. Therefore, the process of learning through operant conditioning can take a vicarious route through observation of the experiences of others. Two key concerns have been raised in relation to psychological learning theories. First, while modeling and operant conditioning make intuitive sense and receive support from anecdotal and case studies, most of the supportive studies rely on correlational analyses and contain serious methodological flaws. A second problem is that modeling and operant conditioning approaches ignore the potential contribution of the individual to behavior. The basic assumption is that the individual is a product of the environment and has little influence over his or her choice of activity.

Personality and Delinquency

Various researchers have proposed that deviants display certain personality characteristics that can be used to explain deviant and criminal behavior.

BOX 3.7 PERSONALITY EXPLANATIONS	
	Key Idea: certain personality characteristics can be used to explain deviant and criminal behavior
The Gluecks	Identified a delinquent personality by comparing delinquent and nondelinquent youths; delinquents are extroverted, impulsive, resentful, defiant, destructive
Antisocial Personality Disorder	A mental-health condition where individuals manipulate and exploit others for their own personal benefit; outlined in the DSM-V
MMPI	Minnesota Multiphasic Personality Inventory; standardized test of personality; based largely on incarcerated individuals

Psychologists have developed a wide array of personality classifications and measures for uncovering personality traits. Indeed, the *Diagnostic and Statistical Manual of Mental Disorders* (5th ed.) of the American Psychiatric Association (known as the DSM-V) includes the classification of "antisocial personality disorder," which refers to individuals who show a continuing pattern of behavior harmful to others.

One of the early attempts to distinguish delinquents from nondelinquents using personality factors was conducted by Sheldon and Eleanor Glueck (1956). Comparing 500 delinquents to 500 matched nondelinquents, Glueck and Glueck claimed that:

> . . . delinquents are more extroverted, vivacious, impulsive, . . . less self-controlled . . . are more hostile, resentful, defiant, suspicious, . . . destructive . . . and are less fearful of failure or defeat than the nondelinquents. They are less concerned about meeting conventional expectations and are more ambivalent toward or far less submissive to authority. They are, as a group, more socially assertive (Glueck & Glueck, 1956:275).

This picture of the delinquent was meant to summarize their overall personality pattern and indicate differences from conventional youths.

While the work of Glueck and Glueck still draws attention today, several concerns have been raised about the findings. First, not all the traits associated with the delinquents are undesirable. For example, being extroverted, assertive, less fearful of failure, and less submissive are traits that many individuals would find valuable. Second,

WEB ACTIVITY

You can read more about the DSM-V at http://www.psych.org/MainMenu/Research/DSMIV.aspx

the authors assume that the individuals had these traits before they exhibited delinquent behavior. It could be argued, however, that the delinquents were hostile, resentful, defiant, and ambivalent to authority due to their contact with the justice system. Finally, the individuals who evaluated the youths were aware of which youths were delinquent and which were not delinquent. Knowing an individual is delinquent and in an institution may prompt an evaluator to expect the subject to be more assertive, more hostile, or have less self-control.

One commonly referenced personality disorder is **Antisocial Personality Disorder (APD)**. The National Center for Biotechnology Information (2010) defines APD as "a mental health condition in which a person has a long-term pattern of manipulating, exploiting, or violating the rights of others." This behavior may be criminal or noncriminal. The actual cause of APD is not clear, but a combination of genetic and environmental factors probably contribute to the condition (Mayo Clinic, 2010). Assessing the presence of APD requires psychological testing and identifying criteria listed in the DSM-V. Treatment is considered very difficult and involves mainly psychotherapy. Unfortunately for juvenile justice, APD typically is not identified until early adulthood and, thus, is most useful in the adult criminal justice system.

A major change in personality research has been to try to develop standardized measures of personality. The **Minnesota Multiphasic Personality Inventory (MMPI)** is one standardized method for uncovering personality traits in individuals. The MMPI is an inventory of over 500 true/false questions that are designed to tap 10 personality dimensions identified in past clinical analyses (Megargee & Bohn, 1979) without the need for extended clinical observation. The MMPI assumes that everyone answers some questions in a deviant manner. Therefore, no single question is associated with deviant behavior. Instead, deviance is considered more likely as the individual answers in a deviant fashion on a number of questions. While the MMPI has been used extensively, it has been challenged on a number of grounds. First, to the extent that the prior clinical evaluations are in error, poorly conceived, or invalid, the MMPI results also are questionable. The results are only as good and useful as the underlying clinical factors. Second, the MMPI is useful primarily in the treatment of offenders, and not for predicting or explaining deviance prior to its occurrence. Finally, because the MMPI has been refined using institutionalized subjects, it is possible that it reflects factors related to institutional life and experiences, rather than a deviant personality. The inventory has been subjected to relatively few tests outside of the institutional setting.

Mental Deficiency and Delinquency

Since the late 1800s, low intelligence has been offered as a prime cause of deviant behavior. The scientific interest in the relation between intelligence and deviance can be traced to the development of IQ testing. **IQ**, or intelligence quotient, was developed by Alfred Binet in the early 1900s as a numerical representation of the mental ability of the individual. The formula for IQ is rather simple:

$$IQ = (\text{mental age/chronological age}) \times 100$$

The mental age of an individual is determined by performance on a standardized test. The test consists of questions geared toward different aged individuals. Persons age 10 and up are expected to be able to answer a certain level of questioning and all those from the easier levels. More difficult questions are assumed to be beyond the ability of the average 10-year-old. Once an individual's mental age is determined, the researcher simply divides that figure by the respondent's actual age and multiplies by the base of 100.

Since the development of the IQ test, many researchers have attempted to show that delinquency and deviance are related to low intelligence. The assumption

BOX 3.8 MENTAL DEFICIENCY EXPLANATIONS

	Key Idea: examination of a person's intelligence as a cause of deviance
IQ	Intelligence Quotient; numerical measure of the mental ability of an individual; attempts to show that delinquency and deviance are related to low intelligence
Nature vs. Nurture	Debate over whether intelligence is inherited (nature) or an outcome of environmental influences (nurture)

that IQ is related to crime is not a surprising one given the knowledge that most incarcerated offenders tend to be less educated and display below-average scores on academic achievement tests. The major source of debate concerning IQ revolves around the question of whether IQ is due to nature or nurture.

The **nature–nurture controversy** refers to the question of whether intelligence is inherited (nature) or whether it is an outcome of environmental influences (nurture). The nature argument views IQ as set at birth and not subject to outside influences, such as the social and physical environment, including education. Conversely, the nurture side of the debate proposes that an individual's IQ is the outcome of complex interactions between the genetic makeup of the person and the environment to which the individual is exposed. This view suggests that IQ can be altered through education and other environmental interventions.

The view that intelligence is genetically determined received a great deal of early support in the United States, where low IQ scores were used as a means of denying immigrants entry to the country. Goddard (1920) argued that most criminals were "feebleminded" (IQ of less than 75) and the government took the position that excluding such individuals was in the best interests of the country. Unfortunately, Goddard (1920) examined only incarcerated "criminals" and had no way of knowing whether they were more or less "intelligent" than anyone else. Wilson and Herrnstein (1985) and Herrnstein and Murray (1994) also have argued that IQ is substantially due to genetics and that IQ is a strong predictor of criminal activity. Hirschi and Hindelang (1977) provide the most widely cited argument in the IQ-delinquency literature. The authors argue that IQ is at least as important in predicting delinquency as social class or race, and is related to delinquency regardless of the race or social class of the individual. Their opinion is that IQ is an indirect cause of delinquency. Specifically, low IQ, through genetics and/or environment, leads to poor school performance, which prompts a lack of concern for education, a rebellious attitude toward the school and societal demands, and, eventually, a heightened chance of deviant behavior. To the extent that environment has a role, individuals with a low IQ who can be encouraged to stay in school, receive special help, or otherwise enhance their abilities may not experience the problems and frustrations that precipitate deviant activity.

Implications of Psychological Theories for Juvenile Justice

Before addressing the impact of psychological theories, it is important to point out some of the criticisms leveled at these explanations. As has been noted throughout the above discussions, psychologically oriented explanations are not particularly good for the prediction of behavior. Many are formulated after the fact and seek, primarily, to explain the observed behavior retrospectively. The emphasis is on why something happened and not predicting what will happen in the future. A second concern with psychological studies is the reliance on subjective interpretations. Most psychological endeavors rest on the opinion of individuals who have been trained in the field of psychology. Unfortunately, there is no single orientation or perspective that drives the entire field, or even subfields, of psychology. The subjective nature of psychology, therefore, often leads to conflicting opinions, even when individuals are looking at the exact same information.

Some commentators criticize what they see as the individualistic nature of psychological explanations. Indeed, many psychological endeavors examine individual subjects, and the precise explanation for deviance could vary from subject to subject. This criticism may be shortsighted, however, given the fact that these individualistic approaches form the basis of other, more general theories. For example, operant conditioning is a key component of differential association-reinforcement theory, and hedonism is at the heart of Gottfredson and Hirschi's general theory of crime (see Chapter 4 for discussions of both of these theories).

Psychological explanations have their greatest impact on the correctional end of the juvenile justice system. Psychology's emphasis on identifying the cause of an individual's behavior fits the general treatment orientation of juvenile justice. As a result, juvenile corrections place heavy emphasis on counseling, education, and other rehabilitative methods. Techniques such as I-level classifications and the MMPI are used to gain insight into a juvenile's problems and subsequently design a response to those problems. Additionally, behavior modification techniques are used to set up token economies in detention centers and training schools. Psychology will more than likely remain primarily a correctional tool in juvenile justice until such time that more precise methods of evaluation are generated or the predictive ability of psychological findings are enhanced.

SUMMARY

The biological and psychological explanations discussed in this chapter represent theories and perspectives developed over many decades. While some have been discounted because of their lack of rigor and relevance, they have engendered discussions that may lead to more applicable and useful theories. Psychological explanations have found a clear place in the juvenile justice system. This is particularly true in the juvenile court and in the correctional phase of processing. Biological explanations have not fared so well. This is due mainly to the poor quality of the early explanations and the current lack of expertise in the physical sciences held by criminologists and criminal justicians. The next chapter turns to a discussion of sociological explanations that hold the dominant position in modern discussions of delinquency and criminality.

DISCUSSION QUESTIONS

1. Compare and contrast the Classical and Positivist schools of thought. What are the basic assumptions each hold about the individual and behavior? What implications do each have for the juvenile justice system?

2. There is a movement to shift the emphasis in the juvenile justice system from the sociological theories and explanations for delinquency to the biosocial perspective. Point out and explain what you see as the more promising biosocial approaches. In addition, project the problems or shortcomings that will result if the emphasis is shifted (that is, what are the problems with the biosocial approach)?

3. Identifying a "criminal or delinquent personality" has proven to be quite difficult. Outline some of the more well-known methods for isolating this personality and what problems exist in these approaches. Which method would you use if you had to pick one and why?

4. Psychological theories are common in correctional practice. Pick specific psychological approaches and illustrate their usefulness and shortcomings for use in correcting juvenile delinquents (i.e., critique the approaches).

CHAPTER 4

Sociological Explanations of Delinquency

WHAT YOU NEED TO KNOW

- Shaw and McKay found that crime and delinquency were concentrated in the center of cities, where lower-SES individuals and immigrants or African Americans lived. The reason they offer for this finding was "social disorganization," meaning the residents did not exert control, thus allowing crime to flourish.

- Differential association argues that deviance is learned just as other behavior is learned. Modifications of differential association include differential identification (which adds the idea of learning from images in the media) and differential reinforcement (which argues we learn from the results of our actions).

- Subcultural theories suggest that youths often act in accordance with a different set of values and beliefs that invariably conflict with the dictates of the larger society, thus leading them to be considered deviant.

- The techniques of neutralization presented by Sykes and Matza allow youths to violate the law while maintaining a positive self-image as a conforming member of society.

- Routine activities theory argues that a criminal act requires a motivated offender and a suitable target to coincide where there is an absence of capable guardianship.

- Strain theory suggests that crime is a logical outcome of the disjunction between the socially prescribed goals and the means available for achieving those goals.

- General strain theory offers a view that strain can come from a wide array of sources besides simply economic strain and inequality.

KEY TERMS

anomie

bond to society

Chicago School

collective efficacy

containment theory

culture conflict

developmental theories

differential association

differential identification

differential reinforcement

drift

ecological fallacy

ecological perspective

elaboration model

external pressures

external pulls

focal concerns

general strain theory

inner containment

internal pushes

labeling

life-course theories

looking-glass self

malicious

mentalistic construct

modes of adaptation

negativistic

non-utilitarian

outer containment

primary deviance

rational choice theory

reintegrative shaming

role-taking

routine activities perspective

secondary deviance

self-control theory

social control theories

social disorganization

strain theory

subculture

symbolic interactionism

tautological

techniques of neutralization

transfer of evil

vertical integration

- ▪ Hirschi's social control theory states that "delinquent acts result when an individual's bond to society is weak or broken." Bond is composed of attachment, commitment, involvement, and belief.

- ▪ Self-control theory argues that behavior is controlled by factors an individual internalizes early in life. Good self-control keeps an individual from violating the law.

- ▪ The labeling perspective proposes that involvement in the juvenile justice system leads to more deviant behavior by labeling the individual as a deviant and forcing him or her to act in accordance with that label.

- ▪ Attempts to integrate theories into more unified, coherent explanations of deviance have met only limited success in advancing sociological theory.

INTRODUCTION

The most prevalent explanations of delinquent behavior are sociologically oriented theories. Indeed, criminology, criminal justice, and juvenile justice have grown around sociological perspectives. The reasons for this are understandable. First, the great changes in society during and after the industrial revolution were accompanied by increased levels of deviant behavior. This behavior, however, was more prevalent in the cities. This led to a natural view that deviant behavior was an outgrowth of social relationships, especially those in urban areas. Second, sociological theories hold a great deal of intuitive appeal. Many of the ideas, as will be seen, are based on common sense and do not require a great deal of education or training for simple understanding. A third reason behind the dominance of sociological explanations entails the ability to test such theories. While tests of biologically oriented theories fail to provide empirical support, and psychological theories often defy empirical testing or are restricted to only individuals, most sociological explanations are accompanied by attempts at empirical research and often find some degree of support.

Sociological theories and perspectives reflect elements of both Classicism and Positivism. From the Positivistic view, sociological theories consider a wide array of social and environmental factors as explanations of deviant behavior. Delinquency is a response to the setting in which the individual finds himself or herself. The neighborhood in which an individual grows up, one's peers, the views of others, social and moral training, the organization of society, economic conditions, and the effect of being processed in the criminal justice system are among the many factors considered in sociological theories. Classical elements appear in discussions of deterrence, control, and routine activities theories where the individual is presumed to have some degree of choice in his or her behavior. This chapter attempts to outline the major points of each theory or view and draw out similarities and differences in the sociological explanations for deviance.

THE ECOLOGICAL PERSPECTIVE

Perhaps the earliest sociological explanation to gain importance in criminology, the **ecological perspective** (or "Chicago School," so named because of the research done using the city of Chicago as a focus) sought to explain deviance as a natural outgrowth of the location in which it occurs, particularly large cities and places within large cities. Research in the early twentieth century recognized the great growth in the number and size of large cities. European immigrants and Southern blacks were flocking to the industrial cities of the north and northeast. These new residents typically moved to the central city areas, where the housing was more affordable and closer to the factories, and jobs were available to lower-skilled and educated individuals. These areas were densely populated, with many of the new residents unable to speak English. The cities could be viewed as a series of concentric circles, or zones, moving out from the original central business district of the community, through areas of growing industry with poor housing, to more affluent areas as the distance from the center increased (Burgess, 1925). Along with the great influx of people came increases in various social problems—including criminal activity.

Shaw and McKay: Social Disorganization

Clifford Shaw and Henry McKay (1942) analyzed where delinquency occurred in Chicago. The researchers identified the location of every recorded delinquent act in the city for two different time periods roughly 20 years apart. Based on

---

BOX 4.1 ECOLOGICAL EXPLANATIONS

	Key Idea: looks at the influence of the environment on where deviance occurs
Concentric Zones	Community grows from the original city center, with inner zone being poor and subsequent zones being more affluent and stable; Burgess
Social Disorganization	Areas in which residents do not concern themselves with a real improvement and fail to take control of behavior in the area; Shaw and McKay
Collective Efficacy	The ability of the neighborhood to regulate or control behavior through both formal and informal means
Sources of Control	Private, Parochial, and Public; Bursik and Grasmick

WEB ACTIVITY

Go to http://www.routledge.com/cw.
whitehead to see how early researchers
saw the layout of the city.

where it occurred, Shaw and McKay (1942) reported that
crime and delinquency was highest:

1. in and around the central business district,
2. in poor areas of the city, and
3. in areas dominated by immigrants and African
    Americans.

All three conclusions pointed to the same physical location in the city,
specifically the city center, where economic conditions were poorest and new
arrivals were able to find affordable housing.

The stability of the delinquency levels in the same areas over time led Shaw
and McKay (1942) to examine what it was about these areas that could explain
the findings. What they uncovered was that these areas were undergoing
constant change. Poor immigrants would settle in the central city areas due to
the availability of cheap housing and the proximity to factory jobs. Over time
the new residents gained employment, were assimilated into American society,
and they would leave the inner city for the more desirable neighborhoods
outside the central city. They were replaced by new immigrants, thus establishing a constant turnover of residents. The delinquency problem was a result
of this turnover. The turnover caused a problem referred to as **social
disorganization** (Shaw & McKay, 1942). Social disorganization referred to the
fact that the people in these core areas did not concern themselves with
improving the area, getting to know one another, or taking control of conditions. They were primarily interested in bettering themselves and getting out
as soon as possible. There was a lack of social organization that could bring
about improvements. The residents were unable to exert control over the
behavior of those living there.

Collective Efficacy

More recent discussions of the ability or inability of residents to control their
neighborhoods and their conditions reference the degree of collective efficacy
of the area. **Collective efficacy** refers to the ability of the neighborhood to
regulate or control behavior through both formal and informal means.
Bursik and Grasmick (1993) identify three primary sources: private, parochial,
and public (see Table 4.1). Unfortunately, marshaling this control is not equal
across neighborhoods. Lower-class, transient, high-crime neighborhoods have
particular trouble developing these sources of control. Areas undergoing a great
deal of change will have an unstable base for private and parochial control
mechanisms. Even stable neighborhoods with strong private and parochial
networks may not be able to marshal the public support needed for effective
delinquency control (Bursik & Grasmick, 1993). Hope (1997) refers to this as
a problem of **vertical integration**. That is, some neighborhoods are unable to

TABLE 4.1 Sources of Neighborhood Control	
Private	Interpersonal relationships: family, friends, and close associates
Parochial	Neighborhood networks and institutions: schools, churches, businesses, social organizations/groups
Public	Agencies and institutions of the city, state, or other governmental unit

Source: See Hunter (1985:230–242); and Bursik and Grasmick (1993).

marshal support from those in power, such as city/government agencies or social service providers.

Critique of the Ecological Approach

While the ecological approach shifted attention away from the biological views of Lombroso to a more sociological orientation, these new ideas also suffered from problems. First, despite the frequent use of "social disorganization" as a theoretical explanation for deviance and social problems, the ecological perspective was not able to measure disorganization independent from the deviance and problems it was supposed to explain. That is, social disorganization explained the problems, and the existence of the problems was used as proof of social disorganization. This is a **tautological**, or circular, explanation. Second, many researchers fell into the trap of attributing results to individuals that are based on grouped data. This is known as the **ecological fallacy**. Just because delinquency may be highest in areas of low income, low average education, and high density does not mean that an uneducated individual from a poor family living in a two-bedroom home with nine people would be delinquent. Indeed, many delinquents in poor inner-city areas may exhibit the exact opposite traits. Knowledge about an area tells little about a specific individual.

Despite problems with the ecological approach, this early work brought crime and delinquency theory squarely into the sociological tradition. For the most part, these early sociological explanations provided a clean break from the biological work of Lombroso and his followers. The ecological studies also provided much of the framework for subsequent theoretical advances.

LEARNING THEORY

Many sociological theorists see deviance as a result of learning. A variety of factors contribute to the learning process, including with whom an individual has contact, what the individual observes, and the consequences of one's behavior. The most prominent of the social learning theories is differential association, which forms the basis of other learning theories.

BOX 4.2 SOCIAL LEARNING EXPLANATIONS

	Key Idea: deviance, like all behavior, is learned
Differential Association	Learning comes from interaction with other people; different interactions have differential impact on an individual; Sutherland
Differential Identification	Personal association not necessary for learning; learning results from taking on a role seen in the media; Glaser
Differential Reinforcement	Operant conditioning argument; people learn from rewards and punishments that come from past behavior: Jeffery

---

Edwin Sutherland (1883–1950) proposed the theory of differential association, a learning theory of delinquency. Sutherland's theory can be considered the first truly sociological effort to explain crime.

CREDIT: Indiana University Archives

Sutherland: Differential Association

Sutherland's (1939) **differential association** views learning as the culmination of various social inputs faced by individuals throughout their lives. Sutherland observed that delinquency was concentrated in the inner-city areas where juveniles came into daily contact with both deviant and conventional ideas. As a result, children could just as easily learn to accept deviance as they could conventional behavior.

In explaining his views, Sutherland proposed nine specific points to differential association (see Table 4.2). Underlying these nine points is the idea that deviance is learned in the same fashion as conforming behavior. The major sources of that learning are the people with whom an individual comes in contact, particularly the family, peers, and religious institutions. Everyone is exposed to both deviant and conforming information. The individual's choice of behavior depends on the relative amount of influence favoring either deviant or conventional activity.

Differential association has been criticized from a variety of perspectives. One of the criticisms revolves around Sutherland's failure to define or operationalize many of his terms. The common definitions of frequency (number of contacts), duration (length of a contact), priority (temporal order of the contacts), and intensity (significance of the contact) have been supplied by other researchers. Sutherland also failed to explicitly define "an excess of definitions." Second, although there have been a large number of studies focusing on differential association (e.g., Adams, 1974; DeFleur & Quinney, 1966; Reiss & Rhodes, 1961; Short, 1960), most of

TABLE 4.2 Sutherland's Differential Association Theory
1. Criminal behavior is learned.
2. Criminal behavior is learned in interaction with other persons in a process of communication.
3. The principal part of the learning of criminal behavior occurs within intimate personal groups.
4. When criminal behavior is learned, the learning includes (a) techniques of the crime, which are sometimes very complicated, sometimes very simple; (b) the specification of motives, drives, rationalizations, and attitudes.
5. The specific direction of motives and drives is learned from definitions of the legal codes as favorable or unfavorable.
6. A person becomes delinquent because of an excess of definitions favorable to violation of law over definitions unfavorable to violation of law.
7. Differential associations may vary in frequency, duration, priority, and intensity.
8. The process of learning criminal behavior by association with criminal and anticriminal patterns involves all of the mechanisms that are involved in any other learning.
9. While criminal behavior is an expression of general needs and values, it is not explained by those general needs and values, because noncriminal behavior is an expression of the same needs and values.

Source: Compiled by authors from Sutherland and Cressey (1974:75–76).

the empirical support is indirect and highly qualified. Sutherland explicitly discounted the influence of factors other than social, face-to-face contacts in differential association. During the early 1900s, television did not exist, movies were silent, and radio and newspapers were the primary form of mass communication. Changes in the modern world prompted researchers to modify and extend the original ideas of differential association. One of the most logical modifications to make in differential association is the inclusion of the mass media and non-face-to-face communication in the theory.

Differential Identification

Glaser's (1956) **differential identification** proposes that personal association is not always necessary for the transmission of behavioral cues. Real and fictional presentations on television and in other mass media provide information concerning acceptable behavior, especially to children. The basic idea is that as an individual observes the activity of a character he begins to imitate or model that behavior. Another term for this is **role-taking**. The child assumes the role that is portrayed. This is especially problematic because many children fail to realize that the media portrayals are in themselves roles and not the actual behavior of the actor. A youth might observe a glorified version of crime from a desirable fictional character and, thus, act in accordance with that portrayal.

Differential Reinforcement

A second set of modifications to learning theory and differential association revolves around the ideas of operant conditioning. **Differential reinforcement** (Jeffery, 1965) and differential association-reinforcement (Burgess & Akers, 1966) theories propose that an individual can learn from a variety of sources besides the social factors found in the ideas of both differential association and differential identification. Individuals can learn from a range of nonsocial factors. In differential reinforcement, nonsocial factors generally refer to the outcome of an individual's behavior. If the behavior results in a pleasurable payoff (e.g., useful stolen goods) the behavior will be repeated. The absence of an acceptable return on the behavior may prompt the person to abandon the activity. Experiencing an undesirable outcome (such as being caught and imprisoned) would prompt a person to cease the activity or avoid the behavior in the future. Burgess and Akers (1966) rewrote differential association using operant conditioning terminology.

SUBCULTURAL THEORIES

Subcultural explanations owe a great deal to the same research that prompted the early ecological and social learning theories. It was the diversity of people in the cities that prompted the idea of social disorganization and provided different inputs to the learning process. Subcultural theorists took these ideas and focused directly on the fact of diversity in the population.

Defining subculture is not an easy task. In the simplest sense, a **subculture** is a smaller part of a larger culture. While it must vary to some degree from the larger culture, it is not totally different. The subculture exists within and is part of the larger culture. More detailed definitions typically refer to differences in values, beliefs, ideas, views, and/or meanings that a group of individuals hold from those of the larger culture.

From a subcultural perspective, delinquency and criminality are the result of individuals attempting to act in accordance with subcultural norms. This can occur in two ways. First, an individual acts according to subcultural mandates that, unfortunately, may be considered deviant by the larger society. This problem could be common for new immigrants who have traditionally acted according to one set of cultural proscriptions and are now faced with a different set of expectations in a new cultural setting. Second, deviance may result from the inability to join or be assimilated into a new culture. Consequently, the

---

BOX 4.3 SUBCULTURAL EXPLANATIONS

	Key Idea: there are variations in values and beliefs; conforming to one set results in violating those of another; culture conflict
Lower-class Gang Delinquency	Lower-class gangs are malicious, negativistic, and nonutilitarian; lower class cannot compete in a middle class world; Cohen
Lower-class Focal Concerns	Lower class has a distinctive set of focal concerns (values); acting in concert with the focal concerns leads to conflict with middle-class norms; Miller
Techniques of Neutralization	Methods used by individuals that allow an individual to accommodate deviant behavior while maintaining a self-image as a conformist; Sykes and Matza

---

individual may strike out against society because of the frustration faced in attempting to live according to the new cultural expectations.

Lower-Class Gang Delinquency

Albert Cohen (1955), recognizing the concentration of delinquency among lower-class boys, argued there was a lower-class gang subculture. Lower-class youths feel ill-equipped to compete in and cannot succeed in a middle-class society. This is compounded by the fact that they are expected to follow the goals and aspirations of the middle class. All youths are measured against a middle-class measuring rod that they cannot meet. The failure to succeed in terms of middle-class values leads to feelings of failure and diminished self-worth among the lower-class youths. As a result, these boys join together in groups and act in concert with the group (subcultural) norms instead of with the mandates of the larger culture. While this provides the youths with some degree of self-worth, status, and success, it also leads to **culture conflict**. That is, by following one set of cultural (or subcultural) values, beliefs and behaviors, the individual is violating the proscriptions of the dominant culture. In Cohen's study, adherence to the subcultural group's mandates means violating the laws of middle-class society.

Cohen (1955) identifies three aspects of the emergent "lower-class gang delinquency." He claims that the subculture is malicious, negativistic, and nonutilitarian. In support of this contention, Cohen points out that the youths often steal items, with the intent of causing trouble and harm for another person, not because they want the item. He sees much of the deviant activity as a means of tormenting others. The behavior brings about an immediate "hedonistic" pleasure instead of supplying any long-term need or solution to a problem. In general, there appears to be little point in the behavior besides causing trouble for the larger middle-class culture.

Lower-Class Focal Concerns

Walter Miller's (1958) subcultural explanation goes beyond the behavior of juveniles to include all lower-class males. Miller views the lower class as operating under a distinct set of cultural values, or **focal concerns** (see Table 4.3). These are: trouble, toughness, smartness, excitement, fate, and autonomy. Adherence to these lower-class focal concerns or values provides status, acceptance, and feelings of belonging for the lower-class individual (Miller, 1958).

At the same time that these values provide positive reinforcement in the lower-class world, they bring about a natural conflict with middle-class values. The goal of the lower-class individual is not to violate the law or the middle-class norms. Instead, the goal is to follow the focal concerns of their class and peers. Deviant behavior, therefore, is a by-product of following the subcultural focal concerns (Miller, 1958). Where Cohen (1955) saw deviance as a conscious reaction of lower-class youths striking out against the middle-class society and value system, Miller (1958) views the focal concerns as an integral part of the lower class.

TABLE 4.3 **Miller's Lower-class Focal Concerns**	
Trouble	Refers to the fact that lower-class males spend a large amount of time preoccupied with getting into and out of trouble. Trouble may bring about desired outcomes such as attention and prestige.
Toughness	Emphasis on physical prowess, athletic skill, masculinity, and bravery. Partly a response of lower-class males raised in [single] female-headed households.
Smartness	Basically the idea of being "streetwise." The concern is on how to manipulate the environment and others to your own benefit without being subjected to sanctions of any kind.
Excitement	Refers to the idea that lower-class individuals are oriented around short-term hedonistic desires. Activities, such as gambling and drug use, are undertaken for the immediate excitement or gratification that is generated.
Fate	The belief that, in the long run, individuals have little control over their lives. Luck and fortune dictate the outcome of behavior. Whatever is supposed to happen will happen regardless of the individual's wishes. This allows for a wide latitude in behavior.
Autonomy	While the individual believes in fate, there is a strong desire to resist outside control imposed by other persons. Individuals want total control over themselves until fate intervenes.

Sykes and Matza: Techniques of Neutralization

Throughout the discussion of subcultural explanations there is a subtle failure to address the fact that no individual operates exclusively in the subculture. Rather, every individual must deal with both the subcultural and the larger cultural expectations. Indeed, many individuals attempt to abide by both sets of values. Juveniles, in particular, often act in accordance with one set of values or rules and still maintain a positive self-image in which they believe they fit into the acceptable behavior of the larger culture. Juveniles who commit delinquent acts often see themselves as no better and no worse than anyone else, despite recognizing their deviant activity.

Sykes and Matza (1957) outlined five **techniques of neutralization** that allow the juvenile to accommodate the deviant behavior while maintaining a self-image as a conformist (see Table 4.4). Each technique requires the individual to admit to the behavior under question. The individual invokes one of the techniques in order to justify his or her behavior in light of confrontation with conventional cultural values. While an exact understanding of how, when, and by whom neutralization techniques are used is not known, evidence shows that such techniques are used in various settings (Agnew, 1994; Agnew & Peters, 1986; Minor, 1981; Thurman, 1984).

TABLE 4.4 Sykes and Matza's Techniques of Neutralization	
Denial of Responsibility	The youth may claim that the action was an accident or, more likely, assert that he or she was forced into the action by circumstances beyond his or her control.
Denial of Injury	Focuses on the amount of harm caused regardless of violating the law. The absence of harm to an individual may involve pointing to a lack of physical injury, the action was a prank, or the person or business could afford the loss.
Denial of the Victim	The juvenile can deny the existence of a victim by claiming self-defense or retaliation, the absence of a victim (such as involving a business and not a person), and/or that characteristics of the victim brought the harm on himself or herself (such as hazing a homosexual).
Condemnation of the Condemnors	The youth turns the tables on those individuals who condemn his or her behavior by pointing out that the condemnors are no better than he or she. In essence, the condemnors are also deviant.
Appeal to Higher Loyalties	Conflict between the dictates of two groups will be resolved through adherence to the ideas of one group. The juvenile may see greater reward and more loyalty to the subcultural group on some issues which, in turn, lead to deviant behavior.

Source: Constructed by authors from Sykes and Matza (1957).

Critique of the Subcultural Approach

The attempt to explain deviance through the use of subcultures faces a number of problems. The greatest problem entails identifying a subculture. Since a subculture means there is a difference in values, beliefs, and norms from those held by the larger culture, it is necessary to measure those domains and show how they differ from the larger culture. Unfortunately, research typically identifies subcultures through the behavior of those in the subculture. That is, those who act in a certain way are in a subculture, which is why they act that way. This is a tautological (or circular) argument. The behavior indicates that a subculture exists, and the subculture is used to explain why the behavior occurs. A related second issue is that this definitional approach results in substituting behaviors for values. It is questionable to what extent you can impute values from behaviors. It is possible that different activities may reflect the same basic values. For example, in order to feed their families (basic value), one individual takes a low-paying job while another robs the local grocery store (different behaviors).

Another concern with subcultural explanations involves a possible middle-class bias. As already noted, many authors, including Cohen and Miller, construct their arguments by observing the behavior of lower-class individuals. Then, these middle-class researchers impute values and beliefs from the behaviors. From a middle-class point of view, the behaviors could appear to be malicious, negativistic, and nonutilitarian (à la Cohen), or indicators of trouble, toughness, or similar traits (à la Miller). The lower-class individuals, however, may be acting as they do for entirely different reasons from those assumed by the researchers. The imputed values are determined by the observers, not the individuals being observed.

ROUTINE ACTIVITIES AND RATIONAL CHOICE

Yet another theoretical area with ties to the ecological perspective is that dealing with routine activities and rational choice. Both of these approaches address the issue of opportunities for delinquency and crime, and the ability/choice of individuals to avail themselves of those opportunities. Two basic assumptions underlie these approaches. First, the movement of offenders and victims over space and time places them in situations in which criminal opportunities will be more or less possible. Second, within these different situations, individuals make choices about what to do and what not to do (see Clarke & Felson, 1993). Routine activities and rational choice arguments, therefore, rest in the arena of Neoclassicism, in which there is an element of choice.

BOX 4.4 ROUTINE ACTIVITIES/RATIONAL CHOICE EXPLANATIONS

	Key Idea: crime and delinquency are largely a result of opportunities and the choice to act on those opportunities
Routine Activities	Crime requires a suitable target, motivated offender, and an absence of guardians; Cohen and Felson
Rational Choice	The individual chooses if, when, and where to commit a crime based on the opportunities that are presented to him or her; Cornish and Clarke

---

Routine Activities

The **routine activities perspective** assumes that the normal behavior of individuals contributes to deviant events. Cohen and Felson (1979) outline three criteria necessary for the commission of a crime: (1) the presence of a suitable target; (2) a motivated offender; and (3) an absence of guardians. The possibility for deviance is enhanced when these three elements coincide. Changes in family life over the past several decades offer one example of how routine activities may impact delinquency. The increase in the number of two-earner households means that many youths are unsupervised after school and at other times. This situation results in a lack of guardianship, while also offering suitable targets (such as other unsupervised youths or unoccupied homes) for potential offenders. Another example appears in schools, particularly large secondary schools, where motivated offenders and suitable targets (both students) are required to be in close proximity with relatively few teachers or staff (guardians) available to oversee what takes place. Research has shown that the routine activities of individuals are related to a wide array of both personal and property offenses (Belknap, 1987; Kennedy & Forde, 1990; Miethe, Stafford, & Long, 1987; Roncek & Maier, 1991).

Rational Choice

Closely tied to routine activities is **rational choice theory**. Rational choice theory assumes that potential offenders make choices based on various factors in the physical and social environments. The individual chooses if, when, and where to commit a crime based on the opportunities that are presented to him or her. Among the factors influencing choices are the payoff, effort, support, and risks involved in the potential behavior (Cornish & Clarke, 1986). There is ample evidence that offenders make choices, but this does not mean that offenders plan their behavior in detail. Rather, unplanned, spontaneous behavior may rest on past observations, experiences, and routine activities that lay the foundation for unconscious decision-making.

The support for rational choice, however, is not without qualification. The factors identified as important in decision-making can vary greatly from situation to situation. Rational choice theory is also criticized for its inability to explain impulsive acts and actions that clearly take place in high-risk settings. It is possible that some individuals will make what appears to be an irrational choice because of limited choices or an inability to identify other options. The neoclassical nature of the theory does not assume total volition by the individual.

Rational choice poses an interesting conundrum for juvenile justice. If one assumes that youths do not have the capacity to make truly informed decisions, to what extent can it be claimed that they are making rational choices? The traditional view of the juvenile justice system is that youths cannot form the requisite intent to be held accountable for their actions. Thus, they are not rational. Instead, their behavior is determined by other factors. At the same time, it is naive to assume no rationality by youths. Coupled with routine activities, rational choice may be helpful for explaining increased delinquency during after-school hours (when there are fewer targets but less supervision) or why theft is more common than robbery.

STRAIN THEORIES

Strain theory views deviance as a direct result of a social structure that stresses achievement but fails to provide adequate legitimate means of succeeding. Unlike many other theories, strain theory removes the onus for deviance from the individual and places it on society. Unacceptable behavior by an individual is seen as a natural (and expected) response to the problems posed by the social structure.

BOX 4.5 STRAIN EXPLANATIONS

	Key Idea: the social structure provides differential access to success which can lead to deviance
Anomie	A state of normlessness or inadequate regulation; the inability of the individual to regulate his or her expectations in accordance with the societal structure
Modes of Adaptation	Each mode of adaptation reflects an individual's acceptance or rejection of culturally prescribed goals and socially institutionalized means of achieving those goals; some result in deviance/delinquency, others in conformity; Merton
General Strain	Strain can arise from many things besides just blocked means to achieve goals; removal of pleasure; presentation of negative stimuli; Agnew

Anomie

An understanding of strain theory begins with an examination of two basic facts. First, man is inherently egoistic (Durkheim, 1933). Happiness is the result of realizing one's expectations. Second, society does not provide equal access to the means of reaching one's wishes and desires. Modern society does not provide everyone with the education and training they need to succeed. It also requires people to fill different roles in society, meaning that some individuals receive more than others despite the fact that everyone aspires to reach the top. The mismatch between the expectations or goals of the individual and the available means to achieve those goals is called anomie. Loosely translated, **anomie** refers to a state of normlessness or inadequate regulation. More specifically, it is the inability of the individual to regulate his or her expectations in accordance with the societal structure. Anomie may result in various forms of deviant behavior, including crime.

Merton: Modes of Adaptation

Robert Merton took the basic ideas of anomie and expanded the discussion to what is known as **strain theory**. Merton (1938) saw anomie as the lack of correspondence between culturally accepted *goals* and socially institutionalized *means* to achieve those goals. The problem is that American society presents everyone with the goals of achieving material success and reaching the top. At the same time, society limits access to the means for achieving those goals. The disjuncture between goals and means is a property of the social structure.

Individuals can respond to the disjuncture between goals and means in various ways. Merton (1938) outlines five **modes of adaptation** (see Table 4.5). Each mode of adaptation reflects an individual's acceptance or rejection of culturally prescribed goals and socially institutionalized means of achieving those goals.

TABLE 4.5 Merton's Modes of Adaptation		
Mode of Adaptation	Cultural Goals	Institutionalized Means
Conformity	+	+
Innovation	+	−
Ritualism	−	+
Retreatism	−	−
Rebellion	±	±

+ means acceptance, − means rejection, ± means rejection and substitution

Source: Merton (1938).

Conformity represents the acceptance of both the goals and means, regardless of whether he or she succeeds. *Innovation* reflects acceptance of the prescribed goals but, when faced with an inability to succeed via acceptable means, the individual resorts to unacceptable or illegitimate methods of achieving success. In *ritualism*, the exact opposite occurs. While the individual gives up on achieving the goals, he or she continues to act in a socially acceptable fashion. A *retreatist* rejects both the goals and the means. This individual retreats from society through such means as alcohol or other drug use, vagrancy, or psychological withdrawal. The final mode of adaptation, *rebellion*, reflects an attempt to replace the existing societal goals and means with a new set that provides more opportunity for everyone in society.

The choice of adaptation varies from individual to individual. The most common response is conformity (Merton, 1938). Conformity presents the individual with the least resistance and does not add the problems of deviance to the problem of not succeeding. In the remaining modes, individuals can be considered deviant either in their outlook or in their actions. Delinquency appears in innovation, retreatism, and rebellion, where accepted modes of behavior (means) are replaced by unacceptable actions. While the root problem of anomie is structurally determined, the choice of adaptation can be understood only in light of individual circumstances.

General Strain Theory

Critics of strain theory have argued that not everyone aspires to the societally prescribed goals underlying Merton's discussion. Rather than focus only on the inability to achieve the societally prescribed goals, Agnew (1992, 2006a, 2006b) has proposed a **general strain theory** that suggests that strain can arise from varying sources, some of which have a greater tendency to lead to crime and delinquency. In his early writings, Agnew (1992) pointed out that strain can come from the removal of desired or valued stimuli (that bring pleasure) or from the presentation of negative stimuli (leading to anger or frustration). The strain may prompt individuals to respond with delinquent or criminal behavior Agnew (2001:338) notes that:

> . . . stressful events and conditions are most likely to lead to crime when they (1) are seen as unjust, (2) are seen as high in magnitude, (3) are associated with low social control, and (4) create some pressure or incentive for criminal coping.

Table 4.6 presents a list of factors most related to criminality and delinquency. Agnew and White (1992) provide empirical support for general strain theory. They report finding a positive relationship between measures of generalized strain and delinquent behavior.

TABLE 4.6 Types of Strain Related to Crime
• Failure to achieve core goals
• Parental rejection
• Erratic, strict, or harsh discipline/supervision
• Child abuse and neglect
• Negative school experiences (e.g., low grades, poor relations with teachers, school seen as boring and a waste of time)
• Work in secondary labor market (unpleasant tasks, physically demanding, low pay, limited opportunities)
• Homelessness
• Abusive peer relationships (insulting, gossiping, ridicule)
• Criminal victimization
• Prejudice and discrimination
• Marital problems
• Residence in poor urban communities

Source: Constructed by authors from Agnew (2001); and Agnew (2006b).

Assessing Strain Theory

The practical implication of strain theory would appear to be alleviating the causes of and conditions leading to strain. In the broadest, Mertonian sense, this would mean changing the structural barriers to success that underlie deviant activity. In a broader sense, it is important to address the myriad inputs that lead to and cause strain for an individual. The social structure and the misalignment of goals and means is not the only cause of strain. Agnew's general strain theory opens the discussion of strain to include many more factors. General strain theory has been subjected to numerous empirical tests. Analyses using both self-report and official data have found strong support for the theory.

SOCIAL CONTROL THEORY

Where most theories look to identify factors that lead or push a juvenile into delinquency, **social control theories** seek to find factors that keep an individual from becoming deviant. Control theorists ask why many people refrain from violating the law even though they are presented with ample opportunity to commit crimes. Reckless (1967) views the main issue as explaining why one individual becomes deviant and another does not when both are faced with the same situations.

BOX 4.6 SOCIAL CONTROL EXPLANATIONS

	Key Idea: considers what keeps an individual from being delinquent, rather than what causes or leads to deviance
Containment Theory	Inner containment (internalized moral codes and factors); outer containment (family, friends, teachers, etc.); internal pushes (discontent, anxiety); external pressures (poverty, unemployment); external pulls (peers, media); Reckless
Hirschi's Control Theory	Deviance results from weak or broken bond to society; attachment, commitment, involvement and beliefs influence behavior
Self-control Theory	Control internalized early in life; mainly parental influence; Gottfredson and Hirschi

---

Containment Theory

One of the earliest control explanations was Reckless's (1962) **containment theory**. Containment theory proposes that there are factors that promote conformity as well as forces promoting deviance. At the same time, the individual may have some control over his or her own behavior. Reckless (1962) outlines two types of containment: **outer containment** and **inner containment**. Outer containment offers direct control over the individual from outside sources. These include family members, friends, teachers, and others who provide supervision, training, and pressure to conform. Conversely, inner containment involves internalized moral codes, tolerance of frustration, and other factors that help the individual refrain from deviance. These play a role when an individual is not under the direct control of outer containment. The combination of these two factors should provide an effective means of avoiding deviant behavior. The factors that promote deviant behavior include **internal pushes** (restlessness, discontent, anxiety), **external pressures** (poverty, unemployment, inequality), and **external pulls** (deviant peers, subcultures, media) (Reckless, 1962). Each of these influences an individual's activity. These factors may lead or push people into deviant activity as a viable form of behavioral response and make deviance an acceptable alternative, while inner and outer containment work to offset their influence.

Hirschi's Control Theory

Perhaps the most well-known control theory is that proposed by Hirschi. Hirschi's (1969:16) theory states that "delinquent acts result when an individual's bond to society is weak or broken." The underlying assumption is that the individual's behavior is controlled by the connections the person has to conventional social order. Deviance shows up when a person's **bond to society** is weak or broken. According to Hirschi (1969), bond is developed through socialization during early childhood and consists of four elements: attachment, commitment, involvement, and belief (see Table 4.7). The failure

TABLE 4.7 **Elements of Hirschi's Bond**	
Attachment	"Sensitivity to the opinion of others" (p. 16)
	The more an individual cares about what others think of himself/herself, the less likely he/she will choose behavior that brings about negative input.
Commitment	A "person invests time, energy, himself, in a certain line of activity" (p. 20)
	As a person builds an investment in conventional endeavors, any choice of deviant behavior will place that investment at risk.
Involvement	"Engrossment in conventional activities" (p. 22)
	Because time and energy are limited, once they are used in the pursuit of conventional activities, there is no time or energy left for deviant behavior.
Belief	"The existence of a common value system within the society or group" (p. 23)
	As a person is socialized into and accepts the common belief system, he/she will be less likely to violate those beliefs through deviant activity.

Source: Constructed by authors from Hirschi (1969).

of an individual to care about what others think about his or her behavior and views (attachment), to work toward acceptable goals (commitment), to use one's energies and time in socially acceptable behaviors (involvement), and/or to accept the common value system in society (belief) opens the door for deviant and delinquent behavior. A weak or broken bond does not *cause* deviance. Rather, *it allows for* deviance. In other words, a weak or broken bond could be viewed as necessary for deviance, but not sufficient. An individual with a weak bond may or may not choose to commit deviant acts.

Numerous tests of Hirschi's social control theory have been undertaken. Hirschi (1969) surveyed more than 4,000 high school boys about their delinquent activity and elements of bond. Consistent with the theory, he found that delinquency was related to weaker attachment to parents, education, and school; lower aspirations (i.e., lacking commitment); more time spent "joy riding" in cars or being bored (involvement); and less respect for the police and the law (belief). Other studies (Hindelang, 1973; Krohn & Massey, 1980; Poole & Regoli, 1979; Wiatrowski, Griswold, & Roberts, 1981) report similar supportive findings.

Despite support for the theory, there are a number of problematic issues. First, the theory does not adequately explain how a bond becomes weak or broken. The theory tries to explain why individuals are deviant and not how they became that way. Second, the relative impact of the four elements of a bond is left unresolved. For example, if attachment is strong and commitment is moderate but involvement and belief are weak, will this permit deviance or not? As a result of this problem, the theory cannot directly offer suggestions on how to avoid the weakening of a bond or how to repair a bond. Third, many youths **drift** between delinquent and conventional behavior. The theory does not explain the vacillation in choices over time and place. Such drift can only be adequately explained by proposing that the bond is strengthened and weakened both easily and often. Finally, the theory assumes that all bonding is to conventional, nondeviant lifestyles. It may be possible that a juvenile is raised in a household in which the parents are deviant and espouse non-traditional behaviors. A juvenile in these circumstances should be bonded to deviance. Indeed, Jensen and Brownfield (1983) report that juveniles will follow the deviant behaviors of their parents as well as the nondeviant themes.

Self-Control Theory

Control theory has undergone its greatest change with the introduction of **self-control theory**. Rather than assume that behavior is controlled by outside forces throughout an individual's life, Gottfredson and Hirschi (1990) argue that self-control, internalized early in life, can serve to keep a person from involvement in deviant behavior. Self-control serves as a restraint from choosing the short-term gratification endemic to most criminal behavior. Self-control theory assumes that people are hedonistic and make choices emphasizing immediate, short-term pleasure.

The primary source of self-control is good parenting (Gottfredson & Hirschi, 1990). Poor self-control is the result of ineffective child-rearing practices by the parents. Good parenting requires exhibiting concern for the child, consistent monitoring of the child's behavior, the ability to identify problematic behaviors, appropriate reactions to inappropriate behavior, and the time and energy to carry through with parental responsibilities. Should the parents fail to build self-control, other social institutions, such as schools, may influence its formation but are typically poor substitutes for the family (Gottfredson & Hirschi, 1990). Once self-control is internalized, it serves to modify an individual's behavior throughout his or her life.

Self-control theory has received both support and criticism. A number of studies have found evidence that a lack of self-control is related to deviant behavior (Grasmick, Tittle, Bursik, & Arneklev, 1993; Piquero, Macintosh, & Hickman, 2000; Piquero, Langton, & Schoepfer, 2008; Pratt & Cullen, 2000; Wood, Pfefferbaum, & Arneklev, 1993). At the same time, the theory has been criticized for its inability to explain significant changes in behavior later in life and to consider the basic social structure as a contributor to parenting and self-control (Lilly, Cullen, & Ball, 1995).

THE LABELING PERSPECTIVE

Another approach that places the blame for deviance on society is the **labeling** perspective. The basic assumption of labeling is that being labeled as deviant by social control agents forces the person to act according to the label. Further deviance is a result of being contacted and sanctioned by the system. For example, being labeled a "delinquent" may lead to exclusion from participation in extracurricular school activities. This inability to participate in conforming activities may prompt further deviant behavior. Continued deviance is a response to the actions of society.

BOX 4.7 LABELING EXPLANATIONS

	Key Idea: people act in accordance with labels placed on them; system intervention causes further offending
Symbolic Interactionism	Every individual develops his or her self-image through a process of interaction with the surrounding world; looking-glass self; Mead; Cooley
Transfer of Evil	When an individual is sanctioned, the evil is often transferred from the act to the actor
Primary and Secondary Deviance	Primary deviance rationalized as part of being normal—no labeling; secondary deviance is acts committed in accordance with accepting the label; Lemert
Reintegrative Shaming	Use sanctions in such a way to shame the individual for the action but to simultaneously reintegrate him to society; no labeling; Braithwaite

---

The Construction of Self-Image

The labeling perspective owes much to the ideas of **symbolic interactionism**. Symbolic interactionism proposes that every individual develops his or her self-image through a process of interaction with the surrounding world (Mead, 1934). How an individual sees himself or herself is determined by how that person thinks others see him or her. That is, a person's self-concept comes out of interaction with other people and the environment. If an individual perceives a positive image of himself or herself from others, the person will hold a positive self-image. A simple way of viewing this process is through what Cooley (1902) calls the **looking-glass self**. The idea is that individuals view themselves in the way other people look at them. Labeling takes these ideas and proposes that individuals mold their behavior in accordance with the perceptions of others. Tannenbaum (1938) saw the sanctioning of deviant behavior as a step in altering a juvenile's self-image from that of a normal, conventional youth to that of being a delinquent. System processing identifies a youth as delinquent, emphasizes the label, and ultimately segregates the youth from normal juvenile behavior. Juveniles begin to view themselves as deviant, which leads to actions consistent with the self-image. Basically, the process of labeling entails a **transfer of evil** from the act to the actor (Tannenbaum, 1938). Instead of viewing the act as deviant and bad, the actor becomes bad and the focus for social action.

Primary and Secondary Deviance

Edwin Lemert (1951) distinguished between two types of deviance—primary and secondary. **Primary deviance** comprises those actions that "are rationalized or otherwise dealt with as functions of a socially acceptable role" (Lemert, 1951). These deviant acts are common and garner minimal attention and mild sanctions. As a result, the individual is not labeled, and his or her self-image is not altered. **Secondary deviance**, however, occurs when an individual "begins to employ his deviant behavior or a role based upon it as a means of defense, attack, or adjustment to the overt and covert problems created by the consequent societal reaction to him" (Lemert, 1951). This means that society has successfully labeled the individual. The individual now views himself or herself as different and/or deviant, and will act accordingly.

It is important to note that primary and secondary deviant acts entail the same types of behavior. What distinguishes secondary from primary deviance is the reason behind the action. The behavior is secondary if the act cannot be rationalized as the outcome of a nondeviant social role *and* is committed as an attack or defense against societal reaction. Secondary deviance, therefore, is a *mentalistic construct*. That is, it relies on the mind-set and attitude of the individual involved.

The reasons for conforming to the label are simple. First, a deviant label makes participation in conventional activity difficult. Societal members expect deviance and react to the individual as a deviant, regardless of whether specific behavior is deviant or conforming. Second, by accepting the label, the individual blunts the impact of any negative feedback provided by society. For example, young children cry when told they are bad because the information is counter to their beliefs. Children would not be affected, however, if they saw themselves as bad. Negative input would simply point out what they already knew and accepted. Finally, individuals conform to labels as a means of striking out against those who are condemning them. Using a kind of "if that is what you think" attitude, individuals decide to show society just how bad they can really be if that is what society wants.

The process by which an individual assumes a negative label is not simple. A single deviant act generally will not lead to the successful application of a label. Lemert (1951) proposes an outline of repeated primary deviant acts followed by increasingly stronger social reactions that eventually culminate in the imposition and acceptance of a deviant label. Lemert notes that this process is not set with any definite number of steps or particular sequence of events. Rather, the process varies by type of offense, offender, and societal response.

Reintegrative Shaming

Where labeling assumes that system intervention and societal reaction to offending invariably lead to a label and further deviance, it is possible to intervene without the imposition of a negative label. Braithwaite (1989) argues that shame can be used in a positive fashion to bring an offender back into society. Under **reintegrative shaming**, society needs to express disapproval of the delinquent activity while forgiving the offender for the action if the offender is willing to learn from the event and make reparations. The key is on "reintegration," thus the label does not carry the negatives outlined in labeling theory. The focus shifts from the negative action of the delinquent to the needs of the victim, the community, and the offender, and a shared response to make things better (Harris, 2003). This type of shaming does not lead to further delinquency, as does shaming aimed at excluding and stigmatizing the delinquent.

THE INTEGRATION AND ELABORATION OF THEORIES

One trend in criminological theorizing is the attempt to integrate various theories into more unified, coherent explanations of deviance. Many writers feel that, rather than attempt to show that any single theory is appropriate in all situations, each theory should be viewed as applicable to different domains of behavior. A number of authors have experimented with linking different explanations into an integrated theory of deviance. This process, also referred to as an **elaboration model**, attempts to take components of various theories and construct a single explanation that incorporates the best parts of the individual theories.

Social control, strain, and differential association theories have been typically used in conjunction with one another. Authors have proposed sequential

BOX 4.8 INTEGRATIVE EXPLANATIONS

	Key Idea: no single theory can explain all behavior; need to use multiple explanations to account for deviance and change over time
Life-course Theories	Life-course perspective incorporates a number of theoretical factors to explain criminality over time; Sampson and Laub
Developmental Theories	Similar to life-course theories, but often include nonsocial factors, such as prenatal and neonatal biological and health factors in explaining behavior

processes leading to deviance. For example, strain is seen as leading to a weakened bond to conventional society, which in turn leads to increased bonding with deviants and subsequent deviant behavior. Mediating this entire process is the influence of learning.

Life-course theories generally reflect efforts that incorporate ideas from several theories and perspectives. Sampson and Laub's (1993) life-course perspective incorporates a number of theoretical factors to explain criminality over time. These authors point to structural conditions as key variables in establishing a base for behavior. Social bonds are an important contributor to actions in response to negative structural factors. Labeling may influence behavior, particularly among younger persons. Later in life, individuals may alter their behavior due to changing life conditions, such as marriage, a family, and employment opportunities.

Using a broader set of potential factors, **developmental theories** often include biological inputs to behavior. Conger and Simons (1997) point out that biological factors, both prenatal and neonatal, play a role in cognitive ability. Cognition impacts on how family, friends, and schools may treat a person, which may then impact on an individual's success in school or in making choices. Throughout this process, the individual faces different demands and opportunities, for which he or she may or may not be adequately prepared.

Braithwaite's (1989) reintegrative shaming incorporates elements of several theories. Labeling and symbolic interaction are important for understanding the risk in shaming someone without concern for reintegration. Social control elements appear in the need to bond the person to society. Additionally, the family is a key actor in teaching proper behavior (learning theory).

Many of these "new" integrated theories have yet to undergo rigorous testing. This is partly due to the complexity of the proposed theoretical models and the lack of appropriate data for testing the full explanation. The advantages of the elaboration/integration approach appear in the attempt to draw together long theoretical traditions, each of which has demonstrated some empirical support. The fact that no single theory has adequately explained deviance suggests that this new direction should be continued.

THE IMPACT OF THEORIES ON JUVENILE JUSTICE

While a good deal of theorizing has been devoted to the causes of delinquent activity, the extent to which these explanations have an impact on the daily operations of the juvenile justice system is highly variable. Court dispositions and correctional treatments display the closest relationships between the theories and justice system action. As noted in Chapter 2, the rhetoric of the juvenile court has consistently emphasized the importance of learning and benevolent care of youths. Social learning theory provides support for interventions that focus on providing proper role models and environments conducive to conforming behavior. Trends toward deinstitutionalization, community corrections, and less restrictive interventions rely on the arguments of labeling theory as well as learning principles. Recent movements toward incarceration and deterrence of juveniles clearly rely on Classical and Neoclassical assumptions of free will and hedonistic choice.

On a larger scale, various theoretical perspectives have helped influence general social movements. The Great Society reforms that began in the mid-1960s attempted to address the social inequities that lead to deviance. Educational programs, economic assistance, vocational training, physical improvement of inner cities, and other efforts can be traced to strain, subcultural, learning, and ecological explanations of social ills. In many of these social actions, delinquency and criminality were only two of many social problems being addressed. The impact of these specific programs is a matter of debate. The consistency in crime, delinquency, and recidivism rates suggests that there was little impact on these problems, but why they did not have an impact is not clear. Some authors argue that the interventions were too short-lived to alter long-standing social problems. Others claim that the implementation of the programs was incomplete or inappropriate. Still others deny the adequacy of the theoretical explanation being utilized. Regardless of past failures, the various theories continue to find their way into the policies and procedures of the juvenile justice system.

SUMMARY

Explanations of delinquent and criminal behavior, whether biological, psychological, or sociological in nature, provide some insight into the reasons for deviance. The diversity in perspectives, however, illustrates the lack of understanding that still exists. Indeed, the search for a single theory that explains all—or almost all—deviance appears to be an effort in futility. The most reasonable consideration is to view deviance as multifaceted. The explanation, therefore, must consider a wide range in variables and influences. Juvenile justice must not ignore theory simply because until this point in time it has failed to arrive at a totally adequate explanation. Rather, the system must take care to select, implement, and evaluate ideas in light of expanding knowledge and research. While the remainder of the text deals with various interventions and system actions, theory forms an implicit base for all discussions.

DISCUSSION QUESTIONS

1. Sociological explanations for deviance are currently the most well known. Pick any sociological theory, outline the argument, and translate those ideas into practical applications for dealing with juveniles.

2. The President has called for a study that will set the tone for future directions in juvenile justice. As a member of the Commission, you have the opportunity to advocate an underlying theory. Which sociological theory will you fight for, and why is it the best possible approach for guiding the juvenile justice system? Present strengths and weaknesses of your choice.

3. A recent trend in delinquency explanations is the integration or elaboration model. Discuss how you can integrate subculture, learning, and control theories. How are they related, and what will the new explanation provide that any single theory cannot?

CHAPTER 5

Gang Delinquency

WHAT YOU NEED TO KNOW

- Many studies note that delinquency is often committed in groups, and that such offending is more recognized by agents of social control.

- There is no one accepted definition of a gang, although common elements of most definitions include persistence over time, congregating in public, self-identifying as a gang, claims over turf, and participation in illegal activity.

- Thrasher provided one of the earliest studies on gangs and viewed them as mainly "spontaneous play groups" in lower-class areas of town.

- Measuring the extent of gang membership is not easy and generally is reliant on reports from police or other social control agencies.

- In the most recent estimates, there are roughly 30,000 active gangs with roughly 782,000 members in the United States.

- Most gang members are young, male, and Hispanic.

- One of the most frequent concerns is that gangs are migrating from the large cities to other locations. There is little evidence of any planned migration, and most movement is actually due to chance or relocation of gang members for non-gang reasons.

- Youths join gangs primarily for a sense of belonging, status, success, self-esteem, and cohesion.

- While most portrayals show gangs as violent and very criminal, actual gang behavior is mainly social and noncriminal. Criminal activity, however, is an important part of gang membership.

- Most gang violence is isolated and between gang members rather than directed at the general public.

KEY TERMS

Boston Gun Project

civil abatement

civil gang injunctions

Community-Wide Approach to Gang Prevention, Intervention, and Suppression Program

detached worker programs

enhancement model

foray

gang

ganging

Gang Resistance Education and Training (G.R.E.A.T.) Program

group hazard hypothesis

hybrid gangs

interstitial areas

National Youth Gang Survey (NYGS)

near group

Project TOUGH

pulling levers

rumble

selection model

social facilitation model

STEP Act

wilding gangs

- Among intervention strategies with gangs, suppression is the most used but considered the least effective, while opportunities provision is the least used but considered the most effective.

- Programs that attempt to place workers in the gangs to help direct their behaviors (i.e., detached workers) have little positive impact and may actually draw youths to the gang.

- Law enforcement/deterrent efforts to address ganging, such as the Boston Gun Project and civil injunctions, can be highly successful, but that success may last only as long as the project operates.

- Classroom-based anti-gang programs such as G.R.E.A.T. are showing promise in limiting gang membership and altering youthful views of gang behavior, although the impact on delinquency and criminality appears limited.

INTRODUCTION

For many individuals, agencies, and communities, the problem of youthful misbehavior is most notably gang delinquency. This is particularly true in large cities where gangs are responsible for 25 percent or more of all homicides (Los Angeles, for instance, attributes half of its homicides to gangs [Howell, Egley, Tita, & Griffiths, 2011]). Law enforcement agencies consistently report that gangs and gang members are heavily involved in drug sales, assaultive behavior, robberies, and burglaries (National Youth Gang Center [NYGC], 2009). A great deal of early research shows that juveniles commit more deviant acts while in the company of other youths than when they are alone (see, e.g., Erickson, 1971; Hindelang, 1971).

The existence of street gangs in the United States can be traced back to the very beginnings of the country. As early as 1783, youthful gangs emerged in New York City (Sante, 1991), with major ganging appearing in the 1820s (Adamson, 1998). The growth of gangs was largely related to the growth of major U.S. cities and the immigration of Eastern Europeans and Southern blacks to the industrial northeast and midwest (Howell et al., 2011). Research on group delinquency dates back to the early twentieth century and the work of Thrasher (1936), Sutherland (1939), and Shaw, Zorbaugh, McKay, and Cottrell (1929).

Early delinquency research often focused on the idea that youthful misconduct was a result of peer influences. Differential association theory (Sutherland,

1939) proposed that much delinquent activity was the result of learning that took place in interactions between youths. Shaw and associates (Shaw et al., 1929; Shaw & McKay, 1942) focused heavily on the idea that juvenile misbehavior took place in groups. This theme of group behavior has persisted throughout the study of delinquency.

While studies claim a propensity for juveniles to act in groups, it is possible that much of the group dimension in offending is due to differential responses by society (Erickson, 1973; Feyerherm, 1980). The **group hazard hypothesis** proposes that delinquency committed in groups has a greater chance of being detected and acted upon by the juvenile and criminal justice systems (Erickson, 1973). In a study of 336 youths, Erickson (1973) reports that the group hazard hypothesis holds for select types of delinquent acts, especially more serious offenses. Group behavior simply may make recognition of a problem easier, thus more youths involved in group delinquency become involved with the juvenile justice system. The finding of high levels of group behavior in self-report surveys, however, suggests that the group hazard hypothesis is not a complete explanation of the group nature of delinquent activity.

Popular concern about gangs can be attributed to the finding that many youthful offenses are committed in concert with other juveniles. Another source for the public's concern may be the portrayal of gang behavior in the mass media. Movies and plays such as *The Blackboard Jungle, West Side Story,* and *Colors* dramatize the lure of gangs for youths and the aggressive nature of these groups of youths.

Interest in gangs has waxed and waned over the years. From the 1950s to the early 1960s there was a great deal of attention paid to gang delinquency. This interest subsided in the late 1960s, possibly due to the shift in attention to broader concerns over the social order, such as the Vietnam War, the economy, and racial unrest (Bookin-Weiner & Horowitz, 1983). New theoretical orientations also shifted interest from the offenders to the structure of society and its systems of social control. As a result, gang problems did not retain their priority as research issues. Not until the late 1980s did we see a renewed interest in gangs and gang behavior. Gang researchers attribute the renewed interest to the escalation of gang violence and the belief that gangs are the driving force behind growing drug problems, particularly crack cocaine.

GANGS DEFINED

While there has been a great deal of interest and research in gang activity, no single definition of a gang has developed. In general, the term **gang** has referred to groups that exhibit characteristics setting them apart from other affiliations of juveniles.

Research Definitions

Various researchers have proposed different definitions of a gang. In one of the earliest gang definitions, Thrasher (1936:57) defined a gang as:

> an interstitial group originally formed spontaneously, and then integrated through conflict. It is characterized by the following types of behavior: meeting face to face, milling, movement through space as a unit, conflict, and planning. The result of this collective behavior is the development of tradition, unreflective internal structure, esprit de corps, solidarity, morale, group awareness, and attachment to a local territory.

This definition introduced a number of key ideas. First, a gang was a specific form of a group. Second, what made these groups different from others was a system of activity and behavior that included conflict and mutual support of members. Finally, gangs were found in those areas of a city that were deteriorating and in a state of disorganization (interstitial areas). Gangs, therefore, were seen by Thrasher as a unique phenomenon of the poor, inner-city, immigrant areas of the early twentieth century.

WEB ACTIVITY

The National Gang Center has a wealth of information on defining and identifying gangs, as well as data on gang behavior. Available at http://www.nationalgangcenter.gov

Today, most definitions include the need for society to recognize the group as a threat and for the group to be involved in some degree of criminal/delinquent activity. The need for official recognition as a threat is evident in the definition used by the National Youth Gang Survey (NYGS) (NYGC, 2000), which defines a youth gang as:

> a group of youths or young adults in [the] jurisdiction that you or other responsible persons in your agency or community are willing to identify or classify as a "gang."

The NYGS specifically excludes motorcycle gangs, hate groups, prison gangs, or gangs composed exclusively of adults.

Klein and Maxson (2006) offer a definition based on input from American and European researchers and policymakers. They note that "a street gang is any durable, street-oriented youth group where involvement in illegal activity is part of its group identity." This definition outlines several key elements:

- The group persists over time despite possible turnover in membership (durability).
- The group spends a great deal of time outside on the street, in parks, or other public places.

- The gang membership is composed primarily of youths, although this does not restrict membership to juveniles.
- There is some degree of illegal activity.
- The group sees itself as having an identity.

This definition, however, has not been universally adopted, and different jurisdictions continue to make up and rely on various definitions.

Curry and Decker (1998) identify six elements typical in most gang definitions: group, symbols, communication, permanence, turf, and crime (see Table 5.1). Being a group is perhaps the easiest of the elements to understand, although most definitions require a minimum number of members. Symbols serve to provide the group with an identity. These elements often are developed for internal use and may not convey meaning outside the group. The symbols also may be used in communication between and among gangs, their members, and others. The development of symbols and unique forms of communication can contribute to the longevity or permanence of the gang. As groups gain permanence, they become harder to combat and dismantle. The element of turf, while common, is not as universal as the other elements because there are many examples of gangs that do not claim a physical territory. The final element, crime, is the most important, because group involvement in criminal activities is key to distinguishing a gang from other groups of people who may use the other elements, such as college fraternities and the Boy Scouts (Curry & Decker, 1998).

TABLE 5.1 Typical Elements of a "Gang" Definition

Group	Usually a specified minimum number of members, certainly more than two
Symbols	Clothes, hand signs, colors, etc., which serve to indicate membership
Communication	Verbal and nonverbal forms, such as made-up words, graffiti, hand signals, etc.
Permanence	Gangs must persist over time, generally at least one year or more
Turf	Territory claimed and/or controlled by the gang (not as common in many definitions)
Crime	Involvement in criminal behavior

Source: Compiled by authors from Curry and Decker (1998).

Statutory Definitions

Beyond definitions used by researchers in studying gangs, many jurisdictions have passed laws specifically dealing with gangs and gang behavior. According to the NGC (2014), 42 states and the District of Columbia have statutes

WEB ACTIVITY

The NGC (2014) has developed a document of statutory definitions that can be downloaded at http://www.nationalgangcenter.gov/legislation. Review this document and see where your state stands and compares to other states. Definitions are available at https://www.nationalgangcenter.gov/Content/Documents/Definitions.pdf

defining a gang, and 14 states define a "gang member." Interestingly, this means that 8 states have no statutes specifically addressing gangs, and 36 fail to define a "gang member." Beyond this, 31 states statutorily define "gang crime." These statutory definitions include many of the same elements noted by Curry and Decker (1998) and others. In terms of "gangs," all statutes require some form of criminal activity or behavior (NYGC, 2014). Thirty-three statutes require gangs to have 3 or more individuals, while 26 require signs, symbols, and a common name (NYGC, 2014). Despite these common elements, there is great diversity among the states. Statutory definitions of "gang members" typically include lists of criteria to use in determining whether an individual is or is not a gang member. The number of different criteria ranges from 2 to 11 (NYGC, 2014). In most states, meeting only two of these is sufficient to determine gang membership. Seven states simply define a "gang member" and do not establish specific criteria that must be met.

That a single definition of a gang has not been agreed upon by either researchers or legislators should be clear to the reader. The term "gang" has different meanings to different individuals, in different locations, at different times. What is common about gangs is the perception that they pose some form of threat to the safety of others.

EARLY GANG RESEARCH

Interest in gangs formed a good portion of the empirical and theoretical research prior to the mid-1960s. Much of the early research on gangs focused on describing the gangs and examining the daily workings of these groups. The research relied to a great extent on participant observation techniques. This research approach involved going out and observing the gangs on a daily basis. Such analysis provided a firsthand look at the structure and behavior of the gangs under study.

Thrasher's Gangs

Perhaps the most noted of the early studies of gangs was that of Frederick Thrasher. Thrasher (1936) studied 1,313 gangs with roughly 25,000 members in Chicago. He noted that the beginnings of gangs were found in spontaneous play groups within the interstitial areas of town that were characterized by a large amount of transience, great numbers of immigrant youths, poor living conditions, and a state of social disorganization. These ideas were simple extensions of the early work of Shaw et al. (1929), Shaw and McKay (1942), and the Chicago School. The gangs supplied needed interaction and social contact for the youths, which were not supplied by families or other social institutions.

Thrasher also viewed gangs as an outgrowth of innocent, everyday behavior among adolescents. Spontaneous play groups provided the basis and possibility for conflict. The groups provided a feeling of belonging and togetherness for the participants. The development of leadership, cohesion, and conflict served to strengthen the spontaneous groups and the establishment of a gang.

Thrasher (1936) did not see gangs as a stable or permanent entity. The development of gangs, or **ganging**, was a continuous process. Gangs were comprised mostly of juveniles between the ages of 11 and 17, and few members remained in gangs past young adulthood due to the movement into marriage and legitimate employment. Change in gangs was due to the maturing of individual members, the movement of members out of the immediate community, and the ability of the gang to provide meaningful activity for its members. While the specific makeup of the gang changed, many gangs would survive by replacing old members with new recruits. The recruits would come from those youths residing in the territory controlled by the gang.

Gang activity very often centered on conflict within the individual gang and between different gangs. According to Thrasher (1936), conflict helped build esprit de corps and unity among the gang's members. Within-group disputes settled through conflict provided a basis for common values, loyalty, and cohesion among the membership. Successful conflict also provided the individual group member with prestige and status. Conflict with other gangs brought about increased cohesion among group members and helped to draw the gang into a more formal, organized, and long-term system of interaction.

The gang was a means for youths in disorganized, inner-city areas to gain acceptance and exert some power over their situation. Gangs were not a planned response to problems in the neighborhoods by the youths. Instead, gangs were formed from the spontaneous play groups in which the youths found themselves.

Bloch and Niederhoffer: Gangs as a Natural Response

Twenty years after Thrasher's (1936) monumental work, Bloch and Niederhoffer (1958) expanded on many of his ideas. Where Thrasher viewed gangs as primarily a lower-class juvenile phenomenon, Bloch and Niederhoffer proposed that gangs were different from other juvenile groups simply by a matter of degree. The gang provided its members with status, success, and feelings of belonging that they were not being provided by the larger society (Bloch & Niederhoffer, 1958). Lower-class youths, who made up most gangs, were simply striving to succeed in the same sense as middle- and upper-class youths. Their social position, however, led them into situations that made gang behavior an acceptable alternative.

The organization of the gang was not greatly different from that portrayed by Thrasher (1936). Gangs developed leadership, cohesion, loyalty, and support through their daily activities. Bloch and Niederhoffer (1958), however, saw gangs as somewhat more fragile in terms of their longevity. The loss of a leader was seen as bringing about the dissolution of the gang. The gang was viewed as having less permanence than those studied by Thrasher. Despite this departure in views, both studies saw the gang as providing needed social support and status for participating youths.

Yablonsky: Near Groups

A different view of gangs is found in Yablonsky's (1962) explanation of gang formation and participation. First, he concentrates mainly on violent gangs whose activity focuses on violence and aggression. The violent gang strives for emotional gratification through hostile actions toward gang members and nonmembers. It also provides a sense of power for the participating individuals. Second, Yablonsky repudiates the idea that a gang is a well-organized group. Instead, he sees the violent gang as a **near group**, characterized by a relatively short lifetime, little formal organization, a lack of consensus between members, a small core of continuous participants, self-appointed leadership (as opposed to group-approved), and limited cohesion. Most "members" of the gang participate on the fringe and become involved only when individual or group violence is indicated. Self-aggrandizement, not group issues, is the major concern for gang members. This near-group view is restricted only to the violent gangs in Yablonsky's (1962) discussion. Other gangs may reflect the more classic portrayal found in other writings, although Yablonsky would argue that the violent "near group" is the dominant form of gang in society.

THE EXTENT OF GANG MEMBERSHIP

Measuring gang delinquency and/or gang involvement is not an easy task. A number of problems arise when attempting to assess the extent of gang membership. First, there is no single, accepted definition of what constitutes a gang. Any attempt to measure gang membership across jurisdictions, therefore, runs the risk of collecting data that reflect different problems or groups. This problem persists even when a survey (such as the NYGS) provides a definition for agencies to use, because the agency records typically reflect a local definition and the information is not reclassified to correspond to the desired definition before it is submitted. Second, many agencies classify individuals as gang members only if the individual self-identifies as such (Egley, Howell, & Major, 2004). Many youths may not claim gang membership, even if they fit a legal or other definition of a gang member.

Third, many jurisdictions may actively deny the existence of gangs and not collect any data on gangs, thus any count would be an under-count. Similarly, jurisdictions may fail to respond to surveys because they do not collect data (even if they recognize they have a problem) or do not keep special enumerations of "gang crime" separate from general crime. Despite these and other problems/issues, many attempts have been made to assess the extent of gangs and gang membership.

Estimates of gang membership typically rely on surveys of key informants, most often criminal justice system personnel. The earliest of these surveys, which was conducted by Miller (1975) and looked at only six cities, found a low estimate of 700 gangs with roughly 28,000 members. Beginning in 1996, the NGC began conducting annual surveys to gauge the extent of gang behavior and responses to that activity. The NGC surveys the police departments of all cities with a population over 50,000, sheriff and police departments of all suburban counties in the United States, and randomly selected police and sheriff's departments serving small towns (between 2,500 and 24,999 population) and rural counties. More than 2,000 law enforcement agencies are surveyed each year (NYGC, 2014).

Based on the 2011 NYGS, roughly one-third of the U.S. jurisdictions experience youth gang problems (NYGC, 2014). This represents approximately 3,400 jurisdictions and has remained relatively stable over the past five years

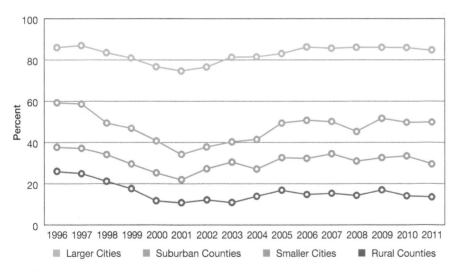

FIGURE 5.1
Prevalence of Gang Problems by Area Type, 1996–2011

Source: National Youth Gang Center (2014). Available at https://www.nationalgangcenter.gov/Survey-Analysis/Prevalence-of-Gang-Problems#prevalenceyouthgangstudy (see Figure 5.1). The gang problem is much more common in cities having a population of 50,000 or more, where more than 8 out of 10 report gang problems. On the other hand, fewer than 2 out of 10 rural counties report gang problems (NGC, 2014).

It is estimated that there are currently almost 30,000 active gangs (NYGC, 2014). This is roughly 50 percent more than in 2003 and roughly the same level as in 1997. There are an estimated 782,500 gang members in the U.S. (NYGC, 2014). The number of gangs and gang members vary greatly from area to area (see Figures 5.2 and 5.3), but they appear in virtually all areas of the country. Table 5.2 provides figures based on the maximum number of reported gangs and gang members in different-size jurisdictions in the 2002–2005 NYGS.

WEB ACTIVITY

A great deal of information on gangs can be found online from the NGC. Explore the information at http://www. nationalgangcenter.gov/survey-analysis

Klein and Maxson (2006) suggest that a better means of measuring gang participation is to survey youths. An important factor to consider in using surveys to gauge gang membership is whether the survey is conducted in areas with higher-than-typical concentrations of gangs and gang members. The use of nationally representative samples would provide more meaningful estimates, although most surveys are conducted using city-wide or

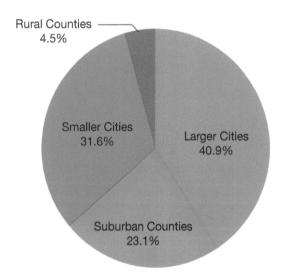

FIGURE 5.2
Distribution of Gangs by Area Type

Source: National Youth Gang Center (2014). Available at https://www.nationalgangcenter.gov/Survey-Analysis/Measuring-the-Extent-of-Gang-Problems#distributiongangsarea

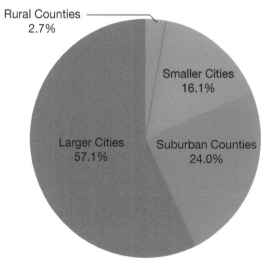

FIGURE 5.3
Distribution of Gang Members by Area Type

Source: National Youth Gang Center (2014). Available at https://www.nationalgangcenter.gov/Survey-Analysis/Measuring-the-Extent-of-Gang-Problems#distributionofgangmembers

TABLE 5.2 Number of Gangs and Gang Members, 2006–2011				
	Large Cities	Suburban Counties	Smaller Cities	Rural Counties
# of Gangs				
<5	13.7%	26.4%	53.8%	55.8%
5–10	31.5	24.8	30.2	23.9
11–25	25.5	21.8	8.8	8.0
>25	26.7	18.6	0.8	0.0
# of Members				
<51	13.9	2.73	54.5	50.7
51–100	12.1	9.8	11.5	9.4
101–250	19.5	11.1	9.5	10.1
251–500	16.5	11.7	4.2	3.6
501–1,000	13.0	6.8	0.8	0.0
1,001–2,500	10.4	5.7	0.0	0.0
>2,500	8.6	4.7	0.0	0.0

Source: Constructed by authors from National Youth Gang Center (2014). Available at http://www.nationalgangcenter.gov/survey-analysis/measuring-the-extent-of-gang-problems

county-wide samples. Based on their review of survey studies since 1990, Klein and Maxson (2006) find 33 different gang prevalence rates, ranging from roughly 5 percent to 20 percent reporting gang membership, with many of the larger figures relating to "ever" belonging to a gang and the smaller figures reflecting younger respondents reporting membership "in the past year."

Three clear results emerge from attempts to measure gang participation. First, gangs are found throughout the United States, in both large and small cities, and both urban and rural areas. Second, the scope of the gang problem is large. Finally, the majority of youths do not belong to gangs and probably never will. While the proportion claiming membership varies from one site to another, a small but significant percentage of youths do claim gang membership.

CHARACTERISTICS OF GANGS

Research has provided a great deal of information on gangs. Unfortunately, there is as much disagreement as agreement on many issues. As with the definition of a gang, questions still exist concerning characteristics of gang membership, gang organizational structure, and gang migration. The following pages attempt to synthesize the diverse literature and provide a general view of gangs in today's society.

Age

Most early research portrayed the typical gang member as a teenage adolescent (Cooper, 1967; Kanter & Bennett, 1968; Klein, 1971; Miller, 1975; Robin, 1967; Short & Strodbeck, 1965). Miller's (1975) national survey showed that the peak age years tend to fall in the mid-teen age group. This fact is borne out in more recent surveys that show that the peak ages for participation are 14 and 15 (Klein & Maxson, 2006). Gangs often use schools as recruiting grounds (Hutchinson & Kyle, 1993), adding to the youthful dominance in most gangs. This does not mean, however, that younger or older individuals have been excluded from gang membership.

Research since the mid-1980s (see, e.g., Hagedorn, 1988; Horowitz, 1983; Howell, 1997; Klein & Maxson, 1989; Moore, 1993; Spergel, Curry, Chance, Kane, Ross, Alexander, Simmons, & Oh, 1990; Toy, 1992) shows that the age range of gang members has expanded, particularly at the older end. Since 1998, NYGS data show that individuals age 18 or older make up roughly 60 percent or more of all gang members (NGC, 2014). This suggests that gangs are retaining their members into young adulthood. The lack of meaningful employment opportunities, coupled with potentially lucrative gang behavior, is one reason for individuals to retain their gang membership into their twenties and thirties (Moore, 1991). The aging of gang membership is also partly a result of older gang members being released from incarceration and returning to their communities and gang roots (Egley & Howell, 2011).

Social Class

Most studies find that the vast majority of gangs are found in lower-class areas and are comprised of lower-class juveniles. The lower-class nature of gangs finds a great deal of support in the early examinations and explanations of ganging behavior. Thrasher's (1936) definition of gangs relies heavily on the physical location of the groups in the lower-class, deteriorating areas of the city. Subsequent analyses paint a similar picture of gang behavior through explanations of deviance heavily reliant on the conflict between lower-class individuals and dominant middle-class society (Cloward & Ohlin, 1960; Cohen, 1955; Miller, 1958). More recent studies suggest that gang delinquency is no longer restricted to the inner city (Johnstone, 1981; Spergel, 1984). The growth of gangs in suburban and rural areas provides further evidence that gang behavior is not restricted to lower-class, inner-city areas.

A separate phenomenon involves middle-class gangs. Such gangs are in opposition to the usual view of gang membership and causes of ganging. Middle-class youths are not faced with the same degree of blocked success as lower-class juveniles. Lowney (1984) views the middle-class gang more as a "near group" along the lines of Yablonsky (1962). **Wilding gangs** fit this "near group" image and, while not as disadvantaged as other youths, these groups strike out at what they perceive as inequalities and infringements on their rights by other ethnic groups (Cummings, 1993). Such middle-class gangs typically do not have well-defined roles, they lack cohesion, and much of the group activity revolves around casual interaction. While many middle-class groups do not fit the traditional image of a gang, the similarity between members and the participation in group-organized behavior leads some to conclude that the youths are a gang (Lowney, 1984). These gangs tend to be less numerous and typically are centered around less violent behavior than their lower-class counterparts.

Race and Ethnicity

Gangs do not appear to be reserved for any particular ethnic or racial groups. Virtually all races and ethnic groups have provided gang delinquents over the years, although different racial/ethnic groups have dominated at different points in time. Thrasher's (1936) gangs consisted mainly of white youths of European descent. Evaluations in the 1950s and 1960s tended to report greater numbers of black gangs. The most recent statistics show that Hispanics comprise about 46 percent of all gang members, with African Americans contributing another 35 percent. Whites make up less than 12 percent of the gang population (NGC, 2014).

Traditionally, gangs tended to be homogeneous in terms of race and ethnicity (Klein, 1971; Short & Strodbeck, 1965; Spergel, 1966; Thrasher, 1936). That is, there were relatively few gangs that had white, black, Hispanic, and Asian members all in the same gang. Today, there is a developing trend toward hybrid gangs. The term **hybrid gangs** generally refers to gangs that are mixed racially or ethnically, but these gangs also can be characterized in other ways. For example, members may belong to more than one gang, or different gangs may cooperate with one another in some endeavor (Starbuck, Howell, & Lindquist, 2001). These gangs also may not fit the traditional definition of a gang and may not claim turf or utilize colors, signs, or other symbols typically considered important in recognizing gang behavior. While most gangs remain racially and ethnically homogeneous, Starbuck et al. (2001) note that roughly one-third of the gangs identified in the 1998 NYGS fit the definition of a hybrid gang.

Females and Gangs

Traditional research on gangs has been devoted almost exclusively to the role of males. This is due primarily to the failure of females to contribute to any large extent to gang membership or activity. Thrasher's (1936) pathbreaking study of 1,313 gangs found only five or six female gangs over the course of his study. Surveys of youths uncover the same basic results, with roughly 10 percent of females reporting gang membership (Klein & Maxson, 2006). The 2010 NYGS reports that only 7.4 percent of all gang members are female

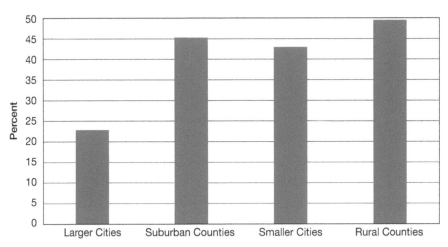

FIGURE 5.4
Percent of Gangs with Female Members, 2009

Source: National Gang Center (2014). Available at https://www.nationalgangcenter.gov/Survey-Analysis/Demographics#anchorgangswithfemalemembers

A U.S. Marshal deputy, left, restrains a female suspect following an early-morning raid on members of an Azusa, California, gang.

CREDIT: AP Photo/Jason Redmond

(NYGC, 2014). Interestingly, the number of gangs with female gang members is notably different by population area (see Figure 5.4), with gangs in rural counties having female members while less than one-quarter of them in large cities having female members (NYGC, 2014).

The overwhelming dominance of male gangs found in law enforcement data (such as the NYGS) is not mirrored in other sources of information. Research shows that there is a great presence of females in gangs. Esbensen and Huizinga (1993) report that at least 20 percent of the gang membership in Denver is female. Fagan (1990), Campbell (1990), and Esbensen and Osgood (1997) claim that females comprise roughly one-third of gang members. Esbensen and Carson (2012) note that girls make up at least one-third of the gang members in their national evaluation of a gang intervention. Curry, Fox, Ball, and Stone (1993) uncovered more than 7,000 female gang members in 27 cities. In many cases the females are part of auxiliary groups and respond to the mandates and activities of their male counterparts (Campbell, 1984, 1990; Monti, 1993). This auxiliary status of female gangs is most clearly seen in the adoption of similar names to the dominant male gangs (i.e., Disciples and Lady Disciples).

There are indications of growing numbers of autonomous female gangs with their own leadership and separate meetings, which operate independently from the male gang in many instances (Campbell, 1984; Fishman, 1988; Moore, 1991). Female gang members tend to participate in many of the same forms of deviance as males, including drug use and violence (Bjerregaard & Smith, 1993; Campbell, 1990; Decker & Van Winkle, 1994; Fishman, 1988).

Organization and Size

Gangs tend to have some type of internal organization that affects the activities of its members, the status of those members, and the decision-making processes of the group (Bloch & Niederhoffer, 1958; Curry & Decker, 1998; Thrasher, 1936; Yablonsky, 1962). The degree of formality and control exercised by the gang varies greatly from gang to gang. Gangs that are more entrepreneurial tend to have a more formal hierarchical structure. Territorial gangs are more loosely organized and have an informal structure (see, e.g., Sanders, 1994). Klein and Maxson (2006) outline five gang types (see Table 5.3). These types indicate that gangs are not all mirror images of one another, and they can be diverse in size, structure, and activity. The most common gang form is the compressed type, followed by the neotraditional (Klein & Maxson, 2006).

At the heart of most gangs is a single core of devoted members. This core may vary in size but is always much smaller than the purported size of the entire gang. The majority of the gang usually reflects a large body of fringe members

TABLE 5.3 **Klein and Maxson's Gang Types**	
Traditional	Very large (over 100 members) with various subgroups; have been in existence for 20+ years; wide range of ages among members; territorial-based; wide range of criminal activity.
Neotraditional	Similar to traditional but not as old; typically 50–100 members; territorial; subgroups.
Compressed	Small gang with no subgroups (less than 50 members); members are close in age; short history; not necessarily territorial.
Collective	Like the compressed but larger (50+); wider age range of members, 10–15 years old; not necessarily territorial.
Specialty	Small gang with no subgroups; narrow age range; short history; very territorial; specializes in few types of crimes.

Source: Constructed by authors from Klein and Maxson (2006).

who rarely take part in decisionmaking and participate in gang activities only at selected times. Gangs that claim memberships of 100 and greater are probably counting a large number of fringe members. The core of the gang provides the leadership and decision-making body of the group.

Not all gangs have the same leadership structure (Kelling, 1975). In some groups, leadership is provided by a single individual determined according to the talents of the core members. Physical prowess often, but not always, determines who becomes the leader of the gang. Other gangs have highly differentiated leadership roles in which different talents call for different leadership. Fights and violence will call on the best fighter. Criminal activity for profit may require youths who knows more about committing the crime and fencing the goods. Internal conflict may necessitate the efforts of someone who can negotiate and come up with alternative solutions. The extent of such specialization is determined by the abilities of the core members and the needs of the group.

Besides the core group, many gangs include a range of different subgroups (Miller, Gertz, & Cutter, 1961). This is especially true in recent years as we see gang members from different age groups, as well as more intergenerational gangs (Hutchinson & Kyle, 1993; Moore, 1991, 1993). Often, the subgroups are based on the age of the gang members. A simple form of organization may have only three membership groups—young "wannabes," the core of the gang, and "old guard" members. The different subgroups of a gang may be identified by various names or labels such as PeeWees, Juniors, Seniors, or Old Heads. It is important to note that this tripartite view of a gang is only a simple presentation. Various gangs may have a more complicated system of subgroups, including female auxiliaries or affiliations with gang chapters in other areas of a city. The actual organization varies greatly from gang to gang and place to place.

Gang Migration

One of the oft-mentioned "facts" about recent gang behavior is that of gangs migrating from place to place. Typically, this discussion centers around the idea that gangs are deliberately moving and setting up chapters in other places for the purpose of selling drugs. Support for this assertion is most often anecdotal and relies on the simple observation of the same or similar gang names, colors, graffiti, or behavior from place to place. Solid proof of gang migration, however, is not available.

For the most part, gang problems are typically "homegrown" and not imported (NYGC, 2014). The apparent migration is more accidental than planned. Skolnick, Bluthenthal, and Correl (1993) note that most gang travel and migration begins with non-gang, non-crime-related activities. Visits to family

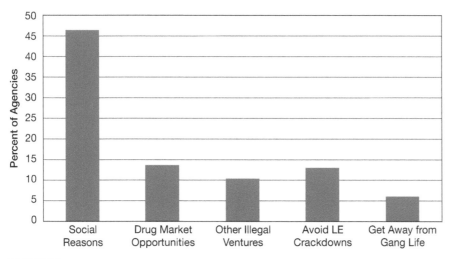

FIGURE 5.5
Factors Influencing Gang Member Migration

Source: National Youth Gang Center (2014). Available at https://www.nationalgangcenter.gov/Survey-Analysis/Gang-Member-Migration#anchorfactors

members in other places or the relocation of a family are typical means by which gang members find themselves in a new environment (Klein & Maxson, 2006). In essence, the gang migration is an unintended consequence of normal family behavior. The connection between gangs in different cities, usually considered a result of planned migration, is more illusory than real (Huff, 1993; Spergel et al., 1990; Valdez, 2000). Figure 5.5 shows that almost half of all migration is related to social factors, while moving to secure illegal opportunities occurs in less than one-quarter of the moves (NGC, 2014). The appearance of established gangs, such as the Crips and Bloods, in cities with no history of gang problems can often be attributed to the arrival of a single gang member who is displaced through family migration.

That there may be gang "chapters" in different cities cannot be totally discounted. Indeed, as competition for drug territory has increased, some gangs have attempted to establish operations in new areas. This movement, however, is typically limited and does not indicate statewide or country-wide organizations of juvenile gangs (Klein & Maxson, 2006). One possible, and plausible, explanation for the apparent "franchising" of gangs in different cities is that more sophisticated drug dealers and organizations recruit youths and emerging gangs as local "employees" in the drug trade. Migration for drug selling, therefore, is more an illusion than a reality. Indeed, low migration levels result in relatively small impacts on a city's existing drug problems (Maxson, Woods, & Klein, 1996). For the most part, juvenile gangs are not as entrepreneurial as the public likes to think.

Summary

We must recognize that gangs, like any other collective of individuals, take on different characteristics based on the desires of the members and the underlying goal of the group. Some gangs may be highly structured with many members, clear leadership, and set agendas. Other gangs may be loose confederations of a few individuals who interact on a sporadic basis. Names, colors, territory, leadership, and other components of gangs are in themselves only potential indicators of ganging. Just as the general characteristics of gangs vary, so do the behavioral tendencies of these groups.

WHY DO YOUTHS JOIN GANGS?

Gang members come together and associate with one another for a wide array of reasons. The early work of Thrasher (1936) suggests that the gang provides inner-city youths with a sense of belonging and acceptance. Several early writers (Bloch & Niederhoffer, 1958; Cohen, 1955; Miller, 1958) argue that the relative disadvantages of being a lower-class youth faced with middle-class goals leads youths to joining gangs as a response to their inability to succeed through normal channels. The lower-class youths find support and unity with others facing similar problems, and gang activity can offer status and a sense of success not available elsewhere. The extent to which the gang is entrepreneurial may provide the members with an income (possibly significant) that is otherwise not available.

Other research dealing with different racial and ethnic gangs (Chin, 1990; Chin, Fagan, & Kelly, 1992; Horowitz, 1983; Huff, 1993; Joe & Robinson, 1980; Moore, 1991, 1993; Sanders, 1994; Toy, 1992; Vigil, 1993, 1997; Zatz, 1985) also portrays gang membership and activity as a result of life in lower-class communities. Many gang members are recent immigrants or are first-generation Americans. The youths often face problems with success in schools and other social situations. Gang behavior is seen as an alternative to the lack of success and status faced by youths. Lower-class youths, regardless of ethnic or racial background, spend a good deal of time on the streets where they meet and interact with other youths. Education is provided through daily street activity. The gang offers its members a sense of belonging and self-esteem, which may not be forthcoming at home (Moore, 1991; Vigil, 1993, 1997).

Similarly, explanations for female ganging have been rare but generally follow the same logic found for

TABLE 5.4 Reasons for Gang Membership

- A Sense of Belonging
- Financial Gain/Rewards
- Status
- Social Support
- Improved Self-esteem
- Feelings of Family
- Group Cohesion
- Acceptance
- Social Activities

male gangs. Brown (1978), Short and Strodbeck (1965), and others have pointed to many of the same social factors associated with male gangs. Blocked opportunity, lack of success at school and home, lack of status, desire for belonging, abuse and family problems at home, and community disorganization were among the cited reasons for female gang participation (Bowker & Klein, 1983; Campbell, 1990; Miller, 2000; Moore, 1988).

Many features of a gang demonstrate that it provides something of value to its members. A sense of belonging, status, feelings of success, and financial gain are examples of what a gang can give its members. The cohesiveness and importance of the gang to the individual can be seen in the names, territory, and other identifiers associated with different gangs. Another way to consider the question of why youths join gangs is to look at potential risk factors (Decker, Melde, & Pyrooz, 2013; Maxson, 2011). Table 5.5 presents five categories of risk factors. These are individual factors, family factors, school factors, peer group influences, and community factors.

Bell (2009) reports that there are few differences between males and females in terms of why they join gangs. Among the factors contributing to gang membership for both sexes is less parental attachment, feeling less safe at school, and more contact with fighting. Some differences are found between the sexes for Hispanics and immigrants, although these differences are not major (Bell, 2009). The increased intergenerational nature of gang membership also contributes to the growth and construction of gangs. Younger members are often siblings or offspring of current or past gang members. "Apprenticeship" periods for "wannabes" and initiation rituals help build the sense of belonging. The gang provides its members with things they do not get at home, school, or elsewhere.

GANG BEHAVIOR

Gangs are portrayed in the media as in constant violent confrontation with one another and with the general public. Contrary to this portrayal, gangs participate in a variety of different behaviors. While gang fights and drive-by shootings do occur, such violent confrontations are rare relative to other gang behavior. Indeed, gangs are involved in many nonviolent activities, including leisure activities,

TABLE 5.5 Risk Factors for Gang Membership

Individual Factors
- Anti-Social Behavior
- Substance Use
- Mental Health Problems
- Victimization
- Negative Life Events

Family Factors
- Poverty
- Weak Family Structure
- Lack of Education
- Gang Involvement

School Factors
- Poor Academic Performance
- Poor School Climate
- Feelings of Being Unsafe at School

Peer Group Factors
- Peer Gang Involvement
- Aggressive Peers

Community Factors
- High-Crime Neighborhoods
- Disadvantaged Neighborhoods
- Poor Neighborhood Collective Efficacy

Source: Compiled by authors from Howell (2010).

drinking and drug use, partying, gambling, and companionship. When gang aggression does occur, it is not necessarily physical in nature. Miller et al. (1961) note that roughly 94 percent of the aggression is verbal, and most does not contain anger.

While physical aggression may not dominate gang behavior, gangs are involved in significant numbers of crimes. Estimates of gang crime from law enforcement data reveal that gangs were responsible for more than 580,000 offenses in 122 cities and 8 counties in 1992 (Curry, Ball, & Decker, 1996). Interestingly, most law enforcement agencies do not note whether offenses are gang-related or not. Except for homicide, less than one-third of law enforcement agencies record aggravated assaults, drug sales, robberies, burglaries, motor vehicle thefts, or larcenies as gang-related (NGC, 2014). At the same time, close to 50 percent report increasing gang violence and property crime in their jurisdictions. The 1998 NYGS revealed that, except for robbery, more than 50 percent of the law enforcement respondents claimed that some or most/all of the gang members in their jurisdictions are involved in aggravated assaults, burglaries, motor vehicle thefts, larcenies, and drug sales. In 2011, the NYGS noted there was almost 2,000 gang-related homicides, with two-thirds of those taking place in cities of at least 100,000 population (NGC, 2014). Clearly, criminal behavior by gangs and gang members is evident in data supplied by law enforcement agencies.

WEB ACTIVITY

The NAGIA offers a number of services and information dealing with gangs. Among these are links to individual state organizations and news reports concerning gang stories from across the country. Available at http://www.nagia.org/

The extent of criminal behavior by gang members also can be addressed through self-report surveys. Thornberry (1998) reported on gang crime as uncovered in the Rochester, Pittsburgh, and Denver youth studies. In every case, gang members accounted for at least 8 out of every 10 violent crimes and 7 out of 10 drug offenses. Gang members do not confine their offending to serious violent crime. They also participate in a large portion of all property crime (Thornberry, 1998). Similarly, Spergel et al. (1990) pointed out that gang members are more criminally active than nonmembers, and commit three times the level of violence.

Drug Activity

Drug activity is a major topic of discussion in relation to gang behavior. The National Alliance of Gang Investigators Associations (NAGIA) notes that "gangs . . . are the primary distributor of drugs throughout the United States" (NAGIA, 2005:1). There is no doubt that many gang members use and sell drugs, and that drug sales are an integral part of some organized gangs. The degree to which gangs are involved in drugs, however, is highly variable. For example, drug sales in one gang may involve sales only among its own members, while another gang may be deeply involved in the drug trade throughout the community. Fagan (1990), in a survey of Los Angeles, San Diego, and Chicago gang members, found that roughly 28 percent are rarely involved in drug use, while 35 percent are seriously involved in both use and sales. Much of the distribution of drugs may be tied to more organized, older gangs. Two examples of this would be outlaw motorcycle gangs (NAGIA, 2005) and Jamaican posses (Gay & Marquart, 1993), which have emerged as organized forces for the distribution and sale of marijuana, cocaine, and other drugs in the United States. Research also shows that, while there is a great deal of drug use among youth gangs, the sale of drugs for profit by local gangs varies greatly from gang to gang (Decker & Van Winkle, 1994; Hagedorn, 1994; Mays, Fuller, & Winfree, 1994; Padilla, 1993).

Gang Violence

Gangs typically evoke images of violence and aggression, and in recent years it is with good cause. The level of violence and physical aggression has clearly changed and increased over time. Where much of the early research attempted to dispel the dominant myth of the centrality of violence in the gangs, more recent studies note that violence is common. Miller (1975, 1982) notes that as early as the late 1970s there was a clear increase in the use of weapons and participation in physical confrontation. While confrontations appeared in the past, they were not a dominant activity and often occurred within the confines of the gang (Miller et al., 1961). Recent research suggests that violence is now a more open activity directed at a greater array of targets, both inside and outside the immediate gang. The bulk of violence, however, is still aimed at other gang members.

The seriousness of the violence is high, as demonstrated by the number of gang-related killings. Based on FBI Supplemental Homicide Reports and information from the NGC, roughly 12 percent of homicides every year are gang-related (NYGC, 2014). Table 5.6 presents 2011 data on gang-related homicides as reported in the NYGS. In large cities of more than 100,000 population, there were 1,242 gang-related homicides accounting for over two-thirds of all gang-related homicides in the country. At the other end, "smaller areas" experienced 46 (or 2.5%) of the gang-related homicides (National Youth Gang Center, 2014). These figures are low estimates due to the fact that they reflect only those homicides occurring in jurisdictions that participate in the NYGS.

Gang violence no longer conforms to the typical image of a **rumble** or gang fight. Rather, most violence appears as forays. A **foray** typically entails an attack by two or three youths upon a single member (or possibly a few members) of a rival gang. A typical form of attack is a "drive-by" shooting. For example, three members of the Bloods drive around a corner, where a member of the Crips lives, they shoot from the car, and then speed away from the scene. A similar

TABLE 5.6 Gang-related Homicides, 2011

	Cities 100,000+	Suburban Counties	Cities 50,000–100,000	Smaller Areas
Number	1,242	338	198	46
Percent	68.1%	18.5%	10.9%	2.5%

Source: Constructed by authors from National Youth Gang Center (2014). Available at http://www.national gangcenter.gov/survey-analysis/measuring-the-extent-of-gang-problems

retaliatory foray by the Crips is the consequence of the Bloods' action. The foray becomes a self-perpetuating activity. Indeed, gang homicides typically take place on the street and involve both firearms and motor vehicles (Klein & Maxson, 2006).

Modern gang violence differs from the earlier portrayals in a number of ways. First, the violence appears to be more random, partly due to the use of automobiles and the willingness to attack when innocent bystanders are present. Second, the violence occurs more frequently through constant small forays rather than in the occasional large rumble. Third, the hit-and-run tactics of the foray make the violence appear more impersonal. Non-gang peers and other individuals who become victims may often be injured as a result of a foray that occurs on the street. Finally, gangs use lethal weapons, particularly firearms, more often (Decker, Pennel, & Caldwell, 1997), and recruit youths who already own guns, and they are more likely to carry guns than are non-gang youths (Bjerregaard & Lizotte, 1995).

Gang Behavior and Types of Gangs

Not all gangs participate in the same types of deviant behavior as other gangs. Indeed, research shows that some gangs tend to specialize their criminal activity. That same research even suggests that a few gangs exist primarily as a forum for criminal behavior, as opposed to a forum for more generalized group behavior. The identification of specific types of offending by gangs, however, is as elusive as identifying a single gang definition. Each gang may do something slightly different from every other gang.

Asian gangs exemplify the type of gang that appears to serve a definitive purpose for its members. A number of studies (Chin et al., 1992; Huff, 1993; Toy, 1992) report that Asian gangs appear to be very profit-oriented and tend to restrict their deviant activities to those that bring a monetary return. Both Huff (1993) and Chin et al. (1992) claim that these gangs often have strong ties to organized crime, which directs both the financial dealings and the use of violence in the Asian communities.

Analyses of Chicano youths suggest they are strongly territorial-based (Moore, 1991; Sanders, 1994; Vigil, 1993, 1997), which provides the gang with a delineated area for which it has almost exclusive rights to gang recruitment. Besides the territorial nature of Chicano gangs, these groups tend to be more heavily involved in drug use (Moore, 1991, 1993) and general deviance (Vigil, 1993).

Skinhead gangs advocate white supremacy and are portrayed as very violent and racist, although this is not true of all skinheads. They also often take an anti-government stance and advocate withdrawal from the dictates of the government, including taxes and all regulatory laws. Skinheads use violence primarily against those who are perceived as a threat to white supremacy (Wooden & Blazak, 2001).

At another extreme are tagger gangs, whose members often view themselves as urban artists. These youths try to have their art seen by as many people as possible, and do not view the graffiti as vandalism, denoting ownership of turf, or harmful to others. It is solely an expression of individuality and a means of gaining status (Wooden & Blazak, 2001).

Explaining Gang Behavior

The reasons behind gang behavior and violence are varied and, to some degree, mirror the reasons for youth participation in most any group. Three of the most prevalent reasons underlying gang behavior appear to be status, control of turf or territory, and financial gain. As noted earlier, most gang members are from the lower classes and where there are few opportunities for legitimate success and for gaining status in the community.

First, the gang serves to provide a means of gaining status. Gang members can prove themselves on the street and are accepted for their contributions to the gang. They can gain honor through their allegiance to other gang members. They are provided with a sense of family and belonging that does not come from the broken, female-headed household. Second, turf or territory provides a sense of ownership and control, which often is denied the gang youth (Vigil, 1993). Overcrowded living conditions, frequent movement from place to place, lack of finances to purchase personal property, and other factors lead youths to feel a lack of control. The turf is a means of exerting control and ownership. While it is not ownership in the legal sense of the term, such control helps provide the feelings of status desired by the gang youth. Attacks on the turf are seen as an attack on the property, honor, and status of the individual gang members, and violence is used to protect the turf (Hutchinson & Kyle, 1993).

Financial gain is a third major reason for gang membership and activity. Faced with a lack of legitimate job opportunities, the gang can provide training in criminal activity (such as robbery and burglary), the opportunity for such criminal actions, and support for this behavior. Trafficking in illegal drugs is a lucrative activity for some gangs. It also brings about contact and opportunities with organized crime and a means of increasing status in the gang and community. At the same time that the drug trade has opened new doors for the gang members, it has also added to the stakes in control of turf and the level of violence between gangs.

While the outward appearance of gang behavior is different from socially acceptable activity, the reasons for the behavior are not much different from those of most other persons. The gang youth values status, belonging, ownership, control, and financial gain. These are major reasons behind the behavior of nondeviant youths and adults. The gang has simply supplied alternative methods for achieving its ends.

DO GANGS CAUSE DELINQUENCY?

Based on the level of gang-member delinquency, one could argue that the elimination of gangs would significantly reduce the level of youthful deviance. An alternative possibility, however, is that gangs simply attract already delinquent youths, rather than causing increased deviance. The delinquency, therefore, is independent of gang membership. Following this argument, Thornberry, Krohn, Lizotte, and Chard-Wierschem (1993) identify three possible models of the delinquency–gang relationship: selection, social facilitation, and enhancement. The **selection model** maintains that gangs recruit or attract already delinquent youths. In this model, the level of delinquency would be independent of gang status. Under the **social facilitation model**, belonging to a gang is the cause of increased deviance. Periods of gang membership, therefore, will result in delinquent activity not found during nonmembership. Finally, the **enhancement model** strikes a middle ground in which gangs recruit delinquency-prone youths and enhance their deviance.

Several studies have sought to test these models of gang influence directly. Using panel data from the Denver Youth Survey, Esbensen and Huizinga (1993) report that gang members are indeed more delinquent while they are actively involved in the gang. At the same time, however, these youths also report higher levels of offending both before and after active gang participation. Thornberry et al. (1993) find that the gang–delinquency relationship varies according to the type of offense and the level of commitment to the gang. The social facilitation model fits for personal and drug-related offenses, while property offenses do not fit any of the models very well. In addition, youths who remain in the gangs for a longer period of time tend to increase their offending (the enhancement model) more than transient gang members (Thornberry et al., 1993).

Melde and Esbensen (2011) investigate the three models in terms of gang membership being a turning point in one's life. The question is what impact joining or leaving a gang has on delinquent activity. Based on survey data for almost 1,400 youths, the authors find that joining a gang reduces informal social controls and increases delinquent behavior, in accord with the facilitation model. At the same time, at-risk youths are more likely to join gangs (Melde & Esbensen, 2011), reflecting selection factors. The fact that both sets of factors appear to be at work suggests an enhancement model.

These studies suggest that the gang is not necessarily the cause of delinquent behavior. Rather, gang membership appears to add to an already established level of deviance by participating youths.

INTERVENTION WITH GANGS

Responding to gangs and gang problems is an area in which much work remains to be done. Unfortunately, the first response by many cities to an emerging gang problem is one of denial (Hagedorn, 1988). Cities often do not want to admit that they have gangs. The outcome of such denial is the emergence of a full-blown problem before the authorities are prepared to deal with it. Once the problem is identified, a number of different responses have been used to address the problem.

Spergel and Curry (1993), in the NYGS, identified five common intervention strategies (see Table 5.7). Most respondents (44%) use suppression (the use of arrest, prosecution, incarceration, and other criminal justice system procedures) as their primary form of response. The intervention ranked second in primacy is social interventions (31.5%), followed by organizational change and development (10.9%) and community organization (8.9%). Opportunities provision is utilized the least by responding agencies. These results indicate that traditional criminal justice system responses to gangs are the most common responses, while efforts to alter the social conditions that cause ganging are addressed the least. Interestingly, in an analysis of the perceived effectiveness of the five types of intervention strategies, Spergel and Curry (1993) report that opportunities provision is viewed as the most effective/promising approach, while suppression is seen as the least effective.

Vigil (2010) argues that effectively responding to gang and gang problems requires a balanced strategy incorporating elements of prevention, intervention, and law enforcement. Rather than lead with enforcement, it is important to consider the varying inputs to ganging and address all of them. This means creating solutions that address the economies of the area, the sociocultural factors surrounding the youths, and the sociopsychological marginality of the youths (Vigil, 2010). The role of law enforcement has got to include the

TABLE 5.7 Gang Intervention Strategies

Suppression	Includes any form of social control in which the criminal justice system (police, courts, or corrections) or society attempt to impose formal or informal limits on behavior
Social Intervention	Basically a social work approach to working with gangs in the neighborhoods (such as detached worker programs)
Organizational Change and Development	Deals with altering the organization(s) that respond(s) to gang problems, such as through the establishment of gang units or specialized training of its personnel
Community Organization	Efforts aimed at mobilizing the community toward self-improvement and change, including both physical and social alterations
Opportunities Provision	Recognizing the lack of meaningful jobs and the training needed to succeed, and taking steps to change the problems; education, vocational training, and job placement are elements

Source: Spergel and Curry (1993).

traditional police functions as well as "soft suppression" interventions, such as youth programs, sports programs, and educational interventions (Vigil, 2010). The following pages will address a number of approaches to gang problems that reflect different elements suggested by Vigil, including detached worker programs, statutory changes, deterrence strategies, the G.R.E.A.T. program, and recent comprehensive initiatives.

Detached Worker Programs

Detached workers have been an integral part of many programs dealing with youths over the years. **Detached worker programs** place gang workers into the community and free the workers from heavy paperwork and administrative requirements (Klein, 1969). The workers are expected to spend considerable time in the neighborhoods, maintain consistent contact with the gangs, and provide immediate assistance and input to the youths. Many programs rely on past gang members for workers although there has been considerable opposition to the use of these individuals from many sources (Vigil, 2010). Klein (1971) notes that the strength of the program includes the ability to reach youths who normally are not contacted, the flexibility of workers to handle situations in unique ways, and the ability to establish confidential relationships with youths.

The impact of detached workers on gangs has been mixed. Klein (1969), in perhaps the most noted evaluation of such programs, claimed that the detached workers in Los Angeles organized 113 sporting events, 90 outings, 16 service projects, and 14 self-help programs. However, in assisting the groups to find alternative behaviors, the project inadvertently caused greater cohesiveness and, indirectly, delinquent behavior (Klein, 1969). Greater contact between the gangs and a worker led to gangs becoming closer and more unified, and the gangs were more successful at recruiting new members. Additionally, these groups participated in greater numbers of delinquent acts after the intervention of the detached workers.

More recent proposals for intervention with gangs typically include a heavy detached worker component, although they may not use that terminology. Spergel's (1984, 1986), Fox's (1985), and Vigil's (2010) discussions of gang interventions reveal a striking similarity with detached worker programs. Emphasis is placed on intimate contact with gang members, providing alternative lines of behavior, and serving as a resource for gangs. Based on Klein's earlier work, it could be argued that this approach is ill-fated.

Statutory Changes

Increased concern about gangs has prompted the passage of new legislation as means of combating gang problems. Many states have passed legislation making gang affiliation a crime, or increasing penalties for gang-related criminal behavior. California's **STEP Act** (Street Terrorism Enforcement and Prevention) of 1988 effectively criminalizes membership in a street gang. Under STEP, the police can invoke civil penalties against gang members for associating with one another in public, promoting their gang, displaying gang symbols, and being involved in other similar gang behavior. As noted earlier in this chapter, many states have passed laws defining gangs and setting penalties for gang-related crimes. Statutes such as those in Florida (Florida Statutes 874.01) and Georgia (Georgia Code 16-16-3) require harsher penalties for gang-related crimes.

In support of such statutes, many police departments, particularly in large cities, have established specialized gang crime units (Curry et al., 1993). Two recent evaluations look at the operations and effectiveness of specialized gang units. Katz and Webb (2003) report on units in Albuquerque (NM), Las Vegas (NV), Phoenix (AZ), and Inglewood (CA). Weisel and Shelly (2004) consider units in San Diego and Indianapolis. In all locations the formation of the units was in response to political pressure, and the operations of the units were generally separate from the rest of the police activities. Katz and Webb (2003) find the units rely mostly on routine police responses and receive little training specific to gangs and gang problems. In both analyses, activities to prevent the formation of gangs is lacking. Rather, most attention seems to be directed at intelligence gathering and investigations aimed at crimes committed by gangs. In general, in neither analysis is there evidence of the units having any significant impact on gangs, gang formation, or gang crime.

Los Angeles City Attorney Office deputy attorneys present a gang injunction removal petition review process to gang intervention activists in Los Angeles. People subject to an injunction often can challenge the decision in court or file a petition asking for it to be removed.

CREDIT: AP Photo/Damian Dovarganes

Another innovative use of legal codes to fight gangs is to employ civil, rather than criminal, codes. **Civil abatement** procedures can be used to control or eliminate locations that gang members frequent or own (Cristall & Forman-Echols, 2009). **Project TOUGH** (Taking Out Urban Gang Headquarters) in Los Angeles is one such program. When an address is identified as a gang headquarters or hang out, the police and civil authorities, including health departments and building code enforcement, will bring lawsuits in civil court against the owners that can result in eviction and/or property forfeiture. Injunctions against gang members can also be used to order them to stay away from the property. The use of civil suits is in some ways easier than invoking the criminal code because the burden of proof is "preponderance of evidence" rather than "proof beyond a reasonable doubt," and there is no right to a jury trial (Cristall & Forman-Echols, 2009). This use of civil abatement is akin to the successful drug abatement projects in Oakland, California (see Mazerolle, Roehl, & Kadleck, 1998).

In a similar fashion, **civil gang injunctions** involve court orders that prohibit certain behaviors linked to criminal activity. These orders may prohibit gang members from associating in public, marking territory, trespassing, loitering, or other similar activities (Los Angeles City Attorney's Office, 2009). These injunctions are typically aimed at specific gangs/gang members, locations, and activities (Hennigan & Sloane, 2013). Violations can result in arrest and fines. Research on civil gang injunctions show generally positive results in terms of reduced crime and fear in the target areas (Grogger, 2002; Maxson, Hennigan, Sloane, & Kolnick, 2004), although Hennigan and Sloane (2013) note that attacking the gang has the potential to build stronger ties among the members if individual attention to gang member needs is not included.

Deterrence Strategies

One approach that has received a great deal of attention in recent years is to have the police strictly enforce any and all codes and regulations (basically a suppression approach) in an attempt to deter gang members and criminal gang behavior. While deterrence is a cornerstone of the interventions, most projects include a strong social service component to later individual and gang activity (Engel, Tillyer, & Corsaro, 2013). Perhaps the most notable deterrence project is the **Boston Gun Project**, which targeted firearms use by gangs. Also known as Operation Ceasefire, the project used an approach referred to as **pulling levers**. Pulling levers simply seeks to deter behavior by taking a zero-tolerance stance with regard to any transgressions (Cook, Moore, & Braga, 2002). For example, if a single gang member commits an offense with a firearm, the police inform the entire gang that they are subject to increased attention from police and the criminal justice system. Officers and other system personnel will enforce trespassing laws and curfews, frequently stop and question gang members, enforce vagrancy and loitering ordinances, check on and enforce probation and parole rules, seize illegal goods obtained through illegal activities, restrict plea bargaining, and impose the highest penalties possible for even the most minor transgressions (Kennedy, 1998). All of this represents a form of "legal harassment" that is meant to influence gangs and gang members to avoid the use of firearms. Evaluation of the Boston Gun Project reveals significant decreases in several offenses, including a 63 percent reduction in homicides, 25 percent reduction in assaults with firearms, and a 32 percent reduction in the number of shots fired (Braga, Kennedy, Piehl, & Waring, 2001).

The success of the Boston Gun Project has prompted several other jurisdictions to adopt similar programs. The Indianapolis Violence Reduction Partnership resulted in a 34 percent drop in homicides (McGarrell, Chermak, Wilson, & Corsaro, 2006). Operation Peacekeeper in Stockton, CA, saw an 35 percent reduction in gun homicides (Braga, 2008) and Project Safe Neighborhoods in Lowell, MA, uncovered a similar 44 percent drop in assaults with a firearm (Braga, Pierce, McDevitt, Bond, & Cronin, 2008). Finally, the Cincinnati Initiative to Reduce Violence, modeled after Operation Ceasefire, was able to reduce gang member involved homicides by roughly 40 percent (Engel et al., 2013). These results illustrate the ability of the criminal justice system to deter gang violence.

The G.R.E.A.T. Program

The **Gang Resistance Education and Training (G.R.E.A.T.) Program** is the most recognizable prevention program targeting gangs. The program began in 1991 under a grant from the Bureau of Alcohol, Tobacco, and Firearms (ATF) (now called the Bureau of Alcohol, Tobacco, Firearms, and Explosives) to the Phoenix police department. Modeled on the Drug Abuse Resistance Education (D.A.R.E.) program, the original G.R.E.A.T. program consisted of nine one-hour lessons taught by local police officers in middle schools. The goal of the program is to:

> prevent youth crime, violence, and gang involvement while developing a positive relationship among law enforcement, families, and our young people to create safer communities (Bureau of Justice Assistance, 2014).

A longitudinal evaluation of the original G.R.E.A.T. programs showed positive outcomes. Esbensen, Peterson, Taylor, Freng, and Osgood (2004), using data for four years following program participation, reported less victimization, less risk-taking behavior, improved attitudes toward the police, increased numbers of prosocial peers, and more negative views about gangs among those youths receiving the G.R.E.A.T. lessons. Unfortunately, the evaluation failed to find any impact on the more important target of the project—reduced gang participation. While this is disappointing, the promising results led the sponsors of the G.R.E.A.T. program to undertake a revision of the curriculum, which resulted in the current 13-lesson scheme (see Box 5.1).

BOX 5.1 G.R.E.A.T. MIDDLE SCHOOL CURRICULUM

1. **Welcome to G.R.E.A.T.: A Gang and Violence Prevention Program**
   - *Lesson Goal*: Students will identify the relationship among crime, violence, drug abuse, and gangs.

2. **What's the Real Deal?: The Real Deal on Gangs and Violence**
   - *Lesson Goal*: Students will analyze information sources and identify realistic, normative beliefs about gangs and violence.

3. **It's About Us: Being Part of the Community**
   - *Lesson Goal*: Students will define their roles and responsibilities in the family, school, and community.

4. **Where Do We Go From Here?: How to Set Goals**
   - *Lesson Goal*: Students will write realistic and achievable goals.

5. **Decisions, Decisions, Decisions: Making the Right Choice**
   - *Lesson Goal*: Students will practice decision-making skills.

6. **Do You Hear What I Am Saying?: How to Communicate Effectively**
   - *Lesson Goal*: Students will practice effective communication skills.

7. **Walk in Someone Else's Shoes: Thinking of Others**
   - *Lesson Goal*: Students will identify active-listening skills, how to recognize the emotional state of others, and how to demonstrate empathy toward victims of crime and violence.

8. **Say It Like You Mean It: Some Ways of Refusing**
   - *Lesson Goal*: Students will practice effective refusal skills.

9. **Getting Along Without Going Along: Dealing With Peers**
   - *Lesson Goal*: Students will practice effective refusal skills (continued).

10. **Keeping Your Cool: Managing Your Anger**
    - *Lesson Goal*: Students will practice anger-management skills.
    - Practice Cooling Off

11. **Keeping It Together: How to Calm Others**
    - *Lesson Goal*: Students will identify how anger-management skills help prevent violence and conflicts.

12. **Working It Out: How to Solve Conflicts**
    - *Lesson Goal*: Students will practice conflict-resolution techniques.

13. **G.R.E.A.T. Days Ahead: Applying Your G.R.E.A.T. Skills**
    - *Lesson Goal*: Students will explain how their G.R.E.A.T. Project helped them develop a feeling of commitment and ownership of their school and their community.

Source: Bureau of Justice Assistance (2014). Gang Resistance Education and Training. Available at: http://great-online.org/Components/MiddleSchool.Aspx

The thrust of the program is to provide youths with the necessary skills for identifying high-risk situations and resisting the pressure/allure of taking part in gangs and gang activity. Beyond targeting just ganging, program curricula are geared toward increasing self-esteem, changing attitudes, and eliminating participation in violent behavior. A key component of G.R.E.A.T. is to teach non-violent conflict resolution techniques to the youths. The program has been adopted by schools throughout the United States. There is currently a six-week program for use in elementary school with 4th and 5th grades, a six-session family program, and a summer component that reinforces the materials learned in school and provides alternative activities to gang participants.

> **WEB ACTIVITY**
>
> More information on G.R.E.A.T. can be found at the program's website: http://www.great-online.org/

The revised curriculum has been the subject of a rigorous national evaluation. A total of 195 classrooms in 31 schools in 7 cities were included in the analysis, with a total of more than 3,800 students. One hundred thirty classrooms received the G.R.E.A.T. training and 93 classrooms served as the controls. Data was gathered over a five-year period of time, including four years post-program participation (Esbensen, Peterson, Taylor, Freng, Osgood, & Matsuda, 2011). Preliminary results based on the first year of follow-up data reveal overall positive results. Results show that participants are more positive about the police, are less positive about gangs, more often use refusal skills they have been taught, are better able to resist peer pressure, and are less involved in gangs (Esbensen, Osgood, Peterson, Taylor, & Carson, 2011). Most importantly, the data reveal 39 percent less gang membership among G.R.E.A.T. participants (Esbensen et al., 2013). These positive results are also sustained at four years post participation. G.R.E.A.T. participants are still 24 percent less likely to be gang members and they maintain positive attitudes toward police, use of refusal skills, and hold more negative attitudes toward gangs (Esbensen et al., 2013). All of these results are significant.

Despite these positive results, the evaluation shows no impact on criminal and violent activity (Esbensen et al., 2013; Pyrooz, 2013). This may be a result of the fact that G.R.E.A.T. targets entire classrooms, which include youths who are both low-risk and high-risk for gang membership. As a result, G.R.E.A.T. may influence a youth's self-identification as a gang member, but it may have little impact on the level of attachment to gangs and criminal gang activity among those who join (Pyrooz, 2013). While G.R.E.A.T. is a promising program, its full impact on behavior is not known.

A Planned Comprehensive Response to Gangs

Where most gang intervention programs focus on a single or limited approach, some efforts have attempted a broader-based set of strategies. In the mid-1990s, the Office of Juvenile Justice and Delinquency Prevention (OJJDP) initiated the **Community-Wide Approach to Gang Prevention, Intervention, and Suppression Program**. In essence, the program aimed to initiate a comprehensive set of strategies mirroring the five strategies outlined by Spergel and Curry (1993) (see Table 5.7). OJJDP funded program implementation and evaluation in five cities (Bloomington-Normal, Illinois; Mesa, Arizona; Riverside, California; Tucson, Arizona; and San Antonio, Texas).

Several factors emerged across the evaluations. First, in San Antonio, the program was never fully implemented (Spergel, Wa, & Sosa, 2004a). Second, suppression remains the primary response in at least three cities (Spergel et al., 2001, 2002, 2003, 2004b). Third, several cities struggled with building programs that included grassroots community organizations. Most of the participants remained official criminal justice agencies and other social service providers (Spergel et al., 2001, 2002, 2004a, 2004b). Finally, the more successful programs offered a wider array of activities that could be considered opportunities provision and social interventions, such as counseling, referrals, and job training.

The program's impact on gang membership and crime is also mixed. The evaluations of the Bloomington-Normal, Mesa, and Riverside programs report reduced offending and reduced arrests among youths in the experimental neighborhoods (Spergel et al., 2001, 2002, 2003). While the Bloomington-Normal program appears to have reduced the level of gang participation (Spergel et al., 2001), there was no apparent impact in Riverside, Tucson, or San Antonio (Spergel et al., 2003, 2004a, 2004b). Despite the mixed results of the programs, the evidence suggests that a successfully implemented program that targets a wider array of interventions than just suppression activities has the ability to impact positively on the level of gang crime and gang membership.

Overview of Interventions

Evidence concerning the effectiveness of dealing with gangs mirrors the research concerning interventions with individual offenders. The basic conclusion is that many methods of intervention have had little impact on deviant activity. Indeed, some evaluations suggest that intervention exacerbates the problem. A large part of past failures may be due to what Klein (1995) refers to as "conceptually misguided, poorly implemented, half-heartedly pursued" responses and programs.

We must recognize that most programs do not address the major underlying cause of ganging and gang behavior—the lack of social opportunities. Despite the recognition that opportunity provision has the most promise, there are few programs that target this area. The more recent OJJDP community-wide approach is an exception to this problem. The lack of education, training, and jobs receives little attention in most gang interventions. Rather, arrest, prosecution, and incarceration remain the mainstay of society's response. Many authors (see, e.g., Cummings & Monti, 1993; Goldstein, 1993; Hagedorn, 1988; Huff, 1990, 1993; Moore, 1991) claim that until major changes are made in the basic social structure, gangs will persist and thrive.

There is room for some hope in dealing with gangs, largely due to recent initiatives that transcend typical narrowly focused local programs. The establishment in 1994 of the NGC has helped coordinate research and know-ledge about gangs. Similarly, programs such as the Chicago Gang Violence Reduction Project and the OJJDP Comprehensive Community-Wide Approach to Gang Prevention, Intervention, and Suppression Program are relying on multiple interventions to address gangs and ganging. These programs incorporate elements of suppression, community organization, social interventions, and other efforts into a unified approach to the problems (Thornberry & Burch, 1997).

SUMMARY

Interest in gang activity has a long history in juvenile justice and appears to have engendered renewed interest in the last few years. The research efforts to date provide striking similarities to one another. The form and explanations for ganging have changed little since Thrasher's (1936) early work. The clearest difference in recent work has been the finding of more serious violence directed against a wider range of victims. Despite the persistent and increasingly dangerous problem, there do not appear to be any clearly successful methods for dealing with gangs.

DISCUSSION QUESTIONS

1. Gang delinquency is apparently on the rise and you are called on to explain to the public about gangs and gang behavior. How would you define a gang? What is the typical gang like? How much danger do gangs pose to the average citizen?

2. Gangs are typically accused of dominating violence and drug use/sales. What can you tell about gang involvement in these actions? How does this compare to the general impression about gangs? What is the G.R.E.A.T. program, and how does it relate to these problems?

3. Due to the apparent increase in gang violence, the police are called on to do something about the problem. As a member of the police department, what programs, interventions, or actions would you suggest for dealing with gangs and/or the public's perception? Be as specific as possible. If past programs form the basis of your suggestions, provide information on the strengths and weaknesses of those programs and how you would improve on them.

CHAPTER 6

Drugs and Delinquency

WHAT YOU NEED TO KNOW

- The Monitoring the Future Project surveys 8th-, 10th-, and 12th-grade students every year to measure drug use. The results show very little drug use beyond alcohol and marijuana and suggest that much use is experimental.

- Trend data for drug use over time had been showing fairly consistent reductions in use, but there has been some increase in use over the last few years.

- The relationship between drug use and delinquency is not entirely clear, with some studies showing that use precedes delinquency and others showing that delinquency precedes drug use. The actual relationship is probably a reciprocal one, with each behavior contributing to the other.

- No one type of drug treatment is effective for every individual or every drug. Treatment needs to vary by the individual circumstances.

- Gauging the effectiveness of drug treatment is very difficult due to the fact that most clients drop out before completion of treatment. What is clear is that treatment can be effective at reducing the need for and abuse of drugs.

- The "Just Say No" approach to prevention is shortsighted and has failed to show any impact on drug use.

- One positive approach is life skills training, which focuses on developing resistance skills for individuals. Evaluations show that this approach can be effective at curbing drug use.

- The popular D.A.R.E. program has failed to have any impact on drug use or abuse.

KEY TERMS

affective interventions

Breaking the Cycle (BTC) program

detoxification

Drug Abuse Resistance Education (D.A.R.E.) program

drug court

incidence

"Just Say No"

knowledge approach

life skills training

maintenance programs

Monitoring the Future (MTF) Project

Multi-dimensional Family Therapy (MDFT)

National Survey on Drug Use and Health

net-widening

outpatient drug-free programs

prevalence

psycho-pharmacological explanations

reciprocal relationship

spurious relationship

systemic violence

therapeutic communities

use, abuse, and addiction

■ Drug courts represent one of the more recent movements for addressing drug use and crime. These courts couple formal court action and intervention with individualized treatment plans involving the offender and his or her family.

INTRODUCTION

Youthful drug use continues to be a societal concern. Beyond the fact that drug use itself is a crime, such behavior is often associated with other criminal actions, including violence and property crime. As noted in the last chapter, drug use and distribution are related to ganging and gang behavior. There is a continuing perception that drug use is problematic in the United States, especially among youths. The authors of *Monitoring the Future* (Johnston, O'Malley, Miech, Bachman, & Schulenberg, 2014) note that current teen drug usage is a complex phenomenon that varies by drug.

There is ample evidence that many youths are under the influence of alcohol or other drugs at the time they commit delinquent acts, or that they recently used alcohol or other drugs. Substance abuse is even more extensive among serious/chronic offenders (Beck, Kline, & Greenfield, 1988; Mulvey, Schubert, & Chassin, 2010). While the causal relationship between drugs and delinquency is the matter of some debate, the indisputable correlation between the two (Huizinga, Loeber, & Thornberry, 1995) raises a variety of issues for the juvenile justice system. This chapter will examine the various issues involved in the drugs–delinquency connection—the extent of drug use, the evidence on the causal relationship, and ways to combat the problem. Before examining these topics, however, it is necessary to define some key terms involved in drug research.

Three common terms used in any discussion of the drug problem are **use, abuse, and addiction**. While definitions for these ideas vary from source to source, we can identify some uniform components in most definitions. Use and abuse are considered to be synonymous by most authors when juveniles are considered. This is true due to the fact that juveniles are legally barred from the recreational use of any drug, including alcohol. Indeed, even medically prescribed drugs are supposed to be administered by an adult following strict guidelines. Abuse generally refers to the use of any drug beyond that legally prescribed for a medical condition. For juveniles, therefore, any use constitutes abuse. Addiction refers to chronic use of a drug to the point at which the individual develops a need to continue use of the drug, increases the amount used over time, and develops a psychological or physical dependence on the drug (World Health Organization, 1964).

GAUGING THE EXTENT OF DRUG USE

Measuring the extent of drug use is somewhat difficult due to the private nature of the behavior. The only individual involved is the user. There is no victim who calls the police and files a complaint. In essence, the victim and offender are the same person. Consequently, the primary source of information on drug use (the extent of it and changes in it) are individual self-reports of behavior. Such self-report surveys have been conducted on both the general population and groups of known offenders. Data from both sources are considered below.

Drug Use Among Adolescents

Drug use by juveniles has been measured on a yearly basis since the 1970s by the **Monitoring the Future (MTF) Project** carried out by Johnston and associates at the University of Michigan. The MTF Project surveys 8th-, 10th-, and 12th-grade students every spring (as well as college students and young adults) (Johnston et al., 2014; Johnston, O'Malley, Bachman, & Schulenberg 2011; Johnston, O'Malley, & Bachman, 1996). The project gathers information on a wide variety of behaviors, including levels and types of drug use. In addition, MTF presents drug use information for different time frames, ranging from "ever" using a drug to "daily use" in the past 30 days.

Table 6.1 presents information on the lifetime, annual, past month, and daily prevalence of drug use for high school seniors graduating in 2013. **Prevalence** indicates how many respondents used the drug during the year, as opposed to how many times (**incidence**) that the drug was used. A number of key observations can be made from this information. First, drug use varies greatly by type of drug. Second, only a small fraction of respondents uses any drug other than alcohol or tobacco on a regular basis. This table clearly supports arguments that much drug use—other than marijuana, alcohol, or cigarettes—is experimental.

An important finding from the data on daily use is that usage varies considerably by drug. Only 6.5 percent claim daily use of marijuana, and about 2 percent claim daily alcohol use. Concerning past month usage, more than 20 percent reported use of marijuana and 39 percent use of alcohol. Seven percent of seniors reported past month use of any prescription drug (not in table), no change from 2012 but down from 8.6 in 2005. Four percent reported past month use of amphetamines. For other drugs, past month use was roughly 1 percent. It is only when annual or lifetime figures are considered that drug use begins to appear to be a serious problem, with several categories of drugs being used by 5 percent or more of the high school senior respondents.

TABLE 6.1 Lifetime, Annual, Past Month, and Daily Drug Use by 12th Graders, 2013

Drug	Lifetime	Annual	Past Month	Daily Use
Any Illicit Drug	50.4	40.3	25.5	
Marijuana	45.5	36.4	22.7	6.5
Inhalants	6.9	2.5	1.0	
Cocaine	4.5	2.6	1.1	
Crack	1.8	1.1	0.6	
Heroin	1.0	0.6	0.3	
Hallucinogens	7.6	4.5	1.4	
Amphetamines	12.4	8.7	4.1	
Methamphetamine	1.5	0.9	0.4	
Barbiturates	7.5	4.8	2.2	
Alcohol	68.2	62.0	39.2	2.2

Source: Compiled by authors from Johnston et al. (2014).

Experts are concerned that marijuana use has been rising in the last two years. In particular, annual prevalence of marijuana use increased for 10th and 8th graders in 2013, but was unchanged for 12th graders and perceived risk associated with marijuana use has been declining sharply. In fact, the National Institute on Drug Abuse (NIDA) argues that teen illicit drug use remains high, citing the 6.5 percent daily use of marijuana figure noted above (NIDA, 2014). Experts also note that recent changes in state laws legalizing recreational marijuana call for careful monitoring of youth behaviors and attitudes in the next few years. One possibility is that such laws will increase youthful marijuana use, but that is not necessarily the case, especially since "[c]urrently, marijuana does not hold the same appeal for youth as it did in the past and today's annual prevalence among twelfth graders of 36% is considerably lower than rates exceeding 50% in the 1970s" (Johnston et al., 2014). The authors of the *Monitoring the Future* report also note that past year use of prescription psychotherapeutic drugs (i.e., amphetamines, sedatives, tranquilizers, or narcotics other than heroin) leveled at 15 percent in 2013, a slight decrease from 17.1 percent in 2005 (Johnston et al., 2014).

These self-report figures, however, must be considered cautiously due to the question of respondent representa-

WEB ACTIVITY

For discussions of drug use trends, see the Monitoring the Future (MTF) website at http://www.monitoringthe future.org; the National Institute on Drug Abuse (NIDA) website at http://www.drugabuse.gov; and the website of the Substance Abuse and Mental Health Services Administration (SAMHSA) at http://www.samhsa.gov

tiveness in the MTF. Specifically, MTF data represent the responses from individuals who were attending school at the time of the survey. This ignores the fact that many youths drop out of school. Dropping out is especially great in the inner city, where the drug trade appears to be most concentrated. Johnston et al. (1987) point out that roughly 15 to 20 percent of students drop out and are not included in the senior survey each year; moreover, they contend that dropouts tend to use drugs more often than those who remain in school. This suggests that the data underreport the level of drug use in the population. Given this caveat, the MTF data are useful from the point of view that the survey is conducted annually and provides a standardized set of data that can be compared over time.

Another source of self-report data on youthful drug use is the **National Survey on Drug Use and Health**, which is conducted by the Substance Abuse and Mental Health Services Administration (SAMHSA). The figures from the survey reflect drug use among a sample of youths ages 12 to 17, as compared to the data on students in individual grades in the MTF project. The SAMHSA survey, therefore, includes a larger number of younger respondents. Table 6.2 presents ever used, past year, and past month use data for the 2012 household survey. The pattern in the results is similar to the MTF data in terms of both use in different time frames and drug categories. Alcohol is the most commonly used substance, followed by tobacco and marijuana. In addition, use is greater when longer time frames are considered. The figures are smaller in most categories compared to the MTF data for high school seniors, primarily due to the inclusion of a wider range of younger respondents.

The data in these tables, particularly those reflecting lifetime or annual use (and to some extent monthly use), often form the basis for claims of a drug problem

TABLE 6.2 Drug Use by 12–17-Year-Olds, 2012

Drug	Ever Used	Past Year	Past Month
Any Illicit Drug	24.2	17.9	10.0
Marijuana/Hashish	17.0	13.5	7.2
Cocaine	1.1	0.7	0.1
Inhalants	6.5	2.6	0.8
Hallucinogens	3.3	2.2	0.6
Psychotherapeutics	10.0	6.6	2.8
Cigarettes	17.4	11.8	6.6
Alcohol	32.4	26.3	12.9

Source: Compiled by authors from SAMHSA (2013). Available at http://www.samhsa.gov/ (Search for "Detailed Tables").

WEB ACTIVITY

The SAMHSA data can be investigated further at http://www.samhsa.gov/ (Search for "Detailed Tables").

or epidemic in the country. Use in the past year should not be used as an indicator of a drug "problem" because such use may simply reflect simple experimentation. When attention is focused on a more accurate indicator of serious abuse (such as daily use within the last 30 days, instead of on any use within the last year or even 30 days), the percentages of adolescents reporting frequent use are much lower and much less alarming.

Trend data for monthly drug use (see Table 6.3) suggest similar conclusions from the preceding discussion. First, use of more serious drugs has been relatively rare and has remained low throughout the years. Only minor fluctuations in use appear in the data over time. Second, alcohol, tobacco, and marijuana have traditionally dominated the drug use data. Of particular note is that the most prevalently used substance (alcohol) has seen a significant decrease in use over the past 30 years (from a high of 72% in 1980 to a much lower figure of 39% in 2013). Use of marijuana/hashish, the second most commonly used substance, has been approximately 20 percent since 1995. Again, recent marijuana law changes may affect teen use in the next few years.

One major concern with the use of the MTF or the SAMHSA data is over the representativeness of the results. Various researchers argue that the level of drug use is much greater than appears in these sources. They claim that if more representative samples of youths and samples of inner-city residents were

TABLE 6.3 Trends in Past Month Prevalence of Use of Various Drugs for 12th Graders, 1975–2013

	Year								
	1975	1980	1985	1990	1995	2000	2005	2010	2013
Any Illicit Drug	30.7	37.2	29.7	17.2	23.8	24.9	23.1	23.8	25.5
Marijuana/Hashish	27.1	33.7	25.7	14.0	21.2	21.6	19.8	21.4	22.7
Inhalants	—	1.4	2.2	2.7	3.2	2.2	2.0	1.4	1.0
Hallucinogens	4.7	3.7	2.5	2.2	4.4	2.6	1.9	1.9	1.4
Cocaine	1.9	5.2	6.7	1.9	1.8	2.1	2.3	1.3	1.1
Crack	—	—	—	0.7	1.0	1.0	1.0	0.7	0.6
Heroin	0.4	0.2	0.3	0.2	0.6	0.7	0.5	0.4	0.3
Amphetamines	8.5	12.1	6.8	3.7	4.0	5.0	3.9	3.3	4.1
Barbiturates	4.7	2.9	2.0	1.3	2.2	3.0	3.3	2.2	2.2
Alcohol	68.2	72.0	65.9	57.1	51.3	50.0	47.0	41.2	39.2

Source: Compiled by authors from Johnston et al. (2014).

used, the figures would be substantially higher. Fagan and Pabon (1990), for example, note that while 30 percent of school students report drug use in the past year, 54 percent of high school dropouts report drug use over the same time period. Similarly, Altschuler and Brounstein (1991) note that while 6 percent of Washington, DC, in-school respondents claim drug use in the past year, 31 percent of the out-of-school respondents make the same claim. Studies such as these illustrate the biased nature of surveys that exclude dropouts or otherwise fail to sample more at-risk populations. At the same time, however, dropout samples are similarly biased toward portraying drug use in its most negative light.

Self-report figures, even those based on samples from high-crime areas, suggest that the drug problem can be blown out of proportion. The data show that the use of illicit drugs is not rampant in society. Relatively few individuals use illicit drugs with even a gross measure of regularity (within 30 days). Figures for daily use fall to almost zero for most illicit drugs. This does not mean that adolescent drug use is not a problem. Indeed, any use of an illicit drug by juveniles is a problem.

Concern over drugs is also justified in light of the availability of illicit substances. Besides asking about drug use, the MTF project also asks students about the ease of availability of different drugs (see Table 6.4). While the figures are lowest for 8th-grade respondents, even among that group drugs appear relatively easy to obtain. This is true not only for alcohol (56% report very easy

TABLE 6.4 Percent Reporting Drugs Very Easy or Fairly Easy to Obtain, 2013

	8th Graders	10th Graders	12th Graders
Marijuana	39.1	69.7	81.4
LSD	7.4	16.3	24.5
PCP	5.8	9.4	15.3
Cocaine Powder	13.5	18.3	28.4
Crack	13.7	17.1	24.6
Heroin	10.0	11.9	22.1
Other Narcotics	9.7	22.5	46.5
Amphetamines	12.8	26.5	42.7
Barbiturates	10.6	18.3	27.9
Tranquilizers	10.4	18.3	15.0
Alcohol	56.1	77.2	89.7
Cigarettes	49.9	71.4	—

Source: Compiled by authors from Johnston et al. (2014).

or fairly easy to obtain), cigarettes (49% very or fairly easy), and marijuana (39% very or fairly easy), but also for serious illicit drugs such as powder cocaine, crack cocaine, and amphetamines. The results for 12th-grade respondents are even more significant: 25 percent or more of respondents claim that each substance is either very easy or fairly easy to obtain.

Self-report data provide some insights. One is that the drug problem has been exaggerated. Relatively few youths use drugs on a regular basis, although many may experiment at some point in their lives. Another is that drug use is a greater problem among those youths who have dropped out of school or are otherwise considered at-risk. Perhaps of greater interest is to what extent drug use causes further deviance. Alternative sources of data are needed to shed light on this issue.

Drug Use Among Offenders

While information on the general population suggests that drug use is not a major problem and that relatively few youths use drugs on a regular basis, data based on offenders presents a different picture. Various data sources suggest that drug use is a critical problem for offenders, including adolescents.

One source for information on drug use among offenders is official data. In 2012, more than 170,000 juveniles were arrested for drug abuse, liquor law, or drunkenness violations in the United States (FBI, 2013). Roughly 14 percent of these violations were committed by juveniles under age 15 (FBI, 2013). According to juvenile court statistics, approximately 165,000 youths entered juvenile court for drug law violations in 2010. About 9,000 juveniles adjudicated delinquent and placed outside the home had been petitioned for a drug offense as their most serious offense (Puzzanchera & Hockenberry, 2013). Self-report data on incarcerated youths also can provide information on the use of illicit drugs. The most recent Survey of Youth in Residential Placement indicated that 28 percent of the youths surveyed said that they were in custody due to a drug offense (Sedlak & Bruce, 2010). Thus, arrest, court, and correctional data provide support for the argument that youthful drug use is highly related to contact with the juvenile justice system.

Youths in custody clearly use alcohol and other drugs at higher rates than youths in the general population. Specifically, almost 75 percent of youths in custody report having tried alcohol compared to 56 percent of youths in the general population. Similarly, 84 percent of youths in custody report using marijuana compared to 30 percent in the general population. Finally, half of youths in custody admit trying illegal drugs other than marijuana, compared to 27 percent of peers in the general population (Sedlak & McPherson, 2010b).

It must be remembered that statistics on youths involved in the juvenile court and institutions represent a worst-case scenario. These youths are not indicative of the majority of juveniles in the population and, therefore, the drug use figures are not applicable to youths not involved in the juvenile justice system. Indeed, this information reflects only those individuals who are caught by the system. It is possible that the use of drugs increases the risk of apprehension. Despite this fact, drug use is integrally related to juvenile justice system involvement.

A Summary of Youthful Drug Use

The fact that relatively few youths use drugs, particularly on a regular basis, does not mean that adolescent drug use is not a problem. At the same time, high levels of drug use by offending youths do not mean that use is a rampant problem in society. Rather, these figures point out that drugs are used by a small but significant number of youths, particularly by offenders, and that the problem needs to be addressed. To repeat the current assessment in the *Monitoring the Future* report, drug use is a complex phenomenon and varies by drug (Johnston et al., 2014). (For updates on use, see periodic reports issued by NIDA, such as *Drug Facts: High School and Youth Trends* [NIDA, 2014].) Use becomes a greater issue if it engenders further delinquent behavior. The degree to which drug use causes delinquency, however, has been the subject of much debate.

THE DRUGS–DELINQUENCY CONNECTION

Statistics showing drug use among delinquent youths (particularly incarcerated individuals) are often pointed to as proof that drug use causes delinquency. The evidence on the drugs–delinquency connection, however, is unclear. A variety of studies note that there is a high degree of correspondence between drug use and delinquent/criminal behavior (Anglin & Speckart, 1986; Ball, Shaffer, & Nurco, 1983; Bennett & Wright, 1984; Brunelle, Tremblay, Blanchette-Martin, Gendron, & Tessier, 2014; Fagan, Weis, & Cheng, 1990; Greenbaum, 1994; Huizinga, Menard, & Elliott, 1989; Inciardi, Horowitz, & Pottieger, 1993; Johnson, Wish, Schmeidler, & Huizinga, 1991; McBride, 1981; Mulvey et al., 2010; Newcomb & Bentler, 1988; Walters, 2014). What is not clear is which one causes which, or whether they are both the result of something else.

Possible Relationships

The actual relationship between drug use and delinquency can take a variety of forms (see Figure 6.1). White (1990) outlines four possible relationships. First, drug use may cause delinquent activity. This argument typically focuses on the high cost of drugs and the need for youths to commit property crimes in order to secure the funds needed to buy drugs. Indeed, various authors point out that drug users often are involved in property offenses (Anglin & Speckart, 1988; Chaiken & Chaiken, 1982; Collins, Hubbard, & Rachal, 1985; Johnson,

FIGURE 6.1
Possible Relationships
between Drug Use and
Delinquency

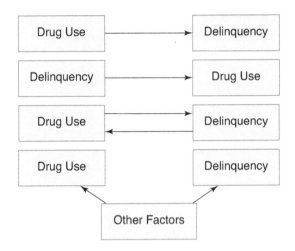

Goldstein, Prebel, Schmeidler, Lipton, Spunt, & Miller, 1985; National Institute of Justice, 1990). Such an "economic need" argument, however, is only one reason that drug use would cause other forms of deviance. Goldstein (1989) suggests that drugs also may cause crime through their psychopharmacological effects and through systemic violence inherent in the drug market. **Psycho-pharmacological explanations** suggest that drugs have a direct effect on the user, either physically or psychologically, that impel him or her to act in a certain way. **Systemic violence** refers to violence due to factors such as competition between dealers, retaliation for the sale of bad drugs, the simple need to obtain a drug, or other factors related to the sale and marketing of drugs.

A second approach to the drugs–delinquency relationship is the view that delinquent activity causes drug use (White, 1990). This line of reasoning argues that delinquency leads to association with deviant peers and that it is within these peer groups that drug use appears (Akers, Krohn, Lonza-Kaduce, & Radosevich, 1979; Elliott, Huizinga, & Ageton, 1985; Johnston, O'Malley, & Eveland, 1978; Kandel, 1973). This explanation views drug use as a form of deviance just like other delinquent acts. As youths associate with others who are involved in deviant behavior, they will participate in the same activities as the other youths. If the group is using drugs, the individual will be more prone to use drugs.

A third possible relationship views drug use and delinquency as feeding one another in a **reciprocal relationship**. This approach is a combination of the first two. The final possibility is that there is a **spurious relationship** involving drug use and delinquency. Under this assumption there would be other factors that cause both drug use and delinquency. In essence, the theoretical explanations for why a youth becomes involved in delinquency would also apply to the reasons for drug use. Drug use and delinquency are simply two manifestations of the same basic problems. Identifying which of the four possible relationships between drug use and delinquency is correct is not an easy task. Most attempts have focused on uncovering the time order between the two variables. That is, which came first, drug use or delinquency?

RESEARCH ON THE DRUGS–DELINQUENCY RELATIONSHIP

Delinquency Causes Drug Use

Research on the temporal (time) order of drug use and delinquency reveals a complex relationship. A variety of studies suggest that the dominant direction in the relationship is from delinquent activity to drug use. In a study using longitudinal data on almost 2,000 high school graduates, Johnston et al. (1978) claim that general delinquency predates most drug use. They argue that youthful drug use is an extension of other deviant behavior. This same pattern of drug use following delinquency is uncovered by Inciardi, Horowitz, and Pottieger (1993) in a study of the behavior of serious inner-city delinquents. They claim that drug use most often appears after youths have become involved in minor delinquency. Other authors (Huba & Bentler, 1983; Johnston et al., 1978; Kandel, Simcha-Fagan, & Davies, 1986; Speckart & Anglin, 1985) also note that delinquent behavior predates actual drug use. That is, the youths commit delinquent acts, join up with other delinquent peers, and enter into drug use along with their peers.

Data from the National Youth Survey (NYS) support this basic argument. The NYS collected data on delinquency, drug use, and demographic factors on a yearly basis from a representative sample of youths. The use of a panel design allows for the inspection of changes in behavior over time and the identification of the temporal order in the data. Elliott et al. (1985) note that minor delinquency and tobacco use typically precede the use of alcohol and other drugs. Similarly, Huizinga et al. (1989) show a general progression from minor delinquency to alcohol use, Index offending, marijuana use, and polydrug use, in that order. With the exception of alcohol, the data show that drug use temporally follows more general delinquent behavior. From these studies, drug use is a product and not a cause of deviant behavior.

Drug Use Causes Delinquency

Other studies lend support to the argument that the relationship is in the opposite direction—that drug use precedes and causes delinquency or crime. Ball et al. (1983) report that heroin addicts commit four to six times as many offenses when they are actively using drugs than when not using drugs. Based on subjects in public drug treatment programs, Collins et al. (1985) point out that daily heroin/cocaine users tend to commit substantially more property offenses than nonusers or weekly users. Anglin and Hser (1987) and Anglin and Speckart (1988) note that both official and self-reported criminal activity, particularly property offenses and drug possession/sales, increase with narcotics use. Other studies report a similar trend of elevated criminality during periods of heavy drug use (Nurco, Kinlock, Hanlon, & Ball, 1988; Watts & Wright, 1990).

Two analyses also provide support for the argument that drug use precedes delinquency. Huizinga et al. (1995), in a summary of the Denver, Pittsburgh, and Rochester youth studies, note that changes in the type and level of substance abuse typically precede significant changes in the level of other delinquent activity. This relationship was found for males and females as well as for different age and ethnic groups. This analysis is especially important because of the longitudinal nature of the data and the use of more than a single research site. Inciardi et al. (1993) arrive at similar conclusions in their study of serious delinquents in Miami, Florida. They point out that regular drug use (and often drug sales) precede other forms of delinquent behavior. Further, they note that the mean age of onset for drug use is younger than the mean age of onset for offending. The early onset of drug use also predicts early participation in serious delinquency (Inciardi et al., 1993). Stevens, May, Rice, and Jarjoura (2011) agree that some youths begin drug use for the immediate internal gratification, but that then involvement in peer groups influences continued use of hard drugs.

Reciprocity and Spuriousness

The fact that no consensus has emerged on the correct causal direction between drug use and delinquency suggests that the more plausible explanation is that the relationship is reciprocal. That is, criminal activity leads to drug use, and drug use leads to criminal activity. Support for a reciprocal relationship can be found in many of the same studies presented above. A number of authors note that increased drug use by already delinquent or criminal individuals leads to higher delinquency levels or more serious offending, not to a first offense (Anglin & Hser, 1987; Anglin & Speckart, 1988; Collins et al., 1985; Huizinga et al., 1995; Inciardi et al., 1993; Nurco et al., 1988). Similarly, Huizinga et al. (1989) point out that while delinquency precedes drug use, polydrug use is a typical precursor of serious persistent delinquency. Van Kammen and Loeber's (1994) analysis of the Pittsburgh youth study data reports that property offending predicted the onset of drug use. At the same time, however, the initiation of drug use was related to escalating participation in personal offenses. From these studies, it would appear that, regardless of which came first, drug use and delinquency contribute to each other. It appears that drug use leads to crime, and crime leads to drug use.

Recent research on serious juvenile offenders also points to a reciprocal relationship. A follow-up study of more than 1,300 serious juvenile offenders over seven years showed that "substance use and serious offending fluctuate in similar patterns over time, suggesting a reciprocal or sequential relationship" (Mulvey et al., 2010).

Similar to the argument for a reciprocal relationship is the view that posits a spurious relationship between drug use and delinquency. This simply means that drug use and crime are contemporaneous—they exist at the same time and vary in a similar fashion, and neither is the ultimate cause of the other. Rather, they are caused by either the same common factors or by different factors. Various authors (Huba & Bentler, 1983; Kandel et al., 1986; White, Pandina, & LaGrange, 1987) argue that there are common causal factors, such as peer and school influences, that underlie both delinquency and drug use. Carpenter, Glassner, Johnson, & Loughlin (1988) claim that the spurious nature of the drugs–delinquency relationship is evident in the fact that few youths routinely use drugs and commit delinquent acts. They further note that the majority of drug use and delinquent actions occur in the absence of the other behavior. The more plausible argument, therefore, is for a spurious relationship. Similarly, the same analysis of the NYS data that points out a sequence of behavior beginning with minor offending and ending with polydrug use (Huizinga et al., 1989) concludes that the actual cause of the behaviors probably lies with a common set of spurious influences. Other research leads to the same conclusion (Collins, 1989; Elliott et al., 1985; Fagan & Weis, 1990; Fagan et al., 1990; Loeber, 1988; White, 1990).

Summarizing the Relationship

The fact that drug use is related to delinquency cannot be disputed. While the causal relationship is unclear, a strong correlation between the two behaviors means that drug use can be used as a predictor of other delinquent behavior (Elliott & Huizinga, 1984; Kandel et al., 1986; Mulvey et al., 2010; Newcomb & Bentler, 1988). The research also suggests that each behavior contributes to the other, thereby providing insight for intervention and treatment. It may be possible to attack delinquency by attacking drug use. Drug use in itself is a delinquent act that can bring about action by the juvenile justice system. By acting on it the system is intervening in the lives of youths who are at a higher risk of participating in other delinquent activities.

INTERVENTIONS

Interventions aimed at drug use and abuse can take a variety of forms and fall under the general categories of treatment and prevention. Treatment programs typically are aimed at those individuals who already have established a pattern of continued drug use. In essence, treatment programs are geared toward addicted individuals and can take a variety of forms, including maintenance programs, detoxification programs, therapeutic/residential communities, and outpatient programs. Prevention programs are geared more at keeping individuals from initial involvement with drugs or, at the least, keeping casual users from more frequent and varied drug use. Drug prevention programs for juveniles often include a variety of approaches, such as information dissemination, affective education, and resistance and social skills training. Each of the various treatment and prevention approaches will be examined below.

Treatment Approaches

What is known about the impact of drug treatment programs comes mainly from the study of programs focusing primarily on adults. This is because there have been relatively few studies of treatment programs for youths and because most juvenile interventions take a more preventive approach. The increased concern over drug use and related problem behavior (such as violence) has resulted in greater attention to treatment programs for juveniles. While programs may have a different emphasis, many similarities and common features appear across programs. For example, counseling and therapy of one sort or another appear in virtually all of the programs. The following discussion offers examples of the more well-known or effective treatment approaches. Other programs appear elsewhere in this book.

Research on treatment programs has led NIDA to list 13 principles of effective treatment (see Box 6.1). Rather than attempt to offer a prescriptive set of activities for an "ideal" program, NIDA's principles address more generalized issues that can be implemented in different ways. Indeed, the second principle notes that no one program is effective for all individuals or situations. In general terms, the principles argue that treatment must be responsive to the multiple needs of each individual.

There appears to be consensus that there are effective drug abuse treatment programs for adolescents in general and for juvenile offenders in particular (see, e.g., Drug Strategies, 2005; Engle and MacGowan, 2009; Henderson, Young, Jainchill, Hawke, Farkas, & Davis, 2007). Elements of effective treatment programs include developmentally appropriate treatment, qualified staff, use of standardized assessment tools, comprehensive services, family involvement in treatment, the need to address co-occurring disorders, continuing care, and the assessment of treatment outcomes. Unfortunately, juvenile offenders with drug problems are often treated in fragmented ways by systems of care that

BOX 6.1 NIDA'S 13 PRINCIPLES OF EFFECTIVE TREATMENT FOR DRUG ABUSE

1. Addiction is a complex but treatable disease that affects brain function and behavior.

2. No single program is appropriate for all individuals.

3. Treatment needs to be readily available.

4. Effective treatment attends to multiple needs of the individual.

5. Remaining in treatment for an adequate period of time is critical.

6. Behavioral therapies—including individual, family, or group counseling—are the most commonly used forms of drug abuse treatment.

7. Medications are an important element of treatment for many patients, especially when combined with counseling and other behavioral therapies.

8. An individual's treatment and services plan must be addressed continually and modified as necessary to ensure that it meets his or her changing needs. Addicted or drug-abusing individuals with coexisting mental disorders should have both disorders treated in an integrated way.

9. Many drug-addicted individuals also have other mental disorders.

10. Medically assisted detoxification is only the first stage of addiction treatment and by itself does little to change long-term drug abuse.

11. Treatment does not need to be voluntary to be effective.

12. Drug use during treatment must be monitored continuously, as lapses during treatment do occur.

13. Treatment programs should test patients for the presence of HIV/AIDS, hepatitis B and C, tuberculosis, and other infectious diseases, as well as provide targeted risk-reduction counseling, linking patients to treatment if necessary.

Source: NIDA (2012).

lack the resources to use evidence-based practices (Henderson et al., 2007). A positive note is that effective programs exist and can produce cost savings. For example, the FIT (Family Integrated Transitions for Probation Youth) Program in Washington State produced approximately $46,000 in benefits per youth served (Barnoski, 2009). (For resources on specific evidence-based practices, see Stephens, 2011.)

Maintenance and Detoxification Programs

Maintenance programs, a common intervention for addicted individuals, seek to establish a steady state in which the individual does not experience withdrawal symptoms when the drug begins to wear off. Consequently, the user will be able to function more normally and participate in everyday activities without the constant need for the drug (Stephens, 1987). The most common maintenance program involves the use of methadone, an oral substitute for heroin. Besides periodic checks (usually urinalysis) to establish abstinence from other drugs, maintenance programs rely heavily on individual and group counseling and the establishment of behavioral guidelines (Anglin & Hser, 1990). Some programs also include incentives/rewards given to clients who test negative for drug use (NIDA, 1999). Evaluations of maintenance programs generally report reduced drug usage and the commission of fewer crimes by patients when they are in the program (Anglin & McGlothlin, 1985; Ball, Corty, Bond, & Tommasello , 1987; Hser, Anglin, & Chou, 1988; Olive, Keen, Rowse, Ewins, Griffiths, & Mathers, 2010). Unfortunately, the impact of these programs tends to disappear after program participation, and patients return to preprogram levels of drug use and criminal activity when they leave the program (Anglin, Speckhart, Booth, & Ryan, 1989; McGlothlin & Anglin, 1981).

Often closely aligned with maintenance programs are programs that emphasize **detoxification**. This approach attempts to remove an individual from an addiction by weaning him or her off drugs. Drugs are used over the short term to minimize the pain and discomfort of withdrawal. Detoxification programs target a wide range of drugs, from alcohol to heroin, and can be found in many hospitals and facilities throughout the country. Anglin and Hser (1990) point out that while short-term follow-ups show that detoxification is successful at eliminating drug use, detoxification has not been adequately evaluated over the long term. Unfortunately, some drug users rely on detoxification to reduce the need for massive amounts of drugs to get high. They then return to more normal drug use until they again reach a point at which small amounts are no longer sufficient to serve their needs (Bellis, 1981).

Evaluations of both maintenance and detoxification programs are somewhat mixed. Sells and Simpson (1979) note that they are effective at lowering arrests and illegal activities among juvenile drug abusers. Other positive support is found in the fact that criminal activity is lower among drug users in treatment than among those receiving no intervention (Kaplan, 1983; Wish, Toborg, & Bellassai, 1988). NIDA (2012), in its list of effective principles for treatment, notes that the use of medications is an important part of treatment for some individuals. Critics, however, allege that they are crutches that do not solve the problem, but instead lead to a nonproductive lifestyle of methadone, alcohol, other drugs, and petty crime (Stephens, 1987). An additional problem is that many maintenance drugs become simple substitutes for the original drug. A prime example of this is the fact that heroin was developed to solve morphine addiction. Today, instead of curing heroin addiction, methadone addiction has itself become an issue.

Therapeutic/Residential Communities and Outpatient Programs

Another major form of treatment, **therapeutic communities**, emphasizes the provision of a supportive, highly structured, family-like atmosphere within which individuals can be helped to alter their personality and develop social relationships conducive to conforming behavior (Anglin & Hser, 1990). Group sessions, called "games," often involve attention on one member because he or she is a new member of the therapeutic community, is suspected of violating a house rule, or is suspected of using drugs. Pressure is exerted to induce the person to admit the particular problem and the need for support from the group (Stephens, 1987). Group counseling is used to explore the reasons for drug use and to suggest alternative methods for dealing with the factors that lead to substance abuse. Therapeutic communities, such as Synanon, Daytop Village, and Phoenix House, boast positive results—including lower levels of drug use and criminal activity (Anglin & Hser, 1990; Coombs, 1981; DeLeon, 1984; DeLeon & Rosenthal, 1989). The KEY/CREST program combines a residential therapeutic community with post-release assistance in the community. Along with the therapeutic community, clients participate in educational activities, HIV education, a 12-step alcohol program, and other activities aimed at preparing the clients for success outside the institution. The New Vision Therapeutic Community program rests primarily on services while the clients are in prison, with an initial aftercare period upon release. Like the KEY/CREST program, clients undergo individual and group counseling, as well as educational activities.

Evaluations of therapeutic communities and residential treatment programs have revealed success in reducing recidivism and drug use. According to MacKenzie (2006), critical elements of effective programs in prisons are a therapeutic community approach and aftercare. It is important to note, however, that even successful programs do not prevent all crime, eliminate all drugs, or graduate all of their initial clients. In a California program, only 28 percent of the offenders completed the program and aftercare, and 22 percent dropped out prior to completing the program (Lipton, 1995). Therapeutic communities can also be cost-effective (Aos & Drake, 2013).

The final treatment modality, **outpatient drug-free programs**, often follows similar approaches to those in therapeutic communities or residential settings. The greatest difference is the lack of a residential component. Individual and group counseling form the cornerstone of these programs. Programs such as Alcoholics Anonymous bring together current and former addicts to help one another stay off drugs. At meetings, members recount their drug histories and how the group is supporting them in their efforts to abstain from drug use. Other components of outpatient programs may include social skills training, vocational programming, social interaction, referral to other sources of assistance, and possibly short-term drug maintenance (Anglin & Hser, 1990).

Several outpatient drug-free programs exist for youthful offenders. **Multidimensional Family Therapy (MDFT)** is centered on the family, peers, and community influences around the youths. Similarly, Multisystemic Therapy addresses the multiple sources of inputs to youthful behavior, including the family, schools, peers, and neighborhoods (NIDA, 1999). The programs assess the needs of the youths and the youths' families, and provide intensive services to the youths within the different social contexts in which they operate. The intent of the programs is to ensure that youths and their needs do not go unaddressed. Each of these programs has been successful at reducing recidivism and drug use (NIDA, 1999; Office of Justice Programs, 2000).

Treatment Summary

There are several problems with the various treatment approaches. First, it is often difficult to motivate addicts and abusers to enter a treatment program. Convincing addicts that they have a problem is often half the battle against the problem. Besides getting drug users into programs, it is also difficult to retain them. Studies of therapeutic communities, for example, have indicated that up to 70 percent of those entering such communities drop out before completing the program (Stephens, 1987; see also Lipton, 1995). One solution to the participation problem may entail mandatory participation as an outcome of either criminal or civil litigation. While research suggests that coerced treatment is less effective than voluntary participation (Anglin, 1988; DeLong, 1972; Maddux, 1988), there is evidence that mandatory treatment does lead to reduced drug use (Anglin & McGlothlin, 1984; Hubbard, Marsden, Rachal, Harwood, Cavanaugh, & Ginzbury, 1989; Leukefeld & Tims, 1988; NIDA, 1999; Visher, 1990). This may be due to the fact that such clients receive more extensive treatment.

Despite various qualifications, treatment appears to be effective at reducing the use of and need for drugs (Fareed, Vayalapalli, Stout, Casarella, Drexler, & Bailey, 2011; Visher, 1990). In one summary evaluation of drug treatment, Simpson and Sells (1982) report lower drug use, lower criminal behavior, and improved employment status for clients as long as six years after the end of treatment. Non-treatment control clients fared significantly worse. MacKenzie's review concludes that "overall, drug treatment is effective in reducing the recidivism of drug-involved offenders" (2006:264; see also MacKenzie & Freeland, 2012). Conversely, Stephens (1987) suggests that maturing out of the addiction cycle may be the most frequent way out of the drug problem. As addicts age, it is simply harder physically to be a drug addict. As a result, some addicts find it easier to give up drugs than to continue addiction. Walker is much more pessimistic about the ability of treatment to have much impact on the drug problem. He notes that treatment is quite effective for those individuals who have decided to quit using drugs, but that treatment programs cannot produce that commitment to quit. So his overall conclusion is that treatment programs "do not have a good record of effectiveness in either reducing drug use or criminal activity" (Walker, 2011:325).

Prevention Approaches

The National Institute on Drug Abuse offers 16 principles of effective drug prevention (see Box 6.2). These include a focus on protective factors; reducing risk factors; including families, peers, and communities in the interventions; dealing with social competence; coupling multiple approaches; and recognizing the long-term

WEB ACTIVITY

As with treatment information, NIDA has a wealth of materials available on drug prevention. See http://www.drugabuse.gov

---

BOX 6.2 NIDA'S 16 PRINCIPLES OF EFFECTIVE PREVENTION FOR DRUG ABUSE

1. Prevention programs should enhance protective factors and reverse or reduce risk factors.

2. Prevention programs should address all forms of drug abuse, alone or in combination, including underage use of legal drugs; the use of illegal drugs; and the inappropriate use of legally obtained substances, prescription medications, or over-the-counter drugs.

3. Prevention programs should address the type of drug abuse problem in the local community, target modifiable risk factors, and strengthen identified protective factors.

4. Prevention programs should be tailored to address risks specific to population or audience characteristics, such as age, gender, and ethnicity, to improve program effectiveness.

5. Family-based prevention programs should enhance family bonding and relationships and include parenting skills; practice in developing, discussing, and enforcing family policies on substance abuse; and training in drug education and information.

6. Prevention programs can be designed to intervene as early as pre-school to address risk factors for drug abuse, such as aggressive behavior, poor social skills, and academic difficulties.

7. Prevention programs for elementary school children should target improving academic and social-emotional learning to address risk factors for drug abuse.

8. Prevention programs for middle or junior high and high school students should increase academic and social competence.

9. Prevention programs aimed at general populations at key transition points, such as the transition to middle school, can produce beneficial effects even among high-risk families and children.

10. Community prevention programs that combine two or more effective programs can be more effective than a single program alone.

11. Community prevention programs reaching populations in multiple settings are most effective when they present consistent, community-wide messages in each setting.

12. When communities adapt programs to match their needs, community norms, or differing cultural requirements, they should retain core elements of the original research-based intervention.

13. Prevention programs should be long-term with repeated interventions to reinforce the original prevention goals.

14. Prevention programs should include teacher training on good classroom management practices such as rewarding appropriate student behavior.

15. Prevention programs are most effective when they employ interactive techniques, such as peer discussion and parent role-playing, that allow for active involvement in learning about drug abuse and reinforcing skills.

16. Research-based prevention programs can be cost-effective.

Source: NIDA (2011).

needs of the clients (NIDA, 2011). Many prevention programs incorporate more than one approach and rely on input from a variety of sources, such as the schools, families, and the community. These approaches can be seen in several of the prevention programs discussed below.

The "Just Say No" Approach

Perhaps the most direct and simplest prevention programs are those that encourage youths to simply say "no" and resist drug use. During the 1980s, the federal government pushed "**Just Say No**" as the cornerstone of its prevention activities. This approach assumes that juvenile drug use develops out of peer interaction and that use occurs mainly in group situations. Children, therefore, are encouraged to make a personal decision in the face of peer influences to refuse any offer to use illicit drugs. Included in this approach is the basic message that drugs are harmful. The emphasis is on total avoidance of drugs.

The total avoidance of illegal drugs in light of peer pressure through a simple "no" response, however, is somewhat shortsighted. Trebach (1987) compares such a prevention approach to related efforts to tell kids to abstain from any premarital sexual activity. As some children are going to use drugs or engage in sex no matter what adult society says, there is an unrealistic naiveté involved in "Just Say No" and similar campaigns. In addition, there may be a certain amount of hypocrisy associated with a total abstinence crusade. Youths recognize drug use by adults and are influenced by the advertising that is aimed at adults. Some "Just Say No" advocates recognize that kids will use drugs anyway, but justify the approach as a way to convey a message against drugs.

Knowledge/Education Programs

A related approach to "Just Say No" programs is the provision of factual knowledge about drugs and their effects. The **knowledge approach** entails providing youths with information on different types of drugs, such as the physical and psychological effects of the drugs, as well as the extent, impact, and possible legal consequences of drug use. In many instances these programs are offered as a part of the normal school curriculum. The basic assumption is that such knowledge will allow the individual to make an informed choice about drug use. It is further assumed that informed youths will opt against using drugs.

Interestingly, evaluations of knowledge/education approaches often suggest that the programs increase drug use by participants. What appears to be happening is that the increased knowledge leads to enhanced curiosity and experimentation by youths in a kind of "I want to find out for myself" attitude (Abadinsky, 1989; Botvin, 1990; Botvin & Dusenbury, 1989; Eiser & Eiser, 1988; Hansen, 1980; Kinder, Pape, & Walfish, 1980; Swadi & Zeitlin, 1987; Weisheit, 1983). Based on information from 143 prevention programs,

Tobler (1986) concluded that knowledge programs fail to show any reductions in drug use behavior. The single point on which these programs can demonstrate success is in their ability to increase a subject's knowledge about drugs (Botvin, 1990).

Affective Approaches

Rather than provide information about different substances and issues related directly to drug use, **affective interventions** focus attention on the individual. The assumption is that by building self-esteem, self-awareness, and feelings of self-worth, the youth will be able to make wise choices and resist pressures to use drugs. Few programs, however, rely solely on affective education elements. Programs such as Here's Looking at You 2000, which purports to use an affective approach, typically also include drug information and social skills training. Consequently, it becomes difficult to isolate the impact of affective elements such as self-esteem on subsequent drug involvement.

One well-known program that incorporates a heavy affective component is the Big Brothers/Big Sisters program. This program matches adult mentors with at-risk children in the community. The goal of the program is to provide positive role models to the youths, help build self-esteem, promote healthy attitudes and behaviors, and prepare the youths for daily living. A key component is helping youths feel good about themselves. The Big Brothers/Big Sisters program can be found in more than 500 communities. Evaluations of the initiative show success at reducing drug use, reducing arrests, increasing educational success, and improving the overall quality of life for youths (Office of Justice Programs, 2000). These results are in contrast to other evaluations of affective programs where the interventions have failed to find any significant impact on substance use (Hansen Johnson, Flay, Graham, & Sobel, 1988; Kim, 1988; Kim, McLeod, & Shantzis, 1993; Newcomb & Bentler, 1988; Tobler, 1986). It is possible that this failure is due to attempts to look at affective interventions separated from other preventive elements, such as those found in Big Brothers/Big Sisters and similar programs.

Life Skills Training Approaches

Perhaps the failure of affective approaches to have an impact on drug use is the failure to include other elements along with building self-esteem. **Life skills training** often includes affective interventions along with a variety of elements, ranging from basic personal and social skills development (which deal with general life situations and how to deal with them) to the provision of specific resistance skills aimed directly at substance abuse issues. This approach assumes that individuals who use drugs are poorly prepared to address the issues and pressures involved in daily decision-making. For example, individuals who find themselves left out of the societal mainstream due to the lack of education

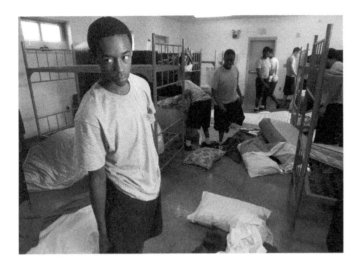

Youths look over a barracks that drill instructors messed up because beds were not made properly at Positive Beginnings camp in Smyrna, Tennessee. Positive Beginnings is a life skills camp used as an alternative disposition for youths whose offenses range from theft and assault to truancy and drug possession.

CREDIT: AP Photo/ *The Tennessean*, John Partipilo

and/or job training need to be taught the skills necessary to obtain a job and succeed in an acceptable manner. Individuals who get into trouble because they simply follow the group need to be taught how to be independent, make decisions for themselves, and resist following others into unwise situations. The key resistance skills taught include how to recognize a problematic situation and what alternatives are available to the individual, how to resist outside pressures (such as peers or advertising), how to identify help, how to cope with stress, and how to make wise choices.

Research on life skills or resistance skills training has shown positive results. Perhaps the best example of this impact comes from a series of studies dealing with tobacco, alcohol, and marijuana use by Botvin and associates (see, e.g., Botvin & Dusenbury, 1989; Botvin, Renick, & Baker, 1983; Botvin, Baker, Renick, Filazzola, & Botvin, 1984; Botvin, Baker, Dusenbury, Botvin, & Diaz, 1995; Botvin, Epstein, Baker, Diaz, & Ifill-Williams, 1997; Botvin, Griffin, Paul, & Macaulay, 2003). In these studies, "life skills training" was successful at reducing the number of youths using drugs. Positive results also appear in evaluations of other programs that focus on life skills, social competence, and related topics (see, e.g., Eisen, Zellman, Massett, & Murray, 2002; Greenberg & Kusche, 1998; Hawkins, Catalano, Kosterman, Abbott, & Hill, 1999). While most of the analyses focus on relatively short-term effects, positive outcomes do appear in longer follow-up assessments.

The D.A.R.E. Program

Perhaps the best-known drug prevention program in existence today is the **Drug Abuse Resistance Education (D.A.R.E.)** program, which incorporates elements of all the previously discussed approaches to prevention. D.A.R.E. is a police-taught, school-based program that began in the Los Angeles United School District in 1983. The program is aimed primarily at elementary students in the fifth or sixth grade, although there are companion programs for younger and older youths as well as for the parents of participating students. The D.A.R.E. curriculum is taught by police officers who have been trained by the program, and it is offered as part of the normal school experience. The topics covered in the program have recently been revised; the current curriculum reflects aspects of affective training, "Just Say No" approaches, peer resistance, and social skills training. The primary focus of the program is on enhancing the social skills of the individual.

Based on its widespread adoption by schools in every state, one would assume that the program has proven successful at combating youthful substance use. Interestingly, this is not the case; the program does not prevent drug use. Based on multiple studies over many years, Rosenbaum recommends policymakers to "Just Say No to D.A.R.E. In light of consistent evidence of ineffectiveness from multiple studies with high validity, public funding of the core D.A.R.E. program should be eliminated or greatly reduced" (Rosenbaum, 2007:815).

In previous editions, we recommended that D.A.R.E. be continued in order to expose youths to positive relations with police officers. While that could be a positive feature of the program, Rosenbaum (2007) raises the concern that police officers have limited teaching experience and may have strained relationships with some communities. A final note is that D.A.R.E. is another example of the panacea phenomenon (Finckenauer, 1982) in which common sense seems to say that a program is exactly what is needed for a particular problem, but evaluation research proves that it is not effective. It is noteworthy that there have been efforts to revitalize D.A.R.E., but Rosenbaum (2007) does not see much improvement in outcomes. (For a different law enforcement issue, namely a proposal about reporting drugs to the police, see Box 6.3.)

BOX 6.3 911 GOOD SAMARITAN LAW

New York State passed a 911 Good Samaritan Law in 2011. The law provides protection against arrest and prosecution for small amounts of drugs for those who call 911 in an overdose emergency situation. Those in possession of large amounts or who are selling drugs would not receive protection. The objective is to encourage reporting of overdoses to prevent loss of life. Proponents argue that no one should fear going to jail if he/she is trying to save a life. Fourteen other states and the District of Columbia have passed such laws. In Washington State, over 60 percent of officers said that they would not arrest someone in an emergency overdose situation.

What do you think? How much protection against arrest and prosecution should there be for someone who reports an overdose?

Sources: Drug Policy Alliance (2014); Banta-Green, Kuszler, Coffin, & Schoeppe (2011).

Prevention Summary

The evidence on prevention programs suggests that drug use can be impacted by certain types of programs. Resistance/life skills training appears to be the most promising at reducing the level of drug use, although more rigorous and extensive testing needs to be completed. On the other hand, programs based on knowledge provision may result in increased curiosity and experimentation with illicit drugs. Programs that stress self-esteem, self-awareness, and interpersonal growth in the absence of other strategies for dealing with life situations, including drugs (typically referred to as affective education programs), also fail to exhibit any strong influence on drug use (Botvin, 1990; Schaps, Moskowitz, Malvin, & Schaeffer, 1986; Tobler, 1986). Interactive programs are more effective than non-interactive programs (Tobler, 1997). In general, while many prevention programs exist and show promise, most still need to be evaluated with longer follow-up periods and better research designs (particularly using adequate comparison groups).

ALTERNATIVE RESPONSES TO DRUG USE

Responses to drug use do not always reflect pure treatment or prevention. The persistence of drug use in society over time, particularly coupled with the failure or modest impact of most prevention and treatment approaches, has prompted various alternate responses. Among the responses are increased enforcement of drug laws, the development of comprehensive programs that combine legal responses with treatment and prevention, and controversial responses, such as the legalization or decriminalization of drugs.

Increased Enforcement

The typical response in the United States is to invoke the legal process. Aggressive police tactics, strict prosecution, and mandatory sentencing are the norm in most communities. Examples of this include police crackdowns on drug markets, drug interdiction at borders, civil abatement procedures in court, and mandatory prison terms for drug possession or sale. This kind of "get tough" orientation permeates the national drug policy, as evidenced in the 2012 National Drug Control Strategy (see Box 6.4) and the funding that accompanies the strategy. While the strategy appears to be heavily oriented toward prevention and treatment, the reality is that enforcement and interdiction are the primary efforts. The total fiscal year budget for drug control in 2013 was almost $25 billion. Of that amount, $9.3 billion (roughly 38%) was clearly for treatment or prevention. The balance is mainly for arrest, interdiction, prosecution, and punishment. An evaluation of a problem-solving, pulling levers police initiative in Rockford, Illinois found that it did reduce drug crimes in the target area. The authors noted that this was consistent with similar positive outcomes for problem-oriented approaches in other cities (Corsaro, Brunson, & McGarrell, 2009).

BOX 6.4 NATIONAL DRUG CONTROL STRATEGY

A. Stopping Use Before it Starts: Education and Community Action

B. Healing America's Drug Users: Getting Treatment Resources Where They are Needed

C. Disrupting the Market: Attacking the Economic Basis of the Drug Trade

---

Source: The White House (2012). *National Drug Control Strategy*. Washington, DC: The White House.

Enforcement Coupled with Treatment

The fact that many offenders use drugs and come to the juvenile justice system with an established pattern of substance use/abuse places the system in the position of needing to respond to the individual as both an offender and someone who needs help. As a result, both the adult and juvenile justice systems have developed processes that couple enforcement with treatment. Two examples of this are drug courts and the Breaking the Cycle program.

Drug Courts. The drug court movement began in 1989, with the first juvenile **drug court** appearing in 1995. Based on the most recent national statistics, there are 2,838 drug courts in operation, of which 447 are juvenile drug courts and 311 are family treatment drug courts (National Drug Court Resource Center, 2014). As of 2003, juvenile drug courts had already handled more than 12,000 youths (Office of Justice Programs, 2003).

The underlying philosophy for drug courts is to use the court's authority to promote participation in and successful completion of treatment aimed at reducing drug use and related criminal behavior. The courts represent a coalition of prosecutors, police, probation, judges, treatment professionals, social service agencies, and other community groups working together to get the offenders off drugs and keep them off drugs (Drug Courts Program Office, 2000). While the drug court process varies from location to location, there is a set of common core strategies that are found throughout most programs (see Box 6.5). Among the common elements are frequent appearances before the court, regular drug testing, treatment assessment, participation in treatment programs, focusing on families, working with schools, aftercare, and providing interventions that are tailored to the individual.

Advocates of drug courts point to a number of potential advantages resulting from the programs. One key advantage is providing treatment to offenders. While most correctional intervention programs, whether residential or nonresidential, offer the opportunity for some types of treatment component, their primary concern with suppression and control often means that treatment is not always available or appropriate. Drug courts, however, are premised upon the need to match offenders with appropriate treatments. The offenders who are admitted to the drug court program are guaranteed to receive some type of treatment. A second advantage is keeping the offender in the community and using community resources to address the offender's needs. The youths are not cut off from their family and community support groups, which are crucial for long-term success.

On the negative side, some critics argue that drug courts can be too quick to intervene with juveniles with no serious drug problems and limited delinquency histories. The critics worry about possible negative effects of court processing instead of allowing them to grow up without the harmful consequences of

BOX 6.5 JUVENILE DRUG COURT STRATEGIES

1. Collaborative Planning—Engage all stakeholders in creating an interdisciplinary, coordinated, and systemic approach to working with youth and their families.

2. Teamwork—Develop and maintain an interdisciplinary, nonadversarial work team.

3. Clearly Defined Target Population and Eligibility Criteria—Define a target population and eligibility criteria that are aligned with the program's goals and objectives.

4. Judicial Involvement and Supervision—Schedule frequent judicial reviews and be sensitive to the effect that court proceedings can have on youth and their families.

5. Monitoring and Evaluation—Establish a system for program monitoring and evaluation to maintain quality of service, assess program impact, and contribute to knowledge in the field.

6. Community Partnerships—Build partnerships with community organizations to expand the range of opportunities available to youth and their families.

7. Comprehensive Treatment Planning—Tailor interventions to the complex and varied needs of youth and their families.

8. Developmentally Appropriate Services—Tailor treatment to the developmental needs of adolescents.

9. Gender-Appropriate Services—Design treatment to address the unique needs of each gender.

10. Cultural Competence—Create policies and procedures that are responsive to cultural differences and train personnel to be culturally competent.

11. Focus on Strengths—Maintain a focus on the strengths of youth and their families during program planning and in every interaction between the court and those it serves.

12. Family Engagement—Recognize and engage the family as a valued partner in all components of the program.

13. Educational Linkages—Coordinate with the school system to ensure that each participant enrolls in and attends an educational program that is appropriate to his or her needs.

14. Drug Testing—Design drug testing to be frequent, random, and observed. Document testing policies and procedures in writing.

15. Goal-Oriented Incentives and Sanctions—Respond to compliance and noncompliance with incentives and sanctions that are designed to reinforce or modify the behavior of youth and their families.

16. Confidentiality—Establish a confidentiality policy and procedures that guard the privacy of the youth while allowing the drug court team to access key information.

Source: Bureau of Justice Assistance (2003).

formalized processing. They also note that many drug courts are small and may only serve a very small number of youths annually (Butts, Roman, & Lynn-Whaley, 2012).

The literature on the effectiveness of drug court programs presents a mixed picture. Various analyses report that drug court participants recidivate at a significantly lower level than comparison groups (Brewster, 2001; Goldkamp & Wieland, 1993; Gottfredson, Najaka, & Kearley, 2003; Harrell, 1998; Listwan, Sundt, Holsinger, & Latessa, 2003; Spohn, Piper, Martin, & Frenzel, 2001; Shaffer, 2011). A cost–benefit analysis of 15 studies of juvenile drug courts showed that such drug courts reduced crime outcomes 3.5 percent and also resulted in overall cost benefits of $11,539 per offender (Aos, Miller, & Drake, 2006; Aos & Drake, 2013). Some analyses, though, find no difference between treatment and comparison groups or higher recidivism for drug court clients (Belenko, Fagan, & Dumanovsky, 1994; Granfield, Eby, & Brewster, 1998; Miethe, Hong, & Reese, 2000). Marlowe (2010) argues that recent studies are finding greater effectiveness in reducing recidivism and that several factors appear to be important, including adhering to evidence-based practices, holding status hearings in court before a judge, requiring parents to attend such hearings, and improving parent or guardian supervision (examples of such research are Henggeler, Halliday-Boykins, Cunningham, Randall, Shapiro, & Chapman [2006]; and Halliday-Boykins, Schaeffer, Henggeler, Chapman, Cunningham, Randall, & Shapiro [2010]). One meta-analysis of 60 outcome evaluations confirmed overall effectiveness, but described the effectiveness as moderate (Shaffer, 2011).

A recent meta-analysis of juvenile drug treatment courts found that graduates have "dramatically lower recidivism rates, both during program participation and in the year following it, than youth who terminate prematurely" (Stein, Deberard, & Homan, 2013). Specifically, only 33.6 percent of graduates recidivated during a one-year follow-up, compared to 52.7 percent of non-graduates. During treatment, 27 percent of eventual graduates recidivated, compared to 51 percent of non-graduates. Disturbingly, the overall premature termination rate was almost half: 46 percent. This shows that drug courts can produce impressive results, but that dropping out prior to graduation is a significant problem. One way to improve graduation rates is to increase parental support, even if it requires entering parents into a drawing for a reward after attending a certain number of family sessions (Alarid, Montemayor, & Dannhaus, 2012).

Sheidow, Jayawardhana, Bradford, Henggeler, and Shapiro (2012) examined the cost-effectiveness of juvenile drug court intervention and found that cost-effectiveness improved with the addition of evidence-based treatments to ordinary family court intervention. However, family court intervention alone was the most cost-effective option for decreasing marijuana use and theft. In fact, simple family court intervention was only about 25 percent of the cost of drug courts that added evidence-based treatments such as Multisystemic Therapy (Sheidow et al., 2012).

WEB ACTIVITY

The popularity of drug courts has resulted in a wealth of information on the approach. One good starting point is the National Drug Court Resource Center at http://www.ndcrc.org/

Despite the fact that evaluations have not been able to declare drug courts an unqualified success, this approach continues to grow and attract attention. The number of drug courts is growing, particularly in terms of juvenile and family drug courts. One driving force behind the movement is the attraction of combining legal sanctions

Chrystal Carreras, one of the first people to graduate from the Lane County Juvenile Drug Court, stands in front of the Lane County Juvenile Justice Center in Eugene, Oregon.

CREDIT: AP Photo/ *The Register-Guard*, Brian Davies

with treatment into a coordinated response. What is still needed is extensive evaluation of the juvenile drug courts in terms of the impact on general delinquent behavior and the use of drugs in particular.

Breaking the Cycle. The **Breaking the Cycle (BTC) program** takes a similar approach to that found in drug courts. The program seeks to identify offenders with substance abuse problems early in their system processing, assess the appropriate treatment needs of the offender, and establish an integrated set of interventions (sanction, treatment, and rewards) for the individual. The key to the BTC program is coordinating services offered by law enforcement, the courts, corrections, families, schools, social service agencies, communities, and substance abuse treatment providers. The court is a pivotal participant because it can provide sanctions if youths fail to comply with the program. The BTC program has been used in several sites with adult offenders.

Lattimore, Krebs, Graham, and Cowell (2005) reported on an evaluation of a juvenile BTC program in Lane County, Oregon. The evaluation of the juvenile BTC program provides mixed results (Lattimore et al., 2005). Comparing program youths to a nonequivalent comparison group, the researchers reported greater access to and use of drug treatment interventions by experimental subjects. Participants also reported reductions in marijuana use, although there were no reductions in any other drug use, including alcohol use. In addition, while there was little impact on subsequent arrest immediately after program participation, there were clear reductions between 6 and 12 months after participation (Lattimore et al., 2005).

Evidence from both juvenile drug courts and the juvenile BTC project show that comprehensive interventions in which the juvenile justice system is heavily involved have the potential to reduce drug use and offending. The impact, however, is not uniformly positive. Further study is needed to identify the keys to success. More consistent positive results are required before either approach receives uncritical acceptance.

Ready Availability of Drugs

A proposal at the other end of the political spectrum from those discussed elsewhere in this chapter is the call for the free (or inexpensive) availability of psychoactive drugs. This is a call to legalize, or to decriminalize at least, the possession of drugs such as heroin and marijuana. Nadelmann (2004), for example, argues that he sees no difference between responsible use of alcohol and responsible use of other drugs. Since the last edition of this book, the states of Colorado and Washington have legalized the possession of recreational marijuana, and more states have legalized the use of medical marijuana.

Proponents argue that such action would have several benefits. First, drug addicts would be less likely to suffer adverse health consequences from adulterated drugs or contaminated needles. Second, it could reduce street crime because addicts would not have to steal to obtain the funds to purchase drugs (Goldstein, 1989). Third, it would reduce the possibility of society alienating adolescents. "Youth may generally lose respect for a society that defines them as criminal because they use marijuana" (Stephens, 1987:119). Fourth, legalization would reduce our law enforcement war on drugs, including the disturbing rates of arrest and incarceration of African Americans.

A major concern with the proposal to legalize drugs is that drug use might escalate at an alarming rate. Nadelmann argues that this is not a problem because most Americans already resist drugs for reasons other than their status as illegal substances. He notes that 70 percent of Americans resist cigarettes, and 90 percent either do not use drugs at all or use them in moderation. Nadelmann concludes that these percentages suggest that Americans "do not really need drug laws to prevent them from entering into destructive relationships with drugs" (Nadelmann, 1997:287). Portugal decriminalized the use and possession of all drugs in 2001. Studies indicate either reductions in problematic use or containment (Greenwald, 2009; Hughes & Stevens, 2010).

Although legalization may be practical for marijuana and in fact has been enacted in some states, it does not seem to be a realistic possibility for many other psychoactive substances. Current attitudes simply do not favor such a liberal approach. For example, even among high school seniors, 97 percent disapprove of taking heroin occasionally and 92 percent disapprove of trying cocaine once or twice. In fact, despite legalization in some states, 74.5 percent disapprove of smoking marijuana regularly (Johnston, O'Malley, Bachman, & Schulenberg, 2013). Thus "our value system, rooted in the Protestant ethic, simply will not permit lawmakers to make freely available such powerful mind-altering and euphoria-producing drugs" (Stephens, 1987:120). (For a debate on the legalization or decriminalization of heroin, see Husak [2003] and Sher [2003].)

SUMMARY: THE RESPONSE OF THE JUVENILE JUSTICE SYSTEM

The juvenile justice system must face several issues concerning drugs and juvenile offenders. First, many of the delinquents committing the worst crimes and the most frequent crimes have drug problems. Statistics clearly demonstrate that offenders tend to have drug problems. It is unclear whether drug use leads to delinquency, delinquency causes drug use, or something else causes both drug use and delinquency. What is clear is that something needs to be done.

The literature on drug treatment and prevention does offer some suggestions for action. As noted earlier, interactive prevention programs fare better than noninteractive programs. Therapeutic communities have had some success in prison settings, especially when followed by aftercare. Multi-dimensional, comprehensive initiatives appear to hold more promise than single-modality programs, and interventions that include the juvenile justice system (such as drug courts) show that coercive programs can have a positive impact. Finally, research shows principles of effective intervention that can and should be implemented for juvenile offenders with drug abuse problems (Drug Strategies, 2005).

The juvenile justice system often attempts to deal with less serious drug users by diverting those youths to other programs. The problem with diverting users of alcohol and other drugs to voluntary programs is that such actions may lead to net-widening. That is, more youths are sent to private programs than really need to be sent. In reaction to this problem, some states, such as Washington, simply opt to divest the juvenile court of its jurisdiction over users of alcohol and other drugs. Unfortunately, such a decision can result in complaints "from disgruntled parents who believed that social control—mandated by the court— was essential for straightening out their children" (Schneider, 1988:123–124).

Beyond the problems directly faced by the juvenile justice system, there is the fact that American society has failed to take a consistent approach toward drug use. For example, while many drugs are illegal, they are still favored by both youths and adults. The most recent change in this area is legalization of recreational marijuana use and medical marijuana use in some states. This puts parents and drug counselors in a bind. Warnings to avoid drugs completely may fall on unreceptive ears. As noted above, however, high percentages of high school seniors express disapproval of drug use, including smoking marijuana on a regular basis.

Efforts to label some drugs as dangerous and criminal and others as socially acceptable lead to problems. Adults can buy and use alcohol and tobacco with little or no restraint but have to break the law to obtain even extremely small amounts of controlled substances. This societal "schizophrenia" (Hills, 1980) leads to conflicts in attitudes and hypocrisy in enforcement. Many interventions focus on certain drugs (such as heroin, cocaine, and marijuana) and ignore the serious problems of alcohol and tobacco abuse. Such slighting occurs even though alcohol and tobacco cause harm to more people than any of the so-called dangerous drugs. It will be important to watch how legalization of marijuana in some states affects overall drug use and drug enforcement.

In summary, there are no easy answers to the question of how the juvenile justice system should deal with drug offenders. Clear, Clear, and Braga (1997) argue that the criminal and juvenile justice systems must be realistic in their efforts. They take the position that any search for a completely drug-free society is unrealistic. A more realistic vision is to limit drug use as much as possible.

DISCUSSION QUESTIONS

1. How would you characterize youths' drug use? Is it an epidemic, a problem, or simply part of teenage experimentation? Offer statistics to support your position.

2. You are asked whether drug use causes delinquency. Discuss the possible relationships between drug use and delinquency and take a position on which one is correct. Justify your position.

3. The state legislature has just appointed you to oversee all treatment and prevention programs dealing with drug use. What programs will you keep or institute to fight the drug problem? Why have you selected these programs?

4. Legislation has been proposed to decriminalize or legalize drug use in your state. Assuming that this legislation passes, what would you expect to happen to drug use and delinquency? What impact would this have on the juvenile justice system? What other impacts will this have in the state? Provide support for your position.

5. The local police department seeks to continue its D.A.R.E. program. Having just completed a degree in criminal justice, you are called upon for advice. What advice would you offer about this issue?

CHAPTER 7

Policing and Juveniles

WHAT YOU NEED TO KNOW

■ In 2011, police arrested an estimated 1.5 million persons under age 18. The majority of these (67 percent) were referred to juvenile court jurisdiction. The police used their discretion to handle and release 22 percent of these youths.

■ A new view of the police role is one of community or problem-solving policing. This view tries to include the community as a partner in defining and solving crime and disorder problems.

■ "Broken windows" policing places emphasis on policing disorder such as loitering and vagrants because this model sees disorder as a factor associated with street crime. The theory is that if police can reduce disorder, crime will also decrease.

■ Research indicates that some departments using traditional police strategies refer to it as community or problem-solving policing. So not all departments are actually following the directions of innovators.

■ African Americans generally hold less positive views of the police than whites. Many youths appear to be either indifferent or less than overwhelming in their support of police.

■ Research on racial profiling has produced mixed results. It is clear, however, that police views on what constitutes a dangerous neighborhood and on what constitutes disrespect can have at least indirect effects on stops and arrests of young black males.

■ Disproportionate minority contact refers to the over-representation of any racial group in arrest and court statistics compared to the proportion of that group in the population.

■ Research indicates that juvenile curfew laws are not effective in reducing crime.

KEY TERMS

"broken windows" policing

community policing

deadly force

disproportionate minority contact

gatekeeper role

juvenile curfew laws

mission distortion

police effectiveness

police use of excessive force

problem-oriented policing

professional policing

racial profiling

restorative justice conferences

School Resource Officers (SROs)

school-to-prison pipeline

INTRODUCTION

Policing brings to mind images of arresting suspects, shooting at criminals, writing traffic tickets, testifying in court, driving on patrol, and interrogating murder suspects in the detective bureau. Police still do these things, but they also engage in activities that many people are not aware of. For instance, today police also lead community meetings to discuss the extent and causes of neighborhood crime and disorder. Together with community members they are searching for solutions to urban problems. Police go to homes of juveniles who are on probation to assist probation officers in making curfew checks and try to determine what can be done to help juvenile probationers stay out of trouble and adjust. Police also facilitate restorative justice conferences, in which, for instance, a burglary victim meets a juvenile burglar and explains precisely how the burglary impacted the victim. Supporters for both sides are present and, with the help of the police officer leader, they work out an agreement on how the youth can make amends for what he or she did.

So policing today means much more than it did 35 years ago. Back then police were wondering how they could adjust car patrol to reduce crime. They were wondering if more cars would reduce crime or if faster response time would reduce crime. Today police are raising questions about the definition of policing. What is policing? What role do the police have in a democratic society? These questions and the solutions raised so far are having important effects on how police interact with juveniles.

In this chapter we will look at police and juveniles. We will discuss the changing police role, particularly as it involves contact with youths. We will also look at attitudes and the police, including both citizen attitudes toward the police and police attitudes toward citizens, some recent developments in policing, the effectiveness of policing, and improper use of police force.

STATISTICS ON POLICE WORK WITH JUVENILES

The FBI's Uniform Crime Reporting (UCR) Program presents the basic picture of what police do with juvenile offenders. Other than traffic and neglect cases, in 2011, police arrested an estimated 1.5 million persons under age 18. The majority of these (68%) were referred to juvenile court jurisdiction. Twenty-two percent were handled within the police department and released. Eight percent were referred to criminal or adult court, and the rest were referred to a welfare agency or to another police agency (FBI, 2013; Puzzanchera, 2013 [Note: This report on juvenile arrests focuses on 2011 data presented in a special annual report issued by the Office of Juvenile Justice and Delinquency Prevention (OJJDP)]; in Chapter 1 we rely on the UCR for 2012 data.]).

Two points are noteworthy. First, the percentage of offenders that police refer to juvenile court (approximately 70%) is a significant increase from 1980, when police referred only 58 percent to juvenile court. Second, the fact that 22 percent of the juveniles taken into custody are simply handled and released shows the discretion that police have with juveniles. Such discretion can have critical consequences for youths. A youth released in this manner does not have to worry that if he or she commits a new delinquent act a year later the first one will be held against him or her and he or she will be treated as someone with a prior record. The juvenile may be treated as someone without any record. If police impose any racial or other biases into their decisions, those racial biases can have serious effects on later decisions by police, prosecutors, and judges. Much of this discretion is hidden and thus difficult to discover.

> **WEB ACTIVITY**
>
> One source of information about juvenile arrest statistics is an annual report put out by the Office of Juvenile Justice and Delinquency Prevention (OJJDP), titled *Juvenile Arrests 2011* (published in 2013; this is the latest one available at the time of writing). Available at www.ojp.usdoj.gov/ojjdp
>
> Arrest statistics can also be found in the FBI's *Uniform Crime Reports*, available at www.fbi.gov

A highlight of the arrest statistics on juveniles is that in 2011 there were an estimated 840 arrests of juveniles for murder. This is a 37 percent decrease compared to 2007. In addition, the 2011 number is down considerably from the peak year of 1993, when there were approximately 3,790 juvenile arrests for murder. In 2011, juvenile arrests for violent crimes were down 27 percent from 2002. Property crime arrests were down 30 percent. Drug abuse violations were down 20 percent (Puzzanchera, 2013).

The overall crime decline that started in the 1990s has yet to be fully explained. Some credit the crime decrease to changes in policing that involved targeting disorder based on a belief that loitering, panhandling, and other types of disorder cause crime (Braga & Bond, 2008). Some credit the decrease to the increase in imprisonment that has been going on for more than 20 years. Others argue that broader trends seem to be at work. Zimring (2007; 2012), for example, argues that crime also decreased in Canada even though that country did not use the police tactics that New York City used. In the next section we will discuss the police role in general and also devote more attention to the effectiveness of police efforts to reduce disorder as a strategy to reduce crime and delinquency.

PROFESSIONAL POLICING AND JUVENILES

For much of the twentieth century, police tried to be professional crime fighters. This often translated into police driving in one- or two-officer patrol cars until they saw something suspicious or received a radio call to respond to a crime or a call for service. The rationale was that quick response to calls would enable the police to apprehend suspects or deal quickly with problems that citizens reported to central dispatch. Many called this the **professional policing** model. Others have called it "911 policing" because 911 is the emergency phone number used to contact police.

There were several problems with this professional or 911 policing model. One was that increased professionalism did not reduce crime. Studies showed, for example, that simply increasing the extent of patrol in a given sector did not reduce crime. In addition, research showed that quicker response time did not have dramatic effects on crime (Walker, 2011), and that much of a police officer's shift did not even involve crime. Citizens call the police for all types of problems that are not directly crime-related. Some of the actions prompting those calls could escalate into crime, but many of the calls occur because people regard the police as government workers who are available seven days a week, 24 hours a day, and thus should be able to deal with their problems.

Another problem with the professional model is that it built barriers between the police and citizens. When officers sit in one- or two-person cars, they do not have the opportunity to interact with citizens. Interaction can have positive consequences. It can alert police to problems in the neighborhood, or it can produce tips about who might be engaged in either criminal activity or disorder. The old-fashioned foot patrol officer could get to know both neighborhood problems and tips about who might be causing the problems by having opportunities to meet with shopkeepers, pedestrians, and people sitting or standing near corners or other gathering places. Professional policing decreased the number of foot patrol officers and put the police car as a barrier between the officer and citizens.

Custody Rules with Youths

Police action in relation to detaining youths has been an interesting problem since the inception of the juvenile court. Under the *parens patriae* doctrine, the use of arrest tactics typically invoked by police in relation to adult offenders would normally be avoided with youths. Fingerprinting, photographing, and incarcerating youths were all either forbidden or severely restricted. The shift to a more punitive orientation in recent years, including mandatory sentencing and more liberal waiver procedures, has resulted in major changes to police procedure and practice with youths.

Perhaps the clearest rules for police handling of youths involve holding juveniles in secure facilities. When a youth is taken into custody there are clear guidelines that must be followed in terms of the custody facility. Youths must be segregated from adults. This segregation has to be physical, visual, and aural (sound) separation. These requirements pose special problems for many police departments. Those that are very small, especially in rural, isolated areas, typically have very small jails where it is often impossible to separate the youths from adults. The choice facing the police, therefore, is either violating the laws on conditions of holding youths in custody or releasing the youths outright.

The rules governing fingerprinting and taking photographs of youths vary from state to state and have changed a great deal over the past several decades. The traditional prohibition against these practices has been replaced with rules outlining who and under what circumstances photos and fingerprints can be gathered, as well as the use and disposition of those records. The state of Ohio, for example, requires judicial consent before fingerprinting and photographing of juveniles is undertaken (Ohio Revised Code [ORC], §2151.313). The law allows the police to obtain these records without judicial consent if the arrest involves a felony or an act besides a traffic offense or minor misdemeanor. The police must immediately inform the juvenile court that this action has been taken, and provide details on the youths and number of fingerprints and photos taken. Further, these materials are to be destroyed within 30 days unless the youth is adjudicated delinquent for an act that is a violent misdemeanor or felony, at which time the judge will set parameters for the retention and/or destruction of the records (ORC, §2151.313). These rules illustrate an attempt to balance protection of the child with the needs of the juvenile and criminal justice systems.

Other states take a more liberal approach to allowing fingerprinting and photographing of youths. Florida, for example, lists a number of specific crimes for which these actions should be taken (Florida Statutes, §985.11). At the same time, fingerprints and photographs can be taken of any child taken into custody, regardless of the offense, at the sole discretion of the agency. These records are considered confidential but can be shared with other agencies and are part of the youth's permanent record that is accessible by the adult court (Florida Statutes, §985.11).

Most states allow some form of fingerprinting and photographing of youths. These requirements, however, vary from state to state and from what are permissible with adults taken into custody. This is one example of how policing youthful misbehavior raises new and unique challenges for the professional police model.

Interrogation Tactics with Juvenile Suspects

As we will see in Chapter 9, the Supreme Court has held that a juvenile suspect can waive the privilege against self-incrimination and the right to consult with an attorney and go ahead and agree to be interrogated. Then a court will judge the voluntariness of any confession by looking at all the circumstances of the interrogation and confession. However, the Court did note in 2011 that police should consider the age of the child as one of the custody factors. In other words, a youth may feel less free in an interrogation situation, and this factor affects how a judge assesses the voluntariness of any apparent waiver (*J.D.B. v. North Carolina*, 2011).

A study by Barry Feld examined the transcripts of 66 police interrogations of juvenile suspects in Minneapolis, Minnesota. Eighty percent of the juveniles waived their *Miranda* rights and agreed to interrogation. On the positive side, police immediately stopped questioning those youths who invoked their rights. On the negative side, police questioned juvenile suspects in much the same manner as they questioned adults. The police often suggested that talking would be beneficial to the suspect, or they phrased the warnings as if they were just a bureaucratic formality instead of a serious constitutional issue with important consequences for the suspect (Feld, 2006). Feld also concluded that the behavior of 16- and 17-year-olds parallels the behavior of most adult suspects; the adult waiver rate is also about 80 percent. So he thinks that 16- and 17-year-olds are about as psychologically mature as adults and understand their rights to the same extent as adults.

In a study of 57 recorded interrogation sessions from 17 police agencies, no attorneys were present for any of the interrogations. The author concludes that this total absence of attorneys "suggests the widespread occurrence that juvenile suspects are making interrogation decisions without the knowledge or advice of counsel" (Cleary, 2013).

An important concern is the danger of false confessions. More than one-third of proven false confessions come from suspects under 18 years of age. In a recent study of 193 14- to 17-year-olds incarcerated for serious offenses, Malloy, Shulman, & Cauffman (2014) found that 17 percent of the youths stated they had made a false confession to police, 81 percent reported having been threatened, and 21 percent experienced force. Feld thinks that 16- and 17-year-olds are similar to adults, but that younger suspects do need greater protection. He argues for recording all confessions as a safeguard (Feld, 2006).

An intriguing issue about police interrogation techniques is that although the police think they are very good at detecting deception in suspects, research indicates that they are not. Although interrogation experts claim 85 percent accuracy, research puts police accuracy at about 50 percent. What is particularly disturbing about juvenile suspects, moreover, is that juveniles often exhibit behaviors that the interrogation experts claim are deceptive, such as slouching and not making eye contact with the interrogator. Therefore, when a youth is just "being youthful," an interrogator will interpret that behavior as evidence that the youth is lying. Another problem is suggestibility. The desire to please or the tendency to trust authority figures, for example, can influence youths to confess falsely (Meyer & Reppucci, 2007).

In their study of more than 300 police investigators in Baltimore, Meyer and Reppucci (2007) found that police used the same interrogation techniques with children under age 14, youths ages 14–17, and adults (age 18 and older). Police believed that children and youths outside the context of interrogation do not understand some words used by adults but then stated that they thought that children, youths, and adults all understand their rights in the interrogation session and the purpose of interrogation. The researchers found that 83 percent of their sample used body language as an indicator of deception despite the problem noted previously that youths are likely to slouch and avoid eye contact. Finally, the Baltimore police also reported using coercive and deceptive interrogation techniques with suspects, regardless of age, even though there is greater likelihood of getting inaccurate reports from youthful suspects (Meyer & Reppucci, 2007). In summary, many juveniles waive their rights, and consent to interrogation. Despite age-related problems with interrogating youthful suspects, many police investigators use techniques, including threats and force, that can lead to inaccurate statements and even false confessions from juvenile suspects.

The Police and Juveniles

A long record of research on the role of police in controlling juveniles has described that role as one of **"gatekeeper"** to the juvenile justice system. This means that police officers exercise considerable discretion with juveniles; officers are often the ones who decide whether a juvenile is processed in the juvenile justice system. Police also experience conflicting feelings toward juveniles. Police want to prevent and control crime, but they also feel a duty to prevent harm to the juvenile and prevent delinquency. These conflicts can result in police taking different actions with juveniles than they would with adults (Brown, Novak, & Frank, 2009).

An observational study of 20 nonurban police departments in southwestern Ohio confirmed the gatekeeper role. Field observation resulted in 195 encounters between police and juveniles ages 13–17 years. In cases involving juveniles initially assuming the role of a suspect or a disputant, only 23 (16%) of those 138 juveniles were actually arrested. In cases in which a juvenile actually committed a crime, only 42 percent of those cases ended in an arrest. As previous research found:

> the deviant behavior of juveniles will more often than not involve less serious offenses, and nonurban police appear to be just as inclined as urban cops to act as "gatekeepers" by resolving juvenile encounters informally without an arrest (Liederbach, 2007:119).

In traditional terminology, much police work with juveniles involves order maintenance rather than crime fighting, as well as discretion (see, e.g., Hurst, Frank, & Browning, 2000; Walker, 1992).

Police officers, patrolling on bicycle and segway, engage with a youth in downtown Cincinnati, Ohio. Police officers exercise considerable discretion with juveniles; officers are often the ones who decide whether a juvenile is processed in the juvenile justice system.

CREDIT: Ellen S. Boyne

An interesting side note from this Ohio study is that the most frequent police encounters with juveniles were traffic-related offenses, including speeding, accidents, violations, and others. Part of the reason for this may be that it was a study of suburban police departments and the automobile is a central feature of suburban life. So while older studies involved police on foot making contact with juveniles, many of the police contacts with juveniles now involve traffic-related problems (Liederbach, 2007). The importance of traffic stops is also seen in an analysis of contacts between the police and the public (age 16 and older) in 2005. About 18 million people—41 percent of all contacts that year—reported that their most recent contact with the police was as a driver in a traffic stop, most frequently for speeding (Durose, Smith, & Langan, 2007). Clearly, we are a nation of drivers, and this affects even contacts with police for both juveniles and adults.

Prior research indicated that gender (being male) and demeanor are important correlates of police officers' decisions to take a youth into custody (see, e.g., Morash [1984]; Lundman [1994]). Most of that research was based on observational study of police. One study took a different approach. Allen (2005) surveyed more than 400 police officers in Cleveland, Ohio, and found that disrespect on the part of a youth, being out late at night, being male, and indicators of suspicious behavior, such as clothing and hair style, were factors influencing the police officers to conclude that the youth should be taken into custody or at least stopped and questioned. Allen (2005) commented that clothing and hair style could result in more black youths being stopped or taken into custody but also noted that there are more black police officers today, which should reduce discrimination against black youths.

Brown et al. (2009) conducted systematic social observation of street-level police officers in Cincinnati, Ohio, from 1997 to 1998. They found that police are more likely to arrest juveniles than adults and more likely to arrest juveniles in distressed communities. A number of factors influenced police to arrest both adults and juveniles, namely, offense seriousness, quantity of evidence, commission of a crime in the officer's presence, race (white), and intoxication. Interestingly, disrespect on the part of an adult suspect but not a juvenile suspect also influenced officers to make an arrest (Brown et al., 2009).

In summary, the police continue to operate as gatekeepers to the juvenile justice system. They exercise considerable discretion in their encounters with juveniles. It is critical that police have guidelines to ensure that such discretion is not abused.

Police Use of Excessive Force (Brutality)

Police use of excessive force is a sensitive topic and thus it is difficult to gain accurate information about its extent. Like any profession, police will not just open up and reveal professional secrets. They will not readily disclose how frequently and under what circumstances they may use excessive force. So researchers often survey citizens to derive estimates of police use of force.

Based on an observational study of police–citizen encounters over three decades ago, Albert Reiss reported that teens were the most likely targets of the least damaging type of police brutality, namely, abusive language and commands to "move on." Such commands were particularly frequent in the summer when youths living in the ghetto were likely to spend more time on the streets. Police told both black youths and white youths to leave or go home (Reiss, 1980). More recent research shows that such problems continue, especially for African-American youths. A 1991 survey of more than 300 Cincinnati youths revealed that almost one-half (46.6%) of the black youths reported having been personally hassled by police, compared to only about 10 percent of white youths. In addition, approximately two-thirds of the blacks said that they knew someone who had been hassled (Browning, Cullen, Cao, Kopache, & Stevenson, 1994).

As noted later in the section on attitudes, a study in Hartford, Connecticut, found that the 132 youths interviewed reported approximately 400 negative experiences (Borrero, 2001). Thirty-nine percent involved physical encounters (force, hitting, injury), 24 percent involved verbal harassment, and 34 percent were categorized as "other."

Geller and Toch (1996) argue that the process of stereotyping can be an important factor leading to the use of force against juveniles. A police officer can stereotype a youth as a "typical gang member," and a youth can stereotype a police officer as a "white cop." This stereotyping very easily leads to a process of arrest, resistance, or actions interpreted as resistance, and excessive force or actions so interpreted that a series of self-fulfilling prophecies are set in motion. The problem is to stop the start of such self-fulfilling prophecies.

BOX 7.1 BAN ON POLICE USE OF TASERS IN SCHOOLS?

When a student tried to break up a fight in a Texas high school, an officer shot the 17-year-old youth to the floor. His head hit the concrete floor so hard that he suffered a severe brain hemorrhage and spent 52 days in a medically induced coma. His parents are suing. Several groups have urged the Texas Education Agency to end the use of Tasers and pepper spray.

Police report that a review of the case showed that the officer followed use of force policy and guidelines. A grand jury declined to indict the officer.

What do you think? Is there a need for such devices in schools? Are they also necessary in elementary schools?

Source: Werner (2014).

A hopeful note is that one review concluded that "physical force is infrequently used by the police and that improper force is used even less" (Worden, 1996:46). One problem with this research conclusion is that it may not be in sync with perceptions on the street, especially perceptions in some of the trouble spots of inner-city areas of cities such as New York and Los Angeles. In such locations, contrary perceptions help to trigger the stereotyping process just noted and lead to tragic results. A national survey on this topic, the Police Public Contact Survey, showed that in 1999 about 3 percent of 16–19-year-old respondents reported force or threat of force, compared to 1.4 percent of 20–29-year-old respondents and less than 1 percent of all age categories 30 or older (Langan, Greenfield, Smith, Durose, & Levin, 2001). Most of those who experienced force (76%) said the force was excessive. Most persons (85%) involved in force incidents said the officer was white. (For a discussion of possible use of force in schools, see Box 7.1.)

Worden (1996) thinks the use of improper force is infrequent, a conclusion supported by the national survey. The hopeful conclusion is that Worden and the national survey are correct. A more pessimistic conclusion is that force is more frequent, especially against minority youths, and that efforts are required to reduce any use of force as much as possible.

An extreme example of the use of excessive force is the use of **deadly force**. About 400 persons annually have been listed as victims of justifiable homicide by law enforcement in recent years (FBI, 2013). In 8 out of 10 such homicides, the victim reportedly used a weapon to threaten or assault the arresting officer(s) and in 17 percent of the cases the arrestee grabbed, hit, or fought with the arresting officer(s) (Mumola, 2007). One study found that:

> officers involved in shootings tend to be younger [w]hite males at the rank of officer and possess a high school diploma. Moreover, officers who have experienced one shooting are more likely to become involved in a future shooting (McElvain & Kposowa, 2008: 519).

BOX 7.2 THE U.S. SUPREME COURT ON DEADLY FORCE

In *Tennessee v. Garner et al.*, the U.S. Supreme Court set down guidelines for the constitutional use of deadly force by police officers. Here are some excerpts from the majority opinion by Justice White:

> The use of deadly force to prevent the escape of all felony suspects, whatever the circumstances, is constitutionally unreasonable. It is not better that all felony suspects die than that they escape. Where the suspect poses no immediate threat to the officer and no threat to others, the harm resulting from failing to apprehend him does not justify the use of deadly force to do so. It is no doubt unfortunate when a suspect who is in sight escapes, but the fact that the police arrive a little late or are a little slower afoot does not always justify killing the suspect. A police officer may not seize an unarmed, nondangerous suspect by shooting him dead . . .

> Where the officer has probable cause to believe that the suspect poses a threat of serious physical harm, either to the officer or to others, it is not constitutionally unreasonable to prevent escape by using deadly force. Thus, if the suspect threatens the officer with a weapon or there is probable cause to believe that he has committed a crime involving the infliction or threatened infliction of serious physical harm, deadly force may be used if necessary to prevent escape, and if, where feasible, some warning has been given.

Source: *Tennessee v. Garner* et al., 1985.

In Philadelphia, however, the race of officer and suspect was not related to contagious fire, that is, multiple officer shootings and multiple shots fired (White & Klinger, 2012). Interestingly, William Geller (1983) describes the typical victim of police shooting as between 17 and 30 years of age. This means that not many juveniles—only the 17-year-olds—are likely to be shot by police officers. All police shootings, however, are not typical; some do involve younger victims. In fact, the primary test case on the use of deadly force involved the shooting of a 15-year-old youth in Memphis, Tennessee. A Memphis police officer shot and killed Edward Garner, a 15-year-old eighth-grade student, under that state's common law "fleeing felon" rule, which authorized police to shoot any fleeing felon—even nondangerous ones. Garner had been prowling inside an empty house and refused to halt in the yard when the police officer warned him to stop. Consequently, the officer shot the youth as he tried to climb a fence to escape. In *Tennessee v. Garner et al.* (1985), the United States Supreme Court ruled that police may not institute a policy to shoot any and all fleeing suspects; rather, they may shoot only those escaping felons who pose a threat to the officer or to others. Box 7.2 presents excerpts from the decision.

COMMUNITY OR PROBLEM-SOLVING POLICING

One response to the shortcomings of the professional policing model is **community policing**, which is also called problem-solving or **problem-oriented policing**. Community policing does not necessarily mean exactly the same thing to everyone who subscribes to it. Some key features do emerge, however, as critical common elements.

One critical factor is problem solving. As Herman Goldstein (1990) has noted, police can and should be problem solvers in the community. Problem solving involves an effort to deal with conditions or factors that lead to crime or disorder. If the police can solve the problem, then they prevent crime from happening. A simple example with juveniles is police in one community leading the community to transform a vacant lot into a skateboard park. This solved the disorder problem of kids skating in the street and on sidewalks (Chaiken, 2004). Another critical element of community policing is community building (Novak, Frank, Smith, & Engel, 2002). An important part of community policing is to strengthen the community and its ability to solve problems and prevent and minimize crime, disorder, and other difficulties. In essence, this involves establishing partnerships between the police and the public (Schnebly, 2008).

In "broken windows" policing, the police also broaden their concerns and actions, compared to traditional 911 policing. Instead of focusing only on crime, the police pay attention to both crime and disorder. Based on the "broken windows" hypothesis, police consider disorder—for example, rowdy teens hanging out on street corners, "squeegee men" offering to wash car windows for cash "contributions," prostitutes plying their trade, youths or adults trying to jump turnstiles to avoid paying subway fare, "winos" urinating on the street or sleeping in public places like subway stations, and so on—as a serious problem that leads to street crime.

> Disorder demoralizes communities, undermines commerce, leads to the abandonment of public spaces, and undermines public confidence in the ability of government to solve problems; fear drives citizens further from each other and paralyzes their normal, order-sustaining responses, compounding the impact of disorder (Kelling & Coles, 1996:242).

"Broken windows" theory holds that disorder creates fear in citizens, causing them to stay off the streets. The more citizens avoid streets, the more deserted the streets get, and the more citizens avoid them. This affects urban trafficking, both auto and pedestrian, hurts business, and can contribute to crime. Some of the strategies used as part of "broken windows" policing are opportunity reduction, problem solving, and crime prevention through environmental design (Kelling & Coles, 1996). Some cities (e.g., Indianapolis, IN) have focused on the "broken windows" model of community policing, while other cities (e.g., St. Petersburg, FL) have focused more on police–community cooperation and problem-solving (Paoline, Myers, & Worden, 2000).

In New York City, police focused broken windows order maintenance activities on stop, question, and frisk actions hoping to catch serious offenders engaging in public marijuana smoking or drinking. Critics see unjustified racial imbalances and constitutional violations that make the strategy "misguided" (Geller & Fagan, 2010). Police argue that proactive police strategies have taken guns off the streets and saved more than 7,000 lives (Kelly, 2013).

Problem solving, community building, and addressing broken windows can directly target youthful problems and concerns. For example, citizens might complain that a particular street corner or bus stop is a center for gang-related activity. After problem identification, police and citizens together explore possible solutions. In Chicago, citizens decided to conduct marches in gang-related areas to discourage gang activity there. Together with police, Chicago citizens also worked with the bus company to relocate a particular bus stop where school children were being harassed. Citizens and police also sought the help of city housing inspectors and housing courts to close down buildings where drug dealers were conducting business.

In another Chicago neighborhood, citizens found that the local juvenile court was so busy that it was ignoring minor offenders. In response to this problem, the community started an alternative-consequence program. This was a program that gave out community service orders for juveniles accused of misdemeanors such as underage drinking, graffiti, vandalism, shoplifting, and bicycle theft. Youthful offenders usually performed between 8 and 100 hours of community service, usually in beautification projects (Skogan & Hartnett, 1997).

In Indianapolis, police act as facilitators at restorative justice conferences. (For a complete discussion of restorative justice, see Chapter 12.) This program is intended for first-time offenders, age 14 and younger, charged with battery, trespass, mischief, conversion, or felony D theft. If the youth is willing to participate, supporters from both sides (offender and victim) meet in a conference. The facilitator tries to get the group to understand what happened. For example, the facilitator asks the youth about the effects of his or her behavior on the victim and asks the victim how the crime affected him or her. After a thorough exploration of the event, the group tries to work out an agreement to repair the harm that was done. Restitution and community service are key elements of agreements. In Indianapolis, police and others (e.g., neighborhood prosecutors, civilian volunteers) have coordinated restorative justice conferences, which have taken place in police stations, schools, libraries, and community centers (McGarrell, Olivares, Crawford, & Kroovand, 2000).

More than 90 percent of victims in conference cases report being satisfied with the way the case was handled. Ninety-eight percent said they would recommend the conference approach. At six months after the initial incident, only 20 percent of the youths who went through restorative justice conferences recidivated, compared to 34 percent in the control group. One year after the initial incident, 31 percent of the restorative justice conference youths had been rearrested, compared to 41 percent of the control group. Both differences were statistically significant (McGarrell et al., 2000).

In Houston, Texas, community police officers provide a "Knock and Talk" service for truants; they visit truants and talk to them about their truancy problems. In Tacoma, Washington, community police officers deliver truants to a community truancy center (Baker, Sigmon, & Nugent, 2001). In Cleveland, Ohio, police converted houses used as crack houses into police substations. In these so-called "RAPP houses" (named for the Residential Area Policing Program) youths could come in and talk to police officers who were there around the clock (Dunworth, 2000). All of these examples are efforts to both solve problems related to crime and disorder and to enhance the ability of the community to participate in policing itself.

Boston police have taken an approach considerably different from the restorative justice approach used in Indianapolis, but it is still considered to be a problem-solving approach. The problem targeted was violence, specifically homicide. In the Boston Gun Project's Operation Ceasefire, police targeted gangs engaged in violent behavior and used a strategy called "pulling levers," which entailed delivering a message to violent gangs that violence will not be tolerated. In Operation Ceasefire, police hold forums with gang members to announce their intent to apply whatever sanctions they can. Police then arrest gang members for trespassing, public drinking, overt drug use, disorder offenses, probation violations, and outstanding warrants. Evaluators report that Operation Ceasefire "was associated with a 63 percent decrease in youth homicides per month, a 32 percent decrease in shots-fired calls for service per month, a 25 percent decrease in gun assaults per month, and a 44 percent decrease in the number of youth gun assaults per month in the highest risk district" (Braga et al., 2001:3). It should be noted, however, that other research indicates that youth gun homicides had begun to decline in 1995 and that they declined 75 percent in other Massachusetts cities during this period (Fagan, 2002).

The Office of Juvenile Justice and Delinquency Prevention has supported the development of comprehensive, community-wide approaches to gang prevention. These programs involve both suppression and services. Suppression means that police—and often probation—work together in surveillance and information sharing. Service means efforts to provide academic, economic, and social opportunities for gang members. One program targeted older members (17 to 24) of two of the most violent gangs in the Little Village neighborhood of Chicago. Results were favorable, including reduced serious gang violence among the targeted gang members, compared to gang members in a comparison group. Specifically, the program resulted in reduced arrests for serious gang crimes (especially aggravated batteries and assaults) among the targeted youths (Howell, 2000).

In summary, community or problem-solving policing tries to solve or prevent problems that contribute to crime and delinquency. Community policing has resulted in a number of innovative strategies in the last 25 years. A recent review of research found that hot spots policing efforts (focusing on high crime locations) with a problem-solving emphasis are effective in crime prevention (Braga, Papachristos, & Hureau, 2014).

CITIZEN ATTITUDES TOWARD POLICE

Contrary to what many police believe, citizens actually hold rather positive attitudes toward the police. For example, a 2012 Gallup Poll reported that 58 percent of those polled rated the honesty and ethical standards of police either very high or high (University at Albany, 2014). In an earlier Gallup Poll respondents rated police below nurses, clergy, druggists, veterinarians, and doctors, but above college teachers, engineers, dentists, psychiatrists, bankers, chiropractors, journalists, lawyers, and others (Maguire & Pastore, 2004). In November of 2001, in the aftermath of the September 11th terrorist attacks, the rating of police jumped; 68 percent of respondents rated police honesty and ethical standards as very high or high (Gallup Organization, 2001). Another survey in 2002 showed that high percentages of the respondents rated the police "excellent" or "pretty good" at solving crime, preventing crime, and being helpful and friendly (Maguire & Pastore, 2004). Recently, almost 60 percent of the respondents said that they had a "great deal of confidence" or "quite a lot of confidence" in the police as one of the institutions in American society (University at Albany, 2014).

Citizens vary considerably, however, in their approval of the police. For example, in the most recent surveys, 59 percent of whites but only 39 percent of blacks rated the honesty and ethical standards of police as high or very high. Similarly, 57 percent of whites but only 32 percent of blacks reported a great deal or quite a lot of confidence in the police. Overall, 17 percent of blacks report having been treated less fairly in the last 30 days (University at Albany, 2014). Similarly, 61 percent of whites but only 43 percent of blacks and 41 percent of Hispanics think that the police treat all races fairly. Less than one-half of young respondents (age 18 to 24 years) think that the police treat all races fairly, compared to more than 50 percent for all other age groups, including 71 percent of senior citizens (age 65 and up). Only 16 percent of whites but 42 percent of blacks and 39 percent of Hispanics fear that the police may stop and arrest them when they are completely innocent (Maguire & Pastore, 2004). In a survey in New York City, "blacks were three times more likely than non-blacks to perceive that racially biased policing was widespread, that it was unjustified, and that it had been experienced personally" (Rice & Piquero, 2005:111). Thus, citizen attitudes toward the police are not uniform. Some citizens are more positive, while others are more negative.

WEB ACTIVITY

The *Sourcebook of Criminal Justice Statistics* contains considerable information on public opinion attitude research about criminal justice topics. Available at http://www.albany.edu/sourcebook/

Of great relevance to the police and juvenile justice is the fact that lower-class youths comprise one group holding negative attitudes toward the police. Anderson (1994) argues that lower-class youths have little faith in the police and subscribe to a street code whereby the "police are most often seen as representing the dominant white society and not caring to protect inner-city residents" (Anderson, 1994:82). As a result of the perception and/or the reality that police do not respond when called, the inner-city youth often relies on self-protection: "taking care of himself" (Anderson, 1994:82) is a critical part of this street code.

Results from a study in St. Louis, Missouri, confirm Anderson's argument. This was a qualitative study that used a purposive sample of 75 African-American youths, a number of whom were highly active in delinquency. High percentages of the youths in St. Louis had been harassed or mistreated by the police. About half of both male and female respondents agreed that the police engage in frequent harassment or mistreatment of people. In summary, young men "described being stopped on a regular basis and treated as suspects. They said officers routinely used disrespectful language, engaged in physically intrusive actions such as strip searches and cavity probes, and assumed young men 'got lucky' rather than were innocent when no evidence of criminal wrongdoing was discovered" (Brunson & Miller, 2006:548). Several of the young men reported that if police lacked enough evidence to arrest them, the officers would drive them to another area, let them out, and make them walk home (Brunson, 2007). Simply being a young black male in a disadvantaged neighborhood put these males at risk of police suspicion of criminal activity (Cobbina, Miller, & Brunson, 2008).

A slightly older study, however, found the issue to be more complicated. Hurst, Frank, and Browning (2000) surveyed more than 800 students in Cincinnati, Ohio. Like prior research, questions about police effectiveness in general showed less positive attitudes for black teens, but black teens were more positive than white teens when asked to consider police behavior in specific encounters. Then, after control variables were added, "the strongest predictor of less positive attitudes was seeing and hearing about the police misconduct aimed at another person (vicarious conduct)" (Hurst et al., 2000:49).

One study offers a suggestion for getting beyond the issue of race and attitudes toward the police. A study of four dimensions of trust in the police found that youths, whether white, black, or Latino, who had less commitment to school and who had seen police stop other youths and treat those other youths with disrespect had significantly less trust in the police. The lesson for police is that their behavior with the public can affect not only those with whom they are interacting but will also affect any witnesses (Flexon, Lurigio, & Greenleaf,

2009). Even delinquent youths who reported that they felt police treated citizens more fairly rated the police higher on legitimacy (Lee, Steinberg, & Piquero, 2010).

A study of more than 5,000 eighth-grade students found that youths were "indifferent" toward the police, that is, they were neither positive nor negative (Taylor, Turner, Esbensen, & Winfree, 2001). Part of the reason for youths' indifference or negative attitudes toward the police is that youths often have negative experiences with the police. A study in Hartford, Connecticut, for example, found that the 132 youths interviewed reported approximately 400 negative experiences. Thirty-nine percent involved physical encounters (force, hitting, injury), 24 percent involved verbal harassment, and 34 percent were categorized as "other." For example, a 15-year-old Hispanic female reported being thrown against the ground and then against a wall when she was hanging out on the street with friends. A black youth suspected of dealing drugs when he was talking to a friend on the street was grabbed, thrown up against the car, and hit with billy clubs. (He admitted possessing but not dealing drugs.) Another youth was driving and was signaled to pull over. The officer smashed his car window and several officers grabbed, beat, and injured the youth (Borrero, 2001).

A national survey of 1,289 youths in middle and high schools found that youths who had been arrested had significantly less positive attitudes toward the police than youths who had not been arrested or who had other types of contact with police. There were no gender differences in attitudes toward the police, but black youths had less favorable attitudes. Based on these findings, the authors suggest that police officers need to be aware of the troubled history between blacks and the police, and "efforts are made to become more inclusive of [b]lack perspectives" (Brick, Taylor, & Esbensen, 2009: 493).

It is interesting to speculate about how changes in the nature of policing might affect attitudes toward the police. Recall that Chicago made a major effort to implement community policing. In four of the five experimental districts, residents reported improved police responsiveness to neighborhood concerns, and African-American residents had improved perceptions about police misconduct (Skogan & Hartnett, 1997). In Boston, where Operation Ceasefire meant a tough, deterrent message and approach to violent gang members, interviews with community members indicated that they felt the deterrence strategy was effective but worried about the long-term effects. They were concerned that simply sending troubled youths to prison was not the complete answer and might just increase youths' hostility and hopelessness (Stoutland, 2001).

These variations in attitudes toward the police help to explain the paradox that police often hold negative or cynical views of citizens while citizen attitudes toward the police are actually rather positive. Part of the explanation for this apparent contradiction is that the police are much more likely to come in contact with citizens with less positive views—minority and younger citizens— than with older citizens who hold more positive views. A second explanation for the paradox is that the police often come into contact with citizens at inopportune times—in instances in which citizens have broken the law (even if only a traffic law), been victimized, or witnessed a crime. At such times, citizens are likely to be under stress. They may react with frustration at receiving a speeding ticket or at hearing an officer say that there is little hope of recovering their stolen property. Citizens may lash out at the available target (i.e., the police officer) much like a frustrated customer reacts to a customer service representative who is not responsible for the problem but has the unpleasant job of trying to rectify it. Repeated contacts with citizens in times of crisis can also lead the police to job burnout (Maslach & Jackson, 1979), cynicism (Niederhoffer, 1967), suspicion (Skolnick, 1966), and/or stress (Crank & Caldero, 1991; Kroes, Margolis, & Hurrell, 1974). In addition, dissatisfaction with a specific police contact leads to lower evaluations of police services in general (Huebner, Schafer, & Bynum, 2004).

One final observation on this matter concerns the fact that any victim of crime views his or her situation as unique while the police view the same situation as routine. The victim often is a first-time victim who is frightened, stunned, and excited about something that is entirely new to him or her. The officer is simply experiencing the third burglary report that night, the twentieth that week, or the one-thousandth in his or her career. Additionally, the officer's realistic judgment that little or nothing can be done to "solve" the crime leads him or her to rush through the encounter with the citizen in order to write up a report so that the victim can file an insurance claim. Based on television or movie stereotypes, the naive citizen may expect the officer to drop everything, spend as much time as possible on the victim's case, and solve it. Realizing that the officer has a very different definition of the situation, the citizen becomes upset and reacts accordingly—possibly accusing the officer of incompetence or laziness. Such negative encounters reinforce officer perceptions of citizens as being negative toward the police, even while the public opinion poll research shows the contrary.

Implications of the Attitudinal Research

Several conclusions can be drawn from this discussion of police attitudes toward citizens and citizen attitudes toward the police. First, both sides could benefit from clarification. The police might benefit from becoming aware that citizens generally are positive about the police. Citizens, on the other hand, need to know why police may be somewhat cynical toward them. Citizens should be aware that police officers have likely seen their problem before and have had contact with some victims who precipitated the crime or were otherwise tainted. More importantly, citizens must be realistic in their expectations of what the police can do. For example, the police often can do little or nothing to recover a stolen television or car. Second, police need to be careful in their dealings with citizens who hold less positive attitudes—namely, youths and minorities. Because these groups may be less favorable in their attitudes toward the police, the police need to target them for more positive treatment. Otherwise, these groups may interpret police indifference and cynicism as evidence of prejudicial attitudes and discriminatory behavior. Furthermore, police sensitivity to the attitudes of youthful and minority citizens can lead to improved police–community relations.

As noted, there has been recent emphasis on the police as problem solvers. Some police experts think that traditional policing can do little more than take reports for many problems. If policing were restructured, however, perhaps more could be done about many of the concerns that citizens have. If police spent less time running from call to call and more time exploring the causes and solutions of various problems, then the police could be more effective and have greater impact (see, e.g., Trojanowicz, Kappeler, Gaines, & Bucqueroux, 1998).

RECENT ISSUES IN POLICING CONCERNING JUVENILES

Police work with juveniles has undergone various changes over the past several decades. Among these initiatives are the introduction of police in schools, the problem of racial profiling and disproportionate minority contact, enforcement of curfew laws, participation in intensive supervision of probationers, and policing of underage drinking.

Police in Schools

Since the early 1990s, police presence in schools has grown considerably. By 2009–10, two-thirds of middle schools and 76 percent of high schools had either security guards or police officers on the premises (Robers, Kemp, Rathbun, & Morgan, 2014). Part of this growth is due to a number of highly publicized shootings in schools such as Columbine and Newtown, Connecticut, which attracted attention and action. Violent crime, drug violations, weapons violations, and bullying have also aroused concern and calls for increased police officer presence in schools (Booth, Van Hasselt, & Vecchi, 2011). One article claimed that both school police and surveillance cameras are in "widespread" use in urban, suburban, and rural schools (Hirschfield & Celinska, 2011). Specifically, 90 percent of schools now control access to school buildings, and 55 percent of schools use security cameras to monitor school buildings

TABLE 7.1 Percentage of Schools with Full-time or Part-time Security at School at Least Once a Week: 2005-06, 2007-08, and 2009-10

Type of Security	Full-time (%)	Part-time (%)
2005–06	27.0	14.6
2007–08	30.4	15.9
2009–10	28.7	14.1

Source: Robers et al. 2014

(Robers, Zhang, Truman, & Snyder, 2010). Student surveys show that more than two-thirds of students report that their school has either a security guard or an assigned police officer (Robers et al., 2010).

The presence of **School Resource Officers** (SROs) has become commonplace. For the 2009–2010 school year, principals in 29 percent of U.S. schools reported having at least one full-time police officer at their school at least once a week. Another 14 percent of schools had only part-time officers. For high schools, the percentages were 62 percent full-time and 15 percent part-time (Robers et al., 2014) (see Table 7.1). In 2011, 70 percent of students reported that their school had either security guards or assigned police officers (Robers et al., 2014).

Most police in schools were involved in traditional police functions, including patrolling, making arrests, and providing security (see Table 7.2). At the same time, many police officers in schools, particularly those in an SRO capacity, provided counseling, mentoring and referrals as well as training to teachers and parents, taught programs such as Drug Abuse Resistance Education (D.A.R.E.), and chaperoned school events (Travis & Coon, 2005). (For discussion of the effectiveness of D.A.R.E., see Chapter 6.)

The introduction of police to schools has not been without controversy. Some observers argue that SROs try to balance their roles as law enforcers and mentors/instructors/problem solvers. Others contend that the widespread introduction of police into the school setting criminalizes school discipline.

At the same time as police have been introduced to school, there has been an introduction of zero-tolerance

TABLE 7.2 Activities of Law Enforcement in Schools

- Law Enforcement Patrol
- Operate Metal Detectors
- Conduct Safety Inspections
- Respond to Crime/Disorder Reports
- Make Arrests
- Write Reports
- Perform Drug Sweeps

- Advise/Mentor Staff
- Mediate Disputes
- Advise Students
- Work with Parent–Teacher Groups
- Advise Athletic Teams
- Mentor Students
- Chaperone Events
- Present Awards

- Teaching D.A.R.E.
- Anti-Gang Classes
- Anti-Hate Classes
- Law-Related Education
- Firearm Safety
- Crime Awareness and Prevention
- Conflict Resolution
- Problem Solving

Source: Travis and Coon (2005).

policies whereby students are suspended or expelled for certain behaviors such as bringing a weapon to school. Critics contend that the introduction of police resource officers and zero-tolerance policies are signs of criminalization in schools. In other words, instead of seeing discipline problems as requiring solutions by teachers and principals, these practices treat students as quasi-criminals and mandate quasi-criminal justice solutions and thereby label youths as criminals. Critics see this as part of a more general trend to ignore problems of poverty and deindustrialization. For example, "the transfer of disciplinary responsibilities from school professionals to the police also supports this purpose given that police are ill-equipped to recognize and address the psychological and social roots of school misconduct" (Hirschfield & Celinska, 2011:7).

Albany police School Resource Officer Curtis Bell talks with a student while greeting teenagers as they arrive at West Albany High School.

CREDIT: AP Photo/*Albany Democrat-Herald*, Mark Ylen

This emphasis on police in schools and zero tolerance policies are part of what is called the **school-to-prison pipeline** (Kim, Losen, & Hewitt, 2010). This refers to a combination of factors that appear to criminalize much youthful behavior and facilitate the eventual placement of youths in our nation's prisons. Kupchik (2014) argues that educational approaches such as tutoring, improved classroom management techniques, and increasing staff diversity are steps that schools could take to reduce problems.

A dramatic example of the school-to-prison pipeline is the Texas practice of handling truancy cases in adult court: 113,000 such cases in 2012. Part of the reason for this is that fines pay for more than half of the operating costs of truancy courts in Dallas County. Dallas County collected $2.9 million in such fines in 2012 (National School Boards Association, 2013). A complaint has been filed with the U.S. Department of Justice to investigate the practice.

One study found that arrest is related to a 20 percent increase in dropping out of high school and thus "hinders the transition to adulthood" (Kirk & Sampson, 2013:54). As a response to the more general problem, Connecticut probation officers are now reviewing each summons to avoid criminalizing "school incidents that are in keeping with normal adolescent behavior" (Bracey, Geib, Plant, O'Leary, Anderson, Herscovitch, O'Connell, & Vanderploeg, 2013:428). More generally, the Council of State Governments Justice Center has recommended that police should not be involved in routine classroom management and minor offenses at school should not be referred to the courts (Morgan, Salomon, Plotkin, & Cohen, 2014).

Na and Gottfredson (2013) found that increasing the presence of police officers in schools is related to increases in weapon and drug crimes but not other types of crime. So they found no evidence that SROs improve school safety. On the other hand, police presence is not related to changes in the use of harsh discipline. They think that further research is needed on this issue and that in the meantime schools should emphasize proven school-based approaches to maintain order in schools.

As in other areas of juvenile justice, diversion programs have been instituted to offer another way to deal with school problems. One program in Florida had misdemeanor school offenders perform community service instead of being processed in juvenile court. The referred students completed 96 percent of the community service hours that they had been ordered to perform and a preliminary analysis of recidivism was promising (Sullivan, Dollard, Sellers, & Mayo, 2010). These positive findings indicate that there are at least some youths who do not need harsh punishment for school infractions but who will respond positively to programs that use more of a problem-solving approach.

Evaluations of effective school–police partnerships also indicate that more is needed than simply placing police officers in schools. First, many schools have problems such as overcrowding, lower attendance rates, larger minority populations, and lower funding than other schools. Second, evaluations of effective partnerships show the need for both parent cooperation and supplementing law enforcement presence "with intensive monitoring, counseling, and other related services that strengthen cooperation and collaboration with other community-based groups having a vested interest in the social justice needs of students attending schools in the community" (Brady, Balmer, & Phenix, 2007). This is congruent with research on Scared Straight (see Chapter 11). Simple solutions such as prison confrontation programs and putting police in schools are not cure-alls for complex problems such as delinquency.

Racial Profiling and System Contact

One issue affecting attitudes and interaction between the police and the public is racial profiling. Racial profiling is defined "as the police use of race as the sole basis for initiating law enforcement activity (e.g., stopping, searching, and detaining a person)" (Meehan & Ponder, 2002:403). Both media depictions (including television news) and political agendas contribute to exaggerated estimates of black criminality (Welch, 2007). One common form of alleged racial profiling is the practice of stopping African-American drivers for "driving while black." In perhaps the most publicized incident of this activity, police on the New Jersey Turnpike were targeting black drivers about twice as often as all other drivers based on claims that blacks were more likely to be carrying drugs. However, searches of white drivers were in fact producing more contraband than searches of black drivers (Roane, 2001). Similarly, a study of profiling in a medium-sized suburban police department found that profiling increased "as African Americans travel farther from 'black' communities and into whiter neighborhoods" (Meehan & Ponder, 2002:422).

It should be noted that charges of racial profiling need thorough investigation. A scientific study of New Jersey State Trooper stops of motorists showed that the troopers were stopping black drivers "in approximate proportion to their representation among speeders" (Lange, Johnson, & Voas, 2005:216). Although this does not automatically rule out profiling, it shows that there is a need to have an accurate measure of the composition of violators and not just a measure of the composition of the population in the jurisdiction (Lange et al., 2005). Similarly, an observational study in Savannah, Georgia, showed that race affected whether police viewed blacks as suspicious, but such non-behavioral suspicion did not influence the officer's decision to stop and question (Alpert, MacDonald, & Dunham, 2005).

A Bureau of Justice Statistics study of police–citizen contacts in 2011 showed that a higher percentage of black drivers (12.8%) than white (9.8%) and Hispanic (10.4%) drivers were stopped by police. Also, that about 6 percent of black drivers, 7 percent of Hispanic drivers, but only 2 percent of white drivers were searched by police. Similarly, a lower percentage of black drivers felt that police had stopped them for a legitimate reason than white drivers (Langton & Durose, 2013). So regardless of the legitimacy of stops of black drivers, black drivers perceive unfairness more frequently than do white drivers. A study in Dade County (Miami), Florida, used both observation and an analysis of 66,000 citizen contact cards that police were required to fill out after a traffic stop. The observation component showed no racial impact. Analysis of the contact cards, however, showed that "in predominantly white and racially mixed areas, black drivers were stopped disproportionately to their representation in the driving population, as estimated through a random sample of not-at-fault drivers in two vehicle crashes" (Alpert, Dunham, & Smith, 2007:48). So part of this study did not support an inference of racial profiling, but the other part did. More generally, however, recent research has shown that blacks and Hispanics are "often overrepresented among stops when compared with the various benchmarks for those groups. Similarly, the research shows that once stopped, blacks and Hispanics are more likely than whites to be searched or arrested" (Alpert, 2007:673). For further discussion of the ethics of profiling, see Box 7.3.

An important part of the controversy over profiling is that it can produce negative consequences. Profiling can reduce deterrence by lowering trust in the police and willingness to report crime.

BOX 7.3 RACIAL PROFILING: DO ONLY OUTCOMES MATTER?

Persico and Todd argue that outcomes are the critical consideration in trying to determine if police are engaging in racial profiling. In an analysis of motorists stopped by the Maryland State Police, 63 percent of those stopped were African Americans, and 29 percent were whites. But the hit rates or outcomes, those found in possession of illegal drugs, were not statistically significantly different: 34 percent for African Americans and 32 percent for whites. Persico and Todd argue that this indicates that the Maryland State Police were not discriminating against blacks (Persico & Todd, 2008).

Engel (2008) notes that legal scholars emphasizing due process argue that procedural equity is an important consideration, as well as outcome equity. This approach

would be concerned that such a disproportionate number of African Americans were stopped even though the outcomes were not significantly different.

What do you think? Are Persico and Todd correct that equal outcomes translate into a conclusion that the police are treating both racial groups fairly? Or are the legal scholars correct that process is a critical consideration? What do you think minority motorists in Maryland would think if they knew about the difference in stop rates versus equality in outcomes?

Sources: Persico and Todd (2008); Engel (2008).

Racial profiling also raises the broader question of the effect of race on police decisions to arrest and juvenile court decisions to detain, petition, and sentence. The outcome of differential decision-making is often called **disproportionate minority contact** (see Chapter 8 for more on disproportionate minority contact in juvenile court decisions). While black youths made up 17 percent of the U.S. population in 2010, they made up 31 percent of arrests, 37 percent of youths petitioned to juvenile court, and 39 percent of those detained (Puzzanchera & Hockenberry, 2013). This disproportionate contact raises the question of possible unfair police action.

A study by Pope and Snyder addressed this question. Using police data from the National Incident-Based Reporting System (NIBRS), they found that in the 17 jurisdictions analyzed there was "no evidence to support the hypothesis that police are more likely to arrest nonwhite juvenile offenders than white juvenile offenders, once other incident attributes are taken into consideration" (Pope & Snyder, 2003:6). Overall, victims identified 69.2 percent of offenders to be white, and 72.7 percent of juvenile offenders arrested were white. The only indication of bias was indirect: "Nonwhite juveniles . . . are more likely to be arrested when the victim is white than when the victim is nonwhite" (Pope & Snyder, 2003:6).

In a report on disproportionate minority contact in Pittsburgh, Rochester, and Seattle, evidence of such contact was found at all three sites. Huizinga, Thornberry, Knight, Lovegrove, Loeber, Hill, & Farrington (2007) did not find evidence that differences in offending behavior explained the disproportionate contact. In other words, it is not the case that minorities clearly commit more delinquency and that this explains why police arrest more minorities. Risk factors such as type of neighborhood, family economic status, and youth education problems did substantially reduce the disproportionate minority contact. These findings do not necessarily prove police bias but are consistent with bias if bias does in fact exist (Huizinga et al., 2007).

In an analysis of disproportionate minority contact in general, Bishop (2005) noted some of the more subtle ways that race can enter into the policing of juveniles. First, police views of neighborhoods as dangerous or having suspicious persons are related to considerations of race and class. Related to this are high crime rates in urban underclass neighborhoods. A result

> ## BOX 7.4 DOES THE OFFICER'S RACE MATTER?
>
> In an observational study of Cincinnati, Ohio police officers, Brown and Frank found that white officers are more likely to arrest suspects in general than black officers. The suspect's race had no effect on white officers' decisions to arrest, but it did have an impact on black officers' decisions. With situational circumstances being equal, the probability that a white officer would arrest a black suspect was 93 percent; the probability that a black officer would arrest a black suspect was 98 percent.
>
> Source: Brown and Frank (2006).

is that police devote more surveillance to such neighborhoods, which leads to more encounters with juveniles and more arrests. Second, race can have an indirect effect via demeanor in police encounters with juveniles. For example, police can interpret a hostile or less cooperative demeanor as a sign of criminal propensity. Complainant preference can also have an effect. Complainants more often press for arrest of African-American suspects. Bishop thus concludes:

> In sum, the literature indicates that, for a number of reasons, minority youths are more likely than whites to be arrested, referred to court, and detained by police [. . .] The overrepresentation of minorities in police arrest data, especially for violent offenses, reinforces racist expectancies (Bishop, 2005:45).

In an attempt to come up with a definitive answer on this question, Kochel, Wilson, and Mastrofski (2011:498) conducted a meta-analysis of 40 research reports and conclude "more definitively than prior nonsystematic reviews that racial minority suspects experience a higher probability of arrest than do Whites." Specifically, a minority suspect's probability of arrest is 30 percent higher than that of a white suspect (Kochel et al., 2011).

The clear lesson is that race is a factor that needs close attention. Police need to be aware of how race can affect decisions to stop and decisions to arrest. They also need to be clear that factors such as a youth's neighborhood and demeanor can bring in race as an indirect influence on those critical decisions. A positive note in this concern about disproportionate minority contact is that a training program in Connecticut did result in significantly more positive police officer attitudes in starting conversations with youths, possessing skills necessary to interact with youths, and the belief that officers could have an impact on youths without neglecting enforcement responsibilities. The study, however, did not measure whether the training actually affected the behaviors of officers after the training was complete (LaMotte, Ouellette, Sanderson, Anderson, Kosutic, Griggs, & Garcia, 2010).

Juvenile Curfew Laws

Juvenile curfew laws have been enacted in numerous cities across the country in an effort to reduce victimization of and by juveniles. The curfew law in Charlotte, North Carolina, included such objectives and also strove to "reinforce and promote the role of parents in raising and guiding children" (City of Charlotte Code, cited in Hirschel, Dean, & Dumond, 2001). To accomplish these goals, children under 16 years of age were prohibited from being on the streets from 11:00 P.M. to 6:00 A.M. during the week and from midnight to 6:00 A.M. on Friday and Saturday nights. Other cities with curfews may have different age or time stipulations. Vernon, Connecticut, for example, enacted a curfew for juveniles under 18 and prohibited them being on the streets from 11:00 P.M. to 6:00 A.M. every night of the week (Males, 2000). In one California city, the curfew applied from 11:00 P.M. to 5:00 A.M. on week nights and from 1:00 A.M. to 5:00 A.M. on weekends. Exceptions involved standing in front of their own homes, returning home within one hour of attending certain activities, working, or being in the company of a parent (Stuphen & Ford, 2001).

Research on the effectiveness of curfews indicates that curfew laws do not reduce crime or victimization. For example, after the implementation of the curfew law in Vernon, Connecticut, Part I crimes did decrease, but the decrease "was similar to or less than the crime declines experienced in similar cities and the state as a whole" (Males, 2000:259). A time-series analysis of victimizations in New Orleans showed that the law was "ineffective for reducing victimizations, victimizations of juveniles, and juvenile arrests" (Reynolds, Seydlitz, & Jenkins, 2000:219). A study of a curfew law in Washington, DC, that included a sophisticated replication design showed that it did not reduce juvenile crime (Cole, 2003). In addition, the laws do not appear to reduce subsequent offending by juveniles who are cited for curfew violations. In Charlotte, for example, 40 percent of the youths cited for curfew violations were arrested for an offense following their first curfew violation (Hirschel et al., 2001). A national evaluation of 52 counties showed that curfew laws only affected significant decreases in 3 of 12 crimes (burglaries, larcenies, and simple assaults). The authors concluded that their research "provides, at best extremely weak support for the hypothesis that curfews reduce juvenile crime rates" and that the "results do not encourage the idea that curfews help prevent juvenile crime" (McDowall, Loftin, & Wiersema, 2000:88).

In a review of studies of teen curfews, Adams (2003) identified 10 empirical studies of juvenile curfews. Adams concluded that the weight of the evidence from these 10 studies overall "fails to support the argument that curfews reduce crime and victimization" (Adams, 2003:155). Adams also questions the fairness of curfew law enforcement, arguing that curfew enforcement relies heavily on officer discretion. Adams worries that curfew enforcement will "fall most heavily on low-income and minority areas" (Adams, 2007:666).

One reason for the ineffectiveness of curfews is that the hours covered by the laws may not be times evidencing high victimization. In Vernon, Connecticut, for example, it was found that juvenile crime was much more likely to occur in the afternoon (Males, 2000). Nationally, it appears that violent offenses and gang crimes peak at approximately 3:00 P.M. (Sickmund, Snyder, & Poe-Yamagata, 1997). One response to this issue is to have daytime curfews for those youths who are not under the jurisdiction of truancy laws. One survey found that 10 percent of the responding jurisdictions had daytime curfews. In fact, some were so restrictive that even a youngster cutting class and not being in the place he was supposed to be in was technically in violation of that city's daytime curfew law (Bannister, Carter, & Schafer, 2001).

Another problem is that juveniles do not necessarily comply with curfew laws. In New Orleans during the first year of the law, more than 3,500 youths were taken into custody just for curfew violations (Reynolds et al., 2000). Most importantly, curfew laws do nothing to improve juveniles' relationships with peers, schools, and family, all of which are important correlates of delinquency. As shown in earlier chapters, parental supervision and attachment to parents are critical factors in preventing delinquency. Curfew laws do nothing to strengthen such supervision or bonding.

It is interesting that police think curfew laws are effective even though they do not have concrete evidence that the curfews are effective in reducing crime (Bannister et al., 2001). Perhaps police enthusiasm for curfews would decrease if they became more familiar with the literature showing that curfews are not effective.

Part of the reality of curfew laws is the panacea phenomenon. As will be noted in Chapter 11 in the discussion of Scared Straight programs, we are often guilty of expecting quick and inexpensive fixes for complicated problems such as delinquency. Unrealistically, we hope that a simple measure such as a curfew law will cure the delinquency problem. We pass curfew laws and expect police enforcement of such laws to magically wipe out juvenile crime. For a note on curfews and high school proms, see Box 7.5.

In England and Wales, curfew orders in community sentences have increased from 1 percent of youth sentences in 2002–2003 to 7.6 percent of youth sentences in 2008–2009. However, two-thirds of youths sentenced to a curfew order in 2009–2010 were reconvicted within a year (Bateman, 2012). A Scottish study found that such curfew orders were not effective unless rehabilitation

BOX 7.5 CURFEWS AND PROMS

In 2001, the Georgia legislature enacted a year-round curfew forbidding anyone under 18 from driving after midnight. So, like Cinderella, prom-goers need to be off the road by the stroke of midnight. Breaking this curfew law can mean a penalty of up to one year in jail or a fine of up to $1,000.

Legislators created this law in response to some highly publicized auto deaths of teenagers in the Atlanta area. Unlike the curfew laws discussed in this chapter, this is a safety curfew more than a crime prevention curfew.

In response, schools are planning to end their proms some time before midnight so that students can get home by 12:00 A.M. One school will end its prom at 11:30 P.M. to allow for plenty of time to beat the curfew. Police say that they are not making any exceptions for prom night.

What do you think? Should there be an exception for prom night?

In Hartford, Connecticut, police decided to step up their enforcement of the city's curfew law after a shooting in which one man died and six young people under 18 were wounded. The curfew prohibited anyone under 18 from being on the streets after 9:00 P.M.

Two points are interesting. First, the police did not have the shooter in custody, and there was no indication of his or her age. Second, this shooting took place after an annual parade and occurred at about 6:30 P.M.

It appears that the Hartford police either are not aware of the research on the ineffectiveness of curfews or they choose to ignore that research. What might influence a police chief to enforce a law that has little empirical support? Might other factors be at work?

Sources: Scott (2002); Associated Press (2008a).

components were also included (Deuchar, 2011). So just as community curfews have not been effective, so also correctional curfews have not worked in the United Kingdom.

Assistance with Intensive Supervision of Probationers

Another way the police have enhanced their activity with juveniles is through their participation in probation. Anchorage, Alaska, has tried using police officers to enhance probation officer supervision of juvenile offenders. Anchorage used police officers to turn regular supervision into intensive supervision. This means that the juvenile probationers received additional contacts, contacts with their probation officers, and contacts with police officers. Like many previous intensive supervision programs, there was no reduction in criminal recidivism; there was no significant difference in the percentage of offenders under intensive supervision who committed any new offense or the percentage of offenders under regular supervision who committed any new offense. However, about 30 percent of the intensive supervision offenders had a probation violation, compared to 17 percent of the regular offenders. Thus, increased supervision translates into increased monitoring and detection of technical violations.

It is interesting that Anchorage tried an intensive supervision effort using police when so much prior research on intensive supervision has not been promising. What is promising is a program such as Operation Eiger in Baton

Rouge, Louisiana. Here police also help probation officers conduct unscheduled evening visits six times per month, but the program involves addressing needs as well as enforcing probation conditions. Services are provided to deal with substance abuse, anger management, academic difficulties, and employment needs (Lizotte & Sheppard, 2001). Hopefully, this combination of intensive supervision and treatment will have greater success than the program in Alaska using intensive supervision alone.

San Bernardino, California, is another example of a police–probation partnership. There a police officer and a probation officer together make a home visit to all new juvenile probationers. They explain the rules of probation and also search the probationer's residence for weapons and drugs. The program has had some effect in reducing serious crimes in the city, but one concern is **mission distortion** for probation. In other words, probation officers may no longer see themselves as service providers or social workers but may instead over-identify with a law enforcement role (Worrall & Gaines, 2006). (See also Chapter 7.)

A survey in Texas showed that most police agencies did not have formal partnerships with juvenile probation agencies. However, 71 percent did report a formal or informal information-sharing partnership with juvenile probation (Kim, Matz, Gerber, Beto, & Lambert, 2013a). This suggests that police–probation partnerships are rather limited at this point in time.

Policing Underage Drinking

The National Minimum Drinking Age Act standardized the legal drinking age at 21 in 1984. Police bear responsibility to enforce this act. Studies show that youths under age 21 are able to purchase alcohol despite the law. Studies in the 1990s using either actual underage buyers or decoy buyers (individuals over 21 who looked younger than 21) showed that purchase rates ranged from 45 percent to 88 percent. A study in a large Midwestern area had an overall sales rate to pseudo-underage buyers of 26 percent (Britt, Toomey, Dunsmuir, & Wagenaar, 2006). The authors concluded that there has been progress in reducing such sales over the last decade, and believed that improved training could result in even lower sales.

Police tend to use compliance checks or "Cops in Shops" programs to combat such underage alcohol purchases. Compliance checks are similar to the research just noted: police use underage decoys to try to purchase liquor. Cops in Shops programs put undercover officers in establishments to detect and cite youths who try to purchase alcohol illegally. Police agencies are twice as likely to use compliance checks as Cops in Shops programs (Montgomery, Foley, & Wolfson, 2006). (For further discussion of the issue of the Legal Drinking Age, see Chapter 9.)

POLICE EFFECTIVENESS WITH JUVENILE CRIME

In examining **police effectiveness**, it is clear that the police are making a variety of efforts to combat juvenile crime. As noted earlier, police are staffing RAPP houses in Cleveland, working in schools in a variety of capacities, facilitating restorative justice conferences in Indianapolis, going to community meetings in Chicago, enforcing curfews all over the country, and participating in demonstration projects such as Operation Ceasefire in Boston.

Overall, how effective are the police in their new efforts against crime and delinquency? For many of these programs, we have already noted specific outcome results. Here a summary is in order.

First, some things simply do not work. Juvenile curfew laws, for example, have been tried in numerous cities. Most evaluations indicate that they are not very effective in the fight against juvenile crime. Related to this, most police encounters with juveniles are for matters such as "hanging out" that are not easily resolved. Even if the police do resolve them, they do not consider that much of an accomplishment. Youths, on the other hand, often see police reprimands as harassment (Watkins & Maume, 2012).

Second, a possible reason that some interventions do not work is that they are simplistic and contrary to what we know. Both the juvenile curfew laws and the Anchorage intensive supervision program, for example, stem from a Scared Straight panacea phenomenon that looks for simple answers: pass a law to keep juveniles off the street or ask a police officer to stop in at a juvenile's house. Human behavior is more complicated than this.

Third, research has indicated what is effective, such as problem-solving approaches, pulling levers strategies, and hot spots policing (Braga et al., 2014). For example, a number of studies have shown that a problem solving/pulling levers strategy reduces youth violence (Corsaro et al., 2009). Concerning hot spots, a Seattle analysis revealed that 50 percent of juvenile arrests took place in less than 1 percent of street segments. In general, much juvenile crime occurs on pathways to school or in areas where kids "hang out," such as playgrounds and malls. Accordingly, one author suggests that school officials be present on walk routes to school, that business owners keep an eye on nearby vacant lots, and that police and communities work to provide safe areas where youths can socialize (Roth, 2013).

Fourth, it is critical to avoid unrealistic expectations. In their study of community policing in Chicago, for example, Skogan and Hartnett (1997) found that some neighborhood conditions improved. Every neighborhood had at least one improvement. Victimization declined in two areas, street crime dropped in two others, drug and gang problems declined in two, and graffiti declined in another. Overall, compared to comparison areas, there were positive changes in 27 of the 51 outcomes that the evaluation measured, an overall success rate of 53 percent (Skogan & Hartnett, 1997:244). Skogan and Hartnett emphasize that communities should have realistic expectations from community policing. A success rate of 50 percent appears to be realistic. Expectations of 95 percent or even 75 percent success rates are fanciful.

Fifth, the police are only part of the picture. Eck and Maguire (2000), for example, contend that the decrease in crime in the last 10 years is the result of communities and the nation mobilizing to fight crime. Such mobilization involves police initiatives such as community policing, increased use of prison, demographic trends (the aging of the population and the decrease in the proportion of young males), and the decline of retail drug markets. A realistic perspective on the police impact on crime can be summarized as follows:

> There is one thing that is a myth: The police have a substantial, broad, and independent impact on the nation's crime rate. Rather than think of the police as an isolated institution that has a distinctive impact on crime, perhaps we should think of the police as part of a network of institutions, some of them formal (e.g., courts and schools) and some of them informal (e.g., families and churches), that respond to crime . . . When considered in isolation, the effectiveness of any one element of this diverse array of people and organizations may be slight. But collectively, the response might be more dramatic (Eck & Maguire, 2000:247–248).

SUMMARY

It is an intriguing time for policing. Both police themselves and outsiders are debating the meaning of policing. Some, like former New York City police commissioner William Bratton, argue that police should take a tough approach (zero tolerance) and arrest even "squeegee men" who harass motorists by foisting unwanted window washing on them. In Boston, this tough approach, called "pulling levers," takes the form of arresting suspected violent gang members for disorder offenses, criminal acts, and outstanding warrants. It appears that SROs are becoming a fixture of the contemporary school. Some critics see SROs and school policies as detracting from traditional approaches to student problems, and some research indicates that arrest can increase high school dropout rates and decrease a student's chances of going to college. The introduction of School Resource Officers and zero tolerance policies are also seen as contributing to the school-to-prison pipeline.

Other developments in policing, however, take a completely different approach. In Indianapolis, for example, police are coordinating restorative justice conferences in which youths, victims, and supporters on both sides sit down and try to repair the harm done by victimizations. Here offenders learn how they harmed their victims and what they can do to repair that harm.

In other places, such as Chicago, police are attending neighborhood meetings and trying to learn what the community considers to be problems and how those problems should be solved. Problems vary from crack houses operating in residential neighborhoods to gangs harassing youths at bus stops after school.

Whatever specific approaches police are taking, many are also following the lead of CompStat (a strategy developed in New York City that directed police resources based on statistical analysis of criminal activity) in attempting to specify their mission and objectives more explicitly and trying to measure how closely they are actually achieving their goals. Accountability is a current emphasis in both business and government.

Many cities continue to use juvenile curfew laws in an attempt to reduce juvenile crime. The goal is to reduce both offending and victimization. Apparently these curfew laws and their enforcement continue despite a lack of supporting research evidence.

Perhaps the answer is to combine both approaches. Perhaps violent gang members need the tough (pulling levers) approach while first offenders charged with certain offenses can benefit from a restorative justice conferencing approach. What is clear, however, is that policing is changing and will continue to change. Many police officers undoubtedly continue to drive patrol cars and respond to 911 calls. In many communities, however, more innovative efforts are underway. Hopefully, such innovation will continue to change our ideas and expectations of what the police can and should do to prevent and control delinquency, disorder, and crime.

An important point to remember in any consideration of the police is that policing is only part of the effort to prevent, reduce, or control crime. When crime increases, much of society reacts, and many institutions and actors try to mobilize against crime. It is erroneous to think that the police alone can reduce crime. It is erroneous to think that SROs and zero-tolerance policies will be a magical solution to problems in schools. So instead of focusing only on the police, we should think of them as part of an interrelated network of responders.

> When violent crime grows into a serious social concern, it is not just the police that focus more attention on the problem. Schools, community groups, businesses, health officials, and many other organizations and individuals also respond to crime [. . .] In summary, as the police mobilize to address crime more effectively, so do many other institutions (Eck & Maguire, 2000:249–250).

So we will repeat our citation of Eck and Maguire at the end of the section on police effectiveness: it is a myth that the "police have a substantial, broad, and independent impact on the nation's crime rate" (Eck & Maguire, 2000:247), but a realistic review of the research shows evidence "for focused policing strategies contributing to the drop in violent crime" (Eck & Maguire, 2000:245). It is also important to note that "[s]ome of the policing strategies that have received the most attention (for example, CompStat and zero-tolerance policing in New York City) are the least plausible candidates for contributing to the reduction in violent crime" (Eck & Maguire, 2000:245).

We need to be realistic in our expectations of the police. Surely the police play a role in combating delinquency, but to expect the police to be the only factor—or even the most important factor—is unrealistic. Many factors contribute to delinquency and crime. All the institutions of society must play a part in addressing the problem.

DISCUSSION QUESTIONS

1. Community policing is based on the assumption that the job of the police is to solve the problems that lead to crime. Do you agree or disagree with this assumption? To what extent can society hold the police responsible for the problems that cause crime?

2. Police are trying new types of policing such as community or problem-solving policing, "broken windows" policing, and CompStat. Which approach do you favor? Discuss. Note any possible problems with the various approaches.

3. What do we know about police attitudes toward citizens? About citizen attitudes toward the police? What can be done to improve attitudes on both sides?

4. What do curfew laws seek to accomplish? Are they effective?

5. What do we know about police use of force with juveniles? What can be done to minimize any improper use of force by police?

6. Schools are adopting School Resource Officers and zero tolerance policies. Some argue that schools should devote more attention to improving classroom teaching and management. The most drastic issue in this area is the so-called school-to-prison pipeline. What can be done to minimize the criminalization of school misbehavior and avoid referring troublesome youths to court?

7. Policing is changing. Would you want to be a police officer in light of all the change that is taking place in policing?

CHAPTER 8

The Juvenile Court Process

WHAT YOU NEED TO KNOW

- In 2010, juvenile courts processed more than 1.3 million delinquency cases and about 137,000 petitioned status offense cases. In addition, approximately 6,000 cases were transferred (waived) to adult court.

- The detention decision concerns whether to keep a juvenile in custody or to allow the youth to go home with his or her parents while awaiting further court action. Two options are secure detention and nonsecure detention.

- When an intake officer does not file a petition against a youth but tries to resolve the matter, that is called informal adjustment.

- Two avenues for youths not petitioned to court are teen court and drug court.

- The prosecutor's role in juvenile court may include approving petitions, deciding to prosecute some juveniles in adult courts, and prosecuting juveniles in juvenile court.

- There are several means for youths to be sent to adult court. The most traditional is transfer or waiver, in which the juvenile court judge makes the decision after a hearing.

- Statutory exclusion means that the state legislature rules that certain offenses automatically go to adult court.

- Prosecutorial waiver gives juvenile and adult court concurrent jurisdiction over certain cases. The prosecutor decides which court to use.

- Research on transfer indicates higher recidivism for youths who were transferred to adult criminal court.

KEY TERMS

adjudication

blended sentencing

concerned adult role

day–evening centers

detention decision

disposition

drug courts

home detention

informal adjustment

intake decision

justice by geography

legislative waiver

nonsecure detention

"once an adult, always an adult" provisions

petition

plea bargaining

prosecutorial waiver

reverse waiver

secure detention

statutory exclusion

teen courts

token economy
programs

training schools

transfer (waiver)

zealous advocate
role

- Adjudication and disposition in juvenile courts are the equivalent of conviction and sentencing in adult courts.

- There are several problems concerning attorney representation of juveniles: many youths waive their right to counsel, many attorneys have high caseloads and are poorly paid, and many defense attorneys are unsure whether they should follow the zealous advocate model of defense with juveniles.

- The trend in juvenile court has been one of increasing punitiveness, but there have now been developments in line with traditional *parens patriae* philosophy, such as recent legislation returning to age 18 as the initial age for criminal court jurisdiction and legislation reducing the possibility of transfer to adult criminal court. A major concern in juvenile court, especially the disposition stage, is the extent of the impact of race on decisions.

INTRODUCTION

Once a police officer takes a youth into custody, it is likely that the police will refer that youth to juvenile court. In 2012, approximately two-thirds of youths (68.1%) taken into custody were referred to juvenile court, and approximately 8 percent of juveniles taken into custody were sent directly to adult criminal court. The other arrests were either handled within the police department and released (approximately 22%) or referred to a social welfare agency or another police agency (about 2%) (Federal Bureau of Investigation, 2013:Table 68).

When police refer a youth to juvenile court, the court personnel must then make one or more critical decisions: whether to detain (jail) the youth, whether to actually file a **petition** (charges) against the youth, whether to find (adjudicate) the youth a delinquent, and how to dispose of the petition. These decisions correspond to the adult court decisions of bail versus jail, formal charge versus dismissal, determination of guilt by plea or by trial, and sentencing. An additional decision is the decision to prosecute the youth as an adult in criminal court or retain jurisdiction in juvenile court. Several juvenile court actors—probation officers, defense attorneys, prosecutors, and judges—are involved in these important decisions. While the judge is often the primary decision-maker, other court personnel play important roles in deciding the fate of juvenile suspects.

This chapter will examine the critical decision points in the juvenile court process: detention, intake, file, transfer (waiver), adjudication, and disposition.

We will look at the roles the various court personnel play and should play in the court process. We will describe what happens when a juvenile suspect goes through the juvenile court process and will compare the ideal with the reality. Finally, we will examine some of the controversial issues facing juvenile court today, such as the question of the impact of race on decision-making and whether juveniles should have the right to a jury trial.

In 2010 (the latest year for which complete figures were available), juvenile courts processed more than 1.3 million delinquency cases (see Figure 8.1). More than half (54%) of the delinquency cases were petitioned, and approximately 6,000 cases were transferred to adult court via judicial waiver (1% of all delinquency cases). More than 425,000 youths were adjudicated delinquent in juvenile court. Juvenile courts also processed an estimated 137,000 petitioned status offense cases. Over half (56%) of these were adjudicated a status offender (see Figure 8.2) (Puzzanchera & Hockenberry, 2013). Finally, several thousand youths were processed in adult court as a result of direct file by

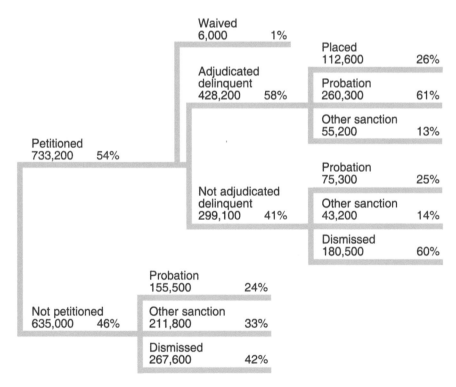

FIGURE 8.1
Juvenile Court Processing of Delinquency Cases, 2010

Source: Puzzanchera and Hockenberry (2013). Reprinted with permission.

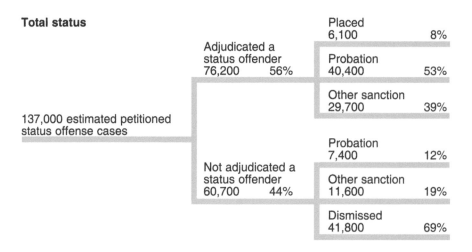

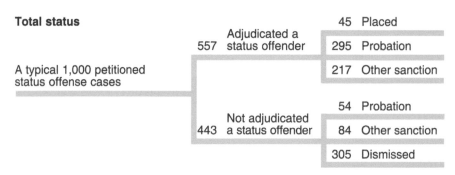

FIGURE 8.2
Juvenile Court Processing of Petitioned Status Offense Cases, 2010

Source: Puzzanchera and Hockenberry (2013). Reprinted with permission.

prosecutors or by statutory exclusion (see below for additional details). (For the latest statistics, go to "Easy Access to Juvenile Court Statistics" online. Available at http://www.ojjdp.gov/ojstatbb/ezajcs/.)

As the figures show, about 61 percent of the adjudicated delinquency cases and 53 percent of the adjudicated status offense cases were placed on probation. Some nonadjudicated cases also were placed on probation. Significant proportions of adjudicated delinquency and status offense cases (26 percent and 8 percent, respectively) were ordered into residential placement (Puzzanchera & Hockenberry, 2013).

DETENTION

The first decision that juvenile court personnel must make is the **detention decision**. It must be decided whether to keep a juvenile in custody or to allow the youth to go home with his or her parents while awaiting further court action. The detention decision is the juvenile court counterpart of the bail decision in adult court. It is very important because it concerns the freedom of the child and, therefore, resembles the disposition decision. In fact, children sent to detention may stay there for an extensive period of time—perhaps even for a longer time than children sent to state **training schools** (i.e., youth prisons for juveniles determined to be delinquent). In 2010, approximately 286,900 delinquency cases involved detention. This number represents approximately 21 percent of delinquency cases, about the same percent as detained in 1985. The offense profile of detained delinquency offense cases was 32 percent person offense cases, 30 percent property cases, 9 percent drug cases, and 29 percent public order cases (Puzzanchera & Hockenberry, 2013). It should be noted that detention can also be used in some states as a disposition for a brief period of incarceration and as a sanction for violations of probation conditions (Griffin & King, 2005).

For status offense cases, in 2010, detention was used in 8 percent of cases, 1 percent higher than 1995. This percentage was similar for whites and blacks. The offense profile of detained status offense cases was 16 percent runaway, 23 percent truancy, 10 percent curfew, 16 percent ungovernability, 24 percent liquor law, and 11 percent miscellaneous. It should be noted that the number of status offense cases involving detention increased 20 percent from 1995 to about 10,400 in 2010 (Puzzanchera & Hockenberry, 2013).

Delinquency cases involving black juveniles were more likely to use detention than cases involving white juveniles. Approximately 19 percent of white delinquency cases and 25 percent of black delinquency cases used detention in 2010 (Puzzanchera & Hockenberry, 2013). In one study, the average IQ score of detainees was 82.5, well below average (Viljoen, Klaver, & Roesch, 2005).

Several years ago it was estimated that it cost about $116 to keep one child in detention for one day in 2005 and just over $200 a day in 2006 (Cohen & Pfeifer, 2011). Crowding is often a problem; 20 percent of public detention facilities were over capacity in 2002 (Snyder and Sickmund, 2006).

Detention workers or probation officers usually make the initial detention decision. State law may stipulate that a detention hearing be held within a specified period of time so that a judge can rule on the continued need for detention. The Model Juvenile Delinquency Act, a guideline for state codes, stipulates that the detention hearing be held within 36 hours and that certain criteria be used to decide whether to detain a particular youngster (Rossum,

BOX 8.1 MODEL JUVENILE DELINQUENCY ACT

Section 26. [Grounds for Pre-Hearing Detention] A youth taken into custody may be detained if there is probable cause to believe that:

- The juvenile is a fugitive from justice;
- The juvenile has committed a felony while another case was pending;
- The juvenile has committed a delinquent act and
- The juvenile will likely fail to appear for further proceedings;
- Detention is required to protect the juvenile from himself or herself;

- The juvenile is a threat to the person or property of others;
- The juvenile will intimidate witnesses or otherwise unlawfully interfere with the administration of justice; or
- There is no person available or capable of caring for the juvenile.

Source: Rossum et al. (1987:33).

Koller, & Manfredi, 1987; see Box 8.1 for the relevant section of the Model Juvenile Delinquency Act).

A troubling feature of detention hearings is that often they are the first opportunity for the juvenile to meet with an attorney. In one study, more than half of the public defenders did not meet their clients prior to the detention hearing. In one site, an unsupervised law student with no background investigations on the youths represented youths at detention hearings (Puritz, Burrell, Schwartz, Soler, & Warboys, 1995). In Pennsylvania, a study found that at detention hearings attorneys did not have much opportunity to confer with their juvenile clients and were not familiar with alternatives to detention (Miller-Wilson & Puritz, 2003).

As noted in Chapter 10, many youths in the juvenile justice system have a mental health disorder (see Skowyra & Cocozza, 2006). A study of almost 2,000 juvenile detainees in Chicago found approximately 10 percent had thought about committing suicide in the six months prior to being interviewed, and 10 percent had attempted suicide in the past. Cutting and drug overdose were the most common methods used in recent suicide attempts (Abram, Paskar, Washburn, & Teplin, 2008). For youths with mental health problems, barriers to receiving mental health services can exist. More than half of such detainees believed that their problem would go away or they could solve it on their own, and about one-third were not sure where to get help (Abram et al., 2008). In addition, more than 90 percent of the detainees had experienced trauma and 11 percent had experienced posttraumatic stress disorder (PTSD) in the previous year (Abram, Teplin, King, Longworth, Emanuel, Romero, McClelland, Dulcan, Washburn, Welty, & Olson, 2013).

Substance use and abuse are also problems. More than three-quarters of detained male juveniles in Cook County (Chicago, Illinois) reported marijuana use in the previous six months, and 4 percent reported cocaine use. Three-quarters of female detainees reported marijuana use, and 10 percent reported cocaine use (McClelland, Teplin, & Abram, 2004). These findings indicate some of the treatment needs in detention facilities. Fortunately, most detention centers do screen for substance abuse, mental health needs, and suicide risk (Snyder & Sickmund, 2006; for details on California, see Cohen & Pfeifer, 2011).

Physical health concerns also need attention. For example, testing at the Harris County (Houston, Texas) juvenile detention center in 2006 and 2007 showed that about 10 percent of the boys and about 25 percent of the girls tested positive for a sexually transmitted disease. More positively, only two boys and no girls tested positive for HIV (Schneider, 2008).

Detention Options

Court personnel have several options at the detention decision point. Releasing a child to his or her parents is the most frequently used option; this is the preferred decision in most states (e.g., Alabama Code 12-15-59). **Secure detention**—placing a child in the juvenile equivalent of a local jail—is another alternative. It involves placement in a locked facility of 10, 20, or more youths who are awaiting further court action or are awaiting transfer to a state correctional facility. In some places, **nonsecure detention** is another option for youths involved in less serious crimes and for those who do not pose much threat to the community or themselves. Such youth may be placed in small group homes that are not locked or not locked as comprehensively as a secure detention facility—hence the term "nonsecure." Youth housed in nonsecure detention centers might even go to regular public school classes during the day. Alternatives to detention, such as home detention, will be discussed later in this chapter.

Detention Decision-making

As noted above, in 2010, delinquency cases involving black youths were placed in detention more frequently than cases involving white youths. This was true for every year from 1985 to 2010 (Puzzanchera & Hockenberry, 2013). Research confirms that minority youths are more likely to be detained than white youths (Bishop, 2005; Piquero, 2008). One reason for this is structural disadvantage, that is, living in disadvantaged areas (Rodriguez, 2010). Many courts are now using risk assessment instruments to base the detention decision on proven risk factors and reduce possible bias. For an example of a risk assessment instrument, see Box 8.2.

BOX 8.2 EXAMPLE OF A RISK ASSESSMENT INSTRUMENT

New York State calculates a Risk Score for a youth's Detention Recommendation based on four factors (one point for each positive answer):

1. A prior delinquency petition;

2. A prior status offense petition;

3. An outstanding delinquency or status offense warrant;

4. The current arrest charges include burglary, grand larceny, autostripping, or motor vehicle theft.

A score of two to four calls for detention. A score of zero calls for release without restrictions and a score of one call for release with restrictions. There is also a list of reasons for not following the risk score recommendation.

Source: Website of the New York State Office of Children and Family Services. Available at http://www.ocfs.state.ny.us/main/rehab/drai/

Amendments in 1992 to the Juvenile Justice and Delinquency Prevention Act were intended to reduce disproportionate minority contact (DMC) in general. The Juvenile Detention Alternatives Initiative (JDAI) was funded by a private foundation in the early 1990s to reduce secure detention and increase the use of community alternatives to detention. It has both reduced the use of detention by as much as 50 percent and also helped to reduce racial disparities in detention in several jurisdictions (Barton, 2012). For example, a study of decision-making in a Virginia court that has been implementing the JDAI found that race was not a significant predictor of detention decisions, apparently due to the use of a risk assessment instrument to help caseworkers make decisions based on relevant criteria. Girls, however, continued to benefit from a degree of leniency as they were less likely to receive secure detention than boys (Maggard, Higgins, & Chappell, 2013). Race, however, did affect override decisions, that is, decisions to go against the outcome determined by one's score on a risk assessment instrument. Thus, policymakers need to review and possibly change instruments if workers believe that numerous override decisions are appropriate (Chappell, Maggard, & Higgins, 2012).

Detention Programming

The psychological technique of behavior modification has inspired many detention centers to use **token economy programs**. With this approach, staff members use points or dollar values to reward detained youths for appropriate behavior and withhold or subtract points for inappropriate behavior. Youths earn credits when they follow the rules and they lose credits when they disobey the rules. If they have more credits than losses, they can "purchase" rewards such as snacks, table games,

WEB ACTIVITY

If you Google "detention risk assessment instrument," you will be able to see a number of instruments in use in various states. Or go to the website of the Annie E. Casey Foundation (http://www.aecf.org/) and search for the report "Juvenile Detention Risk Assessment: A Practice Guide to Juvenile Detention Reform"; the Appendix has risk assessment instruments for Cook County, Illinois; Multnomah County, Arizona; and the Commonwealth of Virginia.

BOX 8.3 DETENTION REWARDS AND FINES

How Dollars May Be Earned

1. School attendance	$10
2. YMCA activities	$10
3. Cleaning room (make beds, sweep, mop, etc.)	$5
4. Extra work (per hour)	$5
5. Good hygiene	$5
6. Attending church, etc.	$5
7. Cleaning unit	$10
8. Good behavior	$5

Fines for Inappropriate Behaviors

1. Body contact (slapping, etc.)	$20
2. Disrespect (sarcastic or abusive speech, not following rules)	$30
3. Profanity	$10
4. Instigating (influencing others to break rules)	$30
5. Arguing (other youth or staff)	$30
6. Lying	$40
7. Complaining (irritating staff with complaints about program, food, other staff, dollars, etc.)	$25
8. Contraband	$50
9. Fighting (another resident)	$100
10. Attempted escape	$150

Source: *Handbook of Procedures, Rules, and Regulations* (Jefferson County Detention Center, Birmingham, Alabama). Items have been renumbered by authors.

and room privacy at the end of the day and/or on the weekend. (See Box 8.3 for examples of rewards, punishments, and costs.) This type of program is based on psychological principles of conditioning that contend that human behavior is learned through reinforcements.

Given the unique needs of girls in detention, it is critical that detention centers develop gender-specific programs for girls. One issue is that about 70 percent of girls in the juvenile justice system have histories of physical abuse compared to only about 20 percent of the boys (Lederman & Brown, 2000). Programming should also include attention to alcohol, drug, and mental disorders. As noted above, significant proportions of detained juveniles have one or more of these problems.

Positive Programs

Research has found that education should be the cornerstone of detention programming. It is important for detention centers to teach basic academic skills, general education development (GED) test preparation, and also special education, employment readiness training, and programs about social, cognitive, and life skills such as problem solving and moral reasoning (Stephens & Arnette, 2000). For example, in Jackson, Mississippi, the detention center is actually an extension of the district public school alternative school. In addition to academic programming, the school also offers vocational training and parent training (an "effective parenting" course) (Stephens & Arnette, 2000).

Arizona has been using character education in its detention and correctional facilities since 2001. Based on programs in regular schools, the "Character Counts!" program teaches character traits that philosophers and religious leaders of all denominations can agree on: trustworthiness, respect, responsibility, fairness, caring, and citizenship. An independent evaluation found an increase in positive behaviors such as taking responsibility and not making excuses (Martinez, 2008).

Often the best programming is to find an alternative to detention. The Maryland Detention Response Unit uses social workers to try to find appropriate community and residential alternatives to detention and to determine the need for mental or educational evaluations. Attorneys also investigate how court-ordered detention can be modified or amended to permit community-based alternatives (National Juvenile Defender Center, 2004).

The survey of youth in residential placement (a survey of youths in various types of placement) gives some indication of what juveniles think about their experiences. The survey showed some problem areas. One-quarter (25%) of the detained youths reported being afraid of being attacked by another resident, and more than 20 percent (22%) reported being afraid of being attacked by a staff member. About one-quarter reported problems with dirty sheets, towels, or clothes, and one-third reported dirty bathrooms. On the positive side, however, one-third of the youths in detention surveyed reported a good recreational program, and 42 percent reported a good school (Sedlak & McPherson, 2010a).

A disturbing issue is that about 33 percent of detained youths have experienced solitary confinement (Rubin, 2013). In addition, a recent investigation found that few detention centers met minimal standards of health care, with wide variability according to race and geography (Barton, 2012).

DETENTION ALTERNATIVES

Because of criticisms of detention programming and because of the high costs of detaining youngsters in secure detention facilities, many jurisdictions have sought alternatives to traditional detention facilities. For example, a few years ago, New York City found that at the time secure detention cost about $58,000 per year per child and that nonsecure detention (foster care and boarding homes) cost about $20,000 per year. Hence, they began using converted stores or lofts as **day–evening centers**. In such centers, mornings involved formal educational programs, early afternoons were devoted to remedial and tutorial work, and late afternoons were reserved for recreational programs (e.g., weekly swimming at YMCA facilities). Two of the four New York City centers also offered evening hours twice a week for children considered to need extra supervision and for those on a waiting list for admission into the day program (Lindner, 1981).

Home Detention

Another popular alternative to traditional detention is **home detention**. This is the juvenile court counterpart of supervised pretrial release for adult criminal defendants. In home detention, the youth awaiting further juvenile court action is allowed to live at home but is also under the supervision of a detention worker who ensures that the youth is attending school (or working on a job) and maintaining a curfew. The detention worker, often a paraprofessional, may check on the home detention youngster up to four times a day if the worker suspects

that the child is getting into new trouble (delinquency). Studies show that 70 to 90 percent of home detention youths do not reoffend and appear in court (Austin, Johnson, & Weitzer, 2005). Similarly, Dallas is now using electronic monitoring for truants instead of detention (Kovach, 2008).

Bail

Bail is not universally available in juvenile court (Rossum et al., 1987:109), but bail for juveniles appears to be an option that is receiving greater attention. New Mexico, for example, authorized bail for serious youthful offenders detained before trial in an adult facility (National Conference of State Legislatures, 1993). This is a reflection of the changing philosophy of juvenile court, from *parens patriae* to punishment. Bail is considered inappropriate in the traditional juvenile court, in which the judge acts like a concerned parent in deciding to detain or release juveniles awaiting further court action. With the changing views of juvenile crime and juvenile court, however, states are beginning to see bail as a reasonable option. The current view that the juvenile is a responsible criminal rather than an immature youth in need of help is consistent with the use of bail as a means to guarantee continued appearance for court hearings.

THE INTAKE DECISION

The second major decision point in juvenile court is the **intake decision**, analogous to the filing decision in adult court. At intake, a court official—either a probation officer or a prosecutor (or both)—decides whether to file a court **petition** of delinquency, status offense, neglect, abuse, or dependency in a particular case. Traditionally, a probation officer has made the intake decision. The *parens patriae* philosophy of the court dictated this approach because its treatment orientation indicated that the probation officer (ideally a trained social worker) should consider the best interests of the child as well as the legal aspects of the case (as an adult court prosecutor might). That is, an intake probation officer is supposed to resolve every case in light of the considerations of the welfare of the child and the legal demands of the police and victim. This tradition is changing; a number of states even allow prosecutors to make the decision to file certain cases directly in adult criminal court and thereby completely bypass the juvenile court.

Informal Adjustment

One frequent decision of the intake officer is not to file a petition alleging delinquency or a status offense, but instead to try to resolve the matter without resorting to a formal petition against the child. As noted above, almost half (46%) of the 1.3 million delinquency cases coming to juvenile court in 2010 were not petitioned (Puzzanchera & Hockenberry, 2013). (Statistics on the number of status offense cases not petitioned are not available.) Many (4 out of 10) of the nonpetitioned cases were dismissed; others were handled informally. Informal handling is usually called adjustment at intake or **informal adjustment**. Examples would include requiring a first-time shoplifter to pay restitution to the store or ordering a vandal to paint the public building he or she has defaced. Similarly, intake probation officers often try to counsel troubled family members on a short-term basis or to refer them to counseling services in the community. As a result, a youth involved in runaway behavior, chronic disobedience ("incorrigibility"), or repeated truancy will not be immediately petitioned to court as a status offender. Instead, the youth receives help in dealing with the problem that brought him or her to the attention of court officials.

It is important to note that such informal adjustment practices occur as frequently as 25 percent of the time (Butts, 1994; McCarthy, 1987) and have been part of juvenile court since its inception. With the emphasis on diversion in the 1970s, informal adjustment practices by intake officers took on added dimensions.

Teen Courts

One diversion option to the traditional juvenile court is the use of **teen courts** (sometimes called youth courts). Here the philosophy is based on restorative justice, and youths act as judge, attorney (prosecutor and defense attorney), and jury in cases involving status offenses, misdemeanors, and occasionally a low-level felony. (About one-half of teen courts use adult judges.) The most common penalty is community service. Other sentences include teen court jury duty, writing essays about offending, writing apologies to victims, community service, and monetary restitution. As of 2010, it was estimated that there were more than 1,050 teen court programs in operation handling more than 100,000 cases per year, making them a primary diversion option (Butts, Buck, & Coggeshall, 2002; National Association of Youth Courts, 2011).

Two studies of the effectiveness of teen courts found no difference between teen courts and comparisons, but three studies found lower recidivism rates in teen court cases than for comparison youths. A study of an Illinois teen court found that most of the offenses handled were low-level infractions such as shoplifting (43% of the cases processed), curfew violation, possession of marijuana, disorderly conduct, and so on. Recidivism was only 12 percent after one year and 19 percent after two years (Rasmussen, 2004).

A multi-site study of teen courts in Alaska, Arizona, Maryland, and Missouri found statistically less recidivism for teen court youths in two of the four sites. In Alaska, 6 percent of teen court youths recidivated, compared to 23 percent of non-teen court youths; in Missouri, 9 percent of teen court youths recidivated, compared to 28 percent of non-teen court youths. The authors of the study concluded that "teen courts represent a promising alternative for the juvenile justice system" (Butts et al., 2002:34). It is also noteworthy that volunteer staff and low budgets mean that teen courts are inexpensive. Two studies using random assignment found no significant effect (Patrick & Marsh, 2005; Stickle, Connell, Wilson, & Gottfredson, 2008). Finally, a study of the Xenia, Ohio, teen court program found no impact on recidivism, and the authors concluded that their finding of no impact and previous systematic research suggests that teen courts are "equivalent to or only slightly better than traditional diversion" (Norris, Twill, & Kim, 2011:215). Butts and his colleagues conclude that "there are still no definitive studies about teen court outcomes" (Butts et al., 2012:613).

Teen court is not intended to deal with serious delinquency, but it appears to be an alternative method for dealing with status offenses, minor delinquent acts such as shoplifting, or problems with alcohol or marijuana. As one author

The oath of office is given to 10 new members of the Kodiak Teen Court in Kodiak, Alaska. Teen courts in cities across Alaska allow juveniles accused of crimes to be judged by their peers while being defended and prosecuted by fellow teens.

CREDIT: AP Photo/ Kodiak *Daily Mirror*, James Brooks

put it, teen court may be a "partial solution to the juvenile justice system's failure to give anything more than a 'slap on the wrist' to first-time offenders" (Rasmussen, 2004:615).

Drug Courts

Another diversion option is juvenile **drug courts** in which the judge, prosecutor, and defense attorney collaborate as a team with drug treatment specialists. Like adult drug courts, juvenile drug courts attempt to intervene in both the criminal activity and the drug usage of clients. The courts use treatment, coordination, and extensive monitoring. The youths must appear in court frequently so that judges can monitor progress and offer encouragement and admonishment to the juveniles. There is frequent drug testing, and there are penalties for failing to test negative. Sanctions for youths that are not following the rules can range from a warning, an order to write a book report or paper or to do household chores, to fines, community service hours, or even detention. There also are incentives such as the dismissal of charges and termination of probation requirements upon graduation. Other rewards include verbal praise and such incentives as gift certificates and tickets to local events. Drug courts usually celebrate completion with a graduation ceremony in court that may include additional features, such as a gift of athletic shoes (Rossman, Butts, Roman, DeStefano, & White, 2004).

As noted in Chapter 6, there is mixed evidence on the effectiveness of juvenile drug courts, but the encouraging news is that recent studies appear to be finding greater effectiveness and that researchers are identifying critical factors such as the use of evidence-based practices, holding status hearings before a judge, and improving parental supervision efforts (Henggeler et al., 2006; Marlowe, 2010; and see Chapter 6). Another reviewer, MacKenzie, concluded that "there is very strong evidence that drug courts reduce the future criminal activities of offenders" (MacKenzie, 2006:234). However, MacKenzie noted that drug courts include both deterrent and rehabilitative strategies, so it is not clear precisely how drug courts achieve their positive results (MacKenzie, 2006). Finally, success is higher for graduates but termination prior to graduation is an alarming 46 percent (Stein et al., 2013).

One problem with drug courts is that they may be reaching the wrong population. If drug courts are actually intended for drug-dependent or addicted youths, they are not capturing many such youths with severe drug problems. "If, on the other hand, juvenile drug courts are designed to deliver prevention services for a broad cross-section of youth involved with alcohol and other drugs, then their current mode of operating may be appropriate, but such a broad mission would raise other questions about the risks of labeling, net-widening, and iatrogenic effects (i.e., the cure may be worse than the disease)" (Butts, Zweig, & Mamalian, 2004:142). Much like the "war" on drugs in general, drug courts often paint a wide stroke that takes in more than is necessary. We worry so much about adolescent drug use that we overreact and do too much.

A related reform is juvenile mental health courts. As of early 2012, there were about 50 such courts in 15 states either in operation or in the plan-ning stages (Heretick & Russell, 2013). As with drug courts, court personnel cooperate with mental health personnel, who are often existing service providers in the community. Some juvenile mental health courts are using evidence-based approaches such as Multi-systemic Therapy (Cocozza & Shufelt, 2006). Given the newness of this approach, it is too early to assess effectiveness. A preliminary study found a reduction in average number of offenses committed prior to admission to the mental health court compared to after admission (Behnken, Arredondo, & Packman, 2009). Preliminary results from Colorado also suggest lower recidivism rates for youths who received mental health court intervention compared to other youths with mental disorders in the juvenile justice system (Heretick & Russell, 2013).

A victim–offender mediation program in Texas emphasizing the offender's accountability is still another type of diversion that has been successful. The mediator is often a trained volunteer. An early evaluation found that 29 percent of referrals ended in successful mediation. A few years later the successful mediation rate was 77 percent (Kurlychek, Torbet, & Bozynski, 1999).

Still another new diversion program is the ACT Now truancy reduction program in Pima County, Arizona. This program combines services to get at the root causes of truancy and even misdemeanor prosecution with criminal fines and penalties for parents who do not do enough to get their children to attend school. In those cases where parents were prosecuted, the usual sanction was community service or a $200 fine (Baker et al., 2001).

These newer programs share several features. Contrasted with diversion programs of 25 years ago, these programs place more emphasis on the account-ability of the offender and concern for the victim. Older diversion programs focused on treating the offender without parallel concern for victims. There is also a tendency to involve community members, either teen or adult or both, in the process whereas older diversion programs relied more on expert staff.

In general, these programs emphasize both accountability and concern for victims whereas older programs emphasized treatment for the offender.

The Prosecutor's Role

If an intake probation officer decides to file a petition against a child, often that decision requires the approval of an attorney, normally the prosecutor. The prosecutor's approval of the probation officer's decision to file a petition ensures that a legally trained official has reviewed the legal criteria for a properly authorized petition. The prosecutor checks the legal wording of the petition, determines that enough evidence is available for establishing the petition (finding the delinquent or status offender "guilty"), and makes sure that the offense occurred in the court's jurisdiction and that the child was of proper age at the time of the offense.

Because of the importance of such legal criteria, and because of the growing emphasis on more punitive juvenile models, some jurisdictions have turned away from the traditional probation-officer model of intake toward models in which the prosecutor is either the first or the sole intake decision-maker. Such models are more consistent with more legalistic views of juvenile court in which the state has abandoned the traditional *parens patriae* philosophy. For example, the state of Washington has switched responsibility for the intake decision to the prosecutor for all felony charges and most misdemeanors. There prosecutors make such decisions on the basis of explicit criteria: offense seriousness, prior record, and the age of the youth. Furthermore, informal adjustments are no longer permitted at intake, although police agencies can still "exercise their traditional discretion regarding whether to refer or adjust incidents involving juveniles" (Schneider & Schram, 1986:214). In place of informal adjustments at intake, minor offenses are supposed to be diverted to restitution programs. This action by Washington represents a radical break with traditional juvenile court thinking and practice and is a close approximation of adult processing with its retributive emphasis. (For a diagrammatic comparison of traditional intake and the Washington State practice, see Box 8.4.) Like the legislation in the state of Washington, the Model Juvenile Delinquency Act also stipulates that the prosecutor shall "[d]irectly supervise all matters relating to intake," although the probation officer may continue to make the file-divert decision in misdemeanor cases if the prosecutor so delegates (Rossum et al., 1987:40). Similarly, the National District Attorneys' Association stipulates a very active role for the prosecutor (Shine & Price, 1992), and Louisiana has given the prosecutor greater authority over the intake process (National Conference of State Legislatures, 1993).

A further development is that the prosecutor is now taking on increased responsibility in juvenile cases as increasingly more states are allowing prosecutors to file cases directly in adult criminal court. In addition to

BOX 8.4 THE INTAKE PROCESS

Traditional Intake

- Police, parents, school officials, or victims bring youths to attention of Intake

- Intake officer files petition *OR* makes an informal adjustment *OR* diverts to a treatment program

- Juvenile Court Hearing

Prosecutorial Model (e.g., Washington State)

- Police, parents, school officials, or victims bring youths to attention of Intake

- Prosecutor files a petition *OR* declines to file a petition *OR* diverts to a restitution program

- Juvenile Court Hearing

traditional waiver (transfer), several mechanisms allow prosecutors to proceed against juveniles in criminal court: concurrent jurisdiction, statutory exclusion, presumptive waiver, reverse waiver, and "once adult/always an adult" statutes. (These prosecutor options will be discussed in greater depth later in this chapter.)

Research on Intake Decision-making

As was the case with police discretion (see Chapter 7), many researchers and analysts have been concerned about the discretion of intake decision-makers either to file or not file petitions. Of particular concern has been the question of whether race is an important factor in the intake decision and whether racial discrimination occurs at intake. Several conclusions can be drawn from the studies that have been conducted on intake decision-making. First, seriousness of the alleged offense clearly influences the decision to file a petition, though it is not necessarily the prime factor. Thus, youths accused of more serious offenses are more likely to be petitioned to court than youths accused of less serious offenses (Bell & Lang, 1985; Bishop & Leiber, 2012; McCarthy & Smith, 1986; Minor, Hartmann, & Terry, 1997). Second, prior record is a factor. Youths with prior records are more likely to be referred (Cohen & Kluegel, 1978; Fenwick, 1982; McCarthy & Smith, 1986). Third, demeanor often has an effect; uncooperative youths are more likely to be petitioned than cooperative youths (Bell & Lang, 1985; Fenwick, 1982). However, demeanor often is not measured in studies because many researchers rely on official records that do not include any record of the attitude of the child when he or she is interviewed by the court official making the intake decision. Finally, variables such as age, race, class, and gender have produced mixed results. As a result, there is considerable controversy surrounding the impact of each of these variables on the intake decision (for a review and analysis, see Bishop, 2005; Bishop & Leiber, 2012).

The methodology used in many previous studies was deficient. Specifically, many early studies looked at small, nonrepresentative samples that made it impossible to generalize to courts nationwide. Other studies used only bivariate rather than multivariate statistical analyses of their data. This means that they examined the independent effects of individual variables (such as race) on intake decisions but did not consider the effects on decisions of several variables at once. In addition, many of the studies were conducted years ago, prior to the introduction of due process guarantees in juvenile court and to the relatively recent civil rights movement focusing on eliminating various forms of discrimination.

Furthermore, at least some researchers (e.g., McCarthy & Smith, 1986; Sampson & Laub, 1993) contend that it is misleading to isolate the intake decision apart from the detention, adjudication, and dispositional decisions. They argue that those decisions are basically parts of one complex whole that must be studied together to avoid possible distortions. An analogy would be studying decisions of college football coaches about what play to call on first down but ignoring strategy decisions on the second, third, and fourth downs. Research on first-down strategy is interesting but incomplete. First-down decisions make the most sense when understood in the context of the other downs.

In summary, race appears to have some effect on the intake decision. Bishop and Leiber (2012) note several reasons for this. First, workers trying to give individualized treatment may consider parental control and supervision factors. Second, economically disadvantaged children may be processed in order to make them eligible for treatment at government expense. Third, stereotypes of minority offenders as dangerous may influence intake officers. Sampson and Laub (1993) have placed the discussion of the impact of race on juvenile court decision-making in a theoretical context. They see race as linked to structural changes in American society, such as the deindustrialization of central cities and the concomitant rise of the underclass. Their research found that "structural contexts of 'underclass' poverty and racial inequality are significantly related to increased juvenile justice processing" (Sampson & Laub, 1993:305). In simple terms, counties with greater poverty and racial inequality showed higher rates of detention and out-of-home placement of juveniles. Their findings are consistent with the notion that "underclass black males are viewed as a threatening group to middle-class populations and thus will be subjected to increased formal social control by the juvenile justice system" (Sampson & Laub, 1993:306).

Pope (1995) concludes that race is a factor, and he suggests that some changes need to be added to the traditional intake process to ensure that race is not a consideration. One suggestion is training. A second suggestion is to have two intake officers decide each case. A third suggestion is to have a review board examine all the decisions to look for any impact of race. If attention is given to such suggestions to improve court processing and if attention is also given to social and economic factors associated with race problems in the United States, race could cease to be a factor in juvenile court decision-making.

PROCESSING JUVENILES IN ADULT CRIMINAL COURT

Many juvenile offenders are now being handled in adult criminal court rather than juvenile court. This is a crucial decision because processing a youth in adult court makes the juvenile subject to adult penalties such as lengthy incarceration in an adult prison as opposed to a relatively short period of incarceration in a juvenile training school. Such a decision also results in the creation of an adult criminal record, which is public and may hinder future opportunities for employment in certain occupations. A juvenile court record, on the other hand, is usually confidential and, therefore, should not harm the child in any way.

There are several methods that states use to place juveniles into adult court jurisdiction: **transfer** or **waiver**, statutory exclusion, prosecutorial waiver, and lowering the age of juvenile court jurisdiction. Traditionally, waiver or transfer was the primary method of placing juveniles into adult criminal court. In 2009, 45 states and the District of Columbia had statutes allowing judicial waiver (Griffin, Addie, Adams, & Firestine, 2011; OJJDP, 2011).

In 2010, approximately 6,000 juveniles were waived to adult criminal court (Puzzanchera & Hockenberry, 2013). This is 55 percent below the peak number of 13,300 cases waived in 1994. The offense profile of waived cases in 2010 was 50 percent person cases, 30 percent property cases, 12 percent drug cases, and 8 percent public order cases (Puzzanchera & Addie, 2014).

Juvenile courts are waiving or transferring fewer cases to adult court because the states have been using other means (statutory exclusion and prosecutorial waiver) to prosecute juveniles in adult criminal court. It is estimated that states use legislative exclusion, prosecutorial discretion, and judicial transfer (waiver) to transfer more than 10,000 youths a year to adult criminal court, and that about 84,000 16- and 17-year-old youths are processed in adult court due to their state's jurisdictional age limits (Butts & Roman, 2014).

Statutory exclusion, also called **legislative waiver**, means that state legislatures rule that certain offenses, such as murder, automatically go to adult court. In 2009, 29 states had exclusion laws (OJJDP, 2011). In Illinois, the list of offenses excluded from juvenile court jurisdiction includes murder, aggravated sexual assault, robbery with a firearm, drug and weapons offenses committed

BOX 8.5 AUTOMATIC TRANSFER (DIRECT FILE): ONE STATE'S EXPERIENCE

The Juvenile Justice Initiative examined three years of data on 257 youths prosecuted and sentenced in adult court in Illinois from January 2010 to December 2012 under the state's automatic transfer (direct file) law. Over half of the cases ended up with convictions for lesser offenses— offenses that could not have triggered transfer. In this group of youths there was only one white youth. Many of the youths could have received longer sentences in juvenile court. Specifically, 18 percent of the transferred youths received a prison sentence of five years or less. A juvenile court sentence for a 15- or 16-year-old would be to age 21, a sentence of five to six years. The report recommended ending automatic transfer and returning to judicial waiver hearings to produce more positive outcomes.

What do you think? Is judicial waiver more appropriate than automatic waiver? Why might it be more appropriate to allow judges to conduct waiver hearings before any youth is transferred to adult criminal court?

Source: Ishida, Clarke, & Reed (2014).

on or near public housing, and gang-related felonies. The law applies to most juveniles 15 and older but includes 13-and 14-year-olds for murder and sexual assault (Bishop, 2000). For a recent critique of the Illinois law, see Box 8.5.

An evaluation of the statutory exclusion law in Washington state (called "direct decline" in that state) found that a sample of youths processed under the law had higher recidivism rates, although not significantly so, than the comparison group on three measures: total recidivism, violent felonies, and all felony convictions. The cost of the policy was estimated to be over $72,000 per youth, although benefits could not be calculated (Drake, 2013).

Prosecutorial waiver (direct file/concurrent jurisdiction) is another method for placing juveniles into adult criminal court. State law gives juvenile and adult court concurrent jurisdiction over certain cases. Depending on the offense, the age of the offender, and/or the youth's prior record, the prosecutor decides whether to file the case in juvenile or adult court. In 2009, prosecutorial waiver (concurrent jurisdiction) was available in 15 states and the District of Columbia (OJJDP, 2011). For example, in Florida, prosecutors can waive 16- and 17-year-olds charged with any felony, 16- and 17-year-olds charged with a misdemeanor if they have one prior felony and at least one prior misdemeanor, and even 14- and 15-year-olds charged with certain offenses (Bishop, 2000).

A report on Florida's experience with its direct file statute indicates serious problems. First, prosecutors have unfettered discretion to choose adult court; there are no criteria to guide the decision, whereas judges have to consider eight statutory factors at a transfer hearing. Second, there is no hearing to allow any challenge of the decision. Third, Human Rights Watch found wide variation in decisions by court district. Others have labeled this "justice by geography" (Feld, 2012). Fourth, there is racial disparity. In one district, 8.8 percent of white youths arrested for drug felonies were processed as adults versus 30.1 percent of black juveniles arrested for drug felonies. Human Rights Watch (2014a) thus recommends repeal of the direct file law.

Another way to direct juveniles to adult court is for state legislatures to lower the maximum age of juvenile court jurisdiction. As of 2014, two states defined age 16 as the beginning age for criminal court jurisdiction, and eight states set age 17 as the age for adult court jurisdiction (Butts & Roman, 2014). One note: three states (Connecticut, Illinois, and Massachusetts) recently went back to age 18 as the age for adult court jurisdiction, and New York was considering the same change. It will be interesting to see if more of the 10 states with ages below 18 for beginning criminal court jurisdiction follow the apparent trend and change back to age 18.

It should be noted that 24 states allow for **reverse waiver**. This means that the criminal courts can return certain cases that they received due to mandatory judicial waiver, legislative exclusion, or prosecutorial waiver back to juvenile court. It is also important to note that 34 states have **"once an adult, always an adult" provisions** (OJJDP, 2011). This means that all or certain categories of youths placed in criminal courts must automatically be processed in adult court for any subsequent offenses (Bishop, 2000).

The waiver decision is made at a hearing that is analogous to the preliminary hearing in adult court. At a waiver hearing, the prosecutor must only show probable cause that an offense occurred and that the juvenile committed the offense. The prosecutor does not have to prove guilt beyond a reasonable doubt. Proof of guilt is reserved for the trial in adult court (if waiver is successful) or for the adjudication stage in juvenile court (if the waiver motion fails). The juvenile transfer hearing differs from an adult court preliminary hearing in that the prosecutor must go further and establish that the juvenile is not amenable to juvenile court intervention or that the juvenile is a threat to public safety. An example of nonamenability would be the case of a youth who is already on parole from a state training school for an earlier delinquent act who then commits another serious offense (e.g., armed robbery). If probable cause were established that the youth committed the robbery, then the judge would have to find that the juvenile court had a history of contacts with the boy dating back several years and that one more juvenile court effort to deal with the boy's problems—either through probation or a training school placement—would be futile. An example of a case involving a threat to public safety would be a murder case or an offender with a history of violent offenses.

Recent Changes to Transfer Laws: Keeping More Juveniles in Juvenile Court

The laws on transfer and direct file discussed in this chapter were those in effect as of 2009. A number of states have made changes since then that are not reflected in the previous discussion. For example, Arizona has expanded the opportunity for "reverse remand" (reverse waiver), Colorado has narrowed direct file eligibility and now provides for a "reverse transfer" hearing for all youth, Nevada has narrowed transfer criteria, and Ohio offers reverse waiver for select youths (Daugherty, 2013). Along with laws restoring 18 as the initial age for criminal court, these laws reflect a softening of the punitive trend that led to the earlier expansion of methods to try juveniles as adults. The reporting of legal provisions as of 2009 follows the latest available summaries from the Office of Juvenile Justice and Delinquency Prevention (OJJDP) at the time of writing.

The Effectiveness of Transfer and Other Methods of Adult Court Processing

Research on transfer and other methods of placing youths into adult court has raised several issues. One concern is what influences the transfer decision; another is that transferred juveniles are receiving harsher sentences than they should. For information on the tragic result of one youth transferred to adult court and sentenced to adult prison, see Box 8.6.

A study of 22 girls who had been tried as adults in Ohio and who were sentenced to an adult prison showed that 5 had no prior record, 10 had never been placed in residential treatment, and most had histories of sexual and physical abuse, neglect, school difficulties, and chemical dependency. Although the sample was small, it suggested that many of the decisions to transfer these girls to adult court had been "questionable decisions" (Gaarder & Belknap, 2004:509).

A study of 1,042 juveniles prosecuted and sentenced in Pennsylvania adult criminal court between 1997 and 1999 showed that juveniles received harsher sentences in adult court than did young adults, even controlling for legal factors such as offense seriousness and prior record. Specifically, the

---

BOX 8.6 THE RESULTS OF ONE TRANSFER DECISION: RAPE AND DEATH

Rodney Hulin was convicted of arson at age 16 in Texas and sentenced to adult prison. Within a week of arriving at the Clemens Unit in Brazoria County, Texas, he was raped. During the following months, he was repeatedly beaten, robbed, and forced to perform oral sex. After he was denied protective custody, he became depressed and attempted suicide. After being in a coma for several months, he died. Rodney was small: 5'2" tall and 125 lbs. Rodney's parents sued. The case was settled out of court. How serious a

crime must be committed for a youth to be transferred to adult court? How serious must the crime be for a youth to be sentenced to an adult prison, where assaults and rapes can occur, especially if the youth is not that strong or not that inclined to defend himself or herself? Based on all the information in the chapter about transfer, is it a positive option?

Source: Adapted from: Human Rights Watch (2001).

juveniles were 10 percent more likely to be incarcerated and received a 29 percent increase in sentence length (average sentence length of 2.18 months per juvenile compared to 1.69 months per adult). These "findings suggest that judges may assign greater levels of culpability and dangerousness to transferred juveniles than to young adult offenders" (Kurlychek & Johnson, 2004).

Similarly, a study of transferred juveniles in Maryland showed that they received harsher sentences in adult court than comparable young adult offenders. For example, a typical 17-year-old drug offender would be 10 percent more likely to be sentenced to prison than a comparable 18-year-old offender and be incarcerated about one year longer. Most disturbing is the conclusion that "the brunt of this disparity is manifest among nonviolent offenders for whom these policies initially were not designed to target" (Kurlychek & Johnson, 2010:747).

One review of the research on transfer concluded that there is need for more research but that "the bulk of the empirical evidence suggests that transfer laws, as currently implemented, probably have little or no general deterrent effect on would-be juvenile offenders" (Redding, 2010:8). Similarly, Steiner and Wright (2006) did a time series analysis of passing direct file waiver laws in 14 states. They found that there was no effect on juvenile homicides and no effect on violent juvenile crime except in one state. Research on specific deterrence, on the other hand, is stronger and has clearer implications. Based on six large-scale studies in five jurisdictions, the results are consistent:

> All of the studies found higher recidivism rates among offenders who had been transferred to criminal court, compared with those who were retained in the juvenile system. . . . Thus, the extant research provides sound evidence that transferring juvenile offenders to the criminal court does not engender community protection by reducing recidivism. On the contrary, transfer substantially increases recidivism (Redding, 2008:3).

Jordan and Myers (2011) agree that the research usually shows either no effect on recidivism (no effect was also found in a recent study of 193 transferred youths in Arizona (Mulvey & Schubert, 2012)), or that transferred youth have higher recidivism than nontransferred youths. Additionally, their study of transfer in Pennsylvania found that it only promoted additional punishment severity, not certainty or swiftness (Jordan & Myers, 2011).

Johnson, Lanza-Kaduce, and Woolard (2011) think that the reason for increased recidivism after transfer to adult court is that the sentence given out in adult court is excessively harsh and represents a failure to use graduated interventions. In other words, a juvenile offender should receive the next most serious punishment. If he or she instead is "leap-frogged" over to a more serious punishment, that will cause increased recidivism. Redding (2010), however, thinks that adult court processing makes juveniles feel that they have been treated unfairly and hardens their self-concept as a criminal and leads to further crimes.

Based on this research and on research that shows that youths are developmentally different from adults, the American Bar Association (ABA) does not favor prosecuting juveniles as adults.

> The ABA opposes, in principle, the trend toward processing more and younger youths as adults in the criminal justice system and urges policymakers at all levels to take the previously mentioned principles into account in developing and implementing policies involving youth under the age of 18 (cited by Mathis, 2007:S1).

Feld and Bishop (2012) argue that current processing of juveniles in adult courts ignores critical developmental differences between youths and adults and that such processing should be extremely rare. Waiver should be used only after a juvenile court waiver hearing with clear criteria and subject to rigorous appellate review.

For a historical note on "passive" transfer in the first juvenile court, see Box 8.7.

BOX 8.7 TRANSFER IN THE FIRST JUVENILE COURT: COOK COUNTY, ILLINOIS

In the first juvenile court in Cook County, Illinois, there was some confusion about the jurisdiction of the court over older teens. There was also some concern that perhaps it was unconstitutional not to give older teens full due process rights. So the juvenile court judges exercised what is called "passive" transfer. This meant that they did not exercise their jurisdiction over older teens who committed serious crimes while on probation in juvenile court. They simply allowed these teens to be treated as adults in criminal court. They hoped that this strategy would prevent either the state legislature or the Illinois Supreme Court from overruling the law authorizing the juvenile court. The strategy worked; the Illinois Supreme Court did not interfere with the operations of the juvenile court.

Source: Tanehaus (2004).

Youth and Worker Attitudes

Research on both youth and worker attitudes toward adult court processing indicates that there are some problems with moving juveniles to adult court jurisdiction.

In interviews with 95 serious and chronic adolescent male offenders in Florida (49 of whom had been transferred to criminal court), Bishop found that almost all described juvenile courts favorably but had criticisms of adult court. Most transferred youths believed that criminal court judges did not show interest in them, saw the proceedings as rushed, and, most importantly, had difficulty understanding everything that took place in criminal court. The transferred youths also perceived the criminal courts to be involved in game playing and felt that the public defenders were more interested in talking the youths into accepting pleas. The youths also perceived the courts to be clearly focused on punishment, based not so much on what they had done but on judgments that "they were depraved or irredeemable" (Bishop, 2000:137).

In a study of 100 juvenile court personnel in three courts, workers—especially defense attorneys and probation officers—expressed prime concern for rehabilitation. Forty-seven percent of judges, 65 percent of public defenders, 80 percent of private attorneys, and 70 percent of probation officers said that rehabilitation was the paramount concern of judges. However, 40 percent of judges and 64 percent of prosecutors rated balancing the interests of child and society as the paramount concern (Sanborn, 2001).

In other words, although the public and politicians may favor transfer as a way to "get tough" on juvenile crime, not all youths and workers agree that this is the best course of action.

ADJUDICATION AND DISPOSITION

For children not sent to adult criminal court, the next steps after the filing of a petition are **adjudication** and **disposition**. In these decisions, a judge determines whether there is enough evidence to establish the petition and then decides what to do if there is enough evidence. These decisions are comparable to the plea, trial, and sentencing decisions in adult court. Refer back to Figures 8.1 and 8.2 for statistics on adjudication and disposition in juvenile court.

Ideally, the determination of the truth of the petition occurs in a rational fashion, with the prosecutor, defense attorney, and judge using their abilities and training to seek justice. In reality, juvenile court sessions often are hectic and hurried, and may reflect the self-interests of the parties involved rather than justice or the best interests of the child. For example, Peter Prescott has described one day in the operations of the Bronx (NY) Family Court as a:

> flow of incompetence and indifference. One court officer perpetually frowns, shaking his head in mute consternation at so much exposure to human fallibility. The court clerk, arrogant and disdainful, speaks as little as possible as if in fear of contamination. When he must speak, his tone is dry and contemptuous, his words chopped short: the burden of dealing with these people and their problems! "I've been here two years," a court officer remarks. "Two years too long. But once you're assigned to Family Court, you're stuck because no one wants to come here" (Prescott, 1981:85–86).

An account of the Los Angeles juvenile court system (Humes, 1996) indicates that numerous problems continue to plague juvenile court, an institution marked by both frustration and heroism.

Attorneys in Juvenile Court

There are several problems concerning attorneys in juvenile court. First, many juveniles do not have attorneys. Many juveniles waive their right to an attorney, often because they do not fully understand their rights, especially the importance of the right to an attorney (see, e.g., Brooks & Kamine, 2003; Feld & Schaefer, 2010; Feld, 2012). A second critical problem is large caseloads for public defenders in juvenile court. Depending on the state, the caseload for the average public defender can range from 360 to 1,000 cases per defender (Jones, 2004). With attorneys being so overworked, many juvenile defendants get the clear impression that "their attorneys do not care about them" (Puritz et al., 1995:47).

Additional problems with public defender systems may include insufficient funding, lack of training, high turnover, low prestige, and low salaries (Feld, 1999; Feld & Schaefer, 2010). Starting salaries for public defenders in Ohio, for example, were as low as $35,000, and hourly rates for appointed counsel in several counties paid only $50 an hour for in-court work and $40 an hour for out-of-court work (Brooks & Kamine, 2003). Similarly, Georgia only pays appointed attorneys $60 per hour for in-court work, and one county has a cap of $300. Maine pays $50 per hour with a cap of $315. In Louisiana, the state only pays public defenders from $22,000 to $30,000 per year (Jones, 2004).

A youth listens to his attorney in juvenile court. Some attorneys assume a concerned adult role rather than a zealous advocate role in juvenile court.

CREDIT: AP Photo/Richard Sheinwald, File

Many attorneys in juvenile court, both public defenders and private attorneys, are reluctant to utilize the **zealous advocate role** that is (at least theoretically) the norm in adult criminal court. Attorneys in adult criminal courts justify such zealous advocacy (where the attorney fights as hard as possible for all defendants, even defendants who have admitted that they are factually guilty) on the grounds that the system is adversarial and that the adversarial process is best for bringing out the truth. In juvenile court, some attorneys, parents, and judges feel that the adult criminal court norm of zealous advocacy is inappropriate.

BOX 8.8 ONE LAWYER'S OBSERVATIONS ABOUT JUVENILE COURT

Thomas Geraghty has defended children in Cook County, Illinois (Chicago), for 28 years. He believes in juvenile court; he thinks it is preferable to an adult criminal court that has "no special focus on the unique problems associated with the adjudication, support, and treatment of children" (Geraghty, 1998:206). He notes that representing children allows lawyers to get to know children and the external forces such as poverty and child abuse that brought them to juvenile court. Geraghty notes that many of these external factors "are factors that our clients did not create and for which they are in no way responsible" (Geraghty, 1998:236).

He notes the important background details that need to be considered before calls are made for the transfer of youths to adult court or for the elimination of juvenile court. For example, consider a 12-year-old who allegedly shot and killed two teenagers. Investigation showed that this youth was trying to impress two older gang members. More importantly,

> [w]hat came out of this investigation was the story of a child's life. It turned out to be a story of a broken home, a child lost to gang culture despite the efforts of his family and school teachers, and access to a snub-nosed .38 caliber gun. The story of this child's life . . . is the product of all of its parts. Unless we focus our efforts on understanding these stories, in a setting supportive of understanding, we are unlikely to provide justice for children (Geraghty, 1998:241).

They may worry that strong advocacy can result in an outcome by which a child who "needs help" will not get it because failure to establish the petition leaves the court with no jurisdiction over the child. As a result, at least some attorneys assume a **concerned adult role** rather than a zealous advocate role, encouraging youths to admit to petitions in cases in which an adversarial approach may have resulted in a dismissal of the petition. Additional problems are that juvenile court is not considered prestigious (it is called "kiddie court") and that judges may pressure attorneys into cooperating rather than being adversarial (Feld, 1999). (For a look at one attorney's thoughts on juvenile court, see Box 8.8.)

A qualitative study indicated that attorneys expressed considerable concern for their youthful clients but that the attorneys were not always sure of the correct course of action. Specifically, interviews with 10 attorneys and 10 clients showed that many of the juveniles did not always understand what was going on either during police interrogation or in court—often they "just didn't get it" (Tobey, Grisso, & Schwartz, 2000:230). For example, one youth waived his *Miranda* rights and talked to the police because he did not understand his right to remain silent. Many of the youths just wanted to "get it over with" (Tobey et al., 2000:234). Attorneys, in turn, felt that their youthful clients were often passive about decisions such as pleading guilty and thus attorneys "spoke of walking an ethical tightrope regarding who, in fact, was making the decision about such matters" (Tobey et al., 2000:237).

Buss (2000) agrees that many juveniles do not understand the role of the attorney as zealous advocate. Youths usually see adults as in control, not as advocates willing to listen to their wishes. Lawyers, in turn, may reinforce inaccurate images. Large caseloads prevent lawyers from devoting sufficient attention to juveniles. In addition, attorney hesitation to embrace the role of zealous advocate instead of concerned parent can influence attorneys to be paternalistic toward youthful clients. The result of any misunderstanding of the lawyer's role is that juveniles often are not fully honest with their attorneys. One way to help juvenile defendants to see their attorneys as zealous advocates is to honor confidentiality, especially by respecting confidentiality in relation to parents. If the attorney shows the youth that he or she will not divulge confidences to the youth's parents, that will demonstrate the attorney's undivided loyalty to the youthful defendant. Another important matter is simply to spend more time with youthful clients to counteract any impression that the youth does not matter (Buss, 2000).

Plea Bargaining

As in adult criminal court, the vast majority of cases in juvenile court are resolved by plea bargains (Feld, 2012). Because of the pressure on youths to plead guilty (admit the allegations in the petition) and because of the problems with **plea bargaining** (see, e.g., Newman, 1986), the American Bar Association has recommended that plea bargaining either be made visible or eliminated entirely (IJA–ABA, 1980). The ABA maintains that if plea bargaining is retained, the judge should not participate in the process. However, the judge "should require disclosure of the agreement reached and explicitly indicate the conditions under which he or she is willing to honor it" (IJA–ABA, 1980:39). If the judge will not accept the plea agreement, he or she should give the juvenile a chance to withdraw his or her plea. Finally, the judge should consult with the juvenile's parents before accepting a plea (IJA–ABA, 1980:47). These regulations (or alternatively, the abolition of plea bargaining) would eliminate many of the traditional abuses of the practice.

The issue of plea bargaining may take on increasing importance. Texas, for example, recently revised its laws to allow more determinate sentencing in juvenile court as an alternative to waiving some youths to adult court. Youths subject to this provision can get longer prison sentences and may complete their sentences, when they turn 21, in the adult system. Mears (2000) found that such increased sentencing options gave prosecutors greater leverage in pressuring juveniles to accept plea bargains.

Attorney Effectiveness

Research has shown some disturbing results concerning the effectiveness of defense attorneys in juvenile court. As we will explain, many of the studies show several problems with attorney representation of juvenile clients.

On the positive side, however, Michael Fabricant's (1983) study of juvenile court public defenders in Brooklyn and the Bronx (New York) found that, contrary to stereotypes, public defenders were more effective (or at least as effective) as private attorneys in defending their juvenile clients. Specifically, the public defenders were very effective in obtaining adjournments, avoiding detention, and gaining dismissals. Such indicators of adversarial effectiveness led Fabricant (1983) to conclude that New York City public defenders were not inadequate. This is an impressive finding because they were representing roughly 75 percent of the delinquency and status offense cases in New York City at the time of the study.

In an analysis of six states, Feld (1988) found that in three states many children did not have attorneys. In all six states, however, "unrepresented juveniles seem to fare better than those with lawyers" (Feld, 1988:418). Juveniles with attorneys were more likely to receive placement outside the home or secure confinement than juveniles without attorneys.

In a study of more than 500 juvenile felony court cases in Missouri, Burruss and Kempf-Leonard (2002) also found an adverse effect of attorneys. In other words, "out-of-home placement was more likely to occur if a youth had an attorney, even when other relevant legal and individual factors were the same" (Burruss & Kempf-Leonard, 2002:60). To be more specific, concerning youths charged with felonies in three Missouri courts (one urban, one suburban, and one rural), suburban youths with counsel were almost three times more likely to be removed from home, and rural youths were two and a half times more likely to get out-of-home placement than youths without attorneys. All the urban youths had counsel (Burruss & Kempf-Leonard, 2002). This negative effect of attorney representation raises an interesting point: Would kids be better off without attorneys? Burruss and Kempf-Leonard think not. They think that the negative impact of attorneys in juvenile court may be due to high caseloads, retaining counsel too late in the process, or other court personnel co-opting the attorneys out of an adversarial role.

In a study of two Midwestern courts, Guevara, Spohn, and Herz (2004) found that "the presence of an attorney (especially a private attorney) was an aggravating factor. Specifically, youth who appeared with a private attorney were the least likely to have the charges dismissed and the most likely to be securely confined" (Guevara et al., 2004:366). Most importantly, these findings about the negative impact of private attorneys call "into question the basic and fundamental right to counsel in juvenile court" (Guevara et al., 2004:366).

An American Bar Association investigation of Ohio juvenile courts produced several disturbing findings. First, "large numbers of poor youth throughout Ohio go unrepresented, even during some of the most critical proceedings that affect their liberty interest" (Brooks & Kamine, 2003:25). In many counties investigators noted that waiver of counsel was common, with as many as 80 percent of juveniles going without counsel. Second, many attorneys (slightly over 40%) saw their role as representing the "best interest" of the youth rather than being the youth's advocate. In some counties this view of the attorney role was so strong that it did not seem important to have an attorney represent the youth. Third, for many youths who did have attorney representation, the quality of that representation was questionable. The report found that many Ohio youths "receive ineffective assistance of counsel from attorneys who are ill-prepared, insufficiently trained, and/or overwhelmed by high caseloads, insufficient resources and low pay" (Brooks & Kamine, 2003:29). Thus, most cases are handled informally or by plea bargaining, and attorneys had little impact at disposition. One specific problem was low compensation. Starting annual salaries for public defenders were as low as $35,000, and hourly rates for appointed counsel in several counties paid only $50 an hour for in-court work and $40 an hour for out-of-court work. Such low rates do not help to attract or retain competent attorneys (Brooks & Kamine, 2003).

An American Bar Association study in Pennsylvania showed similar problems. Significant numbers of youths did not have representation, and many others had ineffective counsel due to lack of preparation or training. At detention hearings attorneys often had little chance to confer with their juvenile clients and were not familiar with alternatives to detention. Most cases were resolved by pleas, and attorneys saw many courts simply interested in dispensing treatment or punishment. Probation officers made disposition recommendations with little challenge from attorneys. At disposition, many attorneys simply were not acting as advocates for their juvenile clients. The investigators found that probation officers were very influential in the juvenile justice system, to the extent that "the system's over-dependence on [probation's] role has tipped the scales toward a 'best interest' system in delinquency cases in lieu of a system that demands the Commonwealth [of Pennsylvania] prove its case" (Miller-Wilson & Puritz, 2003:59).

Thus, the situation in America's juvenile courts appears to be such that some attorneys are adversarial, some are still traditional and act as concerned adults, and some are in between the two extremes. Furthermore, in some states, many juveniles are not represented by attorneys (Brooks & Kamine, 2003; Feld, 1993; Miller-Wilson & Puritz, 2003). Even a new law mandating attorneys in felony and serious misdemeanor cases in Minnesota did not essentially change the rate of representation by counsel (Feld & Schaefer, 2010). One frequent problem is simply that many juveniles waive their right to an attorney (Jones, 2004; Feld, 2012). This state of affairs raises the issue of which is the best approach: zealous advocate, concerned adult, or some compromise between the two alternatives? The chief advantage of the zealous advocate model is that it is probably the best insurance that only truly guilty youths will come under court jurisdiction. Because the attorney does not pressure the child to admit to the petition (plead guilty), there is less danger that the court will attempt some type of intervention program with youths who are not really guilty. An added advantage is that this approach may well generate the most respect from juveniles for the court system. Fewer youths will feel that they have been betrayed or tricked into something that some adult thought was best for them, despite their own wishes.

The biggest danger of the zealous advocate approach is that it may contribute to what Fabricant (1983) calls the contemporary version of benign neglect. That is, because many youths appearing in juvenile court come from families racked with problems, such as low income, public assistance, and/or broken homes, they do need assistance. An adversarial approach may prevent these children from being railroaded into juvenile prisons or other types of intervention due to insufficient legal defense. That adversarial approach, however, does nothing about the real problems faced by these children in their homes and their neighborhoods:

> It must be presumed that these youngsters' fundamental problems will neither be addressed nor resolved through a faithful adherence to process. Just as important, their troubles are likely to be compounded by social indifference. Therefore, a policy of calculated nonintervention may, over time, cause severer and/or increased antisocial behavior from troubled youths who initially are ignored by the court or state (Fabricant, 1983:140).

The advantage of the concerned adult model is that it seeks to address the problems of the child that presumably led the child into delinquency. The problem is that this helping philosophy has been the rationale of the juvenile court since 1899 and, as David Rothman has so aptly phrased it, the rhetoric of individualized attention has always far outstripped the reality of ineffective if not abusive programs (Rothman, 1980).

Jury Trials for Juveniles

Because the U.S. Supreme Court has not mandated the right to a jury trial for all juveniles (see Chapter 9), only 10 states generally allow jury trials as a right for juveniles and another 11 states allow jury trials in special circumstances (Szymanski, 2002). Some contend that it is critical for juveniles to have the right to a jury trial. For example, Rosenberg (2008) notes that judges find guilt about 25 percent more often than juries do. Feld (2012) argues that juries can serve as a check on abuses by both prosecutors and judges and thereby enhance procedural safeguards which "may be even more critical in low-visibility juvenile courts that deal with vulnerable, dependent youths" (Feld, 2012:679). The American Bar Association agrees that judges may be biased, and further states:

A jury trial gives enhanced visibility to the adjudicative process. A jury trial requires the trial court judge to articulate his or her views of the applicable law in the case through jury instructions, thereby facilitating appellate court review of the legal issues involved. Without the focus on legal issues that such an exercise entails, the danger is great that the applicable law may be misperceived or misapplied and that the error will go uncorrected on appeal (IJA–ABA, 1980:53).

Having the right to a jury trial, however, may not make that much difference in juvenile court. In her study of a suburban juvenile court, Mahoney (1985) found that only 7 cases out of the 650 actually went to trial. For those 7 youths, and for 87 other youths who initially requested a jury trial but later settled without a jury trial, there was no impact of setting (scheduling) a case for trial on outcomes. Thus, "in a handful of serious cases in which a child denies charges, it [a jury trial] may be essential to the cause of justice, but it is unclear how much a jury trial benefits a youth or the community in the great majority of cases" (Mahoney, 1985:564). Similarly, relatively recent research in Ohio showed that most attorneys reported that 10 percent or less of cases went to trial and trials were almost nonexistent in some counties (Brooks & Kamine, 2003).

The Recent Emphasis on Punitiveness

Traditionally, the disposition stage of juvenile court has been the epitome of the *parens patriae* philosophy. With the advice of probation officers, social workers, psychologists, and psychiatrists, the judge has tried to act in the best interests of the child. More recently, however, disposition (sentencing) in juvenile justice has taken on an increasingly punitive character.

One indicator of this increasingly explicit focus on punishment is the revision of the purpose clauses of state juvenile codes. In the past, states emphasized prevention, diversion, and treatment. As of 2005, at least six states emphasized "community protection, offender accountability, crime reduction through deterrence, or outright punishment, either predominantly or exclusively," and only four states had traditional child welfare emphases (Griffin, Szymanski, & King, 2005). Sixteen states used the language of balanced and restorative justice, emphasizing public safety, individual accountability to both victims and the community, and offender skill development. Nine states modeled their statutes on the Standard Juvenile Court Act, and six states had a multi-part purpose clause based on the Legislative Guide for Drafting Family and Juvenile Court Acts (Griffin et al., 2005).

A prime indicator of the trend toward punitiveness is the move by many states to expand provisions for processing juveniles in adult criminal court rather than juvenile court. Between 1998 and 2002, 31 states changed their laws governing the prosecution and sentencing of juveniles in adult criminal courts. For example, 18 states expanded their transfer laws, including the addition of new offenses eligible for transfer. Three states (Illinois, Maryland, and North Carolina) legislated "once an adult, always an adult" laws in which processing in criminal court automatically excludes the juvenile from any juvenile court jurisdiction after that (Griffin, 2005). The overall result is that it is easier to process juveniles as adults in criminal court.

Still another development in this direction is **blended sentencing**. In blended sentencing, either the juvenile court or the adult court imposes a sentence that can involve either the juvenile or the adult correctional system or both systems. The adult sentence may be suspended pending either a violation or the commission of a new crime. Fourteen states have juvenile blended sentencing schemes (the juvenile court imposes sentence) and 18 states have criminal blended sentencing laws (the criminal court imposes sentence) (OJJDP, 2011).

One example of a jurisdiction with blended sentencing is New Mexico. That state's "exclusive blend" of sentencing applies to 15-year-olds charged with first-degree murder, 15–17-year-olds charged with serious offenses, or 15–17-year-olds charged with a felony and three prior separate felony adjudications in a two-year period. The juvenile court has jurisdiction and can sentence the youth to a juvenile or an adult sentence. In juvenile-inclusive blended sentencing, the juvenile court has jurisdiction and can sentence to a sanction including both the juvenile correctional system and the adult correctional system. Usually, the adult sanction is suspended unless the youth violates the juvenile sanction (examples of jurisdictions with this are Connecticut, Minnesota, and Montana). Two other options are criminal-exclusive (e.g., California and Florida) and criminal-inclusive blended sentencing (e.g., Arkansas and Missouri), by which the criminal court tries and sentences the youth. In criminal-exclusive systems the sentence can be to juvenile or adult corrections; in criminal-inclusive states the sentence can be to both systems. The other type of blended sentencing is juvenile-contiguous, by which the juvenile court has authority to impose a sanction that goes beyond the age of its jurisdiction. Then differing procedures are used to decide whether the remainder of the sentence is imposed in the adult corrections system (Torbet, Gable, Hurst, Montgomery, Szymanski, & Thomas, 1996).

Still another sign of increasing punitiveness is the passing of statutes concerning the confidentiality of juvenile court records and proceedings. Traditionally, such records and court proceedings were closed to the public. The *parens patriae* rationale dictated that this would protect the juvenile from publicity so that a delinquent act would not stigmatize him or her permanently. In the last few years, however, critics have called for publicity to assure community protection, and legislatures have responded. At the end of 2004, 14 states allowed the public to be present for some cases (e.g., cases of older youths charged with a felony) (Snyder & Sickmund, 2006).

A possible consequence of these punitive developments is that the involved states create two ways of processing juveniles. If a youth is older, commits a serious offense, and/or has a prior record, he or she will be treated as an adult or similar to an adult. If a younger youth commits a less serious offense and lacks a prior record, he or she will be handled in a traditional juvenile court. Much of the rationale behind this division of juveniles into quasi-adults and children is the belief that youths have changed. Youths who commit what appear to be willful violent crimes are considered mature and responsible adults who should be held accountable for their actions. Younger youths who commit less serious offenses are still looked on as wayward youths who can be salvaged by the traditional *parens patriae* juvenile court.

Bishop sees some swing of the pendulum away from punishment and back to rehabilitation. First, she notes that although states have modified their purpose clauses to include both public protection and juvenile account-ability, "45 maintain allegiance to the juvenile court's traditional benevolent mission" (Bishop, 2006:659). Similarly, three states recently passed laws to improve treatment for committed youths, Mississippi ended its boot camp program, and Tennessee passed a law to expunge juvenile records at age 21. As noted above, additional indicators of a de-emphasis on punishment are legis-lation in some states reverting back to age 18 as the initial point of criminal court jurisdiction, legislation restricting transfer, and Supreme Court decisions on life without parole that relied on research on adolescent development. Because of such factors, Bishop and Feld (2012) discern a re-balancing of punishment and treatment concerns in juvenile court. (For further discussion of this re-balancing, see Chapter 14.)

Dispositional Decision-making

A major issue in juvenile justice is the question of which factors influence judges in their dispositional (sentencing) decisions. Research indicates several general conclusions. Legal variables such as seriousness of the offense and prior record have a strong influence on dispositions (e.g., Bishop & Leiber, 2012; Clarke & Koch, 1980; Cohen & Kluegel, 1978; Dannefer & Schutt, 1982; McCarthy & Smith, 1986). The impact of prior record on dispositions, however, may reflect bias amplification (Dannefer & Schutt, 1982; Sampson, 1986). In other words, prior record may mask the influence of race or social class in police decision-making. The impact of offender characteristics such as age, race, social class, and gender has mixed results (for reviews of prior research in this area, especially prior research on the impact of race, see Bishop & Leiber, 2012; Leiber, 2013). Usually, the impact of these variables is weaker than the impact of legal variables. One study, however, indicated that "measures of social class and race become increasingly important as direct influences on the final disposition as youths are selected into the system for further processing" (McCarthy & Smith, 1986:58). Another way to put this is that racial bias at early decision points such as detention hearings can have a cumulative effect at disposition such as being sentenced to residential placement (Guevara et al., 2004; Rodriguez, 2010).

Leiber and Mack (2003) argue that research does suggest a race effect due to decision-makers perceiving minorities, "especially African-Americans, as either dangerous, delinquent, and/or sexually promiscuous, which in turn had an effect on the case processing of these youth" (Leiber & Mack, 2003:37; see also Leiber, 2013). There also appears to be sentencing bias for youths transferred to adult court. Jordan and Freiburger (2010) found that black youths are more likely to be incarcerated than whites, and Hispanic youths are more likely to be sentenced to prison than white youths.

A number of studies report that females receive more severe dispositions than males for minor offenses, especially status offenses, stemming from traditional sex-role expectations. Other studies find leniency for females following the chivalry hypothesis, a paternalistic attitude toward female misbehavior compared to an excusing of boys "sowing their wild oats" (Chesney-Lind, 1977; Chesney-Lind & Shelden, 1992; Cohen & Kluegel, 1979). On the other hand, some studies show no gender bias after controlling for offense type or severity (see Leiber & Mack, 2003).

Prior case processing decisions exert some influence on dispositions. For example, detained youths receive harsher dispositions or are more likely to be formally processed (see Rodriguez [2010] for a discussion) than youths who are not detained. Moreover, prior case dispositions can affect subsequent dispositions (Henretta, Frazier, & Bishop, 1985, 1986; Thornberry & Christenson, 1984). Finally, some authors report that dispositions vary from one jurisdiction to the next (e.g., Belknap, 1984; Dannefer & Schutt, 1982), while others fail to find such differences (e.g., Staples, 1987).

Summarizing the research on the impact of race on dispositions in juvenile court, Bishop and Leiber (2012) argue that race affects police, intake, and detention decisions. Police make decisions to police underclass neighborhoods more extensively, which places minorities at higher risk of arrest; and police also more often perceive minority juveniles to be insolent and uncooperative. Minority juveniles are not diverted as often as whites, but instead more often are referred for formal processing. One reason may be that intake officers make assessments of parental control and supervision. Another may be to opt for court processing to make youths eligible for treatment at state expense. Still another factor is stereotypes of minority offenders as threatening and dangerous. The result is that research shows that "legal variables have the strongest effects on court processing from intake through final disposition, [but] they are contaminated to an unknown degree" (Bishop & Leiber, 2012:471). For example, race may affect the detention decision, which then affects the disposition (see, Bishop & Leiber, 2012 for a thorough review and analysis of the impact of race).

Because the research is often limited to one jurisdiction or state, this may mean that sentencing varies from place to place. Apparently, some jurisdictions have achieved better success than others in making the disposition stage race-neutral. Hopefully, juvenile courts everywhere will make further progress in eliminating race as a factor in juvenile court dispositions. However, a study of Iowa's efforts to reduce DMC showed that there was no change at the intake decision but that judges overcorrected their decisions and treated whites more harshly at disposition (Leiber, Bishop, & Chamlin, 2011).

Piquero's (2008) review of the research on Disproportionate Minority Contact (DMC) concludes that "much data has shown that youth of color have been overrepresented at every stage of the juvenile justice system" (Piquero, 2008:63). Piquero notes that there are three theoretical explanations for DMC. First, the differential involvement hypothesis holds that minorities commit more crimes and more crimes of violence. Second, the differential selection hypothesis holds that police and court officials process minority youths differently than white youths. For example, police focus on minority neighborhoods and use profiling. The third explanation is the mixed-model hypothesis, which contends that differential involvement and selection (processing) operate together to produce DMC. Piquero (2008) concludes that this third model is the most promising explanation (see also Bishop & Leiber, 2012).

Where race is still a factor in juvenile court dispositions, it may be that more is needed than simply addressing the problems of juvenile court. Krisberg and Austin (1993), for example, argue that problems in juvenile court dispositions, especially any findings of possible racial disproportionality, cannot be resolved in isolation but are "tied inextricably to the pursuit of social justice. Reforms will continue to fail, as they have in the past, if they do not address the maldistribution of wealth, power, and resources throughout society" (Krisberg & Austin, 1993:110). For a discussion of judicial attitudes as well as changes intended to improve juvenile court dispositions, see Boxes 8.9 and 8.10.

A final comment on the issue of race: it is clear that there is DMC. Minority youths are more likely to be adjudicated delinquent and placed compared to their proportion of the population. Kempf-Leonard thinks that part of the problem is blocked opportunities and that part of the solution is to improve schools, employment opportunities, and neighborhoods (Kempf-Leonard, 2007). Zimring notes that care must be exercised in addressing the problem of DMC so that the solution does not make the problem worse. By this he

BOX 8.9 JUDGES' ATTITUDES ABOUT REHABILITATION FOR JUVENILES

In a survey of judges, one-third agreed with the statement that the possibility of rehabilitation is reduced for juveniles from poor families. Three-quarters agreed that living with both biological parents enhances chances for rehabilitation. More than one-quarter agreed that juveniles living in the suburbs are more likely to be rehabilitated than inner-city youths.

Attitudes like this can have indirect impact on race. If black youths are more likely to be in such categories, and if

judges rely on such beliefs in their sentencing, the net result is that judges may consider such youths as less likely to be rehabilitated and give them a harsher disposition (sentence) or transfer them to criminal court.

Source: The complete survey results can be found in D'Angelo (2007).

BOX 8.10 SUGGESTIONS FOR REDUCING THE EFFECT OF RACE ON COURT DISPOSITIONS

Bishop and Leiber (2012) offer several suggestions for the problem of minority over-representation in the juvenile justice system. First, since delinquency is related to family, school, and neighborhood factors, juvenile court reforms alone are not enough. Issues such as poverty, unemployment, family disruption, schools, and access to health care all need to be addressed. Second, stereotypes of minority youths, families, and neighborhoods as threatening need to be addressed. A specific recommendation in this area is training criminal justice officials in cultural awareness. Third, to prevent the use of court processing as a method of

providing services for minority youths, Bishop and Leiber suggest alternatives such as vouchers for mental health and other services in the community. Finally, they suggest government attention to such inner-city problems as job creation, efforts to improve schools and efforts at community organization. They conclude: "In the final analysis, reducing minority offending and disparities in the processing of minority offenders will require nothing less than elevating the problems faced by impoverished inner-city families to a national priority" (Bishop & Leiber, 2012:475–476).

means that one possible approach would be to try to get more white juveniles adjudicated and disposed of (sentenced) in juvenile court. He asks, however, whether this is what society wants or if the better solution is to try and have fewer minority youths adjudicated and sentenced. This latter strategy may not result in perfect proportionality, but a reduction in the number of minority youths adjudicated and sentenced is preferable to having higher percentages of youths adjudicated delinquent and receiving harsh dispositions in juvenile court (Zimring, 2005). A dramatic example is "life without parole" sentences. Black youths make up 60 percent of all youths serving such sentences (Human Rights Watch, 2008). Do we simply want less disproportion, or do we really want fewer "life without parole" sentences across the board? Zimring's preference is for harm reduction over simple reduction of disparity.

A final note about dispositions in juvenile court is the issue of **justice by geography**. Apart from the issue of whether courts in some locations disproportionately sentence black youths differently than white youths, the broader issue is that urban courts often lack the mechanisms for informal social control found in rural courts. Urban courts tend to be more formal, focus more on due process, place more youths in detention, appoint attorneys more often, and hand out more severe sentences than either suburban or rural courts. So youths in cities receive harsher sentences than their counterparts in suburban or rural courts, hence the term "justice by geography."

SUMMARY

This chapter has examined the critical decision points in juvenile court: intake, detention, waiver, and other means of getting youths to adult court, adjudication, and disposition. This review has shown that the ideal of a beneficent court system has not always been reached. Sometimes, for example, detention facilities have been deteriorating physical facilities concealing punitive practices. Even though almost 50 years have elapsed since the *In re Gault* decision established due process protections for juveniles (*In re Gault,* 1967), attorneys in juvenile court may be confused about their role and often have high caseloads that prevent effective representation of juveniles. Worse, many juveniles do not even have attorney representation. Despite the history of civil rights legislation and concern, sometimes race appears to be a factor in juvenile court decision-making. Most recently, critics have become concerned about juvenile crime and the adequacy of the juvenile justice system to handle the serious offender. Thus, increased use of waiver, legislative exclusion, and prosecutorial waiver, and of other more punitive measures such as blended sentencing, began to characterize many juvenile court systems. This trend may continue, but there are signs of a return to a treatment orientation.

In light of the ferment in juvenile court and the growing emphasis on harsher measures, concern for the due process rights of juvenile offenders is more critical than ever. In the next chapter, we will discuss due process issues and the rights of juveniles in general.

DISCUSSION QUESTIONS

1. H. Ted Rubin argues that token economies and other detention programs are violations of juvenile detainees' rights because most of the youths have not been adjudicated delinquent. Do you agree, or do you feel that such programs can be justified because they establish order and thereby protect the detainees? Are such practices similar to what "free" youngsters experience every day in a typical school setting?

2. Much of the research described in this chapter concerns the decisions to detain, petition, and dispose of alleged delinquents. One of the basic issues in

all of these decisions is whether the decision-makers should or should not consider social factors in their decision-making. For example, should the attitude of the youth or the quality of parental care influence whether he or she is formally processed or allowed to go home with a warning or a much less severe consequence? Do such social factors have a place in these decisions, or are such social factors so liable to ethnic bias that the decisions should be based solely on legal factors?

3. Do you favor the use of bail in juvenile court? If so, for what sorts of offenders and under what circumstances?

4. Would you consider a career in juvenile detention as an administrator, counselor, teacher, or attendant (guard)?

5. Consider the following: A juvenile is accused of raping a 24-year-old high school teacher. You are a defense attorney and the defendant has asked you to represent him. You are convinced that you could "get the juvenile off" on a technicality. However, several members of your extended family are teachers and feel very strongly about this case. Would you accept the case? Would you pursue the technical defense that would exonerate the defendant, or would you encourage the youth to plead guilty and accept the psychiatric help that an expert feels is needed for the young man?

6. What do you think about the trend toward increased punitiveness (increased criminal court processing of youths, blended sentences, changes in purpose clauses to include punishment and incapacitation as juvenile court objectives, and changes in confidentiality)? Do you favor this trend, or does it represent an abandoning of the ideals of juvenile court? Do you approve of the recent action in some states of returning to age 18 as the age of initial jurisdiction for adult criminal court?

7. Suppose that a 13-year-old youth became extremely agitated and angry. He went to his parents' bedroom and got a pistol that was kept there in case an intruder broke in. He then murdered a family member. If this youth had no prior record but also no evidence of psychiatric disturbance, would you favor or oppose processing this youth as an adult in criminal court? How would the factor of a prior record influence your decision? What details of a prior record would most affect your decision? What are your reasons for your position?

8. The use of blended sentences and the increased processing of juveniles in adult court will probably result in an increase in the number of youths being incarcerated in adult prisons or in new youthful offender prisons instead of traditional training schools. What might be some positive and negative consequences of this? How can we prevent a tragedy such as a young man sent to adult prison where he is raped and eventually dies (see Box 8.6)?

CHAPTER 9

Due Process and Juveniles

WHAT YOU NEED TO KNOW

- The U.S. Supreme Court clarified the rights of juvenile defendants in several landmark cases.
- For example, the *Gault* decision ruled that juveniles have the privilege against self-incrimination and the right to the assistance of counsel in cases with the possibility of a decision to put the juvenile in confinement in a locked facility.
- In *McKeiver v. Pennsylvania,* the Supreme Court ruled that juveniles do not have the right to trial by jury.
- Reasonable corporal punishment is permissible in schools.
- Students do have limited free speech rights at school, but school officials can exercise broad editorial control over student publications.
- School officials can search students when they have reasonable suspicion to do so.
- Carefully drawn curfew laws have been upheld as constitutional. Excessively vague laws have not been upheld.
- Raising the legal drinking age has had positive effects, although a number of college presidents recently expressed concern that the age (21) affects binge drinking on college campuses.

KEY TERMS

Breed v. Jones

consent search

corporal punishment

Fare v. Michael C.

freedom of speech

graduated licensing

In re Gault

In re Winship

Kent v. United States

legal drinking age

McKeiver v. Pennsylvania

New Jersey v. T.L.O.

preventive detention

reasonable doubt standard

Schall v. Martin

school prayer

search and seizure

student search

INTRODUCTION

Juveniles share some—but not all—of the same constitutional rights as adults. While a comprehensive analysis of juvenile rights would require an entire book and is, therefore, beyond the scope of this text, it is important to examine some of the rights pertaining to juveniles. This chapter will first examine the landmark juvenile Supreme Court cases of the 1960s and 1970s (such as *In re Gault*) because those cases fundamentally altered the contours of the juvenile justice system. Then we will examine the Fourth Amendment rights of juveniles in terms of search and seizure by the police. Finally, we will analyze some other important rights of juveniles such as rights in school and rights at home.

THE LANDMARK SUPREME COURT CASES

Between the founding of the juvenile court in 1899 and the *Kent v. United States* case in 1966, the United States Supreme Court basically left the juvenile court alone. In other words, the Supreme Court respected the intentions of juvenile court officials to seek the best interests of the child by allowing juvenile court judges and related personnel a great deal of discretion in attempting to achieve those objectives. In the mid-1960s, however, the Supreme Court was confronted with several cases that indicated that such a hands-off approach was no longer appropriate.

Kent v. United States

In **Kent v. United States** (1966), the Supreme Court was faced with a waiver case appeal wherein a 16-year-old, Morris Kent, had been waived (transferred) to adult criminal court without a hearing, without the assistance of counsel, and without any statement of the reasons for the judge's decision to transfer the matter to the adult court. A judge had decided to transfer Kent, who had been charged with rape, simply on the basis of a review of the youth's social service and probation files. The judge did not allow Kent's privately retained attorney to review any of the files, nor did the judge conduct any hearing on the matter or state the reasons that convinced him to transfer the case. Thus, the waiver decision, a very critical decision that results in the possibility of an adult criminal record and adult penalties, had been made by the judge acting alone, without any concern for Morris Kent's rights.

The Supreme Court justices decided that due process of law entitles a defendant like Morris Kent to certain minimum safeguards, including a hearing, the right to the assistance of an attorney, and a statement of the reasons for transfer if the judge decides to transfer the case to adult court. The Supreme Court reasoned that the juvenile court judge denied Kent his right to the assistance of an attorney. Without a hearing, Kent's attorney had no opportunity to represent the youth. The denial of the assistance of counsel, a Sixth Amendment right, was compounded by the judge's denial of access to the case files. That denial prevented the attorney from raising any challenges to possible errors in social service or probation staff reports about the defendant.

The *Kent* case is important not so much because it corrected the wrongs done to one individual or because it put some order into the waiver (transfer) procedure, but because it marks the Supreme Court's first major examination of juvenile court processing. This examination found serious shortcomings of both the particular juvenile court that had handled Morris Kent and of juvenile courts in general:

> While there can be no doubt of the original laudable purpose of juvenile courts, studies and critiques in recent years raise serious questions as to whether actual performance measures well enough against theoretical purpose to make tolerable the immunity of the process from the reach of constitutional guaranties applicable to adults. There is much evidence that some juvenile courts, including that of the District of Columbia, lack the personnel, facilities and techniques to perform adequately as representatives of the State in a *parens patriae* capacity, at least with respect to children charged with law violation. There is evidence, in fact, that there may be grounds for concern that the child receives the worst of both worlds: that he gets neither the protections accorded to adults nor the solicitous care and regenerative treatment postulated for children (*Kent v. United States*, 1966).

A final comment on the *Kent* case is that many states are now resorting to prosecutor direct file and statutory exclusion (see Chapter 8 for more details) instead of transfer or waiver to prosecute juveniles as adults in criminal courts. Reliance on these other methods means that the affected juveniles do not get the waiver hearing and protections that *Kent* was intended to guarantee.

In re Gault

The case of *In re Gault* was even more significant. Gerald Gault was a 15-year-old Arizona youth who was arrested for allegedly making obscene phone calls to an adult woman. He was adjudicated a delinquent in a court proceeding that resembled a kangaroo court or a dictatorial tribunal rather than a court of law and was sentenced to the state training school for a possible six-year sentence. The maximum penalty for an adult committing the exact same offense was a $50 fine and two months in jail.

Gault, after being accused, was taken into police custody and detained. Within about a week, he was adjudicated a delinquent and committed to the state training school until he was discharged or turned 21 years of age, whichever came first. All of this occurred without the complainant (the target of the obscene phone calls) ever appearing in court to testify, without any detailed and specific charges being filed (Gault was simply accused of being a "delinquent"), without the assistance of an attorney for Gault (his probation officer "represented" him), and without any transcript of the proceedings. The end result was the possibility of a six-year sentence for what was at worst a nuisance offense.

In reviewing the case, Supreme Court Justice Abe Fortas traced the history of the juvenile court and of the *parens patriae* philosophy and found some fundamental problems. Supposedly, due process guarantees such as the assistance of an attorney were to be relaxed in juvenile court so that youths would receive the treatment benefits promised by both the founders and current advocates of the juvenile court. Instead, as the Court observed in the *Kent* case, the child often received the worst of both worlds: lack of procedural fairness and substandard treatment.

Interestingly, the Supreme Court did not go on to discard the juvenile court philosophy of *parens patriae*. Instead, Justice Fortas observed that due process rights would not hinder juvenile court judges from seeking the best interests of the child but actually would assist them in that effort:

> But recent studies . . . suggest that the appearance as well as the actuality of fairness, impartiality, and orderliness—in short, the essentials of due process—may be a more impressive and more therapeutic attitude so far as the juvenile is concerned (*In re Gault*, 1967).

Judge Fortas went on to rule that juveniles do have certain due process rights in delinquency proceedings in which there is the possibility of confinement in a locked facility. Specifically, such juveniles have the Fifth Amendment privilege against self-incrimination (the right to remain silent) and Sixth Amendment rights to adequate notice of the charges against them, to confront and cross-examine their accusers, and to the assistance of counsel.

In re Winship

In 1970, the Supreme Court went a step further. In the case of *In re Winship*, an appeal of a New York case involving a 12-year-old boy who had stolen $112 from a woman's purse from a locker, the Supreme Court turned its attention to the issue of the standard of proof (how strong a case must be to prove delinquency) in juvenile court. The Court made two rulings. First, the Court ruled that the U.S. Constitution requires that adult criminals be convicted only by the standard of "guilty beyond a reasonable doubt" (the **reasonable doubt standard** of proof). This had been standard practice in adult courts; the Court simply stated that the Constitution mandated what the states had been doing all along. Second, the Court extended the reasonable doubt standard of proof to juvenile delinquency proceedings in which there was the possibility of commitment to a locked facility. As was the case in *In re Gault*, the Court reasoned that this safeguard of the reasonable doubt standard would not detract in any way from the noble intentions of the *parens patriae* philosophy. It also suggested that, rhetoric aside, juvenile training schools were the functional equivalents of adult prisons because both resulted in deprivation of liberty—and any such deprivation of liberty requires due process protections. Finally, the Supreme Court noted that New York State's standard of proof in juvenile proceedings (i.e., guilty by a preponderance of the evidence) was open to inaccurate findings. There was a real possibility that youths could be found delinquent when in fact there was insufficient evidence for such findings.

McKeiver v. Pennsylvania

A year later, in 1971, the Supreme Court took up the issue of a juvenile's right to a jury trial in the case of *McKeiver v. Pennsylvania*. In *McKeiver*, the Supreme Court declined to go so far in extending adult rights as to grant juveniles the right to trial by jury. The Supreme Court decided not to grant juveniles the right to jury trials for several reasons. First, the Court did not want to turn the juvenile court process into a fully adversarial process and end "the idealistic prospect of an intimate, informal protective proceeding" (*McKeiver v. Pennsylvania*, 1971). Second, the Court noted that because bench trials (trials decided by a judge rather than by a jury) for adults often result in accurate determinations of guilt, jury trials are not an absolute necessity for accurate determinations of delinquency. The Court also indicated that it was reluctant to impose a federal requirement of a jury trial because such a mandate could prevent individual states from experimenting with different methods. Finally, the Court noted that it had not reached such total disillusionment with the juvenile justice system to warrant abandoning it.

Barry Feld (2012) contends that the denial of the right of a jury trial to juveniles was an important decision because judges and juries view cases differently. The result of the denial of the right to a jury trial is that it is "easier to convict a youth in a juvenile court bench trial than to convict a younger person in a criminal proceeding when the state presents similar evidence to a jury" (Feld, 2012:682). In other words, Feld believes that judges need less evidence to convict than do juries and that delinquents would fare better before juries.

These cases of *Kent, Gault, Winship*, and *McKeiver* constituted a philosophical revolution in juvenile court. Together, they forced juvenile courts to at least pay lip service to the notion that juveniles deserve many of the due process safeguards available to adults. Although the *McKeiver* case ruled against extending the right of trial by jury to juveniles, even this case indicated that the

Supreme Court would not tolerate the whole-sale denial of rights to juveniles. The *McKeiver* case implied that if accurate fact-finding were not available to juveniles, then the Supreme Court might have to impose additional limits on juvenile court discretion.

Still, it must be remembered that a philosophical revolution is not always a revolution in practice. Just because the Supreme Court has ruled that juveniles should be entitled to certain rights, such a pronouncement alone does not guarantee the actual provision of those rights. There is evidence that many children waive their right to counsel and that high caseloads prevent many lawyers representing juveniles from being effective (Miller-Wilson & Puritz, 2003; see also Feld & Schaefer, 2010). Thus, court practices and lack of resources can prevent juveniles from actually benefiting from Supreme Court rulings.

ADDITIONAL SUPREME COURT RULINGS

Since the landmark cases just discussed, the U.S. Supreme Court has decided several cases concerning delinquency proceedings in juvenile court.

Roper v. Simmons: A Ruling on the Death Penalty

In 2005, in *Roper v. Simmons*, the Supreme Court ruled that the death penalty is unconstitutional for juveniles. This case is discussed in detail in Chapter 14.

Two Rulings on Life Without Parole

In *Graham v. Florida* (2010), the Supreme Court ruled that a Life Without Parole (LWOP) sentence is unconstitutional for a juvenile offender who did not commit homicide. This case applied most directly to Florida, which had 77 such offenders in prison at the time of the ruling. It is important to note that the Supreme Court is not ordering states like Florida to release all juvenile offenders. The Court simply has ordered the states to allow such offenders some way to demonstrate sufficient maturity and rehabilitation to justify their release. States may determine that an offender is irredeemable and should not be released. The Court is simply telling the states that they cannot make the decision to keep a juvenile offender in prison for life at the time of sentencing and then deny the offender any opportunity in the future to demonstrate fitness for release. It is important to note that life without parole is constitutional for a juvenile offender who commits murder. In *Miller v. Alabama* (2012), the Court banned the mandatory imposition of LWOP for juveniles. In other words, states can still impose a life without parole sentence on a juvenile, but only after individualized consideration of the juvenile and the juvenile's offense. Some, but not all, states have interpreted *Miller v. Alabama* to apply retroactively to juveniles previously sentenced to LWOP (Rovner, 2014). (See Chapter 14 for a complete discussion of life without parole for juveniles.)

Breed v. Jones: A Ruling on Waiver

In *Breed v. Jones* (1975), the Court made the waiver process more explicit by ruling that states cannot first adjudicate a juvenile a delinquent and then waive or transfer the youth to adult court. The Court ruled that by doing this in a particular case, the state of California violated the youth's Sixth Amendment protection against double jeopardy (being tried twice for the same crime). The state of California had claimed that double jeopardy was not at issue because the juvenile was only punished once, but the Supreme Court ruled that being tried both in juvenile court and then again in adult court did indeed constitute a violation of the double jeopardy provision.

In a sense, the case of *Breed v. Jones* was not much of a victory for juvenile rights. Prior to the case, juveniles were tried in juvenile court, adjudicated delinquent, and then transferred to adult criminal court where they were tried as adults and sentenced. All that the U.S. Supreme Court ruling accomplished was a procedural change by which the juvenile court would now conduct a waiver or transfer hearing to determine if there was probable cause to believe that the juvenile committed the delinquent act. If the juvenile court finds probable cause and also determines that the juvenile is not amenable to juvenile system intervention (for example, the youth is getting too old for juvenile programs or has been in juvenile programs previously without much success), the juvenile court simply transfers the juvenile to the adult system without any final determination of the charge. A few years ago, one of the authors of this text observed such a waiver hearing, which equaled a full trial on the delinquency petition in every respect except that the judge declared a finding of "probable cause" rather than "delinquent" at the end of the hearing. The practical result of such waivers (transfers) to adult criminal court is the same as if the child had been adjudicated a delinquent. *Breed v. Jones* may be more a case of window dressing rather than an influential juvenile justice case.

J.D.B. v. North Carolina and *Fare v. Michael C.*: Rulings on Interrogation

In *J.D.B. v. North Carolina* (2011), the issue was an interrogation of a 13-year-old burglary suspect in a school conference room by police and school administrators. The Court ruled that courts should consider age as a factor in the custody analysis when the child's age was known to the officer or would have been objectively apparent to a reasonable officer. The majority noted that a child may feel pressure to submit to questioning when an adult would feel free to leave the interrogation because children in general are less mature and responsible than adults. The dissent objected that the majority is making the determination of custody too difficult whereas it should be clear and straightforward. The dissent also objected that this could open the door to the Court demanding that police could consider other factors such as intelligence, cultural background, and education. The result of this decision is that police will have to consider age as a possible factor that could affect whether trial and appellate courts will rule on whether a youthful suspect is considered in custody or not for *Miranda* purposes.

As noted above, two of the provisions of the *Gault* case were its explicit endorsements of the Fifth Amendment privilege against self-incrimination and the Sixth Amendment right to the assistance of counsel for juveniles. *Gault* applied to juvenile delinquency suspects the *Miranda* rights granted to adult criminal suspects. Like adults, juveniles may waive these two rights and consent to police interrogation without any attorney being present. A voluntary confession can then be used against the juvenile in court.

Gault left it unclear whether a juvenile could waive these so-called *Miranda* rights without first speaking with at least one parent or an attorney. The American Bar Association has gone so far as to recommend mandatory consultation with an attorney prior to any confession to the police (IJA–ABA, 1982). Most states, however, simply stipulate that the police give *Miranda* warnings in language that is understandable to juveniles (see Holtz, 1987).

The Supreme Court clarified this issue in the case of *Fare v. Michael C.* (1979). In this case, a juvenile murder suspect consented to an interrogation after he was denied the opportunity to consult with his probation officer. The Court ruled that there is no constitutional mandate to allow a suspect to speak with his or her probation officer. The rationale of the Court was that the Sixth Amendment specifies the right to the assistance of counsel, while a probation officer is basically on the side of the police in seeking to prosecute any juvenile who has violated his probation. More importantly, the Court ruled that the child can voluntarily waive his or her privilege against self-incrimination without first speaking to his or her parents and without first consulting an attorney. In such a situation the trial court judge must evaluate the voluntariness of any confession based on the totality of the circumstances rather than on any ironclad rule (called a *per se* rule) mandating the police to bring in at least one parent or an attorney to advise the child about the wisdom of waiving his or her rights. In evaluating the totality of the circumstances of the waiver, the trial court must consider such factors as the age, maturity, experience, and intelligence of the youth. Thus, judges might allow as admissible the waiver of rights by a 17-year-old high school student with a prior record but probably not the waiver of rights by a 13-year-old first offender of below-average intelligence.

It is important to note that there is some controversy about the Supreme Court's wisdom in not requiring more explicit or extensive warnings for juvenile suspects prior to interrogation. First, some research indicates that not all juveniles clearly understand their rights when arrested (Huang, 2001). In one study, about one-third of a sample of institutionalized delinquents thought (erroneously) that they were required to talk to the police (Robin, 1982). Other research has indicated that more than one-half of the youths tested lacked full understanding of all the *Miranda* warnings, and only about one-fifth adequately understood all of the warnings (Holtz, 1987:550; see also Grisso & Schwartz, 2000). Recent neurobiological research confirms difficulties for minors in understanding and asserting their *Miranda* rights (Feld, 2012). Second, parents tend not to be the best protectors of juvenile rights. One study showed that about one-third of the parents would advise their own children to confess criminal involvement to the police (Robin, 1982). Due to considerations such as these, some model juvenile law codes stipulate that police must have juvenile suspects consult with an attorney prior to police interrogation (IJA–ABA, 1982).

Most states follow the "totality of the circumstances" approach outlined in the *Fare* case. A few states put in so-called *per se* rules requiring that juveniles have the opportunity to confer with a parent, guardian, attorney, or other interested adult. Unfortunately, a number of states (Georgia, Louisiana, and Pennsylvania) overturned their *per se* rules as part of the "get tough" movement (Huang, 2001). However, appellate courts in three states—Alaska, Minnesota, and Wisconsin—have ordered that police electronically record all juvenile interrogations in order to assure the voluntariness of confessions and prevent police coercion (Ziemer, 2005). The Pennsylvania Supreme Court ruled that a juvenile can waive his or her right to counsel only after a judge questions the juvenile to determine if the juvenile understands the allegations and that a lawyer can be helpful (Burke, 2005).

In *Yarborough, Warden v. Alvarado* (2004), the U.S. Supreme Court ruled that age was not a factor in determining that a juvenile was not in custody for purposes of police questioning. The case involved a two-hour police interview of a 17-year-old murder suspect in a police station without giving the *Miranda* warnings or allowing the boy's parents to be present in the interview room. Based on his statements to the police, the youth was convicted of murder. The court ruled that the lower court made a correct ruling on the noncustodial status of Alvarado based on objective factors such as: (1) the police did not transport the juvenile to the station; (2) his parents were in the lobby; and (3) at the end of the interview the youth went home. The dissent argued, among other factors, that age is an objective factor that the police and courts should consider in determining custody status.

Feld (2012) observes that, as a whole, Supreme Court rulings on the interrogation of juveniles have excluded statements from youths 15 or younger, but admitted statements of 16- and 17-year-olds. He adds that this follows the developmental research that youths 15 and younger face clear and substantial disabilities in exercising competence in exercising their *Miranda* rights, while 16- and 17-year-olds can function about the same as adults.

Schall v. Martin: A Ruling on Preventive Detention

In *Schall v. Martin* (1984), the U.S. Supreme Court ruled that a juvenile who is awaiting court action can be held in **preventive detention** if there is adequate concern that the juvenile would commit additional crimes while the primary case is pending further court action. The juvenile, however, does have the right to a hearing on the preventive detention decision and a statement of the reasons for which he or she is being detained. The Court justified its decision on the basis that every state permits such preventive detention for juveniles and on the rationale that such detention protects "both the juvenile and society from the hazards of pretrial crime" (*Schall v. Martin*, 1984). Furthermore, the Court majority reasoned that "juveniles, unlike adults, are always in some form of custody" (*Schall v. Martin*, 1984). The three dissenting justices, on the other hand, noted the impossibility of predicting which juveniles will engage in future crime (this is often labeled the "false positive issue") and considered the punitive nature of many detention facilities.

SEARCH AND SEIZURE

Consideration of these landmark U.S. Supreme Court cases demonstrates that juveniles do indeed have basic rights at important stages of the juvenile justice process, especially the waiver (transfer) hearing and the adjudication (trial) stage. Very important are the Fourth Amendment rights of juveniles during investigation or arrest.

The issue of **search and seizure** is a complex one involving a myriad of U.S. Supreme Court interpretations of the Fourth Amendment. This amendment reads:

> The right of the people to be secure in their persons, houses, papers, and effects, against unreasonable searches and seizures, shall not be violated, and no Warrants shall issue, but upon probable cause, supported by Oath or affirmation, and particularly describing the place to be searched, and the persons or things to be seized.

The Fourth Amendment indicates a preference for warrants before the police can search or arrest suspects, but this preference for warrants is riddled with numerous exceptions. This is not the place to describe those exceptions (but see, for example, O'Brien, 1997). Here it is important to examine one question that does affect juveniles: the **consent search** in which a defendant voluntarily allows the police to search someone or one's effects without a search warrant. Since *Schneckloth v. Bustamonte* (1973), the U.S. Supreme Court's ruling on adult consent searches has been that the police may simply ask a person for consent to search the person or his or her house, car, or effects. Unlike the *Miranda* situation, in which the police must advise a person of the right to refuse interrogation, the police do not have to specifically advise an adult suspect that he or she has the right to refuse a search. The police may simply ask an adult, "Do you mind if we take a look around your house?" If the person agrees, then—aware of it or not—the individual has agreed to a consent search. This would be a reasonable search in terms of Fourth Amendment guarantees.

In the case of juveniles, the issue arises whether a juvenile is mature enough to withstand police pressure and intelligent enough to understand his or her rights. The American Bar Association has recommended that juveniles be advised of their right to refuse a consent search and that they also be advised of the opportunity to consult an attorney (IJA–ABA, 1982). The ABA felt that these two safeguards would compensate for any youthful susceptibility to police coercion and any lack of sophistication needed to understand fully one's rights. Another set of standards, the American Law Institute Model Code of Pre-arraignment Procedure, stipulates that if a person about to be asked to consent to a search is under 16 years of age, then a parent should be the one who gives consent. The Model Code further advocates that in any consent search situation involving juveniles or adults, the police should advise the individual that he or she "is under no obligation to give such consent and that anything found may be taken and used in evidence" (Wadlington, Whitebread, & Davis, 1983:301). In other words, the Model Code drafters advocated warnings for consent searches that were similar to the *Miranda* warnings used in interrogation situations. They felt that it should not be assumed that juvenile offenders are aware of their right to refuse a consent search without a clear warning of their right to do so.

A Supreme Court case from 2002 suggests that today's courts are probably inclined to rule on the side of law enforcement rather than to extend offender rights. In *United States v. Mark James Knights* (2002), the Court ruled that a warrantless search of a probationer, supported by reasonable suspicion and authorized by a probation condition, satisfied the Fourth Amendment. This follows *In re Tyrell* (1994), in which a California court ruled that a search of a juvenile on probation (which found marijuana in his pants) did not violate the Fourth Amendment. Police made a pat-down search of the youth when they saw a knife on one of two other youths with him. Even though the police did not have probable cause to conduct the search and even though the youth did not consent to the search, the Court felt the police did not violate the juvenile's expectation of privacy because the boy had been placed on probation, which stipulated the condition that he submit to searches by police, probation officers, or school officials. This probation condition erased any reasonable expectation of privacy (Juvenile Justice Update, 1995).

RIGHTS IN SCHOOL

Because juveniles spend much of their time in school, many questions about juvenile rights have arisen within the context of school policies and procedures.

Corporal Punishment

In *Ingraham v. Wright*, the U.S. Supreme Court ruled that **corporal punishment** (e.g., paddling) of students is permissible so long as it is reasonable. The reasonableness decision depends on:

> the seriousness of the offense, the attitude and past behavior of the child, the nature and severity of the punishment, the age and strength of the child, and the availability of less severe but equally effective means of discipline (*Ingraham v. Wright*, 1977).

The Court noted that corporal punishment could be abused, but observed that common law remedies were effective deterrents to any such abuse of the practice. The Court reasoned that students and their parents could sue school officials or charge them with criminal assault if they went too far in paddling any particular student.

As is often the case, dissenting opinions in Supreme Court cases raise very interesting issues. In fact, dissents sometimes are more noteworthy than the majority or plurality opinions of the Justices. Box 9.1 presents excerpts from the dissenting opinion of Justice White in the case of *Ingraham v. Wright*. These show that there are other sides to the issue of the constitutionality of corporal punishment in schools. The American Bar Association has followed Justice White's dissent and has recommended that "[c]orporal punishment should not be inflicted upon a student" (IJA–ABA, 1982:136). Finally, a review of the research on corporal punishment concluded that it should be banned because children who receive corporal punishment are more prone as adults to various deviant acts. Among the later problems are depression, suicide, physical abuse of children and spouses, commission of violent crime, drinking problems, attraction to masochistic sex, and problems attaining a prestigious occupation (Straus, 1994).

In a Ninth Circuit case, the judges ruled that "no reasonable principal could think it constitutional to intentionally punch, slap, grab, and slam students into lockers" (*P.B. v. Koch*, 1996). (For a note on excessive discipline in schools, see Box 9.2.)

Freedom of Speech for Students

Another school rights issue is the First Amendment right to **freedom of speech**. Here the U.S. Supreme Court has upheld the basic principle that students have at least some degree of constitutional protection in that they do not "shed their constitutional rights to freedom of speech or expression at the schoolhouse gate" (*Tinker v. Des Moines Independent Community School District*, 1969). This does not mean that students can say or express anything they wish in whatever manner they wish. What it means is that the right of free speech is to be balanced with the school's interest in education and discipline. Students are

---

BOX 9.1 EXCERPTS FROM JUSTICE WHITE'S DISSENT IN *INGRAHAM V. WRIGHT*

If there are some punishments that are so barbaric that they may not be imposed for the commission of crimes, designated by our social system as the most thoroughly reprehensible acts an individual can commit, then, *a fortiori*, similar punishments may not be imposed on persons for less culpable acts, such as breaches of school discipline. Thus, if it is constitutionally impermissible to cut off someone's ear for the commission of murder, it must be unconstitutional to cut off a child's ear for being late to class. Although there were no ears cut off in this case, the record reveals beatings so severe that if they were inflicted on a hardened criminal for the commission of a serious crime, they might not pass constitutional muster.

The essence of the majority's argument is that school children do not need Eighth Amendment protection because corporal punishment is less subject to abuse in the public schools than it is in the prison system. However, it cannot be reasonably suggested that just because cruel and unusual punishments may occur less frequently under public scrutiny, they will not occur at all. The mere fact that a public flogging or a public execution would be available for all to see would not render the punishment constitutional if it were otherwise impermissible. Similarly, the majority would not suggest that a prisoner who is placed in a minimum-security prison and permitted to go home to his family on the weekends should be any less entitled to Eighth Amendment protections than his counterpart in a maximum-security prison. In short, if a punishment is so barbaric and inhumane that it goes beyond the tolerance of a civilized society, its openness to public scrutiny should have nothing to do with its constitutionality.

By holding that the Eighth Amendment protects only criminals, the majority adopts the view that one is entitled to the protections afforded by the Eighth Amendment only if he is punished for acts that are sufficiently opprobrious for society to make them "criminal." This is a curious holding in view of the fact that the more culpable the offender the more likely it is that the punishment will not be disproportionate to the offense, consequently, the less likely it is that the punishment will be cruel and unusual. Conversely, a public school student who is spanked for a mere breach of discipline may sometimes have a strong argument that the punishment does not fit the offense, depending upon the severity of the beating, and therefore that it is cruel and unusual. Yet the majority would afford the student no protection no matter how inhumane and barbaric the punishment inflicted on him might be.

This tort action [student lawsuits against teachers who abuse corporal punishment] is utterly inadequate to protect against erroneous infliction of punishment for two reasons. First, under Florida law, a student punished for an act he did not commit cannot recover damages from a teacher "proceeding in utmost good faith . . . on the reports and advice of others"; the student has no remedy at all for punishment imposed on the basis of mistaken facts, at least as long as the punishment was reasonable from the point of view of the disciplinarian, uninformed by any prior hearing. The "traditional common-law remedies" on which the majority relies, thus do nothing to protect the student from the danger that concerned the Court in Goss [v. Lopez] — the risk of reasonable, good-faith mistakes in the school disciplinary process.

Source: *Ingraham v. Wright* (1977).

BOX 9.2 EXCESSIVE DISCIPLINE/CRUEL AND UNUSUAL PUNISHMENT

Cruel and unusual punishment is an issue in prisons. The parallel issue in schools is excessive discipline. For example, recently a teacher ordered a 10-year-old student to clean a toilet. She had mistakenly concluded that the student intentionally put too much toilet paper in the toilet in order to clog the toilet. She made the boy put his hands in the toilet and pull out the paper. He washed his hands and returned to class.

The case made it to the Tenth Circuit. Judges used the "shock the conscience" test. The judges concluded that the teacher had not acted with malice and so her actions were not deliberate, conscience-shocking actions.

The general lesson from cases such as this is that appeals courts use the standard of shock the conscience. But they interpret:

a very high threshold, and that school personnel's conduct must truly be outrageous. Finally, it is of considerable import that both courts focused primarily on the intent of the school personnel to do harm. Therefore, it is important to ask the question: What inspired the school personnel's action? Unless it was malice or sadism or the injury is substantially severe, there is a strong likelihood the school and its personnel will prevail (Colwell, 2002:3).

What do you think? Did this teacher's actions "shock the conscience"? If not, what would she have to do to shock the conscience?

Source: Colwell (2002).

entitled to express themselves as long as their expression does not materially and substantially interfere with school discipline or the educational process.

In the *Tinker* case, for example, at issue was the wearing of black armbands by students to protest United States involvement in the Vietnam conflict. The students doing so were suspended and sent home. When the case reached the U.S. Supreme Court, the majority of the justices ruled that the students' First Amendment rights had been violated, noting that the students had expressed themselves without creating any disturbance or interfering with school discipline. Furthermore, the school system had been inconsistent in that it had allowed some students to wear political campaign buttons and others to wear the traditional symbol of Nazism (the swastika). Writing for the majority, Justice Fortas took serious issue with school system prohibition of student expression of only one particular type:

In our system, state-operated schools may not be enclaves of totalitarianism. School officials do not possess absolute authority over their students. Students in school as well as out of school are "persons" under our Constitution. They are possessed of fundamental rights which the State must respect, just as they themselves must respect their obligations to the State. In our system, students may not be regarded as closed-circuit recipients of only that which the State chooses to communicate. They may not be confined to the expression of those sentiments that are officially approved. In the absence of a specific showing of constitutionally valid reasons to regulate their speech, students are entitled to freedom of expression of their views (*Tinker v. Des Moines Independent Community School District*, 1969).

This case can be misinterpreted as an outstanding victory for children's rights if some cautions are not noted. First, the Court was probably more concerned with the issue of free speech in general rather than with free speech for children. That is, the ruling in favor of the pupils can probably be traced to the Supreme Court's "long tradition of zealous protection of First Amendment rights" (Davis & Schwartz, 1987:58). Second, the case may be interpreted not so much as a children's rights case as a parents' rights case, because the children in this case shared the same views as their parents on governmental involvement in Vietnam (Davis & Schwartz, 1987). If the views of the students and their parents had not been the same, the ruling may have been otherwise. Finally, the case distinguished between passive expression and disruptive expression of views. Passive speech (for example, wearing armbands) is less disruptive than disturbances or other types of expression. The Court is more likely to uphold such passive speech than more rowdy forms of speech. (For a case about free speech by students on the World Wide Web, see Box 9.3.)

More recently the Court addressed the issue of student speech at a school-supervised event that took place off campus. Specifically, in *Deborah Morse, et al., v. Joseph Frederick* (2007), the Court addressed the issue of student speech at an Olympic Torch Rally in Juneau, Alaska, that passed through the street in front of a high school while school was in session. The principal permitted students to watch the relay from the other side of the street and one student unfurled a 14-foot banner reading "BONG HiTS4JESUS." The principal interpreted this message as endorsing drug use and confiscated the banner after the student refused to take it down. Justice Roberts ruled that "schools may

---

BOX 9.3 FREE SPEECH IN SCHOOLS: POSTING A WEBSITE

A Pennsylvania middle school student created a website that had negative comments and pictures about his algebra teacher and school principal. Pictures on the site showed the teacher's head dripping with blood and her face changing into Adolf Hitler. The site also offered money for a hit man to kill the teacher.

In a unanimous decision, the Pennsylvania Supreme Court ruled that school officials could punish the student because the website created a substantial disruption of school activities. The Court reasoned that there was a nexus between the website and the school so that the speech could be considered as occurring on-campus. Following the *Fraser* and *Tinker* cases (see text), the Court concluded that

"the website created disorder and significantly and adversely impacted the delivery of instruction" (see http://www.firstamendmentschools.org).

What do you think? Does the school have the legal authority to punish a student for the contents of a website that the student creates in his or her own home? Should a student be able to create a website and put highly negative content about teachers on that website? Should a student be able to devise a website that criticizes the teaching ability of his or her teachers but does not go so far as to compare the teachers to Hitler or mention anything such as hiring a hit man? What are the limits of free speech for students on websites?

Former Juneau, Alaska, high school principle Deborah Morse, left, accompanied by former drug policy czar Barry McCaffrey, center, and lawyer Kenneth Starr, right, speaks to reporters outside the Supreme Court. Starr argued that Morse was acting reasonably and in accord with the school's anti-drug mission when she suspended a student for displaying a "Bong Hits 4 Jesus" banner.

CREDIT: AP Photo/Evan Vucci

take steps to safeguard those entrusted to their care from speech that can reasonably be regarded as encouraging illegal drug use" (Majority Opinion, *Deborah Morse, et al., v. Joseph Frederick*). In his dissent, Justice Stevens argued that the banner did not infringe on anyone's rights and did not interfere with any of the school's educational programs.

In other First Amendment cases, the Supreme Court has addressed the issue of whether school officials can discipline a student for giving a lascivious speech and who holds editorial control over student publications. In *Bethel School District No. 403 v. Fraser* (1986), the Court addressed the issue of "whether the First Amendment prevents a school district from disciplining a high school student for giving a lewd speech at a school assembly." Matthew Fraser nominated a fellow student for a student office by using "an elaborate, graphic, and sexual metaphor." His obscene language violated a school rule, so he was suspended from school for two days. Both the District Court and the Court of Appeals ruled that the school had violated Fraser's First Amendment right to free speech. They reasoned that the speech was basically the same sort of action as the wearing of the protest armbands in the *Tinker* case. The U.S. Supreme Court, however, reversed the lower courts' decision and determined that the school does have a right to ban sexually explicit language, even if it is couched within a political speech, because it is counter to the basic educational mission of the school (see Box 9.4). The Court also limited the degree of freedom students have in expressing themselves in student publications, again pointing out the educational mission of the schools for justification (see Box 9.5).

In November of 1995, the U.S. Supreme Court declined to hear a case (denied certiorari) involving the right of a Tennessee junior high school teacher to refuse a research paper on the life of Jesus. In 1991, Brittany Settle, a junior high school student in Dickson County, submitted an outline on the life of Jesus for her research paper assignment. The original assignment noted that the topic must be "interesting, research-able, and decent." The teacher rejected Brittany's outline because, among other factors, she failed to get permission for the topic, the teacher thought that Brittany's strong belief would interfere with objectivity in a research assignment, and the assignment required four sources but Brittany used only one source: the Bible. In the U.S. District Court case, Brittany relied

BOX 9.4 LEWD SPEECHES IN SCHOOL

In *Bethel School District No. 403 v. Fraser* (1986), the U.S. Supreme Court argued that students do not have an absolute right to free speech under the First Amendment. They refused to equate lewd language given as part of a political statement with the wearing of protest armbands in the *Tinker* case. The justices distinguished the *Fraser* case from *Tinker* in that, in the *Tinker* case, the speech involved political expression and therefore it merited greater protection; whereas:

> the penalties imposed in this case were unrelated to any political viewpoint. The First Amendment does not prevent the school officials from determining that to permit a vulgar and lewd speech such as respondent's would undermine the school's basic educational mission. A high school assembly or classroom is no place for a sexually explicit monologue directed towards an unsuspecting audience of teenage students. Accordingly, it was perfectly appropriate for the school to disassociate itself to make the point to the pupils that vulgar speech and lewd conduct is wholly inconsistent with the "fundamental values" of public education (*Bethel School District No. 403 v. Fraser*, 1986).

Further, the Court noted that schools play an important role in preparing students for adult citizenship:

The process of educating our youth for citizenship in public schools is not confined to books, the curriculum, and the civics class; schools must teach by example the shared values of a civilized social order. Consciously or otherwise, teachers—and indeed the older students—demonstrate the appropriate form of civil discourse and political expression by their conduct and deportment in and out of class. Inescapably, like parents, they are role models. The schools, as instruments of the state, may determine that the essential lessons of civil, mature conduct cannot be conveyed in a school that tolerates lewd, indecent, or offensive speech and conduct such as that indulged in by this confused boy.

The pervasive sexual innuendo in Fraser's speech was plainly offensive to both teachers and students—indeed to any mature person. By glorifying male sexuality, and in its verbal content, the speech was acutely insulting to teenage girl students. The speech could well be seriously damaging to its less mature audience, many of whom were only 14 years old and on the threshold of awareness of human sexuality. Some students were reported as bewildered by the speech and the reaction of mimicry it provoked (*Bethel School District No. 403 v. Fraser*, 1986).

on *Tinker* for the right of free speech. The Court, however, relied on *Hazelwood School District v. Kuhlmeier*:

> The free speech rights of students in the classroom must be limited because effective education depends not only on controlling boisterous conduct, but also on maintaining the focus of the class on the assignment in question . . . Teachers therefore must be given broad discretion to give grades and conduct class discussion based on the content of speech (*Settle v. Dickson County School Board*, 1995).

Lower courts have ruled on free speech in extracurricular activities. In 2010, the U.S. Court of Appeals for the Fifth Circuit agreed with the District Court that a cheerleader could be removed from the squad for refusing to cheer for a basketball player she claimed had raped her. A grand jury had chosen not to indict the player. The Court stated that the girl's silence was substantially disruptive (*Doe v. Silsbee Independent School District*, 402 F. App'x 852, 853 (5th Cir. 2010), cert. denied 131 S. Ct. 2875 (2011, cited in Zeidel, 2012). In a 2007

BOX 9.5 CENSORSHIP OF STUDENT PUBLICATIONS

In an important First Amendment school case, the Supreme Court ruled that school officials can exercise broad editorial control over student publications:

> Instead, we hold that educators do not offend the First Amendment by exercising editorial control over the style and content of student speech in school-sponsored expressive activities so long as their actions are reasonably related to legitimate pedagogical concerns (*Hazelwood School District v. Kuhlmeier*, 1988).

The case involved a principal's censorship of a high school newspaper. The principal prevented publication of an article describing three students' experiences during pregnancy and of another article describing student reactions to parental divorce. Writing for the majority, Justice White distinguished the *Tinker* case type of speech as "a student's personal expression that happens to occur on the school premises" from "school-sponsored publications, theatrical productions, and other expressive activities" that are "part of the school curriculum" and "are supervised by faculty members and designed to impart particular knowledge or skills" (*Hazelwood School District v. Kuhlmeier*, 1988). For educational reasons, schools have "greater control" over the latter type of speech.

In his dissent, Justice Brennan castigated the majority viewpoint as approving "thought police" and the violation of "the First Amendment's prohibitions against censorship of any student expression that neither disrupts classwork nor invades the rights of others, and against any censorship that is not narrowly tailored to serve its purpose" (*Hazelwood School District v. Kuhlmeier*, 1988). Justice Brennan concluded that "[t]he mere fact of school sponsorship does not . . . license such thought control in the high school, whether through school suppression of disfavored viewpoints or through official assessment of topic sensitivity" (*Hazelwood School District v. Kuhlmeier*, 1988).

case, the Sixth Circuit affirmed the dismissal of high school football players from the team after they circulated a petition expressing dissatisfaction with the coach. The court ruled that the players' actions were disruptive to the coach's efforts to win and were not protected speech. The court distinguished this team goal of winning from the classroom where the focus is on educating students to evaluate competing viewpoints and be informed citizens (Zeidel, 2012).

The Supreme Court has not ruled on the issue of cyberbullying, that is, bullying online. For a discussion of this development, see Box 9.6.

Two additional areas in which freedom of speech in schools has been questioned involve compulsory community service and school prayer. At first glance, the issue of compulsory community service would not appear to be a First Amendment issue. With the advent of programs that require service for high school graduation in several places (such as Dodge City, Kansas; Boston; and the state of Maryland), opponents have argued that such service forces a student to engage in "expressive conduct." That is, the activity serves as an expression of support for the agency receiving the service. For example, a student might object that doing community service at the Girl Scouts sends the message that the student believes in what the Girl Scouts organization represents. This issue was argued in *Steirer v. Bethlehem Area School District* (1994). On appeal the Supreme Court denied certiorari (i.e., the Court declined to

BOX 9.6 CYBERBULLYING AND SCHOOLS

Cyberbullying—online bullying via text messages, Facebook, and other online communications—raises contemporary free speech issues. In traditional bullying, only a few people witnessed the act and the bully's offensive speech only lasted as long as spoken. Now cyberbullying can have the audience of the world wide web and last forever. One in six youths, and 26 percent of youths in a dating relationship, report being a victim of cyberbullying (Zweig, Dank, Lachman, & Yahner, 2013). Cyberbullying can even lead to victims committing suicide, as happened with one 15-year-old when teasing at school escalated into daily online taunts of "fat," "ugly," and worse (Araujo, 2012).

Araujo argues that courts have relied too much on the *Tinker* case standard of "substantial disruption" of school activities, and thereby actually have protected bullies. Instead, Araujo argues, later decisions suggest that a better standard would be that off-campus cyberspeech is protected by the First Amendment, unless it is "(1) directed at an identifiable member of the school; (2) unwanted or uninvited; and (3) lewd, cruel, embarrassing, harassing, or threatening" (Araujo, 2012:371).

What do you think? If a student uses his computer or phone away from school to bully another student by calling him or her offensive names, do you agree with Araujo that such embarrassing or harassing language can and should be subject to school regulation? Or do you think that school officials should only be permitted to step in if the speech substantially disrupts school activities (following the *Tinker* standard)?

Source: Araujo (2012).

---

consider the case, letting the lower court ruling stand). The Court stated that there was no First Amendment free speech issue because expressive conduct was not clearly at stake. The Court noted that engaging in community service is not the same thing as wearing a black armband or burning a draft card, acts that clearly do express a viewpoint. Despite this ruling, Charters (1994) argues that community service can be seen as fostering an ideological viewpoint and that "students have no civic duty to perform acts of altruism and self-sacrifice the omission of which would justify a school district's withholding a student's diploma" (Charters, 1994:613).

School prayer has become a topic of much debate in recent years. The key to the debate is the issue of whether school prayer represents the promotion of religion by the school. The Supreme Court, in *Lee v. Weisman* (1992), ruled that school officials erred in providing guidelines and permitting prayer at a high school graduation ceremony. However, the U.S. Fifth Circuit Court upheld the right of students to plan and lead prayer at school functions (*Jones v. Clear Creek Independent School District*, 1992). The degree to which prayer in school will be permitted has yet to be determined. Box 9.7 provides some insight into this issue.

In May of 1997, the United States Court of Appeals for the Eleventh Circuit affirmed the decision of a federal district court that upheld a 1994 Georgia statute authorizing a "moment of quiet reflection" to begin the school day. The statute noted that this moment of quiet reflection "shall not be conducted as a religious service or exercise but shall be considered as an opportunity for

BOX 9.7 PRAYER AT GRADUATION AND AT FOOTBALL GAMES

God of the Free, Hope of the Brave:

For the legacy of America where diversity is celebrated and the rights of minorities are protected, we thank You. May these young men and women grow up to enrich it.

For the liberty of America, we thank You. May these new graduates grow up to guard it.

For the political process of America in which all its citizens may participate, for its court system where all may seek justice we thank You. May those we honor this morning always turn to it in trust.

For the destiny of America we thank You. May the graduates of Nathan Bishop Middle School so live that they might help to share it.

May our aspirations for our country and for these young people, who are our hope for the future, be richly fulfilled (*Lee v. Weisman*, 1992:2,652–2,653).

A rabbi gave this invocation at graduation for a middle school and a high school in Providence, Rhode Island, in June of 1989. The middle school principal had given the rabbi a guideline for nonsectarian prayers at civic ceremonies and recommended that the invocation and benediction be nonsectarian. The father of one of the students unsuccessfully attempted to get a restraining order prohibiting any invocation or benediction. The District Court held that the actions of the school violated the Establishment Clause of the First Amendment banning governmental advancement of religion. The United States Court of Appeals for the First Circuit affirmed the judgment of the District Court. The case was then appealed to the Supreme Court.

Judge Kennedy's opinion for the court affirmed the lower court decision against the school's actions. Justice Kennedy was concerned about the principal's participation in the composition of the prayer: "our precedents do not permit school officials to assist in composing prayers as an incident to a formal exercise for their students" (*Lee v. Weisman*, 1992:2,657). He was also concerned "with protecting freedom of conscience from subtle coercive pressure in the elementary and secondary public schools" (1992:2,658). He distinguished a graduation ceremony from prayer at the opening of a legislative session "where adults are free to enter and leave with little comment" (1992:2,660).

He concluded that "the prayer exercises in this case are especially improper because the State has in every practical sense compelled attendance and participation in an explicit religious exercise at an event of singular importance to every student, one the objecting student had no real alternative to avoid" (1992:2,661). Thus, "the State, in a school setting, in effect required participation in a religious exercise" (*Lee v. Weisman*, 1992:2,659).

Writing for the dissent, Justice Scalia argued that standing silently during a prayer does not automatically imply that the person is joining in the prayer but may simply signify "respect for the prayers of others." Justice Scalia ridiculed the argument of subtle coercion, noting that the opinion treats students "as though they were first-graders" instead of individuals "old enough to vote" (*Lee v. Weisman*, 1992: 2,682). Theoretically, Justice Scalia lambasted the decision as "the bulldozer of its social engineering" for ignoring historical precedent and laying "waste a tradition that is as old as public-school graduation ceremonies themselves, and that is a component of an even more longstanding American tradition of nonsectarian prayer to God at public celebrations generally" (1992:2,679). Justice Scalia's reading of history showed that the "history and tradition of our Nation are replete with public ceremonies featuring prayers of thanksgiving and petition" (*Lee v. Weisman*, 1992:2,679).

Shortly after the Supreme Court decision, the Fifth Circuit Court ruled that a graduation prayer did not violate the First Amendment because students voted on the prayer, participation was voluntary, and students themselves, rather than a religious official, led the prayer (*Jones v. Clear Creek Independent School District*, 977F.2d 963 [5th Cir. 1992]). Shortly thereafter, several state legislatures introduced bills authorizing student-initiated prayer in the schools (Rossow & Parkinson, 1994). In the spring of 1994, Congress passed an education act that would prevent funds from going to schools adopting "policies designed to prevent students from engaging in constitutionally protected prayer or silent reflection" (cited in Underwood, 1994:1,040).

Similarly, the Santa Fe School District allowed a student to deliver a "non-sectarian, nonproselytizing" prayer over the public address system before each football game. Writing for the majority in *Santa Fe Independent School District v. Doe* (2000), Justice Stevens noted that the invocations were authorized by a government policy and took place on

BOX 9.7 *continued*

government property at a government-sponsored event. In addition, the process of selecting the student to deliver the invocation focused on the majority and denied voicing of minority voices. Justice Stevens ruled that the invocation policy and practice was unconstitutional because:

the realities of the situation plainly reveal that its policy involves both perceived and actual endorsement of religion. In this case, as we found in Lee, the "degree of school involvement" makes it clear that the pre-game prayers bear "the imprint of the State" and thus put school-age children who objected in an untenable

position (*Santa Fe Independent School District v. Doe*, 2000:590).

What do you think? Should prayers such as the one above be permitted at graduation ceremonies? Is such a prayer at graduation improper governmental intrusion into religion? If you were an atheist or a member of a non-mainstream religion, how would you feel during a nonsectarian invocation before a football game? Would it make a difference if each week different students—atheists, Buddhists, Hindus, and so forth—got up to deliver these invocations?

---

a moment of silent reflection on the anticipated activities of the day" (O.C.G.A. 20-2-1050, 1996). The judges noted that there was no coercion in the statute:

All that students must do under this Act is remain silent for 60 seconds; they are not encouraged to pray or forced to remain silent while listening to others' prayers (*Brown v. Gwinnett County School District*, 1997:1,473).

The court also noted that there was no endorsement of religion in the law and no authorization of any prayer. (For a Supreme Court ruling on permitting a religious club to conduct meetings on school premises after school hours, see Box 9.8.)

In 2003, the Secretary of Education issued a directive about constitutionally protected prayer in public elementary and secondary schools. The guidelines address such issues as prayer during noninstructional time, moments of silence, graduation ceremonies, and organized prayer groups. For example, the directive noted that if a school has a "minute of silence" or other quiet times during the school day, then "[t]eachers and other school employees may neither encourage nor discourage students from praying during such time periods" (p. 4 of Directive). Education law attorneys warn that schools should not follow the guidelines blindly because the guidelines are not necessarily an accurate rendering of case law (Colwell, 2003). Opinion poll research, however, shows that the overwhelming majority of students favor at least some form of prayer being allowed in schools, especially a moment of silence but not necessarily a prayer that mentions Jesus Christ (Ott, 2005). Opinion polls of adults show some decline in Catholic and mainline Protestant support for school prayer, but evangelical Protestant support has remained relatively stable (Schwadel, 2013).

BOX 9.8 IS THE GOOD NEWS CLUB GOOD FOR SCHOOL?

The Milford Central School allowed the Good News Club, a private Christian organization for children ages 6–12, to hold weekly meetings in the school cafeteria after school. The club sang songs, heard Bible lessons, memorized scripture, and prayed. Proponents claimed the First Amendment right of free speech. Opponents were concerned about a violation of the Establishment Clause versus the separation of church and state.

The majority concluded that in denying the club the right to meet, the school board denied the Good News Club its right to free speech. Justice Thomas saw this as viewpoint discrimination and argued that no Establishment Clause interpretation justified that restriction. Justice Thomas wrote that there was no indication that the school board was endorsing religion or creed. Justice Thomas saw the club as similar to organizations like the Boy Scouts that rely on "the invocation of teamwork, loyalty, or patriotism . . . to provide a foundation for their lessons" (*Good News Club v. Milford Central School*, 2001).

In their dissent, Justices Souter and Ginsberg cited a sample lesson about how "the Bible tells us how we can have our sins forgiven by receiving the Lord Jesus Christ" and "to trust the Lord Jesus to be your savior from sin." Such content led the dissenting Justices to conclude that:

> It is beyond question that Good News intends to use the public school premises not for the mere discussion of subjects from a particular, Christian point of view, but for an evangelical service of worship calling children to commit themselves in an act of Christian conversion (*Good News Club v. Milford Central School*, 2001).

According to a Gallup Poll, 72 percent of Americans favor allowing the use of school facilities for religious groups, 66 percent favor daily prayer in the classroom, and 80 percent favor graduation speech prayers (Saad, 2001). What do you think? Should religious clubs be allowed to meet on school premises after school hours? Is a club that invites children "to trust the Lord Jesus to be your savior from sin" simply another club that fosters "teamwork" and "loyalty" (in Justice Thomas's terminology)? Or, in the words of the dissent, does opening the school for the Good News Club in effect open the school "for use as a church, synagogue, or mosque"?

Student Searches

Another issue involving students is the right of school officials to conduct searches of students versus the students' right of privacy. This issue was highlighted in the Supreme Court case of *New Jersey v. T.L.O.* (1985), which involved the search of a student's purse by an assistant vice-principal based on a teacher's suspicion that the student had been smoking in the lavatory in violation of school rules. The Court ruled that such a **student search** was legitimate if it was reasonable in its justification and its extent. By this, the Court meant that:

WEB ACTIVITY

To see the directive issued by the Secretary of Education in 2003 about constitutionally protected prayer in public elementary and secondary schools, go to http://www.ed.gov/policy/gen/guid/religionandschools/prayer_guidance.html

Under ordinary circumstances, a search of a student by a teacher or other school official will be "justified at its inception" when there are reasonable grounds for suspecting that the search will turn up evidence that the student has violated or is violating either the law or the rules of the school. Such a search will be permissible in its scope when the measures adopted are reasonably related to the objectives of the search and not excessively intrusive in light of the age and sex of the student and the nature of the infraction (*New Jersey v. T.L.O.*, 1985).

It is important to realize that the Supreme Court explicitly noted that it was not ruling about a student's right to privacy in lockers or desks, about whether it would make a difference if the school was acting in cooperation with or at the suggestion of a police department, or about whether "individualized suspicion" is such an essential element of the reasonableness standard for school searches so as to preclude general searches of students or lockers (*New Jersey v. T.L.O.*, 1985). Thus, the U.S. Supreme Court left open many of the troubling issues surrounding searches on school premises, but it did grant school officials considerable latitude to conduct warrantless searches of students. It gave school officials greater authority to search students than other governmental officials have to search adults. In the case of *New Jersey v. T.L.O.*, Justices Brennan and Marshall concurred in part but also dissented in part. Box 9.9 indicates some of their concerns about the majority opinion.

A 1981 action of the Supreme Court sheds additional light on the Court's attitude toward student searches. Specifically, the Court (*Doe v. Renfrow*, 1981) that year refused to consider an Indiana case in which school officials and police used dogs to sniff students and their possessions for marijuana, searched pockets and purses, and even went so far as to conduct nude body searches

---

BOX 9.9 EXCERPTS FROM THE BRENNAN–MARSHALL PARTIAL CONCURRENCE–PARTIAL DISSENT IN *NEW JERSEY V. T.L.O.*

In this case, Mr. Choplick (the assistant vice-principal who conducted the search) overreacted to what appeared to be nothing more than a minor infraction—a rule prohibiting smoking in the bathroom of the freshmen's and sophomores' building. It is, of course, true that he actually found evidence of serious wrongdoing by T.L.O., but no one claims that the prior search may be justified by his unexpected discovery. As far as the smoking infraction is concerned, the search for cigarettes merely tended to corroborate a teacher's eyewitness account of T.L.O.'s violation of a minor regulation designed to channel student smoking behavior into designated locations. Because this conduct was neither unlawful nor significantly disruptive of school order or the educational process, the invasion of privacy associated with the forcible opening of T.L.O.'s purse was entirely unjustified at its inception.

The schoolroom is the first opportunity most citizens have to experience the power of government. Through it passes every citizen and public official, from schoolteachers to policemen and prison guards. The values they learn there, they take with them in life. One of our most cherished ideals is the one contained in the Fourth Amendment: that the Government may not intrude on the personal privacy of its citizens without a warrant or compelling circumstance. The Court's decision today is a curious moral for the Nation's youth. Although the search of T.L.O.'s purse does not trouble today's majority, I submit that we are not dealing with "matters relatively trivial to the welfare of the Nation. There are village tyrants as well as village Hampdens, but none who acts under color of law is beyond the reach of the Constitution.

Source: *New Jersey v. T.L.O.* (1985).

Savana Redding, right, and lawyer Adam Wolf, stand outside the Supreme Court in Washington, DC, after the court heard the case of Redding, who was strip-searched when she was 13 years old by school officials looking for prescription-strength ibuprofen pills.

CREDIT: AP Photo/Evan Vucci

of a few students. By refusing to hear the case, the Supreme Court let stand the lower court ruling that the school could use a canine team to conduct a general search of classrooms and could legally search pockets and purses, but went too far in requiring nude body searches (*Doe v. Renfrow*, 1981).

In *Safford Unified School District, et al., v. April Redding* (2009), the Supreme Court directly addressed the issue of strip searches. A 13-year-old girl had brought forbidden prescription and over-the-counter drugs to school and her underwear was searched. Delivering the opinion of the Court, Justice David Souter ruled that a strip search, due to its intrusiveness, is permitted but only if there is reasonable suspicion of danger or that the drugs are hidden in the student's underwear. In this case the majority did not see evidence of danger to other students or evidence that the girl was in fact carrying pills in her underwear. Thus, the search of this girl was not reasonable.

Nelson (2011) notes that the Supreme Court has not ruled on strip searches in detention centers. She argues that, following Safford, courts should consider the reasonableness of a strip search in a detention center based on the seriousness of the offense and the intrusiveness of the search considering the age and sex of the juvenile. Greater leeway to strip search should be given in cases of serious crimes.

The stretching of the right to search students has continued to advance. In 1995, the Supreme Court ruled that public schools could make student athletes undergo random drug testing as a condition for playing on school sports teams (*Vernonia School District v. Acton*, 1995). In *Todd v. Rush County Schools* (1998), the Seventh Circuit relied on *Vernonia* to uphold the actions of an Indiana school district that required students to undergo random, unannounced drug tests (urinalysis) before participating in any extracurricular programs or being able to drive to and from school. In a November 1997 case, the U.S. Court of Appeals for the Seventh Circuit upheld a "medical assessment" of a high school student suspected of having smoked marijuana. The "assessment" involved a school nurse taking the student's blood pressure and pulse. In 1996, the Eighth Circuit upheld a search of all male sixth through twelfth graders. The students had to remove their jackets, shoes, and socks; empty their pockets; and be given a metal detector test after a school bus driver informed the principal that there were fresh cuts on the seats of her bus (*Thompson v.*

Carthage School District, 1996). Rossow and Parkinson (1994) had argued that such a ruling would be welcomed by schools using metal detectors at school entrances.

In *Board of Education of Independent School District No. 92 of Pottawatomie County et al. v. Lindsay Earls et al.* (2002), the Supreme Court ruled that random drug tests of students participating in extracurricular activities such as band or Future Farmers of America are not a violation of the Fourth Amendment. The court noted that schools were concerned about the health risks to students from drug use and made note of the voluntary character of participation in such extracurricular activities. Dissenting Justice Ginsburg, however, argued that such drug testing violates the reasonable subjective expectation of privacy that students have about being forced to submit to urine tests. Justice Ginsburg also noted that participation in extracurricular activities is not completely voluntary but rather "a key component of school life, essential in reality for students applying to college, and, for all participants, a significant contributor to the breadth and quality of the educational experience" (*Board of Education of Independent School District No. 92 of Pottawatomie County et al. v. Lindsay Earls et al.*, 2002).

RIGHTS AT HOME AND IN THE COMMUNITY

Not all questions of juvenile rights have emerged in the context of school. Several issues and cases have arisen in the home and community.

The Constitutionality of Curfews

Curfew laws have mushroomed in the United States. Cities have enacted curfews to decrease juvenile crime and to protect juveniles from victimization (Davis, Scott, Wadlington, & Whitebread, 1997). Courts have upheld some curfew laws and struck down others. The recent trend seems to be to uphold the laws if they are narrowly drawn and if they provide exceptions for reasonable activities.

A case involving a curfew law that was challenged and ruled to be constitutional is *Qutb v. Strauss*. This was a 1993 case that concerned the Dallas, Texas, curfew law. That ordinance prohibited juveniles under age 17 from being on the streets from 11:00 P.M. until 6:00 A.M. on weeknights and from midnight until 6:00 A.M. on weekends. Exceptions included being accompanied by a parent, doing an errand for a parent, or attending school, religious, or civic activities. The ordinance also allowed interstate travel or playing on one's own or a neighbor's sidewalk.

The United States Court of Appeals ruled that the law did not violate either equal protection or free association grounds and therefore was not unconstitutional. The Court ruled that the law did serve a compelling state interest, namely, "to reduce juvenile crime and victimization, while promoting juvenile safety and well-being" (*Qutb v. Strauss*, 1993). Here the Court noted that the City of Dallas presented statistics on juvenile crime and victimization during the hours covered by the curfew to substantiate the argument of reducing crime and victimization. Concerning a juvenile's right to free association (a First Amendment right), the Court noted that the law had sufficient exceptions in it so that impositions on association were minor. For example, contrary to arguments that the law prohibited playing midnight basketball, the Court noted that the juvenile could play in such a game as long as it was sponsored by some organization or as long as a parent accompanied the youth to the game.

Similarly drawn curfew laws have stood appeals court challenges, while overly broad laws without exceptions have been struck down. For example, a 1981 case, *Johnson v. City of Opelousas*, was struck down because its only exception was for "emergency errands." Here the judges noted that there was no exception for such associational activities "as religious or school meetings, organized dances, and theater and sporting events, when reasonable and direct travel to or from these activities has to be made during the curfew period" (*Johnson v. City of Opelousas*, 1981).

Thus, clearly drawn curfew laws are withstanding constitutional challenge as long as they allow reasonable exceptions. One author, however, thinks that the constitutional issues merit further review by the Supreme Court in order to clarify some conflicting rulings (Harvard Law Review, 2005). In a related matter, the Supreme Court struck down Chicago's anti-loitering ordinance as vague. The law prohibited two or more people from loitering for "no apparent purpose." The Court said that the law was too vague to give the public adequate notice of the conduct that is prohibited (*Chicago v. Morales*, 1999).

Research indicates that curfew laws do not reduce juvenile crime or victimization. Another problem is that they are inefficient because they take up a great deal of police time (Adams, 2007).

The Legal Drinking Age

An important children's rights issue is the question of the appropriate age for adolescents to drink alcoholic beverages. In fact, because of the actions of groups such as Mothers Against Drunk Driving (MADD) and because of the threat of reduced federal highway funds, all states prohibit the purchase of alcohol by persons under 21 years of age.

Interestingly, raising the **legal drinking age** to 21 is the flip side of the previous historical trend to lower the drinking age. Not too many years ago, lowering the drinking age was very much the norm, and it was part of a more general trend in both the United States and Canada of lowering the age of privilege-responsibility, including lowering the voting age to 18. In Canada the rationale behind this movement was that because "youths paid taxes, could quit school and work, join the military, vote federally, and drive cars, it was felt that they should be allowed to drink" (Vingilis & DeGenova, 1984:163). In the United States, the military draft provided the added argument that if "boys were old enough to be sent to Viet Nam, . . . they were old enough to drink" (Vingilis & DeGenova, 1984:163). Finally, there was some feeling that if "youth had to use substances, alcohol was society's preferred drug" (Vingilis & DeGenova, 1984:163).

Proponents of a high minimum drinking age argue that it reduces automobile accidents and fatalities, especially for adolescents themselves. They reason that teens need to be protected from their immaturity and impulsiveness because they are inexperienced at both driving and drinking alcohol.

It appears that these arguments make good sense because the research suggests that lowering the drinking age is indeed associated with increases in alcohol-related collisions and with higher fatality rates for nighttime and single-vehicle crashes involving young drivers. Conversely, raising the drinking age is associated with a reduced number of collisions (Vingilis & DeGenova, 1984:166–169). Specifically, the Department of Transportation estimates that raising the legal age for drinking to 21 saved more than 29,000 lives between 1975 and 2012, and 525 lives in 2012 (National Highway Traffic Safety Administration, 2014; Walker, 2011; see also Wechsler & Nelson, 2010). In related research, it appears that states with the most restrictive graduated driver licensing laws have lower rates of heavy drinking among drivers ages 15 to 17 than states with the least restrictive laws but that there is no comparable difference in binge drinking (SAMHSA, 2004). (For a summary of research on the effects of underage drinking in general, see OJJDP, 2012).

The issue, however, received attention in 2008 when some college presidents asked for public debate on the minimum legal drinking age. Arguments were made that improvements in car safety were the real reason for fewer traffic deaths and that the age 21 law was forcing college students to drink at private parties with less regulation of drinking than in bars (Wechsler & Nelson, 2010). It now appears that this attention was short-lived.

A problem with raising the drinking age is the question of fairness. That is, the specific issue of raising the drinking age raises the more general issue of the fairness of prohibiting 18-, 19-, and 20-year-olds from drinking, thereby, in effect, treating them as children when the law treats them as adults for other purposes. We have seen,

WEB ACTIVITY

For fact sheets on the legal drinking age issue, see the website of the Centers for Disease Control and Prevention, available at http://www.cdc.gov/alcohol/fact-sheets/mlda.htm

For an online brief in favor of retaining the age of 21, see the website of the Council on Addictions of New York State, available at http://www.canys.net

for example, that all states consider 18-year-olds as adults in terms of their responsibility for criminal actions. In fact, one trend in juvenile justice is toward more liberal waiver and related provisions that allow younger and younger juveniles to be tried as adult criminal suspects (subjecting them to the possibility of imprisonment in adult facilities and even capital punishment). The question arises whether it is fair to subject teens to adult criminal court sanctions while at the same time treating them as immature children in terms of their legal ability to drink alcohol. Additional arguments against a high minimum drinking age include the "forbidden fruit" argument, which maintains that it increases the attraction of alcohol, and the "teach-them-to-do-it-right" argument, which contends that parents can use a lower minimum age as an educational device.

Franklin Zimring (1982) argues that it is fair to prohibit 18-year-olds from drinking, but he does not necessarily agree that it is fair to submit adolescents to criminal court sanctions, especially the death penalty. He states several reasons for his view that age 21 is a fair minimum drinking age. First, he believes that 18-year-olds are not mature but that they are in the process of becoming mature adults. Recall that recent Supreme Court decisions on the death penalty and life without parole for juveniles relied heavily on research that adolescents are not fully developed. Second, he is opposed to a low minimum drinking age because of the leakage problem. Leakage means, for example, that if 18-year-olds can legally purchase alcoholic beverages, then their 16-year-old dates may also drink and be subject to auto accidents and fatalities. Finally, he argues that there are three different aspects to adulthood: liberty, entitlement, and responsibility. Liberty refers to the freedom of choice that adults possess in matters such as making decisions about medical care. An entitlement is a benefit or program offered by government such as the Job Corps, which provides free job training for young persons. Responsibility means "paying the full price for misdeeds and being responsible, as are adults, for self support" (Zimring, 1982:111). It is Zimring's position that it is better to keep the ages for these three aspects of adulthood separate rather than to lump them together. Thus, he sees no inconsistency in permitting adolescents to drive at 16, vote and be drafted at 18, and be able to purchase alcoholic beverages at 21.

Zimring also raises the intriguing issue of raising the drinking age to 25. Based on evidence that single male drivers under 25—not just under 21—are a serious driving risk, he contends that these actuarial facts and logic would argue for an even higher drinking age than 21 to prevent many accidents and fatalities. He notes that there is some precedent for this in that the Constitution does require Senators and the President to be older than 21 years of age. However, Zimring rejects raising the minimum drinking age to 25 because:

> That kind of law is not merely politically implausible and socially divisive, it is also unjust. I have argued elsewhere that our current

deferral of liberties can be justified because adolescence merely seems like forever. But using age-grading to defer common liberty into the mid-20s is exploitation in almost every case. Adding four or seven years onto an already long wait is simply too much of a burden. The twenty-first birthday has a long history of serving as the outer boundary for legal disability based on age. There is no good reason to risk the legal incoherence and social division that pushing beyond this limit imposes (Zimring, 1982:124).

Zimring was writing just before the more recent push to waive increasingly younger juveniles to adult court, so he did not explicitly address the issues of the age of criminal responsibility and the appropriate age for capital punishment. There are strong indications, however, that he would not favor such actions. For example, he clearly believes that even 19- and 20-year-olds are not fully mature and may need some protection from their youthful mistakes. Thus, Zimring is convinced that our legal policy should be one that "preserves the life chances for those who make serious mistakes, as well as preserving choices for their more fortunate (and more virtuous) contemporaries" (Zimring, 1982:91–92).

Zimring's position is worth considering. Contrary to many contemporary voices, he does not advocate a policy that on the one hand would prohibit drinking until 21, but on the other hand would allow waiver to criminal court at 14. Instead, he takes the more consistent view that persons under 21 are not fully mature and responsible, but that certain aspects of adulthood may be more appropriately begun at 18.

In connection with this issue, Barnum (1987) argues that it is false to justify the existence of a separate juvenile court system on the claim that children are less mature and less responsible for their behavior than adults. Rather, "normal intrinsic cognitive development is sufficient for this capacity [to appreciate what they are doing or what effect it will have] by age two or three" (Barnum, 1987:72). Nevertheless, many think there are developmental differences between children and adults that do justify a separate court for juveniles:

> children are less able to be responsible for themselves, . . . adolescents normally experience transient irresponsibility, and . . . even poorly socialized children may have a better prognosis for rehabilitation than do poorly socialized adults (Barnum, 1987:78).

In other words, most children do know right from wrong, just as do most adults. However, there are other differences between children and adults that may justify a separate juvenile court system. (For a discussion of the privacy rights of teen drivers versus parental efforts to track teen driving habits, see Box 9.10.)

BOX 9.10 PARENTAL TRACKING OF TEEN DRIVING

Some parents are installing black boxes in cars that monitor the driving habits of their teenage sons and daughters. The devices record such behaviors as seat belt use and speed of the car. The devices also make a noise when the driver exceeds safety thresholds while driving. AAA's On Board device allows a parent to set speed alerts to notify the parent when the set speed limit is exceeded. Parents can also view their teen's trip history to see date, time, and starting and ending locations of trips.

One teen rights advocate argued that these boxes are an "invasion of privacy" (Davis & O'Donnell, 2005). What do you think? Are automobile black boxes an invasion of privacy or is this simply a reasonable attempt by parents to monitor the driving behavior of teens? Is it legitimate for 16- and 17-year-olds but not for youths 18 or older? Is there any difference between monitoring driving speeds and trip history?

Source: Davis and O'Donnell (2005).

Perhaps a fitting conclusion to this discussion is Davis and Schwartz's observation that there is a fundamental tension in the law between paternalism (protecting children) and autonomy (granting them responsibility) that will not disappear:

> The law is protective of children, for example, in the areas of contracts, employment, and to a great extent, medical decision making in life-threatening cases. The law grants a measure of autonomy to children or their parents in other areas—for example, abortion decision making (but only to a limited extent), torts (but more as a result of a policy favoring compensation of victims than of a desire to grant children greater responsibility), non-life threatening medical decision making, and emancipation decision making. These disparate results stem from an inherent conflict in the law—a kind of schizophrenia—between the desire to accord children a greater degree of control over their lives and freedom of choice, and the need, on the other hand, to protect them from others, their surroundings, and, sometimes, from their own folly (Davis & Schwartz, 1987:201).

It is interesting that at present society is lowering the age of criminal responsibility but at the same time insists on making 21 the age of eligibility to purchase alcohol and is pushing for **graduated licensing**. Davis and Schwartz's description of this as "a kind of schizophrenia" seems most fitting.

Recent developments in juvenile justice—such as some states returning to age 18 as the beginning age of criminal court jurisdiction, and the emphasis on incomplete adolescent development, even at 18, affecting Supreme Court decisions about juveniles—indicate a narrowing of what Davis and Schwartz called "a kind of schizophrenia." It appears that society is becoming more consistent in its view of juvenile maturity issues.

SUMMARY

This chapter has examined the landmark U.S. Supreme Court cases involving juveniles. The Fourth Amendment rights of juveniles and some of the controversial rights issues in school and in the home were examined. There is no perfectly consistent treatment of juveniles and their rights. Sometimes the law treats them as children, and sometimes it treats them as adults. As Zimring (1982) has pointed out, however, because the issue of juveniles' rights is so complex, perhaps a refusal to come up with one magical age for all children's rights issues is the best solution. Finally, as was noted in the discussion of the landmark Supreme Court cases, the mere stipulation of a right by the Court does not guarantee that police or courts will actually or fully protect that right. Practice is not always the same as philosophy.

DISCUSSION QUESTIONS

1. Has the Supreme Court gone too far or not far enough in protecting the rights of juvenile delinquency suspects? If you were on the Supreme Court, what would you seek to change concerning those rights?

2. Your 15-year-old brother has been arrested for the robbery of a movie video rental store. He is of average intelligence but is immature and impulsive. This is his first arrest. Do you think that he should be allowed to waive his privilege against self-incrimination and his right to confer with an attorney, or do you feel that state law should mandate that an attorney be brought in before the police can conduct any interrogation?

3. Assume that you are the editor of the high school newspaper and that one of your best reporters has just completed a lengthy article on drug use in your school. No names are mentioned in the article; in fact, your reporter has gone to great lengths to protect confidentiality. The principal has read the article and has said that she does not want it published in the school paper. What would you do?

4. Do you agree with the Supreme Court's position that corporal punishment is permissible as a school discipline technique? If you became a teacher or principal, would you use corporal punishment? If so, when and under what circumstances? More generally, how would you feel about your children being subjected to corporal punishment?

5. If you were a high school principal, what would your policy on student searches be? The Supreme Court ruled that drug testing of students in band and clubs is permissible. Would you follow the direction of the Supreme Court and initiate testing of band members and the Future Farmers of America?

6. What is your opinion about compulsory community service? Do you think high schools should be allowed to force students to perform community service as a condition for graduation? Why or why not?

7. What is your opinion about school prayer? Should a school be allowed to invite a priest, minister, rabbi, or other religious leader to graduation to offer a nonsectarian invocation? Should the students be allowed to compose and lead their own invocation at graduation? What do you think about a moment of silence to begin (or end) the school day? Should prayer be permissible at athletic events?

8. What do you think should be the response of a school to cyberbullying? If the bullying does not disrupt school activity, should the school stay out of the controversy? Or do you agree with one expert who thinks that school authorities should have more leeway to intervene and protect students?

9. What age do you favor as the minimum legal drinking age? How would you feel about the age being set at 25? What do you think about graduated licensing laws? Do you favor or oppose them?

CHAPTER 10

Institutional/Residential Interventions

WHAT YOU NEED TO KNOW

- 61,423 juvenile offenders were in public, private, or tribal residential placement on the date of the most recent census. In addition, more than 1,300 juveniles were in adult prisons, according to recent data.

- Boot camps can be cost-effective and result in academic progress. They do not reduce recidivism, however, despite the commonsense belief that military-type discipline is beneficial.

- Recent statistics indicate that 70 to 80 percent of juveniles released from state facilities are rearrested. On the other hand, effective programs can reduce recidivism significantly.

- The most prevalent problem in the juvenile justice system is the presence of mental disorders. Studies show that more than two-thirds of juveniles in the juvenile justice system experience mental disorders.

- Estimates of victimization, including sexual victimization, in juvenile facilities vary; some estimates indicate that almost two-thirds of youths are victimized. In a recent government survey, 9.5 percent of youths in state juvenile facilities and large private facilities reported one or more incidents of sexual victimization in the previous year or since their admission to the facility.

- Racial tension has been a problem in juvenile facilities. In 2011, minorities constituted 68 percent of the committed juveniles in custody in public and private facilities nationwide.

- Deinstitutionalization or stopping involuntary placements of status offenders continues; in 2011, only 2,239 committed status offenders were in residential placement.

- Many wilderness programs have not been effective, but a recent evaluation showed that such programs with treatment enhancements can reduce recidivism.

KEY TERMS

behavior modification

boot camps

commonsense corrections

cottage system

deinstitutionalization

institutional life

program effectiveness

racial tension

shock incarceration

state training schools

victimization

wilderness programs

WEB ACTIVITY

For the latest available statistics on juveniles in custody, see Sickmund et al. (2013b). "Easy access to the census of juveniles in residential placement: 1997–2011." Available at http:/www.ojjdp.gov/ojstatbb/ezacjrp/

INTRODUCTION

This chapter will examine juvenile institutional correctional interventions, both public and private. Although more youths are in community correctional programs, residential programs are a critical component of juvenile corrections.

INSTITUTIONAL CORRECTIONS FOR JUVENILES

On the latest one-day count of juveniles in residential placement in 2011, 61,423 juvenile offenders were in detention, correctional, or shelter facilities. Most of these were delinquency offenders. More than 42,500 of the youths were in public facilities, and almost 19,000 (18,839, to be precise) were in private facilities. Sixty-eight percent of these youths were committed (after being tried in court), and 31 percent were being detained prior to a court hearing, adjudication, disposition, or placement elsewhere. About 4 percent of the youths in custody were status offenders. The juvenile custody population dropped 29 percent from 2007 to 2011 (Sickmund, Sladky, & Kang, 2013a). The latest information available indicates that the average length of stay was approximately four months and that the average yearly cost of custody in a public institution was $66,000 to $88,000 (Mendel, 2011). Many juvenile facilities are outdated, built in the 1970s at best (Roush & McMillen, 2000).

According to the most recent report, in 2010, there were 2,295 juveniles in state (adult) prisons. Six states (Florida, New York, Connecticut, North Carolina, Texas, and Arizona) held more than half of all juveniles in state prisons (Guerino, Harrison, & Sabol, 2011). This number reportedly dropped to 1,325 in 2012 (Carson & Golinelli, 2013).

Although probation handles many more youths, institutions involve a significant minority of the offenders who go through the juvenile justice system. They are the costliest part of the system. A recent estimate put the average daily cost of incarcerating one juvenile offender at $241 a day or about $88,000 for one year. In California, the cost to confine one youth for a year is about $250,000 (Mendel, 2011). In 2011, the residential population was 86 percent male and 14 percent female. The racial composition of juvenile offenders in custody was 32 percent white, 40 percent black, and 23 percent Hispanic (the remainder were categorized as "other") (Sickmund et al., 2013b). Thus, blacks are overrepresented in juvenile institutions, one part of the more general problem of disproportionate minority contact.

Correctional managers contend that juvenile correctional facilities seek to serve the "best interests of the child," which means that they attempt to provide educational, therapeutic, and recreational programs staffed by concerned caregivers. Critics argue that, at best, the facilities are warehouses or holding tanks where little, if any, positive change takes place. Both past and more recent critics have contended that juvenile facilities harbor as many horror stories as they do children: tales of neglect, abuse, and even death (Human Rights Watch, 2006; Wooden, 1976).

This chapter examines various types of institutional and residential interventions with juveniles, including state training schools, youth camps, private placements, and group homes. After describing these various placements, we will examine some of the current issues about their operation, such as the determination of appropriate targets for intervention, effectiveness in reducing recidivism, and client and worker adaptations to the pressures of institutional life. The chapter concludes with information on innovative trends in this area such as deinstitutionalization and wilderness programs.

STATE TRAINING SCHOOLS

State training schools are the juvenile justice system's equivalent of the adult prison; they house those delinquents whom juvenile court judges consider unfit for probation or some other lesser punishment. Some training schools actually resemble adult prisons in terms of their architecture: high walls or fences, locked cell blocks, self-sufficiency (they have their own laundry, hospital, and maintenance facility), and solitary confinement for persistent rule breakers. Other training schools have the so-called **cottage system** of architectural design. Unfortunately, the cottage system is often a far cry from the homelike atmosphere intended by its founders. Cottages are often deteriorating dormitories with decrepit plumbing, heating, and lighting, and an accompanying host of social-cultural problems as well.

Missouri, on the other hand, has developed what many consider a model program. In fact, by emphasizing individual and group treatment in small group dormitory settings, such as a converted school building in St. Louis, the state of Missouri has been awarded an Innovations in American Government Award by Harvard University's Ash Institute (Ash Institute, 2008; McGarvey, 2005).

Training School Programs for Residents

The programming at state training schools is often a combination of academic and vocational education and **behavior modification**. Residents attend school much of the day just like their noninstitutionalized counterparts, but the school run by the prison teaches youths who are usually two to three

---

BOX 10.1 SAMPLE OF ONE TRAINING SCHOOL'S RULES

Rules

1. There will be no misuse of any property.
2. There is to be no use of vulgar or profane language.
3. There will be no gambling.
4. There will be no tampering with fire and safety equipment.
5. Students will remain in their assigned areas.
6. Students may not borrow, sell, lend, or trade their property.
7. Students are expected to always be courteous.
8. Students are expected to respect privacy and property of others.
9. Students are expected to follow all dress codes.
10. Students are expected to follow instructions of staff.

Minor Rule Violations

1. Disruptive behavior
2. Failure to follow institutional rules
3. Horseplay
4. Out of assigned area
5. Racial slurs
6. Refusal of a direct order
7. Self-mutilation
8. Sexual slurs
9. Use of obscene language

Source: Student Handbook from a Southeastern state.

---

years below their appropriate grade level in both reading and mathematics. In addition, youths in custody report spending less time in school each day than their free-world counterparts and only 51 percent of youths in custody consider their school program to be a good program (Sedlak & McPherson, 2010a). Further evidence of educational problems is the fact that more than one-half of youths in custody reported skipping classes and having been suspended from school in the year prior to entering custody, and 26 percent reported having repeated a grade (Sedlak & Bruce, 2010). (For a list of the school rules in one training school, see Box 10.1; for a typical daily schedule, see Box 10.2.)

In addition to standard academic subjects, educational programs may include life skills development, remedial reading and writing, conflict resolution skills development, computer literacy, and learning skills assessment. Additional programming may include groups on anger management and substance abuse resistance and recreation such as sports, crafts, board games, reading, and computer games (Roush & McMillen, 2000).

The behavior modification system usually involves the grading of children at one of several levels. The system includes the daily awarding of points for almost every possible action of the child's day, from getting up on time to getting to bed quietly and on time. The points earned each day can be spent on various privileges, ranging from games, television time, and telephone calls home to off-campus group outings and visits home. The higher the child's level, the more extensive the privileges available. (Box 10.3 gives an actual list of

BOX 10.2 TYPICAL WEEKDAY DAILY SCHEDULE AT A RESIDENTIAL PLACEMENT FOR DELINQUENTS

6:30 a.m.	Wake up: dress and clean room
7:00 a.m.	Calisthenics
7:30 a.m.	Hygiene (showers, etc.)
8:00 a.m.	Clean dormitories
8:30 a.m.	Breakfast
9:00 a.m.	Start school
10:30 a.m.	"Rap" half-hour
11:00 a.m.	Return to school
12:00 a.m.	Lunch
12:30 p.m.	"Rap" half-hour
1:00 p.m.	School
3:30 p.m.	Group therapy
5:00 p.m.	Dinner
5:30 p.m.	Work details (kitchen cleanup and dormitory cleanup)
6:00–7:00 p.m.	TV news
7:00–9:00 p.m.	Activities (vary by day; e.g., Values Clarification, Occupational Therapy, Recreational Therapy, etc.)
9:00 p.m.	Bedtime for Phase 1 (9:30 p.m. in the summertime)
10:00 p.m.	Bedtime for Phase 2 and above

Source: Manual from a Midwestern residential facility. Note: In this context, to "rap" is to talk freely and frankly.

opportunities for earning and spending points at a Southeastern training school.) In addition to qualifying for daily privileges, such as television, the points earned also count toward movement from one level to another with additional privilege possibilities. One training school employee characterized the point system as working both as a behavioral control device and as a device to monitor progress within the institution.

Youths in placement report watching an average of 2.9 hours of television on a typical weekday. Fifty percent of youths in residential treatment rated the school program as good and 40 percent rated the recreational program as good, but only 38 percent rated the food as good. Sixteen percent of the youths reported having been offered contraband (alcohol and other drugs, or weapons) since arrival at placement. Nearly one-third profess gang affiliation. Punishments range from removal of privileges, such as television, or being ordered

BOX 10.3 TYPICAL INSTITUTIONAL POINT SYSTEM

Responsibilities	Points	
1. Get self up on time (6:00 a.m.)	+25	−50
2. Locker neat, orderly, clean room or area with bed made	+50	−100
3. Appropriately dressed	+25	−50
4. Brush teeth and comb hair	+25	−50
5. Daily bath and use deodorant	+25	−100
6. Exercise	+25	−50
7. Acts appropriately:		
a. Breakfast	+10	−20
b. Lunch	+10	−20
c. Dinner	+10	−20
8. School (per hour)	+40	
9. Study hour or watching news (per hour)	+25	
10. Daily chores	+50	−100
11. Volunteer work (per hour) (120 maximum per day)	+60	
12. See counselor (per hour)	+25	
13. Attend group (per hour)	+50	−100
14. Attend church or Sunday school services	+25	
15. Bonus points (+100 maximum per day)		

Note: A +25 indicates that a resident can earn up to 25 points for performing the specified behavior. A −100 indicates that a resident can have as many as 100 points deducted if the behavior is not performed or not performed properly.

Spending Opportunities

1. Swimming	25 points	
2. Recreation room	25 points	
3. Parlor games (checkers, cards, etc.)	25 points	
4. Telephone calls	20 points	
5. Use of television room	25 points	
6. Play outside	25 points	
7. Group outing off campus	300 points	
8. Group outing on campus	200 points	
9. Living room	25 points	
10. Movies in dorm	100 points	
11. Home pass	350 points	

Source: Student manual from a Southeastern training school.

to do extra chores to confinement to one's room or solitary confinement (Sedlak & McPherson, 2010a).

Concern for the victim and for crime control has translated into some new programs in juvenile institutions. In California, for example, the Impact of Crime on Victims program combines an educational curriculum with presentations by victims and victims' advocates. In Texas, juvenile murderers receive group psychotherapy and role-playing sessions to help them learn responsibility for their crimes and to imagine what they put their victims through (Bilchik, 1998).

Other Placements

Traditional training schools are not the only means that states use for housing delinquents. In some years, almost 10,000 youths are held in long-term open facilities that allow greater freedom for residents within the facilities and more contacts with the community. The open facilities category of placements includes shelters, halfway houses, group homes, and a few ranches. Group homes are residential facilities for relatively small numbers of youths (perhaps one or two dozen youngsters). The residents often attend regular public schools but participate in group counseling sessions and recreational activities at the group home.

Juvenile court judges also have been known to commit juvenile delinquents to detention centers for a short period of time. Youths are placed on probation, and one condition of probation is a short stay in the local detention facility.

States also utilize private residential placements to house delinquents and some status offenders. In 2011, private facilities held almost 19,000 offenders. This was almost one-third of all juveniles in placement (Sickmund et al., 2013b). Private facilities, like state facilities, range from relatively large institutions to small group homes and even wilderness programs where juveniles camp out. Many were originally started by churches as charitable institutions but have evolved into nonsectarian operations that charge the state thousands of dollars each year for each child they handle.

Boot Camps

A continuing trend is the use of **boot camps** (also called **shock incarceration**). Boot camps are short-term (90-day/120-day/6-month) facilities that are intended to resemble basic training facilities for the military. There is considerable emphasis on discipline and physical training such as marching, running, calisthenics, and other types of conditioning. Usually a "drill instructor" is assigned to each group of offenders. Many boot camp programs also involve aftercare supervision for program graduates. Box 10.4 shows the daily schedule at one boot camp.

BOX 10.4 DAILY SCHEDULE FOR OFFENDERS IN A NEW YORK BOOT CAMP

A.M.	
5:30	Wake up and standing count
5:45–6:30	Calisthenics and drill
6:30–7:00	Run
7:00–8:00	Mandatory breakfast/cleanup
8:15	Standing count and company formation
8:30–11:55	Work/school schedules
P.M.	
12:00–12:30	Mandatory lunch and standing count
12:30–3:30	Afternoon work/school schedule
3:30–4:00	Shower
4:00–4:45	Network community meeting
4:45–5:45	Mandatory dinner, prepare for evening
6:00–9:00	School, group counseling, drug counseling, prerelease counseling, decision-making classes
8:00	Count while in programs
9:15–9:30	Squad bay, prepare for bed
9:30	Standing count, lights out

Source: Clark, Aziz, & MacKenzie (1994).

The rationale behind boot camps is multifaceted. It is claimed that boot camps can protect the public, reduce prison crowding, reduce costs, punish offenders, hold offenders accountable, deter additional crime, and rehabilitate (through counseling and education) (Cronin, 1994).

The effectiveness of boot camps for both adult and juvenile offenders is mixed. There is some indication that boot camps can reduce state correctional costs and that participants rate their experience in camp as positive, but the evidence shows that boot camps have little or no effect on recidivism (Cronin, 1994; Parent, 2003). Based on multiple studies, it is clear that boot camps do not reduce recidivism (Aos et al., 2006; Lipsey, 2009; MacKenzie & Freeland, 2012). Ironically, even though many politicians like boot camps because they appear to be "tough," it appears that the educational and rehabilitative programming is what helps the offenders.

An evaluation of three boot camps in Cleveland, Mobile, and Denver offers insights about their advantages and disadvantages. Eligible youths for these camps were youths ages 13 to 17 who had been adjudicated by the juvenile court and were awaiting disposition. Youths considered eligible could not have any history of mental illness or involvement in violent crime but were rated at "high risk" of chronic delinquency and minimal risk of escape.

The graduation rates were positive, ranging from a low of 65 percent at Denver to 87 percent at Mobile and 93 percent at Cleveland. There was significant academic progress at Cleveland and Mobile: from half to two-thirds of the youths at Cleveland improved at least one grade level in various academic skills. In Mobile about 80 percent of the youths improved at least one grade level (Peters, Thomas, & Zamberlan, 1997). A long-term follow-up of boot camp participants in California also found no impact on recidivism (Bottcher & Ezell, 2005).

The findings on recidivism, however, were discouraging. There were no significant differences in recidivism between boot camp offenders and the control group offenders at Denver or Mobile. In Cleveland, the experimental youths did worse than the controls. Moreover, at all three sites, survival times— time to the commission of a new offense—were shorter for the youths who went through the boot camps than for control cases (Peters et al., 1997).

Concerning cost-effectiveness, the costs per day of the boot camps were similar to one day of institutionalization but more expensive than a day of probation. Costs per offender were lower than controls because boot camp offenders spent less time in the boot camps. The data on annual costs per offender were: Cleveland: $14,021, compared to $25,549 for the Ohio Department of Youth Services; Denver: $8,141, versus $23,425 for a state facility; Mobile; $6,241, versus $11,616 for a state facility (Peters et al., 1997:24–25).

Peters and his colleagues conclude that boot camps are not a panacea, but they do offer some advantages:

> As an intermediate sanction, boot camps are a useful alternative for offenders for whom probation would be insufficiently punitive, yet for whom long-term incarceration would be excessive. As such, under certain conditions, boot camps can free bed space for more hardened offenders, thereby reducing the financial burden on correctional budgets (Peters et al., 1997).

Boot camps are part of a more general trend in society to "get tough" on crime. One author (Clear, 1994) calls this trend the "penal harm movement"; another team of authors calls it "the punishment paradigm" (Cullen & Wright, 1995). These authors contend that since 1980 the United States has operated on the

Inmates at the Department of Youth Services juvenile boot camp in Prattville, Alabama, wait to go outside for physical training.

CREDIT: AP Photo/Rob Carr

premise that more punishment is needed to deter crime and incapacitate offenders. Boot camps are one component of the movement, which includes increased use of prisons and jails, lengthier sentences, determinate sentences, career criminal sentencing provisions, increased use of capital punishment, and harsher community sanctions (intensive supervision, house arrest, and electronic monitoring). For juveniles the punishment paradigm has translated into greater prosecution of juveniles in adult court and blended sentences involving the adult correctional system. Thus, boot camps are not an isolated phenomenon but are part of a broader trend in criminal justice focusing on retribution, deterrence, and incapacitation.

A final word on boot camps comes from Cullen, Blevins, Trager, & Gendreau (2005), who see the boot camp phenomenon as a clear-cut example of the dangers of "commonsense thinking" in corrections and criminal justice. What they mean is that based on the commonsense thinking that military boot camps "made men out of boys" for the army, many individuals were convinced that correctional boot camps would do the same for juvenile offenders. The research on the lack of success of boot camps, however, shows the dangers of relying on such commonsense thinking: "It is dangerous precisely because it seems so correct, leaves our biases unchallenged, and requires virtually no effort to activate" (Cullen et al., 2005:66). Elsewhere, Cullen argues that boot camp interventions fail because they "are based on a limited theory of crime (rational choice) and do not target the known proximate risk factors for reoffending" (Cullen, 2007:720). An incident involving the death of a 14-year-old youth in a Florida boot camp influenced that state to close that particular camp, limit intimidation in the remaining four boot camps in the state, and rename their camps "training and respect programs" (*U.S. News and World Report*, 2006:18).

PROGRAM EFFECTIVENESS

One of the most critical issues facing residential interventions is the effectiveness issue: Do the interventions have any impact on the criminal behavior of their charges? Although much of what follows pertains most directly to publicly run placements (especially state training schools), the problems also affect private placements.

Reviews of Multiple Studies

In the last decade, a number of states have reported recidivism rates for youths released from state juvenile correctional facilities. When rearrest is the measure, on average, 70 to 80 percent of released youths recidivate in two to three years. That figure drops to 40 to 70 percent failure when the measure is reconviction or readjudication. With reincarceration as the measure, the failure rate drops to between 20 and 60 percent (Mendel, 2011). These statistics give no information on what sort or what quality of rehabilitation programs took place in these states.

While much of the **program effectiveness** research has focused on specific programs, some researchers have tried to summarize individual program research into a global conclusion on effectiveness. Most of these studies have used the technique of meta-analysis. Meta-analysis is a technique that allows researchers to re-analyze individual studies and arrive at a summary statistic of effectiveness for each individual study that can then be compared to the summary statistics from the other studies.

Lipsey (2009) conducted a meta-analysis of 548 study samples and found that there were many instances of programs that had positive effects. The most effective treatment types had an impact on recidivism that was equivalent to reducing a control group baseline recidivism rate of 50 percent to 37–39 percent. If the recidivism rate for these juveniles would have been 50 percent without treatment, the most effective programs reduced it by approximately 25 percent. Successful interventions included counseling, multiple services, skill building, and restorative programs. More specifically, cognitive–behavioral therapy, mentoring, and group counseling programs were found to be effective intervention strategies. Deterrence and discipline programs actually made recidivism worse (Lipsey, 2009). (For other reviews of effective correctional interventions, see MacKenzie, 2006; Greenwood, 2008; and see also Chapter 11.)

Because youths in custody report higher drug usage and problems related to substance abuse than youths in the general population, correctional programs need to include substance abuse counseling. For example, 84 percent of youths in custody report having used marijuana at some point in their lives compared to only 30 percent of youths in the general population. Thirty percent of youths in custody report having used cocaine or crack compared to only 6 percent of youths in the general population. More than half of the youths in custody report that they were drunk or high on drugs several times a week or more in the months prior to being taken into custody (Sedlak & McPherson, 2010b).

Conclusions about Program Effectiveness

First, it is clear that certain efforts are not effective. Ineffective programs are those with no theoretical basis or those based on deterrence and control. Second, there are effective programs. Effective programs range from so-called brand name programs such as Multisystemic Therapy (MST) to programs that incorporate proven principles and approaches such as cognitive-behavioral approaches that address transformation in thinking and attitudes (see Chapter 11 for a discussion of those principles; for reviews of effective programs, see MacKenzie, 2006; MacKenzie & Freeland, 2012; Lipsey, 2009). Third, in addition to reducing recidivism, effective programs can also reduce costs (Aos & Drake, 2013). Fourth, unfortunately, often youths simply do not receive the treatment interventions they need, whether during confinement in a residential program or on aftercare status (Schubert & Mulvey, 2014). Fifth, programs that target high-risk delinquents are more effective than those that target low-risk delinquents (for further discussion, see MacKenzie & Freeland, 2012).

Before proceeding to discuss other current issues in juvenile institutions, it is important to note that the measurement of the effectiveness of treatment programs in such settings assumes that the programs are in fact carried out as originally intended. Some call this treatment integrity. Unfortunately, that is not always true. Although Wooden did his research years ago, his observations on this matter apply today. Specifically, Wooden contended that institutions were using behavior modification techniques "to manipulate and control the child for the convenience of the custodians" (Wooden, 1976:101). In a New York facility, "education" actually meant watching movies on the VCR, especially on Friday (Singer, 1996). According to another report, in a facility referred to as "Cottage Blue," staff were chosen to put together notebooks with lesson plans for each week. These staff members simply pulled pages from the Internet and from workbooks. Notebooks were so badly photocopied that it was impossible to read them (Inderbitzin, 2006a). In what was intended to be a new model facility in Arizona, treatment quickly deteriorated. Staff appeared inconsistent and capricious in such matters as scoring youths' behaviors, staff were disrespectful and interrupted youths in group meetings, a few staff made racially insensitive remarks, and youths were shackled when transported to receive medical treatment. A key educational program did not accomplish its objectives and substance abuse treatment was not provided. In short, there was a "repeated and systematic violation of the program's fundamental principles and spirit" (Bortner & Williams, 1997:112). Therefore, impressive terms such as "behavior modification," "model program," and "education" do not necessarily translate into humane and progressive interventions. If such interventions are implemented in such negative ways, it is hardly possible to know what results an evaluation study will find or what sort of confidence can be placed in the results. It is critical to have treatment integrity in order to carry out the intervention as intended.

INSTITUTIONAL LIFE

An important concern in juvenile justice is the effect of institutional life on youths. The theory of institutional placements is that they will provide a caring and nurturing environment that will allow the delinquents to change to prosocial behavior in the institution. This will then carry over into future behavior after release. As we shall see, however, the practice often falls far short of the theoretical ideal.

Mental and Substance Disorders

Research shows that the most prevalent problem in the juvenile justice system is mental disorders. Studies show that more than two-thirds of juveniles in the juvenile justice system experience mental disorders. In fact, a study that looked at more than 1,400 youths in three states found that 70 percent of youths in the system met the criteria for at least one mental health disorder. The most common disorders found were disruptive disorders such as conduct disorders, then substance abuse disorders such as alcohol abuse, then anxiety disorders (e.g., obsessive-compulsive disorder), and then mood disorders (e.g., depression) (Shufelt & Cocozza, 2006).

High rates of disorder persist even if conduct and substance abuse disorders are removed from the equation. If conduct disorders were removed, 66 percent of youths still met the criteria for a mental health disorder. If both disorders were removed, almost one-half (45.5%) of youths still met the criteria for having a mental health disorder (Shufelt & Cocozza, 2006).

Youths themselves report problems. More than 60 percent of youths in custody report anger problems and more than 50 percent report feelings of depression and anxiety such as worry and loneliness. About one-fifth report suicidal feelings and past suicide attempts. Despite these problems, about one-fourth of youths are in facilities that do not screen every child for suicide risk and less than half are in facilities that conduct mental health evaluations or appraisals for all youths (Sedlak & McPherson, 2010b).

Girls involved in the juvenile justice system have higher rates of mental disorder than boys. More than 80 percent of girls met the criteria for at least one mental health disorder compared to 67 percent of boys. Girls were more likely to exhibit internalizing disorders such as anxiety and mood disorders (Shufelt & Cocozza, 2006).

Most importantly, 27 percent of boys and girls in the juvenile justice system had a disorder serious enough to require "significant and immediate treatment"

(Shufelt & Cocozza, 2006:4). In short, many juvenile offenders are suffering from mental health disorders, many need immediate attention, and many others need some type of treatment. On the other hand, a recent study found that a substance abuse disorder (but not mental health problems) was associated with rearrest in a sample of over 1,300 serious youthful offenders. A critical issue was whether youths had criminogenic risk factors. The authors conclude that mental health treatment services for young offenders may be justified on ethical grounds, but may not be justified on claims of a means to reduce recidivism (Schubert & Mulvey, 2014).

Victimization

As is true of adult prisons, probably the most dramatic example of a negative effect of the institution on incarcerated youths is the problem of **victimization**, which ranges from the relatively insignificant act of taking a boy's dessert to forcing a boy to perform fellatio. Such victimization knows no geographic boundaries. In one northern training school, 53 percent of the boys exploited others and 65 percent were exploited at least on occasion (Bowker, 1980). In a study of six southeastern training schools, more than one-third of the whites but less than 25 percent of the blacks reported frequent victimization. In addition, 61 percent of the whites but less than 50 percent of the blacks, reported that other residents "took advantage of them" in the institution (Bartollas & Sieverdes, 1981:538). It appears that institutionalized girls are less subject to forceful sexual attacks but that "attacks sometimes occur, usually involving adolescent inmates who have expressed an unwillingness to participate in homosexuality and who are zealous in ridiculing inmates who engage in this behavior" (Giallombardo, 1974:160). In one New York facility, some guards formed a "wake-up club" which administered regular beatings to misbehaving or disrespectful youths (Singer, 1996).

According to the most recent Survey of Youth in Residential Placement, more than one-third of youths (38%) fear attack by someone, including 25 percent who fear attack by another resident and 22 percent who fear physical attack by a staff member (Sedlak & McPherson, 2010a). It is clear that the institutionalized youngster is deprived of the security that teenagers in positive home environments take for granted.

The Prison Rape Elimination Act (PREA) of 2003 requires facilities to report statistics on sexual violence in both adult and juvenile correctional facilities to the federal Bureau of Justice Statistics. In 2006, juvenile facilities reported 2,025 allegations of sexual violence. Almost 60 percent (57%) involved charges of youth-on-youth violence and the rest (43%) were staff-on-youth incidents. More than one-third of these incidents occurred in state-operated facilities and about two-thirds took place in local or privately operated facilities. The overall rate of sexual violence was 16.8 incidents per 1,000 youths (Beck, Adams, & Guerino, 2008). It must be emphasized that these numbers are based on what officials reported to the federal government.

According to the Survey of Youth in Residential Placement, 46% of youth surveyed in 2003 reported personal property having been stolen and 10 percent reported that someone used force or the threat of force to steal their personal property. Almost 30 percent (29%) reported having been beaten up or threatened with being beaten. Four percent reported having been forced to engage in sexual activity in their current facility. About half of the perpetrators were staff and about half another resident (Sedlak, McPherson, & Basena, 2013).

In another survey, the second National Survey of Youth in Custody, 9.5 percent of youths in custody reported one or more incidents of sexual victimization by another youth or staff member in the previous year. Approximately 2.5 percent reported victimization by another resident; 7.7 percent reported victimization by a staff member. Of those reporting staff sexual misconduct, 89 percent were males who said that they had been victimized by female staff (Beck, Cantor, Hartge, & Smith, 2013).

The federal government also reports on the number of deaths of juveniles in custody. Between October 1, 2009 and September 30, 2010, 11 juveniles died in custody; five deaths were suicides, one was accidental, and one was of unknown cause. For the period 2000–2010, there was an average of 20 deaths and 8 suicides each year (Hockenberry, Sickmund, & Sladky, 2013). As the next paragraph shows, however, there are many more acts of suicidal behavior than actual suicides.

Recent lawsuits and newspaper stories offer further evidence of problems in correctional institutions. According to the Annie E. Casey Foundation, over the last 40 years, 57 lawsuits in 33 states plus the District of Columbia have resulted in court-ordered remedies for physical or sexual abuse, excessive use of isolation or restraint, or failure to provide services such as education and health care. More specifically, the Associated Press reported that 13,000 claims of abuse were reported between 2004 and 2007, and more than 1,300 of these claims had been confirmed (Mendel, 2011). Such abuses have led one authority to summarize the current status of juvenile corrections as "deeply troubled" (Krisberg, 2012:766).

A study of juvenile suicide in confinement found 110 such suicides between 1995 and 1999. Of the suicides analyzed, 42 percent occurred in training schools or secure facilities, 37 percent in detention facilities, 15 percent in residential treatment centers, and 6 percent in reception/diagnostic centers. Seventy percent of the victims had a history of suicidal behavior with prior

BOX 10.5 CONDITIONS AT COTTAGE BLUE: MUCH ADO ABOUT NOTHING OR SOMETHING?

Gresham Sykes coined the phrase "deprivations of imprisonment" to refer to the losses or the pains that prisoners suffer because of incarceration. He listed these deprivations or pains as deprivation or loss of freedom, autonomy, goods and services, security, and heterosexual sexual activity (he was writing of adult prisoners, not juveniles) (Sykes & Matza, 1957).

Inderbitzin's study of Cottage Blue points out some of the deprivations, losses, or pains of imprisonment for contemporary juvenile offenders at one facility.

The youths noted deprivation of autonomy in that they had to ask permission to shave or shower, to make a phone call, to send a letter, or to get paper and pencil. So they felt like helpless children. They also suffered loss of privacy; they complained about irritating roommates who smelled or wet the bed or were just plain annoying by talking all the time or asking questions all the time. Part of the problem was having to live with youths of different races or different ages.

Concerning what Sykes would call loss of possessions (goods and services), the youths complained of "inferior" products such as cheap soap or inferior pizza on Friday nights. More generally, they complained of bland food and too much starch in their meals. Another complaint was boredom. So they often asked staff to rent movies or video games for them or to bring them magazines and books.

What do you think of these complaints? How serious are complaints about cheap soap, bland food, or not enough video games? How much attention should staff and administrators in these facilities give to such concerns? Are these complaints trivial, or is it important to make juvenile facilities as positive as possible?

Source: Adapted by authors from Inderbitzin (2006b).

suicide attempts as the most frequent type of history. Almost all of the suicides were by hanging and more than 70 percent of the victims used their bedding materials to commit suicide. The study recommended that youth facilities have a detailed written suicide prevention policy and effective training programs (Hayes, 2004). For further discussion of living conditions in juvenile prison, see Boxes 10.5 and 10.6.

Despite apparent increases in staff victimization, a study of correctional officers in two juvenile detention facilities in Virginia showed low levels of fear of victimization and perceived risk of victimization. In addition, it did not matter whether the guard was working in a therapeutically oriented detention center or a more traditional detention center (Gordon, Moriarty, & Grant, 2003).

A study of 500 juveniles in institutions (about half were in traditional institutions such as training schools and about half were in boot camps) focused on the psychological states and perceived environments of the residents. First, juveniles perceived their institutional environments to have high levels of both activity and justice. So the juveniles felt that they had things to do and were being treated fairly but they also perceived the environments to be restrictive and controlled. Levels of anxiety and depression both decreased over time. Childhood maltreatment (e.g., coming from an abusive home) increased the levels of depression and anxiety. Therefore, it appears that

BOX 10.6 HUMAN RIGHTS WATCH: GIRLS IN CUSTODY IN NEW YORK

In addition to physical abuse, Human Rights Watch documented three cases in the previous five years of staff having sexual intercourse with girls. The investigation also found less serious sexual abuse, including verbal innuendo, male staff observing girls in different states of undress, and unwanted touching. Some staff also made humiliating comments about the past sexual history of girls or the fact that they had a sexually transmitted disease. Some also harassed girls who were lesbians or did not conform to stereotypes. Staff also used frequent strip searches and inspected girls' genitals. Human Rights Watch concluded that the facilities were often failing to serve or even protect the incarcerated girls. Staff and administrative failure to provide meaningful oversight and lack of outside monitoring meant that the girls had no way to seek assistance to stop the abuses.

What needs to be done to protect girls in custody? What must be done to protect girls from sexual abuse, in any form, by male staff members? Is it necessary to have an independent monitor or inspector visit such facilities on a periodic basis, or can facility administrators ensure the safety of the girls?

Source: Adapted by authors from Human Rights Watch (2006).

institutional staffs should target therapeutic programming for youths with histories of child maltreatment (Gover & MacKenzie, 2003).

Because some juveniles are transferred to adult court and/or subjected to blended sentencing, a number of youths under 18 are being imprisoned in adult facilities. As noted previously, there were over 2,000 such juvenile inmates in state prisons in 2010, but reportedly only 1,325 in 2012 (Carson & Golinelli, 2013) (the Bureau of Justice Statistics does not appear to be updating this statistic any longer). At midyear 2013, there were 4,600 juveniles being held in local jails including those tried or awaiting trial as adults (Minton & Golinelli, 2014). There is evidence that these young prisoners are at heightened risk of assault, including sexual assault. One reason is that young prisoners often lack the coping skills of older prisoners. One study found that juveniles in adult prisons were 21 times as likely to be assaulted or injured as teens in the juvenile system (see Benekos & Merlo, 2008). Suicide risk is also higher for such juveniles (Mumola, 2005).

Girls may face special problems. They report more mental–emotional problems and traumatic experiences than boys (Sedlak & McPherson, 2010b). For example, girls have undergone strip searches and cavity searches in the presence of male guards. This tends to reinforce the belief that they do not have control over their own bodies. Some facilities have not given girls clean clothes and clean towels and washcloths, and some have provided limited hygiene supplies. These abuses and deprivations can be especially important to adolescent girls as they make the transition to womanhood (Acoca, 1998).

A Human Rights Watch investigation found evidence of staff physical abuse of girls in two New York State residential facilities. The investigation alleged that staff frequently applied a technique called "restraint" to girls. Staff would grab a girl from behind, push her on to the floor, push her arms up behind her, and hold or handcuff her. This was used in many situations that did not involve danger or threats—such as talking back or "mouthing off" or not making one's bed correctly. Sometimes the girls got "rug burns" on their faces or all over their bodies. The report noted that excessive force may be especially harmful to girls because past experiences of physical or sexual abuse can lead to intense emotions for them (Human Rights Watch, 2006).

The same investigation also found staff sexual abuse of the residents, ranging from observation of girls in states of undress by male staff, to unwanted touching, all the way to sexual intercourse. Staff abuse also included publicly humiliating comments revealing girls' past sexual histories or their experiences of domestic abuse (Human Rights Watch, 2006).

A study of 22 girls in a large women's prison in the Midwest indicated several problem areas for juvenile girls who had been sentenced to adult women's prisons. One problem was lack of recreation time and equipment. Recreation equipment had been ordered for the under-21 unit but had not arrived by the time of the research. No girl reported having been "raped" by an older woman but some had experienced either name-calling or more serious sexual comments. Four girls indicated that they were in a sexual relationship with an older woman prisoner but that it was consensual. GED education and even college education (an associate degree program in Social Services) were available. Most programs were designed for adult women but anger management, a Girl Scouts program, and a gang awareness program were specifically targeted at the young prisoners. The authors concluded that their research "raises critical questions about the quality of care given to girls in adult prisons, particularly in programming areas such as education, life skills, recreation, and work training" (Gaarder & Belknap, 2004:75). The authors call for improvements in all these areas but they add the cautionary note that their ideal solution is to not put any girls or women in women's prisons because "[w]omen's prisons mirror the regulatory mechanisms and treatment of women in society at large, and we seek to dismantle both" (Gaarder & Belknap, 2004:77).

Schaffner (2006) did qualitative research on girls in California detention centers. She argues that many workers, including probation officers, hold inappropriate notions about contemporary girls and even subtly racist attitudes. She argues that juvenile justice needs to implement more gender-specific programming and also address the needs of girls and women who are gay or other in their sexual orientation. Kempf-Leonard (2012) echoes these concerns about lack of services and lack of gender-appropriate services for girls, and states that the time to address the needs of girls in placement is "past due" (Kempf-Leonard, 2012:515).

Racial Tension

The statistics on victimization also suggest that **racial tension** is a problem in juvenile institutions. For example, Bartollas and Sieverdes found African-American youths to be both more dominant and more aggressive than white inmates: "Twice as many black as white residents were classified by staff members as highly aggressive toward others; over 40 percent of whites were defined by staff as passive" (Bartollas & Sieverdes, 1981:538). Bartollas and Sieverdes attributed this situation to role reversal in the institution, where white Southern youths found themselves in the novel position of being in the minority. White inmates were outnumbered by black inmates (about 60% of the inmates were black) and about half of the staff members were black. The white youths felt threatened because they were in an environment very different from "the southern culture, [where] whites are used to a position of greater superiority in the free society relative to minority groups than are youth elsewhere in the United States" (Bartollas & Sieverdes, 1981:541). Even a model youth prison in Arizona experienced some racial tensions. It was reported that one staff member called a youth a "taco bender" and another staff member called an African-American youth "colored" (Bortner & Williams, 1997).

The fact that training schools continue to be places with significant proportions of several ethnic groups suggests that racial/ethnic tensions will continue into the foreseeable future. As noted at the beginning of this chapter, in 2011 minorities constituted 68 percent of the juveniles in residential placement. Blacks made up 40 percent of those in placement and Hispanics accounted for 23 percent of those in placement (Sickmund et al., 2013b). The federal government, through legislation, research, training, and technical assistance, has been attempting to reduce disproportionate minority confinement. One strategy to reduce such disproportionate confinement is using standardized risk assessments at decision points in the juvenile justice system. Such risk assessment structures decision-making and thus has the potential to reduce racial bias by court officials (Hsia, Bridges, & McHale, 2004). Another strategy is staff training to make staff more aware of possibly unconscious factors that contribute to disproportionate minority confinement (Bishop, 2005).

Inmate Misconduct

Inmate misconduct has been studied more extensively in adult prisons than in juvenile institutions. Recent research, however, has addressed this topic.

A study of 4,686 youths released from a large Southern juvenile correctional system showed that on average each delinquent committed about 53 misconduct incidents while incarcerated. This number was the same for males and females but a higher percentage of males (58%) were considered institutional dangers during their placement than females (35%). One promising note was that risk-score classification was a good predictor of misconduct, suggesting that higher risk youths can be identified and given more attention (Trulson, 2007).

A study that focused on 2,520 serious and violent male delinquents sentenced between 1987 and 2004 in a large Southern youth correctional system under a blended sentencing statute found that overall the delinquents committed an average of 7.64 major misconduct violations during their incarceration for a total of almost 19,000 major violations. On the one hand, 71 percent of the sample was involved in at least one ward assault. On the other hand, 57 percent of the sample had only between zero and four violations and most types of major misconduct were committed by less than one-third of the residents. Variables associated with misconduct included younger age at commitment, number of previous adjudications, substance abuse, gang membership, and a chaotic home environment prior to commitment (Trulson, DeLisi, Caudill, Belshaw, & Marquart, 2010).

As might be expected, research indicates that organizational structure affects the norms and behavior of youthful prisoners. In other words, "[t]he more custodial and punitive settings had inmate cultures that were more violent, more hostile, and more oppositional than those in the treatment-oriented settings" (Feld, 1981:336). This finding on the impact of organizational structure on inmate culture suggests that it is possible for administrators to reduce the negative environments in juvenile prisons by opting for an organizational structure that emphasizes treatment over custody. One specific option that administrators can take is to limit the size of juvenile residential placements. Larger populations are more susceptible to custodial climates than smaller populations. Another option is to facilitate communication between treatment staff and custodial staff so that staff members do not exacerbate potential treatment–custody conflicts.

One final note relates to the increasing presence of juveniles in adult prisons. A recent study of the misconduct of juvenile inmates in an adult prison system (Florida) shows that juveniles are overrepresented in prison misconduct and violence. For example, 16 percent of juveniles threatened a correctional officer compared to 7 percent of adult inmates; 24 percent were charged with fighting compared to 10 percent of the adult inmates; and 21 percent committed assault compared to 5 percent of the adult inmates. Juveniles committed misconduct most frequently in their second year of incarceration (Kuanliang, Sorensen, & Cunningham, 2008).

Deprivation of Heterosexual Contact

Another negative effect of institutions is that incarcerated youths are deprived of heterosexual relationships at a time when such relationships are critical in helping the teenager to define himself or herself as a mature sexual adult. Although written about incarcerated girls, Giallombardo's comments on this matter apply equally well (with the appropriate adjustments) to imprisoned boys:

> They are developing images of themselves as adult women, and they are beset with many anxieties concerning their sexuality and acceptance by males. The exclusion of males in their own age group is a source of confusion for adolescent girls . . . Their confusion is compounded by virtue of the fact that during incarceration they are socialized to view other women as legitimate sex objects (Giallombardo, 1974:244).

In response to this deprivation, many of the girls adjust by participating in kinship role systems and/or homosexual alliances. In the training schools Giallombardo (1974) studied, for example, the girls had affectionate nicknames for one another, wrote love letters to other girls, picked their own special songs, "went steady," and even got married in formal ceremonies (out of staff view). Another study reported that only about 17 percent of the institutionalized girls reported at least one homosexual experience (ranging from kissing to intimate sexual contact) but about half of the girls reported taking a "make-believe family" role (Propper, 1982). Such behavior was clearly not intended by the authorities and has been labeled a "secondary adjustment" (Goffman, 1961: 199). The problem with secondary adjustments is that they divert the youths' attention away from the main aspects of the supposedly rehabilitative programs, such as education and counseling, and direct that attention to making life within the training school as pleasant as possible.

As noted above, Schaffner (2006) claims that concern for deprivation of heterosexual contact needs updating. She argues that some girls are gay, transgender, or questioning of their sexual orientation. If juvenile correctional programs are not aware of this, they are missing a critical component of the lives of the offenders they are trying to help. She also thinks that many correctional workers are not aware of contemporary social habits, even of heterosexual girls, and thus can be overly judgmental of behaviors or remarks that should be seen as nothing out of the ordinary for the contemporary culture.

Other problems faced by incarcerated youths include loss of liberty, deprivation of personal possessions, and boredom. Particularly important in terms of possessions is the loss of clothing articles. This is important because it entails a loss of the opportunity to explore various clothing styles. According to Giallombardo (1974), such exploratory behavior is directly related to a girl's sense of identity as well as her popularity.

In one training school, youths had several complaints: loss of autonomy; they felt like helpless children who had to ask permission to shower or get paper

Joe Clark, then-director of the Essex County Juvenile Detention Center, is shown walking past a group of female inmates. In 2002, Clark was accused by the New Jersey Juvenile Justice Commission of using straitjackets to subdue unruly inmates and keeping some locked in their cells for 37 straight days with just an hour a day to exercise.

CREDIT: AP Photo/Mike Derer

and pencil; loss of privacy; they had roommates who smelled bad or talked all the time; loss of desirable possessions; low-quality soap or toothpaste; and bland food. They hoped staff would rent movies or video games for them or bring them books or magazines to break the boredom (Inderbitzin, 2006b).

An important national study on living conditions in juvenile facilities found "substantial and widespread deficiencies" in four matters: living space, security, control of suicidal behavior, and health care (Abt Associates, 1994). The most recent Survey of Youth in Residential Placement notes that 25 percent of youths report no positive feature about their facility. More specifically, 11 percent of youths in residential treatment report dirty sheets, towels, or clothes; 44 percent report insects or bugs; and 28 percent report dirty bathrooms (Sedlak & McPherson, 2010a).

Many institutions experience problems concerning crowding, safety, prevention of escapes, suicidal behavior, and health screening. That same Survey of Youth in Residential Placement report also advocated collecting systematic data on confined youths' educational and treatment needs. Further evidence of problems in juvenile institutions is the fact that over the last 40 years, 57 lawsuits in 33 states and the District of Columbia have resulted in court-sanctioned remedies for either abuse or unconstitutional conditions in juvenile facilities (Mendel, 2011). Further, a 2008 newspaper investigation found that 13,000 claims of abuse had been reported between 2004 and 2007 (Mendel, 2011). Mendel concludes that the "case against America's youth prisons and correctional training schools can be neatly summarized in six words: dangerous, ineffective, unnecessary, obsolete, wasteful, and inadequate" (Mendel, 2011:5).

NEW DIRECTIONS IN INSTITUTIONAL INTERVENTIONS

Deinstitutionalization of Status Offenders

Since the mid-1970s, there has been a movement away from placing status offenders and delinquents in the same state-operated institutions. It is felt that any mixing of status offenders and delinquents can have harmful consequences on the status offenders. In fact, much of this movement has been one of deinstitutionalization: trying to avoid any involuntary placements of status offenders (the practice of some states to deinstitutionalize delinquents as well as status offenders will be discussed in the next section). The strength of this movement is indicated by the fact that only 2,239 committed status offenders were in residential placement in 2011. This is a considerable decrease from 1985 (Sickmund et al., 2013b).

Deinstitutionalization (Closing Training Schools)

Several states, including Massachusetts, Maryland, Pennsylvania, and Utah, have decreased dramatically their use of training schools by closing some of these facilities. In Massachusetts, for example, only about 15 percent of the approximately 800 youths committed to the State Department of Youth services each year are first placed in a locked treatment program. The other 85 percent of the committed youths are placed in community-based programs such as group homes, forestry camps, day treatment programs, outreach-tracking programs, or foster care. Most of the programs have been privatized; private agencies run the programs on a contract basis with the state. In addition, the residential programs are small in size, with no more than 30 youths housed in a facility (Krisberg & Austin, 1993). What this means for most youths is that they spend only about four weeks in secure placement and then are placed in nonsecure treatment programs. In states with heavy reliance on traditional training schools, most youths spend several months in secure confinement and then are placed on aftercare (parole).

The National Council on Crime and Delinquency evaluated the Massachusetts reform and found it to be successful. Compared to other states still relying on traditional training schools, Massachusetts had similar recidivism results, and the effort was cost-effective. More specifically, depending on how long Massa-chusetts would incarcerate youths in traditional training schools, it would have to spend $10 million to $16.8 million more per year than it was spending in its deinstitutionalization mode (Krisberg, Austin, & Steele, 1989).

An evaluation of the closing of one institution in Maryland, however, found contrary results. Almost three-quarters (72%) of the youths committed to the State Department of Juvenile Services after the institution's closing were rearrested during the one-year follow-up period, whereas only about 45 percent of the youths who had been institutionalized at the training school prior to its closing were rearrested. In a two-and-one-half year follow-up period, 83 percent of the post-closing group were rearrested compared to 66 percent and 69 percent of the two groups that had been incarcerated at the training school under study. The authors concluded that "the alternatives available when Montrose [the state training school] was closed were less effective in reducing crime than institutionalization would have been" (Gottfredson & Barton, 1993:604). The authors suggest that their findings support the conclusion that "neither institutional nor community-based programs are uniformly effective or ineffective. The *design* [emphasis in original] of the intervention rather than its location appears important" (Gottfredson & Barton, 1993:605). In other words, simply closing traditional training schools is only half of the strategy. The other half is to devise effective programs for the youths that would have been committed to the training schools. It appears that Massachusetts was able to devise such effective alternative programming for its delinquent commitments. Maryland apparently did not come up with effective alternative programming so the recidivism rates for the group not sent to the training school were disappointing.

Another state that has tried to reduce its institutional population is Missouri. It closed its only training school in 1983 and has tried to keep newer institutions at 50 beds or fewer with an average population of 20 youths. To accomplish the goal of reduced placements, Missouri uses such strategies as day treatment programs and trackers. Day treatment is intended for youths released from residential confinement; it involves education, counseling, tutoring, and/or community service. Trackers are personnel, often college students completing a degree in social work or a related field, who monitor and support about 800 youths in community supervision. Trackers offer support, mentoring, and assistance. Missouri also uses nonsecure group homes. One benefit has been cost savings. In 2000, Missouri spent about $94 per every youth ages 10 to 17 in the state compared to $140 per youth in surrounding states. The state also reports that only about 11 percent of youths released from custody were rearrested or returned to juvenile custody within one year (Mendel, 2001). Mendel (2001) argues that much of the reason for the apparent success of Missouri's emphasis on community programming is the hiring of high-quality staff. At all times, youths are overseen by at least two educated and highly trained staff members compared to other states, in which less skilled officers supervise youths. An indication of the success of Missouri is the award it received for innovative programming in 2008 (Ash Institute, 2008). Unfortunately, however, there has not been a systematic evaluation of the Missouri model that might specify which aspects of the initiative are related to its apparent success (Bonnies, Johnson, Chemers, & Schuck, 2013).

As noted, the most recent census of juveniles in residential placement showed that there were 61,423 juveniles in public or private facilities in 2011, a drop of almost 30 percent since 2007 and a drop of 44 percent since 1995, when 108,746 youths were in placement. Five states—California, Illinois, Ohio, New York, and Texas—have seen dramatic decreases. For example, California has gone from more than 10,000 youths in custody in 1996 to about 1,200 in 2010. In five years, New York closed 18 facilities. In 2011, Texas closed 3 of 10 youth prisons (Bonnies et al., 2013).

Critics applaud this trend of decreasing institutional placement of youthful offenders, but some call for even greater decreases. The Annie E. Casey Foundation, for example, argues that the "case against juvenile corrections facilities is overwhelming. Countless studies and decades of experience show that these institutions are both dangerous and ineffective" (Mendel, 2011:28). Their recent report suggests more community-based interventions and placement of only very few delinquents in small facilities when considered necessary (Mendel, 2011). The National Research Council argues that "public safety can be well-served—indeed, better served—by abandoning a confinement-oriented correctional approach in favor of community-based services for the majority of juveniles who can be safely supervised in the community" (Bonnies et al., 2013).

Forces behind the decreasing numbers of youths in correctional facilities are the research and criticisms of problems in institutions, research on effective alternatives to incarceration, and calls by even conservatives to reduce spending on prisons (see, e.g., www.rightoncrime.com).

Blended Sentencing

The creation of blended sentencing allows either the juvenile court or the adult court to impose a sentence that can involve either the juvenile or the adult correctional system or both (see Chapter 8 for further discussion of blended sentencing). The adult sentence may be suspended pending either a violation or the commission of a new crime. Texas, for example, allows juveniles convicted of certain violent crimes or of habitual offender status to be sentenced to terms of up to 20 years for a second-degree felony and up to 10 years for a third-degree felony (Feld, 1998). One result of blended sentencing will be a growing number of youthful offenders in adult prisons. Note that juvenile offenders in adult prisons may still be considered "minors" for other purposes. In Wisconsin, for example, 17-year-olds in adult prisons are still subject to mandatory education and require parental consent for medical treatment (Torbet, Griffin, Hurst, & MacKenzie, 2000).

A study on victimization among youthful inmates in adult prisons is important in light of the development of blended sentencing. Maitland and Sluder interviewed 111 inmates ages 17 to 25. They found that less than 1 percent reported that they had been forced to engage in sexual activity, 3 percent had been forced to give up their money, and 5.5 percent had had a weapon used on them. Less serious victimization experiences, however, were much more frequent. Fifty-nine percent had been verbally harassed, approximately 50 percent had had their property stolen, and 38 percent had been hit, kicked, punched, or slapped. The authors concluded that "young, medium-security prison inmates are most likely to be subjected to less serious forms of victimization by peers during their terms of incarceration" (Maitland & Sluder, 1998:68). Thus, any trend toward putting delinquents in adult prisons when they are 17 or 18 can be expected to produce such victimization results for the youthful offenders so incarcerated.

Another negative aspect of blended sentencing and putting juveniles into criminal court and adult institutions is that the youths may have negative perceptions of how they were processed. In research on criminal court processing of youths in Florida, it was found that the court message to the youths was that their behavior was bad and they were bad. Prison staff also communicated a similar negative message; the youthful prisoners heard that "they were lost causes who could never redeem themselves or return to normal personhood" (Bishop, 2000:153).

Wilderness Programs

Another example of what Cullen and his colleagues (Cullen et al., 2005:66) call **commonsense corrections** is the use of various types of **wilderness programs**, ranging from relatively short stays in outdoor settings to rather long wagon train or ocean ship trips. Both private operators and some states have used this type of programming, which places delinquents in settings where they learn survival skills, limits, and self-esteem. The youths are put in natural settings where they must learn to cook, obtain shelter from the elements, tell directions (read a compass), start fires, and so forth. In the process of accomplishing such tasks, the youths learn to depend on both others and themselves. The thinking is that a successful survival experience in a natural setting will then transfer to the youth's normal environment and he or she will turn to more constructive activities than delinquency. The program, then, is based on commonsense notions (perhaps stemming from experience or familiarity with Boy Scouts and Girl Scouts) that outdoors know-how is beneficial.

A wilderness program in Georgia received attention when a 13-year-old boy died. Authorities fired several staff members due to the incident. It is alleged that camp counselors restrained the boy face down and denied him his inhaler (he was asthmatic) (Miller, 2005).

In earlier research, Lipsey and Wilson (1998) concluded that wilderness programs generally had weak effects or no effects on the recidivism rates of the youths who went through the programs compared to control groups. But in a more recent analysis of wilderness and challenge programs for juveniles, they found that programs with more intense physical activities or greater therapeutic enhancements reduced recidivism from 37 percent down to 29 percent (Wilson & Lipsey, 2003).

In conclusion, simply putting teens through a "survivor's" experience as depicted on television is not enough to reduce delinquency. It appears that the wilderness program must have a therapeutic aspect to be effective (Wilson & Lipsey, 2003). Once again, a commonsense belief such as "getting outdoors is what those kids need" is not always accurate (Cullen et al., 2005:66).

SUMMARY

This chapter has examined state and private residential placements, ranging from training schools to wilderness experience programs. An examination of the effectiveness of institutional placements indicates that many children do not really need to be in training schools. Instead, they can be handled in less restrictive settings without any increase in recidivism. This part of the chapter also examined several problematic factors in residential placements, such as victimization, racial tension, and homosexual behavior. Unfortunately, residential placements often translate into horror stories for the children rather than therapeutic havens. Sexual assaults and racial tension have been well-documented components of placements in the past, and they are unlikely to disappear completely. Because of these and related problems, states such as Massachusetts, Maryland, Pennsylvania, and Utah turned to noninstitutional approaches to delinquency, in which fewer youngsters are placed in state training schools. Blended sentencing and increased processing of juvenile offenders in adult court, however, may translate into significant numbers of youthful offenders being incarcerated in adult prisons and to youths serving longer sentences than in the past. The most extreme possibility is that states will abolish juvenile court. If that happens, probably more juveniles will go to adult prisons but some youths will continue to be housed in institutions reserved for offenders under 18. On the other hand, some states have recently returned to setting 18 as the age for youths to be processed as adults. This may indicate a trend to turn away from treating juveniles as adults in light of the psychological research on the development of adolescent brain functioning (see Chapter 14). If such a trend develops, hopefully states will continue the recent practice of sending fewer and fewer youths to institutions, given the many problems associated with institutional placement (for a thorough discussion of problems with institutions, see Mendel, 2011; or Krisberg, 2012).

Based on current practice, one prediction is that the number of juveniles in institutional confinement will continue to decrease. As noted, some call for the end of juvenile prisons or for as much reduction in confinement as possible. Hopeful predictions are that more youths will receive the interventions they need and that there will be continued efforts to make residential placements as safe as possible.

DISCUSSION QUESTIONS

1. Many are calling for harsher punishment for juvenile offenders, especially violent juvenile offenders. Do you think that persons holding that position are aware of the information on victimization in juvenile training schools (prisons)? Would knowledge of victimization risks in juvenile prisons affect calls for tougher measures for juveniles?

2. Do juveniles deserve prisons that are quite different from adult offenders? Should we continue to model juvenile prisons after schools? Should we drop any pretense of lesser punishment for juveniles and make juvenile facilities very similar to adult prisons?

3. Would you consider a career in juvenile corrections, in either public or private facilities?

4. Should corrections for juveniles go back to its roots and try to emphasize rehabilitation, or should it attempt to incorporate more punitive dimensions? What would the ideal residential program for juveniles look like? How can states prevent some of the abuses noted in this chapter, especially sexual abuse of female inmates?

5. Common sense has led to correctional efforts such as boot camps and wilderness experience programs. Evaluation research often indicates that these commonsense solutions are not all that effective. Why is common sense often a poor guide to public policy?

6. How do you envision juvenile corrections in 10 years? What will juvenile prisons look like a decade from now? Do you agree with severe critics of juvenile institutions such as the Annie E. Casey Foundation that juvenile facilities are "both dangerous and ineffective" (Mendel, 2011:28) and that placement in such institutions should be cut back as much as possible?

CHAPTER 11

Juvenile Probation and Community Corrections

WHAT YOU NEED TO KNOW

- In 2010, probation handled more than 500,000 youths who were processed in some way for delinquency or a status offense by the juvenile court.

- In juvenile court, the probation presentence investigation may be called a social history investigation or a predisposition report.

- "Aftercare" is the juvenile court term for parole.

- One current approach in juvenile community corrections is the balanced approach, which attempts to balance offender accountability, competency development, and community safety.

- Police–probation partnerships, including searches of the offender's residence, are an example of a tough approach to juvenile probation.

- Other recent approaches in juvenile probation include restorative justice, peacemaking, and community justice.

- A number of treatment interventions are effective, including cognitive-behavioral and social learning programs.

- Some current concerns about juvenile probation include the problems of goal confusion and some aspects of both restitution and community service.

- Probation managers must attempt to implement programs that are effective in a variety of ways, including reducing recidivism, meeting offender needs, and satisfying the public.

KEY TERMS

aftercare

balanced approach

community justice

community service

effectiveness

emphasis on status offenses

goal confusion

motivational interviewing

peacemaking

probation

Project HOPE

punitive directions in probation

restitution

restorative justice

social history investigation (predisposition report)

INTRODUCTION

Even before the founding of the first juvenile court in Illinois in 1899, community interventions had been a central weapon of those seeking to fight delinquency. This chapter will examine both traditional and nontraditional community interventions and focus on some of the problems with these approaches to the delinquency problem. The chapter will first describe probation and aftercare for juveniles, highlight some of the current trends in community interventions, and then look at some of the concerns in the field. One of the key issues examined in this chapter is the **effectiveness** issue: Do community interventions have any impact on recidivism? In other words, do community interventions help to reduce the number of offenses committed by the juveniles exposed to the programs, or are the programs ineffective in reducing delinquent activity?

PROBATION

Statistics demonstrate that **probation** continues to be a critical part of the juvenile justice system. In 2010 (the most recent year for which complete data are available), an estimated 260,300 youths who were adjudicated delinquent in juvenile court were placed on probation. This represents more than half (61%) of the 428,200 youths who were adjudicated delinquent. Another 75,300 youths who were not adjudicated delinquent agreed to some form of probation and another 155,500 youths who were not petitioned agreed to some form of voluntary probation. So probation handled approximately 500,000 delinquents altogether in 2010. For status offenses, 40,400 cases resulted in probation, 53 percent of all status offense cases that were adjudicated in juvenile court. So probation was the most common disposition for adjudicated status offenders (Puzzanchera & Hockenberry, 2013; see also Livsey, 2010). (Table 11.1 shows the offenses for which delinquents were placed on probation.) Thus, probation continues to be the workhorse of the juvenile court (Torbet, 1996).

Social History (Predisposition) Investigations

When a child has been adjudicated as either a delinquent or a status offender, usually a probation officer conducts a **social history investigation (predisposition report)** of the youngster and his or her family. Similar to the so-called presentence investigation report in adult courts, social history reports offer judges legal and social information. Legal information includes descriptive material about the delinquency or status offense, including the child's, the victim's, and the police officer's (if a delinquent act) version of the offense, and verified data on the child's prior contacts, if any, with the juvenile court and with the police department's juvenile bureau. Social history information

TABLE 11.1 Adjudication Offenses for Juvenile Delinquency Probationers

Adjudicated Delinquent Offender Profiles

Most Serious Offense	2000	2005	2010
Person	23%	26%	26%
Property	40	36	36
Drugs	13	13	13
Public Order	24	26	25
Total	100%	100%	100%

Adjudicated Status Offender Profiles

Most Serious Offense	1995	2005	2010
Runaway	15%	12%	10%
Truancy	37	39	37
Curfew	4	4	5
Ungovernability	16	20	17
Liquor Law	23	19	26
Miscellaneous	5	6	6
Total	100%	100%	100%

Note: Details may not add to total because of rounding.

Sources: Puzzanchera, Stahl, Finnegan, Tierney, and Snyder (2004); Puzzanchera and Sickmund (2008); Puzzanchera and Hockenberry (2013). Reprinted with permission.

includes verification of the child's age (a critical legal condition for court action) and information on the child's development, family, education, and possible problems such as alcohol or other drug abuse.

Probation officers gather such information by interviewing the youth; the youth's family, teachers, and other school personnel; the victim; and the police; and by checking various police, court, and school records. They usually collect information on previous arrests from police and court files. Likewise, they may obtain a copy of the child's cumulative school record which contains information on the child's grades, attendance, disciplinary history, and intelligence testing. If necessary, in probation departments that have the resources, the officer may also see to it that a psychologist and/or a psychiatrist examine the child for any suspected emotional problems and to determine the child's intelligence quotient (IQ) more accurately (by an individual IQ test rather than a group test). The probation officer then summarizes all of this information in a report that provides the judge with a more informed basis for the disposition decision.

WEB ACTIVITY

For the latest available statistics on juveniles and probation, go to the website of the Office of Juvenile Justice and Delinquency Prevention and search for the latest report on juvenile court statistics. Available at http://www.ojjdp. gov. For reports, click on "Publications." For statistics, go to http://www.ojjdp. gov/ojstatbb/ezajcs/

Some adult courts are now omitting all the social history information. Determinate sentencing in many jurisdictions means that only information about the current charges and the prior record of the accused pertains to sentencing.

Racial disparity can enter into probation reports. An examination of more than 200 narrative reports in a Western state indicated that probation officers were more likely to note negative personality factors in reports about black youths but were more likely to note negative environmental factors in reports about white youths. Officers were also more likely to assign a higher risk of reoffending to black youths than white youths. There were no racial differences in sentencing recommendations (Bridges & Steen, 1998). Bishop claims that this study "provides some of the most compelling evidence to date of racial stereotyping by juvenile justice officials and of the power of racial stereotypes to influence decision making" (Bishop, 2005:57).

Probation Supervision

Youths who are placed on formal probation supervision in court must follow various conditions such as reporting regularly to a probation officer, obeying the law, attending school, and remaining within the geographical jurisdiction of the court. Judges may also order specific conditions such as restitution to the victim(s) of the delinquent act or community service restitution (e.g., performing cleanup work at the local park or playground). Another special condition might be to attend counseling sessions with a social worker, psychologist, or psychiatrist, or require the parents to attend the counseling sessions. A judge might also order a short stay (about one month) in detention as a condition of probation (Schwartz, Fishman, Rawson Hatfield, Krisberg, & Eisikovits, 1987).

If a juvenile follows the conditions of the probation disposition and is adjusting favorably at home, in school, and in the community, then the probation officer can request an early discharge from supervision. If a youngster is not abiding by the conditions and is not adjusting well, then the probation officer may request that the judge order that the youth is in violation of the probation agreement. In that case, the judge can either order the probation to continue (perhaps with additional conditions such as more frequent reporting to the probation officer) or can terminate the probation and place the youth under the supervision of the state youth correctional authority for placement in a public facility or place the youth in a private residential setting.

AFTERCARE

Approximately 100,000 youths exit the juvenile justice systems every year (Nellis, 2009). Many states have aftercare or parole programs for youths released from state training schools, group homes, or forestry camp placements. **Aftercare** supervision is very similar to probation supervision. In fact, in some states, probation officers also perform aftercare supervision duties. Just as with probation, youths on aftercare status must follow specific conditions and report on a regular basis to a parole officer. If they do not, parole can be revoked and they can be sent back to an institutional placement. There are also privately operated aftercare programs that have government contracts to provide aftercare services (Dum & Fader, 2013).

As noted in Chapter 10, recidivism statistics for youths released from institutions cause concern; states are reporting that 70 to 80 percent of released youths are arrested for a new offense within two or three years (Mendel, 2011).

A Project Service Achievement Work (SAW) Program coordinator with the Mojave County (Arizona) Probation Department supervises program participants as they install a railing on a museum exhibit. The program, for 16- and 17-year-old juveniles who are on probation and have dropped out of school, puts teens to work in the community.

CREDIT: AP Photo/*Kingman Daily Miner*, Linda Stelp

A national evaluation of intensive juvenile aftercare proved disappointing. Approximately one-half of the youths were arrested for one or more new felonies and, if technical violations (breaking the rules of probation) were included about 80 percent were rearrested for something. The most disturbing conclusion was that "no statistically significant or substantive differences were seen between IAP [intensive aftercare] and control youth on almost all the recidivism measures" (Wiebush, Wagner, McNulty, Wang, & Le, 2005:80). Recidivism measures included percent arrested, number of offenses, severity and frequency of offenses, and time to first arrest. There was some minor evidence that more treatment was associated with less recidivism but this finding was significant in only one of the study sites. So even a program intended to improve post-release performance did not produce the desired results.

Studies on reentry programs and other interventions have not found a clear-cut or simple answer to what makes for successful reentry. However, the research does indicate some suggestions for success. First, mental health services can reduce recidivism. Second, mentoring is related to reduced recidivism, reductions in testing positive for drug usage, and more connections to educational and employment services and mental health treatment (Nellis, 2009).

One study of aftercare workers in a privately contracted program found that the workers were poorly paid, felt pressure to focus on paperwork, and experienced problems with clients such as clients not showing up for appointments or avoiding them. Despite these difficulties, a number of the aftercare workers tried to connect with youths and make a difference in their lives, to provide "proactive caregiving" (Dum & Fader, 2013). Another recent study found that about two-thirds (65%) of the 413 youths in the study had no aftercare services during the critical first six months after release from a juvenile residential setting (Schubert & Mulvey, 2014).

SUPERVISION AND COUNSELING

Probation and aftercare (parole) officers working with juveniles use various combinations of assistance and control (Glaser, 1964; Ward & Kupchik, 2010) to help youthful offenders avoid further trouble. Some officers act like social workers or counselors as they try to understand the youth and his or her problems and assist the youngster in gaining greater self-insight and self-esteem. Such officers also might attempt some family therapy to help parents better understand the family interaction patterns that have contributed to the child's misbehavior. Other officers assume a tougher role: a quasi-police officer who first threatens the youth with punishment and then monitors the compliance of the child to the court conditions. This "surveillance" (Studt, 1973) type of officer typically believes that deterrence and incapacitation are more important goals than rehabilitation. A side note is that most professional social workers abandoned probation work decades ago due to this conflict in the job and because of aversion to working with involuntary clients (Peters, 2011).

Whether oriented toward assistance or control, probation and parole officers tend to use one of several counseling techniques including reality therapy, client-centered (nondirective) therapy, rational emotive therapy, or behaviorism. Assistance-oriented officers utilize these counseling techniques to a greater extent than control-oriented officers but even the latter use some of the basic principles of these approaches to interview probationers and to establish some rapport (for more information on counseling techniques, see Van Voorhis, Braswell, & Lester, 2009). Both cognitive techniques (Chavaria, 1997) and behavior modification have proven effective in community interventions with juveniles (Gendreau, Cullen, & Bonta, 1994; Lipsey, 2009; MacKenzie, 2006).

Recently, attention has also been focused on offender–agent interactions in the supervision process. Experts are suggesting that motivational interviewing can be effective in probation. **Motivational interviewing** refers to "a style of communication that makes it more likely that offenders will listen, will be engaged in the process, and will be more ready to make changes" (Walters, Clark, Gingerich, & Meltzer, 2007:10).

Motivational interviewing does not mean that officers are to become therapists. It simply recognizes the important role that officers play. It is unrealistic to think that officers can simply refer youthful probationers on their caseloads to therapists or programs, or that officers can simply say, "You need to go to counselor X or program X." If the juvenile offender is not motivated to change and is not motivated to go to the counselor or the program, he or she most likely will not go and will not change. In summary, motivational interviewing recognizes that officers interact with probationers and that those interactions can be crucial in the change process (Walters et al., 2007:10).

A study in Maryland evaluated an evidence-based supervision model that included features such as motivational interviewing and other cognitive-behavioral strategies. The program reduced arrest recidivism by 42 percent and technical violations by 20 percent but had no impact on positive drug tests (Taxman, 2008). Taxman's conclusion is that this new model of community supervision, which is a shared decision-making model that involves the offender in the process of determining goals and ways to achieve those goals, can be effective in probation and parole (Taxman, 2008).

A program that provided training in evidence-based practices including service-oriented supervision and motivational interviewing to probation case managers in one state reduced recidivism on two of four measures (Young, Farrell, & Taxman, 2013). A study of probation with heavy reliance on evidence-based practices v. residential placement in Connecticut showed lower likelihood of adjudication and conviction but no significant effect on referral to court or arrest. However, another study of training of probation officers using motivational interviewing found no impact on probationers although the officers became more empathetic. The authors of that study noted that system factors such as lack of time to spend with probationers, scarce resources, and high officer turnover might work against even a positive strategy such as motivational interviewing (Walters, Vader, Nguyen, Harris, & Eells, 2010). These studies offer support for the use of evidence-based practices versus practices not supported by research and versus probation supervision that is so lax that probationers quickly learn that they can ignore the rules (Kleiman, 2011).

CURRENT TRENDS IN COMMUNITY SUPERVISION

Several developments are taking place in community corrections. Many are calling for tougher community corrections with greater attention to punishment and controlling offender risk. Other voices, however, continue to insist that probation and other community interventions need to be more than just strict punishment for crime.

The Balanced Approach

One current approach in juvenile corrections is the **balanced approach**. "This philosophy requires the system to provide balanced attention to the need for competency development, accountability, and community safety and requires efforts to restore, to the greatest extent possible, the victim and community to their precrime status" (Kurlychek et al., 1999:3). It is thought that restitution and community service send out a message that the offender is responsible for his or her crime and is being held accountable for it. It is considered important that the offender come to realize the harm he or she has caused the victim(s). As of 2004, at least 16 states had juvenile court laws with purpose clauses focusing on the balanced approach (Griffin et al., 2005; Snyder & Sickmund, 2006).

As you might guess, the balanced approach is actually a combination of traditional rehabilitation, restorative justice, and classical criminology. One example of the balanced approach is Utah's juvenile restitution program, which includes a restitution work fund. Juveniles without jobs or money can perform community service tasks and thereby earn money for their restitution orders. In Boston, Operation Night Light has police and probation officers together on street patrol checking to ensure that probationers are complying with their probation conditions. St. Louis uses deputy juvenile officers and police to make random home visits to check compliance with court-ordered curfews (Urban, St. Cyr, & Decker, 2003). A similar program in Maryland has the probation officers and police targeting selected crime "hot spots" (Kurlychek et al., 1999).

Another example is the Gang Violence Reduction Program in Chicago, which combines surveillance of violent or potentially violent gang members and the provision of services. Police and probation officers increase their supervision of target youths and provide education, employment, employment training, and some counseling. Evaluation has found decreased serious gang violence and improved perceptions among residents concerning gang crime and police effectiveness in targeting such crime (Howell & Hawkins, 1998).

Pennsylvania has attempted to implement the balanced approach. In fact, the state legislature amended the juvenile law purpose clause in 1995 to include balanced and restorative justice principles. A report on outcome measures in 12 Pennsylvania counties for calendar year 2003 provides a snapshot of what the departments have been attempting to do and what they have achieved. Related to the objective of community protection, the counties report that 87 percent of probation cases had no new offenses and 87 percent also had no serious probation violations. Under the objective of accountability, more than 100,000 hours of community service were completed with 92 percent of probationers ordered to perform community service actually completing such orders. Almost one-half million dollars of restitution was paid ($479,587); 47 percent of the amount ordered. Eighty-four percent of the probationers ordered to pay restitution paid it in full. In summary, more than 75 percent of the juveniles on probation were attending school or GED classes or were working at case closing. Almost 80 percent were closed as "successful" and only 3 percent were closed as "unsuccessful" (Griffin & Thomas, 2004).

This report on juvenile probation in Pennsylvania contrasts very favorably with a federal (GAO) report on adult probation some 20 years ago. That report noted the woeful lack of case plans and treatment objectives and unenforced probation conditions for the adult probationers under study. It was a picture of much not even being attempted. Here there is an accountant-like depiction of activity and outcomes. Reports like this can be used to show both legislators and taxpayers that probation is working—that it is accomplishing something. As one report on probation noted, "The bottom line is results" (Griffin & Torbet, 2002:134).

On the other hand, it is necessary to keep a certain caution about glowing outcome reports. A focus on outcome reporting can lead to attempts to make the statistics as positive as possible, even if those statistics hide deficiencies. Officers can be tempted to close cases as "successful" even where there is less than complete or desired success. The perfect evaluation would be a controlled or quasi-experiment in which probation is compared to a control group that gets supervision from a nonofficial agency or perhaps no supervision at all. This is especially important in analyzing juvenile probation because many of the youths are first-time offenders or less serious offenders and a good scare in court might well deter them from future delinquency.

A specific example of the need for caution is the information on community service. The report notes that in Allegheny County alone (Pittsburgh, PA), probationers completed almost 69,000 hours of community service in 2002, the equivalent of more than $350,000 in labor if the youths had been paid the minimum wage for all those hours. (They simply multiply the number of hours worked times the minimum wage to get this estimate of value.)

This estimate of value makes several critical assumptions. One is that the youths actually worked all those hours and worked them fully—not wasting time. One report suggests that even regular, paid workers waste about two hours a day at work (drinking coffee, gossiping with coworkers, surfing the Internet, etc.). A second assumption is that those hours and the work were truly necessary, not "make-work" projects that somebody devised to fill the time that the youths were supposed to serve. Did the walls the youths painted really need a fresh coat of paint, or was painting those walls a way to "keep those kids from probation busy"? Finally, the estimate of $350,000 in "free" labor does not include any accounting of how much it costs to supervise the youths;

a probation officer or someone else had to make sure the kids got to the work sites and actually did some work. So while reports such as the one from Pennsylvania are encouraging, the actual benefits may not be quite as rosy as depicted (see Box 11.1 about another issue.)

BOX 11.1 TO REGISTER OR NOT TO REGISTER: THE QUESTION OF JUVENILE SEX OFFENDERS

Tennessee does not include persons who committed sex offenses as juveniles on its public sex offender registry. This could result in a 10 percent reduction in federal funding based on provisions of the Adam Walsh Child Protection and Safety Act of 2006.

In Knoxville, Tennessee, over the course of about 10 months, a man raped three women whom he found at coin-operated laundries in the early morning hours. The man had been tried as a sex offender in juvenile court. Tennessee law did not require him to report as a sex offender.

What do you think? Should a juvenile sex offense qualify to place one on a state's sex offender registry? Or does the immaturity and impulsiveness of juveniles (recall the reasoning of the U.S. Supreme Court in the *Roper v. Simmons* case [2005]) argue against such placement?

In answering, consider that one juvenile court in Tennessee has started its own Sex Offender Management Task Force, which tries to keep juvenile sex offenders out of state custody by treating them and then reducing the charges so that the youth is not labeled a sex offender for the rest of his or her life. The child is given a complete assessment, and three treatment plans are submitted to the judge who decides which plan to use. Teens who have committed more serious or violent sex offenses are transferred to adult court. Out of a limited sample of 20 offenders, the program reports no new offenses.

Caldwell (2014) argues that sexual behavior is quite changeable in adolescents and this makes it hard to predict what an adolescent will do in the future. Juvenile sex offenders are very diverse and offend for a variety of reasons. Thus, it is extremely difficult to devise risk assessment instruments that accurately predict who will and who will not be a persistent sexual offender. Another factor is that high percentages of adolescents, especially those 16 or 17, engage in sexual intercourse. The result is that many adults have engaged in criminal sexual activity with a child! Caldwell concludes that the current research "provides no basis for believing that sex offender registration and notification laws or civil commitment policies can generally be applied to adolescents effectively" (Caldwell, 2014:82).

What do you think? Should juvenile sex offenders who are younger and commit less serious offenses be given a second chance? Should juvenile court judges have the discretion to not automatically place a juvenile on a sex offender registry, and the discretion to transfer more serious offenders to adult court? Should sex offender registry and notification laws simply be banned for adolescents?

Sources: Associated Press (2008b); Campbell (2008).

Punitive Directions in Probation

One concern about the balanced approach is whether it in fact "balances" the concerns for competency development, accountability, and community safety or simply places emphasis on accountability. If the balanced approach is not actually balanced, then it might be considered a **punitive direction in probation**. This philosophy is quite direct: the offender, even if a juvenile, deserves to be punished.

As mentioned in Chapter 7 on policing, one recent example of tough probation is police–probation partnerships, as in San Bernardino, California, where a police officer and a probation officer together make a home visit to all new juvenile probationers to explain the rules of probation and search the probationer's residence for weapons and drugs. Although the program has had some effect in reducing serious crimes in the city, one concern is mission distortion for probation—that probation officers may no longer see themselves as service providers or social workers but may instead over-identify with a law enforcement role (Worrall & Gaines, 2006). A study that interviewed probation officers working in partnerships in Washington State found that several officers desired to be more law enforcement oriented (Murphy & Lutze, 2009). However, a study in Pennsylvania found no evidence of mission distortion or role confusion (Alarid, Sims, & Ruiz, 2011).

Another recent development in this direction is Hawaii's Opportunity Probation with Enforcement (HOPE) Program for adult probationers considered to be at high risk of a probation violation. The National Institute of Justice is replicating the project in other jurisdictions. **Project HOPE** involves judicial monitoring of probation that includes frequent drug testing and swift responses to positive drug tests or missed probation appointments. The program is based on the certainty and celerity principles of deterrence theory. An evaluation found that HOPE adult probationers were 55 percent less likely to use drugs, 72 percent less likely to miss appointments and 53 percent less likely to have their probation be revoked, as compared to the control group (Hawken & Kleiman, 2009). While some advocate problem-solving courts/therapeutic jurisprudence for juveniles, Project HOPE is based on a view of offenders as mature and accountable whereas juvenile court recognizes the immaturity of youths. So it is unlikely that similar probation programs will be implemented for juveniles.

A critical question about getting tough/punitive directions is whether such tactics are effective in reducing recidivism. That issue is discussed in the next major section of this chapter. Another interesting question posed by this get-tough movement is whether it is appropriate to use supervision fees in probation. For a discussion of this issue, see Box 11.2.

Renewed Emphasis on Status Offenses

An **emphasis on status offenses** such as truancy is making a comeback in some circles. In 2010, an estimated 137,000 status offense cases were petitioned to juvenile court and about 40,400 juveniles were placed on probation for status offenses. Another 29,700 petitioned status offenders were given another sanction, such as an order to get counseling, to pay restitution or a fine, or do some sort of community service (Puzzanchera & Hockenberry, 2013). About 40 percent of the children were placed on probation due to truancy, about 26 percent for a liquor law violation, and about 27 percent for either runaway

BOX 11.2 SUPERVISION FEES: A NEW DIRECTION?

Adult courts and probation programs are turning to supervision fees to alleviate the costs of the programs. Adult probationers are charged a fee simply for being under supervision and additional fees for treatment programs such as anger management training or drug treatment. It appears that juvenile courts are following suit. A recent study of juvenile probation in Pennsylvania found that fees were imposed in 66 percent of cases and restitution was ordered in 33 percent of cases. In all, judges were ordering economic sanctions in 80 percent of cases (Haynes et al., 2014).

An important issue with such fees is that many probationers earn only minimum wage or a little above minimum wage. If fees go beyond very minimal levels, then it can become very difficult for probationers to keep up with payment schedules, and that can cause revocation to be considered. In the words of some, fees can very easily set probationers up for failure. Since juveniles are normally in school, fees would have to be set up in relation to parental earnings or be limited to juveniles old enough to work. Again, the problem is that many parents of juvenile probationers and juveniles who work earn minimum wage or a little above minimum wage. This could result in late or no fee payment and possible revocation hearings to deal with such problems. One suggestion is to use community service as a sanction, since it does not create problems for adult probationers or parents of juvenile probationers who are struggling to earn enough money to pay for necessities.

What do you think? Should parents who can afford it be required to pay supervision fees for their children on probation? Should juveniles old enough to work be charged fees? What are possible problems with such fees?

or ungovernability. Kern County, California, for example, has instituted a truancy program that uses two deputy probation officers to work with students and families. If initial efforts to resolve truancy fail, the truant youth is referred to one of the deputy probation officers who then meets with the family at least four times. The officer also makes unannounced home visits, monitors attendance, counsels the youth and his or her parents, and refers the family to appropriate service providers. Tracking continues for one year. If unsuccessful, the case is referred back to the school for possible referral to the district attorney for court action (Garry, 1996). What makes this emphasis on status offenses like truancy new is that status offenses are receiving increased attention due to research that indicates that they are risk factors for serious and violent delinquency. So there is a fear that if these troublesome behaviors are not dealt with, then there is a definite possibility of much worse behavior in the future.

Restorative Justice

Bazemore and Maloney argue that restorative justice should be the theme in a new paradigm for criminal justice, juvenile justice in general, and probation in particular. In contrast to retributive justice, which focuses on vengeance, deterrence, and punishment, restorative justice "is concerned with repairing the damage or harm done to victims and the community through a process of negotiation, mediation, victim empowerment, and reparation" (Bazemore & Maloney, 1994:28). In addition to a focus on such repair, restorative justice also emphasizes involving victims, offenders, and community members in the process and rethinking the roles of government and community in trying to achieve justice (Bazemore & Schiff, 2005; see also Bazemore, 2012). As one commentator puts it, "restorative justice is about relationships—how relationships are harmed by crime and how they can be rebuilt to promote recovery and healing for people affected by crime" (Kurki, 2000:266).

As Chapter 12 discusses restorative justice in full, we will end the discussion of restorative justice in probation at this point. We simply note that restorative justice programs can be quite positive. For example, an evaluation of the Community Justice Committee's restorative justice program in Maricopa County, Arizona, showed that youths in the program were .704 times less likely to have a petition filed against them than youths in the comparison group (Rodriguez, 2007). A program that attempted to combine the concept of graduated sanctions with restorative justice did reduce the victimization, but not the criminal activity, of the juvenile probationers, possibly due to the fact that they could not go out in the evening. The restorative justice element involved such features as ordering the youth to perform community service or writing a letter of apology if he or she violated curfew (Urban, 2008). Another impressive piece of evidence in support of restorative justice is a meta-analysis of 35 restorative justice programs that found them to be more effective than traditional programs in improving victim and offender satisfaction, increasing compliance with restitution, and reducing recidivism (Latimer, Dowden, & Muise, 2005). Finally, the Washington State Institute for Public Policy found that restorative justice programs for low-risk offenders reduced recidivism (by 8.7%) and produced cost savings of $7,000 per youth (Aos et al., 2006).

Peacemaking

Like restorative justice, **peacemaking** is a positive philosophy that seeks to go beyond simply criticizing the status quo and beyond a simple focus on recidivism reduction. Peacemaking is a perspective that supports efforts of corrections workers, whether prison counselors or probation officers, to help offenders find greater meaning in their lives. Two proponents, Bo Lozoff and Michael Braswell, contend that all great religions teach four classic virtues: honesty, courage, kindness, and a sense of humor. In this perspective, reductions in recidivism and programs like counseling or vocational training are still important but they are more external. The deeper goal is internal personal change:

> The primary goal is to help build a happier, peaceful person right there in the prison [if working with prisoners], a person whose newfound self-honesty and courage can steer him or her to adjust to the biases and shortcomings of a society which does not feel comfortable with ex-offenders (Lozoff & Braswell, 1989:2).

In a peacemaking perspective, both personal transformation and institutional change are critical but personal change is seen as the basis of social change. It is critical to begin with yourself. It is also a lifetime task that needs constant work (Braswell, Fuller, & Lozoff, 2001).

Community Justice

Another recent development in community corrections is community justice. The mission of **community justice** is to help community residents "to manage their own affairs, solve their own problems, and live together effectively and safely. This goal is best achieved by giving everyone a stake in the quality of community life" (Clear & Karp, 1998:55). To achieve this mission, community justice involves risk assessment and control of offenders, victim restoration, community contracting, and cost sharing.

Like community policing, community justice is based on the principle that the community has a responsibility to deal with offenders. The community cannot simply assume that probation officers will by themselves take care of offenders and offender problems. The community must allow the offender to make reparation to the victim and also enable the offender "to obtain the assistance, supervision, and supports (including treatment intervention programs) necessary to live in the community crime-free" (Clear & Karp, 1998:54).

Community justice is an ideal that sounds plausible and desirable. One question about community justice is just how open communities are to such an ideal. When talk radio and television commentators focus on prosecutors, judges, and even governors that they consider too soft on crime, one has to ask how much room there is for community justice programs? If a sufficient number of observers think such programs are too lenient, will the programs be given a chance to operate? Programs such as community justice inevitably have failures. Whenever you allow offenders to remain in the community, whether on probation, parole, or some new community justice initiative, a percentage will commit new crimes. If community programs are criticized for such recidivism, public outrage may well force the programs to close or to become much more restrictive in the numbers and types of offenders they serve. Public receptivity to such programs is an important issue.

Another question about community justice is one raised in the chapter on policing, namely, whether contemporary communities are cohesive enough and have enough resources to support efforts such as community policing or community justice. In other words, are communities willing to do the work required to make community justice succeed? Are people willing to get involved in programs that help victims and help offenders? Or are most people spending so much time on jobs and family that they simply do not have the time or the willingness to help make something like community justice work? As discussed earlier, Putnam (2000) noted that people are having less and less time to give to voluntary organizations such as Kiwanis and Rotary. And even if people are willing to devote time to community justice, do impoverished communities have sufficient resources to assist juvenile offenders in their midst? On the other hand, Vermont has had considerable success in attracting volunteers to serve on reparative boards in that state (Karp, Bazemore, & Chesire, 2004).

Another concern about community justice is that many of the communities with the worst crime problems are problematic communities in other ways as well. Communities with high crime rates also have low employment rates, lower rates of intact families, more problem schools, and fewer support networks. A community justice center may have many caring judges, prosecutors, and defense attorneys but if the community does not have resources, these caring justice center personnel may not be able to truly assist community residents. Clear and Karp (1998) suggest that cost savings generated by community justice programs be directed to the programs to pay their way. They contend that every person diverted from a prison sentence saves the state about $45,000 a year; such savings could be used to fund community justice. More recently, Clear (2011) calls for any savings to be returned to high-crime communities to be spent on justice reinvestment, that is, on such efforts as improving housing, education and employment in high crime areas that see high numbers of residents being sent to prison. One problem is that such apparent savings are not necessarily real; one less prisoner does not mean that the prison system can fire a guard making $45,000 a year, for example. Even if such savings did result, the state prison system does not have the legal authority to send $45,000 directly to the community justice center. Another problem is that legislators are less willing to reinvest savings in high-crime communities than to spend savings on drug treatment programs or to simply use savings to cut or stabilize taxes (for further discussion, see below).

A PBS documentary, *Red Hook Justice* (Spadola, 2004), inadvertently brought home the problem of lack of community resources. A male youth was back in court on a progress check. The judge asked him where he had looked for a summer job. The youth mentioned some fast food places he had applied to but had not heard back from. The judge then asked the youth if he had applied at Company X because X did a lot of hiring. The youth said that X went out of business some months earlier. Apart from the slight embarrassment on the judge's part for mentioning a company that was out of business, this exchange in court shows that well-intentioned judges and probation officers face a structural battle. Many jobs for teens and young adults now exist in suburban sprawl areas far removed from city districts that are the sites of community justice centers.

A Washington State Juvenile Court Administrator and probation officer hug at a Pierce County Juvenile Court facility in Tacoma, Washington. Pierce County officials say they focus on communities and work toward keeping youths out of state institutions.

CREDIT: AP Photo/Elaine Thompson

Based on restorative justice principles and on concepts about corrections of place, one California jurisdiction started an intensive probation program aimed at providing a wide range of services to both probationers and their families. The study design involved random assignment to either the experimental probation program or a control group that was regular probation (one office visit to the probation officer per month and a home visit by the officer every three months).

Evaluation results showed that program youths received significantly more services than control youths. The program youths experienced an average of 14 contacts per month whereas regular probation officers saw their clients once a month. Despite the dramatic differences in services, there were no significant differences in any of the recidivism measures, including arrest measures and incarceration (Lane, Turner, Fain, & Sehgal, 2005).

The authors give two possible reasons for the failure of this intensive program to show lower recidivism than regular probation. First, they suspect that many of the regular probationers received more services than the records show. Regular probationers were referred out to quite a few services. Second, youths in both groups were at relatively low risk whereas the effectiveness literature indicates that youths at high or medium risk should be the targets of interventions.

On the positive side, because the intensive program youths did no worse, it can be argued that this research showed that a rehabilitative model can be just as effective as a more traditional model: "programs focusing on helping offenders may be as useful as those that focus on a more punishment-oriented, surveillance approach" (Lane et al., 2005:47).

Although this project was supposed to be an implementation of some of Clear's ideas of "corrections of place" (Clear & Cadora, 2003), the evaluation did not measure efforts to affect the community such as community development and community service. It appears that what was measured were the services provided to each probationer and the recidivism of the probationers. As a result, we must caution that the final word is not regarding the effectiveness of community justice efforts.

Current Trends: What Does the Future Hold?

It is difficult to predict where community corrections will go from here. One possible path is to continue down the "get tough" road. A grim reality is that further financial cutbacks will force probation to do less and less. In adult probation, financial pressures have led to dramatic increases in the use of both fees and fines to cover the costs of probation supervision. A recent study indicated that fees were being imposed in two-thirds of juvenile probation cases (Haynes, Cares, & Ruback, 2014). Based on this development in Pennsylvania, it is possible that more and more jurisdictions pressed for revenue might consider assessing supervision fees that juveniles and parents of juveniles on probation would be forced to pay. (For more on probation fees, see Box 11.2.)

Another path is to attempt to return probation to a more traditional focus on trying to rehabilitate offenders. Other departments may seek to implement the balanced approach, restorative justice, or community justice (or some combination of such programs). An important issue in deciding on which direction to take is the effectiveness of community corrections. The next two sections will discuss some important findings from the effectiveness literature. The first section will review major findings on the effectiveness of community sanctions such as probation. The second section will review the research on effective treatments. Together these findings give some assistance in thinking about the most appropriate direction for community corrections to take.

EFFECTIVENESS OF JUVENILE PROBATION AND RELATED SANCTIONS

Although national recidivism statistics on juvenile probationers are not readily available and although the research on juvenile probation has not been as extensive as the research on adult probation, there are considerable research findings available to illuminate the effectiveness issue for juvenile probation. Based on research on both juveniles and adults, several conclusions about the effectiveness of community correctional interventions for juveniles seem sound.

One implication of the research is that simply making probation tougher does not work (Cullen, Wright, & Applegate, 1996). The cumulative research on such get-tough measures as Scared Straight programs, boot camps, and intensive supervision has demonstrated that harsher measures, without more treatment elements, do not reduce recidivism. Experimental evaluations of such programs have shown that these tough measures do not reduce recidivism (new arrests or convictions) (Cullen, 2007; MacKenzie, 2006).

Related to this is the finding that often community supervision may be no worse than incarceration—that is, at least as effective as incarceration (see Krisberg

& Howell, 1998). In fact, Lipsey and Wilson (1998) found that among programs that produced consistent evidence of positive effects for serious offenders, noninstitutional programs showed greater reductions in recidivism than institutional programs. This is important. Although offenders released to community supervision commit some new crimes, the fact that they do no worse (and may do better) than offenders sentenced to training schools and then released on traditional aftercare suggests that society can use community supervision knowing that it is not more harmful than incarceration.

Still another lesson is that intensive supervision can lead to easier detection of technical violations (Petersilia, 1997). In other words, officers are more likely to detect intensive supervision offenders violating the rules of probation such as not reporting to the probation officer, leaving the jurisdiction without permission, breaking curfew, testing positive on a urine drug test, and skipping school. This explains why intensive supervision can be ineffective if the goal is to reduce prison or training school populations. Detection of technical violations often results in revocation of probation. Then the offender is incarcerated as punishment for breaking the conditions of probation. So a sanction (such as intensive supervision) intended to reduce the number of persons being institutionalized can in fact increase the number being institutionalized. This problem can be avoided, however, if a court and correctional agency put in place a system of graduated penalties for technical violations (Altschuler, 1998). A discouraging finding is that some studies have shown that simply being on probation supervision without any officer contacts sometimes is just as effective as being on probation and being seen by an officer (National Council on Crime and Delinquency, 1987). This finding questions whether probation officers have much impact on their clients. One explanation is that perhaps officers are not doing much for their clients. Another explanation is that some offenders do not need much supervision. Perhaps being caught and being placed on probation sent a clear message to these probationers and they have learned their lesson and will not reoffend.

An encouraging finding in recent research is that intensive supervision that includes treatment components can reduce recidivism by an average of more than 20 percent, but that surveillance-only programs have no impact on recidivism (Aos et al., 2006; Petersilia, 1997). This suggests that although being tough is not enough, addressing offender needs can make a difference. Recall also that a national evaluation of intensive juvenile aftercare did not show effectiveness but that in one of the study sites treatment was associated with less recidivism (Wiebush et al., 2005 [see discussion earlier in this chapter]). Contrary to this claim, one study of aftercare with treatment did not show any effectiveness. The study, however, involved a sample of all substance-abusing offenders (Sealock, Gottfredson, & Gallagher, 1997). Because research indicates that treatment is critical, the next section will review the treatment research to show which types of treatment appear to offer promise and which seem to be ineffective.

EFFECTIVE AND INEFFECTIVE TREATMENT INTERVENTIONS WITH OFFENDERS

Although many politicians and citizens favor get-tough approaches to crime and delinquency, there is considerable consensus that correctional interventions are effective and cost-effective.

Lipsey (1999; 2009) has done extensive meta-analysis research on effective programming for juvenile offenders. Recall that meta-analysis is a research technique that studies the overall effects of interventions based on grouping together individual studies. If five studies have looked at the impact of individual counseling programs, for example, meta-analysis would convert the individual findings of each study into an overall effect size for all the studies combined. Using this technique, Lipsey has reported that, on average, counseling, skill building, and restorative interventions reduce recidivism by at least 10 percent. Specific interventions reduce recidivism by more than 20 percent. For example, cognitive–behavioral skill building programs reduce recidivism by 26 percent and mentoring programs reduce recidivism by 21 percent (Lipsey, 2009). Similarly, an evaluation of an adult probation program called "Citizenship" which incorporated the principles of effective interventions, found that it reduced recidivism by 31 percent (Pearson, McDougall, Kanaan, Bowles, & Torgerson, 2011). (For details on the recidivism reductions of various interventions for noninstitutionalized offenders, see Table 11.2. For a summary of the research findings on successful intervention principles, see Box 11.3. This is only a brief summary of the effectiveness literature, but it gives an outline of effective intervention principles.)

Greenwood and Turner (2012) argue that the most successful programs focus on family interactions, since parents are the ones supervising and training juveniles. They specifically mention Functional Family Therapy (FFT) and Multisystemic Therapy (MST), both of which address effective parenting skills. Another recommended intervention is Aggression Replacement Therapy (ART), a form of cognitive-behavioral therapy that teaches anger control and moral reasoning skills. All three have produced both recidivism reductions and cost savings. (For a complete list of both effective and ineffective interventions, see Greenwood & Turner, 2012.)

Gendreau and his colleagues have spearheaded much of the treatment research. They have concluded that there are several principles of effective interventions. First, interventions need to be intensive and behavioral. Intensive means that

TABLE 11.2 Effective Types of Intervention and Estimated Effects on Recidivism		
Intervention Philosophy (N)	Recidivism Reduction	Treatment/Control Recidivism Contrast*
Counseling Programs	13%	.43/.50
Individual Counseling (12)	5%	.48/.50
Family Counseling (29)	13%	.44/.50
Mentoring (17)	21%	.39/.50
Group Counseling (24)	22%	.39/.50
Skill Building Programs	12%	.44/.50
Social Skills (18)	13%	.43/.50
Behavioral (30)	22%	.39/.50
Cognitive–Behavioral (30)	26%	.37/.50

Numbers in parentheses represent number of studies in that category.

*Recidivism of intervention group in comparison to assumed control group recidivism of .50. For example, mentoring would produce a recidivism rate of 39 percent compared to the control group without mentoring having a recidivism rate of 50 percent (for a reduction of 22 percent).

Source: Lipsey (2009).

the intervention takes up at least 40 percent of the offender's time and goes on for three to nine months. Behavioral interventions are based on the principles of operant conditioning, especially reinforcement. Simply, there must be rewards for desirable behaviors. Some examples are token economies, modeling, and cognitive-behavioral interventions such as problem solving, reasoning, self-control, and self-instructional training. Successful programs target criminogenic needs such as antisocial attitudes, peer associations, substance-abuse problems, and self-control issues rather than noncriminogenic needs such as low self-esteem, anxiety, or depression. The responsivity principle means that attention needs to be paid to matching offenders, therapists, and programs. For example, offenders who prefer structure do better in a more structured program such as a token economy. More anxious offenders do better with therapists who show more interpersonal sensitivity. Programs need to enforce their rules in a firm but fair manner and positive reinforcers should outnumber punishers by a ratio of at least four to one. Therapists need to be sensitive and adequately trained and supervised. Relapse prevention and advocacy and brokerage with other community agencies are also necessary (Gendreau, 1996; see also Andrews, 2006).

An additional principle is attention to risk; intensive programs should target high- or medium-risk youths rather than low-risk youths and should not mix

BOX 11.3 SUMMARY OF RESEARCH FINDINGS ABOUT SUCCESSFUL CORRECTIONAL INTERVENTIONS

Research indicates that correctional interventions should:

1. Concentrate on changing negative behaviors by requiring juveniles to recognize and understand thought processes that rationalize negative behaviors.

2. Promote healthy bonds with, and respect for, prosocial members within the juvenile's family, peer, school, and community network.

3. Have a comprehensible and predictable path for client progression and movement. Each program level should be directed toward and directly related to the next step.

4. Have consistent, clear, and graduated consequences for misbehavior and recognition for positive behavior.

5. Recognize that a reasonable degree of attrition must be expected with a delinquent population.

6. Provide an assortment of highly structured programming activities, including education and/or hands-on vocational training and skill development.

7. Facilitate discussions that promote family problem solving.

8. Integrate delinquent and at-risk youths into generally prosocial groups to prevent the development of delinquent peer groups.

To update these principles, in her analysis of effective treatment interventions, Doris MacKenzie emphasizes that punishment and deterrence interventions are not effective. Individual change is critical, especially the offender's cognitive reasoning, antisocial attitudes, and attitudes toward drug use and vocational skills. Most importantly, "[t]here is sufficient evidence to reject the 'nothing works' mantra. Correctional programs do reduce recidivism. Specifically, effective programs provide human service treatment and focus on changing the individual."

Sources: Kurlychek et al. (1999); MacKenzie (2006: 334–346).

---

high- and low-risk offenders (Andrews, 2006). An encouraging note, however, is that there are effective interventions for low-risk youths. For example, a program in Michigan targeted shoplifters. Although not a serious, violent crime, shoplifting accounts for about one-quarter of all property offense petitions in juvenile court. A diversion program using probation officers incorporated such restorative justice components as community service, restitution to charities, and victim apology letters, as well as other elements. The study used random assignment and a two-year follow-up period. Ten percent of the treatment group youths had new petitions filed versus 25 percent of the control group (Kelley, Kennedy, & Homant, 2003).

One note about intervention principles is that programs or jurisdictions seeking to start effective programs have two choices. They can adopt proven programs completely. In fact, some programs are commercial or "brand name" in the sense that they are copyrighted and are for sale. Alternatively, a jurisdiction (e.g., a probation department) can review the literature and start its own program incorporating many of the principles noted above that contribute to successful programs. Greenwood (2008) calls this the choice between brand-name and generic programs. One problem is that although the programs reduce recidivism, they can be expensive. MST, for example, costs more than $7,500 per offender, but produces net benefits of $27,000 per offender

(Aos & Drake, 2013). Many probation departments simply may not have the monies to fund such a costly program, even if it has been proven to reduce recidivism and provide cost benefits in the long run. On the other hand, there are less expensive programs; or a probation department can opt for a "generic" program (for details on costs and benefits, see Aos et al., 2006; and Aos & Drake, 2013). Clear (2011) argues that if governments reduced the use of ineffective interventions such as excessive incarceration, they could use the savings to reinvest in rebuilding community resources which would prevent much crime and delinquency (see below and Chapter 14 for a further discussion of Clear's proposal).

As noted earlier, Lipsey (2009) notes that mentoring programs can reduce recidivism by as much as 21 percent (see Table 11.2). It bears emphasizing that mentoring programs will not be extremely expensive because they rely on volunteers. On the other hand, it is critical that a successful mentoring program includes such factors as establishing goals for the relationship and providing training, supervision, and support for the mentors (Rhodes, 2008). So either a probation department or a community agency will need to provide proper oversight. Moreover, additional research on mentoring is needed to clarify which aspects of mentoring make it effective (Tolan, Henry, Schoeny, & Bass, 2008).

One balancing observation is that although the research shows that interventions that use evidence-based principles and practices are effective, there is no panacea or cure-all for delinquency. For example, as Table 11.2 shows, even a 22 percent reduction in recidivism means that 39 percent of the offenders who received the effective intervention recidivated compared to a higher base of 50 percent for the control group (50 – 39 = 11; 11 percent × 2 = a 22 percent reduction). So while there is reason for optimism, proponents of correctional interventions have to remind both politicians and the public that it is erroneous to think that even effective interventions will wipe out all delinquency. The warning of Finckenauer (1982) against expecting a panacea or cure-all for crime or delinquency is as true today as it was when he first noted the "panacea phenomenon."

In summary, there are effective interventions that can reduce recidivism. Second, effective interventions are also cost-effective; they save money. Third, many get-tough or deterrent approaches are not effective. Fourth, effective interventions can reduce recidivism but they are not cure-alls or panaceas; they do not wipe out or prevent delinquency completely.

Additional Factors Related to Effectiveness

The effectiveness research is critical. It is imperative to know what works and what does not work. It is also important, however, to recall some additional factors about successful intervention with offenders.

One point to note is that often programs are simply not available for offenders. An assessment of the gap between needs and services provided in Texas found that only 57 percent of those juveniles with high mental health needs received any mental health services. Only one-third of those youths with high needs for substance abuse services received substance abuse treatment (Kelly, Macy, & Mears, 2005). A study of more than 1,300 serious youthful offenders found that many did not receive services while in placement, and only 35 percent reported receiving services during the first six months after release (Schubert & Mulvey, 2014). So although research indicates that resolving criminogenic needs such as substance-abuse problems is critical in changing offenders and reducing recidivism, the programs to change such offenders are not always readily available. Part of the problem is that the public and politicians are reluctant to increase government spending, even for worthy projects.

A second factor that probation officers need to consider is that youths on probation may have more serious or more prevalent problems than official records indicate. In a study of juvenile probationers in Southern Illinois, official records indicated that only 20 percent of the youths were truant and only 6 percent were involved in drug usage, whereas almost one-half of the youths themselves admitted to truancy and 43 percent admitted to drug usage (Cashel, 2003). This reflects the strong possibility that juvenile probationers have problems that are more extensive than officers know.

Another factor to consider is that interventions that would appear to offer benefits for offenders do not always do so. For example, many people assume that part-time employment for teens reduces their chances of committing delinquent acts. These people assume that having a job teaches important life lessons in responsibility. Some research, however, shows that employment is not always beneficial. Wright and his colleagues found that the "number of hours employed had an indirect effect in increasing delinquency across the sample" (Wright, Cullen, & Williams, 1997:215). In fact, much of the delinquency of working teens is occupationally related (Wright & Cullen, 2000). So it may not always be productive for probation officers to help teenage probationers get part-time jobs. Instead it may be productive to provide teens with "modest" cash incentives to graduate. In one study such incentives prevented approximately the same amount of crime as a three-strikes law at one-tenth the cost (Wright et al., 1997).

This issue is complex, however. Several programs for older adolescents that included an emphasis on employment or advanced skills training had very positive effects. Thus, Krisberg, Currie, Onek, and Wiebush (1995) argue that such programs are effective for older teens.

An Australian study confirmed the oft-repeated observation that workers perceive working with delinquent girls to be more difficult than working with delinquent boys. Baines and Alder interviewed youth workers in Victoria, Australia, and found that perceptions of girls were that they were "more 'devious,' 'full of bullshit,' and 'dramatic' contrasted with their understanding of young men as 'open' and 'honest' and therefore easier to engage" (Baines & Alder, 1996:481). A distressing implication of this study is that workers dislike working with girls. Thus, female offenders, who have very real and serious needs, are not getting the attention and treatment that they need. This is especially distressing given that this "may be a last chance opportunity for many of the young women who are clients of these services" (Baines & Alder, 1996:483).

Another study of officer attitudes toward girls found that many probation officers see girls as manipulative yet the officers do not take the next appropriate step. They do not try to understand if such manipulative behaviors may be a reasonable response to real problems and then seek out appropriate programs to address the girls' problems. Instead, they just write off the girls (Gaarder, Rodriguez, & Zatz, 2004).

Many also thought that alternative education programs that have distinct school schedules intended for students not doing well in traditional classrooms would be beneficial for delinquents. One meta-analysis of alternative schools found that they could have positive effects on school performance and attitude but they did not reduce delinquent behavior (Cox, Davidson, & Bynum, 1995).

Recent budgetary problems may affect probation. As jurisdictions struggle with the effects of a struggling economy on budgets, many are reconsidering how many offenders they are sending to prisons and juvenile correctional centers. One possibility is that cost concerns may influence legislators and system officials to try to utilize more cost-effective interventions. As noted above, the state of Washington has been a leader in this direction and its policy research office has studied the costs and benefits of various interventions (Aos & Drake, 2013).

As previously noted, criminologist Todd Clear (2011) has called for justice reinvestment. This means reducing spending on incarceration because it does not reduce crime and is expensive. Instead, Clear calls for redirecting the cost savings derived from less spending on prisons to investment in communities so as to prevent more crime and delinquency. Clear had a very idealistic vision of tax savings going to disadvantaged communities to improve housing, education, and employment for neighborhood residents. A recent report indicates that states have been using savings from justice reinvestment for victims' services, prison and community-based supervision, probation and parole supervision, electronic monitoring, transitional housing, and mental health and drug accountability courts, among other things. One state even raised monthly supervision fees for offenders (LaVigne, Bieler, Cramer, Ho,

Kotonias, Mayer, McClure, Pacifici, Parks, Peterson, & Samuels, 2014). Clear would definitely oppose such a fee increase, and although many of the expenditures from cost savings are positive, they do not represent the considerable investment in troubled communities that many prisoners come from and that were Clear's intended focus for investment.

CONTINUING CONCERNS IN COMMUNITY CORRECTIONS

As juvenile court and probation enter into their second century of formal existence since the historic founding of the Illinois juvenile court in 1899, several concerns continue. This section will discuss the concerns of goal confusion, restitution, and community service.

Goal Confusion

Goal confusion, also known as "mission distortion" (Worrall & Gaines, 2006), means that judges, probation and aftercare officers, probation directors, state legislators, and juvenile justice experts disagree about the purposes and objectives of juvenile court and community supervision. Part of the reason for such goal confusion is that we have conflicting images of juvenile offenders. At times we see them as "kids gone wrong"—as victims who are not completely evil. At other times we see them as "hostile predators" and "full-fledged" criminals (Morse, 1999). These conflicting images influence how we treat juveniles. Thus, what was once a rather clear institution for supplementing parental concern by means of adult advice and psychological/social work skill has become a matter of controversy. Some courts, officers, and experts still advocate a *parens patriae* and rehabilitation philosophy. In Glaser's (1964) terminology, the emphasis is on assistance to the probationer rather than on controlling the offender. As noted above, however, developments such as punitive probation, including police–probation partnerships, see the juvenile as a criminal to be patrolled and arrested rather than as a youth in need of assistance. They indicate that many no longer adhere to a pure assistance model. Moreover, advocates of restorative justice argue that it is time to go beyond the stale debates of the past and place new attention on the concerns of the victim. Proponents of the balanced approach would second that suggestion and add that community safety should also be a prime concern.

A trend that may reduce goal confusion is increasing emphasis on the use of evidence-based practices to achieve measurable outcomes. Probation, like other government agencies, is beginning to focus on practices that research evidence demonstrates are successful in achieving measurable outcomes such as reductions in drug usage and recidivism and increases in positive outcomes such as payment of restitution and fines and higher employment rates.

The federal probation system has turned to such an outcome-based focus (Alexander & Vanbenschoten, 2008), and it is likely that many local and state probation agencies will do so in the near future. In fact, a number of states now mandate that juvenile correctional services use evidence-based practices (e.g., Tennessee).

Restitution

Restitution occurs when juvenile offenders pay for all or part of the damage inflicted on crime victims or property. Restitution can take the form of either the payment of money or the performance of work (chores) for the victim. Restitution may be part of victim–offender reconciliation in which the offender and victim meet to express their concerns and feelings. In some cases probation officers or restitution officers help juveniles find jobs so they can afford to make restitution payments.

The costs of victimization show the importance of restitution to victims. For 2006, the FBI reported that the average dollar value loss per robbery was $1,268, per burglary was $1,834, and per larceny-theft (e.g., shoplifting) was $855. Even thefts of bicycles and coin-operated machines and purse snatching resulted in average losses of $263, $317, and $440, respectively (FBI, 2007).

Although restitution has many positive features, especially concern for the victim, there are some problems. Some critics think that it is unfair to law-abiding juveniles to help law-breaking youths find jobs. From this viewpoint, job assistance seems like a reward for delinquency. Second, the claims made about the amounts of money paid back to victims are often exaggerated. Victims may be told that all of their losses will be recouped but actual restitution often falls short.

A study in California found that approximately 15 percent of youths in an intensive program and control group youths completed their court-ordered restitution. For the intensive program juveniles, the mean restitution paid was $55 while the mean restitution ordered was $777; for the control group, the mean paid was $42 out of an average order of $321 (Lane et al., 2005). A review of a juvenile restitution program in Vermont showed that only about one-third of the youths were ordered to pay restitution and enforcement of all conditions (not just restitution) was a problem (Karp et al., 2004). As noted above, almost one-half million dollars of restitution was paid ($479,587) in 12 counties in Pennsylvania in 2003, 47 percent of the amount ordered (Griffin & Thomas, 2004). More positively, in 2006, in Reading, Pennsylvania, almost all of the restitution ordered for juvenile probationers ($204,720 or 94 percent of the $217,787

WEB ACTIVITY

For further details on the latest crime trends and costs (as well as additional reports), go to the FBI's Uniform Crime Reports, available at http://www.fbi.gov/stats-services/crimestats

ordered) was paid (*Reading Eagle*, 2008). Third, restitution advocates often neglect to consider all of the costs involved in administering a restitution program such as the salaries of those who oversee the program.

Some evaluation research on restitution has been promising. In one study, in two of four sites, about 10 percent fewer offenders sentenced to restitution recidivated than offenders not ordered to pay restitution (Schneider, 1986). Restitution also resulted in clear suppression effects. Those juveniles ordered to pay restitution had lower arrest rates in the year after their sentences compared to the year prior to their sentences (Schneider, 1990). A study of more than 7,000 cases handled informally and more than 6,000 cases placed on formal probation in Utah showed that "the use of restitution is associated with significant reductions in recidivism among certain juvenile offenders" (Butts & Snyder, 1992:4). In a New Hampshire program cited as a model program by the Office of Juvenile Justice and Delinquency Prevention, more than 80 percent of the offenders completed their community service and restitution obligations. The recidivism rate was below 30 percent (Allen, 1994). Recall that a meta-analysis of 35 restorative justice programs found them to be more effective in improving victim and offender satisfaction, increasing compliance with restitution, and reducing recidivism than traditional programs (Latimer et al., 2005).

Some juveniles have been unable to pay restitution because they could not find jobs or because of family circumstances. To deal with such problems, Utah established a restitution work fund that allows juveniles to work in community service projects. Victims receive restitution from the state fund. Youths have cleaned buses, removed graffiti, cleaned up parks, and worked in public libraries (Kurlychek et al., 1999).

Community Service

Community service is similar to restitution. It means that offenders perform unpaid work for government or private agencies as payment for crimes without personal victims (e.g., vandalism of public property). Community service could include cutting grass at local parks, doing volunteer work in hospitals, or painting the clubhouse of a Boys Club.

Advocates argue that community service helps delinquents realize the extent of the damage they have done and feel they have paid their debt to society. Proponents also argue that cost benefits result from the "free" labor of the youths. Critics argue that extensive use of community service could take away jobs from law-abiding citizens and that the actual cost benefits of community service are not as impressive as claimed. More specifically, critics contend that the work done is not always necessary (e.g., the clubhouse did not really need a new coat of paint) and that many of the hours of community service labor included such nonproductive activities as learning the job, work breaks, and dawdling if an adult supervisor is not in constant watch over the work. These criticisms do not mean that restitution or community service is worthless but that claims about their worth should be realistic rather than exaggerated.

As noted in the earlier discussion of restorative justice, an important question is whether the community service is simply busy work or has some relationship to the delinquent's offense. If a delinquent can see the connection between his or her community service order and the harm he or she has done, or can see that the community service is a meaningful contribution to the community, he or she is then more likely to see the importance of such service. The offender is then more likely to learn something positive from the community service assignment rather than merely see it as a boring burden to finish as quickly as possible. Community service needs to be taken seriously by both the juvenile justice system and the juvenile so that it is a teaching tool and not just something to keep a youth busy for a few hours a week.

SUMMARY

Probation is under scrutiny. One author has gone so far as to state that in the 1990s, probation faced a "crisis of legitimacy" (Corbett, 2002:175). By this, Corbett meant that in light of the alarming statistics on juvenile violence at that time, many were questioning whether probation could do anything to stem the tide. Like all government programs, probation is under pressure to show results. Two well-researched studies, one on intensive probation and one on aftercare, showed no differences in recidivism despite hopes that increased services in both programs would produce such differences. On the other hand, the research on Pennsylvania probation demonstrates that probation agencies can show that they are producing outcomes such as hours of community service, restitution dollars, and probationers who are engaged in meaningful activities such as education. More importantly, research on effective interventions (e.g., Lipsey, 2009; Greenwood & Turner, 2012) and on cost–benefit analyses of effective interventions (Aos et al., 2006; Aos & Drake, 2013) shows that probation programs and other programs that incorporate evidence-based principles and practices can both reduce recidivism and save money. As noted above and also in Chapter 12, restorative justice programs have many positive features such as paying attention to crime victims and involving the community in the justice process. Tough programs such as Boston's Operation Night Light and San Bernardino's Operation Nightlight offer statistics on homicide reduction and other street crimes that are at least compelling in a public relations sort of way, even if not scientifically compelling.

The future of probation will probably include increased reliance on the use of evidence-based practices and greater attention to cost-effectiveness. Current

> ## BOX 11.4 A CONTEMPORARY VISION STATEMENT FOR JUVENILE PROBATION
>
> We envision the role of juvenile probation as that of a catalyst for developing safe communities and healthy youth and families. We believe we can fulfill this role by:
>
> - Holding offenders accountable;
> - Building and maintaining community-based partnerships;
> - Implementing result-based and outcome-driven services and practices;
>
> - Advocating for and addressing the needs of victims, offenders, families, and communities;
> - Obtaining and sustaining sufficient resources; and
> - Promoting growth and development of all juvenile probation professionals.
>
> Source: Griffin and Torbet (2002).

problems with the economy and state budgets would seem to indicate such a direction. (See Box 11.4 for a contemporary mission statement for probation.) Although Clear (2011) has called for reducing spending on prisons so as to reinvest in communities, it is questionable that legislators will follow his advice. As we note in Chapter 14, there is "pervasive public antipathy" to helping the poor, disadvantaged, disproportionately minority youths who are often the clients of the juvenile justice system (Feld, 1999). A safer prediction is that legislators will be more willing to turn to evidence-based, cost-effective practices than to reinvest huge sums of money in low-income communities that do not receive the attention that they deserve. Although deterrence-based probation (e.g., Project HOPE) is gaining momentum in adult probation, it seems that this model is not well-suited for juveniles. It is hoped that juvenile probation will not turn to supervision fees and treatment fees to the extent that some adult probation departments have in order to raise revenues (see Human Rights Watch, 2014b). Adopting such fees in juvenile probation to the same extent would be devastating for many disadvantaged families.

A safe prediction is that juvenile corrections of the future will not be the same as they were 25 years ago. It is likely that changes will continue as society attempts to minimize youth crime.

DISCUSSION QUESTIONS

1. Many are calling for harsher punishment for juvenile offenders, especially violent juvenile offenders. Do you think that community corrections can supervise such offenders and protect the public? Will the public support community corrections for violent juvenile offenders?

2. Would you consider a career in juvenile corrections, either training schools or community corrections?

3. What measures should community corrections take to best serve juveniles? Give specific suggestions. Is there any indication that new measures can also be cost-effective?

4. Should community corrections for juveniles go back to its roots and try to emphasize rehabilitation, or should it attempt to incorporate more punitive dimensions? Do advocates of restorative justice or the balanced approach have the answer to the question of how we can make juvenile probation better? What would the ideal probation program for juveniles look like?

5. Probation is placing increasingly more emphasis on outcomes and outcomes assessment and research on effective interventions. What are the positive implications of this emphasis? Are there any possible problems with greater attention to outcomes, outcomes assessment, and effectiveness?

6. How important are considerations such as costs? Adult probation has moved to the use of fees and fines to pay for at least part of the cost of community corrections. Should juvenile probation departments start charging parents for the costs of supervising juveniles on probation?

7. Where do you envision juvenile community corrections in 10 years? What will juvenile probation and aftercare look like a decade from now?

CHAPTER 12

Restorative Justice

WHAT YOU NEED TO KNOW

- Restorative justice seeks to repair the harm done to both the victim and the community, while simultaneously changing the behavior of the offender.

- A primary argument used to explain restorative justice is the idea of reintegrative shaming which argues that shame can be used in a positive fashion to bring offenders back into society.

- Restorative justice takes four primary forms: victim–offender mediation, family group counseling, neighborhood reparative boards, and sentencing/peacemaking circles.

- Victim–offender mediation, also called victim–offender reconciliation programs, involves bringing the victim and offender together with a mediator to try to arrive at an understanding of all positions and find a solution agreeable to both parties.

- Family group/community conferencing includes involving family members, friends, and support groups with the victim and offender in trying to find a solution to the issues.

- Neighborhood reparative boards do not require victim participation and require the offender to make amends, restore the victim and community to the pre-offense state, and help the offender understand what he or she did.

- Sentencing/peacemaking circles are open to anyone in the community and are often a part of the court. The sentences can include virtually anything, including jail time.

- Evaluations of restorative justice reveal a great deal of satisfaction among participants and some reduced recidivism, although a great deal of additional research is needed.

KEY TERMS

collective efficacy

community group conferencing (CGC)

conflict resolution programs

dispute resolution

exchange theory

family group conferencing (FGC)

neighborhood reparative boards (NRBs)

peacemaking circles

peer mediation programs

reintegrative shaming

reparative justice

restorative justice

retributive justice

sentencing circles

social disorganization

victim–offender mediation (VOM)

INTRODUCTION

Bazemore and Maloney (1994) argue that restorative justice should be the theme in a new paradigm for criminal and juvenile justice in general and probation in particular (see also, Bazemore & Schiff, 2005). In contrast to the dominant theme of retributive justice, which focuses on vengeance, deterrence, and punishment, restorative justice "is concerned with repairing the damage or harm done to victims and the community through a process of negotiation, mediation, victim empowerment, and reparation" (Bazemore & Maloney, 1994:28; for a similar definition, see Ward & Langlands, 2008). As one commentator puts it, "restorative justice is about relationships—how relationships are harmed by crime and how they can be rebuilt to promote recovery and healing for people affected by crime" (Kurki, 2000:266).

This chapter examines the idea of restorative justice as a means of addressing the needs of youthful offenders, victims, and the community. Restorative justice is a major shift from existing practices. Consequently, it is important to define and discuss the philosophical and practical differences between restorative justice and most juvenile justice system activity. This chapter also examines precursors to restorative justice that attempt to shift some problems out of the formal justice system, as well as historical practices used by different cultural groups to handle social problems. These various efforts include victim–offender mediation, family-group conferencing, and circle sentencing. This chapter examines the emergence of these and other restorative justice alternatives for addressing the needs of offenders, victims, and the community.

BACKGROUND OF RESTORATIVE JUSTICE

Over the past 30 years, there has been an increasing call for programs that pay more attention to the combined needs of victims, offenders, and the community. There is a recognition that juvenile justice processing of offenders is not effective at deterring crime and reducing victimization (McLaughlin, Fergusson, Hughes, & Westmarland, 2003). Consequently, there has been a growing demand for new methods of working with offenders. These apparent competing concerns (i.e., finding an alternative to the system for some offenses, assisting the victim, intervening with offenders, and addressing community needs) suggest that any new intervention needs to serve a broader audience. The concept of restorative or **reparative justice** seeks to use interventions that return the victim and offender to their pre-offense states. For offenders, it means assuring that the action will not be repeated. For victims, this means repairing the harm done. For the community, it means returning things to their state prior to the offensive behavior.

Discussions of restorative justice often begin with a comparison between this new idea and that of retributive justice. **Retributive justice** generally focuses on

TABLE 12.1 Assumptions of Retributive and Restorative Justice	
Retributive Justice	Restorative Justice
Crime is an act against the State, a violation of a law, an abstract idea.	Crime is an act against another person or the community.
The criminal justice system controls crime.	Crime control lies primarily in the community.
Offender accountability defined as taking punishment.	Accountability defined as assuming responsibility and taking action to repair harm.
Crime is an individual act with individual responsibility.	Crime has both individual and social dimensions of responsibility.
a. Punishment is effective. Threat of punishment deters crime. b. Punishment changes behavior.	Punishment alone is not effective in changing behavior and is disruptive to community harmony and good relationships.
Victims are peripheral to the process.	Victims are central to the process of resolving crime.
The offender is defined by deficits.	The offender is defined by capacity to make reparations.
Focus on establishing blame, on guilt, on past (did he/she do it?).	Focus on problem solving, on liabilities/obligations, on future (what should be done?).
Emphasis on adversarial relationship.	Emphasis on dialogue and negotiation.
Imposition of pain to punish and deter/prevent.	Restitution as a means of restoring both parties; goal of reconciliation/restoration.
Community on sideline, represented abstractly by the state.	Community as facilitator in restorative process.
Response focused on offenders' past behavior.	Response focused on harmful consequences of offenders' behavior; emphasis on the future.
Dependence upon proxy professionals.	Direct involvement by participants.

Sources: Adapted by authors from Bazemore and Umbreit (1994); and Zehr (1990).

the lawbreaker and the imposition of sanctions for the purposes of deterrence, vengeance, and/or punishment. The formal criminal justice system operates primarily from a retributive justice approach. **Restorative justice** seeks to repair the harm that was done to both the victim and the community, while simultaneously changing the behavior of the offender. Table 12.1 contrasts some of the basic assumptions underlying both retributive and restorative justice.

A major difference between retributive and restorative justice is the role of victims and the community in addressing the harm caused by the criminal/delinquent act. Under retributive justice, a criminal act is viewed as an offense against society or the state and the victim is nothing more than a witness for the state. Zehr and Mika (2003:41) note that "crime is fundamentally a violation of people and interpersonal relationships." Restorative justice sees crime as an act against the victim and community and the focus shifts from what is best for the state to repairing the harm that has been committed against the victim and community.

This shift in focus to the victim, community, and harm done means that the typical retributive response to crime of punishment and deterrence is no longer appropriate. Instead, restorative approaches seek to repair the harm done to the victim and community (Zehr & Mika, 2003). This requires a focus on the type of harm done and the desire of the victim and community for actions such as restitution and conciliation. The victim and community must be involved in the process in order to identify the harm and the appropriate responses desired by those victimized.

The entire focus of restorative justice, however, is not on the victim and the community. There is also a belief that the offender is in need of assistance in recognizing the impact of his or her actions and identifying what needs to change in order to avoid such behavior in the future. Rather than focusing on punishment and deterrence as the major approach to dealing with the offender, restorative interventions seek to understand the causes of the behavior and eliminate those factors.

A quick review of the assumptions in Table 12.1 demonstrates the centrality of the harm done to the victim and community and the need for the entire community, including the offender and victim, to participate in repairing the harm. The community, rather than the juvenile justice system alone, should shoulder the burden of dealing with crime (Nicholl, 1999). Braithwaite (2003) points out that restorative justice seeks to restore the victims, restore harmony in society, restore social support for all parties, and restore the offenders.

WEB ACTIVITY

There are several organizations that offer information on restorative justice. Two of the leaders are the International Institute for Restorative Practices (http://www.restorativepractices.org/) and the Restorative Justice Online Blog (http://www.restorativejustice.org)

This is accomplished by bringing together a range of interested parties in a nonconfrontational setting including the victim and the offender as well as family members or friends, criminal justice system personnel, and members of the general community. The participants, as a group, seek to understand the actions that led to the criminal or antisocial behavior, reveal the feelings and concerns of all parties, negotiate or mediate a solution agreeable to everyone, and assist in implementing that solution (Bazemore & Maloney, 1994). Kurki (2000:266) notes that "restorative justice is about relationships—how relationships are harmed by crime and how they can be rebuilt to promote recovery and healing for people affected by crime."

PRECURSORS TO RESTORATIVE JUSTICE

The basic elements of restorative justice can be found throughout history. Braithwaite (1999:2) argues that: "Restorative justice has been the dominant model of criminal justice throughout most of human history for all the world's peoples." There was no formal criminal or juvenile justice system as we know it today throughout most of history. There were no authorities to turn to for help if an individual was victimized. Victims and their families were expected to take action themselves to address the problems and repair the harm from the offense. The earliest codified laws, such as the Law of Moses, the Code of Hammurabi, and Roman laws, all outlined the responsibility of individuals to deal with criminal acts committed against them. The development of formal justice systems, particularly the police and criminal courts, shifted the emphasis for taking redress from the victim to the state. It was at this point that the victim became little more than a witness for the state and the response to crime and delinquency became punishment rather than addressing the harm that was inflicted.

Many restorative justice practices being used today, however, can be traced directly to historical traditions that have survived in indigenous cultures (Weitekamp, 1999). Of particular note are the practices of the Maori in New Zealand, the Aboriginal tribes in Australia, the Inuits in Alaska, and the First Nations tribes in Canada (Crawford & Newburn, 2003). While there is some debate over the degree to which restorative justice comes directly from the traditions of these groups (see Daly, 2002), there is little doubt that the ideas underlying restorative justice are not new in the last quarter century.

In many respects, it could be argued that the very bases for the development of a juvenile court and juvenile justice system are found in restorative justice principles. The *parens patriae* philosophy of the juvenile court focuses not on the offense but the offender and the actions needed to help the youth. The emphasis was not on punishment. Rather, the emphasis was on correcting the deficiencies in the family and community in order that the youth could lead a productive life while at the same time making society safer. As seen in earlier chapters in this book, the juvenile justice system (at least according to its rhetoric) focuses on fixing problems for the offender and society.

Dispute Resolution

An immediate precursor to restorative justice is dispute resolution or dispute mediation, which can be found operating in the United States, Canada, Great

Britain, Australia, Denmark, Germany, and many other countries (Umbreit, 1997). One can trace modern dispute resolution back to the early 1970s. During this time, a number of jurisdictions started programs to divert minor disputes out of the formal court system. While many programs were adjuncts to prosecutors' offices and the judiciary, others were sponsored by outside groups or organizations. These initial programs provided an arena in which victims and offenders could meet and work out mutually agreeable solutions. The goal, of course, was to avoid going to court.

Dispute resolution is a mechanism for achieving a number of goals simultaneously. First, the parties involved in the situation work together to resolve the problem rather than having some outside authority impose a solution. Second, any dispute that reaches a settlement is one less case with which the formal justice system must contend. This alternative alleviates some congestion in the court system. Third, this informal approach empowers victims by giving them a direct voice in their own matters. Victims retain complete veto power over the final outcome. Finally, dispute resolution provides the victim with a face-to-face encounter with the offender. This meeting enables the victim to vent anger and seek understanding—something that many victims deeply desire.

The basic idea behind dispute resolution is to bring opposing parties together in an attempt to work out a mutually agreeable solution. While dispute resolution programs can vary in terms of the cases they handle or the procedures they use, they typically share five traits in common (see Table 12.2) (Garofalo & Connelly, 1980).

These programs involve a third-party mediator who monitors participant interaction, keeps the discussion focused, and makes suggestions whenever the need arises. A second characteristic is that many disputants have known each other over a period of time and typically are neighbors, friends, or family members (although store owners and customers can utilize such a program). While this familiarity can be helpful when trying to forge a compromise, it can be a challenge if the dispute is the result of a long-term, interpersonal issue or problem. Third, most programs require voluntary participation by all disputants. If either party declines to take part, the dispute moves back to the realm of more formal legal action. Fourth, the actual resolution process is very informal. Rules of evidence are not enforced and attorneys are not permitted. Instead, the process relies on discussion rather than rigid fact-finding and the mediator has a free hand to conduct each meeting as he or she sees fit. The fifth and final common aspect is that most participants are referred to the program by a member of the criminal justice system. Most often, the prosecutor has reviewed the case and decided that the interests of justice can be better served in a nontraditional manner.

TABLE 12.2 Common Traits of Dispute Resolution
• A third-party mediator is involved.
• Disputants usually know each other.
• Participation must be voluntary.
• Processes are informal.
• Disputants are usually referred to the process by someone in the criminal justice system.

Source: Compiled by authors from Garofalo and Connelly (1980).

The types of cases found in dispute resolution take a variety of forms. Interpersonal disputes between family members and friends comprise a large portion of the cases brought to mediation. Domestic disputes, harassment, neighborhood nuisances, and landlord/tenant problems make up the bulk of the disputes. Merchant/customer disputes are more evident in programs that rely heavily on prosecutors' offices for referral. Mediation with juveniles is an attempt to keep the youth out of the formal system and eliminate the negative consequences of formal processing (Veevers, 1989).

Peer Mediation

Dispute resolution in school settings often takes the form of peer mediation or conflict resolution. **Peer mediation programs** bring together disputing parties with a peer mediator to discuss the situation and attempt to resolve the dispute to the satisfaction of both parties. In many cases, there is no clear victim and offender. Instead, the two parties are involved in an argument or disagreement that, left unchecked, could escalate into a physical confrontation. The goal of the mediation is to defuse the situation before it reaches that stage and to keep it from occurring again in the future. Many schools have instituted **conflict resolution programs**. These programs may include peer mediation. The most important element of conflict resolution in schools is teaching youths alternative methods for resolving conflicts before they occur.

THE THEORETICAL BASIS OF RESTORATIVE PRACTICES

The basic argument underlying restorative justice is that reactions to crime and harmful behavior should seek to repair the harm done to the individual and society. At the same time, restorative justice should reintegrate and address the needs of the offender. Specific goals of restorative justice include making amends, building relationships, exchanging ideas, and taking ownership of community problems (Bazemore & Schiff, 2005). All of these goals rely on a number of different theories.

Reintegrative Shaming

The explanation most often proffered is Braithwaite's (1989) reintegrative shaming. **Reintegrative shaming** rests on the assumption that typical processing of offenders through the criminal justice system serves to isolate the offender and stigmatize him or her. This action marginalizes the offender (even more than he or she may already be in society). In addition, it does nothing to correct the behavior or repair the harm done to the victim. Basically, typical system processing serves only to exact a punishment (retribution) for the criminal act.

The underlying premise of Braithwaite's (1989) theory is that shame can be used in a positive fashion to bring the offender back into society. Under reintegrative shaming, the system needs to express its disapproval of the criminal activity while simultaneously forgiving the offender for the action if the offender is willing to learn from the event and make reparations to the victim and society. The key is "reintegration" rather than "stigmatization" (Braithwaite, 1989). The ability to employ reintegrative shaming effectively rests on shifting the sole focus of societal response from the offender to a shared focus on the offending behavior, social disapproval (often by family, friends, and significant others), the needs of the victim and community, and a shared response to make things better (Harris, 2003).

Exchange Theory

A second theoretical explanation involves exchange theory. **Exchange theory** proceeds from the assumption that equal reciprocity is a cornerstone of social interaction. Parties to a confrontation (such as an offense and subsequent restorative justice program) are looking to establish a balance in the relationship. The offender is expected to make amends for the harm caused in exchange for reintegration back into society (Bazemore & Schiff, 2005). Under the retributive system of justice, the offender is punished and, while this may be accepted by the victim and community as payment, the punishment can be seen as harmful in itself and not appropriate for truly repairing the harm and ensuring that the problem does not occur again. Bazemore and Schiff (2005) argue that the offender needs to actually make amends in order to be accepted back into society by the victim and the community.

Social Disorganization

A third theoretical perspective in restorative justice involves the need to develop community resources to address social problems. Many communities display a level of **social disorganization** that mitigates the ability of residents to effect change and control in the area. Restorative justice offers a mechanism to build the social capital necessary to address youthful offenders and the causes of misbehavior (Bazemore & Schiff, 2005). Bazemore and Schiff suggest the need to transform communities into active participants in controlling problem youths and socialize them into proper societal roles. Community members need to feel empowered to do something about problems, that is, they need **collective efficacy**.

It should be apparent that principles of restorative justice rest on a wide array of theories and theoretical perspectives. This is attributable to the fact that restorative justice seeks to do more than just punish offenders, assist victims, or control the community. Instead, it offers opportunities to do all of these things simultaneously as well as accomplish other related tasks.

TYPES OF RESTORATIVE JUSTICE

Restorative justice takes a variety of different forms, although they all attend to the same basic tenets. Indeed, "restorative justice" is often referred to as

A detainee in the Florida Parishes Juvenile Detention Center works in the center's garden in Goodbee, Louisiana. Juvenile detainees are experiencing restorative justice with programs that teach new skills and encourage them to give back to the community.

CREDIT: AP Photo/*Daily Star*, Kari Wheeler

"transformative justice," "social justice," "balanced and restorative justice," "peacemaking," or other terms. Braithwaite (2002) notes that many of these terms and programs have been incorporated into the more general idea of restorative justice.

The diversity in restorative programs can be seen in the extent to which they address the different goals of empowerment, restoration, reintegration, and emotional and social healing for the varied participants in the restorative process (Harris, 2003). *Empowerment* reflects the need for all interested parties to be involved in the process. This provides a sense of legitimacy for both the victim and the offender. *Restoration* simply refers to repairing the harm done to all participants. At the same time, retribution is disavowed as a legitimate response to the behavior. Restorative justice also seeks to *reintegrate* both the offender and the victim into the community without the stigma of being an offender or being different from the other community members. Finally, there is a clear need to address the *emotional harm* that accompanies the behavior. Figure 12.1 presents a graphic depiction of the types of restorative justice programs and the degree to which they can be considered fully restorative.

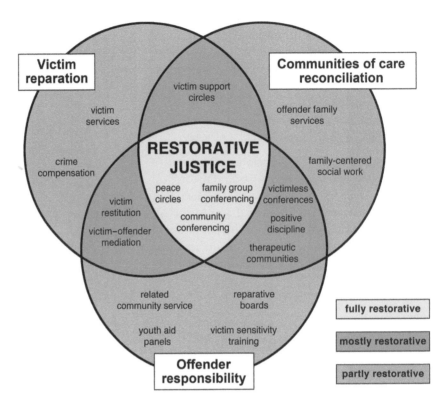

FIGURE 12.1
Restorative Practices Typology

Source: McCold and Wachtel (2002). Reprinted with permission.

The restorative practices typology shown in Figure 12.1 represents an inter-section of three different dimensions—a victim reparation orientation, an offender responsibility focus, and a communities of care domain—all indicated by a separate circle. Each of these dimensions contributes something to address crime and victimization although each dimension alone offers only limited restoration. Victim reparation, for example, focuses exclusively on the needs of the immediate crime victim, through things like victim compensation and victim services and excludes concerns for the community or the offender. Similarly, the offender responsibility dimension relates to activities that help the offender understand his or her actions and take responsibility.

The intersection of different dimensions brings about greater restoration, with the greatest level of restoration occurring where all three dimensions overlap. It is within this intersection that full restoration can take place. Typical restorative justice practices that appear in this area are victim–offender mediation, family group conferencing, and circle sentencing. Each of these is discussed below.

Bazemore and Schiff (2005) outline a variety of objectives/foci addressed by different restorative justice processes in juvenile justice. As can be seen in Table 12.3, restorative justice seeks to achieve multiple aims ranging from preventing offending to repairing harm to providing a voice for victims in the formal justice system to rehabilitating the offender. These goals can be realized through various practices and programs located throughout the community and the formal justice system.

TABLE 12.3 Restorative Justice Objectives, Practice, and Typical Location

Objective/Focus	Practice	Typical Location/Use
Prevention, peace-making, youth development, community building, family and school discipline	School and neighborhood conferencing, youth development circles, victim awareness education, restorative discipline family support and discussion groups	Schools, neighborhoods, churches, civic groups
Provide decision-making alternative to formal court or other adversarial process for determining obligations for repairing harm	Victim–offender dialogue, family group conferencing, circles, neighborhood accountability boards, other restorative conferencing approaches	Police and community diversion, court diversion, dispositional/sentencing alternatives, post-dispositional planning, residential alternative discipline, conflict resolution, post-residential reentry
Victim and community input to court or formal decision-making	Written or oral impact statement to court or other entity	Court, probation, residential facilities
Provide reparative sanctions or obligation in response to crime or harmful behavior	Restitution, restorative community service, service to victims, service for surrogate victims, payment to victim service funds	Diversion, court sanction, probation condition, residential program, reentry
Offender treatment/rehabilitation/educated	Victim impact panels, victim awareness education, drunk driving panels, community service learning projects	Probation, residential facilities, diversion program, jails
Victim services and support groups	Volunteer support groups, faith community groups, counseling	Multiple settings
Reentry	Reentry conferences, support circles, restorative community service	Neighborhood and community

Source: Bazemore and Schiff (2005:31). Reprinted with permission.

TABLE 12.4 Restorative Conferencing Models Administration and Process

	Victim–offender Mediation	Family Group Conferencing	Neighborhood Board	Peacemaking Circles
Who normally participates	Mediator, victim, offender (family)	Facilitator, offender, family (victim)	Board chair, volunteers, offender, family (victim)	Keeper, offender, volunteers, family, victim and offender supporters
Common permanent structure/staffing	Program coordinator, volunteer mediators (some paid mediators)	Program coordinator, facilitator (volunteer)	Coordinator, volunteer board chair, volunteer board members	Coordinator, volunteer circle members
Facilitation and dominant process	Victims option to speak first; mediator facilitates open-ended dialogue with minimal interference	In most programs facilitator follows script or outline in which offender speaks first, followed by victim and other participants; seeks to move process through phases	Board chair initiates member deliberation after questioning offender and parents, though some variation emerging toward circle or family group conferencing process	Keeper opens session and closes session, person allowed to speak when talking piece is passed to them. Shared leadership and consensus decision-making
Dominant philosophy	Meeting victim and offender needs, healing dialogue as transformative	Family group as essential problem-solver; respectful, normative, disapproval with support; offender empathy and emotion key	Neighborhood social support and community norm affirmation; neighborhood problem-solving focus	Collective healing; community focus; broad problem-solving, community building focus beyond individual offense

Source: Bazemore and Schiff (2005:38). Reprinted with permission.

Four broad types of restorative conferencing are victim–offender mediation, family/community group conferencing, neighborhood reparative boards, and peacemaking/sentencing circles. Each of these approach restorative justice in slightly different ways using the involvement of different individuals and groups (see Table 12.4).

Victim–Offender Mediation

Victim–offender mediation (VOM), also referred to as victim–offender reconciliation programs (VORPs), is a direct outgrowth of the early dispute resolution/dispute mediation programs of the early 1970s and is considered the oldest form of restorative justice (Umbreit, 1999). VOM is typically a post-conviction process (although pre-conviction programs exist) in which the victim and the offender are brought together to discuss a wide range of issues. A trained mediator attends these meetings.

The basic premise of VOM is that the criminal incident and its consequences are complex and beyond the ability of the criminal code to address on its own (Nicholl, 1999). Where the formal criminal justice response to crime is to simply impose the sanction outlined in the statutes, VOM seeks to deal with the needs of both the victim and the offender. The VOM meetings identify for the offender the types and level of harm suffered by the victim as a result of the crime. The victim is given the opportunity to express his or her concerns about the crime and his or her loss. At the same time, the offender is given the chance to explain why he or she committed the act and the circumstances that may underlie the behavior.

The focus of the meetings is on repairing the harm done to the victim, helping the victim heal (both physically and emotionally), restoring the community to the pre-crime state, and reintegrating the offender into society (Umbreit, Vos, Coates, & Brown, 2003). Among the potential tangible outcomes for the victim may be the offender making monetary restitution or providing service to repair the harm done. Perhaps of equal importance are changes in behavior and attitude on the part of the offender.

Participation in VOM is voluntary for the victim but the offender may be required by the court to participate as a part of the court process (Umbreit, 1999). Some programs allow for mediation to occur without the need for a face-to-face meeting between the victim and offender. This typically takes place only when the victim desires to participate in mediation but is reluctant to have any further direct contact with the offender.

Victim–offender mediation programs may be a part of the formal criminal justice system or may be run by other

WEB ACTIVITY

More information on VOM can be obtained from the Victim Offender Mediation Association at http://www.voma.org/

agencies that are not directly connected to the system. In some jurisdictions, mediation may be ordered by the judge in lieu of formal sentencing. A successful mediation may mean that the original conviction is vacated or expunged. On the other hand, the failure of an offender to participate in mediation or the failure of the mediation to reach an agreeable resolution may result in the offender being returned to the court for formal sentencing.

Family/Community Group Conferencing

Family group conferencing (FGC) finds its roots in indigenous practices of the Maori in New Zealand. Family group conferencing came to prominence in 1989 when New Zealand, responding to the increasing number of Maori youths being handled in the formal justice system, passed the Children, Young Persons and Their Families Act (Crawford & Newburn, 2003). This Act removed all youths ages 14–17 (with only a few exceptions for very serious offenders) from formal court processing and mandated that they be diverted to family group conferencing (Kurki, 2000). The basic ideas of FGC were adapted by the police in Wagga-Wagga, Australia, in 1991 into a process known as **community group conferencing (CGC)** (McCold, 2003).

The greatest difference between group conferencing and VOM is the inclusion of family members, close friends, other support groups and community members in the conferences (McCold, 2003). There is also the possibility of including criminal justice system personnel, including social workers, police officers, and an offender's attorney (Van Ness & Strong, 2015). Figure 12.2 graphically depicts the potential involvement of different individuals and support groups in FGC and CGC. The expansion of participants from the victim,

FIGURE 12.2
Parties Involved in Conferencing

Source: Nicholl (1999).

offender, and mediator in VOM to support persons and community representatives is very important in a variety of ways.

Another difference between group conferencing and VOM is the absence of a mediator who participates in constructing a resolution to the issues. Instead, group conferences are led by a trained facilitator who serves in various roles. Most often the facilitator will make contact with all participants prior to the conference. At that time he or she will explain the process and the role of each individual. The facilitator will also emphasize the fact that the conference should conclude with a resolution to which all parties are in agreement.

Once the conference begins, the facilitator leads the participants through a discussion of the facts of the case, the impact of the victimization on the parties, the feelings of all participants toward the action and the offender, and the development of a mutually agreed-upon resolution (Nicholl, 1999). The families and support persons are very important to this process. They are expected to voice their feelings about the harm that was committed, their concern for the victim of the crime, their disappointment about the offender's behavior, and their suggestions for how to resolve the problem. Of great importance is that the support groups are expected to take some responsibility in monitoring the offender and making certain that any agreements are carried out after the conference (Kurki, 2000). Conferences can be held either pretrial or post-trial, and have become a part of police and pretrial diversion programs in many countries (McGarrell et al., 2000; Moore & O'Connell, 1994).

Neighborhood Reparative Boards

Neighborhood reparative boards (NRBs), or neighborhood accountability boards, have existed since the mid-1990s and typically deal with nonviolent youthful offenders. Not unlike other restorative practices, NRBs seek to restore the victims and community to pre-offense states, require the offender to make amends, and aid the offender in understanding the impact of his or her actions on the victim and community. Cases are referred to the boards by the court, most often prior to formal adjudication.

Despite the philosophical similarities between NRBs and other types of restorative conferencing, there are several key differences in how this approach operates. First, victims are not required to participate. Indeed, many early boards frowned on victim participation (Strickland, 2004), although victim participation is becoming more common. Second, while the conferences are often open to the public, actual participation is limited by the board and who they wish to interview. The board questions the offender and examines statements made by members of the offender's family and others knowledgeable about the event (Bazemore & Umbreit, 2001). Third, the boards are composed of a small group of citizens who have been specially trained in conducting hearings and constructing appropriate sanctions.

At the conclusion of the hearing, the board undertakes private deliberations and outlines a suggested set of actions to be followed by the offender. If the offender agrees with the plan, the board oversees the offender's compliance with the terms and reports to the court about the success or failure of the offender (Bazemore & Umbreit, 2001). Typical conditions of agreements include restitution, apologies, and community service (Karp, 2001).

Peacemaking/Sentencing Circles

The final type of restorative justice program to be discussed is peacemaking/sentencing circles. **Peacemaking/sentencing circles** are based on Canadian First Nation practices and began formal operation in the early 1990s. Circles invite members from across the community to participate in determining the appropriate sanctions for offenders (Van Ness & Strong, 2015). As a sentencing procedure, this process typically occurs after a case is concluded and the offender is found guilty in court. Participants in circles typically include all of the parties found in FGCs as well as general community members who wish to be included.

Peacemaking/sentencing circles may function as either a part of the court or separate from the court. In many jurisdictions, this sentencing alternative is used at the discretion of the trial judge and is not provided for under any statutory authority (Crawford & Newburn, 2003). Most cases handled by sentencing circles involve minor offenses although some programs will consider more serious crimes (Stuart, 1996). Because of the fact that this process takes place post-conviction and can include a wide array of participants, circles normally require a great deal of preparation before they actually convene (Kurki, 2000).

A facilitator meets with all participants prior to the actual circle to explain the process, outline the facts of the case for those who have more limited knowledge, answer any questions the parties may have, and make plans for the actual meeting. In many cases the offender will work on an initial plan to address the harms he or she committed which will be presented when the circle meets (Nicholl, 1999). This extensive preparation may mean that the circle takes place months after the crime occurred and the court case concluded. Every participant in the sentencing circle is given the opportunity to speak, express his or her feelings about the crime, and offer opinions and rationales about the outcome of the discussion. The intended outcome of the circle is consensus on a plan of action that may include a wide array of activities.

Outcomes of the circles may include further meetings between the victim and offender, apologies by the offender, restitution, community service, treatment/rehabilitation programs (such as counseling or drug/alcohol treatment), and/or explicit sentencing recommendations to the trial judge (Nicholl, 1999; Van Ness

& Strong, 2015) including possible jail or prison time (Stuart, 1996). The decision of the circles is often binding on the offender (and may be specifically incorporated into the official court record). Failure to adhere to the decision may result in further criminal justice system processing or being returned to the circle (Van Ness & Strong, 2015).

Beyond the reparative plan for the offender, sentencing circles are meant to bring about action by all parties to the crime. The victim is supposed to receive support and be an active participant in healing himself or herself. The community is to identify factors that led to the offending behavior and seek ways to eliminate those problems. These causal factors may be specific to the individual offender (such as lack of parental supervision or underage alcohol use) or may be larger social-structural issues (such as unemployment or the presence of gangs in the community).

Summary

While each of the forms of restorative justice take a slightly different approach to repairing the harm done by the criminal act, all are considered restorative because they seek to address the needs of the victim, the offender, and the community. The various approaches bring about restoration by attempting to build understanding between the parties, identifying the factors at work in the behavior, and arriving at a plan of action that is agreed to by all parties. The extent to which these restorative justice programs are successful is addressed next.

THE IMPACT OF RESTORATIVE JUSTICE

Restorative justice programs are intended to have a number of different possible outcomes, including rehabilitating the offender and repairing the harm done to the victim. Assessing the impact of the interventions, however, is more difficult to do. Many evaluations focus on victim and offender satisfaction with the process and the level of compliance or completion of the agreed-upon settlement. Less common are analyses of the impact of the programs on subsequent offending by the offender.

Satisfaction, Fairness, and Compliance

Assessments of the impact of restorative justice have most often relied on outcomes such as victim satisfaction, feelings of fairness by victims, and compliance with the agreements. With very few exceptions, participants express satisfaction with the restorative process in which they have participated (Braithwaite, 1999). This is true of VOM, FGC, and circle sentencing. Evaluations of VOM typically reveal that between 75 and 100 percent of the participants express satisfaction with the mediation (Kurki, 2000). Similarly high levels of satisfaction arise from FGCs (Bazemore & Umbreit, 2001; Moore & O'Connell, 1994; Umbreit et al., 2003). The level of satisfaction is also reflected in feelings by participants that the process is fair (McCold, 2003; McGarrell et al., 2000; Umbreit, 1999; Umbreit & Coates, 1992; Umbreit et al., 2003). McCold and Wachtel (2002), rating restorative justice programs according to the degree to which they were fully restorative, mostly restorative, or not restorative, find that participants in fully restorative programs report higher levels of satisfaction and perceived fairness, followed by those in mostly restorative programs. Individuals from programs rated as not restorative report the lowest levels of satisfaction and fairness (McCold & Wachtel, 2002). These results contrast greatly with those found in analyses of formal criminal justice system processing in which victims and offenders report lower satisfaction and feelings of fairness.

The success of restorative justice programs is also measured in terms of the ability of the meetings to achieve consensus on a solution and whether the parties carry through with the agreement. Again, there is evidence that most meetings culminate in an agreement and most parties comply with the settlement (Braithwaite, 1999; Kurki, 2000; Schiff, 1999; Umbreit & Coates, 1992). Restitution is a common component of many agreements and evaluations reveal that 90 percent or more of the offenders in FGC comply with the ordered restitution (Wachtel, 1995). McGarrell et al. (2000) note that participants in a conferencing program completed the program at a significantly higher rate than normal diversion clients.

This information on satisfaction and compliance must be tempered somewhat by the fact that participation in the programs is voluntary. The fact that a program is voluntary may mean that only those individuals who are more amenable to the process to begin with are included in the programs. There may be a built-in bias in favor of positive results. Umbreit et al. (2003), for example, point out that only 40 to 60 percent of the victims and offenders who are asked to participate in VOM agree to do so. McCold and Wachtel (1998) report that almost 60 percent of the cases never materialize due to a refusal to participate. Similarly, an analysis of youth conferencing panels in England and Wales finds that only 20 percent of the victims participate (Crawford & Newburn, 2003). There is no way of knowing if positive results are actually a function of the willingness to participate and effect change rather than of the program itself.

Recidivism

Reducing reoffending is an important restorative goal, particularly in a discussion of juvenile justice. It appears that earlier studies of recidivism did not show consistent reductions in recidivism but that more recent studies have shown recidivism reductions (Rodriguez, 2007). In fact, a meta-analysis of 35 restorative justice programs found that two-thirds of the effect sizes showed such reduction in recidivism. The restorative justice programs also resulted in higher victim satisfaction and that offenders were more likely to comply with restitution orders (Latimer et al., 2005).

Most evaluations of recidivism have appeared in relation to VOM programs. In an early evaluation, Umbreit and Coates (1992) uncovered significantly less recidivism on behalf of the youthful VOM sample. Umbreit, Coates, and Vos (2001) provide evidence that youths completing VOM projects in two Oregon counties reduced their offending by at least 68 percent in the year after program participation compared to the year before the intervention. Nugent, Umbreit, Wiinamaki, and Paddock (1999) note that both the level of reoffending and the seriousness of subsequent offenses is lower for youths who enter and complete VOM programs.

Positive results also appear in numerous evaluations of group conferencing. In their analysis of restorative justice conferences for youths in Indianapolis, McGarrell et al. (2000) report a 40 percent reduction in recidivism for the program youths compared to those undergoing normal system processing. Bonta, Wallace-Capretta, Rooney, and McAnoy (2002) report that youths in conferencing recidivate less than those in traditional processing particularly when subjects are matched on risk. McGarrell and Hipple (2007), as well as deBeus and Rodriguez (2007), find that restorative justice program participants are less likely to reoffend than other youths.

Daly (2002), examining juvenile conferencing in South Australia, finds significantly less recidivism by participants in the conferences. This is particularly true for conferences that are rated as highly restorative. Similarly, Hayes and Daly (2004) uncover reduced recidivism levels after conferencing. The results are strongest for first-time offenders who are participating in the programs. The results also vary by other characteristics of the offenders, suggesting that conferencing is not equally effective with all individuals and cases (Hayes & Daly, 2004). Hayes and Daly (2004) note that reductions in recidivism are strongly related to the ability of a conference to achieve a genuine consensus on a plan of action.

Rodriguez (2005) reports reduced recidivism from FGC, particularly for older offenders and cases involving property crimes. An evaluation of FGC in Indianapolis showed a nonsignificant difference in prevalence (only 48% of the FGC group failed compared to 54% of the control group, but this was not statistically significant) but a longer survival time (more time crime free) and a reduction in incidence (the average number of arrests) for the FGC group. Jeong, McGarrell, and Hipple (2012) report that graduates of group conferencing exhibit lower recidivism as long as 12 years post intervention although the statistical significance of the results wanes over time. Calhoun and Pelech (2010) note that the Calgary (Canada) Community Conferencing program (a mediation and dialogue model) was effective in producing positive intermediate outcomes such as helping the offender assume more account-ability and repairing the relationship between the offender and the victim. Bergseth and Bouffard (2012) note that youths participating in restorative justice stay offense free longer than other youths and this result holds more for younger youths, males and first-time offenders. Finally, a meta-analysis of 35 restorative justice programs (27 victim–offender mediation programs and 8 conferencing programs) reported that the restorative programs were more effective in reducing recidivism than traditional criminal justice programs (Latimer et al., 2005).

In summary, positive results on recidivism appear in several analyses. There is still room for additional research. This is especially true for group conferencing and peacemaking/sentencing circle programs, which have not undergone as extensive evaluations as VOM. There remains a need to identify and understand the conditions under which different restorative justice programs work and do not work (Braithwaite, 2002).

PROBLEMS AND ISSUES WITH RESTORATIVE JUSTICE

Despite the growing popularity of restorative justice approaches, there are a number of problems and concerns that remain unanswered. Box 12.1 presents a number of concerns with restorative justice. Because a full discussion of critical issues is available elsewhere (see Ashworth, 2003; Feld, 1999; Kurki, 2000), only a few of the major concerns are presented here.

One problem is that restorative justice programs attempt to solve very complex societal problems (Kurki, 2000). These programs simply gather common citizens together to talk about a problem and brainstorm possible solutions.

BOX 12.1 KEY CONCERNS WITH RESTORATIVE JUSTICE

- Lack of Victim Participation
- Emphasis on Shaming and Not Enough on Reintegration/Reconciliation
- Inadequate Preparation
- Inability to Engender Participation
- Problems with Identifying Appropriate Participants
- Problems Recruiting Representative Panels
- Coercive Participation (particularly coercion of offenders)

- Inadequate Screening of Cases
- Inability of Participants (e.g. Families, Communities) to Meaningfully Contribute
- Lack of Neutrality by Participants and/or Facilitator
- Inability to Address Serious Violent Crimes
- Inability to Address Long-Standing Interpersonal Disputes
- Too Victim-Oriented
- Inability to Protect Constitutional Rights of Offenders

This represents a very simplistic approach to addressing much more complex processes that may cause crime. Many problems involve long-standing inter-personal disputes that may not be amenable to simple mediation or conferencing. Furthermore, structural inequalities in society that affect juvenile offenders and delinquency are simply not addressed (Ward & Langlands, 2008).

A second concern, related to the first, is that restorative justice has been used primarily with less serious and property crimes. There is a great deal of debate over whether this approach can be used successfully with serious violent offenses such as spousal abuse, sexual assault, aggravated assault, and murder (see Bannenberg & Rössner, 2003). While few programs have directly assessed this question, there is some evidence that restorative justice can be used in more serious personal crime cases. For example, Umbreit et al. (2003) report success using VOM with murderers and the families of their victims. Corrado, Cohen, and Odgers (2003) also find positive results (mostly in terms of satisfaction) for a VOM program dealing with serious and violent offenses in British Columbia, Canada. The strongest finding in these studies is the need for very lengthy and extensive preparation prior to the intervention. Despite the fact that most cases involve more minor offenses, Bazemore and Schiff's (2005)

TABLE 12.5 Charges Accepted by Type of Restorative Conferencing Program (Percentages)

Charges	Program Type					
	VOM/D	Multiple Practice	Circle	FGC	Board	Total
Minor assault	79.3	81.8	100.0	67.6	91.7	78.8
Property damage	76.9	77.3	83.3	70.3	61.5	74.5
Personal theft	70.4	81.8	50.0	73.0	92.3	73.1
Business theft	51.9	59.1	33.3	73.0	76.9	59.5
Breaking and entering	41.8	86.4	66.7	45.9	61.5	51.9
Vandalism	50.0	59.1	33.3	48.6	61.5	51.6
Serious assault	40.7	45.5	66.7	29.7	23.1	38.8
Minor drug	14.6	18.2	33.3	32.4	52.8	23.6
Domestic violence	23.1	21.7	33.3	12.8	21.4	21.3
Serious drug	4.9	4.5	16.7	13.5	7.7	8.1
Other*	44.4	36.4	33.3	64.9	23.1	45.6

*Other charges include arson, harassment, loitering, alcohol, behavior issues, auto theft, bomb threat, disorderly conduct, DUI, forgery, weapons, menacing, trespass, possession of stolen property, and various other charges and combination of charges.

Source: Bazemore and Schiff (2005:112). Reprinted with permission.

survey of juvenile conferencing programs in the United States reveals that many programs accept serious personal crimes for settlement (see Table 12.5).

Third, there is an underlying level of coercion in most programs. What makes this problematic is that many programs do not allow (or at least frown upon) the presence of defense attorneys, thus raising the issue of an accused's constitutional rights and procedural safeguards (Feld, 1999; Levrant, Cullen, Fulton, & Wozniak, 1999). In some instances, the participation of the offender is actually coerced by the fact that he or she is required to participate under threat of being processed in court. Compounding this problem is the need for the offender to admit to the act during the process. This is especially problematic if the intervention is taking place pre-adjudication. Thus, the process can violate the rights of offenders (Ward & Langlands, 2008).

A fourth concern with restorative justice is over how the "community" is defined and who is allowed to represent the community (Kurki, 2000). This is important because the participants help mold the outcome and the expectations for the solution. Unfortunately, they may also bring a wide array of differing expectations. This may not be a problem in smaller, more homogeneous communities, such as Maori or Native American communities, but it can certainly be problematic in large, diverse cities. Related to this, restorative justice assumes communities in which concerned parties are willing and able to work with both victims and offenders (Takagi & Shank, 2004). In many cities, extensive poverty, unemployment, problem-ridden schools, and drug abuse may make it extremely difficult to find capable adults who can take part in conferencing or sentencing practices. Restorative justice presumes the existence of caring communities and caring adults, presumptions that simply are not true in many large cities with high delinquency rates.

Fifth, Feld (1999) notes that there is a distinct imbalance of power in most restorative justice programs. This is especially problematic when juvenile offenders must face not only the victim but also the victim's support groups, members of the criminal justice system, and strangers from the general community. The power differential must be a prime consideration in meetings. A related concern is that restorative justice often ignores the victimization of the offender. Many offenders themselves experience victimization but the focus on the recent crime means a focus on the victimization they caused and overlooks the fact that they may have experienced victimization themselves (Ward & Langlands, 2008).

A final criticism is that there is confusion about how to define restorative justice. Some see restorative justice as a call for a fundamental shift in how society pursues justice. As noted at the very beginning of this chapter, some restorative justice thinkers want a radical shift in how society deals with crime, criminals, and victims—a change from a punitive system focused on blame to a system that seeks accountability, repair of harm to victims, and building offender competence (Ward & Langlands, 2008). Others see restorative justice as making minor adjustments to the criminal justice system such as adding more restitution to sentences or simply giving victims a greater voice in the process. It does not equate to total overhaul of the adult or juvenile systems. (For a more complete discussion of this concern, see Gavrielides, 2008.)

Despite these and other concerns, restorative justice is receiving a great deal of increased attention. Within a relatively short time frame restorative programming has spread to countries around the world and is being used with a wide array of problems and events. While used most commonly with youthful offenders and property or minor offenses, advocates are working to include serious and violent acts under the umbrella of restorative justice programming. The increased interest in restorative justice is evident in the recommendation of the Commission on Crime Prevention and Criminal Justice of the United Nation's Economic and Social Council in 2002 that restorative justice practices be used whenever feasible.

SUMMARY

Restorative justice programs offer another method for handling youths after an offense has occurred. The intent of these programs is multifaceted. The programs attempt to repair the more general harm that has been done to both the victim and the larger community. Equally important is rehabilitating the offender so that he or she does not commit future offenses. There is also a desire to build the community's capacity to address social issues before or as they emerge.

Restorative justice involves various constituencies (Bazemore & Umbreit, 2001; Umbreit, 1997; Van Ness, 1990; Van Ness & Strong, 2015). Under this approach, victims are compensated through restitution, are given a voice in the case handling, and become an integral part of the treatment or intervention provided to the offender. The offender is held accountable for his or her transgressions and may be subjected to a wide array of possible interventions.

The restorative justice model is very attractive for juvenile justice because it offers an alternative to popular get-tough approaches and legislation. It focuses on the victim as well as the offender and the community. It seeks to make the offender more competent and productive in an effort to bond the offender more closely to the community. Finally, the public has a more favorable attitude about such programs with juvenile rather than adult offenders (see Chapter 14 for more details).

DISCUSSION QUESTIONS

1. Restorative justice programs are appearing throughout the United States. Do you think this approach is the most appropriate direction for the juvenile justice system to pursue? If so, what form of restorative justice practice should be emphasized (VOM, FGC, NRB, or peacemaking/sentencing circles)? If not, what should be done instead of restorative justice?

2. Advocates of restorative justice point to an array of potential advantages. What features or advantages are there in the restorative justice approach, and which of these should be considered as most important from a juvenile justice perspective?

3. To what extent do you see restorative justice practices meeting the philosophical goals of juvenile justice? Discuss specific features of restorative justice that do and do not correspond to the philosophy of the juvenile justice system.

4. Compare and contrast the different types of restorative justice (i.e., VOM, FGC, NRB, peacemaking/sentencing circles). Which appear to be best suited for use in the juvenile justice system?

CHAPTER 13

The Victimization of Juveniles

WHAT YOU NEED TO KNOW

- Victimization of youths is a very common occurrence and a problem that needs to be addressed by the juvenile justice system.

- According to the NCVS, between 4 and 6 percent of all youths are victims of a violent crime each year, with a very large portion of that crime taking place at school.

- Counter to popular belief, the killing of students at school is an extremely rare event.

- Youths are also victimized within family settings. Child maltreatment, either as abuse or neglect, is a major problem.

- Youths may adopt an array of responses to victimization, ranging from fear, to avoidance, to carrying weapons and joining a gang.

- Formal agencies that respond to child maltreatment include child protective services, the juvenile court, family court, and the adult criminal justice system.

KEY TERMS

abuse

avoidance

child maltreatment

child protective services

Children's Advocacy Centers (CAC)

Court-Appointed Special Advocate (CASA)

cycle of violence

domestic relations court

family courts

guardian *ad litem*

in camera testimony

intraindividual theories

lifestyle explanations

National Child Abuse and Neglect Data System (NCANDS)

National Crime Victimization Survey (NCVS)

neglect

INTRODUCTION

The juvenile justice system does not deal exclusively with delinquent youths. As has already been seen, the juvenile court is tasked with handling noncriminal misbehavior by juveniles, typically considered as status offenders or unruly/ungovernable. In many jurisdictions, it also has the responsibility of handling youths who are the victims of maltreatment. Beyond the fact that the juvenile justice system must deal with more than just juvenile offenders is the reality that most victims of juvenile offenders are themselves juveniles and these youths are also in need of assistance.

routine activities
theory

social learning
approaches

sociocultural
explanations

victim-blaming

victim precipitation

This chapter turns the orientation of the book on its head and focuses on youths as victims rather than offenders. Several topics are explored. First, the chapter presents evidence on the extent of juvenile victimization, as depicted in both victimization survey data and data on child abuse and neglect. The chapter also discusses explanations for the different forms of victimization. What will become apparent is that there is no single explanation for victimization just as there is no single explanation for delinquency. Individuals also respond to victimization in different ways and these methods are explored. Finally, the chapter addresses the roles of the juvenile and criminal justice systems in dealing with youthful victims.

THE EXTENT OF VICTIMIZATION

Gauging the extent of victimization can be accomplished through the use of various data collection techniques. Official records, such as the Uniform Crime Reports, provide some indication of the overall extent of victimization in society through counts of offenses brought to the attention of social control agencies. In discussions of victimization, however, most attention turns to surveys that ask respondents about their experiences as a victim of crime. Victim surveys are only about 40 years old and were developed in response to criticisms that official measures underreport the level of crime in society. Consequently, most victim surveys tend to address offenses similar to those found in the Uniform Crime Reports. Victim surveys, however, have been used to address crimes occurring in specific locations such as in schools and at work as well as other types of activities such as abuse and neglect. Beyond victim surveys, organizations such as the American Humane Association and various medical groups also collect information on specific types of victimization.

General Victimization in the Community

The most well-known source of victimization data is the **National Crime Victimization Survey (NCVS)**. The current version of the NCVS is the direct descendant of early work in the 1960s and 1970s that explored both the extent of self-reported victimization and the best ways to survey the public. Among the earliest victimization surveys were those commissioned by the 1967 President's Commission on Law Enforcement and Administration of Justice. Those early surveys indicated that, on the average, there was twice as much crime occurring as reflected in police records. The NCVS (originally called the National Crime Survey, which began in 1972) provides a great deal of information about the extent of victimization; characteristics of the victim; known information about the offender; data on the time, place, and circumstances of the offense; the economic and physical impact of the crimes; responses by victims; and contact with the criminal justice system.

One important piece of information provided by the NCVS is the breakdown of crimes by victim age and demographic characteristics. Table 13.1 presents estimated 2012 victimization rates for youths ages 12–14 and 15–18. For these age groups, the estimated rate of all personal violent crime victimizations is approximately 61 per 1,000 youths ages 12–14, and 36 per 1,000 youths ages 15–18. This means that 4 to 6 percent of all youths ages 12–18 are victims of a personal crime in a single year. Note that almost all of these offenses entail physical confrontations with an assailant.

WEB ACTIVITY

You can view additional information on victims of crimes on the Bureau of Justice Statistics website, where you can request a variety of analyses through the interactive analysis tool available at http://www.bjs.gov/index.cfm?ty=nvat

Compared to victimization figures for persons age 25 and older, youths are victimized at much higher rates. Violent crime victimization rates are 34.2 per 1,000 for persons 25–34 years of age, 29.1 for persons 35–49 years of age, 15.0 for 50–64 years of age, and only 5.7 for those 65 and over (Bureau of Justice Statistics, 2014). What these data show are that youths contribute disproportionately to the ranks of crime victims.

Breakdowns by race and sex (see Table 13.1) reveal some interesting results. In terms of race, younger black juveniles are violent crime victims less often than young whites in all categories but robbery. Older black youths, however, experience similar violent victimization to older white youths. Comparisons of younger males and females reveal higher violent victimization for males, although data for older males and females reveal higher overall violent victimization and simple assaults for females.

TABLE 13.1 Estimated Personal Crime Victimization Rates for Youthful Age Groups (per 1,000), 2012

Age	Total 12–15	16–19	White 12–15	16–19	Black 12–15	16–19	Male 12–15	16–19	Female 12–15	16–19
Crimes of Violence	60.6	36.0	63.2	35.6	49.2	42.2	78.3	33.9	42.2	38.2
Rape/Sexual Assault	2.1	1.0	2.5	0.4	0.0	2.0	0.5	0.0	0.0	3.8
Robbery	2.7	3.5	2.2	2.8	4.8	7.0	4.9	5.5	0.3	1.5
Aggravated Assault	7.0	3.5	9.3	3.2	0.0	2.4	12.2	5.3	1.5	1.6
Simple Assault	48.9	28.0	49.2	29.2	44.5	30.9	60.6	23.1	36.6	33.1
Personal Larceny/Theft	0.9	0.4	0.7	0.6	2.3	0.0	1.8	0.8	0.0	0.0

Source: Compiled by authors from Bureau of Justice Statistics (2014).

The NCVS figures demonstrate that a significant number of youths are victims of crimes ranging from simple larceny to aggravated assault and robbery. A number of other facts are also apparent from the NCVS. First, youths are more likely to be victimized by offenders of the same age, race, and sex as the victim. Second, youths also know the offender more often than do adults. Third, juveniles are less likely to report their victimization experience to the police. Many youths report the offense to someone other than the police.

Victimization in Schools

Whitaker and Bastian (1991) note that many youths are victimized at school. Because youths spend more than one-third of their waking hours at school, it should not be surprising that they experience victimization at school. Unfortunately, victimization at school has only been a major concern over the past 20 years, mostly due to media portrayals of violence and weapon use on school grounds.

The United States Departments of Education and Justice issue an annual report on school crime and safety based on multiple indicators. Some of the indicators are from the NCVS, and some are from other sources. Students ages 12 through 18 reported almost 1.4 million victimizations (thefts and violent crimes) at school in 2012 (see Table 13.2). This translates into 52 victimizations per 1,000 youths at school. Students are almost equally victims of theft and violence at school. Interestingly, these figures are larger than student reports of victimization away from school. This should not be surprising since youths spend a majority of their waking hours at school during the school year. In addition, schools bring together potential victims with potential offenders, thus enhancing the possibility for victimizations.

TABLE 13.2 Victimization at Schools, 2012		
	Number	Rate*
Theft	615,600	23.6
Violence	749,200	28.8
Serious Violence	89,000	3.4
Total	1,364,900	52.4

*Rate per 1,000 students

Source: Compiled by authors from Robers et al. (2014).

WEB ACTIVITY

Extensive information on crime and victimization at school is compiled each year by the Departments of Justice and Education. Their findings appear in the annual Indicators of School Crime and Safety report that can be accessed at http://nces.ed.gov/programs/crime indicators/crimeindicators2013/

Data on victimization of youths at school also provide insight to differences by gender and race/ethnicity. The most striking result in the data is the relative uniformity in the results across almost every student characteristic. Males report higher violent and overall victimization at school than females, but similar levels of theft (Robers et al., 2014). The overall level of victimization is similar across different racial/ethnic groups, although blacks experience more thefts but fewer violent acts. In terms of age, the results show that younger youths are victimized at higher levels than are older youths at school. One attention-grabbing form of victimization at school has been killings of students by other students. The killings in Jonesboro, Arkansas, Columbine High School, Sandy Hook Elementary, and other places attract a great deal of media attention and claims of "crises" facing schools. The reality, however, is that such actions are rare. The data in Table 13.3 show that the number of homicides at school is very low, both in terms of absolute levels and relative to the numbers occurring away from school. It is also important to note that the figures in Table 13.3 subsume the multiple homicides that occur in many cases (such as at Columbine). The data clearly demonstrate that youths are safer at school than in the community.

Victimization at school raises a number of perplexing problems. First, the schools are failing to protect the youths who are legally required to attend school. This raises potential issues of liability. Second, the level of victimization at school may have a direct impact on the quality of education received by the students. This may result from students missing days of school because of the offense or fear of being victimized. It also may occur because school officials must spend time trying to establish discipline and control or because the level of crime makes the staff feel that the students are not interested in receiving an education. Crime and victimization, therefore, may replace educating as the primary concern of the school. Consequently, victimization has both immediate and long-term impacts on students.

TABLE 13.3 Homicides of Youths at and away from School		
School Year	At School	Away from School
1992–1993	34	2,741
1993–1994	29	2,942
1994–1995	28	2,696
1995–1996	32	2,545
1996–1997	28	2,221
1997–1998	34	2,100
1998–1999	33	1,777
1999–2000	14	1,567
2000–2001	14	1,509
2001–2002	16	1,498
2002–2003	18	1,553
2003–2004	23	1,474
2004–2005	22	1,554
2005–2006	21	1,697
2006–2007	32	1,801
2007–2008	21	1,744
2008–2009	17	1,605
2009–2010	19	1,410
2010–2011	11	1,336

Source: Compiled by authors from Robers et al. (2014).

Bullying

A major topic of concern for many youths and their parents is the problem of bullying. The issue of bullying has received a great deal of attention over the past decade. This is partly due to events at schools where part of the blame/explanation for violent behavior is attributed to past bullying. While most bullying does not lead to such levels of retaliatory violence, it clearly has an impact on the victim.

Bullying behavior can be classified into four types: verbal, physical, social, and cyberbullying. Too often it is assumed that bullying is primarily verbal such as teasing and name calling. It is important to note that many forms of bullying involve physical confrontations that are actually forms of criminal victimization. Included here are hitting, shoving, and punching. Starting rumors about someone or ostracizing them from participating in events are examples of social bullying. The final major form, cyberbullying, involves the use of the Internet

The issue of bullying has gained attention in recent years. Protesters hold signs at Hamilton Middle School in Cypress, Texas, to bring attention to the suicide of Asher Brown, an eighth grader who killed himself at home. His parents blamed his suicide on two years of bullying they say he had suffered at the school.

CREDIT: AP Photo/*Houston Chronicle*, Karen Warren

and other technologies to attack the victim. This can occur through posts on social media (such as MySpace and Facebook), texts, sexting, and unwanted Internet contacts.

Information on the extent of bullying generally comes from survey data. The 2011 NCVS provides a breakdown of types of bullying at school as reported by youths ages 12–18 (see Table 13.4). Over one-quarter of the students report being the victim of at least one form of bullying at school. The most common form of reported bullying is being the subject of rumors (18.3%), closely followed by being made fun of, insulted, or being called names (17.9% of respondents). Almost 8 percent are physically bullied.

Cyberbullying is a growing problem in recent years and is not restricted to one location or setting. Table 13.5 presents data on cyberbullying from the

TABLE 13.4 Student Reports of Bullying at School, 2012

Total	27.8%
Made fun of/called names/insulted	17.6
Subject of rumors	18.3
Threatened with harm	5.0
Pushed/shoved/tripped/spit on	7.9
Tried to make do things they did not want to do	3.3
Excluded from activities on purpose	5.6
Property destroyed on purpose	2.8

Source: Compiled by authors from Robers et al. (2014).

TABLE 13.5 Student Reports of Cyberbullying, 2012	
Total	9.0%
Harmful information on Internet	3.6
Private information purposefully shared on Internet	1.1
Subject of harassing instant messages	2.7
Subject of harassing text messages	4.4
Subject of harassing emails	1.9

Source: Compiled by authors from Robers et al. (2014).

2011 NCVS: School Crime Supplement. A total of 9 percent of the student respondents reported being the victim of some form of cyberbullying. This is up from less than 4 percent in 2007. Different forms of cyberbullying reported by students include harmful information posted on the internet, the distribution of private information on the internet, and various forms of harassment.

Child Maltreatment

Victimization surveys and most official sources of crime data generally miss a major form of victimization against youths, namely child maltreatment. **Child maltreatment** is a term encompassing a variety of actions in which children are harmed, either intentionally or unintentionally. According to the Federal Child Abuse Prevention and Treatment Act of 1974 (CAPTA), child abuse and neglect is defined as:

> Any recent act or failure to act on the part of a parent or caretaker which results in death, serious physical or emotional harm, sexual abuse or exploitation, or an act or failure to act which presents imminent risk of serious harm (42 U.S.C.A. §5106g).

This definition incorporates a number of different actions, including physical abuse, neglect, sexual abuse, emotional abuse, abandonment, and substance abuse. Definitions of each of these can be found in Box 13.1. Broadly stated, **abuse** is the intentional commission of an act upon a child, while **neglect** refers to the omission of a caretaker to provide what a child needs. Neglect can be physical (e.g., failing to provide food or shelter), medical (i.e., failing to provide medical care), emotional, or educational.

What makes child maltreatment especially noteworthy is the fact that the offender is typically a parent or other relative. While not a new phenomenon, it is only since the 1960s that child abuse and neglect have been seen as a social problem. Prior to that time, these types of actions were primarily considered private problems that were best dealt with by the family.

BOX 13.1 MAJOR TYPES OF CHILD ABUSE AND NEGLECT

Physical abuse is nonaccidental physical injury (ranging from minor bruises to severe fractures or death) as a result of punching, beating, kicking, biting, shaking, throwing, stabbing, choking, hitting (with a hand, stick, strap, or other object), burning, or otherwise harming a child, that is inflicted by a parent, caregiver, or other person who has responsibility for the child. Such injury is considered abuse regardless of whether the caregiver intended to hurt the child. Physical discipline, such as spanking or paddling, is not considered abuse as long as it is reasonable and causes no bodily injury to the child.

Neglect is the failure of a parent, guardian, or other caregiver to provide for a child's basic needs. Neglect may be:

- Physical (e.g., failure to provide necessary food or shelter, or lack of appropriate supervision)

- Medical (e.g., failure to provide necessary medical or mental health treatment)

- Educational (e.g., failure to educate a child or attend to special education needs)

- Emotional (e.g., inattention to a child's emotional needs, failure to provide psychological care, or permitting the child to use alcohol or other drugs).

Sexual abuse includes activities by a parent or caregiver such as fondling a child's genitals, penetration, incest, rape, sodomy, indecent exposure, and exploitation through prostitution or the production of pornographic materials.

Emotional abuse (or psychological abuse) is a pattern of behavior that impairs a child's emotional development or sense of self-worth. This may include constant criticism, threats, or rejection, as well as withholding love, support, or guidance. Emotional abuse is often difficult to prove and, therefore, child protective services may not be able to intervene without evidence of harm or mental injury to the child. Emotional abuse is almost always present when other forms are identified.

Abandonment is now defined in many states as a form of neglect. In general, a child is considered to be abandoned when the parent's identity or whereabouts are unknown, the child has been left alone in circumstances where the child suffers serious harm, or the parent has failed to maintain contact with the child or provide reasonable support for a specified period of time.

Substance abuse is an element of the definition of child abuse or neglect in many states. Circumstances that are considered abuse or neglect in some states include:

- Prenatal exposure of a child to harm due to the mother's use of an illegal drug or other substance

- Manufacture of methamphetamine in the presence of a child

- Selling, distributing, or giving illegal drugs or alcohol to a child

- Use of a controlled substance by a caregiver that impairs the caregiver's ability to adequately care for the child.

Source: Compiled by authors from Child Welfare Information Gateway (2013). What is Child Abuse and Neglect?: Recognizing the Signs and Symptoms. Washington, D.C.: U.S. Department of Health and Human Services, Children's Bureau. Retrieved on June 20, 2014, from https://www.childwelfare.gov/pubs/factsheets/whatiscan.cfm

Measuring child abuse and neglect is difficult due to the nature of the actions and the victim–offender relationship. First, abuse and neglect typically do not take place in public. Instead, they occur at home where there are no witnesses besides the victim, offender, and other family members. Second, in many cases, the victim may not recognize the action by the parent as wrong. The child is either too immature to understand the nature of what is happening, cannot adequately verbalize the events, or does not know who to tell about the abuse or neglect. Third, despite the abuse, children often still express love and affection for the parent/relative and may not want to do something that will get the offender into trouble. As a result, the child will not report, and may even deny, the existence of maltreatment.

Due to these problems, no firm figures on abuse and neglect are available. What is known is that the problem is widespread. One source of data on child abuse and neglect is child protective services (CPS) agencies in each state. Data from these agencies are collected and compiled by the National Child Abuse and Neglect Data System (NCANDS). In 2009, there were over 870,000 documented cases of child abuse or neglect in the United States (see Table 13.6) (Administration on Children, Youth, and Families, 2010). Over three-quarters of the maltreated children (78.3%) experienced some form of neglect. Less than 18 percent experienced physical abuse while more than 9 percent experienced sexual abuse, and more than 7 percent psychological maltreatment (Administration on Children, Youth, and Families, 2010). Unfortunately, child maltreatment often leads to the death of the victim. According to NCANDS data, 1,676 children were killed in 2009 as a result of maltreatment.

The figures for the extent of abuse and neglect are only estimates. There is no accurate count for this type of victimization. The fact that most such acts occur behind closed doors between relatives means that we may never have a complete picture of the problem. What can be concluded is that these are baseline figures and that the real extent of abuse and neglect is probably much higher.

WEB ACTIVITY

More information on what constitutes child maltreatment and how you can identify potential maltreatment can be found at http://www.childwelfare.gov/pubs/factsheets/whatiscan.cfm

TABLE 13.6 Number, Percent, and Rate (per 100,000) of Child Maltreatment, 2012

Type	Number	%*	Rate
Physical Abuse	124,544	18.3	168.0
Neglect	531,241	78.3	720.0
Medical Neglect	15,705	2.3	21.3
Sex Abuse	62,936	9.3	85.3
Psychological Maltreatment	57,880	8.5	78.4
Other Abuse	71,846	10.6	97.4
Unknown	1,326	0.2	1.8
TOTAL	865,478		1,173.0

*Percentage does not equal 100 due to multiple types in some incidents

Source: Compiled from the Administration on Children, Youth, and Families (2013).

EXPLAINING JUVENILE VICTIMIZATION

Attempts to explain why an individual is a victim can take a variety of forms. Certainly, one way to explain victimization is to turn the equation over and focus on the offender. The various theories addressed earlier in this text (Chapters 3 and 4) follow this more traditional approach to understanding unacceptable behavior. Because the perpetrator is the one who has violated the law, it is natural to focus attention on that individual, rather than the victim. There must be something about the offender that led to the victimization. The realm of victimology, however, does not rely exclusively on the theories already presented in this text. Rather, attempts to explain juvenile victimization range from those that attempt to blame the victim for the action to others targeted at specific forms of victimization.

From Victim-Blaming to Lifestyle

Early research on victims paid considerable attention to who the victims were and the circumstances surrounding the events. Throughout these works was an underlying theme that individuals became victims because of something they did, did not do, or could not do. For example, von Hentig (1941) outlined 13 categories of victims, including the young, females, the elderly, minorities, and mentally defective individuals. What made these people victims was the fact that they were somehow vulnerable. Some people cannot physically ward off an attack, others do not recognize they are being victimized, and others see themselves outside the societal mainstream and accept the victimization.

Wolfgang (1958) argued that substantial numbers of offenses are victim-precipitated. **Victim precipitation** posits that the victim is actively involved in the offense. The victim, therefore, holds some responsibility for his or her own status due to his or her actions or inactions. While this early idea of victim culpability has been referred to as **victim-blaming** and subjected to much criticism (see Curtis, 1974; Franklin & Franklin, 1976; Weis & Borges, 1973), the idea that the actions of individuals may contribute to their victimization has not been completely discounted.

Today, **lifestyle explanations** and **routine activities theory** are commonly employed to show how individual behavior contributes to victimization. These theories argue that where individuals go, who they go with, and when they go all define their lifestyle and their chances of victimization (Cohen & Felson, 1979; Hindelang, Gottfredson, & Garofalo, 1978). If one's choices for behavior places him or her in an area where crime is common, at a time when there is no one to provide protection, then the chances for victimization are enhanced. That person's lifestyle, therefore, contributes to becoming a victim.

Examples and support for a lifestyle explanation of juvenile victimization are plentiful. The fact that juveniles are disproportionately represented among offenders would suggest that juveniles would also be the victims for a variety of reasons. First, other youths are available to victimize—at school, out-of-doors in the neighborhood, in play groups, and as acquaintances. Second, juvenile offenders will view other youths as more physically vulnerable than most adults. Third, interaction with other youths provides knowledge and opportunities for offending. Fourth, individuals who engage in deviant behavior are themselves at higher risk of being a victim (Clark & Lab, 1995; Esbensen & Huizinga, 1991; Lauritsen, Sampson, & Laub, 1991). In essence, the juvenile lifestyle includes more youths to victimize than adults. As youths either find themselves or place themselves in situations in which delinquency is more likely, they will invariably be victimized.

Explanations of Child Abuse and Neglect

Where the lifestyle approach emphasizes the behavior and choices of the victim as contributors to victimization, explanations of child maltreatment focus exclusively on the offender and society. The victim is not considered culpable. In general, explanations for child maltreatment can be divided into three categories: intraindividual theories, sociocultural explanations, and social learning theories (Doerner & Lab, 2012). **Intraindividual theories** view child maltreatment as an internal flaw or defect of the abuser. Abusers are considered to exhibit some form of psychopathological condition (Steele & Pollock, 1974). Intraindividual theories have been used to absolve society of any responsibility for child abuse and lay the blame on a few "sick" individuals.

Sociocultural explanations shift the emphasis from the individual to society and the environment. The abuser may be stressed by any number of factors, such as unemployment, conflicts at work or home, family size, social isolation, and economic problems (Belsky, 1978; Garbarino & Gilliam, 1980; Gelles, 1980; Gil, 1971). This stress may lead the individual to strike out against a child who has neither the physical stature nor the social standing to resist maltreatment. A child, therefore, becomes the recipient of abuse as a proxy outlet for stress.

Social learning approaches to child maltreatment rest on the assumption that an individual has learned to be abusive by observing past abusive behavior. This observation includes the possibility that the abuser was himself or herself abused as a child. The idea that a child who is abused or who witnesses abuse will grow up to be an abuser is often referred to as the **cycle of violence** (Schwartz, 1989; Straus, 1983). Widom (1989, 1995), following abused/neglected youths and a control group into adulthood, reports a significant relationship between abuse/neglect as a child and deviant behavior later in life.

Explanations for child abuse and neglect are still in their infancy. Indeed, scholarly interest in this form of victimization is relatively new, with most work dating since the 1960s. Consequently, little consensus exists on the explanations for maltreatment or how to best attack the problem.

RESPONSES TO VICTIMIZATION

Victimization, whether direct or vicarious, has the potential of eliciting a number of responses from the victim. While victims may view the responses as beneficial, they are often debilitating and may lead the victims into criminal or delinquent behavior. Youthful responses can range from raised levels of fear of crime to various actions aimed at reducing the risk of initial or further victimization. Carrying weapons for protection or joining gangs may be responses chosen by youthful victims. In both cases, however, the response may be illegal and/or lead to more victimization.

Fear of Crime as a Response

Whether or not a victim takes an action at the time of an offense, there will probably be some changes in beliefs or behavior subsequent to the victimization experience. While many studies show that roughly 40 to 50 percent of the population is fearful of crime (Hindelang, 1975; Skogan & Maxfield, 1981; Toseland, 1982), there is relatively little research that assesses fear among juveniles. This is particularly interesting because youths are among the most victimized.

When research does look at youths, fear does not appear to be a minor concern. Lab and Clark (1994), in their study of junior and senior high school students, found that 30 percent of the students claimed to fear being attacked at school, independent of whether they had ever been victimized in the past. Similarly, the 2011 NCVS reports 3.7 percent of youths are fearful of being attacked at school, and 2.4 percent are fearful of attack or harm away from school (Robers et al., 2014). These levels of fear are relatively stable across gender, race, and location.

Fear can be debilitating, regardless of whether it is a result of past victimization. Fear leads some people to avoid other persons and places. It makes others decide to carry a weapon for protection, and still others to join groups to fight crime. The very fact that fear can cause people to change their normal routine is evidence that it is something to be addressed. This is not to suggest that fear is always a bad thing. Indeed, to the extent that fear alters a person's behavior and chances of being victimized, fear is a useful tool.

Avoidance

A common reaction to actual or potential victimization and fear is **avoidance** of certain places or people. Avoidance is possibly the leading response to fear of victimization (Gates & Rohe, 1987; Skogan, 1981). Reasonable avoidance behavior for a youth may include staying away from a playground where gang members are known to hang out or refraining from walking alone at night in an area with a high crime rate.

For youths, avoidance is problematic when the school is the location of victimization. Victimization at school raises the option of staying home from school or avoiding certain places at school. Avoidance at school, however, means that school work is missed, the student is distracted from work while at school, and/or there is discomfort and inconvenience involved in avoiding important parts of the school (such as a restroom or the cafeteria). The 2011 NCVS: School Crime Supplement reports that 5.5 percent of students avoid school, school activities, and/or specific places at school due to fear of attack or harm (Robers, Zhang, Truman & Snyder, 2012). A variety of other studies have reported similar proportions of youths who skip school due to fear (Lab & Clark, 1996; Lab & Whitehead, 1994; Metropolitan Life, 1993; Ringwalt, Messerschmidt, Graham, & Collins, 1992). While the youths may be attending school, the quality of the education they receive is diminished. Some students may go hungry, suffer discomfort because they are afraid to use restrooms, arrive late for classes due to using only certain stairways or hallways, or refrain from taking part in enriching extracurricular activities. In essence, the school experience is far from an ideal nurturing atmosphere. The ultimate form of this avoidance is quitting school. Students who drop out are not included in surveys of students. Thus, the number of youths who report avoiding school due to fear in most studies is an undercount of who is taking this action.

TABLE 13.7 Avoidance Responses of Students to Victimization and Fear in School, 2011

Avoidance Behavior	
Any place at school	5.5%
School activities	2.0
Stayed home from school	0.8
Avoided places	4.7
Entrances	0.9
Hallways or stairs	2.5
School cafeteria	1.8
Restrooms	1.7
Other places	1.1

Source: Compiled by authors from Robers et al. (2014).

Resorting to Weapons

Another form of response involves self-defense actions, particularly carrying weapons for protection. An inescapable fact about youths in recent years is their ability to obtain and use weapons. According to data from the Youth Risk Behavior Survey conducted by the Centers for Disease Control and Prevention, 5.4 percent of high school students reported carrying a weapon to school at least once in the past 30 days (Dinkes, Kemp, Baum & Snyder, 2009). Lab and Clark (1996) found that 24 percent of the respondents carried a weapon to school

A student at Brainerd High School in Chattanooga, Tennessee, walks through a metal detector as she enters the building.

CREDIT: AP Photo/*Chattanooga Times Free Press*, Tim Barber

for protection at least once over a six-month time period. Even higher levels of weapon possession at school emerge in studies of inner-city schools (see, for example, Sheley, McGee, & Wright, 1995). Among the weapons carried for protection are guns, knives, brass knuckles, razor blades, spiked jewelry, and mace (Lab & Clark, 1996).

Unfortunately, while bringing a weapon to school may make a youth feel safer, such devices have the potential of causing more problems than they solve. One negative outcome is that being caught with a weapon can lead to expulsion, criminal prosecution, and other sanctions against the student who is trying to protect himself or herself. A second possibility is that if the student is attacked and does try to use the weapon, the level of violence and victimization may escalate. That is, a fistfight can become a shooting or a theft can result in an aggravated assault. The victim may be more seriously harmed or the victim may become the offender. Yet another consequence is that schools can become armed camps where the administration is forced to take progressively intrusive measures to keep weapons out of school.

Gangs as Protection

In times of crisis or turmoil, it is natural for people to seek out support from those around them. Most victims will turn to family members for such assistance. Another source of support is close friends and peers. For many youths, the friends and peers include gang members. This is particularly true for youths in large inner-city areas. The response to victimization, therefore, may entail joining a gang for protection. Some youths see joining a gang as a means of restoring a feeling of security. If a youth is victimized by gang members, either directly or by mistake, joining a gang further becomes a self-defense mechanism.

Joining gangs as a response to victimization, however, is a double-edged sword. While the gang may supply some sense of protection, it typically demands participation in illegal behavior and conflict with other gangs and individuals. These demands often result in further victimization of the individual rather than protection from victimization. At the same time that gang membership may alleviate victimization, joining a gang can also contribute to ongoing victimization, albeit as a member of a group and not just as an individual.

Summary of Victimization Responses

Juveniles can respond to victimization in a variety of ways. At the same time, many of the potential responses have negative aspects that can exacerbate problems for the youth. Fear, which may serve as a protective measure, can lead to withdrawal from other people and the community. It can also prompt a youth to stay home from school or avoid certain places at school. Still other victims may purchase and carry weapons for protection. Victimization also may drive a youth to join a gang as a means of feeling safe. While each of these may appear reasonable, they can lead to further victimization, more serious situations, and, certainly, a deterioration in the general quality of life.

THE ROLE OF FORMAL SOCIAL CONTROL AGENCIES

Various social control agencies can become involved in youthful victimization. Most social control agencies, however, focus on juvenile victims of abuse and neglect and ignore the victim status as it emerges from other forms of offending. Clearly, a juvenile who loses money due to a theft or is hurt from an assault tends to be considered a witness more so than a victim by the justice system. Assistance to these victims is relatively limited to mediation and similar programs already discussed. On the other hand, victims of abuse and neglect receive a great deal of attention by various formal control agencies, particularly child protective services and the different court systems.

Perhaps the only agency that will have contact with all forms of youthful victims will be the police. This is because they are typically the ones called whenever someone is in need of help. The police, however, are geared toward identifying offenders, making arrests, and preparing cases for prosecution. Except for initial contacts, providing immediate protection, referrals to other sources of assistance, and work with prevention programs, law enforcement officers spend little time dealing with the victim. This is true whether the victim is an adult or a juvenile. Consequently, the balance of this section looks at how other system components deal with youthful victims.

Child Protective Services

An alternative point of system entry besides the police that has been established for the purposes of protecting youths is child protective services. **Child protective services** are mandated in every state as a direct result of the Child Abuse Prevention and Treatment Act of 1974 (Wiehe, 1992). This federal act required states to set up rules for the reporting and handling of abused children. States not conforming to the Act would be denied various forms of federal funding. Because the exact nature of how a state would provide protective services was left to the state, these services appear under various state agencies such as Social Services and Departments of Human Services.

Child protective service agencies fill a variety of roles and have diverse powers. First, in virtually all jurisdictions, these agencies are responsible for accepting reports of abuse and neglect cases and undertaking or coordinating the investigation of such allegations. While many investigations are done by employees of the child protective service, others may be assigned to other agencies, such as the police or prosecutor's office. A second common function of child protective services is the removal of children from suspected (or documented) abusive situations. This removal may last for only a short time or can last for an extended period, depending on the facts of the case. The protection of the child from further possible harm is the goal of any decision to remove a child from his or her parents. Child protective services often provide oversight to foster care, adoption, and other forms of custodial arrangements for the state.

Finally, child protective services focus on the preservation of the family unit. Underlying this approach is the belief that the family setting is the most appropriate for raising a child. Stabilizing the family situation, removing the problematic elements in the home, and improving the quality of life for the child guide the decisions made by the agency. Given this preoccupation with family preservation, most child protective agencies do not need court orders or sanctions to work with families. Much like diversion programs or informal probation, child protective services will work with families to solve problems without resorting to formal court procedures if all parties agree. In some cases the agency will actually provide the recommended intervention, and in others the agency may act as more of a referral source than service provider.

Child protective services reach a large number of victims and families each year. An estimated 6.3 million children were referred for preventive measures in 2012 (Administration on Children, Youth, and Families, 2014). Almost two-thirds of these referrals received post-investigative services, of which roughly 20 percent were victims of crimes (Administration on Children, Youth, and Families, 2014). Roughly 146,000 youths were removed from their homes in 2012 as a result of abuse or neglect (Administration on Children, Youth, and Families, 2014). These figures reveal two things. First, CPS agencies reach a substantial number of abuse and neglect victims. Second, these agencies handle many youths for an array of problems beyond just victimization.

Child protective services personnel work very closely with different courts. While these agencies often generate cases for the criminal and juvenile courts, the courts also call on these services for assistance as cases work their way through the system. This referral from the courts to protective services can range from taking custody of children when parents are incarcerated for a crime to investigating allegations of abuse and neglect that emerge in the course of divorce proceedings.

Children's Advocacy Centers

A **Children's Advocacy Center** (CAC) is an umbrella organization, independent of the criminal justice system, that brings together child protective services workers, law enforcement officers, the prosecutor's office, educators, mental health counselors, and medical personnel in an effort to provide a coordinated response and seamless service delivery to maltreated children. This multidisciplinary team approach is designed to keep children from being shuttled from one agency to the next, and to provide a variety of services under one roof. The first CAC opened its doors in 1985 in Huntsville, Alabama. Since then, the concept has expanded, and there are now more than 700 CACs operating throughout the country (National Children's Alliance, 2013).

The goals of a CAC are to minimize the trauma child victims undergo, and to provide a safe and comfortable atmosphere. One notable service CACs provide is videotaped forensic interviews. Among other things, videotaping reduces the number of interviews/interviewers, preserves testimony for later use, documents the tone of the session and the conditions under which the interview took place, and allows an assessment of the child's veracity (Chandler, 2000). In fact, an independent assessment of "best practices" specifically praised a multidisciplinary team approach, trained forensic interviewers, videotaping interviews, and the CAC model as being among the "best practices" to utilize when conducting child maltreatment investigations (Jones, Cross, Walsh, & Simone, 2005).

WEB ACTIVITY

More information about the National Children's Advocacy Center is available at http://www.nationalcac.org/

More than 5,000 silver pinwheels glittering on the front lawn of the Kentucky Capitol, in Frankfort, Kentucky, represent child victims of sexual abuse served by the children's advocacy centers across Kentucky in 2011.

CREDIT: AP Photo/LRC Public Information

The Juvenile Court

The juvenile court deals with a wide variety of issues related to youths. Besides handling delinquents and status offenders, it faces cases of dependency, abuse, and neglect. In these cases, the court must consider the protection and needs of the juvenile victim, the needs of the entire family unit, and the possible sanctioning and needs of the (typically adult) offender.

Cases of abuse and neglect force the juvenile court to assume more of a conflict orientation than presumed under the *parens patriae* philosophy. Because of the diverse issues in abuse and neglect cases, many juvenile courts are affiliated with (or even part of) what are more generally known as **family courts**. Larger family courts may designate certain judges to handle delinquency matters and others to deal with abuse and neglect cases. These latter cases typically follow a more rigorous set of procedural guidelines, including evidentiary safeguards, the presence of attorneys, and formal examination and cross-examination of witnesses. This is required because of the due process rights of the accused.

In every case of abuse and neglect, the primary concern of the juvenile court is the well-being of the juvenile and the family unit. Other youths in the home also become a focal point along with the individual victim, based on the assumption that they are potential victims. Because abuse and neglect cases place the interests of the child in conflict with that of an accused parent, the court typically appoints someone to be an advocate for the needs and interests of the child. Two common names for such an advocate would be a **Court-Appointed Special Advocate (CASA)** or a **guardian** *ad litem*. The CASA program began in Seattle in the late 1970s and has since spread to all states (National CASA, 2014). According to National CASA (2014), in 2012 there were roughly 77,000 CASA volunteers handling roughly 234,000 children in the United States. These advocates usually serve in a voluntary capacity, although some courts provide office space, supplies, and travel expenses. The exact role and responsibility of a CASA volunteer and a guardian *ad litem* varies across jurisdictions, although their general duty is to protect the interests of the child in virtually any legal proceeding (see Box 13.2). These individuals typically receive training in the functioning of the juvenile court, the needs of youths, the availability of resources, and how to investigate the circumstances of the case.

WEB ACTIVITY

Look up the statutory guidelines for a guardian *ad litem* in your state.

Court-appointed advocates often fulfill some of the same functions as other actors in the criminal and juvenile justice systems. These individuals, because of their focus on youths, can undertake a more thorough investigation of a case than can an overburdened police force. They can also spend the time to identify potential sources of treatment for the child, offender, and family that is not a role of law enforcement investigators. In some places these individuals also serve in the place of an attorney on the child's behalf. One key difference, however, between an attorney and a CASA volunteer or guardian *ad litem* involves their orientation toward the case. Whereas an attorney argues in accordance with the client's wishes, a court-appointed advocate is supposed to argue in the best interests of the child, even if that conflicts with the desires of the child (Sagatun & Edwards, 1995). These court volunteers provide a vital source of information and recommendations to the juvenile or family court.

BOX 13.2 EXCERPTS FROM OHIO'S GUARDIAN *AD LITEM* STATUTE

(A) The court shall appoint a guardian *ad litem*, subject to rules adopted by the supreme court, to protect the interest of a child in any proceeding concerning an alleged or adjudicated delinquent child or unruly child when either of the following applies:

(1) The child has no parent, guardian, or legal custodian.

(2) The court finds that there is a conflict of interest between the child and the child's parent, guardian, or legal custodian.

(B)(1) The court shall appoint a guardian *ad litem*, subject to rules adopted by the supreme court, to protect the interest of a child in any proceeding concerning an alleged abused or neglected child . . .

(2) The guardian *ad litem* appointed for an alleged or adjudicated abused or neglected child may bring a civil action against any person who is required . . . to file a report of child abuse or child neglect that is known or reasonably suspected or believed to have occurred if that person knows, or has reasonable cause to suspect or believe based on facts that would cause a reasonable

person in a similar position to suspect or believe, as applicable, that the child is the subject of child abuse or child neglect and does not file the required report and if the child suffers any injury or harm as a result of the child abuse or child neglect that is known or reasonably suspected or believed to have occurred or suffers additional injury or harm after the failure to file the report . . .

(I) The guardian *ad litem* for an alleged or adjudicated abused, neglected, or dependent child shall perform whatever functions are necessary to protect the best interest of the child, including, but not limited to, investigation, mediation, monitoring court proceedings, and monitoring the services provided the child by the public children services agency or private child placing agency that has temporary or permanent custody of the child, and shall file any motions and other court papers that are in the best interest of the child . . .

Source: Anderson's Ohio Online Docs. Available at: http://codes.ohio.gov/orc/2151.281v2

CASA volunteers have had a big impact on abuse and neglect cases. An evaluation conducted by the U.S. Department of Justice's (2006) Inspector General noted that cases in which CASA was involved tended to receive more and longer services and arrive at better position outcomes than cases without their intervention (see Table 13.8). The only surprise was the fact that cases involving CASA had a lower rate of family reunification. The reason for this is probably due to the fact that CASA handles more complex and difficult cases.

WEB ACTIVITY

More information about CASA can be found at the national website at http://www.nationalcasa.org/

The Criminal Court

The criminal court holds a difficult position when faced with youthful victims, particularly abuse and neglect victims. This is because of its orientation toward determining guilt or innocence of the accused and imposing sentences on the convicted. The victim in the criminal court holds no more stature than does any witness. It is the state that is the aggrieved party and the state that is pursuing the prosecution of the offender (Doerner & Lab, 2012). As a consequence of this situation, the criminal court focuses on providing the accused with his or her due process rights. Besides the victim's role as a witness, the court's only other concern for a victim is to protect him or her from further harm.

TABLE 13.8 Outcomes of CASA Involvement

- Youths spend a longer time in foster care.
- More youths are placed in foster care.
- Youths receive more case services.
- More cases are permanently closed before the youth reaches the age of majority.
- Less likelihood youths will reenter the juvenile justice system.
- Higher likelihood of a successful "permanent plan" being implemented.
- Lower chance of family reunification—more adoptions.

Source: U.S. Department of Justice (2006).

A juvenile victim in the criminal court is especially problematic due to his or her lack of maturity. The process can be very traumatic for a child, particularly if the accused is an abusive or neglectful parent. In the past, many cases never reached trial, or the prosecution was unsuccessful due to problems with youthful victims/witnesses. In recent years, however, criminal courts have started to make accommodations for youthful victims. For example, some jurisdictions provide victim counselors as a means of minimizing the trauma of a court appearance and assisting youths with recall problems (Burgess & Laszlo, 1976; Geiselman, Bornstein, & Saywitz, 1992). These counselors can serve in a fashion and capacity similar to CASA workers and guardians *ad litem*. Other courts have relaxed the hearsay rule (Levine & Battistoni, 1991) or allowed *in camera* testimony (Bjerregaard, 1989; Melton, 1980) as a means of entering testimony while protecting the victim. The relaxed hearsay rule allows third-party testimony, such as from a counselor or psychiatrist. *In camera* testimony entails testimony outside the courtroom, such as in a judge's chambers or by means of closed-circuit television or on tape. While these efforts are not allowed in all jurisdictions, they are gaining acceptance as a way to protect the youthful victim while still prosecuting the accused.

On a related note, both juvenile and adult victims hold few rights in the criminal court. As noted earlier, there have been some accommodations made for juveniles as witnesses. Other inroads to the court appear in legislation that provides victims with rights such as the right to be informed about court proceedings, the right to protection from intimidation, and the right to address the court at the time of sentencing (Doerner & Lab, 2012). Unfortunately, there is little discussion of youthful victims in any of the arguments for these changes or in the enacting legislation.

Domestic Relations Court

A final court in which juvenile victims may find themselves is a **domestic relations court**. These are civil courts devoted to the issues involved in divorce, child support, and related matters. As with juvenile courts, domestic relations may be configured as a special court within a larger family court setting in some jurisdictions. Youthful victims appear in these courts primarily in cases in which allegations of abuse or neglect are made by one parent against another. The child does not have a separate standing in the court, despite the possibility of abuse or neglect. When such allegations are made, the court will order an investigation (often by protective services agencies) for the purpose of making a determination with regard to the question before the court (i.e., divorce, support payments, etc.). It is possible that the court will provide a CASA worker or a guardian *ad litem* to the child when such allegations are made. If evidence of abuse or neglect is uncovered in the case, those issues are turned over to the criminal or juvenile courts for action. Therefore, while youthful victimization may emerge in domestic relations courts, those problems are outside of the court's jurisdiction and will be turned over to another court.

SUMMARY: THE NEED TO RECOGNIZE THE VICTIM

Addressing children as victims of crime has long been a component of the juvenile justice system and, to a minimal extent, other courts; but this fails to garner much attention in discussions of juvenile justice. This is unfortunate, because most youthful offenders prey on other youths and significant numbers of youths are victims of abuse and neglect. While the juvenile court has long standing in the areas of abuse and neglect, youthful victims have few coping mechanisms available for dealing with other forms of victimization. This is especially true outside the juvenile justice system. To what can this anonymity of juvenile victimization be attributed? One major source of blame has to be the fact that too often the emphasis on juvenile offenders ignores the other half of the offense dyad—the juvenile victim. We have attempted to begin to rectify this shortcoming in this chapter. It is also important, however, that more emphasis be placed on research and programming for juvenile victims. Without those efforts, juvenile victims will continue to receive little attention.

DISCUSSION QUESTIONS

1. You have recently been hired to work for an agency that deals with abused and neglected youths. Research your state statutes and report on the legal definitions of abuse and neglect, and what is mandated in terms of dealing with these victims (such as mandatory reporting, treatment, etc.). What gaps do you see in the statutes? What changes would you make?

2. You have been asked to draw up new legislation dealing with child abuse and neglect. Define the terms, outline the issues you would include in the legislation, and discuss the role you see for the juvenile court and how, if at all, it would alter the court's philosophy.

3. Discuss the responses youths make when victimized. What are the positive and negative consequences of the various responses? What types of services are available to handle victimized juveniles (not including abuse and neglect)? What services are in your town? What services would you like to see initiated?

4. Your local Parent Teacher Association (PTA) is clamoring for increased security measures at school. The PTA wants to prevent homicides and other violent crimes. What information should the PTA and the school be aware of in order to make reasonable choices?

CHAPTER 14

Future Directions in Juvenile Justice

WHAT YOU NEED TO KNOW

- Reform proposals for juvenile court include reemphasizing and reinvigorating the rehabilitative orientation of juvenile court, changing juvenile court into a scaled-down version of criminal court, and abolishing juvenile court.

- Another model is to adopt a restorative justice model for juvenile court.

- Social issues that affect juveniles include race (disproportionate minority confinement and contacts), the need to rebuild community, the role of the family, character education, and the political economy.

- In *Roper v. Simmons* (2005), the U.S. Supreme Court ruled that the death penalty is unconstitutional for juveniles. Like the dissenting Justice Scalia, some would argue that the death penalty is appropriate for juveniles.

- The Supreme Court has ruled that life without parole sentences cannot be given to juveniles for a non-homicide offense (*Graham v. Florida* [2010]) and that mandatory life without parole sentences are unconstitutional for juveniles (*Miller v. Alabama* [2012]). Both rulings were based on the incomplete adolescent psychological development and impulsiveness of juveniles.

- There is some confusion over the proper role of juvenile court concerning status offenders. Petitioned cases are increasing while many call for ending jurisdiction.

- Although many would like an easy solution, that is not possible. The answer is to address the problems of youths who break the law.

KEY TERMS

capital punishment

criminalized juvenile court

divestiture

jurisdiction over status offenders

political economy

positive youth development

restorative justice juvenile court

Roper v. Simmons

spiritual dimension in corrections

therapeutic jurisprudence

youth justice system

INTRODUCTION

The juvenile court continues to be under scrutiny. Critics point out numerous problems and suggest either change or elimination. State legislators and prosecutors have taken away many of the clients of juvenile court. New state laws mandate handling many juveniles in adult criminal court. Prosecutors today have increased authority to direct juveniles to adult court. A contrary direction is that some states have returned the age of criminal court jurisdiction to 18. Some developments involve turning away from traditional juvenile court philosophy while others suggest a return to that philosophy.

This chapter will examine several proposals about the future of juvenile court. One drastic proposal is to abolish juvenile court. Other proposals call for new types of courts. We will outline these proposals and assess them. This chapter will also look at some broader issues affecting the treatment of juvenile offenders. For example, we will look at the role of community and family in dealing with delinquency. We will question whether steps can be taken to improve the ways in which both community and family try to prevent delinquency.

PROPOSALS FOR REFORMING JUVENILE COURT

Rehabilitating the Rehabilitative *Parens Patriae* Court

One approach to the problems of the juvenile court is try to return to the rehabilitative and *parens patriae* roots of the court. Reformers who support this option think that the failures of juvenile court are failures of implementation: the juvenile court has not delivered the rehabilitation that it initially promised. A major factor behind this failure of implementation is lack of funding. Legislators have not provided the money needed to help youths obtain education, individual counseling, family counseling, and vocational training.

If juvenile courts received adequate funding and if they followed the advice of the research on effective rehabilitation programs (see Chapters 10 and 11 for summaries of those findings), then juvenile court could be the ideal youth court envisioned by the Progressives at the beginning of the twentieth century. Juvenile court judges could act like concerned parents trying to help children.

A leader in the drive to get juvenile court to deliver rehabilitation is Lipsey (2009; also see Cullen, 2007). Lipsey has done meta-analysis research on effective interventions. He believes that such research shows that there are effective interventions for both institutionalized and noninstitutionalized offenders. The best programs have the capability to "reduce recidivism by 40–50 percent, that is, to cut recidivism rates to very nearly half of what they would be without such programming" (Lipsey, 1999:163). Furthermore, these programs "do not entail exceptional efforts or costs" (Lipsey, 1999:163); they are doable and affordable. (For recent reviews of effective correctional interventions for both juveniles and adults, see Greenwood, 2008; Lipsey, 2009; or MacKenzie, 2006.)

Krisberg uses the term "redemption" and offers the moral argument that we need to be concerned about redeeming all children:

> Moreover, it is patently clear that most of us would seek a justice system that is founded on core principles of charity and redemption if it were our own children who were in trouble. This, of course, is the key issue. If we recognize the truth that all children are our children, the search for the juvenile justice ideal is our only moral choice (Krisberg, 2005:196).

Corbett (2001) agrees with the call to implement the findings on effective interventions and adds that it is important to focus on early intervention instead of late intervention. Parent training, for example, has been shown to be effective. Another suggestion is to emphasize "the paying of just debts": "Restitution and community service programs repay and restore victims and harmed communities and counter the prevalent notion that juvenile offenders are immune from any real penalties . . ." (Corbett, 2001:149). He also suggests that probation officers should act as moral educators who help juveniles build character. He maintains that setting an example is crucial:

> Every occasion where self-restraint is exercised in the face of a probationer's provocation, where kindness and courtesy is extended to a probationer's family in defiance of the juvenile's expectation, and every effort by the officer to insure fair treatment in dispositional and revocational proceedings are opportunities for character building and moral education (Corbett, 2001:149).

His final suggestion is to attempt violence prevention through anger management skills training and similar social skills education programs.

A slight variation of this focus on the return to rehabilitation is the concept of **positive youth development**. Proponents of this concept argue that most youths can grow up properly and stay out of trouble if they can be attached to the proper social resources, especially prosocial, caring adults. For youths under juvenile court supervision, probation would include linking the youth with an adult mentor, involving the youth in a community engagement project and in appropriate recreation, and ensuring that the youth has some sort of paid employment. This would be different from the current philosophy of juvenile court that sees minor offenders as not really needing anything until they escalate into more serious delinquency (Butts, Mayer, & Ruth, 2005).

For a review and analysis of early intervention efforts in general, see Farrington and Welsh (2007) and Welsh (2012).

Bishop claims that many states have actually passed legislation to continue rehabilitation in juvenile court. Purpose clauses continue to include treatment as a primary purpose of the court. Three states have recently passed legislation to improve individualized treatment plans for youths in custody, four states have passed laws providing mental health assessment and treatment, and several states have passed laws to establish teen courts and other diversion programs. Still other states operate drug and/or mental health courts with a clear treatment focus. Mississippi ended its boot camp program, and Connecticut raised the age of jurisdiction from 16 to 18. Bishop argues that such legislative actions are evidence that "the juvenile justice system is less punitive and more treatment-oriented than is commonly assumed" (Bishop, 2006:659).

None of these suggestions requires a radical reshaping of probation or the juvenile justice system. The suggestions build on the history and tradition of probation as caring individuals (probation officers in the tradition of probation founder John Augustus). What Corbett proposes is that today's officers utilize both social science findings (e.g., parent education and anger management training) and common sense, such as setting a character-building example, to attempt to induce juveniles to become prosocial.

Another note in favor of a rehabilitative juvenile court is that public opinion supports it. For example, in a survey of 1,308 Florida residents, Mears and his colleagues Hay, Gertz, and Mancini found that more than 80 percent of the public disapproves of abolishing the juvenile justice system. In fact, even "many conservatives . . . view violent juvenile offenders as capable of being rehabilitated" (Mears et al., 2007:249; for an additional suggestion from Mears and his colleagues, see Box 14.1.) Similarly, Applegate, Davis, and Cullen (2009) found that more than three-quarters of their sample of Florida residents thought that having a juvenile justice system "makes good sense."

A final argument in favor of a rehabilitative juvenile court is that effective interventions can also be very cost-effective. A cost–benefit study has reported the following benefits per juvenile offender: Functional Family Therapy: $58,043; Multisystemic Therapy: $26,545; and Aggression Replacement Training: $55,821. Deterrence-based programs, however, such as surveillance-oriented parole and Scared Straight, result in additional costs per offender, for example, almost $13,000 for each youth in Scared Straight (Aos & Drake, 2013). Given current budget constraints on governments, such cost considerations are a powerful argument to use evidence-based treatment interventions with juvenile offenders.

BOX 14.1 A UNIFORM UPPER AGE FOR JUVENILE COURT

Mears et al. (2007) suggest that the time is right to revisit the question of the upper age limit in juvenile court and to settle on one uniform age for all the states. As Chapter 1 noted, states vary in their upper age limits, with most states having 18 as the age at which adult criminal court jurisdiction begins (except for transfer).

Mears and his colleagues first note that the *Roper* capital punishment decision would fit with the age of 18. That decision relied heavily on psychological research, demonstrating that most juveniles under 18 are not fully developed psychologically. Second, their research on public opinion in Florida found that there is considerable variation in public opinion about age and juvenile court jurisdiction. About one-third said that 17 or older should be the lowest age for

trying youths as adults, 28 percent said 16, 13 percent said 15, and 28 percent said 14 or lower (Mears et al., 2007).

Mears and his colleagues think that the current variation in ages needs to end; states should have a uniform age that is consistent with the psychological research on adolescent development (Mears et al., 2007). Recall that some states have recently gone back to age 18.

What do you think? Should the states be uniform in setting the upper age limit for juvenile court? If so, which age is best? As noted above, public opinion is divided on the opposite question about the appropriate lower limit for treating juveniles as adults.

A Criminalized Juvenile Court

A solution to the problems of juvenile court is to "criminalize" juvenile court: to attempt to make it a scaled-down version of adult criminal court. In order to do this, two things need to be done. First, a **criminalized juvenile court** would entail providing juveniles with all the procedural protections of criminal court. Thus, children would have the right to a jury trial and would have fully adversarial defense attorneys, not attorneys who often slip into the role of a concerned parent trading off zealous advocacy for promises of treatment. A second action that needs to be taken to transform juvenile court into a criminal court for youths would be to scale down penalties out of concern for the reduced culpability of children. Sentences would be shorter in such a juvenile court compared to adult criminal court. This reform was suggested about 30 years ago by the American Bar Association and the Institute of Judicial Administration. The suggestion was published in the Juvenile Justice Standards (IJA–ABA, 1982).

The major problem with the suggestion for a criminalized juvenile court is that it may not satisfy calls for a more punitive approach to juvenile offenders. Critics of the current juvenile justice system do not want reduced penalties; they want adult penalties for what they perceive as adult offenses: "adult crime, adult time," in the words of one governor (see Vandervort & Ladd, 2001:229). Such critics contend that violent offenses indicate culpability and should be punished with lengthy prison terms, and that is not the vision of the Juvenile Justice Standards.

Abolishing Juvenile Court

Barry Feld (1999) points out flaws with the argument that juvenile court failure is simply a failure of implementation and that all that is needed is a rededication to the original rehabilitative ideals of juvenile court. Feld agrees that adequate funds have not been devoted to juvenile court, but he argues that funds will always be inadequate. One reason is that there is "pervasive public antipathy" to helping the poor, disadvantaged, disproportionately minority youths who are the clients of juvenile court. Another reason is that because committing a crime is the condition for receiving "help" from juvenile court, there is a built-in punishment focus. Feld argues that providing for children is a societal responsibility, not just a responsibility of juvenile court. In fact, the mere existence of juvenile court is an excuse or alibi for not providing for poor, minority youths. In Feld's words:

> A society collectively provides for the welfare of its children by supporting families, communities, schools, and social institutions that nurture all young people and not by cynically incarcerating its most disadvantaged children "for their own good" (Feld, 1999:296).

Feld also argues that juvenile court does not provide procedural fairness to children. Traditionally, some of the procedural protections of adult court, such as the right to jury trial, have been denied to children on the justification that the juvenile court was not a punitive court like adult court. Even worse than denying procedural protections, juvenile courts have treated children in similar circumstances who commit similar offenses in unequal and disparate fashion. This individualized handling was originally justified on the supposed rehabilitative foundation of juvenile court. However, because juvenile court is punitive and does not provide rehabilitation, this denial of due process safeguards makes juvenile court unfair and unjust.

In summary, Feld thinks that efforts to return the juvenile court to its rehabilitative ideal are doomed to failure: "The current juvenile court provides neither therapy nor justice and cannot be rehabilitated" (Feld, 1999:297). Because juvenile court provides neither help nor crime control, now is the time to abolish it. In its place Feld proposed adult criminal court for all, both juveniles and adults.

Adult court would mean that juveniles would receive adult procedural protections. Juveniles would have the right to a jury trial, and defense attorneys would act as zealous adversaries. In addition, Feld argued that juveniles should still get shorter sentences because shorter sentences have been a saving feature of juvenile court and they "enable most young offenders to survive the mistakes of adolescence with a semblance of their life chances intact" (Feld, 1999:304). He argued that adult courts could "discount" sentences for youths. Specifically,

14-year-olds would receive 25 to 33 percent of the adult penalty; 16-year-olds, 50 to 66 percent; and 18-year-olds, the full adult penalty.

Feld failed to note that adult court sentencing for juveniles would also require some type of protection of the youth's record. The state of New York, for example, has a "youthful offender" provision that makes convictions and sentences under its provisions like juvenile court adjudications and dispositions in that they do not count against the individual. In other words, one benefit of juvenile court is that a youth can legally say that he or she has not been "arrested" or "convicted"; instead, he or she has been "taken into custody" and "adjudicated." Such legal protections against arrest and conviction records can be extremely important if one is applying for a job, graduate school, or the military.

Vandervort and Ladd (2001) raise a serious objection to Feld's proposal. They argue that Michigan has changed its juvenile code to the point that many juveniles are now handled in adult court, and the results have been harmful for juveniles. They contend that procedural rights are eroding in adult court. A juvenile transferred to adult court actually receives fewer due process protections in adult court than he or she would have in juvenile court. Juveniles are simply getting punishment in adult court, not treatment. Their conclusion is far more pessimistic than Feld's:

> Realistically, the adult criminal system has little or nothing positive to offer young people; it serves few, if any, elements of the public's interest, other than the impulse for retribution (Vandervort & Ladd, 2001:230).

One example illustrates their point. In 1997, Nathaniel Abraham, then 11 years old, was charged with murder. The juvenile court trial judge suppressed Nathaniel's confession to the police because the youth did not understand the *Miranda* warnings. The trial judge also chose a juvenile disposition; Nathaniel could only be under juvenile justice system control until age 21. The appellate court reversed the judge's ruling on understanding *Miranda* because it felt that the trial judge had placed too much emphasis on the child's youth and emotional impairment and not enough emphasis on the facts of the crime. Likewise, both the governor and other politicians criticized the judge's sentence; this is when the governor invoked the slogan "adult crime, adult time" (Vandervort & Ladd, 2001:229).

Exemplifying the deficiencies of Feld's suggestion is the case of *In re LeBlanc* (1988). LeBlanc was a 16-year-old who was charged with murdering his father. He had lived an exemplary life and been a good student but was immature mentally. He was waived to adult court where the likely sentence was life in prison. If he had been kept in juvenile court, he could be confined only until age 21, and he would have received high school and college education. The only possible "benefit" of adult court processing would be that the adult correctional system would teach LeBlanc a trade, but the lengthy prison sentence meant that "it would be decidedly unlikely that he would ever have been able to use that trade beyond the walls of the prison in which he would be housed" (Vandervort & Ladd, 2001:250).

Research, too, shows problems with adult court processing. Bishop and her colleagues interviewed juveniles who had been transferred to adult court in Florida. Juveniles were negative about adult court and adult corrections. They did not fully understand what transpired in adult court and perceived the process to be one of gamesmanship. They felt that criminal court judges had "little interest in them or their problems" whereas juvenile court judges "expressed interest in their problems and concern for their well-being" (Bishop, 2000:136). Similarly, the juveniles felt that juvenile correctional staff "cared for them, understood what troubled them, and believed in their potential," whereas they perceived staff in adult correctional facilities as hostile, derisive, and uncaring workers who thought the juveniles were incapable of change (Bishop, 2000:144).

Kerbs (1999) notes two other problems with Feld's suggestion to switch juveniles to adult criminal court. First, politicians are not saying "discount"; they are crying out "adult crime, adult time." Politicians are mouthing a simplistic formula that suggests that they regard youthful offenders as simply younger but fully responsible offenders. Second, Kerbs fears that African-American juveniles transferred to adult court will continue to receive unfair treatment compared to whites—"unequal justice under law" (Kerbs, 1999:120). Thus, there is reason to believe that abolishing juvenile court would not have the positive effects Feld envisioned and might well produce very negative effects.

Attitudinal research indicates that public opinion is not as simple as some think. On the one hand, a recent study of Florida residents found that more than 75 percent favored a separate court system for juveniles, but 73 percent of the same sample reported favoring transfer to adult court for juveniles who commit violent crimes. More specific questions found that 50 percent favored juvenile court for a juvenile burglar, and 25 percent even favored juvenile court processing for a juvenile murderer (Applegate et al., 2009). Further analysis indicates that respondents seem to want several outcomes: accountability, fair handling, and rehabilitation. A final complicating factor is that respondents are not necessarily fully aware of some of the choices they favor. For example, many respondents favor adult court processing in the mistaken belief that adult court will provide both greater fairness and effective rehabilitation when the adult court may simply provide more punitive handling (Applegate et al., 2009).

In 2007, Feld changed his position that juvenile court should be abolished, because at that point he thought that juvenile courts could do less harm than trying juveniles in adult criminal court. But he still thought that juvenile court was not achieving its rehabilitative mission, and that black youths were receiving unfair treatment (Feld, 2007). Most recently, he has changed his position again, and he and Bishop have a new proposal (Bishop & Feld, 2012; see below in section titled "A New Balance").

Creating a New Juvenile Court

Still another suggestion is to make a new juvenile court. Claude Noriega (2000) suggests that we create a new juvenile court that has two branches: one for children and one for adolescents. The children's court would be rehabilitative and would presume that children are inculpable, that is, they do not have criminal responsibility. The adolescent court would presume partial culpability and would be more punitive than the children's court. Of course, adult court would continue to presume that adults are culpable and would be the most punitive of the three courts.

Waiver would be by judicial hearing only. There would be no prosecutorial or legislative waiver, and waiver would be only to the next step. Thus, children could only be waived to adolescent court, and only adolescents could be waived to adult court. Juveniles (children and adolescents) would not be allowed to waive their right to counsel. Noriega's reasoning for this is that children and adolescents are generally presumed not competent; they are not allowed to enter into contracts, cannot drink alcohol, and cannot vote or drive (until late adolescence).

This is an interesting proposal. Noriega disagrees with Feld that abolishing juvenile court is the best course of action. Noriega argues that abolishing juvenile court will not guarantee that adult courts treat children/adolescents properly. He argues that it will be hard to treat a juvenile as a juvenile after he has been designated an "adult" and that it will be difficult to actually give discounts, à la Feld, to juveniles in adult court "as if they were getting their sentence on sale from Kmart" (Noriega, 2000:692–693).

An attractive feature of this proposal is that it offers a more complex and realistic view of development. Instead of assuming that one day a juvenile is a child and the next day he is an adult, it recognizes the intermediate stage of adolescence. Noriega is also probably more realistic than Feld about the actual results of abolishing juvenile court and letting adult court handle juvenile matters. Adult courts are probably not going to be as caring and protective or concerned about youth discounts as Feld hopes.

Unfortunately, Noriega just gives a sketchy outline. He says that states should have a children's court and an adolescent's court. He does not give us specific age limits for each. Nor does he specify punishment limits (e.g., incarceration terms) for each. Still another problem is that this could result in yet another bureaucracy—adolescent court and adolescent corrections—when the current juvenile and adult bureaucracies both have myriad problems. To note just one issue, will states be willing to create a new adolescent court and corrections system (assuming the current juvenile court becomes children's court)? Will they be willing to hire more personnel? Build more courtrooms? Build more prisons? As Garland (2001—and see below) so aptly points out, the recent trend has been to cut back the welfare state in general. Noriega's proposal goes against that trend; governmental bodies are looking to cut expenditures, not embrace new spending initiatives.

A "Youth Justice System" Within Adult Criminal Court

Jeffrey Butts (2000) offers still another variation: a **youth justice system** within adult court. As we observed at the beginning of the chapter, Butts notes that the juvenile justice system is disappearing before our very eyes. Presumptive waiver provisions, mandatory waiver, blended sentencing, mandatory minimums and other sentencing guidelines, open hearings, and the use of juvenile records in adult court (e.g., to count as first or second strikes in three-strikes cases) are all nails in the coffin of the traditional juvenile court. Thus "[i]t is too late to save the traditional [juvenile justice] system because the traditional system is already gone" (Butts, 2000:52). He also notes that widespread opposition to the idea of delinquency dictates the end of delinquency cases in juvenile court. When the public hears "delinquent," they think "weak and lenient" (Butts, 2000:55).

His suggestion is to transfer all delinquency matters to adult court but to create a separate arm of adult court to deal with criminal acts allegedly committed by juveniles. He argues that adult courts are creating new specialized courts such as drug courts and mental health courts that do specialized intake and treatment. He thinks that specialized youth justice courts could do the same for juveniles. The benefit would be to stop fighting over which court—juvenile or adult—gets which offender and to start focusing "on ensuring the quality of the process used for all youth" (Butts, 2000:56). Because Butts is proposing a specialized court like drug and mental health courts, his proposal can be considered an extension of the movement called **therapeutic jurisprudence**: "an interdisciplinary perspective that urges us to consider the therapeutic and anti-therapeutic consequences of legal rules, of legal procedures, and of the roles of lawyers, judges, and others acting within the legal arena" (Wexler, 2002:205).

Butts is accurate that many of the changes in juvenile court in the last 10 years have taken away many of the clientele (via some type of waiver/transfer). He is also accurate that some of the new drug courts and mental health courts (therapeutic jurisprudence) have made significant strides in dealing with their particular clients. A major question, however, is whether most jurisdictions would in fact start such courts and would devote the resources needed to allow them to carry out their mission. Creating new youth services courts in the adult system without adequate funding and resources would be a sham.

A New Balance

Bishop and Feld (2012) argue that the current juvenile court is showing signs of re-balancing, or a new balance. They argue that the punitive strains of the "get tough" era of the 1980s and 1990s are softening and they "see signs of a counterbalance to the repressive policies of the recent past" (Bishop & Feld, 2012:921).

There are several factors behind this softening of the "get tough" era. First, the famous crime decline (see Chapter 7) of the 1990s has eased calls for harsh treatment of juveniles. Second, advances in both neuroscience and developmental psychology have provided scientific support for the proposition that youth are less mature and less responsible. Third, advocacy groups have worked to soften punitive demands of the "get tough" era.

One sign of the re-balancing is a trend to return the lower bound of criminal court jurisdiction to age 18. Connecticut, Illinois, and Massachusetts did so recently, and New York is considering the move. Second, other states have restricted the offense or offender criteria for transfer, or have mitigated the possible sentences for transferred youth (for details, see Daugherty, 2013). The trend is not perfect, as some states have expanded offender or offense criteria for transfer. A third sign is that the Supreme Court ruled against life without parole sentences for youths convicted of non-homicide offenses (*Graham v. Florida*, 2010) and ruled against mandatory life without parole sentences for juveniles (*Miller v. Alabama*, 2012). More important than the holdings, in these decisions the Court extended the *Roper* rationale that juveniles are not as culpable as adults. Also, a number of states are giving greater protection to the right to counsel for juveniles by prohibiting or dissuading waivers of counsel.

Some states are leading the way while some states resist, but the changes noted above "raise hope for continuing shifts toward more sensible and humane practices" (Bishop & Feld, 2012:921). Economics may help this trend. A cost–benefit analysis in North Carolina estimated that raising the age of criminal court jurisdiction to 18 would save the state about $50 million a year, a saving of approximately 40 percent (Butts & Roman, 2014).

In a separate piece, Feld (2013) reaffirms his earlier proposal for a youth discount in sentencing based on the recognition of youthfulness as mitigating culpability in the *Roper*, *Graham*, and *Miller* decisions (see sections on the death penalty and life without parole below). Specifically, he suggests that a 14-year-old might receive a sentence that is only 20 or 25 percent of the sentence an adult would get; a 16-year-old, 50 percent of an adult sentence; and that the harshest penalty available for a youth would be 20 or 25 years, instead of life without parole (Feld, 2013).

A Developmental Approach

The National Research Council of the National Academies of Science recently completed a comprehensive study on the implications of the research on adolescent development for the juvenile justice system. The resulting report recommended that juveniles be held accountable for offending, but that condemnation, control, and lengthy confinement are not necessary to do so. Instead, restorative justice programs and restitution are two examples of developmentally appropriate methods. A second focus should be to prevent reoffending by implementing evidence-based programs after appropriate risk/needs assessment. Intervention efforts should engage the youth's family and draw on neighborhood resources. A third emphasis is on procedural fairness, including attorney representation and reducing racial/ethnic disparities via reduced processing or structured decision-making. Attention needs to be devoted to making sure that adolescents are competent to understand all proceedings and to ensure that juveniles perceive that they have been treated fairly. An interesting note to this report is that the report authors argued that juvenile court is based on seeing juveniles as children, while recent "get tough" measures see juveniles as adults. The research on adolescent development, however, sees juvenile offenders as between the two (Bonnies et al., 2013). (For additional voices focusing on the need to base policy on what we know about adolescent development, see Sullivan, Piquero, & Cullen, 2012; and Zimring & Tanenhaus, 2014).

The National Research Council report edited by Bonnies et al. (2013) is based on a wide range of research, and is comprehensive. In contrast to the other reform proposals in this chapter, this set of suggestions has the added weight of being written by a panel of experts from a nationally recognized body of scientists. Thus, no one can claim that this report and its recommendations are simply one person's viewpoint.

A Restorative Justice Juvenile Court

Gordon Bazemore (1999) suggests that now is the time to take the "fork in the road," to try a new path for juvenile court. As noted in Chapter 12, Bazemore is one of the main proponents for adopting a restorative justice model in the juvenile justice system.

In Pittsburgh, young offenders are involved in service projects such as home repair for the elderly and voter registration drives. In Utah, offenders are paying victim restitution out of wages from public service jobs. In Oregon, offender work crews cut firewood and deliver it to the elderly. More than 150 cities are utilizing victim–offender mediation. In Colorado and Florida, offenders work with Habitat for Humanity building homes for lower-income families. In Florida, probation officers are walking neighborhood beats to help promote local guardianship of communities. In Boston and in Florida, probation officers are helping police monitor probationers at night.

What all of these efforts have in common is a restorative justice focus that emphasizes the victim and the community. The approach is "focused less on achieving public safety by incarcerating individual offenders and more on reducing fear, building youth-adult relationships, and increasing the capacity of community groups and institutions to prevent crime and safely monitor offenders in the community" (Bazemore, 1999:98; see also Takagi & Shank, 2004).

This represents a radical rethinking of the role of juvenile court. Instead of sanctioning and supervising offenders, the role of the **restorative justice juvenile court** would be to build community so that neighborhoods can better respond to—but also prevent—delinquency. Communities would be more involved in sentencing through community panels or conferences or dispute resolution programs. Communities would return to their role of being responsible for youths. Bazemore argues that the community must address socialization needs with "caring adults who spend time with young people not because they are paid to do so but because they share a commitment to the idea that youth development is a community responsibility" (Bazemore, 1999:101).

A positive feature of Bazemore's proposal is that it is not a hypothetical proposal; many restorative justice programs are already in place. As noted, numerous communities already are working at restorative justice. A major question, however, is how far restorative justice can go. How willing are citizens to assume the responsibilities that restorative justice would give them in deciding cases and monitoring sanctions such as community service? If people are not available to staff the restorative justice programs, they will not work. Proving that it is possible to implement such programs, Vermont has a system of 49 restorative justice boards with almost 300 volunteer board members in operation (Karp et al., 2004). These boards use 30- to 60-minute meetings to negotiate restorative justice contracts between victims and offenders. So it is possible to implement such programs.

A survey of juvenile court judges found overall support for victim involvement in the juvenile court process. For example, 60 percent of the judges agreed that victims should have input into the sanctioning and dispositional decisions of juvenile court, and 44 percent thought that victims should have input into diversion decisions. Focus group discussions with judges, however, showed some ambivalence about victim involvement. Some judges thought that involving victims in juvenile court decisions might introduce some bias into juvenile court. Some judges thought that greater victim involvement might detract from judges' attempts to remain neutral in juvenile court (Bazemore & Leip, 2000).

On the one hand, restorative justice is a reality in many juvenile courts. As of a few years ago, Bazemore and Schiff (2005) noted that there were well over 700 restorative justice programs, some adult and some juvenile, in operation across the country. While most of these programs do address the core restorative justice principle of repairing harm, not all of the programs have addressed community and government role transformation. In other words, many operate within the traditional framework of government programs rather than trying to achieve community-building. So a probation department may start a restitution program or a community service program or even some type of victim–offender mediation, but it may not take the next step of involving community members to a much greater extent in seeking justice and making both victims and offenders whole once again (Bazemore & Schiff, 2005).

Another concern about restorative justice is the reliance on communities to get involved in programs such as mediation and conferencing. Takagi and Shank (2004), for example, note that in Oakland, California, the black youth unemployment rate approaches 50 percent, more than half the people in homeless shelters are African-American, and three black high schools in Oakland consistently rank at the bottom of the state in academic performance. So what does community mean for the unemployed, the homeless, and the poorly educated? Is restorative justice possible if community is so fractured?

Bazemore's (2012) most recent comment on restorative justice is that it is in danger of being perceived as being a "boutique" program, or having the "Oprah" effect. What he means is that Oprah Winfrey has featured restorative conferences on her show, and Bazemore fears that restorative justice may be seen as something "often viewed as 'perfect for' just the right (unfortunately rare) case" (Bazemore, 2012:713). So it is seen as "interesting" and fine for minor offenses, instead of being found useful for almost all delinquency cases, as it has been used in New Zealand.

Zimring's Caution

Franklin Zimring (2000) adds a cautionary note to the various proposals about keeping, abolishing, or modifying juvenile court. He reminds us that even juvenile court is in the business of imposing punishment. As rehabilitative as the intentions of the founders may have been, the truth, as noted in *In re Gault*, is that juvenile court "dispositions" often deprive youths of their freedom. For Zimring, this truth of punishment means that a crucial element, even if we abolish juvenile court, is reduced punishment. In other words, even if all juveniles went to adult court, there still would be a legitimate issue of deciding on lesser punishments for such offenders. Second, Zimring points out that the United States is inconsistent about juveniles. It prohibits them from voting until age 18 and from drinking until age 21 because they are considered immature, yet submits them to adult court and punishment at increasingly lower ages. Zimring agrees that youths are immature and argues that states need to address this inconsistency and not just ignore it.

Summary

Juvenile justice is at a crossroads. Critics have pointed out serious flaws with juvenile court, and many states have already removed many youths from juvenile court jurisdiction. Some have advocated the end of juvenile court. On the other hand, research on the development of juvenile brain functioning, Supreme Court decisions relying on that research to ban life without parole sentences for non-homicide offenses and mandatory life without parole sentencing schemes, and research on the effectiveness of treatment programs (e.g., Kim, Merlo, & Benkos, 2013b) suggest that a current trend is to reaffirm the need for juvenile court. Evidence of such a trend is recent legislation in some states, such as Connecticut, Illinois, and Massachusetts, to return the age of beginning criminal court jurisdiction to 18; and legislation narrowing transfer laws and offering reverse transfer hearings (Daugherty, 2013). There has even been a call to extend juvenile court jurisdiction to 21 or even 24 (Bulman, 2014)! As will be noted below (see section below titled "Jurisdiction Over Status Offenses"), many are calling for juvenile court to stay away from processing status offenders in favor of community treatment programs. In summary, one current emphasis seems to be to keep and possibly expand the ability of juvenile court to deal with delinquents, but to reduce if not eliminate court interactions with status offenders.

BROADER ISSUES

Beyond the need to make changes in juvenile court, there are additional issues that need to be addressed if American society is to help juveniles grow into mature, responsible, law-abiding adults. We will note several such issues here and show how they relate to juvenile justice. We will consider the issues of race and juvenile court, the possible decline of community and social capital, the role and needs of American families, and the political economy.

Race and Juvenile Court

Several sources note that race is a problem in juvenile justice. The harshest criticism is that the public is not as concerned about disadvantaged children as middle- and upper-class children (Feld, 1999; Krisberg, 2012). The consensus is that the juvenile justice system has a problem of disproportionate minority contacts (see, e.g., Bishop, 2005; Piquero, 2008; Rovner, 2013).

A number of writers argue that juvenile justice must fight the influence of racism. The federal government, for example, has made the elimination of disproportionate minority confinement in juvenile correctional facilities a priority.

Rovner (2013) notes that there are racial disparities throughout the juvenile justice system. In 2010, black youths made up 31 percent of all arrests, but only 17 percent of all juveniles. In juvenile court, black youths are more likely to be referred to court, less likely to be diverted, and more likely to be sent to secure confinement; they accounted for 33 percent of delinquency cases (Puzzanchera & Robson, 2014). Studies show that race effects persist even after controlling for legal variables such as offense seriousness, and that early decisions to arrest and detain contaminate decisions at later stages to an unknown degree (Bishop & Leiber, 2012). In other words, police decisions to focus on certain neighborhoods, police tendencies to react to the attitudes of minority suspects, and decisions to not divert and to detain that are affected by such factors as resources available to lower-class children, begin early in the process and have indirect effects later on.

Perhaps most disturbing of all is Feld's (1999) assertion that there is pervasive public antipathy to the problems of disadvantaged and minority children. If society does not really care for poor minority children, then it may not matter all that much which court—juvenile rehabilitative, juvenile criminal, or adult criminal—is designated to process juvenile delinquency. Unless society is truly committed to the problems of all youths, and especially disadvantaged youths, then youth crime will persist.

An analysis of three major studies of delinquency in Pittsburgh, Rochester, and Seattle found clear evidence of greater contact/referral of minorities in the juvenile justice system. This differential minority contact cannot be accounted for by higher offending by minorities. However, the researchers could not conclude that differential minority contact proves racial bias (Huizinga et al., 2007). This report suggests that race continues to be an issue that merits concern in the juvenile justice system.

Similarly, recent reviews of the research on juvenile justice system processing concludes that race is still a factor in processing (Bishop, 2005; Piquero, 2008). One reason for the influence of race is at the very heart of the juvenile justice system. As noted in Chapter 2, juvenile court was founded to treat children with problems. This intent put discretion into the system. Because officials have discretion, they often focus on minority juveniles because they think that minority youths need the help that the juvenile justice system is supposed to offer. So the positive intention of offering assistance to minority children has resulted in a disproportionate share of minority youths being subjected to juvenile court processing and dispositions such as placement. While the intent may have been positive, the result has been a disproportionate share of minorities at all stages of the juvenile justice system, starting with police and ending with custodial placements (Bishop, 2005).

This is not the place for a thorough analysis of racism in the juvenile justice system (for a discussion, see Bishop & Leiber, 2012; for an analysis of racism in the adult criminal justice system, see Tonry, 2011b). We simply note that most analysts see disproportionate processing of minority youths. The federal government has been supporting efforts to eliminate or reduce disproportionate minority contacts. It is critical to eliminate any traces of racism or perceived racial inequities in juvenile court so that all youths will regard the juvenile justice system as fair. Without the perception of fair treatment, minority youths will be suspicious and resentful, and those emotions doom any hope of reclaiming problem youths.

The Need to Rebuild Community

As noted in the discussion of community policing in Chapter 7, Robert Putnam (2000) argues that we are "bowling alone;" that is, social capital is eroding. In other words, civic participation and other measures of community involvement are declining. If accurate, this decline of social capital has implications for juvenile justice.

One measure of the decline of community is religious participation. Between the 1960s and the 1990s, church membership declined by approximately 10 percent. Similarly, church attendance has declined by approximately 10–12 percent over the last quarter century, most markedly from the mid-1980s to the mid-1990s (Putnam, 2000). Participation in civic clubs has also declined. In 1975–1976, about two-thirds (64%) of Americans had attended at least one club meeting in the previous year. That slipped to about 38 percent by 1999 (Putnam, 2000).

What do Americans do with their time now? It appears that much of our time is now spent watching screens, either television screens (about four hours per day) or computer or smartphone screens. So we watch things as individuals and have less time to do things together such as participate in community organizations (Putnam, 2000).

As noted in Chapter 7, if community is in fact declining, then the future of community policing is not as optimistic as its proponents proclaim. Decline of community would have other repercussions as well. If community is declining and if that decline cannot be stopped, then restorative justice efforts also will face difficulties. If we want citizens to participate in restorative justice conferencing, victim–offender mediation programs, sentencing circles, and other restorative justice programs (see the earlier section on restorative justice), we need a solid community base as the foundation for those efforts. If people do not join together socially, how can we realistically expect them to come together for restorative justice initiatives? As noted earlier, if communities such as Oakland have staggering unemployment and homelessness rates, and their high schools are the worst in the state, then is it realistic to expect community members to have the time and resources to participate in restorative justice programs (Takagi & Shank, 2004)?

While Putnam discusses reduced civic club membership as a sign of community decline, some criminal justice analysts see more profound problems. For example, homicide rates in certain dangerous neighborhoods are alarmingly high: for black males in one Rochester neighborhood, the homicide rate was 520 per 100,000 African-American males aged 15–19, 65 times the national rate (Travis, 2012). Currie (2012) links such high crime areas to the recent economic crisis which has left many urban communities "even more bereft of resources, opportunities, and social supports than they were before" (Currie, 2012:46). Clear and others have argued for justice reinvestment (see, e.g., Clear, 2011). By this they mean that if we decreased our reliance on such expensive options as mass imprisonment, we could and should use the savings to invest in programs that would bring jobs and housing to neighborhoods that currently have high crime rates and high imprisonment rates. One problem with justice reinvestment is that when states cut back on expenses such as imprisonment, the savings often go to reduce budget deficits or to reduce taxes (Currie, 2012). So Currie sees the problem as more serious than Putnam does. Currie sees both concentrated poverty and joblessness as getting worse in America while we use prison "as a costly and ineffective alternative to serious efforts to address those enduring social deficits" (Currie, 2012:46).

Another issue is that the decline of community may even make delinquency worse and increase the need for juvenile justice interventions. If civic clubs are disbanding due to lack of interest and participation, we can expect reduced sponsorship of youth sports teams, scout troops, and Boys and Girls Clubs. Many civic clubs sponsor such programs for neighborhood youths. If the clubs are disappearing, either the parents will have to pick up the tab or the youth teams and programs will not survive.

There is hope, however. Putnam points out, for example, that Americans seem to want to reverse the trend of declining civic participation and social capital: "We tell pollsters that we wish we lived in a more civil, more trustworthy, more collectively caring community" (Putnam, 2000:403). He offers some steps that could be effective in restoring social capital. One is for employers to be more family- and community-friendly. Some firms, for example, offer release time to some employees to volunteer for community service such as serving on United Way campaigns. Because part-time workers participate more in community, Putnam urges employers to make greater allowance for part-time employment opportunities. He urges urban planners to design living areas that are more pedestrian-friendly and urges church leaders to revivify spiritual community. He calls for electronic entertainment that fosters community engagement rather than passive sitting in front of television sets. He suggests using the arts to foster community. He urges greater civics education and other efforts to foster political participation (Putnam, 2000).

The challenge is great. Many forces are at work to isolate us from our neighbors. Contemporary trends, such as the proliferation of personal computers, smartphones, Internet usage, personal MP3 players, and a TV and DVD player for each household member, are all working to drive us apart. In the 1950s, even television watching was a family activity. There was only one television set and only three major networks. Today we have multiple sets in even the poorest of households and hundreds of cable or satellite stations to choose from. Families may watch the Super Bowl together, but little else.

It is important not to idealize a past that was far from perfect. The 1950s were not idyllic for African Americans, who had to sit at the back of the bus and could not get into the college of their choice. Nor were they idyllic for women, who could not enter jobs and professions that they aspired to. However, it is important to note that we need to restore social capital. If we wish to prevent delinquency and to pursue new avenues such as restorative justice, then citizens must be willing to contribute to their communities. As noted above, states such as Vermont are proving that there are citizens willing to step up and serve on restorative justice boards; that is, there are people willing to do something about delinquency and victimization (Karp et al., 2004).

Bazemore and Schiff have a different opinion about Putnam's argument that individuals are abandoning community clubs like Kiwanis and Rotary and spending increasingly more time in solitary/individual pursuits, such as surfing the web or playing video games. They think that there is truth in Putnam's assessment, but they also think that there is a real hunger for community. Bazemore and Schiff feel that many citizens are frustrated with justice systems for professionalizing and taking over tasks and responsibilities that are really community responsibilities. It is hoped that restorative justice practices can build on community resolve "to deal with what can no longer be viewed simply as individual problems of offenders or victims" (Bazemore & Schiff, 2005:351). In other words, Bazemore and Schiff think that the community really wants to be involved and that restorative justice programs can be successful in the difficult task of reengaging citizens in the juvenile justice process (Bazemore & Schiff, 2005).

Social Support for Families

All agree that family is critical for child and adolescent development and delinquency prevention. Many think, however, that society is not as supportive of families as it could be. The problem is not that parents are abandoning family values, but that there are social, economic, and political forces at work that weaken the ability of families to do their job. The answer is to provide more assistance to families.

Alida Merlo noted that 13 percent of American children live in conditions that are considered to make them "high-risk" children. About one-third of U.S. children live in one-parent families, about 20 percent live in a home headed by a high school dropout, about 20 percent grow up in poverty, almost 30 percent live with parents who do not have a full-time job, about 12 percent of families receive public assistance, and about 15 percent of children do not have health insurance (Merlo, 2000). (In a partial update of Merlo's case, in 2010 about 30 percent of children lived in one-parent families or with no parent, and about 10 percent had no health insurance. In 2009, 21 percent of all children were living in poverty [Federal Interagency Forum on Child and Family Statistics, 2010].) In 1996, about 1,000 children died of maltreatment (abuse or neglect), yet in "all the political rhetoric about preventing youth violence, any reference to these fatalities, or the conditions that may increase their likelihood, is conspicuously absent" (Merlo, 2000:649). The proponents of tough juvenile policies also ignore the developmental stages that youths go through and instead simply assume that adolescents are completely adult in all respects. Merlo concludes that we need "a moratorium on punitive, reactionary juvenile justice reform" in favor of "a more rational, less political, more observant, more humane manner" (Merlo, 2000:658–659).

Merlo is right for two reasons. First, she is right because it is simply wrong to ignore these high-risk children. The second reason is that there is an "emerging consensus" that "coercion causes crime and social support prevents crime" (Colvin, Cullen, & Vander Ven, 2002:19). To be more specific, the research clearly shows that childhood conduct disorders can lead to delinquency, especially for high-rate offenders. It is also clear that "supportive programs—programs that invest in at-risk children and in at-risk families—work to reduce crime" (Cullen, Wright, & Chamlin, 1999:198–199). Social support for families includes such assistance as parent-effectiveness training, paid family leave, health care insurance, and visiting nurse programs. There is also clear evidence that early prevention programs such as preschool intellectual enrichment, home visitation and parent management training, and community-based mentoring programs can prevent delinquency and crime (Welsh & Farrington, 2007).

In conclusion, a number of conservative and liberal writers agree that there are important problems pertaining to families and their ability to raise healthy and law-abiding children. Conservatives argue that families need to return to traditional values (Bennett, 2001) and character education (Sommers, 2000), whereas liberals argue that families need more social and economic support to help them to do their job.

The Political Economy and Juvenile Court, and Possible Directions

David Garland (2001) makes an intriguing and complex assessment of today's criminal justice policy. He argues that the **political economy**—social, political, and economic changes in the last 30 years—has had important effects on how we view and treat crime, criminals, and delinquents.

To summarize a complex argument, forces such as the proliferation of consumer goods and the decline of guardianship (watchers) due to more women entering the workplace were increasing crime at the same time that government funds were decreasing the provision of treatment programs for delinquents and criminals (due to such factors as the globalization of the economy). Thus, popular sentiment was developing against the poor in general and against delinquents and criminals in particular. Governments were waging war on crime and tending to incarcerate more and more and treat less and less. In juvenile court, this movement has translated into increasing transfer of youths to adult court, sentencing youthful offenders to adult corrections or blended corrections (a combination of juvenile and adult sanctions), and even use of the death penalty for juveniles.

The net result is that instead of devising initiatives to help these groups, politicians are practicing welfare reform for the poor and tough justice for youthful delinquents. These policies coincide with economic realities in twenty-first-century America (and Britain) and they also comfort the middle and upper classes with their fear of street crime—no matter how exaggerated that paranoia may be.

Garland does not have the answers to the scene he so well describes. Inattention to the real needs of youths (especially poor youths) is not a new phenomenon in the United States. In the mid-nineteenth century, for example, the Children's Aid Society in New York City dealt with the urban poor by getting rid of them rather than by actually dealing with the poverty that afflicted them. Specifically, Charles Loring Brace, founder of the Children's Aid Society, began the "orphan trains" that shipped New York City youths west to farmers and whomever else would accept these youths. This practice grew, even though many of the youths suffered abuse in their new environments equal to or worse than what they had suffered at the hands of their own parents in New York. The policy was attractive because it visibly removed problem youths from New York and put them out of sight in placements out West (O'Connor, 2001).

Part of the solution may mean a re-ordering of priorities. If the global economy and the recent economic recession mean that there is only a limited amount of money available for social spending programs in our postmodern economy, perhaps we need to re-evaluate our entitlement programs. Just as Western democracies re-evaluated welfare spending in the 1990s and enacted "welfare reform," perhaps we need to re-evaluate other entitlement programs to see if we are spending enough money on programs that benefit youths.

Maybe the easiest way to follow Garland's suggestions, however, is to use his analysis to clarify some of the true purposes of the current system. He argues that the current passion for punishment is politically generated. It coincides with many of the social and economic changes of the last 25 years and addresses much of the fear of crime generated by the proliferation of consumer goods, the reduction of guardianship in sprawling suburban housing developments spawned by the interstate highway system, the absence of anyone home during working hours due to dual-income households, and a perception that traditional values are eroding. Garland clearly shows that much of America's passion for punishment is a grasping for straws in the face of threatening changes and perceptions of high crime rates.

One strategy is to seek solutions to the crime-delinquency problem that are both politically and economically feasible. An entire issue of *Criminology & Public Policy* in 2011 did precisely this. The lead article (Durlauf & Nagin, 2011) centered on three main points: research indicates that deterrent policies such as increasing prison sentences do not reduce crime; imprisonment is criminogenic—it increases crime among released offenders; and hiring more police and certain police practices do reduce crime through deterrence. A panel of experts responded to these points. In a broader-based perspective, as briefly mentioned in an earlier chapter, Clear (2011) calls for justice reinvestment. By this he means cutting back on costly imprisonment policies and investing the savings into building or re-building neighborhood infrastructures—schools, healthcare, parks, job training, and other services. Clear even endorsed the suggestion for an "urban justice corps," first put forth by Tucker and Cadora (2003), in which youths would be diverted from incarceration to work on rebuilding their urban communities. His argument is that such reinvestment would improve communities that currently have high crime and delinquency rates and that also see many adults and youths arrested and sent to prison or training schools. He thinks his proposal is feasible because it would not require new expenditures but simply re-direct current spending to more productive outlays.

Sections of this textbook echo much of this debate. We have discussed how several deterrence programs—such as Scared Straight, capital punishment, and direct file waiver to adult court—simply do not reduce or prevent delinquency (see previous chapters). We have also seen how certain police practices have been found to be effective. Going beyond Durlauf and Nagin (2011), we have also discussed the findings on the effectiveness of rehabilitation (e.g., Greenwood, 2008; Lipsey, 2009) and on the cost-effectiveness of such rehabilitative interventions (Aos & Drake, 2013).

In this concluding chapter, therefore, we argue for the abandonment of deterrence-based strategies that do not work and that do not reflect optimism in human potential. We argue for the adoption of rehabilitative strategies that do work and do reflect belief in human potential. What writers like Garland—and Durlauf and Nagin—add to this is the realistic reminder that the public and politicians also enter the picture. Any solution to juvenile delinquency needs to pass the test of being acceptable to the public and to politicians. The Durlauf and Nagin article (2011) contributes by pointing out the lack of evidence for a deterrent impact of imprisonment and the harmful effects of imprisonment on offenders, including increased criminal activity upon release. In the past, criminologists have not done a good job of conveying research findings to the public and to legislators. Now is the time to try to correct that. Perhaps the current budgetary crises in governments can make a difference. Perhaps both the public and legislators will be more attentive to discussions of what works and the cost–benefits of what works versus what is ineffective. A definition of insanity is doing the same thing over and over and expecting different results. The current budgetary crises in most government jurisdictions should help both the public and the legislators to think twice before committing the insanity of repeating deterrent strategies that much research has proven ineffective, as well as the comparative sanity of adopting evidence-based strategies that work, are cost-effective, and speak to the positive side of humanity.

Reintroducing the Spiritual Dimension into Corrections

As noted above, some think that the answer to delinquency is character education. Going even further than this, Ron Powers (2002) argues that the basic problem facing today's youths is apocalyptic nihilism. By this he means that American youths face a gnawing gap in their lives, that they seek "a community that satisfied their longing for worth-proving ritual, meaningful action in the service of a cause, and psychological intimacy" (Powers, 2002:65). Similarly, Staples (2000) argues that one explanation for school violence is the emptiness of our consumer culture, which does not satisfy the deeper longings of the heart. In Staples's words, both youths and adults possess a "fundamental yearning for significance through engagement in the processes of reflection, creativity, compassion, and the gift of self to others" (Staples, 2000:33). So Powers, Staples, and others believe that youths are searching for a deeper sense of meaning in their lives.

Instead of providing such meaning, American policy offers problem youths punishment. The answer, says Powers, is "respectful inclusion: through a reintegration of our young into the intimate circles of family and community life. We must face the fact that having ceased to exploit children as laborers, we now exploit them as consumers. We must find ways to offer them useful functions tailored to their evolving capacities" (Powers, 2002:74).

John Whitehead and Michael Braswell (2000) argue that what is needed is to re-introduce the **spiritual dimension in corrections**. This would entail efforts of corrections workers, whether prison counselors, chaplains, or probation officers, to help offenders find greater meaning in their lives.

Both residential institutions and probation can try to address the spiritual needs of juvenile offenders. Prisons and jails have always had chaplains and religious services as part of their programming. That can and should continue but institutions and probation/parole can take additional steps to incorporate the spiritual dimension into correctional practice.

First, correctional workers—correctional counselors, probation officers, parole officers, correctional officers—can all attempt to help offenders focus on the question of meaning in their lives. In group sessions and individual reporting, these workers can encourage offenders to think about the meaning of their lives.

Second, correctional workers have the simple but potentially profound example of their own lives. They can come to work each and every day showing a sense of purpose and meaning in their lives and in their interactions with prisoners that will influence those who come in contact with them. All of us can attest to persons who show by the example of their lives that there is something that energizes them and inspires them despite the difficulties they face. This is in stark contrast to workers who exert a negative influence in the prison or in the parole office. For example, in one women's prison, some guards came in and plopped down in front of the television set to watch hours of sports programming (Girshick, 1999), and in some Canadian correctional facilities, guard supervisors were found to create an environment rife with sexual harassment (McMahon, 1999). At the very least, workers need to refrain from abuse, harassment, and anything else that detracts from prison as a place where offenders can think about the meaning of their lives.

A concrete suggestion is to adopt an intervention strategy such as the "Making Life Choices" program, which is a participatory learning strategy that focuses "on creating contexts in which young people themselves can discover their own competence for influencing the direction of their lives" (Ferrer-Wreder, Lorente, Briones, Bussell, Berman, & Arrufat, 2002:170). The goal is "accepting control and responsibility of one's life" (Ferrer-Wreder et al., 2002:171). More generally, Christian Hoff Sommers argues that parents and schools need to emphasize character education, that is, "habituating children to the exercise of self-control, temperance, honesty, courage" (Sommers, 2000:191).

A similar suggestion is to start faith-based training schools for juveniles. The state of Florida has started faith-based prisons for adult prisoners, and the federal government started some faith-based programming in 2002 (Camp, Klein-Saffran, Kwon, Daggett, & Joseph, 2006). A recent evidence-based assessment of faith-based programs found some evidence that the programs reduced recidivism. The authors noted that much of the research in this area is weak but concluded that it would be "premature to abandon faith-based programs" (Dodson, Cabage, & Klenowski, 2011:381). So at this point it appears that definitive results are not yet available. One concern about faith-based prisons is that they could divert money away from important programs for all prisoners, such as education and vocational training (Jablecki, 2005).

Corrections officials tour the Lawtey Correctional Institution in Lawtey, Florida. In 2004, Lawtey became a male Faith- and Character-Based Institution (FCBI), which seeks to encourage the spirituality of inmates of all faiths.

CREDIT: AP Photo/Oscar Sosa

One reason for raising the issue of introducing the spiritual dimension into corrections is that there is evidence that it matters. In a study of offenders ages 15 to 24, Benda (2002) found that religion was inversely related to carrying a weapon, violence, the use of illicit drugs, and the selling of illicit drugs. Religion was measured by church attendance, religious expressions, and forgiveness.

So one task of corrections may be to help that segment of offenders who are open to asking and seeking answers to the perennial questions about life: Why am I here? What is the meaning of life? What is happiness? Should I just seek more money and prestige or are there other more important goals in life? Do I just consider myself or should I think about others? Am I making moral or immoral choices? As one thinker puts it, am I seeking "significance through engagement in the processes of reflection, creativity, compassion, and the gift of self to others" (Staples, 2000:33)? None of this should lead to proselytizing or to erasing the separation of church and state. No correctional worker should impose his or her religious beliefs on inmates or probationers.

Some may object that attempting to inject the spiritual into correctional practice is too ambitious a project. If corrections cannot accomplish the basic objective of keeping offenders crime-free, then how can it be expected to help offenders become better persons spiritually? However, this objection may have it backwards. Perhaps one reason that corrections has had such an uninspiring record with recidivism is that it makes no effort to help offenders in a search for meaning and purpose in their lives. If the implicit objective of corrections is that offenders only need to buy into the American Dream, and if that dream is questionable and uninspiring and one that ignores the deeper potential of human living, then it may be no surprise that probation does little to improve recidivism.

A final note is that research has shown the importance of religion in delinquency causation. In a study of boot camp inmates, Benda (2002) found that religion was clearly correlated (inversely) with crimes against persons. In fact, religion was the fifth largest correlate in the model. So the more religious these inmates, the less likely they were to be involved in violence. Similarly, an analysis of the National Youth Survey found that religiosity affected adolescent use of illicit drugs (Jang & Johnson, 2001). These studies confirm the importance of religion and suggest its usefulness in preventing delinquency (see also, Dodson et al., 2011).

CAPITAL PUNISHMENT FOR JUVENILES

In 2012, there were 14,827 homicides in the United States, and 443 juveniles were arrested for homicide (FBI, 2013). This is dramatically lower than the approximately 3,800 juveniles who were arrested for murder in 1993, the peak year for murders by juveniles (Snyder, 2005). Despite this decrease, however, we will probably see continued media attention on juveniles who kill.

For adult murderers, **capital punishment** has been debated for years (see, e.g., van den Haag & Conrad, 1983; and Costanzo, 1997, for further discussion). The questions in the debate have been both philosophical and empirical. Some of the philosophical questions involve the moral issue of the state taking a human life (for viewpoints on this issue, see Boxes 14.2 and 14.3) and the morality of capital punishment in the face of the possibility of mistakes (i.e., executing someone who has been mistakenly convicted). The empirical questions include the deterrent impact of capital punishment (does it prevent individuals from committing murder because they fear being sentenced to die?) and the issue of racial or class bias (is the death penalty more likely to be imposed on minorities than on whites?). These same issues apply to the question of the appropriateness of the death penalty for juveniles.

WEB ACTIVITY

For extensive information on the death penalty, including current statistics, go to the website of the Death Penalty Information Center: http://www.death penaltyinfo.org

In 2005, the Supreme Court ruled that the death penalty is unconstitutional for juveniles. In *Roper v. Simmons* (2005), writing for the majority, Justice Arthur Kennedy wrote that "[t]he Eighth and Fourteenth Amendments forbid imposition of the death penalty on offenders who were under the age of 18 when their crimes were committed." The ruling came in a case in which Christopher Simmons, age 17, with two accomplices, broke and entered a home at 2:00 A.M., took a woman captive, drove away, and threw the woman from a railroad trestle into a river.

BOX 14.2 SOME ARGUMENTS AGAINST CAPITAL PUNISHMENT

Two voices against capital punishment are Mark Costanzo and Donald Cabana.

One of Costanzo's arguments is that if society considers killing to be wrong, then it is just as wrong for the state to kill as it is for an individual to kill. The only exceptions are "self-defense, imminent danger, or the protection of society" (Costanzo, 1997:135). None of these exceptions apply to the capital offender because he "has already been captured and waits in a prison cell safely isolated from the community" (Costanzo, 1997:136).

Costanzo is very empathetic to the victim's family, but he argues that an execution will not bring back the victim for the family. Furthermore, an execution is "a state-sanctioned killing [that] will debase us all and create a new set of victims: the murderer's family" (Costanzo, 1997:143). This is to be avoided because, for one thing, the murderer's family members are innocent of wrongdoing. An interesting suggestion of Costanzo's is to stop trying to abolish the death penalty, at least for a period of time. Instead, opponents should try a "detour" strategy of trying to get state lawmakers to limit the death penalty to multiple or serial murder cases. There are several advantages to this strategy. First, because it would reduce the number of capital punishment cases, it would save both court trial time and appellate time. Second, it would reduce the possibility of mistakes because the evidence in multiple murder cases is "often overwhelming" (Costanzo, 1997:155). Third, it would reduce racial bias because most serial killers are white. The overall result would be that "[w]e could finally claim that only the worst of the worst are executed" (Costanzo, 1997:155).

Finally, Costanzo aptly expresses the argument of many that killing a murderer seems an extremely illogical way for society to convey the message that killing is wrong:

Killing is an odd way to show that killing is wrong, an odd way to show that society is just and humane . . . we also send the message that killing is an acceptable way of solving the problem of violence, that a life should be extinguished if we have the power to take it and the offender has taken a life. We lend legal authority to the dangerous idea that if someone has committed a depraved crime, we should treat him or her as a nonhuman who can be killed without remorse (Costanzo, 1997:166–167).

Donald Cabana is a former warden who carried out a number of executions in the state of Mississippi. He has written about the execution of one man, Connie Evans, whom he executed and had come to know was a changed individual:

> This was not the same cold-blooded murderer who had arrived on death row six years before. His tears were not just those of a young man fearful of what lay beyond death's door; I was convinced they were also tears of genuine sorrow and pain for the tragic hurt and sadness he had caused so many people (Cabana, 1996:15).

Cabana argued to the governor for a stay, but there were no legal grounds to do so. Cabana had to carry out the execution even though he felt that "as a society we were supposed to be better than the Connie Ray Evanses of the world" (Cabana, 1996:15). Cabana eventually resigned his warden's position and went on to become a college professor.

The majority opinion reasoned that the juvenile death penalty is rejected by the majority of the states and is used infrequently in states that authorize it. This suggests that today, American society views juveniles as less culpable than adults. The majority went on to cite scientific evidence that juveniles under 18 are less mature and responsible than adults, more susceptible to peer pressure, and have characters that are less well formed than those of adults. The majority recognizes that there is no perfect decision about the appropriate

BOX 14.3 AN ARGUMENT IN FAVOR OF CAPITAL PUNISHMENT

Ernest van den Haag is one of the leading proponents of the death penalty. Here are some of his arguments in favor of the death penalty.

First, he thinks that many critics of the death penalty are cowards who are afraid to impose the penalty:

> Aware of human frailty they shudder at the gravity of the decision and refuse to make it. The irrevocability of a verdict of death is contrary to the modern spirit that likes to pretend that nothing ever is definitive, that everything is open-ended, that doubts must always be entertained and revisions made. Such an attitude may be proper for inquiring philosophers and scientists. But not for courts. They can evade decisions on life and death only by giving up their paramount duties: to do justice, to secure the lives of the citizens, and to vindicate the norms society holds inviolable (van den Haag, 1978:67–68).

Second, van den Haag argues that murder—the most serious crime—cries out for the most serious penalty: execution. Otherwise, society is failing to carry out the proper affirmation of common values:

> In all societies, the degree of social disapproval of wicked acts is expressed in the degree of punishment threatened. Thus, punishments both proclaim and enforce social values according to the importance given to them. There is no other way for society to affirm its values. To refuse to punish any crime with death, then, is to avow that the negative weight of a crime can never exceed the positive value of the life of the person who committed it. I find that proposition implausible (van den Haag, 1978:68).

Third, van den Haag is not persuaded by arguments that the death penalty is wrong because it is carried out in a discriminatory fashion. If discriminatory use of the death penalty is a problem, eliminate the discrimination, not the death penalty. Furthermore, van den Haag cautions against any unfounded cries of discrimination:

> It is true that most of those currently under sentence of death are poor and a disproportionate number are black. But most murderers (indeed, most criminals) are poor and a disproportionate number are black. (So too are a disproportionate number of murder victims.) One must expect therefore that most of our prison population, including those on death row, are poor and a disproportionate number black (van den Haag & Conrad, 1983: 206–207).

Finally, van den Haag thinks that the average person favors capital punishment, while the average college-educated judge opposes it. There are two reasons for this:

> First, the college-educated, including judges, usually do not move in circles in which violence, including murder, is a daily threat. Not feeling threatened by murder, they can afford to treat it leniently . . . Second, . . . students tend to absorb and to be victimized by the intellectual fashions of their college days. Uneducated people more often accept tradition and their own experience . . . The idea of the criminal as a sick victim of society thrives among intellectuals. The fashion in intellectual circles for the last fifty years has been to regard criminals as victims of society, sick people who should be treated and rehabilitated. People who are executed cannot be rehabilitated (van den Haag & Conrad, 1983:159).

age for the death penalty, but that a line has to be drawn somewhere. They choose age 18. "The age of 18 is the point where society draws the line for many purposes between childhood and adulthood" (*Roper v. Simmons*, 2005).

Dissenting, Justice Antonin Scalia pointed out that only 18 states actually prohibit executions for juveniles. Unlike the majority, Justice Scalia argued that one cannot reason that states without the death penalty prohibit it for juveniles; he contended that those states should not be considered because they have not addressed the issue of the appropriate age for the death penalty. He also

BOX 14.4 MAJORITY AND DISSENTING OPINIONS IN THE *ROPER* CASE

Justice Kennedy's Majority Opinion:

> The susceptibility of juveniles to immature and irresponsible behavior means "their irresponsible conduct is not as morally reprehensible as that of an adult." *Thompson, supra*, at 835 (plurality opinion). Their own vulnerability and comparative lack of control over their immediate surroundings mean juveniles have a greater claim than adults to be forgiven for failing to escape negative influences in their whole environment. See *Stanford*, 492 U.S., at 395 (Brennan, J. dissenting). The reality that juveniles still struggle to define their identity means it is less supportable to conclude that even a heinous crime committed by a juvenile is evidence of irretrievably depraved character. From a moral standpoint it would be misguided to equate the failings of a minor with those of an adult, for a greater possibility exists that a minor's character deficiencies will be reformed.

Justice Scalia's Dissent:

> Murder, however, is more than just risky or antisocial behavior. It is entirely consistent to believe that young people often act impetuously and lack judgment, but, at the same time, to believe that those who commit premeditated murder are—at least sometimes—just as culpable as adults. Christopher Simmons, who was only seven months shy of his 18th birthday when he murdered Shirley Crook, described to his friends *beforehand*—"[i]n chilling, callous terms," . . . the murder he planned to commit. He then broke into the home of an innocent woman, bound her with duct tape and electrical wire, and threw her off a bridge alive and conscious.

What do you think? Is Justice Kennedy correct that minors are still immature and struggling with their identity? Is there greater chance that they can be reformed? Or is Justice Scalia correct that some individual juveniles are just as culpable as adults—that some youths commit heinous crimes and should be held fully accountable for them? Do you agree with Justice Kennedy that all youths should be ineligible for the death penalty, or do you agree with Justice Scalia that some youths may deserve the death penalty?

noted that psychological studies about maturity and recklessness give us a picture of juveniles in general. Some particular juveniles, however, may be culpable and may commit particularly heinous crimes that merit the death penalty. He thinks that a jury can and should decide whether a particular juvenile is indeed culpable and has committed a crime that is so horrible as to deserve capital punishment. (See Box 14.4 for quotes from the majority opinion and from Justice Scalia's dissent.)

The Supreme Court's *Roper* decision has ended the debate over the death penalty for practical purposes. An unintended consequence of the decision was an increase in the number of juveniles serving life without parole sentences. The Supreme Court has issued two rulings on this practice. The next section discusses this issue.

LIFE WITHOUT PAROLE FOR JUVENILES

The most recent estimate is that there are over 2,500 persons serving life without parole (LWOP) sentences who were under 18 when they committed their crimes; this is up from 2,225 in 2005 (The Sentencing Project, 2014;

Human Rights Watch, 2010). A few years ago, youths serving such sentences were 97 percent male and 60 percent black. Sixteen percent were 15 or younger at the time of their crimes (Human Rights Watch, 2008). Some of these juveniles were sentenced prior to *Roper*, and some were sentenced after *Roper* made it impossible to sentence a juvenile to death.

As noted in Chapter 9, the Supreme Court has issued two recent decisions concerning juvenile LWOP. In *Graham v. Florida* (2010), the Court banned LWOP for juveniles not convicted of homicide. In *Miller v. Alabama* (2012), the Court banned the mandatory imposition of LWOP for juveniles. In other words, states can still impose a life without parole sentence on a juvenile, but only after individualized consideration of the juvenile and the juvenile's offense. Some but not all states have interpreted *Miller* to apply retroactively to juveniles previously sentenced to LWOP. Thirteen states have passed legislation (as of 2014) to address the *Miller* ruling and now set the minimum sentence for juveniles convicted of homicide between 25 and 40 years. For example, Michigan still allows LWOP but sets the minimum sentence at 25 years. Texas no longer allows LWOP but also has a 40-year minimum sentence (Rovner, 2014). Feld (2012) labels sentences such as these *de facto* life sentences. In effect, some states have complied with the letter of the *Miller* ruling but not necessarily the spirit. See Table 14.1 for selected state legislative responses to the *Miller* decision.

The growth in the use of LWOP sentences for juveniles was expected, given the *Roper* decision banning the death penalty for juveniles. Absent the death penalty, LWOP is arguably the harshest sentence a state can impose. So if a juvenile is convicted of a heinous murder, it is logical that judges, responding to prosecutors, juries, the public, and the press, would impose the harshest alternative available: LWOP.

Critics, however, see problems. One problem is unfair implementation. For example, one report showed that in 11 states, black youths arrested for murder were more likely to be sentenced to such a sentence than white youths arrested for murder (Human Rights Watch, 2008). That report also noted that in both California and Connecticut, the ratio of black youths arrested for murder sentenced to LWOP was more than five times higher than that for white youths arrested for murder. Just as some criticized racial discrimination in the administration of the death penalty, critics see racial problems continuing in the use of LWOP sentences.

Critics also point to other problems in meting out LWOP sentences to juveniles. First, one report showed that the majority—59 percent—of juveniles with LWOP sentences were first-time offenders with no prior adult criminal record or juvenile adjudication record. Second, it is estimated that a quarter (26%) of the juveniles with LWOP sentences were convicted of felony murder.

TABLE 14.1 Select State Legislative Responses to *Miller* Decision				
State	Year of Law	Minimum Sentence	Allows LWOP?	Retroactive?
Delaware	2013	25 years	Yes	Yes
Florida	2014	35 years	Yes	Not addressed
Michigan	2014	25 years	Yes	No
Pennsylvania	2012	Under age 15: 25 yrs Age 15–17: 35 yrs	Yes	No
Texas	2013	40 years	No	No
Washington	2014	25 years	Yes	Yes

Source: Adapted by authors from Rovner (2014).

That is, they were an accomplice; for example, their co-defendant actually committed the murder during another felony crime. Third, frequently the juvenile committed the crime with an adult, and in many cases the adult received a more lenient sentence.

A recent study of 1,579 juvenile lifers found that many had suffered from socioeconomic disadvantages, school failure, and abuse. Specifically, 79 percent had witnessed violence in their homes, almost half (47 percent) had been physically abused, and 77 percent of the girls had been sexually abused. About a third were raised in public housing, and 18 percent were not living with a close relative just prior to their incarceration. Only 47 percent had been attending school at the time of their offense, and 84 percent had been either suspended or expelled from school at some point in their past (Nellis, 2012). Another problem is that youths sentenced to LWOP are experiencing severe trauma in prison including knifings, threats, and suicidal thoughts (Human Rights Watch, 2008).

Still another criticism is that while sentences usually serve multiple goals, including rehabilitation, LWOP has no rehabilitative aspects. It simply gives up on any hope of change for the offender. In fact, many prisons deny access to programs such as education to inmates serving life sentences. With juveniles, however, there is usually considerable chance for change.

Perhaps the most serious criticism of LWOP sentences for juveniles is the question of responsibility. Barry Feld, for example, argues that the reasoning behind the *Roper* decision that made the death penalty unconstitutional for juveniles applies with equal vigor to LWOP sentences. If a juvenile is too immature and too susceptible to peer pressure to be executed, argues Feld, the same logic dictates that he or she is not mature enough for a sentence of LWOP.

WEB ACTIVITY

Human Rights Watch has reports critical of LWOP for juveniles, available at http://www.hrw.org

The Heritage Foundation sponsored a major report in favor of LWOP for juveniles, available at http://www.heritage.org (Search for "Adult Time for Adult Crimes.")

In Feld's words: "Adolescents' personalities are in transition and it is unjust and irrational to continue harshly to punish a fifty- or sixty-year old person for the crime that an irresponsible child committed several decades earlier" (Feld, 2008:36). Most recently, Feld (2013) has argued that the reasoning in *Roper, Graham,* and *Miller* is sound rationale to have a youth discount for all juvenile sentences, and that the harshest sentence available should be no more than 20 or 25 years.

A number of authorities concur with Feld that LWOP is overly harsh for juveniles. Human Rights Watch, for example, notes that the United States is "an international anomaly" as the only country in the world that imposes LWOP sentences on juveniles (Human Rights Watch, 2008:8). Michael Tonry argues that LWOP is one of several American inhumane policies that is "unimaginable in most other Western countries" (Tonry, 2008:3). On the other side, some argue that LWOP sentences are reasonable and should be available for those juveniles who commit extremely violent murders and are a danger to society (Stimson and Grossman, 2009).

Still another problem is that mistakes can be made. This is due to "the inability of judges and juries to accurately render individualized assessments about whether a teenager's immaturity and developmental deficits attenuates his or her culpability" (Fagan, 2007:742). Part of the problem is that juries sometimes treat youthful age as a factor characterizing juveniles as more dangerous, rather than seeing incomplete development as making them less responsible.

LWOP for juveniles has not attracted the same outcry that capital punishment for juveniles did. The death penalty is dramatic because it is so extreme. LWOP can be seen as a considerable improvement over the death penalty and can lull juvenile justice reform advocates into a sense of victory that they have stopped a horrible injustice. However, if Barry Feld is correct that the same reasoning that destroys the justification for a juvenile death penalty also destroys that for a juvenile LWOP, then juvenile justice advocates need to get ready for another fight—the fight to overturn LWOP for juveniles.

JURISDICTION OVER STATUS OFFENSES

Also related to the fundamental issue of the philosophy and continued existence of juvenile court is the issue of **divestiture**, that is, eliminating juvenile court **jurisdiction over status offenders**. Assuming that a state chooses not to eliminate juvenile court completely, should it continue to exercise control over disobedient, runaway, and truant adolescents? As noted, the state of Washington has opted to continue juvenile court but to eliminate jurisdiction over status offenses. Maine has written full divestiture into law. Most states have retained jurisdiction but implemented policies of deinstitutionalization (stopped confining status offenders in state institutions). In many places, private drug treatment and mental health facilities have stepped in to fill the void that juvenile court previously occupied (Feld, 1999).

Despite such efforts, status offenses and status offenders continue to take up a considerable portion of juvenile court time and effort. In 2010, juvenile courts handled an estimated 137,000 petitioned status offense cases, an increase of 6 percent over 1995. In 2008, the number was 156,300 cases. Truancy cases doubled between 1995 and 2007 but then declined 31 percent from 2007 to 2010. Curfew cases increased 56 percent from 1995 to 2000 but then declined 35 percent from 2000 to 2010. Ungovernability cases decreased 12 percent below the 1995 level. Despite more than a decade of discussion about ending juvenile court jurisdiction over status offenses, approximately 6,000 youths were adjudicated status offenders and placed in out-of-home placements in 2010 (Puzzanchera & Hockenberry, 2013). The 2011 census of juveniles in custody showed 2,239 youths in custody for a status offense (Sickmund et al., 2013b).

Michel (2011) suggests that jurisdictions stop using probation officers in initial work with status offenders. Instead, states should set up a new program that hires recent college graduates and trains them to produce more favorable outcomes for youths and avoid all the negative labeling of juvenile court processing.

Arguments for Ending Jurisdiction

There are several arguments in favor of complete divestiture. First, it allows the juvenile court more time and resources to deal with juvenile delinquents—especially violent and chronic delinquents. Because the court does not have to process or supervise status offenders, probation officers, prosecutors, public defenders, judges, and correctional program employees are able to focus on more serious delinquents. Second, the elimination of status offense jurisdiction prevents any possible violations of the due process rights of status offenders, such as being prosecuted for very vague charges. For example, how disobedient does a child have to be before he or she is "incorrigible," or how truant before he or she is eligible for a truancy petition? Status offense statutes typically are unclear and vague. Third, elimination of this jurisdiction recognizes the reality that juvenile courts are not adequately staffed and equipped to deal with status offenders. Most probation officers often have only bachelor's degrees and are not qualified to do the social work and psychological counseling necessary to assist troubled teenagers and their families. Thus, status offenders should be diverted to private agencies with trained social workers and counselors who are better equipped to handle the complex problems of these youths and their families. Furthermore, eliminating juvenile court jurisdiction would force any intervention to be voluntary, which some argue is the proper way to deal with status offenders.

Another argument for elimination is that jurisdiction over status offenses has "weakened the responsibility of schools and agencies to arrange out-of-court interventive services and solutions" (Rubin, 1985:63). What Rubin means is that status offense laws have allowed schools to run inadequate and boring programs that promote truancy and, in turn, blame parents and children for the problem. Instead of petitioning youths to juvenile court, schools should be improving instructional programs or offering innovative approaches such as alternative schools where children attend school half a day and then work half a day for pay. In other words, prosecuting status offenders often is a blame-the-victim approach that ignores the real causes of the problems: inferior schools, ineffective parents, and insensitive communities (see Rubin, 1985; and Schur, 1973, for further discussion of this issue). Meda Chesney-Lind (1987) believes that status offenses are intricately intertwined with the place of women in American society. She questions whether the concern over maintaining jurisdiction is one of concern or control:

> What is really at stake here is not "protection" of youth so much as it is the right of young women to defy patriarchy. Such defiance by male youth is winked at, both today and in the past, but from girls such behavior is totally unacceptable (Chesney-Lind, 1987:21).

Much of the concern, therefore, about status offenders is not so much for the children as for maintaining a patriarchal society. Thus, like the critics of the child savers discussed in Chapter 2, Chesney-Lind questions the intentions of those concerned with the protection of status offenders.

Simmons (2006) argues that mandatory mediation for status offenses is superior to processing such children in juvenile court and can better address the root problems behind status offending. Simmons reports on three programs that had considerable success in dealing with status offenders (Simmons, 2006). On the other hand, recent experience in juvenile court shows that a number of courts charge status offenders with violations of court orders (VCOs) as a way to "bootstrap" them into delinquency charges and even to place them in secure confinement.

In fiscal year 2006–07, Connecticut reformed how it handled status offenders in an attempt to reduce court handling, to eliminate detention for status offenders, and to direct status offenders to community services and the education system. A study of results in fiscal years 2007–08 and 2008–09 showed that complaints declined over 40 percent, there were no Families with Service

Needs youth confined in a secure detention facility in FY 2008–09, and that juvenile courts only handled 4 percent of status offense complaints in 2009. Subsequent referrals and arrests also dropped (Ryon, Devers, Early, & Hand, 2012). This indicates that states can be successful in drastically reducing juvenile court involvement in status offense cases if they set up community services and educational interventions for such cases.

Arguments for Continuing Jurisdiction

Some still think, however, that juvenile court jurisdiction over status offenses is both desirable and necessary. Proponents of continued jurisdiction contend that parents and schools need the court backing to impress adolescents with the need to obey their parents, attend school, and not run away from home. Concerning truancy, Rubin argues that repeal of status offense jurisdiction would "effectively eradicate compulsory education" and that "children will be free to roam the streets with impunity" (Rubin, 1985:65). Furthermore, such total freedom would "deny children the necessary preparation for achievement in a complex technological society" (Rubin, 1985:65). Second, proponents of court jurisdiction argue that private agencies in the community will not handle (or will not be able to handle) all of the status offense cases if the juvenile court cannot intervene. Private agencies intervene only with willing clients, and many status offenders taken to such agencies simply refuse assistance. Moreover, some agencies do not provide the services they claim to provide (Schneider, 1985).

Proponents also contend that status offenders often escalate into delinquent activity, and note that truants are linked with daytime burglary and vandalism (Baker et al., 2001). Therefore, they claim, early intervention can prevent current and future delinquency. However, the escalation hypothesis is controversial. Some proportion of status offenders do indeed escalate or progress, but most do not (Lab, 1984; Rojek & Erickson, 1982; Shannon, 1982). Hence, it is questionable whether all status offenders should be subject to juvenile court jurisdiction. A similar argument is that many status offenders become involved in very dangerous situations that can cause serious harm to the child. For example, one study of runaways found that more than 50 percent dealt drugs and about 20 percent (including 19% of the male runaways) engaged in acts of prostitution to support themselves (Miller, Miller, Hoffman, & Duggan, 1980). Research on street children has shown that many turn to theft, prostituting, rolling johns, and selling drugs to survive (Hagan & McCarthy, 1997). Proponents of court jurisdiction argue that courts might prevent some children from running away and becoming involved in associated dangerous behaviors. A related argument is that because states intervene "to protect adults from their own harmful conduct" (Ryan, 1987:64), they should protect juveniles from the harmful consequences of their actions.

Another argument in favor of continued jurisdiction is that it prevents status offenders from being processed as delinquents. That is, where divestiture has occurred, there is some evidence of treating status offenders as minor delinquents (Schneider, 1985). Finally, there is concern that total removal of status offense jurisdiction from juvenile court "changes the character of the court and may substantially weaken attempts to consider the child status of delinquent" (Mahoney, 1987:29). In other words, Mahoney fears that removal of status offense jurisdiction, with a concentration on delinquency only, may lead to a view of the juvenile court as concerned with crime only and, hence, a belief that adult criminal courts can exercise that function. Thus, removal of status offense jurisdiction may very well be the beginning of the end of the juvenile court.

At present, the debate over divestiture has changed. In the Justice Department's research and writing on delinquency, there is little mention of status offenses as such. Instead of debate about divestiture, the Office of Juvenile Justice and Delinquency Prevention emphasizes prevention strategies that help youngsters at risk of becoming delinquent by building up protective factors. Such protective factors include caring parents who supervise their children, personal attributes such as conventional beliefs and conflict resolution skills, and schools that have caring teachers and help youths succeed in school (Coordinating Council on Juvenile Justice and Delinquency Prevention, 1996). The Coordinating Council is concerned with such programs as truancy reduction programs that have the police round up truants so that parents can be notified and come pick up their children (see also Chapter 8). Also mentioned are mentoring programs including Bigs in Blue, which matches high-risk youths with police officer mentors who try to help youths cope with peer pressure and also do well in school. Noted as well are conflict resolution programs in schools and community efforts such as community policing cooperative arrangements that attack community risk factors such as easy availability of drugs and firearms (Coordinating Council on Juvenile Justice and Delinquency Prevention, 1996; see also Baker et al., 2001).

Unlike a decade ago, the emphasis is not so much on the status offender as a distinct problem, but on those risk factors that can lead to serious, violent, or chronic delinquency. Attention to reducing risk factors and enhancing protective factors is considered to be the way to prevent such problematic delinquency.

CONCLUSION

Most of the proposals for the future of the juvenile justice system have some merit. The authors of these proposals care about juveniles and about how the juvenile court system should attempt to prevent and control delinquency.

The suggestion to get the juvenile justice system to return to its *parens patriae* roots—to attempt to get juvenile court to truly implement rehabilitation efforts based on valid empirical research findings—is a positive one. The goal is noble: genuine assistance for juveniles. Obstacles include funding problems, lack of societal commitment to the disadvantaged youths that are the clientele of juvenile court, vestiges of racism, and punitive strains in some politicians.

Bazemore's call to make a drastic change and pursue the path of restorative justice (Bazemore, 2012) is also positive. Advantages of this proposal are that it can appeal to both liberals and conservatives. Both parties like the fact that restorative justice puts renewed emphasis on the victim. Restitution, for example, is desirable because it restores the victim to the condition he or she was in prior to the crime. Perhaps the major question about this proposal is whether citizens will commit to participate. Putnam's (2000) concerns about the decline of community in America raise the question that citizens are not as civically involved today as they were even 50 years ago. A number of communities, including the state of Vermont (Karp et al., 2004), have implemented restorative justice practices, though, so this does not appear to be a pipedream.

In the last decade, developmental psychology has examined the incomplete development of adolescent brain functioning and maturity, the Supreme Court has issued rulings on the death penalty and life without parole for juveniles based in part on those findings, and several states have reverted to age 18 for initial criminal court jurisdiction and/or limited transfer provisions and sentencing. As noted, Bishop and Feld (2012) see these developments as signs of re-balancing or a new balancing between traditional juvenile court *parens patriae* philosophy and the "get tough" movement of the 1990s and early 2000s. If they are correct, then the call to abolish juvenile court may have run its course and the future may see more states following this new trend to mitigate the harsh reforms enacted in response to what now appears to have been a baseless moral panic over an imagined juvenile crime spree by "superpredators" that never should have been predicted in the first place.

Some of the broader suggestions noted in this chapter also merit mention in this concluding section. For instance, Garland's analysis that the decline of the rehabilitative ideal is tied in with broader economic changes, such as the globalizing economy and the eroding of the welfare state (Garland, 2001), deserves serious attention. This analysis suggests that trying to return juvenile court to its rehabilitative roots and even trying to set up youth justice courts that address youth needs within the adult court system are both doomed to failure unless it can be shown that there is funding available for such efforts. One way to do this is to point to cost–benefit analyses of evidence-based interventions, as was done in Washington state (Aos & Drake, 2013). A related strategy is to call for the end of ineffective and costly strategies. Clear (2011) suggested that cost savings be re-invested in either effective interventions or in rebuilding disadvantaged communities so as to prevent crime and delinquency in the first place.

Character education or the reintroduction of the spiritual dimension into juvenile corrections also merits serious consideration. If Staples (2000) is correct that problems such as school violence stem, at least in part, from excessive emphasis on the consumer culture and inattention to the search for meaning, creativity, and engagement, then superficial changes in juvenile court are not critical. If such terms as "character education" or a "search for the spiritual" are simply ploys to avoid funding meaningful programs for youths in trouble, then they are hypocritical and dangerous. However, if calls for character education and the reintroduction of the spiritual dimension go along with education, job training, substance abuse counseling, and other efforts to address all the needs of problem youths, both material and spiritual, then they hold promise. Critics of our consumer culture are accurate that there is more to life than purchasing increasingly more goods.

A unique voice for change is Michael Tonry's call for fundamental change. He argues that many of the proposals to improve the adult criminal justice system and the juvenile justice system miss the need for fundamental change. He thinks these systems are "profoundly unjust" because they are "unduly harsh." So he calls for harsh penalties such as three-strikes, life without parole, and mandatory minimums to be narrowed or abolished and for a commitment to focus on justice. For the juvenile justice system, he specifically recommends turning back the adult criminal age in all states to 18 because "[y]oung people are in important respects different from adults; processing them in adults courts does unnecessary harm to them and their prospects of growing up to become successful adults" (Tonry, 2011a: 639). Tonry does not focus on the economic costs of his proposal because he feels that justice demands such fundamental change.

The founders of the juvenile court had it at least half right: kids do need help. That was true back in 1899 and is as true today in the twenty-first century. The problem is that in seeking solutions for youth problems and problem youths, we prefer to ignore this truth and seek refuge in simplistic slogans like "adult time" and "Scared Straight." We are a lot like dieters seeking to lose weight; we want the easy way out. Just as persons trying to lose weight have to face the hard facts of diet and exercise, American society has to face the facts of delinquency. There is no easy solution. Whatever proposal for the future of juvenile court wins out, it will not be an answer unless it addresses the problems of youths who break the law.

DISCUSSION QUESTIONS

1. Discuss the reform proposals for juvenile court. Which proposal(s) do you favor? Why? What might the consequences be of abolishing juvenile court? Do you agree with Bishop and Feld that a re-balancing movement seems to be taking place in juvenile justice?

2. How does the status of community life affect juvenile delinquency and juvenile justice? How much does reform of the juvenile justice system depend on strong communities? Is Putnam correct that community life seems to be having problems as individuals seem to turn to more solitary pursuits? Can this trend be reversed? Is Clear's suggestion to use savings from reduced use of prison sentences on community development realistic?

3. How do current political and economic events affect juvenile justice? For example, do you think that the war on terrorism will have any effects on juvenile justice? What will be the effect of current economic difficulties on juvenile justice?

4. Do you favor the death penalty for juveniles? Discuss this in light of the recent Supreme Court decision making the juvenile death penalty unconstitutional.

5. Discuss LWOP for juveniles. Although the Supreme Court did not completely abolish this sentence for juvenile murderers, it expressed the hope that such sentences would be very rare. Do you think states should abolish LWOP for juveniles altogether? In *Graham v. Florida*, dissenting Chief Justice Roberts raises the question of what an appropriate sentence would be for a juvenile who rapes an 8-year-old girl and leaves her to die, or juveniles who gang-rape a woman and force her to perform oral sex on her own 12-year-old son [real cases]? Justice Roberts thinks that a LWOP sentence might be the appropriate sentence in such cases. What do you think?

6. What role, if any, should juvenile court have with status offenders? Do you agree with some experts that all status offenders should be handled in diversion programs or other community treatment programs, and that juvenile court should have no control over status offenses and status offenders?

Bibliography

Abadinsky, H. (1989). *Drug abuse: An introduction*. Chicago: Nelson-Hall.

Abram, K. M., Paskar, L. D., Washburn, J. J., & Teplin, L. A. (2008). Perceived barriers to mental health services among youths in detention. *Journal of the American Academy of Child and Adolescent Psychiatry, 47*, 291–300.

Abram, K. M., Teplin, L. A., King, D. C., Longworth, S. L., Emanuel, K. M., Romero, E. G., McClelland, G. M., Dulcan, M. K., Washburn, J. J., Welty, L. J., & Olson, N. D. (2013). *PTSD, trauma, and comorbid psychiatric disorders in detained youth*. Washington, DC: Office of Juvenile Justice and Delinquency Prevention.

Abt Associates. (1994). *Conditions of confinement: Juvenile detention and corrections facilities: Research report*. Washington, DC: U.S. Department of Justice.

Acoca, L. (1998). Outside/inside: The violation of american girls at home, on the streets, and in the juvenile justice system. *Crime & Delinquency, 44*, 561–589.

Adams, K. (2003). The effectiveness of juvenile curfews at crime prevention. *Annals of the American Academy of Political and Social Science, 587*, 136–159.

Adams, K. (2007). Abolish juvenile curfews. *Criminology & Public Policy, 6*, 663–670.

Adams, L. R. (1974). The adequacy of differential association theory. *Journal of Research in Crime and Delinquency, 11*, 1–8.

Adamson, C. (1998). Tribute, turf, honor and the American street gang: Patterns of continuity and change since 1820. *Theoretical Criminology, 2*, 57–84.

Administration on Children, Youth, and Families. (2010). *Child maltreatment, 2009*. Washington, DC: U.S. Department of Health and Human Services.

Administration on Children, Youth, and Families. (2013). *Child Maltreatment, 2012*. Washington, DC: U.S. Department of Health and Human Services. Available at http://www.acf.hhs.gov/programs/cb/resource/child-maltreatment-2012

Administration on Children, Youth, and Families. (2014). *Child Maltreatment, 2013*. Washington, DC: U.S. Department of Health and Human Services.

Agnew, R. (1992). Foundation for a general strain theory of crime and delinquency. *Criminology, 30*, 47–87.

Agnew, R. (1994). The techniques of neutralization and violence. *Criminology, 32*, 555–580.

Agnew, R. (2001). Building on the foundation of general strain theory: Specifying the types of strain most likely to lead to crime and delinquency. *Journal of Research in Crime and Delinquency, 38*, 319–361.

Agnew, R. (2006a). *Pressured into crime: An overview of general strain theory.* Los Angeles: Roxbury.

Agnew, R. (2006b). General strain theory: Current status and directions for future research. In F. T. Cullen, J. P. Wright & K. R. Blevins (Eds.), *Taking stock: The status of criminologial theory* (pp. 101–123). New Brunswick, NJ: Transaction.

Agnew, R., & Peters, A. A. R. (1986). The techniques of neutralization: An analysis of predisposing and situational factors. *Criminal Justice and Behavior, 13,* 81–97.

Agnew, R., & White, H. R. (1992). An empirical test of general strain theory. *Criminology, 30,* 475–499.

Akers, R. L., Krohn, M. K., Lonza-Kaduce, L., & Radosevich, M. (1979). Social learning and deviant behavior: A specific test of a general theory. *American Sociological Review, 44,* 636–655.

Alarid, L. F., Montemayor, C. D., & Dannhaus, S. (2012). The effect of parental support on juvenile drug court completion and postprogram recidivism. *Youth Violence and Juvenile Justice, 10,* 354–369.

Alarid, L. F., Sims, B. A., & Ruiz, J. (2011). Juvenile probation and police partnerships as loosely coupled systems: A qualitative analysis. *Youth Violence and Juvenile Justice, 9,* 79–95.

Alexander, M., & Vanbenschoten, S. (2008). The evolution of supervision within the federal probation and pretrial system. *Journal of Offender Rehabilitation, 47,* 319–337.

Allen, P. (1994). *OJJDP model programs 1993.* Washington, DC: U.S. Department of Justice.

Allen, T. T. (2005). Taking a juvenile into custody: Situational factors that influence police officers' decisions. *Journal of Sociology and Social Welfare, 32,* 121–129.

Alpert, G. P. (2007). Eliminate race as the only reason for police-citizen encounters. *Criminology & Public Policy, 6,* 671–678.

Alpert, G. P., Dunham, R. G., & Smith, M. R. (2007). Investigating racial profiling by the Miami-Dade police department: A multimethod approach. *Criminology & Public Policy, 6,* 25–56.

Alpert, G. P., MacDonald, J. M., & Dunham, R. G. (2005). Police suspicion and discretionary decision making during citizen stops. *Criminology, 43,* 407–434.

Altschuler, D. M. (1998). Intermediate sanctions and community treatment for serious and violent juvenile offenders. In R. Loeber & D. P. Farrington (Eds.), *Serious and violent juvenile offenders: Risk factors and successful interventions* (pp. 367–385). Thousand Oaks, CA: Sage.

Altschuler, D., & Brounstein, P. J. (1991). Patterns of drug use, drug trafficking, and other delinquency among inner city adolescent males in Washington, DC. *Criminology, 29,* 589–622.

American Correctional Association. (2008). *2008 Directory: Adult and Juvenile Correctional Departments, Institutions, Agencies, and Probation and Parole Authorities.* Alexandria, VA: American Correctional Association.

American Dietetics Association. (1984). Position paper of the American Dietetics Association on diet and criminal behavior. *Journal of the American Dietetics Association, 85,* 361–362.

Anderson, E. (1994). The code of the streets. *Atlantic Monthly, 273*(5), 81–94.

Anderson, G. S. (2007). *Biological influences on criminal behavior.* Boca Raton, FL: CRC Press.

Andrews, D. A. (2006). Enhancing adherence to risk-need-responsivity: Making quality a matter of policy. *Criminology & Public Policy, 5*, 595–602.

Anglin, M. D. (1988). The efficacy of civil commitment in treating narcotics addiction. *Journal of Drug Issues, 18*, 527–547.

Anglin, M. D., & Hser, Y. (1987). Addicted women and crime. *Criminology, 25*, 359–397.

Anglin, M. D., & Hser, Y. (1990). Treatment of drug abuse. In M. Tonry & J. Q. Wilson (Eds.), *Drugs and crime* (pp. 393–460). Chicago: University of Chicago Press.

Anglin, M. D., & McGlothlin, W. H. (1984). Outcome of narcotic addict treatment in California. In F. M. Tims & J. P. Ludford (Eds.), *Drug abuse treatment evaluation: Strategies, progress and prospects* (pp. 106–128). Washington, DC: National Institute on Drug Abuse.

Anglin, M. D., & McGlothlin, W. H. (1985). Methadone maintenance in California: A decade's experience. In L. Brill & C. Winnick (Eds.), *Yearbook of substance use and abuse* (pp. 219–280). New York: Human Sciences Press.

Anglin, M. D., & Speckhart, G. R. (1986). Narcotics use, property crime, and dealing: Structural dynamics across the addiction career. *Journal of Quantitative Criminology, 2*, 355–375.

Anglin, M. D., & Speckhart, G. R. (1988). Narcotics use and crime: A multisample, multimethod analysis. *Criminology, 26*, 197–233.

Anglin, M. D., Speckhart, G. R., Booth, M. W., & Ryan, T. M. (1989). Consequences and costs of shutting off methadone. *Addictive Behaviors, 14*, 307–326.

Annie E. Casey Foundation. (2013). *2013 Kids Count Data Book*. Baltimore, MD: Annie E. Casey Foundation.

Aos, S., & Drake, E. (2013). *Prison, police, and programs: Evidence-based options that reduce crime and save money* (Doc. No. 13-11-1901). Olympia, WA: Washington State Institute for Public Policy.

Aos, S., Miller, M., & Drake, E. (2006). *Evidence-based public policy options to reduce future prison construction, criminal justice costs, and crime rates* (Washington State Institute of Public Policy Report: # 06-10-1201). Olympia, WA: Washington State Institute for Public Policy. Available at http://www.wsipp.wa.gov/

Applegate, B. K., Davis, R. K., & Cullen, F. T. (2009). Reconsidering child saving: The extent and correlates of public support for excluding youths from the juvenile court. *Crime & Delinquency, 55*, 51–77.

Araujo, W. (2012). Punishing cyberbullies: Using Supreme Court guidance beyond *Tinker* to protect students and school officials. *Thomas Jefferson Law Review 34*, 325–372.

Aries, P. (1962). *Centuries of childhood*. New York: Knopf.

Ash Institute. (2008). *Division of youth services honored as innovations in American Government award winner*. Cambridge, MA: Harvard University Press.

Ashworth, A. (2003). Is restorative justice the way forward for criminal justice? In E. McLaughlin, R. Fergusson, G. Hughes & L. Westmarland (Eds.), *Restorative justice: Critical issues*. Thousand Oaks, CA: Sage.

Associated Press. (2008a, August 12). *Hartford police to beef up teen curfew after shooting. Johnson City Press*, 6A.

Associated Press (2008b, August 18). *State sex offender registry exempts juvenile offenses. Johnson City Press*, 5A.

Austin, J., Johnson, K. D., & Weitzer, R. (2005). *Alternatives to the secure detention and confinement of juvenile offenders*. Washington, DC: U.S. Department of Justice.

Baines, M., & Alder, C. (1996). Are girls more difficult to work with? Youth workers' perspectives in juvenile justice and related areas. *Crime & Delinquency, 42*, 467–485.

Baker, M. L., Sigmon, J. N., & Nugent, M. E. (2001). *Truancy reduction: Keeping students in school*. Washington, DC: Office of Juvenile Justice and Delinquency Prevention.

Ball, J. C., Corty, E., Bond, R., & Tommasello, A. (1987). *The reduction of intravenous heroin use, nonopiate abuse and crime during methadone maintenance treatment—further findings*. Paper presented at the Annual Meeting of the Committee on Problems on Drug Dependency, Philadelphia, PA.

Ball, J. C., Shaffer, J. W., & Nurco, D. N. (1983). The day-to-day criminality of heroin addicts in Baltimore: A study in the continuity of offense rates. *Drug and Alcohol Dependence, 12*, 119–142.

Bandura, A., & Walters, R. H. (1963). *Social learning and personality development*. New York: Holt, Rhinehart and Winston.

Bannenberg, B., & Rössner, D. (2003). New developments in restorative justice to handle family violence. In E. Weitkamp & H. Kerner (Eds.), *Restorative justice in context: International practice and directions* (pp. 51–79). Portland, OR: Willan.

Bannister, A. J., Carter, D. L., & Schafer, J. (2001). A national police survey on juvenile curfews. *Journal of Criminal Justice, 29*, 233–240.

Banta-Green, C. J., Kuszler, P. C., Coffin, P. O., & Schoeppe, J. A. (2011). *Washington's 911 Good Samaritan Drug Overdose Law—Initial Evaluation Results*. Seattle, WA: Alcohol & Drug Abuse Institute, University of Washington.

Barnoski, R. (2009). *Providing evidence-based programs with fidelity in Washington state juvenile courts: Cost analysis*. Olympia, WA: Washington State Institute for Public Policy. Available at http://www.wsipp.wa.gov/

Barnum, R. (1987). The development of responsibility: implications for juvenile justice. In F. X. Hartman (Ed.), *From children to citizens: Volume II: The role of the juvenile court* (pp. 67–79). New York: Springer-Verlag.

Bartollas, C., & Sieverdes, C. M. (1981). The victimized white in a juvenile correctional system. *Crime & Delinquency, 27*, 534–543.

Barton, W. H. (2012). Detention. In B. C. Feld & D. M. Bishop (Eds.), *The Oxford handbook of juvenile crime and juvenile justice* (pp. 637–663). New York: Oxford University Press.

Bateman, T. (2012). Concern that courts in England and Wales may impose curfews in 'inappropriate situations.' *Youth Justice, 12*, 258–268.

Bazemore, G. (1999). The fork in the road to juvenile court reform. *Annals of the American Academy of Political and Social Science, 564*, 81–108.

Bazemore, G. (2012). Restoration, shame, and the future of restorative practice. In B. C. Feld & D. M. Bishop (Eds.), *The Oxford handbook of juvenile crime and juvenile justice* (pp. 695–722). New York: Oxford University Press.

Bazemore, G., & Leip, L. (2000). Victim participation in the new juvenile court: Tracking judicial attitudes toward restorative justice reforms. *Justice System Journal, 21*(2), 199–226.

Bazemore, G., & Maloney, D. (1994). Rehabilitating community service: Toward restorative service in a balanced justice system. *Federal Probation, 58*, 24–35.

Bazemore, G., & Schiff, M. (2005). *Juvenile justice reform and restorative justice: Building theory and policy from practice*. Portland, OR: Willan.

Bazemore, G., & Umbreit, M. (1994). *Balanced and restorative justice: Program models*. Washington, DC: Office of Juvenile Justice and Delinquency.

Bazemore, G., & Umbreit, M. (2001). *A comparison of four restorative conferencing models*. Washington, DC: U.S. Department of Justice, Office of Juvenile Justice and Delinquency Prevention.

Beaver, K. M., & Connolly, E. J. (2013). Genetics and environmental influences on the development of childhood anti-social behavior: Current evidence and directions for future research. In C. L. Gibson & M. D. Krohn (Eds.), *Handbook of life-course criminology*. New York: Springer.

Beck, A. J., Adams, D. B., & Guerino, P. (2008). Sexual violence reported by juvenile correctional authorities, 2005–2006. *Bureau of Justice Statistics Special Report*. Washington, DC: U.S. Department of Justice.

Beck, A. J., Cantor, D., Hartge, J., & Smith, T. (2013). *Sexual victimization in juvenile facilities reported by youth, 2012*. Washington, DC: Bureau of Justice Statistics.

Beck, A. J., Kline, S. A., & Greenfield, L. A. (1988). Survey of youth in custody, 1987. *Bureau of Justice Statistics Special Report*. Washington, DC: US Department of Justice.

Behnken, M. P., Arredondo, D. E., & Packman, W. L. (2009). Reduction in recidivism in a juvenile mental health court. *Juvenile and Family Court Journal, 60*(3), 23–44.

Beldon, E. (1920). *Courts in the U.S. Hearing children's cases*. Washington, DC: U.S. Children's Bureau.

Belenko, S., Fagan, J. A., & Dumanovsky, T. (1994). The effects of level sanctions on recidivism in special drug courts. *Justice System Journal, 17*, 53–80.

Belknap, J. (1984). The effect of local policy on the sentencing patterns of state wards. *Justice Quarterly, 1*, 549–561.

Belknap, J. (1987). Routine activity theory and the risk of rape: Analyzing ten years of national crime survey data. *Criminal Justice Policy Review, 2*, 337–356.

Bell, D., & Lang, K. (1985). The intake dispositions of juvenile offenders. *Journal of Research in Crime and Delinquency, 22*, 309–328.

Bell, K. E. (2009). Gender and gangs: A quantitative comparison. *Crime and Delinquency, 55*, 363–387.

Bellis, D. J. (1981). *Heroin and politicians: The failure of public policy to control addiction in America*. Westport, CT: Greenwood.

Belsky, J. (1978). Three theoretical models of child abuse: A critical review. *Child Abuse & Neglect, 2*, 37–49.

Benda, B. B. (2002). Religion and violent offenders in boot camp: A structural equation model. *Journal of Research in Crime and Delinquency, 39*, 91–121.

Benekos, P. J., & Merlo, A. V. (2008). Juvenile justice: The legacy of punitive policy. *Youth Violence and Juvenile Justice, 6*, 28–46.

Bennett, T., & Wright, R. (1984). The relationship between alcohol and burglary. *British Journal of Addiction, 79*, 431–437.

Bennett, W. J. (2001). *The broken hearth: Reversing the moral collapse of the American family*. New York: Doubleday.

Bentham, J. (1948). *An introduction to the principles of morals and legislation.* New York: Hafner.

Bergseth, K. J., & Bouffard, J. A. (2012). Examining the effectiveness of a restorative justice program for various types of juvenile offenders. *International Journal of Offender Therapy and Comparative Criminology, 57,* 1,054–1,075.

Bilchik, S. (1998). *A juvenile justice system for the 21st century.* Washington, DC: U.S. Department of Justice.

Bishop, D. M. (2000). Juvenile offenders in the adult criminal justice system. In M. Tonry (Ed.), *Crime and justice: A review of research* (Vol. 27, pp. 81–167). Chicago: University of Chicago Press.

Bishop, D. M. (2005). The role of race and ethnicity in juvenile justice processing. In D. F. Hawkins & K. Kempf-Leonard (Eds.), *Our children, their children: Confronting racial and ethnic differences in American juvenile justice* (pp. 23–82). Chicago: University of Chicago Press.

Bishop, D. M. (2006). Public opinion and juvenile policy: Myths and misconceptions—reaction essay. *Criminology & Public Policy, 5,* 653–664.

Bishop, D. M. & Feld, B. C. (2012). Trends in juvenile justice policy and practice. In B. C. Feld & D. M. Bishop (Eds.), *The Oxford handbook of juvenile crime and juvenile justice* (pp. 898–926). New York: Oxford University Press.

Bishop, D. M. & Leiber, M. J. (2012). Racial and ethnic differences in delinquency and justice system responses. In B. C. Feld & D. M. Bishop (Eds.), *The Oxford handbook of juvenile crime and juvenile justice* (pp. 445–484). New York: Oxford University Press.

Bjerregaard, B. (1989). Televised testimony as an alternative in child sexual abuse cases. *Criminal Law Bulletin, 25,* 164–175.

Bjerregaard, B., & Lizotte, A. (1995). Gun ownership and gang membership. *Journal of Criminal Law and Criminology, 86,* 37–58.

Bjerregaard, B., & Smith, C. (1993). Gender differences in gang participation, delinquency, and substance use. *Journal of Quantitative Criminology, 4,* 329–355.

Bloch, H. A., & Niederhoffer, A. (1958). *The gang: A study in adolescent behavior.* New York: Philosophical Library.

Bohman, M. (1996). Predisposition to criminality: Swedish adoption studies in retrospect. *Ciba Foundation Symposium, 194,* 99–109.

Bonnett, P. L., & Pfeiffer, C. L. (1978). Biochemical diagnosis for delinquent behavior. In L. J. Hippchen (Ed.), *Ecologic-biochemical approaches to treatment of delinquents and criminals* (pp. 183–205). New York: Van Nostrand Reinhold.

Bonnies, R. J., Johnson, R. L., Chemers, B. M., & Schuck, J. A. (Eds.). (2013). *Reforming juvenile justice: A developmental approach.* Washington, DC: The National Academies Press.

Bonta, J., Wallace-Capretta, S., Rooney, J., & McAnoy, K. (2002). An outcome evaluation of a restorative justice alternative to incarceration. *Contemporary Justice Review, 5,* 319–338.

Bookin-Weiner, H., & Horowitz, R. (1983). The end of the youth gang: Fad or fact? *Criminology, 21,* 585–602.

Booth, A., & Osgood, D. W. (1993). The influence of testosterone on deviance in adulthood: Assessing and explaining the relationship. *Criminology, 31,* 93–118.

Booth, B., Van Hasselt, V. B., & Vecchi, G. M. (2011). Addressing school violence. *FBI Law Enforcement Bulletin, 80*(5), 1–9.

Borrero, M. (2001). The widening mistrust between youth and police. *Families in Society: The Journal of Contemporary Human Services, 82,* 399.

Bortner, M. A., & Williams, L. M. (1997). *Youth in prison: We the people of unit four.* New York: Routledge.

Bottcher, J., & Ezell, M. E. (2005). Examining the effectiveness of boot camps: A randomized experiment with a long-term follow-up. *Journal of Research in Crime and Delinquency, 42,* 309–332.

Botvin, G. J. (1990). Substance abuse prevention: Theory, practice and effectiveness. In M. Tonry & J. Q. Wilson (Eds.), *Drugs and crime* (pp. 461–520). Chicago: University of Chicago Press.

Botvin, G. J., Baker, E., Dusenbury, L., Botvin, E., & Diaz, T. (1995). Long-term follow-up results of a randomized drug-abuse prevention trial in a white middle class population. *Journal of the American Medical Association, 273,* 1,106–1,112.

Botvin, G. J., Baker, E., Renick, N., Filazzola, A. D., & Botvin, E. (1984). A cognitive-behavioral approach to substance abuse prevention. *Addictive Behaviors, 9,* 137–147.

Botvin, G. J., & Dusenbury, L. (1989). Substance abuse prevention and the promotion of competence. In L. A. Bond & B. E. Compas (Eds.), *Primary prevention and promotion in the schools* (pp. 146–178). Newbury Park, CA: Sage.

Botvin, G. J., Epstein, J. A., Baker, E., Diaz, T., & Ifill-Williams, M. (1997). School-based drug abuse prevention with inner-city minority youth. *Journal of Child and Adolescent Substance Abuse, 6,* 5–19.

Botvin, G. J., Griffin, K. W., Paul, E., & Macaulay, A. P. (2003). Preventing tobacco and alcohol use among elementary school students through life skills training. *Journal of Child and Adolescent Substance Abuse, 12,* 1–18.

Botvin, G. J., Renick, N., & Baker, E. (1983). The effects of scheduling format and booster sessions on a broad spectrum psychological approach to smoking prevention. *Journal of Behavioral Medicine, 6,* 359–379.

Bowker, L. H. (1980). *Prison victimization.* New York: Elsevier.

Bowker, L. H., & Klein, M. W. (1983). The etiology of female juvenile delinquency and gang membership: A test of psychological and social structural explanations. *Adolescence, 18,* 739–751.

Bracey, J. R., Geib, C. F., Plant, R., O'Leary, J. R., Anderson, A., Herscovitch, L., O'Connell, M., & Vanderploeg, J. J. (2013). Connecticut's comprehensive approach to reducing in-school arrests: Changes in statewide policy, systems coordination and school practices. *Family Court Review, 51,* 427–434.

Brady, K. P., Balmer, S., & Phenix, D. (2007). School-police partnership effectiveness in urban schools: An analysis of New York City's impact schools initiative. *Education and Urban Society, 39,* 455–478.

Braga, A. A. (2008). Pulling levers focussed deterrence strategies and the prevention of gun homicide. *Journal of Criminal Justice, 36,* 332–343.

Braga, A. A., & Bond, B. J. (2008). Policing crime and disorder hot spots: A randomized controlled trial. *Criminology, 46,* 577–607.

Braga, A. A., Kennedy, D. M., Piehl, A. M., & Waring, E. J. (2001). *The Boston gun project: Impact evaluation findings.* Washington, DC: National Institute of Justice.

Braga, A. A., Papachristos, A. V., & Hureau, D. M. (2014). The effects of hot spots policing on crime: An updated systematic review and meta-analysis. *Justice Quarterly, 31,* 633–663.

Braga, A. A., Pierce, G. L., McDevitt, J., Bond, B. J., & Cronin, S. (2008). The strategic prevention of gun violence among gang-involved offenders. *Justice Quarterly, 25*,132–162.

Braithwaite, J. (1989). *Crime, shame and reintegration*. Cambridge, England: Cambridge University Press.

Braithwaite, J. (1999). Restorative justice: Assessing optimistic and pessimistic accounts. In M. Tonry (Ed.), *Crime and justice: A review of research* (Vol. 25, pp. 1–127). Chicago: University of Chicago Press.

Braithwaite, J. (2002). *Restorative justice and responsive regulation*. New York: Oxford University Press.

Braithwaite, J. (2003). Restorative justice and a better future. In E. McLaughlin, R. Fergusson, G. Hughes & L. Westmarland (Eds.), *Restorative justice: Critical issues*. Thousand Oaks, CA: Sage.

Braswell, M., Fuller, J., & Lozoff, B. (2001). *Corrections, peacemaking, and restorative justice: Transforming individuals and institutions*. Cincinnati: Anderson.

Brennan, P. A., Mednick, S. A., & Jacobsen, B. (1996). Assessing the role of genetics in crime using adoption cohorts. *Ciba Foundation Symposium, 194*, 115–123.

Brennan, P. A., Mednick, S. A., & Volavka, J. (1995). Biomedical factors in crime. In J. Q. Wilson & J. Petersilia (Eds.), *Crime* (pp. 65–90). San Francisco: ICS Press.

Brenzel, B. M. (1983). *Daughters of the state: A social portrait of the first reform school for girls in North America, 1856–1903*. Cambridge, MA: MIT Press.

Brewster, M. P. (2001). An evaluation of the Chester County (PA) drug court program. *Journal of Drug Issues, 31*, 171–206.

Brick, B. T., Taylor, T. J., & Esbensen, F. (2009). Juvenile attitudes towards the police: The importance of sub-cultural involvement and community ties. *Journal of Criminal Justice, 37*, 488–495.

Bridges, G. S., & Steen, S. (1998). Racial disparities in official assessments of juvenile offenders: Attributional stereotypes as mediating mechanisms. *American Sociological Review, 63*, 554–570.

Britt, H., Toomey, T. L., Dunsmuir, W., & Wagenaar, A. C. (2006). Propensity for and correlates of alcohol sales to underage youth. *Journal of Alcohol and Drug Education, 50*(2), 25–42.

Brooks, K., & Kamine, D. (2003). *Justice cut short: An assessment of access to counsel and quality of representation in delinquency proceedings in Ohio*. Columbus: Ohio State Bar Association.

Brown, R. A., & Frank, J. (2006). Race and officer decision making: Examining differences in arrest outcomes between black and white officers. *Justice Quarterly, 23*, 96–126.

Brown, R. A., Novak, K. J., & Frank, J. (2009). Identifying variation in police officer behavior between juveniles and adults. *Journal of Criminal Justice, 37*, 200–208.

Brown, W. K. (1978). Black gangs as family extension. *International Journal of Offender Therapy and Comparative Criminology, 22*, 39–45.

Browning, S. L., Cullen, F. T., Cao, L., Kopache, R., & Stevenson, T. J. (1994). Race and getting hassled by the police: A research note. *Police Studies, 17*(1), 1–11.

Brunelle, N., Tremblay, J., Blanchette-Martin, N., Gendron, A., & Tessier, M. (2014). Relationships between drugs and delinquency in adolescence: Influence of gender and victimization experiences. *Journal of Child & Adolescent Substance Abuse, 23*, 19–28.

Brunner, H. G. (1996). MAOA deficiency and abnormal behavior. Perspectives on an association. In G. R. Bock & J. A. Goode (Eds.), *Genetics of criminal and antisocial behavior* (pp. 155–163). Chichester, England: John Wiley and Sons.

Brunson, R. K. (2007). 'Police don't like black people': African-American young men's accumulated police experiences. *Criminology & Public Policy, 6*, 71–102.

Brunson, R. K., & Miller, J. (2006). Gender, race, and urban policing: The experience of African American youths. *Gender and Society, 20*, 531–552.

Bulman, P. (2014). *Young offenders: What happens and what should happen.* Washington, DC: Office of Juvenile Justice and Delinquency Prevention.

Bureau of Justice Assistance. (2003). *Juvenile Drug Courts: Strategies in Practice.* Washington, DC: Bureau of Justice Assistance.

Bureau of Justice Assistance. (2005). *Gang resistance education and training.* Washington, DC: Bureau of Justice Assistance.

Bureau of Justice Statistics. (2014). NCVS Victimization Analysis Tool (NVAT). Available at http://www.bjs.gov/index.cfm?ty=nvat

Burgess, A. W., & Laszlo, A. T. (1976). When the prosecutrix is a child: The victim consultant in cases of sexual assault. In E. C. Viano (Ed.), *Victims & Society.* Washington, DC: Visage Press.

Burgess, E. W. (1925). The growth of the city. In R. E. Park, E. W. Burgess & R. D. McKenzie (Eds.), *The City.* Chicago: University of Chicago Press.

Burgess, R. L., & Akers, R. L. (1966). A differential association-reinforcement theory of criminal behavior. *Social Problems, 14*, 128–147.

Burke, M. N. (2005). Juvenile justice supreme court provides uniformity in juvenile procedure rules. *Pennsylvania Law Weekly, 28*(17), 5.

Burruss, G. W., & Kempf-Leonard, K. (2002). The questionable advantage of defense counsel in juvenile court. *Justice Quarterly, 19*, 37–68.

Bursik, R. J., & Grasmick, H. G. (1993). *Neighborhoods and crime: The dimensions of effective community control.* New York: Lexington.

Buss, E. (2000). The role of lawyers in promoting juveniles' competence as defendants. In T. Grisso & R. G. Schwartz (Eds.), *Youth on trial: A developmental perspective on juvenile justice* (pp. 243–265). Chicago: University of Chicago Press.

Butts, J. A. (1994). Offenders in juvenile court, 1992. *Juvenile Justice Bulletin.* Washington, DC: U.S. Department of Justice.

Butts, J. A. (2000). Can we do without juvenile justice? *Criminal Justice, 15*(1), 50–57.

Butts, J. A., Buck, J., & Coggeshall, M. B. (2002). *The impact of teen court on young offenders.* Washington, DC: Urban Institute Press.

Butts, J. A., Mayer, S., & Ruth, G. (2005). *Focusing juvenile justice on positive youth development—issue brief.* Chicago: Chapin Hall Center for Children.

Butts, J. A. & Roman, J. K. (2014). *Line drawing: Raising the minimum age of criminal court jurisdiction in New York.* New York: Research & Evaluation Center, John Jay College of Criminal Justice, City University of New York.

Butts, J. A., Roman, J. K., & Lynn-Whaley, J. (2012). Varieties of juvenile court: Nonspecialized courts, teen courts, drug courts, and mental health courts. In B. C. Feld & D. M. Bishop (Eds.), *The Oxford handbook of juvenile crime and juvenile justice* (pp. 606–635). New York: Oxford University Press.

Butts, J. A., & Snyder, H. N. (1992). *Restitution and juvenile recidivism.* Washington, DC: U.S. Department of Justice.

Butts, J. A., Zweig, J. M., & Mammalian, C. (2004). Defining the mission of juvenile drug courts. In J. A. Butts & J. Roman (Eds.), *Juvenile drug courts and teen substance abuse* (pp. 137–184). Washington, DC: Urban Institute Press.

Cabana, D. A. (1996). *Death at midnight: The confession of an executioner.* Boston: Northeastern University Press.

Caldwell, M. F. (2014). Juvenile sexual offenders. In F. E. Zimring & D. S. Tanenhaus (Eds.), *Choosing the future for American juvenile justice* (pp. 55–93). New York: New York University Press.

Calhoun, A., & Pelech, W. (2010). Responding to young people responsible for harm: A comparative study of restorative and conventional approaches. *Contemporary Justice Review, 13,* 287–306.

Camp, S. D., Klein-Saffran, J., Kwon, O., Daggett, D. M., & Joseph, V. (2006). An exploration into participation in a faith-based prison program. *Criminology & Public Policy, 5,* 529–550.

Campbell, A. (1984). Girls' talk: The social representation of aggression by female gang members. *Criminal Justice and Behavior, 11,* 139–156.

Campbell, A. (1990). Female participation in gangs. In C. R. Huff (Ed.), *Gangs in America* (pp. 163–182). Newbury Park, CA: Sage.

Campbell, B. (2008, September 13). DCS picks up funding of program that helps juvenile sex offenders. *Johnson City Press,* 4A.

Carpenter, C., Glassner, B., Johnson, B. D., & Loughlin, J. (1988). *Kids, drugs, and crime.* Lexington, MA: Lexington Books.

Carson, E. A. & Golinelli, D. (2013). *Prisoners in 2012: Trends in admissions and releases, 1991–2012.* Washington, DC: U.S. Department of Justice.

CASA. (2014). *Court appointed special advocates for children.* Available at http://www.casafor children.org/site/c.mtJSJ7MPIsE/b.5301295/k.BE9A/Home.htm

Cashel, M. L. (2003). Validity of self-reports of delinquency and socio-emotional functioning among youth on probation. *Journal of Offender Rehabilitation, 37,* 11–23.

Cavan, R. S., & Ferdinand, T. N. (1981). *Juvenile delinquency* (4th ed.). New York: Harper and Row.

Chaiken, J. M., & Chaiken, M. R. (1982). *Varieties of criminal behavior.* Santa Monica, CA: RAND.

Chaiken, M. R. (2004). *Community policing beyond the big cities.* Washington, DC: National Institute of Justice.

Chandler, N. (2000). *Best practices for establishing a children's advocacy center program* (3rd ed.). Washington, DC: National Children's Alliance. Available at http://www.fncac.org/file. php/2129/BEST+PRACTICES.pdf

Chappell, A. T., Maggard, S. R., & Higgins, J. L. (2012). Exceptions to the rule? Exploring the use of overrides in detention risk assessment. *Youth Violence and Juvenile Justice, 11,* 332–348.

Charters, C. A. (1994). Volunteer work assumes a new role in public high school: *Steirer v. Bethlehem Area School District. Journal of Law and Education, 23,* 607–613.

Chavaria, F. P. (1997). Probation and cognitive skills. *Federal Probation, 61*, 57–60.

Chesney-Lind, M. (1977). Judicial paternalism and the female status offender: Training women to know their place. *Crime & Delinquency, 23*, 121–130.

Chesney-Lind, M. (1987). *Girls' crime and woman's place: Toward a feminist model of female delinquency.* Paper presented at the Annual Meeting of the American Society of Criminology, New Orleans, LA.

Chesney-Lind, M., & Shelden, R. G. (1992). *Girls, delinquency, and juvenile justice.* Pacific Grove, CA: Brooks/Cole.

Child Abuse Prevention and Treatment Act. (1974). 42 U.S.C.A. §5106g. Available at http://uscode.house.gov/view.xhtml?req=child+abuse+prevention+and+treatment+act&f=treesort&fq=true&num=102&hl=true&edition=prelim&granuleId=USC-prelim-title42-section5101

Child Welfare Information Gateway (2013). *What is child abuse and neglect? Recognizing the signs and symptoms.* Washington, DC: U.S. Department of Health and Human Services, Children's Bureau. Available at https://www.childwelfare.gov/pubs/factsheets/whatiscan.cfm

Chin, K. (1990). *Chinese subculture and criminality: Nontraditional crime groups in America.* Westport, CT: Greenwood.

Chin, K., Fagan, J., & Kelly, R. J. (1992). Patterns of Chinese gang extortion. *Justice Quarterly, 9*, 625–646.

Christiansen, K. O. (1974). Seriousness of criminality and concordance among Danish twins. In R. Hood (Ed.), *Crime, criminology, and public policy.* New York: Free Press.

Clark, C. L., Aziz, D. W., & MacKenzie, D. L. (1994). *Shock incarceration in New York: Focus on treatment.* Washington, DC: U.S. Department of Justice.

Clark, R. D., & Lab, S. P. (1995). *The relationship between victimization and offending among junior and senior high school students.* Paper presented at the Annual Meeting of the Academy of Criminal Justice Sciences, Boston, MA.

Clarke, J. P., & Tifft, L. L. (1966). Polygraph and interview validation of self-reported deviant behavior. *American Sociological Review, 31*, 516–523.

Clarke, R. V., & Felson, M. (1993). *Routine activities and rational choice.* New Brunswick, NJ: Transaction.

Clarke, S. H., & Koch, G. G. (1980). Juvenile court: Therapy or crime control, and do lawyers make a difference. *Law and Society Review, 14*, 263–308.

Clear, T. R. (1994). *Harm in American penology: Offenders, victims, and their communities.* Albany, NY: SUNY Press.

Clear, T. R. (2011). A private-sector, incentives-based model for justice reinvestment. *Criminology & Public Policy, 10*, 585–608.

Clear, T. R., & Cadora, E. (2003). *Community justice.* Belmont, CA: Wadsworth.

Clear, T. R., Clear, V. B., & Braga, A. A. (1997). Correctional alternatives for drug offenders in an era of overcrowding. In M. McShane & F. P. Williams (Eds.), *Criminal justice: Contemporary literature in theory and practice* (pp. 24–44). New York: Garland.

Clear, T. R., & Karp, D. R. (1998). Community justice: An essay. *Corrections Management Quarterly, 2*(3), 49–60.

Cleary, H. M. D. (2013). Police interviewing and interrogation of juvenile suspects: A descriptive examination of actual cases. *Law and Human Behavior, 38*, 272–282.

Cloward, R., & Ohlin, L. (1960). *Delinquency and opportunity: A theory of delinquent gangs.* New York: Free Press.

Cobbina, J. E., Miller, J., & Brunson, R. K. (2008). Gender, neighborhood danger, and risk-avoidance strategies among urban African-American youths. *Criminology, 46,* 673–707.

Cocozza, J. J., & Shufelt, J. L. (2006). *Juvenile mental health courts: An emerging strategy.* Delmar, NY: The National Center for Mental Health and Juvenile Justice.

Cohen, A. K. (1955). *Delinquent boys: The culture of the gang.* Glencoe, IL: Free Press.

Cohen, E., & Pfeifer, J. (2011). Mental health services for incarcerated youth: Report from a statewide survey. *Juvenile and Family Court Journal, 62*(2), 22–34.

Cohen, L. E., & Felson, M. (1979). Social changes and crime rate trends: A routine activities approach. *American Sociological Review, 44,* 588–608.

Cohen, L. E., & Kluegel, J. R. (1978). Determinants of juvenile court dispositions: ascriptive and achieved factors in two metropolitan courts. *American Sociological Review, 44,* 588–608.

Cohen, L. E., & Kluegel, J. R. (1979). Selecting delinquents for adjudication: An analysis of intake screening decisions in two metropolitan juvenile courts. *Journal of Research in Crime and Delinquency, 16,* 143–163.

Cole, D. (2003). The effect of a curfew law on juvenile crime in Washington, DC. *American Journal of Criminal Justice, 27,* 217–232.

Collins, J. J. (1989). Alcohol and interpersonal violence: Less than meets the eye. In N. A. Wiener & M. E. Wolfgang (Eds.), *Pathways to criminal violence* (pp. 49–67). Newbury Park, CA: Sage.

Collins, J. J., Hubbard, R. L., & Rachal, J. V. (1985). Expensive drug use and illegal income: A test of explanatory hypotheses. *Criminology, 23,* 743–764.

Colvin, M., Cullen, F. T., & Vander Ven, T. (2002). Coercion, social support, and crime: An emerging theoretical consensus. *Criminology, 40,* 19–42.

Colwell, B. (2002). Shocking the conscience: Excessive discipline of elementary and secondary students. *School Law Reporter, 44*(1), 1–3.

Colwell, B. (2003). Student speech at graduation: When does it violate the establishment clause? *School Law Reporter, 45*(5), 75–78.

Conger, R. D., & Simons, R. L. (1997). Life-course contingencies in the development of adolescent antisocial behavior: A matching law approach. In T. P. Thornberry (Ed.), *Advances in criminological theory* (pp. 55–99). New York: Aldine.

Cook, P. J., Moore, M. H., & Braga, A. A. (2002). Gun control. In J. Q. Wilson & J. Petersilia (Eds.), *Crime: Public policies for crime control* (pp. 291–330). Oakland, CA: ICS Press.

Cooley, C. H. (1902). *Human nature and the social order.* New York: Scribner.

Coombs, R. H. (1981). Back on the streets: Therapeutic communities' impact upon drug abusers. *American Journal of Alcohol Abuse, 8,* 185–201.

Cooper, C. N. (1967). The Chicago YMCA detached workers: Current status of an action program. In M. W. Klein (Ed.), *Juvenile gangs in context* (pp. 183–193). Englewood Cliffs, NJ: Prentice Hall.

Coordinating Council on Juvenile Justice and Delinquency Prevention. (1996). *Combating violence and delinquency: The national juvenile justice action plan: Report.* Washington, DC: U.S. Department of Justice.

Corbett, R. P. (2001). Juvenile probation on the eve of the next millennium. In J. L. Victor & J. Naughton (Eds.), *Annual edition: Criminal justice 01/02* (pp. 141–151). Guilford, CT: Dushkin.

Corbett, R. P. (2002). Reinventing probation and reducing youth violence. In G. S. Katzmann (Ed.), *Securing our children's future: New approaches to juvenile justice and youth violence* (pp. 175–199). Washington, DC: Brookings Institution Press.

Cornish, D. B., & Clarke, R. V. (1986). *The reasoning criminal.* New York: Springer-Verlag.

Corrado, R. R., Cohen, I. M., & Odgers, C. (2003). Multi-problem violent youths: A challenge for the restorative justice paradigm. In E. G. M. Weitekamp & H. Kerner (Eds.), *Restorative justice in context: International practice and directions.* Portland, OR: Willan.

Corsaro, N., Brunson, R. K., & McGarrell, E. F. (2009). Problem-Oriented Policing and Open-Air Drug Markets: Examining the Rockford Pulling Levers Deterrence Strategy. *Crime and Delinquency, 59,* 1,085–1,107.

Cortes, J. B. (1972). *Delinquency and crime.* New York: Seminar Press.

Costanzo, M. (1997). *Just revenge: Costs and consequences of the death penalty.* New York: St. Martin's Press.

Cox, S. M., Davidson, W. S., & Bynum, T. S. (1995). A meta-analytic assessment of delinquency-related outcomes of alternative education programs. *Crime & Delinquency, 41,* 219–234.

Crank, J. P., & Caldero, M. (1991). The production of occupational stress in medium-sized police agencies: A survey of line officers in eight municipal departments. *Journal of Criminal Justice, 19,* 339–349.

Crawford, A., & Newburn, T. (2003). *Youth offending and restorative justice: Implementing reform in youth justice.* Portland, OR: Willan.

Cristall, J., & Forman-Echols, L. (2009). *Property abatements—the other gang injunction: Project T.O.U.G.H.* National Gang Center Bulletin 2. Washington, DC: Bureau of Justice Assistance.

Cronin, R. C. (1994). *Boot camps for adult and juvenile offenders: Overview and update.* Washington, DC: National Institute of Justice.

Crowe, R. R. (1972). The adopted offspring of women criminal offenders. *Archives of General Psychiatry, 27,* 600–603.

Cullen, F. T. (2007). Make rehabilitation corrections' guiding paradigm. *Criminology & Public Policy, 6,* 717–728.

Cullen, F. T., Blevins, K. R., Trager, J. S., & Gendreau, P. (2005). The rise and fall of boot camps: A case study in common sense corrections. *Journal of Offender Rehabilitation, 40,* 53–70.

Cullen, F. T., & Wright, J. P. (1995). The future of corrections. In B. Maguire & P. Radosh (Eds.), *The past, present, and future of American criminal justice* (pp. 198–219). New York: General Hall.

Cullen, F. T., Wright, J. P., & Applegate, B. K. (1996). Control in the community: The limits of reform. In A. T. Harland (Ed.), *Choosing correctional options that work: Defining the demand and evaluating the supply* (pp. 69–116). Thousand Oaks, CA: Sage.

Cullen, F. T., Wright, J. P., & Chamlin, M. B. (1999). Social support and social reform: A progressive crime control agenda. *Crime & Delinquency, 45,* 188–207.

Cummings, S. (1993). Anatomy of a wilding gang. In S. Cummings & D. J. Monti (Eds.), *Gangs: The origins and impact of contemporary youth gangs in the United States* (pp. 49–73). Albany, NY: SUNY Press.

Cummings, S., & Monti, D. J. (1993). Public policy and gangs: Social science and the urban underclass. In S. Cummings & D. J. Monti (Eds.), *Gangs: The origins and impact of contemporary youth gangs in the United States* (pp. 305–320). Albany, NY: SUNY Press.

Currie, E. (2012). Reaping what we sow: The impact of economic justice on criminal justice. In M. Mauer and K. Epstein (Eds.), *To build a better criminal justice system: 25 experts envision the next 25 years of reform* (pp. 46–47). Washington, DC: The Sentencing Project.

Curry, G. D., Ball, R. A., & Decker, S. H. (1996). Estimating the national scope of gang crime from law enforcement data. *Research in Brief*. Washington, DC: U.S. Department of Justice, Office of Justice Programs, National Institute of Justice.

Curry, G. D., & Decker, S. H. (1998). *Confronting gangs: Crime and community*. Los Angeles: Roxbury.

Curry, G. D., Fox, R. J., Ball, R. A., & Stone, D. (1993). *National assessment of law enforcement anti-gang information resources—Final report*. Washington, DC: U.S. Department of Justice, Office of Justice Programs, National Institute of Justice.

Curtis, L. A. (1974). *Criminal violence: National patterns and behavior*. Lexington, MA: D.C. Heath.

Dabbs, J. M., Carr, T. S., Frady, R. L., & Riad, J. K. (1995). Testosterone, crime and misbehavior among 692 male prison inmates. *Personality and Individual Differences, 18*, 627–633.

Daly, K. (2002). Restorative justice: The real story. *Punishment and Society, 4*, 5–79.

D'Angelo, J. M. (2007). The complex nature of juvenile court judges' transfer decisions: A study of judicial attitudes. *Social Science Journal, 44*, 147–159.

Dannefer, D., & Schutt, R. K. (1982). Race and juvenile justice processing in court and police agencies. *American Journal of Sociology, 87*, 1,113–1,132.

Daugherty, C. (2013). *State trends: Legislative victories from 2011–2013 removing youth from the adult criminal justice system*. Washington, DC: Campaign for Youth Justice.

Davis, R., & O'Donnell, J. (2005). Some teenagers call tracking driving an invasion of privacy. *USA Today, 1B*.

Davis, S. M., & Schwartz, M. D. (1987). *Children's rights and the law*. Lexington, MA: D.C. Heath.

Davis, S. M., Scott, E. S., Wadlington, W., & Whitebread, C. H. (1997). *Children in the legal system: Cases and materials* (2nd ed.). Westbury, NY: Foundation Press.

deBeus, K. & Rodriguez, N. (2007). Restorative justice practice: An examination of program completion and recidivism. *Journal of Criminal Justice, 35*, 337–347.

Decker, S., Melde, C. , & Pyrooz, D. C. (2013). What do we know about gangs and gang members and where do we go from here? *Justice Quarterly, 30*, 369–402.

Decker, S., Pennel, S., & Caldwell, A. (1997). *Illegal firearms: Access and use by arrestees*. Washington, DC: National Institute of Justice.

Decker, S., & Van Winkle, B. (1994). Slinging dope: The role of gangs and gang members in drug sales. *Justice Quarterly, 11*, 583–604.

DeFleur, M. L., & Quinney, R. (1966). A reformulation of Sutherland's differential association theory and a strategy for empirical verification. *Journal of Research in Crime and Delinquency, 3*, 1–22.

DeLeon, G. (1984). Program-based evaluation research in therapeutic communities. In F. M. Tims & J. P. Ludford (Eds.), *Drug abuse treatment evaluation: Strategies, progress and prospects* (pp. 69–87). Washington, DC: National Institute on Drug Abuse.

DeLeon, G., & Rosenthal, M. S. (1989). Treatment in residential therapeutic communities. In T. B. Karasu (Ed.), *Treatment of psychiatric disorders: A task force report of the American Psychiatric Association* (Vol. 2, pp. 1,379–1,396). Washington, DC: American Psychiatric Association.

DeLong, J. V. (1972). Treatment and rehabilitation. *Dealing with drug abuse: A report to the Ford Foundation* (pp. 173–254). New York: Praeger.

Deuchar, R. (2011). The impact of curfews and electronic monitoring on the social strains, support and capital experienced by youth gang members in the west of Scotland. *Criminology & Criminal Justice, 12,* 113–128.

Dinkes, R., Kemp, J., Baum, K., & Snyder, T. D. (2009). *Indicators of school crime and safety: 2009.* Washington, DC: U.S. Department of Education and U.S. Department of Justice. Available at http://nces.ed.gov/pubs2010/2010012.pdf

Dodson, K. D., Cabage, L. N., & Klenowski, P. M. (2011). An evidence-based assessment of faith-based programs: Do faith-based programs work to reduce recidivism? *Journal of Offender Rehabilitation, 50,* 367–383.

Doerner, W. G., & Lab, S. P. (2012). *Victimology* (6th ed.). Burlington, MA: Routledge (Anderson Publishing).

Drake, E. (2013). *The effectiveness of declining juvenile court jurisdiction of youthful offenders* (Doc. No. 13-12-1902). Olympia, WA: Washington State Institute for Public Policy.

Drug Courts Program Office. (2000). *About the drug courts program office.* Washington, DC: U.S. Department of Justice.

Drug Policy Alliance (2014). *911 Good Samaritan laws: preventing overdose deaths, saving lives.* New York: Drug Policy Alliance.

Drug Strategies. (2005). *Bridging the gap: A guide to drug treatment in the juvenile justice system.* Washington, DC: Drug Strategies.

Dum, C. P. & Fader, J. J. (2013). These are kids' lives!: Dilemmas and adaptations of juvenile aftercare workers. *Justice Quarterly, 30,* 784–810.

Dunworth, T. (2000). *National evaluation of the youth firearms initiative.* Washington, DC: U.S. Department of Justice.

Durkheim, E. (1933). *The division of labor in society.* New York: Free Press. (Translated by G. Supson.)

Durlauf, S. N., & Nagin, D. S. (2011). Imprisonment and crime: Can both be reduced? *Criminology & Public Policy, 10,* 13–54.

Durose, M. R., Smith, E. L., & Langan, P. A. (2007). *Contacts between police and the public, 2005: Bureau of Justice Statistics Special Report.* Washington, DC: U.S. Department of Justice.

Eck, J., & Maguire, J. (2000). Have changes in policing reduced violent crime? An assessment of the evidence. In A. Blumstein & J. Wallman (Eds.), *The crime drop in America* (pp. 207–265). Cambridge, England: Cambridge University Press.

Egley, A., & Howell, J. C. (2011). *Highlights of the 2009 National Youth Gang Survey.* Washington, DC: Office of Juvenile Justice and Delinquency Prevention. Juvenile Justice Fact Sheet.

Egley, A., Howell, J. C., & Major, A. K. (2004). Recent patterns of gang problems in the United States: Results from the 1996–2002 national youth gang survey. In F. Esbensen, S. G. Tibbetts & L. Gaines (Eds.), *American youth gangs at the millennium* (pp. 90–108). Long Grove, IL: Waveland.

Ehrenkranz, J., Bliss, E., & Sheard, M. H. (1974). Plasma testosterone: Correlation with aggressive behavior and social dominance in man. *Psychosomatic Medicine, 36,* 469–475.

Eisen, M., Zellman, G. L., Massett, H. A., & Murray, D. L. (2002). Evaluating the lions-quest 'skills for adolescence' drug education program: First year behavior outcomes. *Addictive Behaviors, 27,* 619–632.

Eiser, C., & Eiser, J. R. (1988). *Drug education in schools.* New York: Springer-Verlag.

Elliott, D. S., & Huizinga, D. (1984). *The relationship between delinquent behavior and ADM problems.* Boulder, CO: Behavioral Research Institute.

Elliott, D. S., Huizinga, D., & Ageton, S. S. (1985). *Explaining delinquency and drug use.* Beverly Hills: Sage.

Ellis, L., & Walsh, A. (2000). *Criminology: A global perspective.* Boston: Allyn and Bacon.

Empey, L. T. (1982). *American delinquency: Its meaning and construction.* Homewood, IL: Dorsey Press.

Engle, B., & MacGowan, M. J. (2009). A critical review of adolescent substance abuse group treatments. *Journal of Evidence-Based Social Work, 6,* 217–243.

Engel, R. S. (2008). A critique of the 'outcome test' in racial profiling research. *Justice Quarterly, 25,* 1–36.

Engel, R. S., Tillyer, M. S., & Corsaro, N. (2013). Reducing gang violence using focused deterrence: Evaluating the Cincinnati initiative to reduce violence (CIRV). *Justice Quarterly, 30,* 403–439.

Erickson, M. L. (1971). The group context of delinquent behavior. *Social Problems, 19,* 114–129.

Erickson, M. L. (1973). Group violations and official delinquency: The group hazard hypothesis. *Criminology, 11,* 127–160.

Esbensen, F., & Carson, D. C. (2012). Who are the gangsters? An examination of the age, race/ethnicity, sex, and immigration status of self-reported gang members in a seven-city study of American youth. *Journal of Contemporary Criminal Justice, 28,* 465–481.

Esbensen, F., & Huizinga, D. (1991). Juvenile victimization and delinquency. *Youth and Society, 23,* 202–228.

Esbensen, F., & Huizinga, D. (1993). Gangs, drugs and delinquency in a survey of urban youth. *Criminology, 31,* 565–590.

Esbensen, F., & Osgood, D. W. (1997). National evaluation of G.R.E.A.T. *NIJ Research in Brief.* Washington, DC: National Institute of Justice.

Esbensen, F., Osgood, D. W., Peterson, D., Taylor, T. T., & Carson, D. C. (2013). Short- and long-term outcome results from a multisite evaluation of the G.R.E.A.T. program. *Criminology and Public Policy, 12,* 375–412.

Esbensen, F., Peterson, D., Taylor, T. J., Freng, A., & Osgood, D. W. (2004). Gang prevention: A case study of a primary prevention program. In F. Esbensen, S. G. Tibbetts & L. Gaines (Eds.), *American youth gangs at the millennium* (pp. 274–351). Long Grove, IL: Waveland.

Esbensen, F., Peterson, D., Taylor, T. J., Freng, A., Osgood, D. W., Carson, D. C., & Matsuda, K. N. (2011). Evaluation and evolution of the gang resistance education and training (G.R.E.A.T.) program. *Journal of School Violence, 10*, 53–70.

Eysenck, H. J., & Gudjonsson, G. H. (1989). *The causes and cures of criminality.* New York: Plenum.

Fabricant, M. (1983). *Juveniles in the family courts.* Lexington, MA: Lexington Books.

Fagan, J. (1990). Social process of delinquency and drug use among urban gangs. In C. R. Huff (Ed.), *Gangs in America* (pp. 183–219). Newbury Park, CA: Sage.

Fagan, J. (2002). Policing guns and youth violence. *Children, Youth and Gun Violence, 12*, 133–151.

Fagan, J. (2007). End natural life sentences for juveniles. *Criminology & Public Policy, 6*, 735–746.

Fagan, J., & Pabon, E. (1990). Contributions of delinquency and substance use to school dropout among inner-city youths. *Youth and Society, 21*, 306–354.

Fagan, J., & Weis, J. G. (1990). *Drug use and delinquency among inner city youth.* New York: Springer-Verlag.

Fagan, J., Weis, J. G., & Cheng, Y. (1990). Delinquency and substance use among inner city students. *Journal of Drug Issues, 20*, 351–402.

Fareed, A., Vayalapalli, S., Stout, S., Casarella, J., Drexler, K., & Bailey, S. P. (2011). Effect of methadone maintenance treatment on heroin craving: A literature review. *Journal of Addictive Diseases, 30*, 27–38.

Farrington, D. P., & Welsh, B. C. (2007). *Saving children from a life of crime: Early risk factors and effective interventions.* New York: Oxford University Press.

Faust, F. L., & Brantingham, P. J. (1979). *Juvenile justice philosophy: Readings, cases and comments.* St. Paul, MN: West Group.

Federal Bureau of Investigation. (2007). *Crime in the United States, 2006.* Washington, DC: Federal Bureau of Investigation. Available at http://www.fbi.gov/ucr/cius2006/index. html/

Federal Bureau of Investigation (2013). *Crime in the United States, 2012.* Washington, DC: Federal Bureau of Investigation. Available at http://www.fbi.gov/about-us/cjis/ucr/crime-in-the-u.s/2012/crime-in-the-u.s.-2012

Federal Interagency Forum on Child and Family Statistics. (2010). *America's children: Key national indicators of well-being, 2011.* Available at http://www.childstats.gov/pdf/ac2011/ac_11.pdf

Feld, B. C. (1981). Legislative policies toward the serious juvenile offender: On the virtues of automatic adulthood. *Crime & Delinquency, 27*, 497–521.

Feld, B. C. (1988). *In re Gault* revisited: A cross-state comparison of the right to counsel in juvenile court. *Crime & Delinquency, 34*, 393–424.

Feld, B. C. (1993). *Justice for children: The right to counsel and the juvenile courts.* Boston: Northeastern University Press.

Feld, B. C. (1998). Juvenile and criminal justice systems' responses to youth violence. In M. Tonry & M. H. Moore (Eds.), *Youth violence* (pp. 189–261). Chicago: University of Chicago Press.

Feld, B. C. (1999). *Bad kids: Race and the transformation of the juvenile court.* New York: Oxford University Press.

Feld, B. C. (2006). Juveniles' competence to exercise *Miranda* rights: An empirical study of policy and practice. *Minnesota Law Review, 91*, 26–100.

Feld, B. C. (2007). A century of juvenile justice: A work in progress or a revolution that failed? *Northern Kentucky Law Review, 34*, 189–256.

Feld, B. C. (2008). A slower form of death: Implications of *Roper v. Simmons* for juveniles sentenced to life without parole. *Notre Dame Journal of Law, Ethics & Public Policy, 22*(1), 9–65.

Feld, B. C. (2012). Procedural rights in juvenile courts: Competence and consequences. In B. C. Feld & D. M. Bishop (Eds.), *The Oxford handbook of juvenile crime and juvenile justice* (pp. 664–691). New York: Oxford University Press.

Feld, B. C. (2013). Adolescent criminal responsibility, proportionality, and sentencing policy: *Roper, Graham, Miller/Jackson* and the youth discount. *Law and Inequality, 31*, 263–330.

Feld, B. C. & Bishop, D. M. (2012). Transfer of juveniles to criminal court. In B. C. Feld & D. M. Bishop (Eds.), *The Oxford handbook of juvenile justice* (pp. 801–842). New York: Oxford University Press.

Feld, B., & Schaefer, S. (2010). The right to counsel in juvenile court: Law reform to deliver legal services and reduce justice by geography. *Criminology & Public Policy, 9*, 327–356.

Fenwick, C. R. (1982). Juvenile court intake decision making: The importance of family affiliation. *Journal of Criminal Justice, 10*, 443–453.

Ferrer-Wreder, L., Lorente, C. C., Briones, E., Bussell, J., Berman, S., & Arrufat, O. (2002). Promoting identity development in marginalized youth. *Journal of Adolescent Research, 17*, 168–187.

Feyerherm, W. (1980). The group hazard hypothesis: A reexamination. *Journal of Research in Crime and Delinquency, 17*, 58–68.

Finckenauer, J. O. (1982). *Scared straight! and the panacea phenomenon.* Englewood Cliffs, NJ: Prentice-Hall.

Fishbein, D., Miller, S., Winn, D. M., & Dakof, G. (2009). Biopsychological factors, gender, and delinquency. In M. Zahn (Ed.), *The delinquent girl*. Philadelphia: Temple University Press.

Fishman, L. T. (1988). *The vice queens: An ethnographic study of black female gang behavior.* Paper presented at the Annual Meeting of the American Society of Criminology, Chicago, IL.

Flexon, J. L., Lurigio, A. J., & Greenleaf, R. G. (2009). Exploring the dimensions of trust in the police among Chicago juveniles. *Journal of Criminal Justice, 37*, 180–189.

Fox, J. R. (1985). Mission impossible? Social work practice with black urban youth gangs. *Social Work, 30*, 25–31.

Franklin, C. W., II, & Franklin, A. P. (1976). Victimology revisited: A critique and suggestions for future direction. *Criminology, 14*, 177–214.

Gaarder, E., & Belknap, J. (2004). Little women: Girls in adult prison. *Women & Criminal Justice, 15*(2), 51–80.

Gaarder, E., Rodriguez, N., & Zatz, M. (2004). Criers, liars, and manipulators: Probation officers' views of girls. *Justice Quarterly, 21*, 547–578.

Gallup Organization (2001). Firefighters top Gallup's 'honesty and ethics' list. *The Gallup Poll Monthly, 435*, 46–48.

Garbarino, J., & Gilliam, G. (1980). *Understanding abusive families*. Lexington, MA: Lexington Books.

Garland, D. (2001). *The culture of control: Crime and social order in contemporary society*. Chicago: University of Chicago Press.

Garofalo, J., & Connelly, K. J. (1980). Dispute resolution centers, part I: Major features and processes. *Criminal Justice Abstracts, 12*, 416–436.

Garry, E. M. (1996). *Truancy: First step to a lifetime of problems*. Washington, DC: U.S. Department of Justice.

Gates, L. B., & Rohe, W. M. (1987). Fear and reactions to crime: A revised model. *Urban Affairs Quarterly, 22*, 425–453.

Gavrielides, T. (2008). Restorative justice—the perplexing concept: Conceptual fault-lines and power battles within the restorative justice movement. *Criminology & Criminal Justice, 8*, 165–183.

Gay, B. W., & Marquart, J. W. (1993). Jamaican posses: A new form of organized crime. *Journal of Crime and Justice, 16*, 139–170.

Geary, D. P. (1983). Nutrition, chemicals and criminal behavior: Some psychological aspects of anti-social conduct. *Juvenile and Family Court Journal, 34*, 9–13.

Geiselman, R. E., Bornstein, G., & Saywitz, K. J. (1992). *New approach to interviewing children: A test of its effectiveness*. Washington, DC: U.S. Department of Justice.

Geller, A., & Fagan, J. (2010). Pot as pretext: Marijuana, race, and the new disorder in New York City street policing. *Journal of Empirical Legal Studies, 7*, 591–633.

Geller, W. A. (1983). Deadly force: What we know. In C. B. Klockars (Ed.), *Thinking about police: Contemporary readings* (pp. 313–331). New York: McGraw-Hill.

Geller, W. A., & Toch, H. (1996). Understanding and controlling police abuse of force. In W. A. Geller & H. Toch (Eds.), *Police violence: Understanding and controlling police abuse of force* (pp. 292–328). New Haven, CT: Yale University Press.

Gelles, R. J. (1980). Violence in the family: a review of research in the 70s. *Journal of Marriage and the Family, 42*, 873–885.

Gendreau, P. (1996). The principles of effective intervention with offenders. In A. T. Harland (Ed.), *Choosing correctional options that work: Defining the demand and evaluating the supply* (pp. 117–130). Thousand Oaks, CA: Sage.

Gendreau, P., Cullen, F. T., & Bonta, J. (1994). Intensive rehabilitation supervision: The next generation in community corrections? *Federal Probation, 58*(1), 72–78.

Geraghty, T. F. (1998). Justice for children: How do we get there? *Journal of Criminal Law and Criminology, 88*, 190–241.

Giallombardo, R. (1974). *The social work of imprisoned girls*. New York: John Wiley.

Gil, D. (1971). *Violence against children: Physical child abuse in the United States*. Cambridge, MA: Harvard University Press.

Girshick, L. B. (1999). *No safe haven: Stories of women in prison*. Boston: Northeastern University Press.

Glaser, D. (1956). Criminality theories and behavioral images. *American Journal of Sociology, 61*, 434–444.

Glaser, D. (1964). *The effectiveness of a prison and parole system.* Indianapolis: Bobbs-Merrill.

Glueck, S., & Glueck, E. (1956). *Physique and delinquency.* New York: Harper.

Goddard, H. H. (1920). *Efficiency and levels of intelligence.* Princeton, NJ: Princeton University Press.

Goffman, E. (1961). *Asylums: Essays on the situation of mental patients and other inmates.* Garden City, NY: Anchor Books.

Gold, M. (1970). *Delinquent behavior in an American city.* Belmont, CA: Brooks/Cole.

Goldkamp, J. S., & Weiland, D. (1993). Assessing the impact of Dade County's felony drug court. *NIJ Research in Brief*, Washington, DC: U.S. Department of Justice.

Goldstein, A. P. (1993). Gang intervention: A historical review. In A. P. Goldstein & C. R. Huff (Eds.), *The gang intervention handbook* (pp. 21–51). Champaign, IL: Research Press.

Goldstein, H. (1990). *Problem-oriented policing.* New York: McGraw-Hill.

Goldstein, P. J. (1989). Drugs and violent crime. In N. A. Weiner & M. E. Wolfgang (Eds.), *Pathways to criminal violence* (pp. 16–48). Newbury Park, CA: Sage.

Gordon, J. A., Moriarty, L. J., & Grant, P. H. (2003). Juvenile correctional officers' perceived fear and risk of victimization: Examining individual and collective levels of victimization in two juvenile correctional centers in Virginia. *Criminal Justice and Behavior, 30,* 62–84.

Goring, C. (1913). *The English convict: A statistical study.* Montclair, NJ: Patterson Smith.

Gottfredson, D. C., & Barton, W. H. (1993). Deinstitutionalization of juvenile offenders. *Criminology, 31,* 591–611.

Gottfredson, D. C., Najaka, S. S., & Kearley, B. (2003). Effectiveness of drug treatment courts: Evidence from a randomized trial. *Criminology & Public Policy, 2,* 171–198.

Gottfredson, M. R., & Hirschi, T. (1990). *A general theory of crime.* Stanford, CA: Stanford University Press.

Gover, A. R., & MacKenzie, D. L. (2003). Child maltreatment and adjustment to juvenile correctional institutions. *Criminal Justice and Behavior, 30,* 374–396.

Granfield, R., Eby, C., & Brewster, T. (1998). An examination of the Denver drug court: The impact of a treatment-oriented drug-offender system. *Law and Policy, 20,* 183–202.

Grasmick, H. G., Tittle, C. R., Bursik, R. J., & Arneklev, B. J. (1993). Testing the core empirical implications of Gottfredson and Hirschi's general theory of crime. *Journal of Research in Crime and Delinquency, 30,* 5–29.

Gray, G. E., & Gray, L. K. (1983). Diet and juvenile delinquency. *Nutrition Today, 18,* 14–21.

Greenbaum, S. (1994). Drugs, delinquency and other data. *Juvenile Justice, 2*(1), 2–8.

Greenberg, M. T., & Kusche, C. (1998). *Promoting alternative thinking strategies (paths): Blueprints for violence prevention.* Boulder, CO: Institute of Behavioral Science.

Greenwald, G. (2009). *Drug decriminalization in Portugal: Lessons for creating fair and successful drug policies.* Washington, DC: Cato Institute.

Greenwood, P. (2008). Prevention and intervention programs for juvenile offenders. *The Future of Children, 18,* 185–210.

Greenwood, P. W., & Turner, S. (2012). Probation and other noninstitutional treatment: The evidence is in. In B. C. Feld & D. M. Bishop (Eds.), *The Oxford handbook of juvenile justice* (pp. 723–747). New York: Oxford University Press.

Griffin, P. (2005). National overviews. *State Juvenile Justice Profiles.* Pittsburgh: National Center for Juvenile Justice. Available at http://www.ncjj.org/stateprofiles/

Griffin, P., Addie, S., Adams, B., & Firestine, K. (2011). Trying juveniles as adults: An analysis of state transfer laws and reporting. Washington, DC: Office of Juvenile Justice and Delinquency Prevention.

Griffin, P., & King, M. (2005). National Overviews. *State Juvenile Justice Profiles*. Pittsburgh: National Center for Juvenile Justice. Available at http://www.ncjj.org/stateprofiles/

Griffin, P., Szymanski, L., & King, M. (2005). National Overviews. *State Juvenile Justice Profiles*. Pittsburgh: National Center for Juvenile Justice. Available at http://www.ncjj.org/stateprofiles/

Griffin, P., Szymanski, L., & King, M. (2006). National overviews. *State Juvenile Justice Profiles*. Pittsburgh: National Center for Juvenile Justice. Available at http://www.ncjj.org/stateprofiles/

Griffin, P., & Thomas, D. (2004). The good news: Measuring juvenile outcomes at case closing. *Pennsylvania Progress, 10*(2), 1–6.

Griffin, P., & Torbet, P. (2002). *Desktop guide to good juvenile probation practice*. Pittsburgh: National Center for Juvenile Justice.

Grisso, T. P., & Schwartz, R. G. (2000). *Youth on trial: A developmental perspective on juvenile justice*. Chicago: University of Chicago Press.

Grogger, J. (2002). The effects of civil gang injunctions on reported violent crime: Evidence from Los Angeles County. *Journal of Law and Economics, 4*, 69–90.

Guerino, P., Harrison, P. M., & Sabol, W. J. (2011). *Prisoners in 2010*. Washington, DC: U.S. Department of Justice.

Guevara, L., Spohn, C., & Herz, D. (2004). Race, legal representation, and juvenile justice: Issues and concerns. *Crime & Delinquency, 50*, 344–371.

Guo, G., Roettger, M. E., & Cai, T. C. (2008). The integration of genetic propensities into social-control models of delinquency and violence among male youths. *American Sociological Review, 73*, 543–568.

Hagan, J., & McCarthy, B. (1997). *Mean streets: Youth crime and homelessness*. New York: Cambridge University Press. (In collaboration with P. Parker and J. Climenhage.)

Hagedorn, J. M. (1988). *People and folks: Gangs, crime and the underclass in a rustbelt city*. Chicago: Lakeview Press.

Hagedorn, J. M. (1994). Homeboys, dope fiends, legits, and new jacks. *Criminology, 32*, 197–220.

Halliday-Boykins, C. A., Schaeffer, C. M., Henggeler, S. W., Chapman, J. E., Cunningham, P. B., Randall, J., & Shapiro, S. B. (2010). Predicting nonresponse to juvenile court drug interventions. *Journal of Substance Abuse Treatment, 39*, 318–328.

Hansen, D. J. (1980). Drug education: Does it work? In F. S. Scarpitti & S. K. Datesman (Eds.), *Drugs and youth culture* (pp. 251–282). Beverly Hills: Sage.

Hansen, W. B., Johnson, C. A., Flay, B. R., Graham, J. W., & Sobel, J. L. (1988). Affective and social influence approaches to the prevention of multiple substance abuse among seventh grade students: Results from project SMART. *Preventive Medicine, 17*, 135–154.

Hardt, R. H., & Peterson-Hardt, S. (1977). On determining the quality of delinquency self-report method. *Journal of Research in Crime and Delinquency, 14*, 247–261.

Harrell, A. (1998). Drug courts and the role of graduated sanctions. *NIJ Research Preview*. Washington, DC: National Institute of Justice.

Harris, J. A. (1999). Review and methodological considerations in research on testosterone and aggression. *Aggression and Violent Behavior, 4,* 273–291.

Harris, N. (2003). Evaluating the practice of restorative justice: The case of family group conferencing. In L. Walgrave (Ed.), *Repositioning restorative justice.* Portland, OR: Willan.

Harvard Law Review. (2005). Juvenile curfews and the major confusion over minor rights. *Harvard Law Review, 118,* 2,400–2,421.

Hawken, A. & Kleiman, M. (2009). *Managing drug involved probationers with swift and certain sanctions: Evaluating Hawaii's HOPE.* Report submitted to the National Institute of Justice. Available at https://www.ncjrs.gov

Hawkins, J. D., Catalano, R. F., Kosterman, R., Abbott, R., & Hill, K. G. (1999). Preventing adolescent health-risk behaviors by strengthening protection during childhood. *Archives of Pediatric and Adolescent Medicine, 153,* 226–234.

Hayes, H., & Daly, K. (2004). Conferencing and re-offending in Queensland. *Australian and New Zealand Journal of Criminology, 37,* 167–191.

Hayes, L. M. (2004). *Juvenile suicide in confinement: A national survey.* Baltimore, MD: National Center on Institutions and Alternatives.

Haynes, S. H., Cares, A. C., & Ruback, R. B. (2014). Juvenile economic sanctions: An analysis of their imposition, payment, and effect on recidivism. *Criminology & Public Policy, 13,* 31–60.

Henderson, C. E., Young, D. W., Jainchill, N., Hawke, J., Farkas, S., & Davis, R. M. (2007). Program use of effective drug abuse treatment practices for juvenile offenders. *Journal of Substance Abuse Treatment, 32,* 279–290.

Henggeler, S. W., Halliday-Boykins, C. A., Cunningham, P. B., Randall, J., Shapiro, S. B., & Chapman, J. E. (2006). Juvenile drug court: Enhancing outcomes by integrating evidence-based treatments. *Journal of Consulting and Clinical Psychology, 74,* 42–54.

Hennigan, K. M., & Sloane, D. (2013). Improving civil gang injunctions: How implementation can affect gang dynamics, crime, and violence. *Criminology and Public Policy, 12,* 7–42.

Henretta, J. C., Frazier, C. E., & Bishop, D. M. (1985). *Juvenile justice decision-making: An analysis of the effects of prior case outcomes.* Paper presented at the Annual Meeting of the American Society of Criminology, San Diego, CA.

Henretta, J. C., Frazier, C. E., & Bishop, D. M. (1986). The effect of prior case outcomes on juvenile justice decision-making. *Social Forces, 65,* 554–562.

Heretick, D. M. L., & Russell, J. A. (2013). The impact of juvenile mental health court on recidivism among youth. *OJJDP Journal of Juvenile Justice, 3,* 1–14.

Herrnstein, R. J., & Murray, C. (1994). *The bell curve: Intelligence and class structure in American life.* New York: Free Press.

Hills, S. L. (1980). *Demystifying social deviance.* New York: McGraw-Hill.

Hindelang, M. J. (1971). The social versus solitary nature of delinquent involvement. *British Journal of Criminology, 11,* 167–175.

Hindelang, M. J. (1973). Causes of delinquency: A partial replication and extension. *Social Problems, 20,* 470–487.

Hindelang, M. J. (1975). *Public opinion regarding crime, criminal justice, and related topics.* Washington, DC: U.S. Department of Justice.

Hindelang, M. J., Gottfredson, M. R., & Garofalo, J. (1978). *Victims of personal crime: An empirical foundation for a theory of personal victimization.* Cambridge, MA: Ballinger.

Hindelang, M. J., Hirschi, T., & Weis, J. G. (1981). *Measuring delinquency.* Beverly Hills: Sage.

Hippchen, L. J. (1978). *Ecologic-biochemical approaches to treatment of delinquents and criminals.* New York: Van Nostrand Reinhold.

Hippchen, L. J. (1981). Some possible biochemical aspects of criminal behavior. *International Journal of Biosocial Research, 2,* 37–48.

Hirschel, J. D., Dean, C. W., & Dumond, D. (2001). Juvenile curfews and race: A cautionary note. *Criminal Justice Policy Review, 12,* 197–214.

Hirschfield, P. J., & Celinska, K. (2011). Beyond fear: Sociological perspectives on the criminalization of school discipline. *Sociology Compass, 5,* 1–12.

Hirschi, T. (1969). *Causes of delinquency.* Berkeley: University of California Press.

Hirschi, T., & Hindelang, M. J. (1977). Intelligence and delinquency: A revisionist review. *American Sociological Review, 42,* 572–587.

Hockenberry, S., Sickmund, M., & Sladky, A. (2013). *Juvenile residential facility census, 2010: Selected findings.* Washington, DC: Office of Juvenile Justice and Delinquency Prevention.

Holtz, L. E. (1987). *Miranda* in a juvenile setting: A child's right to silence. *The Journal of Criminal Law and Criminology, 78,* 534–556.

Hope, T. (1997). Inequality and the future of community crime prevention. In S. P. Lab (Ed.), *Crime prevention at a crossroads* (pp. 143–158). Cincinnati: Anderson.

Horowitz, R. (1983). *Honor and the American dream: Culture and identity in a Chicano community.* New Brunswick, NJ: Rutgers University Press.

Howell, J. C. (1997). Youth gangs. *OJJDP Fact Sheet #72.* Washington, DC: Office of Juvenile Justice and Delinquency Prevention.

Howell, J. C. (2000). *Youth gang programs and strategies: Summary.* Washington, DC: Office of Juvenile Justice and Delinquency Prevention.

Howell, J. C. (2010). *Gang prevention: An overview of research and programs.* Juvenile Justice Bulletin. Washington, DC: Office of Juvenile Justice and Delinquency Prevention.

Howell, J. C., Egley, A., Tita, G. E., & Griffiths, E. (2011). *U.S. gang problem trends and seriousness, 1996–2009.* National Gang Center Bulletin No. 6. Washington, DC: National Gang Center.

Howell, J. C., & Hawkins, J. D. (1998). Prevention of youth violence. In M. Tonry & M. H. Moore (Eds.), *Youth violence* (pp. 189–261). Chicago: University of Chicago Press.

Hser, Y., Anglin, M. D., & Chou, C. (1988). Evaluation of drug abuse treatment: A repeated measure design assessing methadone maintenance. *Evaluation Review, 12,* 547–570.

Hsia, H. M., Bridges, G. S., & McHale, R. (2004). *Disproportionate minority confinement 2002 update: Summary.* Washington, DC: U.S. Department of Justice.

Huang, D. T. (2001). Less unequal footing: State courts' per se rules for juvenile waivers during interrogation and the case for their implementation. *Cornell Law Review, 86,* 437.

Huba, G. J., & Bentler, P. M. (1983). Causal models of the development of law abidance and its relationship to psychosocial factors and drug use. In W. S. Laufer & J. M. Day (Eds.), *Personality theory, moral development and criminal behavior* (pp. 165–215). Lexington, MA: D.C. Heath.

Hubbard, R. L., Marsden, M. E., Rachal, J. V., Harwood, H. J., Cavanaugh, E. R., & Ginzbury, H. M. (1989). *Drug abuse treatment: A national study of effectiveness*. Chapel Hill, NC: University of North Carolina Press.

Huebner, B. M., Shafer, J. A., & Bynum, T. S. (2004). African American and white perceptions of police service: Within- and between-group variation. *Journal of Criminal Justice, 32*, 123–135.

Huff, C. R. (1990). Denial, overreaction, and misidentification: A postscript on public policy. In C. R. Huff (Ed.), *Gangs in America* (pp. 310–317). Newbury Park, CA: Sage.

Huff, C. R. (1993). Gangs in the United States. In A. P. Goldstien & C. R. Huff (Eds.), *The gang intervention handbook* (pp. 3–20). Champaign, IL: Research Press.

Hughes, C. E., & Stevens, A. (2010). What can we learn from the Portuguese decriminalization of illicit drugs? *British Journal of Criminology, 50*, 999–1022.

Huizinga, D., Loeber, R., & Thornberry, T. P. (1995). *Urban delinquency and substance abuse: Research summary*. Washington, DC: Office of Juvenile Justice and Delinquency Prevention.

Huizinga, D., Menard, S., & Elliot, D. (1989). Delinquency and drug use: Temporal and developmental patterns. *Justice Quarterly, 6*, 419–456.

Huizinga, D., Thornberry, T. P., Knight, K. E., Lovegrove, P. J., Loeber, R., Hill, K., & Farrington, D.P. (2007). *Disproportionate minority contact in the juvenile justice system: A study of differential minority arrest/referral to court in three cities*. An unpublished report submitted to the Office of Juvenile Justice and Delinquency Prevention. Available from the National Criminal Justice Reference Service.

Human Rights Watch. (2001). *No escape: Male rape in U.S. prisons*. Available at http://www.hrw.org/

Human Rights Watch. (2006). *Custody and control: Conditions of confinement in New York's juvenile prisons for girls*. New York: Human Rights Watch.

Human Rights Watch. (2008). *The rest of their lives: Life without parole for youth offenders in the United States in 2008*. New York: Human Rights Watch.

Human Rights Watch (2010). *Distribution of estimated 2,589 juvenile offenders serving juvenile life without parole*. Available at http://www.hrw.org/

Human Rights Watch (2014a). *Branded for life: Florida's prosecution of children as adults under its "direct file" law*. New York: Human Rights Watch.

Human Rights Watch (2014b). *Profiting from probation: America's "offender funded" probation industry*. New York: Human Rights Watch.

Humes, E. (1996). *No matter how loud I shout: A year in the life of juvenile court*. New York: Simon & Schuster.

Hunter, A. (1985). Private, parochial and public school orders: The problem of crime and incivility in urban communities. In G. D. Suttles & M. N. Zald (Eds.), *The challenge of social control: Citizenship and institution building in modern society*. Norwood, NJ: Ablex.

Hurst, Y. G., & Frank, J. (2000). How kids view cops: The nature of juvenile attitudes toward the police. *Journal of Criminal Justice, 28*, 189–202.

Hurst, Y.G., Frank, J., & Browning, S. L. (2000). The attitudes of juveniles toward the police: A comparison of black and white youth. *Policing: An International Journal of Police Strategies & Management, 23*, 37–53.

Husak, D. (2003). Four points about drug decriminalization. *Criminal Justice Ethics, 30,* 21–29.

Hutchings, B., & Mednick, S. A. (1977). Criminality in adoptees and their adoptive and biological parents: A pilot study. In S. A. Mednick & K. O. Christiansen (Eds.), *Biosocial bases of criminal behavior* (pp. 127–141). New York: Gardner Press.

Hutchinson, R., & Kyle, C. (1993). Hispanic street gangs in Chicago's public schools. In S. Cummings & D. J. Monti (Eds.), *Gangs: The origins and impact of contemporary youth gangs in the United States* (pp. 113–136). Albany, NY: SUNY Press.

Inciardi, J. A., Horowitz, R., & Pottieger, A. E. (1993). *Street kids, street drugs, street crime: An examination of drug use and serious delinquency in Miami.* Belmont, CA: Wadsworth.

Inderbitzin, M. (2006a). A look from the inside: Balancing custody and treatment in a juvenile maximum-security facility. *International Journal of Offender Therapy and Comparative Criminology, 51,* 348–362.

Inderbitzin, M. (2006b). Lessons from a juvenile training school: Survival and growth. *Journal of Adolescent Research, 21,* 7–26.

Institute of Judicial Administration–American Bar Association. (1980). *Juvenile justice standards project: Standards relating to adjudication* (2nd ed.). Cambridge, MA: Ballinger.

Institute of Judicial Administration–American Bar Association. (1982). *Juvenile justice standards project: Standards for juvenile justice: A summary and analysis* (2nd ed.). Cambridge, MA: Ballinger.

Ishida, K., Clarke, E., & Reed, D. (2014). *Automatic adult prosecution of children in Cook County, Illinois.* Evanston, IL: Juvenile Justice Initiative.

Jablecki, L. T. (2005). A critique of faith-based prison programs. *The Humanist, 65,* 11–16.

Jang, S. J., & Johnson, B. R. (2001). Neighborhood disorder, individual religiosity, and adolescent use of illicit drugs: A test of multilevel hypotheses. *Criminology, 39,* 109–144.

Jeffery, C. R. (1965). Criminal behavior and learning theory. *Journal of Criminal Law, Criminology and Police Science, 56,* 294–300.

Jensen, G. F., & Brownfield, D. (1983). Parents and drugs. *Criminology, 21,* 543–554.

Jeong, S., McGarrell, E. F., & Hipple, N. K. (2012). Long-term impact of family group conferences on re-offending: The Indianapolis restorative justice experiment. *Journal of Experimental Criminology, 8,* 369–385.

Joe, D., & Robinson, N. (1980). Chinatown's immigrant gangs: The new young warrior class. *Criminology, 18,* 337–345.

Johnson, B. D., Goldstein, P. J., Prebel, E., Schmeidler, J., Lipton, D. S., Spunt, B., & Miller, T. (1985). *Taking care of business: The economics of crime by heroin abusers.* Lexington, MA: Lexington Books.

Johnson, B. D., Wish, E. D., Schmeidler, J., & Huizinga, D. (1991). Concentration of delinquent offending: Serious drug involvement and high delinquency rates. *Journal of Drug Issues, 21,* 205–229.

Johnson, K., Lanza-Kaduce, L., & Woolard, J. (2011). Disregarding graduated treatment: Why transfer aggravates recidivism. *Crime & Delinquency, 57,* 756–777.

Johnston, L. D., Bachman, J. G., & O'Malley, P. M. (2013). *Monitoring the Future: Questionnaire responses from the nation's high school seniors, 2011.* Ann Arbor, MI: Institute for Social Research.

Johnston, L. D., O'Malley, P. M., & Bachman, J. G. (1987). *National trends in drug use and related factors among American high school students and young adults, 1975–1986.* Rockville, MD: National Institute on Drug Abuse.

Johnston, L. D., O'Malley, P. M., & Bachman, J. G. (1996). *National survey results on drug use from the monitoring the future study, 1975–1995.* Washington, DC: U.S. Department of Health and Human Services.

Johnston, L. D., O'Malley, P. M., Bachman, J. G., & Schulenberg, J. E. (2011). *Monitoring the future: National results on adolescent drug use: Overview of key findings, 2010.* Ann Arbor: Institute for Social Research, The University of Michigan. Available at http://monitoringthefuture.org/

Johnston, L. D., O'Malley, P. M., Bachman, J. G., & Schulenberg, J. E. (2013, December 18). American teens more cautious about using synthetic drugs. University of Michigan News Service: Ann Arbor, MI. Available at http://www.monitoringthefuture.org/

Johnston, L. D., O'Malley, P. M., & Eveland, L. K. (1978). Drugs and delinquency: A search for causal connections. In D. B. Kandel (Ed.), *Longitudinal research on drug use: Empirical findings and methodological issues* (pp. 137–156). Washington, DC: Hemisphere.

Johnston, L. D., O'Malley, P. M., Miech, R. A., Bachman, J. G., & Schulenberg, J. E. (2014). *Monitoring the future: National results on drug use: 1975–2013: Overview, key findings on adolescent drug use.* Ann Arbor: Institute for Social Research, The University of Michigan. Available at http://www.monitoringthefuture.org/

Johnstone, J. W. C. (1981). Youth gangs and black suburbs. *Pacific Sociological Review, 58,* 355–375.

Jolicoeur, M., & Zedlewski, E. (2010). *Much ado about sexting.* Washington, DC: National Institute of Justice.

Jones, J. B. (2004). *Access to counsel.* Washington, DC: U.S. Department of Justice.

Jones, L. M., Cross, T. P., Walsh, W. A., & Simone, M. (2005). Criminal investigations of child abuse: The research behind "best practices." *Trauma, Violence, & Abuse, 6,* 254–268.

Jordan, K. L., & Freiburger, T. L. (2010). Examining the impact of race and ethnicity on the sentencing of juveniles in adult court. *Criminal Justice Policy Review, 21,* 185–201.

Jordan, K. L., & Myers, D. (2011). Juvenile transfer and deterrence: re-examining the effectiveness of a 'get tough' policy. *Crime and Delinquency, 57*(2), 247–270.

Juvenile Justice Update. (1995). Juveniles subject to warrantless search as a probation condition have no expectation of privacy. *Juvenile Justice Update, 2,* 8.

Kandel, D. B. (1973). Adolescent marijuana use: Role of parents and peers. *Science, 181,* 1,067–1,070.

Kandel, D. B., Simcha-Fagan, O., & Davies, M. (1986). Risk factors for delinquency and illicit drug use from adolescence to young adulthood. *Journal of Drug Issues, 16,* 67–90.

Kanter, D., & Bennett, W. (1968). Orientation of street-corner workers and their effects on gangs. In S. Wheeler (Ed.), *Controlling delinquents.* New York: Wiley.

Kaplan, J. (1983). *The hardest drug: Heroin and drug policy.* Chicago: University of Chicago Press.

Karp, D. R. (2001). The offender/community encounter: Stakeholder involvement in the Vermont reparative boards. In D. R. Karp & T. Clear (Eds.), *What is community justice? Case studies of restorative justice and community supervision* (pp. 61–86). Thousand Oaks, CA: Sage.

Karp, D. R., Bazemore, G., & Chesire, J. D. (2004). The role and attitudes of restorative board members: A case study of volunteers in community justice. *Crime & Delinquency, 50,* 487–515.

Katz, C. M., & Webb, V. J. (2003). *Police response to gangs: A multi-site study—final report.* Washington, DC: National Institute of Justice.

Katz, J., & Chamblis, W. J. (1995). Biology and crime. In J. F. Sheley (Ed.), *Criminology: A contemporary handbook* (pp. 275–304). Belmont, CA: Wadsworth.

Kelley, T. M., Kennedy, D. B., & Homant, R. J. (2003). Evaluation of an individualized treatment program for adolescent shoplifters. *Adolescence, 38,* 725–733.

Kelling, G. (1975). Leadership in the gang. In D. S. Cartwright, B. Tomson & H. Schwartz (Eds.), *Gang delinquency* (pp. 111–126). Monterey: Brooks/Cole.

Kelling, G. L., & Coles, C. M. (1996). *Fixing broken windows: Restoring order and reducing crime in our communities.* New York: Touchstone.

Kelly, R. (2013, July 22). The NYPD: Guilty of saving 7,383 lives. *Wall Street Journal* online. Available at http://online.wsj.com/news/articles/SB1000142412788732444810457861633588719320

Kelly, W. R., Macy, T. S., & Mears, D. P. (2005). Juvenile referrals in Texas: An assessment of the criminogenic needs and the gap between needs and services. *Prison Journal, 85,* 467–489.

Kempf-Leonard, K. (2007). Minority youths and juvenile justice: Disproportionate minority contact after nearly 20 years of reform efforts. *Youth Violence and Juvenile Justice, 5,* 71–87.

Kempf-Leonard, K. (2012). The conundrum of girls and juvenile justice processing. In B. C. Feld & D. M. Bishop (Eds.), *The Oxford handbook of juvenile crime and juvenile justice* (pp. 485–525). New York: Oxford University Press.

Kennedy, D. (1998). Pulling levers: Getting deterrence right. *National Institute of Justice Journal, 236,* 2–8.

Kennedy, L. W., & Forde, D. R. (1990). Routine activities and crime: An analysis of victimization data in Canada. *Criminology, 28,* 137–152.

Kerbs, J. J. (1999). (Un)equal justice: Juvenile court abolition and African Americans. *Annals of the American Academy of Political and Social Science, 564,* 109–125.

Kim, B., Matz, A. K., Gerber, J., Beto, D. R., & Lambert, E. (2013a). Facilitating police-probation/parole partnerships: An examination of police chiefs' and sheriffs' perceptions. *Policing: An International Journal of Police Strategies & Management, 36,* 752–767.

Kim, B., Merlo, A. V., & Benekos, P. J. (2013b). Effective correctional intervention programmes for juveniles: Review and synthesis of meta-analytic evidence. *International Journal of Police Science and Management, 15,* 169–189.

Kim, C. Y., Losen, D. J., & Hewitt, D. T. (2010). *The School-to-Prison Pipeline: Structuring Legal Reform.* New York: NYU Press.

Kim, S. (1988). A short- and long-term evaluation of here's looking at you alcohol education program. *Journal of Drug Education, 18,* 235–242.

Kim, S., McLeod, J. H., & Shantzis, C. (1993). An outcome evaluation of here's looking at you 2000. *Journal of Drug Education, 23,* 67–81.

Kim-Cohen, J., Caspi, A., Taylor, A., Williams, B., Newcombe, R., Craig, I., & Moffitt, T. E. (2006). MAOA, maltreatment, and gene-environment interaction predicting children's mental health: New evidence and a meta-analysis. *Molecular Psychiatry, 11,* 903–913.

Kinder, B. N., Pape, N. E., & Walfish, S. (1980). Drug and alcohol education programs: A review of outcome studies. *International Journal of the Addictions, 15*, 1,035–1,054.

Kirk, D. S., & Sampson, R. J. (2013). Juvenile arrest and collateral educational damage in the transition to adulthood. *Sociology of Education, 86*, 36–62.

Kleiman, M. A. R. (2011). Justice reinvestment in community supervision. *Criminology & Public Policy, 10*, 651–659.

Klein, M. W. (1969). Gang cohesiveness, delinquency, and a street-work program. *Journal of Research in Crime and Delinquency, 6*, 135–166.

Klein, M. W. (1971). *Street gangs and street workers*. Englewood Cliffs, NJ: Prentice Hall.

Klein, M. W. (1995). *The American street gang: Its nature, prevalence and control*. New York: Oxford University Press.

Klein, M. W., & Maxson, C. L. (1989). Street gang violence. In N. A. Weiner & M. E. Wolfgang (Eds.), *Violent crime, violent criminals* (pp. 198–234). Newbury Park, CA: Sage.

Klein, M. W., & Maxson, C. L. (2006). *Street gang patterns and policies*. New York: Oxford University Press.

Kochel, T. R., Wilson, D. B., & Mastrofski, S. D. (2011). Effect of suspect race on officers' arrest decisions. *Criminology, 49*, 473–512.

Kohlberg, L. (1981). *The philosophy of moral development*. San Francisco: Harper and Row.

Kornhauser, R. R. (1978). *Social sources of delinquency*. Chicago: University of Chicago Press.

Kovach, G. C. (2008, May 12). To curb truancy, Dallas tries electronic monitoring. *New York Times* online. Available at http://www.nytimes.com/2008/05/12/education/12dallas.html?_r/1&partner/rssnyt&emc/rss&ore/slogin/&_r=0

Kreuz, L. E., & Rose, R. M. (1972). Assessment of aggressive behavior and plasma testosterone in a young criminal population. *Psychosomatic Medicine, 34*, 321–332.

Krisberg, B. (2005). *Juvenile justice: Redeeming our children*. Thousand Oaks, CA: Sage.

Krisberg, B. (2012). Juvenile corrections: An overview. In B. C. Feld & D. M. Bishop (Eds.), *The Oxford handbook of juvenile justice* (pp. 748–770). New York: Oxford University Press.

Krisberg, B. (2012). There is no juvenile crime wave: A call to end the war against children. In M. Mauer & K. Epstein (Eds.), *To build a better criminal justice system: 25 experts envision the next 25 years of reform* (pp. 32–33). Washington, DC: The Sentencing Project.

Krisberg, B., & Austin, J. (1978). *The children of Ishmael*. Palo Alto, CA: Mayfield.

Krisberg, B., & Austin, J. (1993). *Reinventing juvenile justice*. Newbury Park, CA: Sage.

Krisberg, B., Austin, J., & Steele, P. A. (1989). *Unlocking juvenile corrections: Evaluating the Massachusetts Department of Youth Services*. San Francisco: National Council on Crime and Delinquency.

Krisberg, B., Currie, E., Onek, D., & Wiebush, R. G. (1995). Graduated sanctions for serious, violent, and chronic juvenile offenders. In J. C. Howell, B. Krisberg, J. D. Hawkins & J. J. Wilson (Eds.), *Serious, violent, and chronic juvenile offenders: A sourcebook* (pp. 142–170). Thousand Oaks, CA: Sage.

Krisberg, B., & Howell, J. C. (1998). The impact of the juvenile justice system and prospects for graduated sanctions in a comprehensive strategy. In R. Loeber & D. P. Farrington (Eds.), *Serious and violent juvenile offenders: Risk factors and successful interventions* (pp. 313–345). Thousand Oaks, CA: Sage.

Kroes, W. H., Margolis, B. L., & Hurrell, J. J. (1974). Job stress in policemen. *Journal of Police Science and Administration, 2*, 145–155.

Krohn, M., & Massey, J. (1980). Social control and delinquent behavior: An examination of the elements of the social bond. *Sociological Quarterly, 21*, 529–543.

Kuanliang, A., Sorensen, J. R., & Cunningham, M. D. (2008). Juvenile inmates in an adult prison system: Rates of disciplinary misconduct and violence. *Criminal Justice and Behavior, 35*, 1,186–1,201.

Kupchik, A. (2014). The school-to-prison pipeline: Rhetoric and reality. In F. E. Zimring & D. S. Tanenhaus (Eds.), *Choosing the future for American juvenile justice* (pp. 94–119). New York: New York University Press.

Kurki, L. (2000). Restorative and community justice in the United States. In M. Tonry (Ed.), *Crime and justice: A review of research* (Vol. 27, pp. 235–303). Chicago: University of Chicago Press.

Kurlychek, M., & Johnson, B. D. (2004). The juvenile penalty: A comparison of juvenile and young adult sentencing outcomes in criminal court. *Criminology, 42*, 485–515.

Kurlychek, M. C., & Johnson, B. D. (2010). Juvenility and punishment: Sentencing juveniles in adult criminal court. *Criminology, 48*, 725–757.

Kurlychek, M., Torbet, P. M., & Bozynski, M. (1999). *Focus on accountability: Best practices for juvenile court and probation.* Washington, DC: U.S. Department of Justice and Delinquency Prevention.

Lab, S. P. (1984). Patterns in juvenile misbehavior. *Crime & Delinquency, 30*, 293–308.

Lab, S. P., & Allen, R. B. (1984). Self-report and official measures: A further examination of the validity issue. *Journal of Criminal Justice, 12*, 445–456.

Lab, S. P., & Clark, R. D. (1994). *Gauging crime and control in the schools.* Paper presented at the Annual Meeting of the American Society of Criminology, Miami, FL.

Lab, S. P., & Clark, R. D. (1996). *Discipline, control and school crime: Identifying effective intervention strategies. Final Report.* Washington, DC: National Institute of Justice.

Lab, S. P., & Whitehead, J. T. (1994). Avoidance behavior as a response to in-school victimization. *Journal of Security Administration, 17*(2), 32–45.

LaMotte, V., Ouellette, K., Sanderson, J., Anderson, S. A., Kosutic, I., Griggs, J., & Garcia, M. (2010). Effective police interactions with youth: A program evaluation. *Police Quarterly, 13*, 161–179.

Lane, J., Turner, S., Fain, T., & Sehgal, A. (2005). Evaluating an experimental intensive probation program: Supervision and official outcomes. *Crime & Delinquency, 51*, 26–52.

Langan, P. A., Greenfield, L. A., Smith, S. K., Durose, M. R., & Levin, J. J. (2001). *Contacts between police and the public: Findings from the 1999 national survey.* Washington, DC: U.S. Department of Justice.

Lange, J. E., Johnson, M. B., & Voas, R. B. (2005). Testing the racial profiling hypothesis for seemingly disparate traffic stops on the New Jersey turnpike. *Justice Quarterly, 22*, 193–223.

Langton, L., & Durose, M. (2013). Police behavior during traffic and street stops, 2011. Washington, DC: U.S. Department of Justice.

Latimer, J., Dowden, C., & Muise, D. (2005). *The effectiveness of restorative justice practices: A meta-analysis.* Ottawa, Canada: Canada Department of Justice. (Cited in Rodriguez, N. (2007). Restorative justice at work: Examining the impact of restorative justice resolutions on juvenile recidivism. *Crime & Delinquency, 53,* 355–379.)

Lattimore, P. K., Krebs, C. P., Graham, P., & Cowell, A. J. (2005). *Evaluation of the juvenile breaking the cycle program—final report.* Washington, DC: National Institute of Justice.

Lauritsen, J. L., Sampson, R. J., & Laub, J. H. (1991). The link between offending and victimization among adolescents. *Criminology, 29,* 265–292.

LaVigne, N., Bieler, S., Cramer, L., Ho, H., Kotonias, C., Mayer, D., McClure, D., Pacifici, L., Parks, E., Peterson, B., & Samuels, J. (2014). *Justice reinvestment initiative state assessment report.* Washington, DC: Urban Institute.

Lederman, C. S., & Brown, E. N. (2000). Entangled in the shadows: Girls in the juvenile justice system. *Buffalo Law Review, 48,* 909–925.

Lee, J. M., Steinberg, L., & Piquero, A. R. (2010). Ethnic identity and attitudes toward the police among African American juvenile offenders. *Journal of Criminal Justice, 38,* 781–789.

Legal Clips. (2013, June 20). Advocacy groups file DOJ complaint claiming truancy enforcement at Dallas area districts violates civil rights of disabled and LEP students. Available at http://legalclips.nsba.org/2013/06/20/advocacy-groups-file-doj-complaint-claiming-truancy-enforcement-at-dallas-area-districts-violates-civil-rights-of-disabled-and-lep-students/

Leiber, M. J. (2013). Race, pre- and postdetention, and juvenile justice decision making. *Crime & Delinquency, 59,* 396–418.

Leiber, M., Bishop, D., & Chamlin, M. B. (2011). Juvenile justice decision-making before and after the implementation of the Disproportionate Minority Contact (DMC) mandate. *Justice Quarterly, 28,* 460–492.

Leiber, M. J., & Mack, K. Y. (2003). The individual and joint effects of race, gender, and family status on juvenile justice decision-making. *Journal of Research in Crime and Delinquency, 40,* 34–70.

Lemert, E. M. (1951). *Social pathology: A systematic approach to the theory of sociopathic behavior.* New York: McGraw-Hill.

Leukefeld, C. G., & Tims, F. M. (1988). *Compulsory treatment of drug abuse: Research and clinical practice.* Rockville, MD: National Institute on Drug Abuse.

Levine, M., & Battistoni, L. (1991). The corroboration requirement in child sex abuse cases. *Behavioral Sciences and the Law, 9,* 3–20.

Levrant, S., Cullen, F. T., Fulton, B., & Wozniak, J. F. (1999). Reconsidering restorative justice: The corruption of benevolence revisited? *Crime & Delinquency, 45,* 3–27.

Liederbach, J. (2007). Controlling suburban and small-town hoods: An examination of police encounters with juveniles. *Youth Violence and Juvenile Justice, 5,* 107–124.

Lilly, J. R., Cullen, F. T., & Ball, R. A. (1995). *Criminological theory: Context and consequences* (2nd ed.). Thousand Oaks, CA: Sage.

Lindner, C. (1981). The utilization of day-evening centers as an alternative to secure detention of juveniles. *Journal of Probation and Parole, 13,* 12–18.

Lipsey, M. W. (1999). Can intervention rehabilitate serious delinquents? *Annals of the American Academy of Political and Social Science, 564,* 142–166.

Lipsey, M. W. (2009). The primary factors that characterize effective interventions with juvenile offenders: A meta-analytic overview. *Victims and Offenders, 4*, 124–147.

Lipsey, M. W., & Wilson, D. B. (1998). Effective intervention for serious juvenile offenders: A synthesis of research. In R. Loeber & D. P. Farrington (Eds.), *Serious and violent juvenile offenders: Risk factors and successful intervention* (pp. 313–345). Thousand Oaks, CA: Sage.

Lipton, D. L. (1995). *The effectiveness of treatment for drug abusers under criminal justice supervision*. Washington, DC: U.S. Department of Justice.

Listwan, S. J., Sundt, J. L., Holsinger, A. M., & Latessa, E. J. (2003). The effects of drug court programming on recidivism: The Cincinnati experience. *Crime & Delinquency, 49*, 389–411.

Livsey, S. (2010). *Juvenile delinquency probation caseload*. OJJDP Fact Sheet. Washington, DC: Office of Juvenile Justice and Delinquency Prevention.

Lizotte, A., & Sheppard, D. (2001). Gun use by male juveniles: Research and prevention. *Juvenile Justice Bulletin*. Washington, DC: U.S. Department of Justice.

Loeber, R. (1988). Natural histories of conduct problems, delinquency and related substance abuse. In B. B. Lahey & A. E. Kazdin (Eds.), *Advances in clinical child psychology* (Vol. 11, pp. 73–124). New York: Plenum.

Lombroso, C. (1876). *On criminal man*. Milan, Italy: Hoepli.

Los Angeles City Attorney's Office. (2009). *Gang injunctions: How they work (The City Attorney's report)*. Available at http://www.atty.lacity.org/stellent/groups/electedofficials/@atty_contributor/documents/contributor_web_content/lacityp_006877.pdf

Lounsbury, K., Mitchell, K. J., & Finkelhor, D. (2011). The true prevalence of "sexting." Durham, NH: University of New Hampshire Crimes Against Children Research Center.

Lowney, J. (1984). The wall gang: A study of interpersonal process and deviance among twenty-three middle-class youths. *Adolescence, 19*, 527–538.

Lozoff, B., & Braswell, M. (1989). *Inner corrections: Finding peace and peace making*. Cincinnati: Anderson.

Lubow, B. (2012). Juvenile justice in 25 years: A system that passes the "my child" test. In M. Mauer & K. Epstein (Eds.), *To build a better criminal justice system: 25 experts envision the next 25 years of reform* (pp. 34–35). Washington, DC: The Sentencing Project.

Lundman, R. J. (1994). Demeanor or crime? The midwest city police encounters study. *Criminology, 32*, 631–656.

Lyons, M. J. (1996). A twin study of self-reported criminal behavior. In G. R. Bock & J. A. Goode (Eds.), *Genetics of criminal and antisocial behavior* (pp. 61–69). Chichester, England: John Wiley and Sons.

Mack, J. W. (1909). The juvenile court. *Harvard Law Review, 23*, 104–119.

MacKenzie, D. L. (2006). *What works in corrections: Reducing the criminal activities of offenders and delinquents*. New York: Cambridge University Press.

MacKenzie, D. L., & Freeland, R. (2012). Examining the effectiveness of juvenile residential programs. In B. C. Feld & D. M. Bishop (Eds.), *The Oxford handbook of juvenile justice* (pp. 771–798). New York: Oxford University Press.

Maddux, J. F. (1988). Clinical experience in civil commitment. In C. G. Leukefeld & F. M. Tims (Eds.), *Compulsory treatment of drug abuse: Research and clinical practice* (pp. 35–56). Washington, DC: National Institute on Drug Abuse.

Maggard, S. R., Higgins, J. L., & Chappell, A. T. (2013). Pre-dispositional juvenile detention: An analysis of race, gender, and intersectionality. *Journal of Crime and Justice 36*, 67–86.

Maguire, K. (2014). *Sourcebook of criminal justice statistics [online]*. Washington, DC: Bureau of Justice Statistics. Available at http://www.albany.edu/sourcebook/

Maguire, K., & Pastore, A. L. (2004). *Sourcebook of criminal justice statistics, 2003*. Washington, DC: Bureau of Justice Statistics. Available at http://www.albany.edu/sourcebook/

Mahoney, A. R. (1985). Jury trial for juveniles: Right or ritual? *Justice Quarterly, 2*, 553–565.

Mahoney, A. R. (1987). *Juvenile justice in context*. Boston: Northeastern University Press.

Maitland, A. S., & Sluder, R. D. (1998). Victimization and youthful prison inmates: An empirical analysis. *Prison Journal, 78*, 55–73.

Males, M. A. (2000). Vernon, Connecticut's juvenile curfew: The circumstances of youths cited and effects on crime. *Criminal Justice Policy Review, 11*, 254–267.

Malloy, L. C., Shulman, E. P., & Cauffman, E. (2014). Interrogations, confessions, and guilty pleas among serious adolescent offenders. *Law and Human Behavior, 36*, 181–193.

Marlowe, D. B. (2010). *The facts on juvenile drug treatment courts*. Alexandria, VA: National Association of Drug Court Professionals. Available at http://www.nadcp.org/

Martin, G. E. (2012). Marching upstream: Moving beyond reentry mania. In M. Mauer & K. Epstein (Eds.), *To build a better criminal justice system: 25 experts envision the next 25 years of reform* (pp. 48–49). Washington, DC: The Sentencing Project.

Martinez, J. Y. (2008). Character education in juvenile detention. *Corrections Today, 70*, 150–154.

Maslach, C., & Jackson, S. E. (1979). Burned-out cops and their families. *Psychology Today, 12*(12), 59–62.

Mathis, K. J. (2007). American Bar Association: Adult justice system is the wrong answer for most juveniles. *American Journal of Preventive Medicine, 32*, S1–S2.

Mause, L. (1974). *The history of childhood*. New York: Psychohistory Press.

Maxson, C. L. (2011). Street gangs. In J. Q. Wilson & J. Petersilia (Eds.), *Crime and public policy*. New York: Oxford University Press.

Maxson, C. L., Hennigan, K. M., Sloane, D. C., & Kolnick, K. A. (2004). *Can civil gang injunctions change communities? A community assessment of the impact of civil gang injunctions*. Washington, DC: National Institute of Justice.

Maxson, C. L., Woods, K., & Klein, M. W. (1996). Street gang migration: How big a threat? *NIJ Journal, 230*, 26–31.

Mayo Clinic. (2010). *Antisocial personality disorder*. Available at http://www.mayoclinic.com/health/antisocial-personality-disorder/DS00829/

Mays, G. L., Fuller, K., & Winfree, L. T. (1994). Gangs and gang activity in southern New Mexico: A descriptive look at a growing rural problem. *Journal of Crime and Justice, 17*, 25–44.

Mazerolle, L. G., Roehl, J., & Kadleck, C. (1998). Controlling social disorder using civil remedies: Results from a randomized field experiment in Oakland, California. In L. G. Mazerolle & J. Roehl (Eds.), *Civil Remedies and Crime Prevention*. Monsey, NY: Criminal Justice Press.

McBride, D. (1981). Drugs and violence. In J. A. Inciardi (Ed.), *The drugs/crime connection* (pp. 105–124). Beverly Hills: Sage.

McCarthy, B. R. (1987). Preventive detention and pretrial custody in the juvenile court. *Journal of Criminal Justice, 15,* 185–200.

McCarthy, B. R., & Smith, B. L. (1986). The conceptualization of discrimination in the juvenile justice process: The impact of administrative factors and screening decisions on juvenile court dispositions. *Criminology, 24,* 41–64.

McClelland, G. M., Teplin, L. A., & Abram, K. M. (2004). Detection and prevalence of substance use among juvenile detainees. *Juvenile Justice Bulletin.* Washington, DC: U.S. Department of Justice, Office of Juvenile Justice and Delinquency Prevention.

McCold, P. (2003). A survey of assessment research on mediation and conferencing. In L. Walgrave (Ed.), *Repositioning restorative justice* (pp. 67–120). Portland, OR: Willan.

McCold, P., & Wachtel, T. (1998). *Restorative policing experiment: The Bethlehem, Pennsylvania, police family group conferencing project.* Pipersville, PA: Community Service Foundation.

McCold, P., & Wachtel, T. (2002). Restorative justice theory validation. In E. G. M. Weitekamp & H. Kernere (Eds.), *Restorative justice: Theoretical foundations.* Portland, OR: Willan.

McDowall, D., Loftin, C., & Wiersema, B. (2000). The impact of youth curfew laws on juvenile crime rates. *Crime & Delinquency, 46,* 76–91.

McElvain, J. P., & Kposowa, A. J. (2008). Police officer characteristics and the likelihood of using deadly force. *Criminal Justice and Behavior, 35,* 505–521.

McGarrell, E. F., Chermak, S., Wilson, J. M., & Corsaro, N. (2006). Reducing homicide through a "lever-pulling" strategy. *Justice Quarterly, 23,* 214–231.

McGarrell, E. F., & Hipple, N. K. (2007). Family group conferencing and re-offending among first-time juvenile offenders: The Indianapolis experiment. *Justice Quarterly, 24,* 221–246.

McGarrell, E. F., Olivares, K., Crawford, K., & Kroovand, N. (2000). *Returning justice to the community: The Indianapolis juvenile restorative justice experiment.* Indianapolis: Hudson Institute.

McGarvey, A. (2005, September). A culture of caring. *The American Prospect,* A12–A14.

McGlothlin, W. H., & Anglin, M. D. (1981). Shutting off methadone: Costs and benefits. *Archives of General Psychiatry, 38,* 885–892.

McLaughlin, E., Fergusson, R., Hughes, G., & Westmarland, L. (2003). Introduction: Justice in the round—contextualizing restorative justice. In E. McLaughlin, R. Fergusson, G. Hughes & L. Westmarland (Eds.), *Restorative justice: Critical issues.* Thousand Oaks, CA: Sage.

McMahon, M. (1999). *Women on guard: Discrimination and harassment in corrections.* Toronto, Canada: University of Toronto Press.

Mead, G. H. (1934). *Mind, self and society.* Chicago: University of Chicago Press.

Mears, D. P. (2000). Assessing the effectiveness of juvenile justice reforms: A closer look at the criteria and the impacts on diverse stakeholders. *Law and Policy, 22,* 175–202.

Mears, D. P., Hay, C., Gertz, M., & Mancini, C. (2007). Public opinion and the foundation of the juvenile court. *Criminology, 45,* 223–257.

Mednick, S. A., & Christiansen, K. O. (1977). *Biosocial bases of criminal behavior.* New York: Gardner.

Meehan, P. J., & Ponder, M. C. (2002). Race and place: The ecology of racial profiling African American motorists. *Justice Quarterly, 19,* 399–430.

Megargee, E. I., & Bohn, M. J. (1979). *Classifying criminal offenders: A new system based on the MMPI*. Beverly Hills: Sage.

Melde, C., & Esbensen, F. (2011). Gang membership as a turning point in the life course. *Criminology, 49*, 513–552.

Melton, G. B. (1980). Psycholegal issues in child victims' interaction with the legal system. *Victimology, 5*, 274–284.

Mendel, R. A. (2001). *Guiding lights for reform in juvenile justice*. Washington, DC: American Youth Policy Forum.

Mendel, R. A. (2011). *No place for kids: The case for reducing juvenile incarceration*. Baltimore: MD: The Annie E. Casey Foundation.

Merlo, A. V. (2000). Juvenile justice at the crossroads: Presidential address to the Academy of Criminal Justice Sciences. *Justice Quarterly, 17*, 639–661.

Merton, R. K. (1938). Social structure and anomie. *American Sociological Review, 3*, 672–682.

Metropolitan Life (1993). *Violence in America's public schools*. New York: Louis Harris and Associates.

Meyer, J. R., & Reppucci, N. D. (2007). Police practices and perceptions regarding juvenile interrogation and interrogative suggestibility. *Behavioral Sciences and the Law, 25*, 757–780.

Mezzacappa, E. S. (1999). Epinephrine, arousal and emotion: A new look at a two factor theory. *Cognition and Emotion, 13*, 181–199.

Michel, D. A. (2011). The CHINS don't stand a chance: The dubious achievements of child in need of services ("CHINS") jurisdiction in Massachusetts & a new approach to juvenile status offenses. *Boston University Public Interest Law Journal, 20*, 321–352.

Miethe, T. D., Hong, L., & Reese, E. (2000). Reintegrative shaming and recidivism risks in drug court: Explanations for some unexpected findings. *Crime & Delinquency, 46*, 522–541.

Miethe, T. D., Stafford, M. C., & Long, J. S. (1987). Social differentiation in criminal victimization: A test of routine activities lifestyle theory. *American Sociological Review, 52*, 184–194.

Miller, D., Miller, D., Hoffman, F., & Duggan, R. (1980). *Runaways—illegal aliens in their own land: Implications for service*. New York: Praeger.

Miller, J. (2000). *One of the guys? Girls, gangs and gender*. New York: Oxford University Press.

Miller, J. Y. (2005, May 14). Six aides lose jobs after a boy dies. *Atlanta Journal-Constitution*, A9–A10.

Miller, W. B. (1958). Lower class culture as a generating milieu of gang delinquency. *Journal of Social Issues, 15*, 5–19.

Miller, W. B. (1975). *Violence by youth gangs and youth groups as a crime problem in major American cities*. Washington, DC: National Institute for Juvenile Justice and Delinquency Prevention.

Miller, W. B. (1982). *Crime by youth gangs and groups in the United States*. Washington, DC: Office of Juvenile Justice and Delinquency Prevention.

Miller, W. B., Gertz, H., & Cutter, H. S. G. (1961). Aggression in a boys' street-corner group. *Psychiatry, 24*, 283–298.

Miller-Wilson, L. S., & Puritz, P. (2003). *Pennsylvania: An assessment of access to counsel and quality of representation in delinquency proceedings.* Washington, DC, and Philadelphia: American Bar Association Juvenile Justice Center and Juvenile Law Center in collaboration with the National Juvenile Defender Center and the Northeast Juvenile Defender Center. Available at http://www.jlc.org/sites/default/files/publication_pdfs/ PA%20Assesment%20of%20Access%20to%20Counsel.pdf

Minor, K. I., Hartmann, D. J., & Terry, S. (1997). Predictors of juvenile court actions and recidivism. *Crime & Delinquency, 18,* 295–318.

Minor, W. W. (1981). Techniques of neutralization: A reconceptualization and empirical examination. *Journal of Research in Crime and Delinquency, 18,* 295–318.

Minton, T. D., & Golinelli, D. (2014). *Jail inmates at midyear 2013—statistical tables.* Washington, DC: U.S. Department of Justice.

Moffitt, T. E., Brammer, G. L., Caspi, A., Fawcett, J. P., Raleigh, M., Yuwiler, A., & Silva, P. (1998). Whole blood serotonin relates to violence in an epidemiological study. *Biological Psychology, 43,* 446–457.

Montgomery, J. M., Foley, K. L., & Wolfson, M. (2006). Enforcing the minimum drinking age: state, local and agency characteristics associated with compliance checks and Cops in Shops programs. *Addiction, 101,* 223–231.

Monti, D. J. (1993). Origins and problems of gang research in the United States. In S. Cummings & D. J. Monti (Eds.), *Gangs: The origins and impact of contemporary youth gangs in the United States* (pp. 3–26). Albany, NY: SUNY Press.

Moore, D., & O'Connell, T. (1994). Family conferencing in Wagga Wagga: A communitarian model of justice. In C. Adler & J. Wundersitz (Eds.), *Family conferencing and juvenile justice: The way forward or misplaced optimism?* Canberra, Australia: Australian Institute of Criminology.

Moore, J. (1988). Introduction: Gangs and the underclass: A comparative perspective. In J. M. Hagedorn (Ed.), *People and folks: Gangs, crime and the underclass in a rustbelt city* (pp. 3–18). Chicago: Lake View Press.

Moore, J. (1991). *Going down to the barrio: Homeboys and homegirls in change.* Philadelphia: Temple University Press.

Moore, J. (1993). Gangs, drugs, and violence. In S. Cummings & D. J. Monti (Eds.), *Gangs: The origins and impact of contemporary youth gangs in the United States* (pp. 27–46). Albany, NY: SUNY Press.

Morash, M. (1984). The establishment of a juvenile police record: The influence of individual and peer group characteristics. *Criminology, 22,* 97–112.

Morgan, E., Salomon, N., Plotkin, M., & Cohen, R. (2014). *The school discipline consensus report: Strategies from the field to keep students engaged in school and out of the juvenile justice system.* New York: The Council of State Governments Justice Center.

Morse, S. (1999). Delinquency and desert. *Annals of the American Academy of Political and Social Science, 564,* 56–80.

Mulvey, E. P., & Schubert, C. A. (2012). *Transfer of juveniles to adult court: Effects of a broad policy change in one court.* Washington, DC: Office of Juvenile Justice and Delinquency Prevention.

Mulvey, E. P., Schubert, C. A., & Chassin, L. (2010). *Substance use and delinquent behavior among serious adolescent offenders.* Washington, DC: Office of Juvenile Justice and Delinquency Prevention.

Mumola, C. J. (2005). Suicide and homicide in state prisons and local jails. *Bureau of Justice Statistics Special Report.* Washington, DC: U.S. Department of Justice.

Mumola, C. J. (2007). Arrest-related deaths in the United States, 2003–2005. *Bureau of Justice Statistics Special Report.* Washington, DC: U.S. Department of Justice.

Murphy, D., & Lutze, F. (2009). Police-probation partnerships: Professional identity and the sharing of coercive power. *Journal of Criminal Justice, 37,* 65–76.

Na, C., & Gottfredson, D. C. (2013). Police officers in schools: Effects on school crime and the processing of offending behaviors. *Justice Quarterly, 30,* 619–650.

Nadelmann, E. A. (1997). Thinking seriously about alternatives to drug prohibition. In M. McShane & F. P. Williams (Eds.), *Criminal justice: Drug use and drug policy* (pp. 269–316). New York: Garland.

Nadelmann, E. A. (2004). Criminologists and punitive drug prohibition: To serve or to challenge? Reaction essay. *Criminology & Public Policy, 3,* 441–450.

Nassi, A., & Abramowitz, S. I. (1976). From phrenology to psychosurgery and back again: Biological studies of criminality. *American Journal of Orthopsychiatry, 46,* 591–607.

National Alliance of Gang Investigators Associations. (2005). *National gang threat assessment.* Washington, DC: Bureau of Justice Assistance.

National Association of Youth Courts. (2011). *Youth courts.* Baltimore: National Association of Youth Courts. Available at http://www.youthcourt.net/

National Campaign to Prevent Teen and Unplanned Pregnancy. (2009). *Sex and tech: Results from a survey of teens and young adults.* Available at http://thenationalcampaign.org/resource/sex-and-tech

National CASA. (2014). *Court appointed special advocates for children.* Available at http://www.casaforchildren.org/site/c.mtJSJ7MPIsE/b.5301303/k.6FB1/About_Us__CASA_for_Children.htm

National Center for Biotechnology Information. (2010). *Antisocial personality disorder.* Available at http://www.ncbi.nlm.nih.gov/pubmedhealth/PMH0001919/

National Children's Alliance. (2013). *History of National Children's Alliance.* Washington, DC: National Children's Alliance. Available at http://www.nationalchildrensalliance.org/

National Conference of State Legislatures. (1993). *1993 state legislature summary.* Washington, DC: National Conference of State Legislatures.

National Council on Crime and Delinquency. (1987). *The impact of juvenile court sanctions: A court that works: Executive summary.* San Francisco: National Council on Crime and Delinquency.

National Dairy Council. (1985). Diet and behavior. *Dairy Council Digest, 56,* 19–24.

National Drug Court Resource Center. (2014). *How many drug courts are there?* Alexandria, VA: National Drug Court Resource Center. Available at http://www.ndcrc.org/

National Highway Traffic Safety Administration. (2014). *Traffic safety facts: 2012 data: Young drivers.* Washington, DC: NHTSA's National Center for Statistics and Analysis.

National Institute on Drug Abuse. (1999). *Principles of drug addiction treatment: A research-based guide.* Washington, DC: National Institute on Drug Abuse.

National Institute on Drug Abuse. (2011). *Lessons from prevention research.* Washington, DC: National Institute on Drug Abuse.

National Institute on Drug Abuse. (2012). *Principles of drug addiction treatment: A research-based guide* (3rd ed.). Washington, DC: National Institute on Drug Abuse.

National Institute on Drug Abuse. (2014). *Drug facts: High school and youth trends.* Washington, DC: National Institute on Drug Abuse.

National Institute of Justice. (1990). *Drugs and crime: 1989 drug use forecasting report.* Washington, DC: National Institute of Justice.

National Juvenile Defender Center. (2004). *The use and abuse of juvenile detention: Understanding detention and its uses.* Washington, DC: National Juvenile Defender Center.

National School Boards Association. (2013, June 12). Advocacy groups file DOJ complaint claiming truancy enforcement at Dallas area districts violates civil rights of disabled and LEP students. *San Francisco Chronicle.* Available at http://legalclips.nsba.org/2013/06/20/advocacy-groups-file-doj-complaint-claiming-truancy-enforcement-at-dallas-area-districts-violates-civil-rights-of-disabled-and-lep-students/

National Youth Gang Center. (2000). *1998 National youth gang survey: Summary.* Washington, DC: Office of Juvenile Justice and Delinquency Prevention.

National Youth Gang Center. (2009). *National youth gang survey analysis.* Available at http://www.nationalgangcenter.gov/Survey-Analysis/

National Youth Gang Center. (2014). *National Youth Gang Survey Analysis.* Washington, DC: Office of Juvenile Justice and Delinquency Prevention.

Nellis, A. (2009). *Back on track: Supporting youth reentry from out-of-home placement to the community.* Washington, DC: Juvenile Justice and Delinquency Prevention Coalition: The Sentencing Project.

Nellis, A. (2012). *The lives of juvenile lifers: Findings from a national survey.* Washington, DC: The Sentencing Project.

Nelson, E. J. (2011). Custodial strip searches of juveniles: How *Safford* informs a two-tiered standard of review. *Boston College Law Review, 52,* 339–374.

Newcomb, M. D., & Bentler, P. M. (1988). *Consequences of adolescent drug use.* Newbury Park, CA: Sage.

Newman, D. J. (1986). *Introduction to criminal justice* (3rd ed.). New York: Random House.

Newman, H. H., Freeman, F. H., & Holzinger, K. J. (1937). *Twins: A study of heredity and environment.* Chicago: University of Chicago Press.

Nicholl, C. G. (1999). *Community policing, community justice, and restorative justice: Exploring the links for the delivery of a balanced approach to public safety.* Washington, DC: Office of Community Oriented Policing Services.

Niederhoffer, A. (1967). *Behind the shield: The police in urban society.* Garden City, NY: Anchor Books.

Noisette, L. E. (2012). Resetting our moral compass: Devastated communities leading the fight for a just system. In M. Mauer & K. Epstein (Eds.), *To build a better criminal justice system: 25 experts envision the next 25 years of reform* (pp. 22–23). Washington, DC: The Sentencing Project.

Noriega, C. (2000). Stick a fork in it: Is juvenile justice done? *New York Law School Journal of Human Rights, 16,* 669–698.

Norris, M., Twill, S., & Kim, C. (2011). Smells like teen spirit: Evaluating a midwestern teen court. *Crime & Delinquency, 57,* 199–221.

Novak, K. J., Frank, J., Smith, B. W., & Engel, R. S. (2002). Revisiting the decision to arrest: Comparing beat and community officers. *Crime & Delinquency, 48,* 70–98.

Nugent, W. R., Umbreit, M. S., Wiinamaki, L., & Paddock, J. (1999). Participation in victim-offender mediation and severity of subsequent delinquent behavior: Successful replications? *Journal of Research in Social Work Practice, 11,* 5–23.

Nurco, D. N., Kinlock, T. W., Hanlon, T. E., & Ball, J. C. (1988). Nonnarcotic drug use over an addition career—a study of heroin addicts in Baltimore and New York City. *Comprehensive Psychiatry, 29,* 450–459.

O'Brien, D. M. (1997). *Constitutional law and politics* (Vol. 2) (3rd ed.). New York: W.W. Norton.

O'Brien, R. M. (1985). *Crime and victimization data.* Beverly Hills: Sage.

O'Connor, S. (2001). *Orphan trains: The story of Charles Loring Brace and the children he saved and failed.* Boston: Houghton Mifflin.

Office of Justice Programs. (2000). *Promising strategies to reduce substance abuse.* Washington, DC: Office of Justice Programs.

Office of Justice Programs. (2003). *Juvenile family drug courts: Summary of drug court activity by state and county.* Washington, DC: Office of Justice Programs.

Office of Juvenile Justice and Delinquency Prevention. (2011). *Statistical Briefing Book.* Available at http://www.ojjdp.gov/ojstatbb/

Office of Juvenile Justice and Delinquency Prevention. (2012). *Effects and consequences of underage drinking.* Washington, DC: Office of Juvenile Justice and Delinquency Prevention.

Office of Juvenile Justice and Delinquency Prevention. (2013). *Statistical Briefing Book: Juveniles in Court.* Available at http://www.ojjdp.gov/ojstatbb/court/JCSCR.asp?qa Date=20130417

Olds, D., Henderson, C. R., Cole, R., Eckenrode, J., Kitzman, H., Luckey, D., Pettitt, L., Sidora, K., Morris, P., & Powers, J. (1998). Long-term effects of nurse home visitation on children's criminal and antisocial behavior: 15 year follow-up of a randomized controlled trial. *JAMA, 280,* 1,238–1,244.

Olive, P., Keen, J., Rowse, G., Ewins, E., Griffiths, L., & Mathers, N. (2010). The effect of time spent in treatment and dropout status on rates of convictions, citations and imprisonment over 5 years in a primary care-led methadone maintenance service. *Addiction, 105,* 732–739.

Ott, B. (2005, July 26). School prayer: Teen support hinges on type. *Gallup poll Tuesday briefing,* 1–2.

Owen, T. (2012). The biological and the social in criminological theory. In S. Hall & S. Winslow (Eds.), *New directions in criminological theory.* New York: Routledge.

Padilla, F. (1993). The working gang. In S. Cummings & D. J. Monti (Eds.), *Gangs: The origins and impact of contemporary youth gangs in the United States* (pp. 173–192). Albany, NY: SUNY Press.

Paoline, E. A., Myers, S. M., & Worden, R. E. (2000). Police culture, individualism, and community policing: Evidence from two departments. *Justice Quarterly, 17,* 575–605.

Parent, D. G. (2003). *Correctional boot camps: Lessons from a decade of research.* Washington, DC: National Institute of Justice.

Parsloe, P. (1978). *Juvenile justice in Britain and the U.S.: The balance of needs and rights.* London: Routledge and Kegan Paul.

Patrick, S., & Marsh, R. (2005). Juvenile diversion: Results of a 3-year experimental study. *Criminal Justice Policy Review, 16,* 59–73.

Pearson, D. A. S., McDougall, C., Kanaan, M., Bowles, A., & Torgerson, D. J. (2011). Reducing criminal recidivism: Evaluation of citizenship, an evidence-based probation supervision process. *Journal of Experimental Criminology, 7,* 73–102.

Persico, N., & Todd, P. E. (2008). The hit rates test for racial bias in motor-vehicle searches. *Justice Quarterly, 25,* 37–53.

Peters, C. M. (2011). Social work and juvenile probation: Historical tensions and contemporary convergences. *Social Work, 56,* 355–365.

Peters, M., Thomas, D., & Zamberlan, C. (1997). *Boot camps for juvenile offenders: Program summary.* Washington, DC: U.S. Department of Justice.

Petersilia, J. (1997). Probation in the United States. In M. Tonry (Ed.), *Crime and justice: A review of research* (Vol. 22, pp. 149–200). Chicago: University of Chicago Press.

Piquero, A. R. (2008). Disproportionate minority contact. *The Future of Children, 18,* 59–79.

Piquero, A. R., MacIntosh, R., & Hickman, M. (2000). Does self-control affect survey response? *Criminology, 38,* 897–930.

Piquero, N. L., Langton, L., & Schoepfer, A. (2008). *Completely out of control or the desire to be in complete control? An examination of low self-control and the desire-for-control.* Unpublished.

Pisciotta, A. W. (1979). *The theory and practice of the New York house of refuge, 1857–1935.* Florida State University. Unpublished Ph.D. dissertation.

Pisciotta, A. W. (1982). Saving the children: The promise and practice of *parens patriae,* 1838–98. *Crime & Delinquency, 28,* 410–425.

Pisciotta, A. W. (1983). Race, sex and rehabilitation: A study of differential treatment in the juvenile reformatory, 1825–1900. *Crime & Delinquency, 29,* 254–269.

Platt, A. M. (1977). *The child savers: The invention of delinquency.* Chicago: University of Chicago Press.

Podolsky, E. (1964). The chemistry of murder. *Pakistan Medical Journal, 15,* 9–14.

Poole, E. D., & Regoli, R. M. (1979). Parental support, delinquent friends and delinquency. *Journal of Criminal Law and Criminology, 70,* 188–193.

Pope, C. E. (1995). Equity within the juvenile justice system: Directions for the future. In K. K. Leonard, C. E. Pope & W. H. Feyerherm (Eds.), *Minorities and the juvenile justice system* (pp. 201–216). Thousand Oaks, CA: Sage.

Pope, C. E., & Snyder, H. N. (2003). *Race as a factor in juvenile arrests.* Washington, DC: U.S. Department of Justice.

Powers, R. (2002). The apocalypse of adolescence. *Atlantic Monthly, 89*(March), 58–74.

Pratt, T., & Cullen, F. T. (2000). The empirical status of Gottfredson and Hirschi's general theory of crime: A meta-analysis. *Criminology, 38,* 931–964.

Prescott, P. S. (1981). *The child savers: Juvenile justice observed.* New York: Knopf.

President's Commission on Law Enforcement and the Administration of Justice. (1967). *The challenge of crime in a free society.* Washington, DC: United States Government Printing Office. Available at https://www.ncjrs.gov/pdffiles1/nij/42.pdf

Propper, A. M. (1982). Make-believe families and homosexuality among imprisoned girls. *Criminology, 20*, 127–138.

Puritz, P., Burrell, S., Schwartz, R., Soler, M., & Warboys, L. (1995). *A call for justice: An assessment of access to counsel and quality of representation in delinquency proceedings.* Washington, DC: American Bar Association Juvenile Justice Center.

Putnam, R. D. (2000). *Bowling alone: The collapse and revival of American community.* New York: Simon & Schuster.

Puzzanchera, C. (2013). *Juvenile Arrests 2011.* Washington, DC: Office of Juvenile Justice and Delinquency Prevention.

Puzzanchera, C. & Addie, S. (2014). *Delinquency cases waived to criminal court, 2010.* Washington, DC: Office of Juvenile Justice and Delinquency Prevention.

Puzzanchera, C. & Robson, C. (2014). *Delinquency cases in juvenile court, 2010.* Washington, DC: Office of Juvenile Justice and Delinquency Prevention.

Puzzanchera, C., & Sickmund, M. (2008). *Juvenile court statistics, 2005.* Pittsburgh: National Center for Juvenile Justice.

Puzzanchera, C., Stahl, A. L., Finnegan, T. A., Tierney, N., & Snyder, H. N. (2004). *Juvenile court statistics, 2000.* Pittsburgh, PA: National Center for Juvenile Justice.

Puzzanchera, M. & Hockenberry. S. (2013). *Juvenile court statistics 2010.* Pittsburgh, PA: National Center for Juvenile Justice.

Pyrooz, D. C. (2013). Gangs, criminal offending, and an inconvenient truth: Considerations for gang prevention and intervention in the lives of youth. *Criminology and Public Policy, 12*, 427–436.

Rada, R. T., Laws, D. R., & Kellner, R. (1976). Plasma testosterone levels in the rapist. *Psychosomatic Medicine, 38*, 257–268.

Raine, A., Venables, P. H., & Williams, M. (1995). High autonomic arousal and electrodermal orienting at age 15 years as protective factors against criminal behavior at age 29 years. *American Journal of Psychiatry, 152*, 1,595–1,600.

Rasmussen, A. (2004). Teen court referral, sentencing, and subsequent recidivism: Two proportional hazards models and a little speculation. *Crime & Delinquency, 50*, 615–635.

Reading Eagle. (2008, January 26). Berks County juveniles pay off fines by serving community. Available at http://www2.readingeagle.com/article.aspx?id=77795

Reckless, W. C. (1962). A non-causal explanation: Containment theory. *Excerpta Criminologica, 1*, 131–134.

Reckless, W. C. (1967). *The crime problem.* New York: Appleton, Century, Crofts.

Redding, R. E. (2008). Juvenile transfer laws: An effective deterrent to delinquency? *OJJDP Juvenile Justice Bulletin.* Washington, DC: Office of Juvenile Justice and Delinquency Prevention.

Redding, R. E. (2010). Juvenile transfer laws: An effective deterrent to delinquency? *OJJDP Juvenile Justice Bulletin.* Washington, DC: Office of Juvenile Justice and Delinquency Prevention.

Reiss, A. J., Jr. (1980). Police brutality. In R. J. Lundman (Ed.), *Police behavior: A sociological perspective* (pp. 274–296). New York: Oxford University Press.

Reiss, A. J., Jr., & Rhodes, A. L. (1961). The distribution of juvenile delinquency in the social class structure. *American Sociological Review, 26*, 720–732.

Reiss, A. J., Jr., & Roth, J. A. (1993). *Understanding and preventing violence* (Vol. 1). Washington, DC: National Academy Press.

Reynolds, K. M., Seydlitz, R., & Jenkins, P. (2000). Do juvenile curfew laws work? A time-series analysis of the New Orleans law. *Justice Quarterly, 17,* 205–230.

Rhee, S. H., & Waldman, I. D. (2002). Genetic and environmental influences on antisocial behavior: A meta-analysis of twin and adoption studies. *Psychological Bulletin, 128,* 490–529.

Rhodes, J. E. (2008). Improving youth mentoring interventions through research-based practice. *American Journal of Community Psychology, 41,* 35–42.

Rice, S. K., & Piquero, A. R. (2005). Perceptions of discrimination and justice in New York City. *Policing, 28,* 98–117.

Ringwalt, C. L., Messerschmidt, P., Graham, L., & Collins, J. (1992). *Youth's victimization experiences, fear of attack or harm, and school avoidance behaviors. Final report.* Washington, DC: National Institute of Justice.

Roane, K. R. (2001). A risky trip through white man's pass. *U.S. News and World Report, 130,* 24.

Robers, S., Kemp, J., Rathbun, A., and Morgan, R. (2014). *Indicators of school crime and safety: 2013.* National Center for Education Statistics, U.S. Department of Education, and Bureau of Justice Statistics, Office of Justice Programs, U.S. Department of Justice. Washington, DC. Available at http://nces.ed.gov/pubsearch/pubsinfo.asp?pubid=2014042

Robers, S., Zhang, J., Truman, J., & Snyder, T. D. (2010). *Indicators of school crime and safety: 2010.* Washington, DC: Bureau of Justice Assistance.

Robers, S., Zhang, J., Truman, J., & Snyder, T. D. (2012). *Indicators of school crime and safety, 2011.* Washington, DC: Bureau of Justice Statistics. Available at http://nces.ed.gov/pubs2012/2012002.pdf

Robin, G. D. (1967). Gang member delinquency in Philadelphia. In M. W. LeKlein (Ed.), *Juvenile gangs in context* (pp. 15–24). Englewood Cliffs, NJ: Prentice Hall.

Robin, G. D. (1982). Juvenile interrogations and confessions. *Journal of Police Science and Administration, 10,* 224–228.

Rodriguez, N. (2005). Restorative justice, communities, and delinquency: Whom do we reintegrate? *Criminology & Public Policy, 4,* 103–130.

Rodriguez, N. (2007). Restorative justice at work: Examining the impact of restorative justice resolutions on juvenile recidivism. *Crime & Delinquency, 53,* 355–379.

Rodriguez, N. (2010). The cumulative effect of race and ethnicity in juvenile court outcomes and why preadjudication detentions matters. *Journal of Research in Crime and Delinquency, 47,* 391–413.

Rojek, D. G., & Erickson, M. L. (1982). Juvenile diversion: A study of community cooptation. In D. G. Rojek & G. F. Jensen (Eds.), *Readings in juvenile delinquency* (pp. 316–321). Lexington, MA: D.C. Heath.

Roncek, D. W., & Maier, P. A. (1991). Bars, blocks, and crimes revisited: Linking the theory of routine activities to the empiricism of 'hot spots'. *Criminology, 29,* 725–753.

Rosenbaum, D. P. (2007). Just say no to D.A.R.E. *Criminology & Public Policy, 6,* 815–824.

Rosenberg, I. M. (2008). Gault turns 40: Reflections on ambiguity. *Criminal Law Bulletin, 44,* 330–354.

Rossman, S. B., Butts, J. A., Roman, J., DeStefano, C., & White, R. (2004). What juvenile drug courts do and how they do it. In J. A. Butts & J. Roman (Eds.), *Juvenile drug courts and teen substance abuse* (pp. 55–106). Washington, DC: Urban Institute Press.

Rossow, L. F., & Parkinson, J. R. (1994). Yet another student strip search: *Cornfield by Lewis v. Consolidated High School District No. 230. School Law Reporter 36*(3), 1–2.

Rossum, R. A., Koller, B. J., & Manfredi, C. P. (1987). *Juvenile justice reform: A model for the states.* Clairmont, CA: Rose Institute of State and Local Government and the American Legislative Exchange.

Roth, J. J. (2013). Commentary: Place-based delinquency prevention: Issues and recommendations. *OJJDP Journal of Juvenile Justice, 3,* 110–119.

Rothman, D. J. (1971). *The discovery of the asylum: Social order and disorder in the new republic.* Boston: Little, Brown.

Rothman, D. J. (1980). *Conscience and convenience: The asylum and its alternatives in progressive America.* Boston: Little, Brown.

Roush, D. M., & McMillen, M. (2000). *Construction, operations, and staff training for juvenile confinement facilities.* Washington, DC: Office of Juvenile Justice and Delinquency Prevention.

Rovner, J. (2013). *Disproportionate minority contact in the juvenile justice system.* Washington, DC: The Sentencing Project.

Rovner, J. (2014). *Slow to act: State responses to 2012 Supreme Court mandate on life without parole.* Washington, DC: The Sentencing Project.

Rowe, D. C. (2002). *Biology and crime.* Los Angeles: Roxbury.

Rubin, H. T. (1985). *Juvenile justice: Policy, practice, and law* (2nd ed.). New York: Random House.

Rubin, H. T. (2013). Juveniles in solitary confinement. *Juvenile Justice Update, 19,* 1–10.

Ryan, C. M. (1987). Juvenile court jurisdiction: Intervention and intrusion. In F. X. Hartmann (Ed.), *From children to citizens: Volume II: The role of the juvenile court* (pp. 56–64). New York: Springer-Verlag.

Ryerson, E. (1978). *The best-laid plans: America's juvenile court experiment.* New York: Hill and Wang.

Ryon, S. B., Devers, L., Early, K. W., & Hand, G. A. (2012). Changing how the system responds to status offenders: Connecticut's families with service needs initiative. *Juvenile and Family Court Journal, 63,* 37–46.

Saad, L. (2001). Fear of crime at record lows. *Gallup Poll Monthly, 433,* 2–10.

Sagatun, I. J., & Edwards, L. P. (1995). *Child abuse and the legal system.* Chicago: Nelson-Hall.

SAMHSA. (2004). *Graduated driver licensing and drinking among young drivers.* Washington, DC: Substance Abuse and Mental Health Services Administration. Available at http://www.drugabusestatistics.samhsa.gov/

Sampson, R. J. (1986). Effects of socioeconomic context on official reaction to juvenile delinquency. *American Sociological Review, 51,* 876–885.

Sampson, R. J., & Laub, J. H. (1993). *Crime in the making: Pathways and turning points through life.* Cambridge, MA: Harvard University Press.

Sanborn, J. (2001). A *parens patriae* figure or impartial fact finder: Policy questions and conflicts for the juvenile court judge. *Criminal Justice Policy Review, 12,* 311–332.

Sanders, W. B. (1994). *Gangbangs and drive-bys: Grounded culture and juvenile gang violence.* New York: Aldine de Gruyter.

Sante, L. (1991). *Low life: Lures and snares of old New York.* New York: Vintage Books.

Schaffner, L. (2006). *Girls in trouble with the law.* New Brunswick, NJ: Rutgers University Press.

Schaps, E., Moskowitz, J. M., Malvin, J. H., & Schaeffer, G. A. (1986). Evaluation of seven school-based prevention programs: A final report of the Napa project. *International Journal of the Addictions, 21,* 1,081–1,112.

Schauss, A. G. (1980). *Diet, crime and delinquency.* Berkeley, CA: Parker House.

Schiff, A. (1999). The impact of restorative interventions on juvenile offenders. In G. Bazemore & L. Walgrave (Eds.), *Restorative juvenile justice: Repairing the harm of youth crime.* Monsey, NY: Criminal Justice Press.

Schlossman, S. L. (1977). *Love and the American delinquent: The theory and practice of "progressive" juvenile justice, 1825–1920.* Chicago: University of Chicago Press.

Schnebly, S. M. (2008). The influence of community-oriented policing on crime-reporting behavior. *Justice Quarterly, 25,* 223–251.

Schneider, A. L. (1985). *The impact of deinstitutionalization on recidivism and secure confinement of status offenders.* Washington, DC: U.S. Department of Justice.

Schneider, A. L. (1986). Restitution and recidivism rates of juvenile offenders: Results from four experimental studies. *Criminology, 24,* 533–552.

Schneider, A. L. (1988). A comparative analysis of juvenile court responses to drug and alcohol offenses. *Crime & Delinquency, 34,* 103–124.

Schneider, A. L. (1990). *Deterrence and juvenile crime: Results from a national policy experiment.* New York: Springer-Verlag.

Schneider, A. L., & Schram, D. D. (1986). The Washington State juvenile justice reform: A review of findings. *Criminal Justice Policy Review, 2,* 211–235.

Schneider, M. E. (2008). HIV rates are low in high-risk adolescent group studied. *Pediatric News, 42,* 10.

Schubert, C. A., & Mulvey, E. P. (2014). *Behavioral health problems, treatment, and outcomes in serious youthful offenders.* Washington, DC: Office of Juvenile Justice and Delinquency Prevention.

Schulsinger, F. (1972). Psychopathy: Heredity and environment. *International Journal of Mental Health, 1,* 190–206.

Schur, E. M. (1973). *Radical nonintervention: Rethinking the delinquency problem.* Englewood Cliffs, NJ: Prentice Hall.

Schwadel, P. (2013). Changes in Americans' views of prayer and reading the bible in public schools: Time periods, birth cohorts, and religious traditions. *Sociological Forum, 28,* 261–282.

Schwartz, I. M., Fishman, G., Rawson Hatfield, R., Krisberg, B. A., & Eisikovits, Z. (1987). Juvenile detention: The hidden closets revisited. *Justice Quarterly, 4,* 219–235.

Schwartz, M. D. (1989). Family violence as a cause of crime: Rethinking our priorities. *Criminal Justice Policy Review, 3,* 115–132.

Scott, M. (2002, May 1). Georgia prom-goers to face curfew thanks to recent legislation. *Johnson City Press,* 6.

Sealock, M. D., Gottfredson, D. C., & Gallagher, C. A. (1997). Delinquency and social reform: A radical perspective. In L. Empey (Ed.), *Juvenile justice* (pp. 245–290). Charlottesville: University of Virginia Press.

Secretary of Education. (2003). *Guidance on constitutionally protected prayer in public elementary and secondary schools.* Available at http://www2.ed.gov/policy/gen/guid/religionand schools/prayer_guidance.html

Sedlak, A. J., & Bruce, C. (2010). *Youth's characteristics and backgrounds: Findings from the survey of youth in residential placement.* Washington, DC: U.S. Department of Justice.

Sedlak, A. J., & McPherson, K. S. (2010a). *Conditions of confinement: Findings from the survey of youth in residential placement.* Washington, DC: U.S. Department of Justice.

Sedlak, A. J., & McPherson, K. S. (2010b). *Youth's needs and services: Findings from the survey of youth in residential placement.* Washington, DC: U.S. Department of Justice.

Sedlak, A. J., McPherson, K. S., & Basena, M. (2013). *Nature and risk of victimization: Findings from the survey of youth in residential placement.* Washington, DC: Office of Juvenile Justice and Delinquency Prevention.

Sells, S. B., & Simpson, D. D. (1979). Evaluation of treatment outcomes for youths in the drug abuse reporting program (DARP): A follow-up study. In G. M. Beschner & A. S. Friedman (Eds.), *Youth drug abuse* (pp. 571–628). Lexington, MA: Lexington Books.

Shaffer, D. K. (2011). Looking inside the black box of drug courts: A meta-analytic review. *Justice Quarterly, 28,* 493–529.

Shah, S. A., & Roth, L. H. (1974). Biological and psychophysiological factors in criminality. In D. Glaser (Ed.), *Handbook of criminology* (pp. 101–173). New York: Rand McNally.

Shannon, L. W. (1982). *Assessing the relationship of adult criminal careers to juvenile careers.* Iowa City: Iowa Urban Community Research Center.

Shaw, C. R., & McKay, H. D. (1942). *Juvenile delinquency and urban areas.* Chicago: University of Chicago Press.

Shaw, C. R., Zorbaugh, F. M., McKay, H. D., & Cottrell, L. S. (1929). *Delinquency areas.* Chicago: University of Chicago Press.

Sheidow, A. J., Jayawardhana, J., Bradford, W. D., Henggeler, S. W., & Shapiro, S. B. (2012). Money matters: Cost-effectiveness of juvenile drug court with and without evidence-based treatments. *Journal of Child and Adolescent Substance Abuse, 21,* 69–90.

Sheldon, W. H. (1949). *Varieties of delinquent youth: An introduction to correctional psychiatry.* New York: Harper and Brothers.

Sheley, J. F., McGee, Z. T., & Wright, J. D. (1995). *Weapon-related victimization in selected inner-city high school samples.* Washington, DC: National Institute of Justice.

Sher, G. (2003). On the decriminalization of drugs. *Criminal Justice Ethics, 22,* 30–33.

Shine, J., & Price, D. (1992). Prosecutors and juvenile justice: new roles and perspectives. In I. M. Schwartz (Ed.), *Juvenile justice and public policy: toward a national agenda* (pp. 101–133). New York: Lexington Books.

Short, J. F. (1960). Differential association as a hypothesis: Problems of empirical testing. *Social Problems, 8,* 14–25.

Short, J. F., & Nye, I. (1958). Extent of unrecorded delinquency: Tentative conclusions. *Journal of Criminal Law, Criminology and Police Science, 49,* 296–302.

Short, J. F., & Strodbeck, F. L. (1965). *Group process and gang delinquency.* Chicago: University of Chicago Press.

Shufelt, J. S., & Cocozza, J. C. (2006). *Youth with mental health disorders in the juvenile justice system: Results from a multi-state prevalence study*. Delmar, NY: National Center for Mental Health and Juvenile Justice.

Sickmund, M., Sladky, A., & Kang, W. (2013a). *Easy access to juvenile court statistics: 1985–2011*. Available at http://www.ojjdp.gov/ojstatbb/ezajcs/

Sickmund, M., Sladky, T. J., Kang, W., & Puzzanchera, C. (2013b). *Easy access to the census of juveniles in residential placement: 1997–2011*. Available at http://www.ojjdp.gov/ojstatbb/ezacjrp/

Sickmund, M., Snyder, H. N., & Poe-Yamagata, E. (1997). *Juvenile offenders and victims: 1997 update on violence*. Washington, DC: Office of Juvenile Justice and Delinquency Prevention.

Simmons, T. J. (2006). Mandatory mediation: A better way to address status offenses. *Ohio State Journal of Dispute Resolution, 21*, 1–31.

Simpson, D. D., & Sells, S. B. (1982). Effectiveness of treatment for drug abuse: An overview of the darp research program. *Advances in Alcohol and Substance Abuse, 2*, 7–29.

Singer, S. I. (1996). *Recriminalizing delinquency: Violent juvenile crime and juvenile justice reform*. New York: Cambridge University Press.

Skinner, B. F. (1953). *Science and human behavior*. New York: Macmillan.

Skogan, W. G. (1981). On attitudes and behavior. In D. A. Lewis (Ed.), *Reactions to crime*. Beverly Hills: Sage.

Skogan, W. G., & Hartnett, S. M. (1997). *Community policing, Chicago style*. New York: Oxford University Press.

Skogan, W. G., & Maxfield, M. G. (1981). *Coping with crime: Individual and neighborhood reactions*. Beverly Hills: Sage.

Skolnick, J. (1966). *Justice without trial*. New York: John Wiley and Sons.

Skolnick, J., Bluthenthal, R., & Correl, T. (1993). Gang organization and migration. In S. Cummings & D. J. Monti (Eds.), *Gangs: The origins and impact of contemporary youth gangs in the United States* (pp. 193–218). Albany, NY: SUNY Press.

Skowyra, K., & Cocozza, J. J. (2006). A blueprint for change: Improving the system response to youth with mental health needs involved with the juvenile justice system. *National Center for Mental Health and Juvenile Justice Research and Program Brief*. Delmar, NY: National Center for Mental Health and Juvenile Justice.

Snyder, H. N. (2005). Juvenile arrests, 2003. *OJJDP Juvenile Justice Bulletin*. Washington, DC: U.S. Department of Justice, Office of Juvenile Justice and Delinquency Prevention.

Snyder, H. N., & Sickmund, M. (2006). *Juvenile offenders and victims: 2006 national report*. Pittsburgh, PA: National Center for Juvenile Justice.

Soler, H., Vinayak, P., & Quadagno, D. (2000). Biosocial aspects of domestic violence. *Psychoneuroendocrinology, 25*, 721–739.

Sommers, C. H. (2000). *The war against boys: How misguided feminism is harming our young men*. New York: Touchstone.

Spadola, M. (2004). *Red Hook Justice*. Produced in association with the Independent Television Service (ITVS) by Sugar Pictures LLC.

Speckart, G. R., & Anglin, M. D. (1985). Narcotics and crime: A causal modeling approach. *Journal of Quantitative Criminology, 2*, 3–28.

Spergel, I. A. (1966). *Street gang work: Theory and practice.* Reading, MA: Addison-Wesley.

Spergel, I. A. (1984). Violent gangs in Chicago: In search of social policy. *Social Service Review, 58,* 199–226.

Spergel, I. A. (1986). The violent gang problem in Chicago: A local community approach. *Social Service Review, 60,* 94–131.

Spergel, I. A., & Curry, G. D. (1993). The national youth gang survey: A research and development process. In A. P. Goldstein & C. R. Huff (Eds.), *The gang intervention handbook* (pp. 359–400). Champaign, IL: Research Press.

Spergel, I. A., Curry, G. D., Chance, R., Kane, C., Ross, R., Alexander, A., Simmons, E., & Oh, S. (1990). *National youth gang suppression and intervention program: Executive summary, stage 1: Assessment.* Arlington, VA: National Youth Gang Information Center.

Spergel, I. A., Wa, K. M., & Sosa, R. V. (2001). *Evaluation of the Bloomington-Normal comprehensive gang program—Final report.* Washington, DC: Office of Juvenile Justice and Delinquency Prevention.

Spergel, I. A., Wa, K. M., & Sosa, R. V. (2002). *Evaluation of the Mesa gang intervention program (MGIP)—Final report.* Washington, DC: Office of Juvenile Justice and Delinquency Prevention.

Spergel, I. A., Wa, K. M., & Sosa, R. V. (2003). *Evaluation of the Riverside comprehensive community-wide approach to gang prevention, intervention and suppression—Final report.* Washington, DC: Office of Juvenile Justice and Delinquency Prevention.

Spergel, I. A., Wa, K. M., & Sosa, R. V. (2004a). *Evaluation of the Tucson comprehensive community-wide approach to gang prevention, intervention and suppression—Final report.* Washington, DC: Office of Juvenile Justice and Delinquency Prevention.

Spergel, I. A., Wa, K. M., & Sosa, R. V. (2004b). *Evaluation of the San Antonio comprehensive community-wide approach to gang prevention, intervention and suppression—Final report.* Washington, DC: Office of Juvenile Justice and Delinquency Prevention.

Spohn, C., Piper, R. K., Martin, T., & Frenzel, E. D. (2001). Drug courts and recidivism: The results of an evaluation using two comparison groups and multiple indicators of recidivism. *Journal of Drug Issues, 31,* 149–176.

Staples, J. S. (2000). Violence in schools: Rage against a broken world. *Annals of the American Academy of Political and Social Science, 567,* 30–41.

Staples, W. G. (1987). Law and social control in juvenile justice dispositions. *Journal of Research in Crime and Delinquency, 24,* 7–22.

Starbuck, D., Howell, J. C., & Lindquist, D. J. (2001). Hybrid and other modern gangs. *OJJDP Juvenile Justice Bulletin.* Washington, DC: Office of Juvenile Justice and Delinquency Prevention.

Steele, B. F., & Pollock, C. B. (1974). A psychiatric study of parents who abuse infants and small children. In R. E. Helfer & C. H. Kempe (Eds.), *The battered child* (2nd ed.; pp. 80–133). Chicago: University of Chicago Press.

Stein, D. M., Deberard, S., & Homan, K. (2013). Predicting success and failure in juvenile drug treatment court: A meta-analytic review. *Journal of Substance Abuse Treatment, 44,* 159–168.

Steiner, B., & Wright, E. (2006). Assessing the relative effects of state direct file waiver laws on violent juvenile crime: Deterrence or irrelevance? *Journal of Criminal Law and Criminology, 96,* 1451–1477.

Stephens, D. J. (2011). Substance abuse and co-occurring disorders among criminal offenders. In T. J. Fagan & R. K. Ax (Eds.), *Correctional mental health: From theory to best practice* (pp. 235–256). Thousand Oaks, CA: Sage.

Stephens, R. C. (1987). *Mind-altering drugs: Use, abuse, and treatment.* Newbury Park, CA: Sage.

Stephens, R. D., & Arnette, J. L. (2000). *From the courthouse to the schoolhouse: Making successful transitions.* Washington, DC: Office of Juvenile Justice and Delinquency Prevention.

Stevens, J., May, D., Rice, N., & Jarjoura, G. R. (2011). Nonsocial versus social reinforcers: Contrasting theoretical perspectives on repetitive serious delinquency and drug use. *Youth Violence and Juvenile Justice, 9,* 295–312.

Stickle, W. P., Connell, N. M., Wilson, D. M., & Gottfredson, D. (2008). An experimental evaluation of teen courts. *Journal of Experimental Criminology, 4,* 137–163.

Stimson, C. D., & Grossman, A. M. (2009). *Adult time for adult crimes: Life without parole for juvenile killers and violent teens.* Washington, DC: The Heritage Foundation.

Stoutland, S. E. (2001). The multiple dimensions of trust in resident/police relations. *Journal of Research in Crime and Delinquency, 38,* 226–253.

Straus, M. A. (1983). Ordinary violence, child abuse, and wife battering: What do they have in common? In D. Finkelhor, R. J. Gelles, G. T. Hotaling & M. A. Straus (Eds.), *The dark side of families: Current family violence research.* Beverly Hills: Sage.

Straus, M. A. (1994). Should the use of corporal punishment by parents be considered child abuse? In M. A. Mason & E. Gambrill (Eds.), *Debating children's lives: Current controversies on children and adolescents* (pp. 196–222). Newbury Park, CA: Sage.

Strickland, R. A. (2004). *Restorative justice.* New York: Peter Lang.

Stuart, B. (1996). Circle sentencing: Turning swords into ploughshares. In B. Galaway & J. Hudson (Eds.), *Restorative justice: International perspectives.* Monsey, NY: Criminal Justice Press.

Studt, E. (1973). *Surveillance and service in parole: A report of the parole action study.* Washington, DC: National Institute of Corrections.

Stuphen, R. D., & Ford, J. (2001). The effectiveness and enforcement of a teen curfew law. *Journal of Sociology and Social Welfare, 28,* 55–78.

Substance Abuse and Mental Health Services Administration. (2013). *Results from the 2012 National Survey on Drug Use and Health: Summary of national findings,* NSDUH Series H-46, HHS Publication No. (SMA) 13-4795. Rockville, MD: Substance Abuse and Mental Health Services Administration.

Sullivan, C., Grant, M. Q., & Grant, J. D. (1957). The development of interpersonal maturity: Applications to delinquency. *Psychiatry, 20,* 373–385.

Sullivan, C. J., Dollard, N., Sellers, B., & Mayo, J. (2010). Rebalancing response to school-based offenses: A civil citation program. *Youth Violence and Juvenile Justice, 8,* 279–294.

Sullivan, C. J., Piquero, A. R., & Cullen, F. T. (2012). Like before, but better: The lessons of developmental, life-course criminology for contemporary juvenile justice. *Victims and Offenders, 7,* 450–471.

Sutherland, E. H. (1939). *Principles of criminology* (3rd ed.). Philadelphia: Lippincott.

Sutherland, E. H., & Cressey, D. R. (1974). *Criminology* (9th ed.). Philadelphia: Lippincott.

Swadi, H., & Zeitlin, H. (1987). Drug education to school children: Does it really work? *British Journal of Addiction, 82,* 741–746.

Sykes, G. M., & Matza, D. (1957). Techniques of neutralization: A theory of delinquency. *American Sociological Review, 22,* 664–670.

Szymanski, L. A. (2002, September). Juvenile delinquents' right to a jury trial. *NCJJ Snapshot, 7*(9). Pittsburgh: National Center for Juvenile Justice.

Takagi, P., & Shank, G. (2004). Critique of restorative justice. *Social Justice, 31,* 147–163.

Tanehaus, D. S. (2004). *Juvenile justice in the making.* New York: Oxford University Press.

Tannenbaum, F. (1938). *Crime and the community.* New York: Columbia University Press.

Taxman, F. S. (2008). No illusions: Offender and organizational change in Maryland's proactive community supervision efforts. *Criminology & Public Policy, 7*(2), 275–302.

Taylor, T. J., Turner, K. B., Esbensen, F., & Winfree, T. (2001). Coppin' an attitude: Attitudinal differences among juveniles toward police. *Journal of Criminal Justice, 29,* 295–305.

The Sentencing Project. (2014). *Juvenile life without parole: An overview.* Washington, DC: The Sentencing Project.

Thornberry, T. P. (1998). Membership in youth gangs and involvement in serious and violent offending. In R. Loeber & D. P. Farrington (Eds.), *Serious and violent offenders.* Newbury Park, CA: Sage.

Thornberry, T. P., & Burch, J. H. (1997). *Gang members and delinquent behavior.* Washington, DC: Office of Juvenile Justice and Delinquency Prevention.

Thornberry, T. P., & Christenson, R. L. (1984). Unemployment and criminal involvement: An investigation of reciprocal causal structures. *American Sociological Review, 49,* 398–411.

Thornberry, T. P., Krohn, M. D., Lizotte, A. J., & Chard-Wierschem, D. (1993). The role of juvenile gangs in facilitating delinquent behavior. *Journal of Research in Crime and Delinquency, 30,* 55–87.

Thrasher, F. M. (1936). *The gang.* Chicago: University of Chicago Press.

Thurman, Q. C. (1984). Deviance and the neutralization of moral commitment: An empirical analysis. *Deviant Behavior, 5,* 291–304.

Tobey, A., Grisso, T., & Schwartz, R. (2000). Youths' trial participation as seen by youths and their attorneys: An exploration of competence-based issues. In T. Grisso & R. G. Schwartz (Eds.), *Youth on trial: A developmental perspective on juvenile justice* (pp. 225–242). Chicago: University of Chicago Press.

Tobler, N. S. (1986). Meta-analysis of 143 adolescent drug prevention programs: Quantitative outcome results of program participants compared to a control or comparison group. *Journal of Drug Issues, 16,* 537–567.

Tobler, N. S. (1997). Meta-analysis of adolescent drug prevention programs: Results of the 1993 meta-analysis. In W. J. Bukoski (Ed.), *Meta-analysis of drug abuse prevention programs* (pp. 5–68). Rockville, MD: National Institute on Drug Abuse.

Tolan, P., Henry, D., Schoeny, M., & Bass, A. (2008). *Mentoring interventions to affect juvenile delinquency and associated problems.* Oslo, Norway: The Campbell Collaboration. Available at http://www.campbellcollaboration.org/

Tonry, M. (2008). Crime and human rights—how political paranoia, protestant fundamentalism, and constitutional obsolescence combined to devastate black America: The American Society of Criminology 2007 presidential address. *Criminology, 46,* 1–33.

Tonry, M. (2011a). Making peace, not a desert: Penal reform should be about values not justice reinvestment. *Criminology & Public Policy, 10,* 637–649.

Tonry, M. (2011b). *Punishing race: A continuing American dilemma*. New York: Oxford University Press.

Torbet, P. M. (1996). *Juvenile probation: The workhorse of the juvenile justice system*. Washington, DC: U.S. Department of Justice.

Torbet, P., Gable, R., Hurst, H., Montgomery, I., Szymanski, L., & Thomas, D. (1996). *State responses to serious and violent juvenile crime*. Washington, DC: Office of Juvenile Justice and Delinquency Prevention.

Torbet, P., Griffin, P., Hurst, H., & MacKenzie, L. R. (2000). *Juveniles facing criminal sanctions: Three states that changed the rules*. Washington, DC: U.S. Department of Justice.

Toseland, R. W. (1982). Fear of crime: Who is most vulnerable? *Journal of Criminal Justice, 10*, 199–210.

Toy, C. (1992). A short history of Asian gangs in San Francisco. *Justice Quarterly, 9*, 647–666.

Travis, J. (2012). Summoning the superheroes: Harnessing science and passion to create a more effective and humane response to crime. In M. Mauer & K. Epstein (Eds.), *To build a better criminal justice system: 25 experts envision the next 25 years of reform* (pp. 5–13). Washington, DC: The Sentencing Project.

Travis, L. F., & Coon, J. K. (2005). *The role of law enforcement in public school safety: A national survey*. Washington, DC: National Institute of Justice.

Trebach, A. S. (1987). *The great drug war and radical proposals that could make America safe again*. New York: Macmillan.

Trojanowicz, R., Kappeler, V. E., Gaines, L. K., & Bucqueroux, B. (1998). *Community policing: A contemporary perspective* (2nd ed.). Cincinnati: Anderson.

Trulson, C. R. (2007). Determinants of disruption: Institutional misconduct among state-committed delinquents. *Youth Violence and Juvenile Justice, 5*, 7–34.

Trulson, C. R., DeLisi, M., Caudill, J. W., Belshaw, S., & Marquart, J. W. (2010). Delinquent careers behind bars. *Criminal Justice Review, 35*, 200–219.

Tucker, S., & Cadora, E. (2003). Justice reinvestment: To invest in public safety by reallocating justice dollars to refinance education, housing, healthcare, and jobs. *Ideas for an Open Society, 3* (Monograph).

Umbreit, M. S. (1997). Victim-offender dialogue: From the margins to the mainstream throughout the world. *The Crime Victims Report, 1*(35–36), 48.

Umbreit, M. S. (1999). Avoiding the marginalization and McDonaldization of victim offender mediation: A case study in moving toward the mainstream. In G. Bazemore & L. Walgrave (Eds.), *Restorative juvenile justice: Repairing the harm of youth crime* (pp. 213–234). Monsey, NY: Criminal Justice Press.

Umbreit, M. S., & Coates, R. B. (1992). *Victim offender mediation: An analysis of programs in four states of the U.S.* St. Paul, MN: Center for Restorative Justice and Peacemaking.

Umbreit, M. S., Coates, R. B., & Vos, B. (2001). *Juvenile offender mediation in six Oregon counties*. Salem, OR: Oregon Dispute Resolution Commission.

Umbreit, M. S., Vos, B., Coates, R. B., & Brown, K. A. (2003). *Facing violence: The path of restorative justice and dialogue*. Monsey, NY: Criminal Justice Press.

Underwood, J. (1994). Prayer in the schools. *Schools and the Courts, 20*(May), 1,039–1,050.

University at Albany. (2014). *Sourcebook of criminal justice statistics*, Tables 2.21.2011, 2.12.2012, and 2.0046.2013. Albany, NY: Hindelang Criminal Justice Research Center. Available at http://www.albany.edu/sourcebook/

Urban, L. S. (2008). Court-ordered curfew: The application of graduated sanctions for juvenile offenders. *Justice Policy Journal, 5,* 1–35.

Urban, L. S., St. Cyr, J. L., & Decker, S. H. (2003). Goal conflict in the juvenile court: The evolution of sentencing practices in the United States. *Journal of Contemporary Criminal Justice, 19,* 454–479.

U.S. Bureau of the Census (2011). *Annual population estimates 2002 to 2009.* Washington, DC: U.S. Bureau of the Census. Available at http://www.census.gov/popest/

U.S. Department of Justice. (2006). *National CASA program—audit report 07-04.* Washington, DC: U.S. Department of Justice, Office of the Inspector General.

U.S. News and World Report. (2006, May 8). Florida boots harsh tactics, 18.

Valdez, A. (2000). *Gangs: A guide to understanding street gangs* (3rd ed.). San Clemente, CA: LawTech.

van den Haag, E. (1978). In defense of the death penalty: a legal-practical-moral analysis. *Criminal Law Bulletin,* 14, 51–68.

van den Haag, E., & Conrad, P. (1983). *The death penalty: A debate.* New York: Plenum.

Vandervort, F. E., & Ladd, W. E. (2001). The worst of all possible worlds: Michigan's juvenile justice system and international standards for the treatment of children. *University of Detroit Mercy Law Review, 78,* 202–258.

Van Kammen, W. B., & Loeber, R. (1994). Are fluctuations in delinquent activities related to the onset and offset in juvenile illegal drug use and drug dealing? *The Journal of Drug Issues, 24,* 9–24.

Van Ness, D. W. (1990). Restorative justice. In B. Galaway & J. Hudson (Eds.), *Criminal justice, restitution, and reconciliation.* Monsey, NY: Criminal Justice Press.

Van Ness, D. W., & Strong, K. H. (2015). *Restoring justice: An introduction to restorative justice* (5th ed.). Boston: Elsevier (Anderson Publishing).

Van Voorhis, P., Braswell, M., & Lester, D. (2007). *Correctional counseling and rehabilitation* (6th ed.). Newark, NJ: LexisNexis Matthew Bender.

Van Voorhis, P., Braswell, M., & Lester, D. (2009). *Correctional counseling and rehabilitation* (7th ed.). Newark, NJ: LexisNexis Matthew Bender.

Van Voorhis, P., & Salisbury, E. (2014). *Correctional counseling and rehabilitation* (8th ed.). Boston: Elsevier (Anderson Publishing).

Veevers, J. (1989). Pre-court diversion for juvenile offenders. In M. Wright & B. Galaway (Eds.), *Mediation and criminal justice: Victims, offenders and community.* Newbury Park, CA: Sage.

Vigil, J. D. (1993). The established gang. In S. Cummings & D. J. Monti (Eds.), *Gangs: The origins and impact of contemporary youth gangs in the United States* (pp. 95–112). Albany, NY: SUNY Press.

Vigil, J. D. (1997). Learning from gangs: The Mexican American experience. *ERIC Digest* Document No. RC020943.

Vigil, J. D. (2010). *Gang redux: A balanced anti-gang strategy.* Long Grove, IL: Waveland.

Viljoen, J. L., Klaver, J., & Roesch, R. (2005). Legal decisions of preadolescent and adolescent defendants: Predictors of confessions, pleas, communication with attorneys, and appeals. *Law and Human Behavior, 29,* 253–277.

Vingilis, E. R., & DeGenova, K. (1984). Youth and the forbidden fruit: Experiences with changes in legal drinking age in North America. *Journal of Criminal Justice, 12,* 161–172.

Virkkunen, M., Goldman, D., & Linnoila, M. (1996). Serotonin in alcoholic violent offenders. In G. R. Bock & J. A. Goode (Eds.), *Genetics of criminal and antisocial behavior* (pp. 168–176). Chichester, England: John Wiley and Sons.

Visher, C. A. (1990). Incorporating drug treatment in criminal sanctions. *NIJ Reports #221.* Washington, DC: National Institute of Justice.

Vold, G. B., & Bernard, T. J. (1986). *Theoretical criminology* (3rd ed.). New York: Oxford University Press.

von Hentig, H. (1941). Remarks on the interaction of perpetrator and victim. *Journal of Criminal Law, Criminology and Police Science, 31,* 303–309.

Wachtel, T. (1995). Family group conferencing: Restorative justice in practice. *Juvenile Justice Update, 1*(4), 1–2, 13–14.

Wadlington, W., Whitebread, C. H., & Davis, S. M. (1983). *Cases and materials on children in the legal system.* Mineola, NY: Foundation Press.

Walker, S. (1992). *The police in America: An introduction.* New York: McGraw-Hill.

Walker, S. (2011). *Sense and nonsense about crime, drugs, and communities* (7th ed.). Belmont, CA: Wadsworth Cengage Learning.

Walsh, A. (2009). *Biology and criminology: The biosocial synthesis.* New York: Routledge.

Walters, G. D. (1992). A meta-analysis of the gene-crime relationship. *Criminology, 30,* 595–613.

Walters, G.D. (2014). Crime and substance misuse in adjudicated delinquent youth: The worst of both worlds. *Law and Human Behavior, 38,* 139–150.

Walters, S. T., Clark, M. D., Gingerich, R., & Meltzer, M. L. (2007). *A guide for probation and parole: Motivating offenders to change.* Washington, DC: U.S. Department of Justice, National Institute of Corrections.

Walters, S. T., Vader, A. M., Nguyen, N., Harris, T. R., & Eells, J. (2010). Motivational interviewing as a supervision strategy in probation: A randomized effectiveness trial. *Journal of Offender Rehabilitation, 49,* 309–323.

Ward, A. C. (2000). *Evidentiary use of biological disorder: Ethics and justice.* Burnaby, BC: Simon Fraser University. Thesis.

Ward, G. & Kupchik, A. (2010). What drives juvenile probation officers? Relating organizational contexts, status characteristics, and personal convictions to treatment and punishment orientations. *Crime & Delinquency, 56,* 35–69.

Ward, T., & Langlands, R. L. (2008). Restorative justice and the human rights of offenders: Convergences and divergences. *Aggression and Violent Behavior, 13,* 355–372.

Watkins, A. M., & Maume, M. O. (2012). Rethinking the study of juveniles' attitudes toward the police. *Criminal Justice Studies, 25,* 279–300.

Watts, W. D., & Wright, L. S. (1990). The relationship of alcohol, tobacco, marijuana, and other illegal drug use to delinquency among Mexican-American, black, and white adolescent males. *Adolescence, 25,* 171–181.

Wechsler, H., & Nelson, T. F. (2010). Will increasing alcohol availability by lowering the minimum legal drinking age decrease drinking and related consequences among youths? *American Journal of Public Health, 100,* 986–992.

Weis, K., & Borges, S. S. (1973). Victimology and rape: The case of the legitimate victim. *Issues in Criminology, 8*, 71–115.

Weisheit, R. A. (1983). The social context of alcohol and drug education: Implications for program evaluations. *Journal of Alcohol and Drug Education, 29*, 72–81.

Weitekamp, E. G. M. (1999). The history of restorative justice. In G. Bazemore & L. Walgrave (Eds.), *Restorative juvenile justice: Repairing the harm of youth crime*. Monsey, NY: Criminal Justice Press.

Welch, K. (2007). Black criminal stereotypes and racial profiling. *Journal of Contemporary Criminal Justice, 23*, 276–288.

Welsh, B. C. (2012). Delinquency prevention. In B. C. Feld & D. M. Bishop (Eds.), *The Oxford handbook of juvenile crime and juvenile justice* (pp. 395–415). New York: Oxford University Press.

Welsh, B. C., & Farrington, D. P. (2007). Save children from a life of crime. *Criminology & Public Policy, 6*, 871–880.

Werner, A. (2014, April 16). Don't tase students at school, activists say. *CBS News*. Available at http://www.cbsnews.com/news/tasers-plus-teenagers-equal-a-dangerous-mix-activists-say/

Wexler, D. B. (2002). Some reflections on therapeutic jurisprudence and the practice of criminal law. *Criminal Law Bulletin, 38*, 205–215.

Whitaker, C., & Bastian, L. (1991). *Teenage victims: A national crime survey report*. Washington, DC: U.S. Department of Justice.

White, G. F. (1990). The drug use-delinquency connection in adolescence. In R. Weisheit (Ed.), *Drugs, crime and the criminal justice system*. Cincinnati: Anderson.

White, H. R., Pandina, R. J., & LaGrange, R. L. (1987). Longitudinal predictors of serious substance use and delinquency. *Criminology, 25*, 715–740.

White, M. D., & Klinger, D. (2012). Contagious fire? An empirical assessment of the problem of multi-shooter, multi-shot deadly force incidents in police work. *Crime & Delinquency, 58*, 196–221.

Whitehead, J. T. (1991). The effectiveness of felony probation: Results from an eastern state. *Justice Quarterly, 8*, 525–543.

Whitehead, J. T., & Braswell, M. C. (2000). The future of probation: Reintroducing the spiritual dimension into correctional practice. *Criminal Justice Review, 25*, 207–233.

White House. (2012). *National drug control strategy*. Washington, DC: The White House.

Wiatrowski, M., Griswold, D., & Roberts, M. (1981). Social control theory and delinquency. *American Sociological Review, 46*, 525–541.

Widom, C. S. (1989). Child abuse, neglect and violent criminal behavior. *Criminology, 27*, 251–271.

Widom, C. S. (1995). *Childhood victimization and violent behavior*. Paper presented at the Annual Conference on Criminal Justice Research and Evaluation, Washington, DC.

Wiebush, R. G., Wagner, D., McNulty, B., Wang, Y., & Le, T. N. (2005). *Implementation and outcome evaluation of the intensive aftercare program—Final report*. Washington, DC: Office of Juvenile Justice and Delinquency Prevention.

Wiehe, V. R. (1992). *Working with child abuse and neglect*. Itasca, IL: F.E. Peacock.

Weisel, D. L., & Shelley, T. O. (2004). *Specialized gang units: Form and function in community policing—final report.* Washington, DC: National Institute of Justice.

Wilson, J. Q., & Herrnstein, R. J. (1985). *Crime and human nature.* New York: Simon & Schuster.

Wilson, S. J., & Lipsey, M. W. (2003). Wilderness challenge programs for delinquent youth: A meta-analysis of outcome evaluations. *Evaluation and Program Planning, 23,* 1–12.

Wish, E. D., Toborg, M. A., & Bellassai, J. P. (1988). *Identifying drug users and monitoring them during conditional release.* Washington, DC: U.S. Department of Justice.

Wolfgang, M. E. (1958). *Patterns in criminal homicide.* Montclair, NJ: Patterson Smith. (Reprinted 1975.)

Wood, P. B., Pfefferbaum, B., & Arneklev, B. J. (1993). Risk-taking and self-control: Social psychological correlates of delinquency. *Journal of Crime and Justice, 16,* 111–130.

Wooden, K. (1976). *Weeping in the playtime of others: America's incarcerated children.* New York: McGraw-Hill.

Wooden, W. S., & Blazak, R. (2001). *Renegade kids, suburban outlaws: From youth culture to delinquency* (2nd ed.). Belmont, CA: Wadsworth.

Worden, R. E. (1996). The causes of police brutality: Theory and evidence on police use of force. In W. A. Geller & H. Toch (Eds.), *Police violence: Understanding and controlling police abuse of force* (pp. 23–51). New Haven, CT: Yale University Press.

World Health Organization. (1964). *WHO expert committee on addiction producing drugs: 13th Report. #23.* Geneva: World Health Organization.

Worrall, J. L., & Gaines, L. K. (2006). The effect of police-probation partnerships on juvenile arrests. *Journal of Criminal Justice, 34,* 579–589.

Wright, J. P., & Beaver, K. M. (2005). Do parents matter in creating self-control in their children? A genetically informed test of Gottfredson and Hirschi's theory of low self-control. *Criminology, 43,* 1,169–1,202.

Wright, J. P., & Cullen, F. T. (2000). Juvenile involvement in occupational crime. *Criminology, 38,* 863–896.

Wright, J. P., Cullen, F. T., & Williams, N. (1997). Working while in school and delinquent involvement: Implications for social policy. *Crime & Delinquency, 43,* 203–221.

Yablonsky, L. (1962). *The violent gang.* New York: Macmillan.

Young, D. W., Farrell, J. L., & Taxman, F. S. (2013). Impacts of juvenile probation training models on youth recidivism. *Justice Quarterly, 30,* 1,068–1,089.

Youth Online Safety Working Group. (2009). *Interdisciplinary response to youths sexting.* Alexandria, VA: National Center for Missing and Exploited Children.

Zatz, M. S. (1985). Los Cholos: Legal processing of Chicano gang members. *Social Problems, 33,* 13–30.

Zehr, H. (1990). *Changing lives: A new focus for crime and justice.* Scottdale, PA: Herald Press.

Zehr, H., & Mika, H. (2003). Fundamental concepts of restorative justice. In E. McLaughlin, R. Fergusson, G. Hughes & L. Westmarland (Eds.), *Restorative justice: Critical issues.* Thousand Oaks, CA: Sage.

Zeidel, R. L. (2012). Forecasting disruption, forfeiting speech: Restrictions on student speech in extracurricular activities. *Boston College Law Review, 53,* 303–343.

Ziemer, D. (2005, July 13). Juvenile interrogations must be recorded. *Wisconsin Law Journal* online. Available at http://wislawjournal.com/2005/07/13/juvenile-interrogations-must-be-recorded/

Zimring, F. E. (1982). *The changing legal world of adolescence.* New York: Free Press.

Zimring, F. E. (2000). Penal proportionality for the young offender: Notes on immaturity, capacity, and diminished responsibility. In T. Grisso & R. G. Schwartz (Eds.), *Youth on trial: A developmental perspective on juvenile justice* (pp. 271–289). Chicago: University of Chicago Press.

Zimring, F. E. (2005). Minimizing harm from minority disproportion in American juvenile justice. In D. F. Hawkins & K. Kempf-Leonard (Eds.), *Our children, their children: Confronting racial and ethnic differences in American juvenile justice* (pp. 413–427). Chicago: University of Chicago Press.

Zimring, F. E. (2007). *The great American crime decline.* New York: Oxford University Press.

Zimring, F. E. (2012). *The city that became safe: New York's lessons for urban crime and its control.* New York: Oxford University Press.

Zimring, F. E. & Tanenhaus, D. S. (Eds.). (2014). *Choosing the future for American juvenile justice.* New York: New York University Press.

Zweig, J. M., Dank, M., Lachman, P., & Yahner, J. (2013). *Technology, teen dating violence and abuse, and bullying.* Washington, DC: Urban Institute.

Bethel School District No. 403 v. Fraser, 478 U.S. 675, 106S.Ct. 3159, 92 L.Ed.2d 549 (1986).

Board of Education of Independent School District No. 92 of Pottawatomie County et al. v. Lindsay Earls et al., 536 U.S. 822 (2002).

Breed v. Jones, 421 U.S. 519, 95S.Ct. 1779, 44 L.Ed.2d 346 (1975).

Brown v. Gwinnett County School District, 112 F.3d 1464 (11th Cir. 1997).

Chicago v. Morales, 527 U.S. 41 (1999).

Commonwealth v. Fisher, 213Pa. 48 (1905).

Cornfield by Lewis v. Consolidated High School District No. 230, 991 F.3d 1316, 1326-1327 (7th Cir. 1993).

Deborah Morse, et al., v. Joseph Frederick, 551 U.S. 393 (2007).

Doe v. Renfrow, 451 U.S. 1022 (1981).

Doe v. Silsbee Independent School Disrict, 402 F. App'x 852, 853 (5th Cir. 2010).

Ex parte Crouse, 4 Wheaton (Pa.) 9 (1838).

Fare v. Michael C., 442 U.S. 707, 99 S.Ct. 2560, 61 L.Ed.2d 197 (1979).

Gonzalez v. Mailliard, Civ. No. 50424, N.D. Cal. 2/9/71, Appeal U.S. No. 70-120 4/9/71 (1971).

Good News Club v. Milford Central School, 533 U.S. 98 (2001).

Graham v. Florida, 560 U.S. (2010).

Hazelwood School District v. Kuhlmeier, 484 U.S. 260, 108 S.Ct. 562, 98 L.Ed.2d 592 (1988).

Ingraham v. Wright, 430 U.S. 651, 97 S.Ct. 1401, 51 L.Ed.2d 711 (1977).

In re Gault, 387 U.S. 1, 87 S.Ct. 1428, 18 L.Ed.2d 527 (1967).

In re LeBlanc, 430 N.W.2d 780, Mich. Ct. App. (1988).

In re Tyrell, 8 Cal.4th 68 (1994).

In re Winship, 397 U.S. 358, 90 S.Ct. 1068, 25 L.Ed.2d 368 (1970).

J.D.B. v. North Carolina. (2011).

Johnson v. City of Opelousas, 658 F.2d 1065 (5th Cir. 1981).

Jones v. Clear Creek Independent School District, 977 F.2d 963 (5th Cir. 1992).

Kent v. United States, 383 U.S. 541, 86 S.Ct. 1045, 16 L.Ed.2d 84 (1966).

Lee v. Weisman, 112 S. Ct. 2649 (1992).

McKeiver v. Pennsylvania, 403 U.S. 528, 91S.Ct. 1976, 29L.Ed.2d 647 (1971).

Miller v. Alabama, 132 S. Ct. 2455 (2012).

New Jersey v. T.L.O., 469 U.S. 325 (1985).

P.B. v. Koch, 96 F.3d 1298 (9th Cir. 1996).

People v. Turner, 55 Ill. 280 (1870).

Qutb v. Strauss, 11 F.3d 488 (5th Cir. 1993).

Roper v. Simmons, 543 U.S. 551 (2005).

Safford Unified School District v. Redding, 557 U.S. 364 (2009).

Santa Fe Independent School District v. Doe, 530 U.S. 290 (2000).

Schall v. Martin, 467 U.S. 253, 104 S.Ct. 2403, 81 L.Ed.2d 207 (1984).

Schneckloth v. Bustamonte, 412 U.S. 218, 93 S.Ct. 2041, 36 L.Ed.2d 854 (1973).

Settle v. Dickson County School Board, 53 F.3d 152 (6th Cir. 1995).

Steirer v. Bethlehem Area School District, 987 F.2d 989 (3rd Cir. 1994).

Tennessee v. Garner et al., 83 U.S. 1035, 105 S.Ct. 1694, 85 L.Ed.2d 1 (1985).

Thompson v. Carthage School District, 87 F.3d 979 (8th Cir. 1996).

Tinker v. Des Moines Independent Community Schools District, 393 U.S. 503, 89 S.Ct. 733, 21 L.Ed.2d 731 (1969).

Todd v. Rush County Schools, 133 F.3d 984 (7th Cir. 1998).

United States v. Mark James Knights, 278 F.3d 920 (9th Cir. 2002).

Vernonia School District v. Acton, 515 U.S. 646 (1995).

Yarborough, Warden v. Alvarado, 541 U.S. 652 (2004).

Combined Glossary Index

Page numbers in italics followed by **b**, **t** or **f** refer to boxes (**b**), tables (**t**) or figures (**f**).

A

abandonment: the permanent desertion of a child; an acceptable practice from the fourth to the thirteenth centuries when a child was an economic burden to a household 31, 182, 365, 403

Abraham, Nathaniel 387

abuse: any nonaccidental infliction of injury that seriously impairs a child's physical or mental health 365, 369–70, 375

accountability in policing 202

ACT Now truancy reduction program 219

adjudication: the process of determining whether there is enough evidence to find a youth to be a delinquent, a status offender, or a dependent 229–30

adoption studies 59–60

adult criminal court 223–9, *224b,* *226b, 228b*

adult criminal offenders 35, 272

affective interventions: an approach to drug use prevention that focuses attention on the individual in order to build self-esteem, self-awareness, and feelings of self-worth 159

African Americans
  delinquency cases 15, 209
  gangs 117
  police use of excessive force 179
  racial profiling 192–6, *194b, 195b*
  youth attitudes toward police behavior 186

aftercare: mandatory programming for youths after release from training schools or other placements, similar to parole in adult courts 309–10

age distribution 7, 9

age factors in gang delinquency 116

Aggression Replacement Therapy (ART) 323

American Bar Association (ABA) 228, 232–6, 255, 256

American Indians 15

American Law Institute Model Code of Pre-arraignment Procedure 255

androgen hormone 62

Annie E. Casey Foundation 291, 301

anomie: Emile Durkheim's concept of the state of normlessness in society 93, 94

anti-loitering ordinance 270

anti-social activities 66

Antisocial Personality Disorder (APD): a mental health condition in which a person has a long-term pattern of manipulating, exploiting, or violating the rights of others 73–4

apprenticeship: a situation in which one is bound by indenture to serve another for a prescribed period with a view to learning an art or trade 31–2, 34–6, 123

atavistic: a term describing ape-like physical qualities of the head and body that were supposed by Cesare Lombroso to be indicative of the individual's developmental state 56–7

Attention Deficit Hyperactivity Disorder (ADHD): disorder characterized by being persistently disruptive, acting impulsively, easily frustrated, experiencing wide mood swings, and acting inappropriately 60

attorneys
  effectiveness 232–5
  in juvenile court 230–2, *230f, 231b*
  mandatory consultation with 252

Augustus, John 36

avoidance: a common reaction to actual or potential victimization in which an individual stays away from particular locations where or individuals by whom victimization is anticipated 66, 158, 371, *371t*

B

bail and detention 215–16

balanced approach: a recent approach in juvenile corrections that places emphasis on the offender, the victim, and community safety. One aim is to restore the victim and the community, as much as possible, to his or her pre-crime status 311–14

Bazemore, Gordon 392–4

Beccaria, Cesare Bonesana Marchese de 53

behavior
  African Americans' attitudes toward police behavior 186
  continuum of 5, *5f*
  as determined 54
  gang delinquency and 123–8, *126t*
  of police toward youths 186–7
  runaway behavior 216

behavior modification: a therapeutic approach based on the work of B.F. Skinner and Hans J. Eysenck that entails the use of reinforcements to increase the probability of desired behaviors and a lack of reinforcement, or punishment stimuli, to decrease the probability of undesirable behaviors 279–80, 288

Bentham, Jeremy 53

bias in making arrests 14

Binet, Alfred 74

biological influences and deviance 65–6

biosociology: also known as sociobiology, the idea that the biological makeup of the organism and the surrounding

environment are intimately related 61–5, *61b*, *65t*

blended sentencing: a development in juvenile justice in which either the juvenile court or the adult court imposes a sentence that can involve either the juvenile or the adult correctional system or both 236, 301–2

Board of Education of Independent School District No. 92 of Pottawatomie County et al. v. Lindsay Earls et al. (2002) 269

bond to society (also called social bond): in Travis Hirschi's control theory, the connections an individual has to the social order; the four elements of the bond are attachment, commitment, involvement, and belief 96

boot camp: a short-term program that resembles basic military training by emphasizing physical training and discipline; boot camps often include educational and rehabilitative components 283–6, *284b*

born criminals 56

Boston Gun Project: a project that targeted firearms use by gangs by using a "pulling levers" (zero-tolerance) approach 132–3

Boston Gun Project's Operation Ceasefire 184, 187

Brace, Charles Loring 401

Braswell, Michael 317, 404

Bratton, William 201

Breaking the Cycle (BTC) program: a program that seeks to identify offenders with substance abuse problems early in their system processing, assess the appropriate treatment needs of the offender, and establish an

integrated set of interventions (sanction, treatment, and rewards) for the individual 162, 166

Breed v. Jones (1975) 251

Bridewell Institution: early English institution to handle youthful beggars 34

"broken windows" policing: policing strategies based on the belief that signs of urban decay, such as broken windows, in a neighborhood serve to make the neighborhood more conducive to crime and more fear-inducing; police attend to both crime and disorder 182–3

bullying
  cyberbullying *263b*, 364–5, *364t*, *365t*
  sexting and 24
  as victimization 363–5, *364f*, *364t*, *365t*

Bureau of Alcohol, Tobacco, and Firearms (ATF) 133

Bureau of Justice Statistics 193

Butts, Jeffrey 390–1

C

capital punishment: the death penalty. The Supreme Court recently ruled that capital punishment is unconstitutional for juveniles 406–9, *407b*, *408b*, *409b*

censorship of student publications *262b*

Centers for Disease Control and Prevention 371

Chancery Court: a body concerned with property matters in feudal England; responsible for overseeing the financial affairs of orphaned juveniles who were not yet capable of handling their own matters 40

Chicago School: a perspective explaining deviance as the natural outgrowth of the location in which it occurs; named for the work performed by social scientists at the University of Chicago 81

Chicano youth gangs 127

Child Abuse Prevention and Treatment Act of 1974 (CAPTA) 365, 373

child maltreatment: a variety of actions in which children are harmed, either intentionally or unintentionally 292–3, 365–7, *366b, 367t*

child protective services: a state's agency for handling child abuse cases; usually responsible for accepting and investigating reports of abuse and neglect and for removing children from potential or actual abusive situations 367, 373–4

child saver: Anthony Platt's term for a person involved in the development of the juvenile court during the Progressive Era 44, 414

child-raising practices 39

Children's Advocacy Center (CAC): an umbrella organization, independent of the criminal justice system, that brings together child protective services workers, law enforcement officers, the prosecutor's office, educators, mental health counselors, and medical personnel in an effort to provide a coordinated response and seamless service delivery to maltreated children 375

Children's Aid Society 401

CHINS (child in need of supervision) 3

chronic disobedience ("incorrigibility") 216

citizen attitudes toward police 185–9

civic club membership 398

civil abatement: procedures to control or eliminate locations that gang members frequent or own 132, 162

civil gang injunctions: court orders that prohibit certain behaviors linked to criminal activity 132

Clark, Joe *298f*

Classicism: a school of thought that sees humankind as having free will, that is, humans calculate the pros and cons of an activity before choosing what to do (compare to **Positivism**) 53–5, 80

Clear, Todd 328, 418

Cohen, Albert 87

collective efficacy: the empowerment of the community to do something about problems (e.g., crime) 82–3, 343

commonsense corrections: the use of various types of wilderness programs, ranging from relatively short stays in outdoor settings to long wagon train or ocean ship trips 302

commonsense thinking 286

community group conferencing (CGC): a strategy involving the community of people most affected by the crime in deciding the resolution of a criminal or delinquent act. It is much like family group conferencing, except that it includes a broader set of support groups and community members 348–9, *348f*
see also **family group conferencing**

community justice: an approach to justice that focuses on helping community residents manage their own affairs, solve their own problems, and live together effectively and safely 318–20, 321

community policing: problem-oriented policing that relies on input from the public to define problems and establish police policy 181–7, 200–1, 318, 397, 416

community rebuilding 397–9

community service: the practice of having offenders perform unpaid work for government or private agencies as payment for crimes without personal victims
alternative-consequence program 183
as balanced approach 312–13
day treatment services and 300
First Amendment issues over 263
monitoring of 393–4
overview 331–2
as penalty 217–19
under probation 308, 320
reforming juveniles through 383
release time for 398
as restorative justice 317, 325, 350
by school offenders 192, 262
for status offenders 315, 414–15

community supervision, current trends
balanced approach 311–14
community justice 318–20
emphasis on status offenses 315–16
future of 321
juvenile sex offenders *314b*
overview 311
peacemaking 317–18
punitive direction in probation 314–15
restorative justice 316–17

community truancy center 184

Community-Wide Approach to Gang Prevention, Intervention, and Suppression Program: a program aimed to initiate a comprehensive set of strategies: mobilizing communities, providing youth opportunities, suppressing gang violence, providing social intervention (services) and street outreach, and facilitating organizational change and development in community agencies 135

complainant preference 195

CompStat strategy 202

concerned adult role: a role assumed by some attorneys in juvenile cases in which the attorney acts as a "concerned adult" rather than a zealous advocate, sometimes encouraging youths to admit to petitions in cases in which an adversarial approach may have resulted in a dismissal of the petition 230f, 231

concordance: similarity among groups in a study 59

conflict resolution programs: programs in which the most important element is teaching youths alternative methods for resolving conflicts before they occur 341, 416

conformity 5, 94

consent search: a search in which a defendant voluntarily allows the police to search person or effects without a search warrant 254–5

containment theory: Walter Reckless's social control theory holding that behavior is controlled through outer containment (influences of family, peers, etc.) and inner containment (strengths within an individual), working in opposition to external pushes, external pressures, and external pulls 96

continuum of behavior 5, 5f

Conventional Level of moral development 70

Cops in Shops programs 199

corporal punishment: physical punishment 256

cost-effectiveness of boot camps 285

Cottage Blue 292b

cottage setups 36

cottage system: a training school design that attempts to simulate home life more closely than would a prison-like institution; it divides the larger prison into smaller "cottages" for living 279

Court-Appointed Special Advocate (CASA): a voluntary advocate for children in child abuse and neglect cases 376–7, 378t

criminal court 377–8

criminal law definitions of delinquency 2, 3b

criminalized juvenile court: a suggested reform of juvenile court that advocates providing juveniles with all the procedural protections of adult criminal court and offering reduced penalties for juvenile offenders 385, 385b

criminaloids 57

Crouse, Mary Ann 41

culture conflict: the conflict resulting when one set of cultural or subcultural practices necessitates violating the norms of a coexisting culture 87

curfews, constitutionality 269–70

custody rules with youths 174–5

cyberbullying and schools 263b, 364–5, 364t, 365t

cycle of violence: the idea that a child who is abused or who witnesses abuse will grow up to be an abuser 369

D

dark figure of crime: crimes that are unreported to the police 13–14

Darwin, Charles 56

day treatment services 300

day–evening center: a detention alternative in which a center was formed to devote time to formal education and remedial and tutorial work in the day and recreational programs in the evening 215

deadly force: police actions that have the potential to cause the death of the offender 180–1, 181b

Deborah Morse et al., v. Joseph Frederick (2007) 259–60, 260f

deinstitutionalization: the practice of avoiding any involuntary residential placements of status offenders; also, the general idea of removing any youths from institutional control 298–301

delinquency: in general, conduct that subjects a juvenile individual to the jurisdiction of the juvenile court (for more on the various definitions comprised under this term, see Chapter 1)
comparison of measures 25–6
criminal law definitions 2, 3b
introduction 2
juvenile, defined 6
lower-class gang delinquency 87
mental deficiency and 74–6, 75b
personality and 72–4, 72b
self-report comparisons 22–5
self-report measures 18–22, 19b
social/criminological definitions 4–5
status offense definitions 3–4, 3b
summary 26–7
trends in 9, 10–11t, 12, 12f
UCR and 7–18

delinquency, sociological explanations
ecological perspective 81–3, 81b, 83t
integration and elaboration of theories 101–2, 101b
introduction 80–1

labeling perspective 99–101, *99b*

learning theory 83–6, *84b, 84f, 85t*

routine activities and rational choice 90–2, *91b*

social control theory 95–8, *96b, 97t*

strain theories 92–5, *92b, 93t, 95t*

subcultural theories 86–90, *87b, 88t, 89t*

summary 103

Denver Youth Survey 128

Depo-Provera (drug) 66, *66f*

detached worker program: a program designed to place social workers into the environment of the gang 130–1

detention

    bail 215–16

    decision-making 211–12

    home detention 215

    introduction 209–11, *210b*

    options for 211

    positive programs 214

    rewards and fines *213b*

detention decision: the decision whether to keep a juvenile in custody or to allow the youth to go home while awaiting further court action 209, 211–12, 239–40, 254

determinism: a theory or doctrine holding that acts of the will, occurrences in nature, and social or psychological phenomena are causally determined by preceding events or natural laws 55

deterrence-based programs 333, 384, 403

detoxification: a treatment approach that attempts to remove an individual from an addiction by weaning him or her off drugs 152–4

developmental approaches to deviance 69–70, *69b, 70t*

developmental theories: theories that explain the changes and stability that characterize the trajectory of an individual's behavior or[s1] time 102

deviance

    biological and sociobiological theories 56–66

    biosocial factors 61–5, *61b, 65t*

    genetic-inheritance studies 58–61, *59b*

    introduction 52

    learning theory and deviance 83–6, *84b, 84f, 85t*

    physical appearance and 56–8, *57b, 58t*

    primary and secondary 100–1

    secondary deviance 100–1

    summary 77

    theoretical schools of thought 52–5

    trauma and 66, 210, 293, 375, 378, 411

    see also psychological explanations of deviance

Diagnostic and Statistical Manual of Mental Disorders (5th ed.) (DSM-V) 73

differential association: Edwin Sutherland's theory suggesting that criminal behavior is learned when an individual encounters an excess of definitions favoring deviant definitions over those that conform to the law 84–5, *84f, 85t*, 106–7

differential identification: a concept proposing that personal association is not always necessary for the transmission of behavioral cues; fictional presentations provide information concerning acceptable behavior 85–6

differential reinforcement: a theory that proposes that an individual can learn from a variety of sources, both social and nonsocial, and that the differing levels of reinforcement received will help shape future behavior 86

disorder and crime 182

disposition: the process of determining what intervention to give a juvenile offender upon his or her adjudication as a delinquent 229–30

disposition stage of juvenile court 236, 240

dispositional decision-making 222, 238–42, 393

disproportionate minority contact: the fact that minority youths are more likely to be arrested or adjudicated delinquent compared to their proportion of the population 194, 212, 240–1

dispute resolution: bringing together adversarial parties in an attempt to arrive at a mutually agreeable solution 339–41, *341t*

diversion: attempting to find alternative forms of dealing with problem youth outside of normal system processing

    child protective services 374

    conferences as part of 349

    juvenile court 215–19, 384

    with probation 325

    restorative justice and 352, 393

    school problems and 192

    state juvenile codes and 236

divestiture: elimination of juvenile court jurisdiction over status offenses 412–16

dizygotic (DZ) twins 58–9, *59b*

domestic relations court: a civil court devoted to issues involved in divorce, child support, and related matters 378–9 dopamine: hormone that acts in the opposite way from serotonin; higher dopamine levels result in greater action and pleasure-seeking behaviors; aggression is similarly enhanced from higher dopamine levels in the body 63–4

dowry: the money, goods, or estate that a woman would bring to her husband in marriage 31

drift: the concept that individuals are pushed and pulled toward different modes of activity at different times in their lives (that is, a person can "drift" in and out of crime) 98

Drug Abuse Resistance Education (D.A.R.E.) program: a school-based, police-taught program aimed at elementary students that attempts to reduce drug use by focusing on enhancing the social skills of the individual 133, 160–1, 190

drug court: a specialized court that attempts to help drug offenders stop using drugs by providing services and judicial supervision 163, 218–20, *218f*

drugs and delinquency
alternative responses to 162–7, *162b, 164b, 166f*
among offenders 146–7
connection between 147–9, *148f*
drug availability 166–7
gangs and 124–5
gauging extent of 141–7, *142t, 143t, 144t, 145t*
interventions 151–62, *153b, 157b, 160f, 161b*
introduction 140–1
maintenance programs 153–4
marijuana use 142, 149, 160, 168, 211
neurotransmitters and 63–4
research on 149–51
treatment approaches 152–6, *153b*

drunkenness violations 146
due process and juveniles
additional rulings 250–4
curfews, constitutionality 269–70
introduction 246
legal drinking age 270–4
rights at home and community 269–74
rights in school 256–69
search and seizure 254–5
summary 275
Supreme Court cases 246–50
Due Process Period: period from 1967 to the early 1980s when due process was emphasized in juvenile proceedings 47

E
ecological fallacy: the fallacy of attributing results based on grouped data to the individual level 83
ecological perspective: an approach that seeks to explain deviance as a natural outgrowth of the location in which it occurs 81–3, *81b, 83t*
effectiveness: whether interventions have an impact on any measure of the crime problem 306
ego: in Freudian theory, the social identity of an individual; actual behavior; conscious activity 68
Eighth Amendment *257b*
elaboration model: a perspective that takes components of various theories in order to construct a single explanation that incorporates the best parts of the individual theories 101
electroencephalography (EEG) 64
Elmira Reformatory 37
emotional harm 343, 365
emphasis on status offenses: a focus on status offenses such as truancy 315–16
see also status offense

empowerment 316, 336, 343
English Chancery Court 40
enhancement model: a model of the delinquency–gang relationship that strikes a middle ground in which gangs recruit delinquency-prone youths and enhance their deviance 128, 129
epinephrine: hormone that increases adrenaline; influences fight or flight reactions 62
evidence-based supervision model 311
Ex parte Crouse (1838) 41, 42
excessive discipline *258b*
exchange theory: a theory that proceeds from the assumption that equal reciprocity is a cornerstone of social interaction. Parties to a confrontation (such as an offense and subsequent restorative justice program) seek to establish a balance in the relationship 342
external pressures: poverty, unemployment, inequality 96
external pulls: deviant peers, subcultures, media 96

F
Fabricant, Michael 232–3
faith-based programs 405
family courts: courts designated to deal with family matters 165, 229, 376, 379
family group conferencing (FGC): a strategy involving the community of people most affected by the crime in deciding the resolution of a criminal or delinquent act 348–9, *348f*
Fare v. Michael C. (1979) 252–3
"feebleminded" 75
Feld, Barry 176, 249, 253–4, 386–7, 411–12

females
    detention and 212
    gang delinquency and 117–19, *118f*, 122–3
    juvenile institutions for 37
fingerprinting youths 175
First Amendment 258, 259
FIT (Family Integrated Transitions for Probation Youth) Program 153
focal concerns: the concerns designated by Walter Miller to represent the cultural values of the lower class; they include, trouble, toughness, smartness, excitement, fate, and autonomy 88, *88t*
foray: an attack, usually by two or three youths, upon one or more rival gang members (e.g., a drive-by shooting) 125–6
Fortas, Abe 43, 248
foster homes 36
Fourth Amendment 255, 275
fraternal twins *see* dizygotic (DZ) twins
free will: the tenet that people choose to act the way that they do after calculating the pros and cons of an activity 53, 55, 103
freedom of speech: the right to speak freely without censorship or limitation; for students, the Supreme Court has ruled that the right of free speech is to be balanced with the school's interest in education and discipline 256–63, *259b*
Freud, Sigmund 67–8, *68t*
Functional Family Therapy (FFT) 323
Future Farmers of America 269

G

gang: in general, a group that exhibits characteristics that set them apart from other affiliations of juveniles, often involved in deviant activity (for more on the various definitions comprised under this term, see Chapter 5)
    age factors 116
    behavior and 123–8, *126t*
    characteristics of 115–22, *118f*, *118t*, *119t*, *121f*
    defined 107–10, *109t*
    deterrence strategies 132–3
    deviance causes with 128–9
    drug activity in 124–5
    early gang research 110–12
    extent of 112–15, *113f*, *114f*, *115t*
    females and 117–19, *118f*, 122–3
    hybrid gangs 117
    in institutions 281
    intervention programs 129–37, *130t*, *132f*, *134b*
    introduction 106–7
    migration and 120–2, *121f*
    as natural response 111–12
    organization and size 119–20, *119t*
    as protection from victimization 372
    race and ethnicity 117
    reasons to join 122–3, *122t*, *123t*
    social class and 116–17
    summary 137
    types of 126–7
    violence and 125–6, *126t*
Gang Resistance Education and Training (G.R.E.A.T.) Program: a program operated by the Bureau of Alcohol, Tobacco, Firearms, and Explosives in which local police officers present a curriculum to middle-school children designed to induce them to resist the pressure to join a gang 133–5, *134b*
Gang Violence Reduction Program (Chicago) 312
ganging: the process of developing gangs 106, 111, 116, 122, 135–7, 140
Garner, Edward 181
gatekeeper role: means that police officers exercise considerable discretion with juveniles and are often the ones who decide whether a juvenile is processed in the juvenile justice system or not 177, 179
Gault, Gerald 247–8
    see also In re Gault
Geller, William 181
general education development (GED) 214
general strain theory: Robert Agnew's theory positing that the removal of valued stimuli or the presentation of negative stimuli can lead to strain and, perhaps, deviance 94, 95
generic control theory: a theory that proposes that control can come from several sources that vary over time and situation; four categories of control mechanisms are bonding, unfolding, modeling, and constraining
genetic-inheritance studies of deviance 58–61, *59b*
"get tough" movement 417
goal confusion: the state of affairs in which judges, probation and aftercare officers, probation directors, state legislators, juvenile justice experts, and others in the system disagree about the objectives of juvenile court and community supervision 329–30
Goldstein, Herman 182
Good News Club *266b*
Good Samaritan Law *161f*
graduated licensing: a strategy in which young drivers acquire on-the-road driving experience in lower-risk settings, then learning time is increased and drivers are gradually introduced to more difficult driving

situations; they "graduate" to greater driving responsibility as they master the previous steps 274

Graham v. Florida (2010) 250, 391, 410

Great Society reforms 103

group delinquency 106, 107

group hazard hypothesis: a contention that delinquency committed in groups has a greater chance of being detected and acted upon by the juvenile and criminal justice systems 107

guardian *ad litem:* an individual appointed by the court to serve as an advocate for a child in a child abuse or neglect case 376, *377b,* 379

see also **Court-Appointed Special Advocate**

H

health care insurance 400

Healy, William 40

hedonistic calculus: the belief that individuals seek to maximize pleasure 53

heterosexual relationships in institutions 296–8

Highfields Project 47, *47f*

high-rate offenders 24, 400

high-risk children/youths 288, 315, 400, 416

high-risk settings 92, 135, 285

Hirschi's Control Theory 96–8, *97t*

Hispanics
    attitudes toward police 185
    as gang members 117, 123
    juvenile correction statistics 16–17, 295
    racial profiling and 193

home detention: programs that supervise juveniles at home instead of in custody while they are awaiting further court action 211, 215

hormones and aggression 62

houses of refuge: early institutions for children that were designed to separate the youth from the detrimental environment of the city 34–6

Hulin, Rodney *226b*

Human Rights Watch 293–4, *293b,* 412

hybrid gangs: gangs that are mixed racially or ethnically or gangs whose members may belong to more than one gang 117

hypoglycemia: a condition of low blood sugar 62–3

I

id: in Freudian theory, unconscious desires, drives, instincts 67

identical twins *see* monozygotic (MZ) twins

I-levels: *see* **Interpersonal Maturity Levels**

immigrants
    benevolence *vs.* self-interest 44, 45
    ecological perspective on 81
    gangs and 106, 122–3
    IQ scores of 75
    juvenile court and 33, 39
    migration and gang delinquency 120–2, *121f*
    subculture of 86
    turnover issues 82

in camera **testimony:** testimony given outside the courtroom, often used for the testimony of children in abuse and neglect cases 378

In re Gault (1967) 242, 246, 247–8, 394

In re LeBlanc (1988) 387–8

In re Tyrell (1994) 255

In re Winship (1970) 248–9

incidence: how many times something (e.g., a drug) was used 141

Index crime: an offense included in Part I of the Uniform Crime Reports. The eight crimes

included are murder, rape, robbery, aggravated assault, burglary, larceny, motor vehicle theft, and arson 7

infanticide: the deliberate killing of young children, a common practice prior to the fourth century when a child was an economic burden to a household 30–1

informal adjustment: informal handling of an offense without the filing of a petition (e.g., a probation intake officer orders the payment of restitution) 216–17

Ingraham v. Wright (1977) 256, *257b*

inmate misconduct 295–6

inner containment: direct control over the individual from inside sources 96

innovation 94, 202

insane criminals 57

institutional life: refers to the demands of daily life in institutions such as detention centers and state training schools where all aspects of life are regulated. Inmates typically make adjustments to such institutions that often work against the objectives of staff defined 289
    heterosexual relationships 296–8
    inmate misconduct 295–6
    mental and substance disorders 289–90
    victimization 290–4, *292b, 293b*
    see also juvenile institutions

institutional/residential interventions
    blended sentencing 301–2
    boot camps 283–6, *284b*
    institutional corrections 278–9
    institutional life 289–98
    introduction 278
    new directions 298–302
    program effectiveness 286–9
    state training schools 279–86

summary 303
training school programs for
residents 279–83, *280b, 281b,
282b*
intake decision: the decision
whether to file a court petition
of delinquent, status offense,
abuse or dependency 216–23,
218f, 221b
intelligence quotient (IQ): a test,
developed by Alfred Binet,
that provides a numerical
representation of the mental
ability of an individual [the
formula is IQ = (mental
age/chronological age) × 100]
74–5, 307
internal pushes: restlessness,
discontent, anxiety 96
**Interpersonal Maturity Levels
(I-levels):** developed by
Sullivan et al., the seven levels
that reflect the progressive
development of social and
interpersonal skills 69, *70t*
interrogation tactics of youths
175–7
interstitial areas: areas that are
deteriorating and in a state of
disorganization 108, 110
intervention programs
drugs and delinquency 151–62,
153b, 157b, 160f, 161b
gang delinquency 129–37, *130t,
132f, 134b*
intraindividual theories: in
explanations of child
maltreatment, theories that
view child maltreatment as an
internal defect of the abuser
369
involuntary servitude: selling or
trading a youth to another for
service 31–2, 45

J
J.D.B. v. North Carolina (2011)
251–2
Job Corps 272

Johnson v. City of Opelousas (1981)
270
judicial waiver *see* **waiver**
jurisdiction over status offenders:
the juvenile court's authority to
exercise control over juveniles
who have committed status
offenses (e.g., disobedient,
runaway, and truant
adolescents) 412–16
see also **status offense**
jury trials for juveniles 235–6
"Just Say No": a school- and media-
based program designed to
encourage children to make a
personal decision to refuse
any offer to use illicit drugs in
the face of peer influences
158
justice by geography: Juvenile
courts vary from jurisdiction
to jurisdiction in how they
process cases. For example,
rural courts may vary
considerably from urban courts
224–5, 241–2
juvenile: a minor. (The precise
definition of a juvenile varies
from jurisdiction to
jurisdiction, currently ranging
from under age 16 to under age
18) 6
juvenile correction statistics 16–17,
17t, 18
juvenile court
abolishment of 386–9
attorneys in 230–2, *230f, 231b*
creation of new 389–90
developmental approach 392
drug strategies *164b*
establishment of 37–44
general purpose clauses *48t*
growth of 38–40
legal philosophy of 40–3
major milestones *38b*
new balance within 391–2
parens patriae and 40–2, *41t,*
49
police referrals to 173

political economy 401–3
problems of 43–4
race issues and 45, 395–7
rehabilitative juvenile court
382–4
restorative justice juvenile court
392–4
as social control agency 375–7,
377b
summary 395
youth demographics in *15t*
youth justice system 390–1
juvenile court process
adjudication and disposition
229–41
adult criminal court and 223–9,
224b, 226b, 228b
criminalized juvenile court 385,
385b
dispositional decision-making
238–42
drug courts 218–20, *218f*
informal adjustment 216–17
intake decision 216–23, *218f,
221b*
introduction 206–8, *207f,
208f*
prosecutor's role 220–1
punitiveness 236–8
summary 242
teen courts 217–18
transfer decisions 223–8, *224b,
226b, 228b*
see also **detention**
juvenile curfew laws: laws that
state that juveniles must stay
inside their houses at specific
times, enacted in an effort to
reduce victimization of and by
juveniles 196–8, *198b*
Juvenile Detention Alternatives
Initiative (JDAI) 212
juvenile institutions
detention facilities *48f*
for females 37
houses of refuge 34–6
new reformatories 36–7
rise of 33–7
see also **institutional life**

juvenile justice
  broader issues 395–406
  capital punishment 406–9, *407b,*
    408b, 409b
  conclusion 416–18
  drugs and delinquency 168–9
  introduction 382
  jurisdiction over status offenders
    412–16
  life without parole 409–12,
    411t
  proposals for reforming 382–95
  rehabilitating *parens patriae* court
    382–4
  spiritual dimension in corrections
    403–6
  theories of delinquency impact
    102–3
juvenile justice history
  benevolence *vs.* self-interest
    44–6
  comparative terms *39t*
  establishment of juvenile court
    37–44
  introduction 30
  juvenile institutions 33–7
  major milestones *33b*
  1920s to 1960s 46–7
  property and person 30–3
  since 1960s 47–9
  summary 49
juvenile probation and community
    corrections
  aftercare 309–10
  community service 331–2
  continuing concerns 329–32
  current trends 311–21
  effective and ineffective treatment
    323–9, *324t, 325b*
  effectiveness of 321–3
  goal confusion 329–30
  introduction 306
  probation 306–8, *307t*
  restitution 330–1
  summary 332–3, *333b*
  supervision and counseling with
    probation 310–11
juvenile sex offenders *314b*
juvenile suicide 291–2

K
Kennedy, Arthur 406
Kent, Morris 246–7
Kent v. United States (1966) 43,
  246–7
KEY/CREST program 155
"Knock and Talk" service 184
knowledge approach: an approach
  to drug use prevention that
  entails providing youths with
  information on different types
  of drugs and the possible legal
  consequences of using them
  158–9
Kohlberg's moral development
  69–70, *71t*

L
labeling: the contention that the
  fact of being labeled deviant by
  society leads an individual to
  act in accordance with that
  label 99–101, *99b*
Lancaster State Industrial School:
  early industrial school for girls
  in Massachusetts 37
leadership structure of gangs 120
learning theories
  delinquency and 70–2, *71b, 71t*
  deviance and 83–6, *84b, 84f, 85t*
  social learning theory 86, 102–3,
    369
Lee v. Weisman (1992) 263
legal drinking age: the age at which
  a person is allowed to legally
  purchase and consume alcohol
  199, 270–4
Legislative Guide for Drafting
  Family and Juvenile Court Acts
  236
legislative waiver: state laws that
  provide for automatic transfer
  of juvenile to adult court, as
  opposed to judicial waiver or
  transfer 223–4, 389
  see also **waiver**
Lemert, Edwin 100
lewd speeches in school 260, *261b*
lie-detector tests 24

life expectancy of youths 30, 32, 67
life skills training: educational
  programs that include basic
  personal and social skills
  development (which deal with
  general life situations and how
  to deal with them) as well as
  specific resistance skills aimed
  directly at substance abuse
  issues 159–60
life without parole (LWOP) 250,
  409–12, *411t*
life-course theories: *see*
  developmental theories
lifestyle explanations: *see* **routine
  activities theory**
Lindsey, Ben 38
Lombroso, Cesare 56–7, 83
looking-glass self: the idea that
  individuals view themselves in
  the way other people look at
  them 99
lower-class focal concerns 88, *88t*
lower-class gang delinquency 87
lower-class youths 122
Lozoff, Bo 317
Lyman School for Boys: opened in
  1848 by the state of
  Massachusetts and eliminated
  the housing of adult and
  juvenile offenders 35–6

M
Mack, Julian W. 39
McKay, Henry 81–2
McKeiver v. Pennsylvania (1971)
  249–50
magnetic resonance imaging (MRI)
  64
maintenance programs: drug
  treatment programs that seeks
  to establish a state in which the
  individual does not experience
  withdrawal systems 153–4
"Making Life Choices" program 404
malicious: term used by Cohen to
  denote that gang behavior is
  meant to cause trouble or harm
  87, 90

mandatory waiver 390

marijuana use 142, 149, 160, 168, 211

Maryland Detention Response Unit 214

medical model: a perspective that approaches the deviant act as a symptom of a larger problem (or "disease") 54

mental deficiency and delinquency 74–6, *75b*

mental disorders 289–90

mentalistic construct: relies on the mindset and attitude of the individual involved 100

mentoring programs
    effectiveness 287, 309, 323, 326, 400
    for high-risk youths 416
    in institutions 300
    in schools 190

Merlo, Alida 400

Merton, Robert 93

meta-analysis: a statistical technique that uses data from a number of studies to compute a common statistic in order to compare results across studies
    defined 60, 287
    intervention effectiveness 323, 382
    outcome evaluations 165
    racial profiling 195
    restorative justice programs 331, 352, 354

middle-class gangs 116–17

migration and gang delinquency 120–2, *121f*

Miller, Walter 88, *88t*

Miller v. Alabama (2012) 250, 391, 410, *411t*

Minnesota Multiphasic Personality Inventory (MMPI): a 556-question inventory that serves as a standardized method for tapping personality traits in individuals 74

Miranda rights 176, 231, 253, 387

mission distortion: in probation, the phenomenon describing what happened when probation officers no longer see themselves as service providers or social workers but instead over-identify with a law enforcement role 199, 329–30

Model Juvenile Delinquency Act 209, *210b*

modeling: a form of learning that entails copying the behavior of others 70–1, 85–6

modes of adaptation: according to Merton, the various ways of adapting to strain; the five modes of adaptation are conformity, innovation, ritualism, retreatism, and rebellion 93–4, *93t*

Monitoring the Future (MTF) Project: a self-report survey, administered annually to high school seniors, college students, and young adults, that includes both serious and less serious offenses, such as robbery, aggravated assault, hitting teachers, use of weapons, group fighting, and drug usage
    demographic data from 23
    overview 19, 20, *21–2t*
    teen drug use 140, 141–3

Monoamine oxidase A (MAOA) gene: facilitates or inhibits the transfer of information from neuron to neuron, thus altering possible reactions to inputs 60–1

monozygotic (MZ) twins 58–9, *59b*

moral development: Kohlberg's theory that individuals progress through six stages of "moral development," which are arranged into three levels: preconventional, conventional, and postconventional (principled) 69–70, *71t*

Mothers Against Drunk Driving (MADD) 270

motivational interviewing: a style of communication designed to make it more likely that offenders will listen, will be engaged in the process, and will be more ready to make changes 310–11

motorcycle gangs 108, 125

Multi-Dimensional Family Therapy (MDFT): therapy centered on the family, peers, and community influences around youths 155–6

multiple causation: the belief that delinquency is caused by multiple factors in conjunction with one another 54, 55

Multisystemic Therapy (MST) 219, 288, 323, 325

N

National Academies of Science 392

National Alliance of Gang Investigators Associations (NAGIA) 124–5

National Center for Biotechnology Information 73

National Child Abuse and Neglect Data System (NCANDS): a voluntary national data collection and analysis system created in response to the requirements of the Child Abuse Prevention and Treatment Act 367

National Council on Crime and Delinquency 299

National Crime Victimization Survey (NCVS): a victim survey administered by the U.S. Census Bureau 360–2

National Drug Control Strategy 162, *162b*

National Incident-Based Reporting System (NIBRS) 194

National Institute on Drug Abuse (NIDA) 142, 157–8, *157b*

National Minimum Drinking Age Act 199

National Research Council 301, 392

National Survey on Drug Use and Health: a survey of the prevalence, patterns, and consequences of alcohol, tobacco, and illegal drug use and abuse of the general U.S. civilian noninstitutionalized population, age 12 and older, conducted by the Substance Abuse and Mental Health Services Administration (SAMHSA) 143

National Youth Gang Center (NYGC) 106

National Youth Gang Survey (NYGS): a survey administered by Spergel and Curry (1993) that identified the five common gang-intervention strategies of suppression, social intervention, organization change and development, community organization, and opportunities provision 108, 129

National Youth Survey (NYS): a self-report survey administered to 11- to 17-year-old youths that taps information on Index offenses 19–20, *20b*, 149, 151

nature–nurture controversy: the debate as to whether intelligence is inherited (nature) or whether it is an outcome of growth in the environment (nurture) 75

near group: an assembly of individuals characterized by a relatively short lifetime, little formal organization, a lack of consensus between members, a small core of continuous participants, self-appointed leadership, and limited cohesion 112, 116

negativistic: term used by Cohen to denote gang behavior as having no positive value or intent 87, 90

neglect: the failure to provide life's essentials (e.g., affection, food, shelter, clothing, etc.) to a child 365, 369–70, 375

neighborhood reparative boards (NRBs): boards made up of community members that seek to restore victims and community to pre-offense states, require the offender to make amends, and aid the offender in understanding the impact of his or her actions on the victim and community 349–50

Neoclassicism: the middle ground between classicism and positivism, the contention that humankind exercises some degree of free will, but that choices are limited by a large number of factors both within and outside of the individual (also called soft determinism) 55, 90, 92, 103

net-widening: the practice of handling youths (or other offenders) who normally would have been left alone 168

neurotransmitters: chemicals involved in the transmission of electrical impulses through the nervous system 63–4

New Jersey v. T.L.O. (1985) 266, 267, *267b*

new reformatories 36–7

nonsecure detention: the placement of a delinquent youth in a small group home that is not as securely locked to await further court action (compare to **secure detention**) 211

non-utilitarian: term used by Cohen

to denote gang behavior as supplying no long-term need or solution to a problem 87, 90

norepinephrine: hormone that leads to increased heart rates and energy levels; influences fight or flight reactions 62

Noriega, Claude 389–90

nullification: a refusal to enforce the law or impose a punishment 32

Nye, Ivan 18, *19b*

NYS Family Study (NYSFS) 20

O

offense rate: the number of offenses per 100,000 persons 12

Office of Juvenile Justice and Delinquency Prevention (OJJDP) 6, 134–7, 172, 184, 226

"once an adult, always an adult" provisions: state laws that mandate that certain juvenile offenders be processed in adult court after an initial processing in adult criminal court 225

operant conditioning: the reinforcement of behavior through a complex system of rewards 71–2, 76, 86, 324

Operation Ceasefire 184, 187

Operation Eiger 198–9

Operation Night Light (Boston) 312

orthomolecular factors: chemicals that are introduced to the body or altered through diet or other influences 62–3, 66

outer containment: direct control over the individual from outside sources 96

out-of-home placement of juveniles 222

outpatient drug-free program: a nonresidential form of drug treatment that emphasizes the provision of a supportive, highly structured, family-like atmosphere within which a patient can be helped to alter his or her personality and develop social relationships conducive to conforming behavior 155

P

panel design: a study design in which the same set of individuals are interviewed repeatedly over an extended number of years 19–20, 149

parens patriae: a legal doctrine under which the state is seen as a parent
    arrest tactics under 174
    conflict orientation under 375
    detention and 215, 216
    disposition stage of juvenile court 236, 238
    due process rights and 248–9
    "get tough" movement 417
    juvenile court and 40–2, *41t,* 49
    rehabilitation and 329, 382–4
parental discipline 34–6
parental tracking of teen driving *274*
parent-effectiveness training 400
Parishes Juvenile Detention Center *343f*
Part I offenses *see* **index crime**
P.B. v. Koch (1996) 256
peacemaking: a perspective that supports efforts of corrections workers, whether prison counselors or probation officers, to help offenders find greater meaning in their lives 317–18, 343, 350–1
peacemaking circles: *see* **sentencing circles**
peer mediation: a program in which disputants in a matter are brought together with a third-party peer (youth)

mediator in an effort to resolve the dispute to the satisfaction of both parties 341
Pennsylvania Supreme Court 41, 43
People v. Turner (1870) 42
personality and delinquency 72–4, *72b*
petition: the document filed in juvenile court alleging that a juvenile is a delinquent, status offender, or dependent 206, 216
phrenology: the study of the shape of a person's skull 56, *56f*
physical appearance of offenders 56–8, *57b, 58t*
physiognomy: the study of facial features 56
PINS (person in need of supervision) 3
Platt, Anthony 44–5
plea bargaining: negotiation between the prosecutor and the defense attorney concerning the petition (charge) and/or the disposition (sentence) 232, 234
pleasurable response (positive reinforcer) 72
point system in institutions *282b*
police effectiveness: whether police are accomplishing their objectives such as controlling crime, improving the quality of life, or solving problems 200–1
police in schools 189–92, *190t, 191f*
Police Public Contact Survey 180
police use of excessive force: intentional use of brutality by police 179–81, *180b, 181b*
policing and juveniles
    citizen attitudes toward police 185–9
    community or problem-solving policing 181–5
    custody rules with youths 174–5
    interrogation tactics 175–7
    introduction 172

juvenile curfew laws 196–8, *198b*
    police effectiveness 200–1
    police use of excessive force 179–81, *180b, 181b*
    probationer supervision 198–9
    professional crime fighters and 173–81, *178f, 180b, 181b*
    racial profiling 192–6, *194b, 195b*
    recent concerns 189–99, *190t, 191f, 194b, 195b, 198b*
    research implications 188–9
    statistics on 172–3
    summary 201–3
    underage drinking 199
    see also **problem-oriented policing; professional policing**
political economy: writers such as Garland contend that both politics and economics affect the operation of the criminal and juvenile justice systems. For example, Garland argues that current political and economic pressures dictate less emphasis on rehabilitation and greater emphasis on punishment, deterrence, and incapacitation 401–3
positive youth development: the concept that most youths can grow up properly and stay out of trouble if they can be attached to the proper social resources, especially prosocial, caring adults 383
Positivism: a school of thought based upon determinism, wherein what an individual does is determined by factors beyond the control of the individual (compare to **Classicism**) 52–5, *54t,* 80
positron emission tomography (PET scans) 64
postconventional level of moral development 70
posttraumatic stress disorder (PTSD) 210
Powers, Ron 403

Preconventional Level of moral development 70

Prescott, Peter 229

presumptive waiver 221

prevalence: how many respondents report the use of something (e.g., a drug) 141

preventive detention: detention to prevent further delinquency while awaiting court action on an earlier charge 254

primary deviance: those actions that are rationalized or otherwise dealt with as functions of a socially acceptable role (compare to secondary deviance) 100–1

Principled Level of moral development 70

Prison Rape Elimination Act (PREA) 290

private juvenile facilities 16

probation: a type of community corrections in which an offender is under the supervision of a probation officer. The court orders the offender to follow certain rules and to report regularly to a probation officer 36, 306–8, 307t

see also juvenile probation and community corrections

probation supervision 198–9, 308

problem-oriented policing: addressing the underlying causes of problems (such as delinquency) rather than simply addressing the symptoms 181–5

professional policing: also known as the 911 model of policing, a model of policing that emphasizes rapid response to citizen calls for service. This model includes greater emphasis on police patrol in cruisers rather than foot patrol 173–81, *178f, 180b, 181b*

program effectiveness: the question of whether programs achieve their objectives 286–9

Progressive Era 44

Project HOPE 315

Project Service Achievement Work (SAW) *309f*

Project TOUGH: (Taking Out Urban Gang Headquarters–Los Angeles) this project entails the employment of civil abatement procedures to control or eliminate locations that gang members frequent or own 132

prosecutorial waiver: a waiver or transfer by the prosecutor of a juvenile case to adult court 224, 225, 242

psychoanalysis: pioneered by Freud, an approach to understanding human behavior, the major premise of which is that unconscious, and perhaps instinctual, factors account for much of the behavior displayed by individuals 67

psychological explanations of deviance
developmental approaches 69–70, *69b, 70t*
implications of 76
learning theories 70–2, *71b, 71t*
mental deficiency 74–6, *75b*
overview 66–7
personality and 72–4, *72b*
psychoanalytic explanations 67–8, *67b, 68t*

psychopharmacological perspective: the perspective that drugs have a direct causal impact on crime by inducing the user to act out in a certain way 63, 148

psychotherapeutic interventions 46–7

pulling levers: an approach wherein the police strictly enforce any and all codes and regulations (i.e., zero tolerance) in an attempt to change the behavior of a target group 133, 162, 184, 200–2

punitive models in probation: Probation models that emphasize punishment and control of probationers over treatment 314–15

Punitive Period: started in the 1980s when increased use of waiver, mandatory sentencing, and less emphasis on rehabilitation and treatment was evident 47

punitiveness 236–8

Putnam, Robert 397–9, 417

Q

Qutb v. Strauss (1993) 270

R

race concerns
dispositional decision-making 239–40, *241b*
distribution of delinquency 9, 17
in institutions 294, 295
intake decisions 222
juvenile courts 45, 395–7

racial composition of juvenile offenders 278

racial disparity in probation reports 308

racial profiling: the practice of using race as the sole indicator of suspicion of criminal activity 192–6, *194b, 195b*

racial tension: discord based on differences in racial background 295, 303

rational choice theory: the theory that potential offenders make choices based on various factors in the physical and social environments 91–2, *91b*

reactive hypoglycemia: changes in the blood sugar level, both higher and lower, as a result of dietary intake 62–3

reasonable doubt standard: the standard of proof used in both adult criminal cases and juvenile delinquency cases: doubt based on reason that a reasonable man or women might entertain 248

recidivism
  boot camps 284–5
  criminogenic risk factors and 290
  drug treatment programs and 165
  drug use and 329
  effectiveness of therapy and *324t*
  with intervention programs 219, 306, 315, 323–7, *324t*
  juvenile court and 43, 217
  juvenile *vs.* adult court 227
  probation and 320, 321–2, 332
  rates of 103, 287, 300, 302, 309, 311
  reduction of 155–6, 279, 288, 382–3
  restitution use 331
  restorative justice and 317–18, 323, 352–4
  statutory exclusion law 224
  supervision programs 192, 198
  training schools 299, 303
reciprocal relationship: a relationship in which two behaviors being studied (e.g., drug use and delinquency) feed one another 148, 150–1
Red Hook Justice (documentary) 319
rehabilitation
  balanced approach to 312
  belief in 47, 49, 55
  curfew orders and 197–8
  deterrence and incapacitation 310
  effectiveness 403
  judges' attitudes toward *241b*
  juvenile court and 229, 382–4, 386, 388, 417
  parens patriae and 329
  prognosis for 273

punishment *vs.* 238
quality of 287
release justification 250
sentencing circles 350
reintegrative shaming: an idea postulated by Braithwaite that offers shaming as a key mechanism for showing societal disapproval. The shaming needs to be imposed in such a fashion as to draw the offending party into conforming society 101, 342
Reintegrative Shaming Experiments (RISE): a study conducted in Australia that compared the effects of standard court processing with the effects of conferencing on victims and offenders involved in drunk driving, juvenile property offenses, juvenile shoplifting, and violent youthful offenses
Reiss, Albert 179
religious training 34, 35
reparative justice: *see* **restorative justice**
research definitions of gangs 108–9, *109t*
Residential Area Policing Program (RAPP) houses 184, 200
restitution: the practice of offenders paying for all or part of the damage inflicted on persons or property damaged by the offense
  as accountability 357
  compliance with 353
  in developmental approach 392
  first-time offenses 216
  goal confusion 329
  importance of 183, 312–13, 315, 317, 417
  in juvenile court 217, 308
  mediation and 347, 350, 352
  overview 330–1, 332
  programs 220, 325, 338, 383

restorative justice: a model of justice that is concerned with repairing the damage or harm inflicted through processes of negotiation, mediation, empowerment, and reparation
  background of 336–9, *337t*
  community group conferencing 348–9, *348f*
  defined 316–17
  dispute resolution 339–41, *341t*
  exchange theory 342
  family group conferencing 348–9, *348f*
  impact of 351–4
  introduction 336
  neighborhood reparative boards 349–50
  peacemaking/sentencing circles 350–1
  precursors to 339–41
  problems and issues with 354–7, *354b, 355t*
  reintegrative shaming 342
  as reparative justice 336, *337t*, 344
  social disorganization 342–3
  summary 357
  theoretical basis of 341–3
  types of 343–51, *344f, 345t, 346t*
  victim–offender mediation 347–8
restorative justice conferences: meetings in which victims and offenders face one another in an attempt at restorative justice, for example, a burglary victim meets a juvenile burglar and explains precisely how the burglary impacted the victim. Supporters for both sides are present and, with the help of a leader, they work out an agreement on how the offender can make amends 172, 183, 200–2, 353, 397

restorative justice juvenile court: a juvenile court focused on building community so that neighborhoods can better respond to and prevent delinquency. With such a court, communities would be more involved in sentencing through community panels or conferences or dispute resolution programs 392–4

retribution 47, 49, 53, 286, 343, 387

retributive justice: justice that focuses on the lawbreaker and the imposition of sanctions for the purposes of deterrence, vengeance, and/or punishment 336–7, *337t*

reverse waiver: the act of the adult criminal court returning certain cases received from juvenile court via waiver back to the juvenile court 221, 225, 226

right to intervention: *Commonwealth v. Fisher* determined that a juvenile has a right to intervention rather than a right to freedom; the juvenile court was granted a free hand in dealing with youths 42

rights in school
    corporal punishment 256
    due process and 256–69
    freedom of speech 256–63, *259b*
    student searches 266–9

risk assessment instrument 211, *212b*

role-taking: the process in which an individual (a child) assumes the role of a person or character whom they have observed *see* **modeling**

Roper v. Simmons (2005) 250, 406, 409, *409b*, 410

routine activities perspective 90, 91, *91b*

routine activities theory: a perspective that assumes that the normal, day-to-day behavior of individuals contributes to deviant events; that is, the convergence of motivated offenders, suitable targets, and an absence of guardians allows for the commission of crime 81, 368

rumble: a gang fight 125, 126

runaway behavior 216, 415

S

Safford Unified School District, et al., v. April Redding (2009) 268, *268f*

Scalia, Antonin 408–9

Schall v. Martin (1984) 254

Schneckloth v. Bustamonte (1973) 254–5

school prayer: prayer that takes place in the school setting; it is debated whether school prayer represents the promotion of religion by the school 263, *264–5b*

School Resource Officers (SRO): police officers in schools who provide traditional police activity as well as mentoring and referrals, training to teachers and parents, teaching programs such as Drug Abuse Resistance Education (D.A.R.E.), and chaperoning school events 190–1, *190t*, 201

school victimization 362–3, *362t*, *363t*

school–police partnerships 192

school-to-prison pipeline: refers to a combination of factors that appear to criminalize much youthful behavior and facilitate the eventual placement of youths in our nation's prisons 191

search and seizure: can include searches of persons, places, and

things and actions such as taking into custody (arrest); Fourth Amendment protects against unreasonable searches and seizures 246, 254–5

secondary deviance: deviance that occurs when deviant behavior is used as a means of adjusting to society's reactions (compare to **primary deviance**) 100–1

secure detention: the placement of a youth in a locked facility with other youths who are awaiting either further court action or transfer to a state correctional facility 211–12, 215, 415

security cameras in schools 189

selection model: a model of the delinquency–gang relationship that maintains that gangs recruit or attract already delinquent youths 128

self-aggrandizement 112

self-control theory: Gottfredson and Hirschi's theory holding that self-control, internalized by individuals early in life, is what constrains a person from involvement in deviant behavior 98

self-image construction 89, 99–100

self-report measures: surveys that attempt to gauge the level of delinquency by asking individuals to tell of their own participation in deviant activity
    comparisons of delinquency 22–5
    critique of 24–5, *25b*
    measures of delinquency 18–22, *19b*
    new directions from 23–4

self-restraint 383

sentencing circles: a community-directed process, conducted in partnership with the criminal justice system, to develop consensus on an appropriate sentencing plan that addresses the concerns of all interested parties; the process takes place post-conviction to determine a sentence 347, 350–1, 354

September 11th terrorist attacks 185

serotonin: hormone that is an inhibitor of behavior, particularly aggressive and impulsive behaviors 63–4

Settle, Brittany 260–1

sexting: the sending of sexually explicit texts or nude or partially nude images of minors by minors 23–4, 364

sexual orientation 294, 297

Shaw, Clifford 81–2

shock incarceration: alternatives to traditional incarceration in which participants are involved in an intensive curriculum of discipline, work, strenuous physical activities, education, and other programs; boot camps are a common form 283

Short, James 18, *19b*

Short–Nye instrument: developed by James Short and Ivan Nye, this early self-report survey asked youths to note the frequency with which they committed each of 23 items, dominated by status and minor offenses 19, *19b*

Simmons, Christopher 406

Sixth Amendment 247–8, 251–2

skinhead gangs 127

slave labor 35, 36

social bond: *see* bond to society

social class and gang delinquency 116–17

social control agencies 23, 99, 360, 373–9

social control theories: theories that seek to find factors that keep an individual from becoming deviant 95–8, *96b*, *97t*

social disorganization: the state of a community in which the people in that community are unable to exert control over those living there 81–3, 86, 110, 342–3

social facilitation model: a model of the delinquency–gang relationship that maintains that belonging to a gang is the cause of increased deviance 128

social history investigation: an investigation performed by a probation officer into the legal and social history of a delinquent youth and his or her family, similar to a presentence investigation in adult court 306–8

social learning approaches: in explanations of child maltreatment, approaches that contend that an individual learns to be abusive or neglectful by observing past behavior of that type 369

social learning explanations 84

social learning theory 86, 102–3, 369

social support for families 399–401

social/criminological definitions of delinquency 4–5

sociocultural explanations: in explanations of child maltreatment, explanations that emphasize the role of society and the environment in leading to deviant behavior 369

sociopsychological marginality of youths 129

soft determinism *see* Neoclassicism

solitary confinement 214, 279, 283

somatotypes: physiques (e.g., ectomorph, endomorph, and mesomorph) supposedly corresponding to particular temperaments 57–8, *58t*

Souter, David 268

spiritual dimension in corrections: a suggestion that corrections should go beyond providing education and counseling to also focus on such issues as the meaning of life and the importance of personal values in one's life 403–6

spiritualistic/demonological explanations: the belief that deviant acts are the result of the battle between good and evil, God and the devil 52

spurious relationship: a relationship in which two occurrences have no causal connection yet it may be inferred that they do, due to a certain third factor that causes both behaviors being studied (e.g., drug use and delinquency) 148, 151

State Department of Juvenile Services 299

state training schools: residential placement centers for juveniles who have been adjudicated delinquent. They are youth prisons that may have a cottage structure and educational programming 279–86

status offense: an action illegal only for persons of a certain status (i.e., juveniles); an action for which only a juvenile can be held accountable (e.g., runaway behavior, truancy) defined 2, 3–4, *3b*, 7
deinstitutionalization of 298–9
delinquency comparisons 25, 26
detention and 209
emphasis on 315–16
institutional corrections and 278
intake decision 216, 217, 220
jurisdiction over 412–16
juvenile court and 14–19, 39, 207, *208f*, 375
noncriminal misbehavior 359

probation 306
processing of 395
rates of 233
serious offending *vs.* 13
sex-role expectations 239
training schools 283
statutory definitions of gangs 109–10
statutory exclusion: a state legislature's rule that certain offenses, such as murder, automatically go to adult court 208, 221, 223–4, 247
see also **legislative waiver**
Steirer v. Bethlehem Area School District (1994) 262
STEP Act: California's Street Terrorism Enforcement and Prevention Act of 1988, which effectively criminalizes membership in a street gang 131
strain theory: Robert Merton's theory that deviance results from a disjuncture between the goals approved by a culture and the means approved for reaching those goals 92–5, *92b, 93t, 95t*
street gangs 106
student search: search of a student's possessions or person in a school 266–9
subcultural theories 86–90, *87b, 88t, 89t*
subculture: a smaller part of a larger culture that exists within and is part of the larger culture 86–7, 89–90, 96
Substance Abuse and Mental Health Services Administration (SAMHSA) 143
substance disorders 289–90
suicide *see* juvenile suicide
superego: in Freudian theory, learned values, behaviors; moral character of the individual; outlines the acceptable and unacceptable;

may be conscious or unconscious 67–9
supervision and counseling with probation 310–11
supervision fees 315, *316b*
surveillance-only programs 322
Survey of Youth in Residential Placement 290–1
Sutherland, Edwin 84–5, *84f, 85t*
symbolic interactionism: the process through which an individual creates his or her self-image through interaction with the outside world 99, 102
systemic violence: violence due to factors related to the sale and marketing of drugs 148

T

tagger gangs 127
Taser use *180b*
tautological: leading to circular reasoning 83, 90
techniques of neutralization: techniques outlined by Sykes and Matza that allow a juvenile to accommodate deviant behavior while maintaining a positive self-image 89, *89t*
teen courts: a diversion option in which youths act as judge, prosecutor, defense attorney, and jury in minor cases such as status offenses and misdemeanors. The most common penalty is community service 217–18
see also **juvenile court**
Tennessee v. Garner et al. (1985) 181, *181b*
testosterone hormone 62, 66
theory: an attempt to answer the question "why?" 52
see also specific theories
therapeutic communities: a residential form of drug treatment that emphasize the provision of a supportive,

highly structured, family-like atmosphere within which a patient can be helped to alter their personality and develop social relationships conducive to conforming behavior 154–6, 168
therapeutic jurisprudence: courts that go beyond adjudicating and sentencing issues to consider the therapeutic role that the court can take. A prime example is drug courts, which attempt to use the court setting to motivate the offender and offer the offender services that will help solve his/her drug problem 315, 390
Thrasher, Frederick (Thrasher's gangs) 110–11
Tinker v. Des Moines Independent Community School District (1969) 257–9
Todd v. Rush County Schools (1998) 268
token economy programs: a behavior modification strategy, often used in training schools and other residential facilities, in which point or dollar values are assigned to particular behaviors and are used as a way of rewarding appropriate behavior 76, 212, 324
Tonry, Michael 412
training school: an institution that houses delinquents considered to be unfit for probation or another lesser punishment 209, 279–83, *280b, 281b, 282b*
transfer 6, 223–8, *224b, 226b, 228b*
see also **waiver**
transfer of evil: moving the attribution of evil from the act to the actor 100
trauma and deviance 66, 210, 293, 375, 378, 411

truancy
  juvenile court and 415
  laws for 197
  petitions 413
  rates of 209
  renewed emphasis on 184,
    315–16
  repeated truancy 216
  services for 184, 191, 219, 327,
    416
  as status offenses 4, *4f*, 315–16,
    414
twins studies on deviance 58–9,
  59b

U

underage drinking 183, 189, 199,
  271
underconformity 5
Uniform Crime Reports (UCR):
  data collected yearly by the
  Federal Bureau of Investigation,
  which provides information
  on 29 categories of offenses
  known to the police. It includes
  two offense subgroups: the first
  eight offenses are known as the
  Part I crimes or Index crimes;
  all remaining offenses fall
  within the Part II category
  age distribution 7, 9
  critique of 13–14, *14b*
  defined 7
  delinquency and 7–18
  juvenile correction statistics
    16–17, *17t*
  official statistics, summary
    17–18
  overview 172
  percent of clearances *8t*
  race distribution 9, 17
  sex distribution 9
  summary 26
United States v. Mark James Knights
  (2002) 255
unusual punishment *258b*
urban justice corps 402
U.S. Children's Bureau 40
U.S. Justice Department 16

use, abuse, and addiction: three
  common terms used in
  discussing the drug problem.
  Use means the utilization of a
  drug. *Abuse* refers to the use of
  any drug beyond that legally
  prescribed for a medical
  condition. *Addiction* refers to
  chronic use of a drug to the
  point at which the individual
  develops a need to continue
  use of the drug, increases the
  amount used over time, and
  develops a psychological or
  physical dependence on the
  drug 140

V

Vernonia School District v. Acton
  (1995) 268
vertical integration: stable
  neighborhoods with strong
  private and parochial networks
  may not be able to marshal the
  public support needed for
  effective delinquency control
  82–3
victim precipitation: a situation in
  a victimization experience in
  which the victim may have
  struck the first blow or
  somehow initiated the
  victimization 368
victim-blaming: assigning some of
  the responsibility for a
  victimization to the victim 368
victimization: in general, being
  victimized by a crime or
  delinquent act such as assault
  or theft. In reference to
  institutional life, victimization
  refers to an assault (physical or
  sexual) or theft experienced in
  a facility such as a state training
  school
  avoidance and 370, *371t*
  bullying 363–5, *364f*, *364t*, *365t*
  child abuse and neglect 365,
    369–70

child maltreatment 365–7, *366b*,
  367t
cost of 330
explanations of 368–70
extent of 360–70
fear of crime and 370
gangs as protection from 372
in general community 360–2
introduction 359–60
overview 290–4, *292b*, *293b*
rates of *361t*
responses to 370–3
in schools 362–3, *362t*, *363t*
social control agencies 373–9
summary 379
weapons and 371–2
victim–offender mediation (VOM):
  a formal mediation program in
  which victim and offender are
  clearly identified and the
  participation of the offender is
  often a requirement of the
  court; also known as
  Victim–Offender
  Reconciliation Programs
  (VORPs) 219, 347–8, 353

W

waiver: the process by which an
  individual who is legally a
  juvenile is sent to the adult
  criminal system for disposition
  and handling (also called
  judicial waiver or **transfer**)
  adult waiver rate 176
  defined 6, 223
  legislative waiver 223–4, 389
  mandatory waiver 390
  presumptive waiver 221
  prosecutorial waiver 224, 225,
    242
  reverse waiver 221, 225, 226
  transfer as 6, 207, 221, 223–8,
    224b, *226b*, *228b*
Washington State Institute for
  Public Policy 317
Washington State Juvenile Court
  320f
weapons and victimization 371–2

wet nursing: the practice of
employing a surrogate mother
to care for and suckle a child 31
wilderness program: a program in
which youths undergo an
outdoor experience that is
designed to teach self-reliance,
independence, and self-worth
302–3
wilding gangs: middle-class gangs
that strike out at what their
members perceive to be
inequalities and infringements
on their rights by other ethnic
groups 116–17
worker attitudes toward adult court
processing 228–9

Y

Yarborough, Warden v. Alvarado
(2004) 253
youth attitudes toward adult court
processing 228–9
youth justice system: a suggestion
to process juveniles in adult
courts that are a type of
therapeutic jurisprudence.
These juvenile courts would
be similar to drug courts in
their emphasis on treatment
within a court framework
390–1
see also juvenile court
Youth Online Safety Working Group
(YOSWG) 23

Z

zealous advocate role: defense
attorney role that emphasizes
strong tactics to prove the
juvenile defendant innocent or
get the least severe penalty
(contrasted to the concerned
adult model in which the
attorney acts like a parent
seeking the best treatment
outcome for the youth) 230,
235
zero-tolerance policies 133, 190–1,
201–3
Zimring, Franklin 272–3, 394–5